GOREN'S
HOYLE
ENCYCLOPEDIA
of GAMES

GOREN'S HOYLE

ENCYCLOPEDIA *of* GAMES

With Official Rules and Pointers on Play

INCLUDING

The Latest Laws of Contract Bridge

BY

Chas H Goren

A *Chancellor Hall* BOOK

GREYSTONE PRESS

NEW YORK

HAWTHORN BOOKS, INC.

W

THIS BOOK IS
DEDICATED TO THE MEMORY OF MY FRIEND

Geoffrey Mott-Smith

WHOSE INVALUABLE CONTRIBUTION TO GAMES OF SKILL
WILL EVER BE REMEMBERED

FOREWORD

"ACCORDING TO HOYLE" has become a phrase generally applied to give firm assurance to all concerned that everything in a dispute has been fairly resolved and consistent with the existent rules and laws. Such is the authority that Edmond Hoyle's books have gained over the last two centuries.

It all began in 1742 when Mr. Edmond Hoyle, K. C., a middle-aged English barrister, fortunately addicted to coffee houses and what went on there, published *A Short Treatise on the Game of Whist*. His book immediately became so great a success that it had to be reprinted and finally enlarged to include most of the then known games of skill. Because the playing of cards and games is a universal diversion, there have been innumerable editions ever since, in all western languages, of one or another *Hoyle*—the most comprehensive of which up to now was the previous edition of the present book: CULBERTSON'S HOYLE, published eleven years ago.

By coincidence, I too am a lawyer, and middle-aged. I am not addicted to coffee houses, but have been interested in and written about many games of skill, particularly one whose acquaintance poor Mr. Hoyle was prevented from making, namely Contract Bridge.

It seems, at least to me, quite appropriate that I should have the opportunity of remedying history's error and bringing Contract Bridge at its most recent development to Mr. Hoyle, if not in the flesh, at least in this latest edition of his book.

My book, of course, has taken into consideration the passing of two centuries and, therefore, also other games which have come into being since Mr. Hoyle have been included while others have been adjusted to our changed times or dropped entirely if they have become obsolete.

Particularly helpful to me in the preparation of GOREN'S HOYLE were two friends, Albert H. Morehead and the late Geoffrey Mott-Smith, who, in collaboration and independently, have written many books and articles on all types of games of skill. Mr. Morehead is known here and abroad for his many books on virtually every kind of game. He is bridge editor of *The New York Times*. Mr. Mott-Smith was editor of *Games Digest,* and was a renowned games mathematician and consultant to the American Playing Card Association. I can safely say that they are perhaps the most widely acknowledged arbiters of games in the truest sense of the word.

I believe you will discover many valuable nuggets in the bridge section to which I have given particular emphasis, and all through the book you will find the most comprehensive advice on all games from top experts that has withstood the test of time. If I may be indulged in a bit of back-slapping, GOREN'S HOYLE today, in the middle of the Twentieth Century, can well claim the position of authority that Hoyle did in the Eighteenth Century. It is a fascinating book, and I think you will find it rewarding.

Charles H. Goren

CONTENTS

The following table lists the main divisions of this book and the games most popular today. It does not attempt to list every one of the hundreds of games described in the text, all of which are listed in the Dictionary of Games and Terms, beginning on page 589.

⇀ RUMMY ⇀

Rummy (or Rum) is believed to be an American adaptation of a Spanish game, Conquian, which crossed the border from Mexico in the middle of the last century. Today, polls show that more Americans know the rules of Rummy than of any other card game. A vast number of variants have developed. They are here grouped into five sub-families: Rummy, the basic game; 500 Rummy, which includes Canasta, Oklahoma and other popular new games; Contract Rummy; Knock Rummy, the parent of Gin Rummy; and Conquian, from which sprang "Pan," the favorite of card clubs in the far west.

BASIC RUMMY

Definitions. 1. The following terms are used in Rummy:

BREAK. In some forms of Rummy, the act of making the first meld; in other forms, the point at which the stock has one card for each player, at which point the top discard can no longer be taken.

DEADWOOD. Unmatched cards remaining in a hand.

DISCARD PILE. The heap of cards successively discarded.

GO DOWN. End the play by placing the remainder of one's cards face up on the table.

GO OUT. Get rid of the last card in the hand.

GO RUMMY. Go out by melding the whole hand in one turn, having made no previous meld.

GROUP. Matched set; especially a set of three or four cards of the same rank, as distinguished from a sequence.

LAY DOWN. Meld a set.

LAY OFF. Meld separate cards by adding them to sets already on the table.

MATCHED CARD. One that forms part of a valid set.

MELD. Place one or more cards face up on the table, as provided by the rules, whether in a set or in laying off; any card or cards melded; a valid set.

ROPE. A set in sequence.

SEQUENCE. Three or more cards of the same suit in consecutive order of rank, as ◇7 ◇8 ◇9.

SET. Three or more cards of the same rank (group) or of the same suit in sequence (sequence). Also called matched set, meld.

SPREAD. Melded set; to meld.

STOCK. The rest of the pack after the hands are dealt.

UNMATCHED CARDS. Those not included in sets; deadwood.

UPCARD. The top card of the stock, turned over to commence the discard pile.

1

Number of players. 2. From two to six may play, each for himself. Four to six make a better game than two or three.

The pack. 3. A regular pack of 52 cards.

Rank of cards. 4. King (high), Q, J, 10, 9, 8, 7, 6, 5, 4, 3, 2, A. (In some of the Rummy games the ace ranks either high or low.)

The shuffle and cut. 5. Spread the pack face down. Each player draws a card, but not from the four at top or bottom. The player drawing the lowest card deals first.

6. The dealer shuffles the pack and the player at his right cuts it.

The deal. 7. The dealer distributes cards one at a time face down, in clockwise rotation, beginning with eldest hand (the player at his left). Each player receives: ten cards, when two play; seven cards, when three or four play; six cards, when five or six play.

8. The undealt remainder of the pack is placed face down in the center of the table, becoming the stock. The top card of the stock is turned face up and placed beside it; this upcard starts the discard pile.

9. When two play, the winner of a hand deals the next. When more than two play, the turn to deal rotates clockwise.

Object of play. 10. The player strives to get rid of all his cards by melding them on the table. To meld, he must form some or all of his hand into matched sets.

11. A matched set may comprise either:

(a) three or four cards of the same rank, as ♠7 ♡7 ◇7 ♣7; or

(b) three or more cards of the same suit in sequence, as ♠Q ♠J ♠10. (In basic Rummy the ace is in sequence with the two, but not with the king, so that a sequence round-the-corner, as 2-A-K, is barred.)

The play. 12. Eldest hand plays first, and thereafter the turn to play rotates clockwise. Each player must begin his turn with a draw and end it with a discard. (In basic Rummy and other variants, the discard may be omitted if the player goes out.) After his draw and before the discard, he may, if able and willing, meld any number of cards.

13. In drawing, the player always has the choice of taking the top card of the stock or the top card of the discard pile. He adds this card to his hand. He may discard any card then in his hand, placing the card face up on the upcard or discard pile. If he draws from the discard pile, he may not discard the same card in the same turn. The discard pile is kept squared up, and previous discards may not be examined.

14. In melding, the player may (a) lay down one or more matched sets, each of three or more cards; and/or (b) lay off any number of cards on melds already on the table—opponents' melds as well as his own. [Examples: If three jacks have been melded, he may add the fourth jack; if ◇9 ◇8 ◇7 has been melded, he may add the ◇10 or ◇6 or ◇10 ◇J or ◇6 ◇5.]

15. The player who first goes out by getting rid of all cards from his hand wins the deal. If all his remaining cards are matched or playable, he may lay them down without making a final discard.

16. If no player goes out by the time the last card of the stock is drawn, the discard pile is turned over (without shuffling) to form a new stock, and play continues. The next player in turn after the last card is drawn has choice between the discard and the top of the new stock.

17. *Optional rule.* If a card that could be laid off is discarded, any other player may call "Rummy!" as a claim to the discard. The claimant may lay off the card and make a discard, after which the turn reverts to the rightful player. The first to call rummy has priority; if two or more call simultaneously, the card goes to the player nearest the left of the discarder.

Scoring. 18. Each other player pays to the winner the index value of the cards remaining in his hand, whether they form matched sets or not. Face cards count 10 each, aces 1. When a player goes out, every player shows his full hand.

19. If a player goes rummy by melding his entire hand in one turn, having made no previous meld, he collects double from every other player.

20. Each deal is a complete game, as regards the scoring. (*Optional rule:* A game ends when any player's total score reaches 100.)

Irregularities. 21. *Play out of turn.* If a player draws out of turn and attention is not called to it before he has discarded, it stands as a play in turn and intervening players lose their turns.

22. If the offender has drawn the top discard and correction is required in time, he restores that card and play reverts to the player whose turn it was. The offender must retract any meld he made after his illegal draw. There is no penalty.

23. If the offender has drawn from the stock and has added the card to his hand before attention is called to the irregularity, he keeps the card drawn; play reverts to the player whose turn it was; and when the offender's turn comes he must discard without drawing and may not meld. The offender must retract any meld he made after the illegal draw.

24. If the offender has drawn from the stock and correction is required before he adds the card to his hand, paragraph 25 applies.

25. *Illegal draw.* If, in consequence of a play out of turn or by drawing more than one card from the stock, a player sees a card to which he is not entitled, and if correction is required before he has added that card to his hand, he must place it face up on the stock. If it was the offender's turn, he must discard if necessary to reduce his hand to the proper number of cards, but he may not meld. The next player in turn may draw the exposed card, or may have it put in the middle of the stock, face down (see paragraph 38), and proceed to play as if no irregularity had occurred.

26. If a player has drawn more than one card from the stock and has added them to his hand before correction is required, he must discard without melding; and in each subsequent turn he must discard without drawing or melding until his hand is correct.

27. If a player draws any discard but the last, and if correction is required before he has discarded, he must restore that card to its proper place in the discard pile. If he has not added the card to his hand, he may proceed to play without penalty. If he has added the card to his hand, he must retract any meld he may have made and his turn ends. If correction is not required before the offender has discarded, his play stands as regular.

28. *Incorrect hand.* If a player is dealt an incorrect number of cards and calls attention to it before drawing in his first turn, there must be a redeal. Thereafter, a player with too many cards discards without drawing, a player with too few cards draws without discarding (but only one card in each turn), until his hand is correct. A player who begins a turn with an incorrect hand may not meld in that turn.

29. If the player who goes out has too few or too many cards, and if it is discovered before any cards have been mixed together for the next shuffle, the offender draws a card from the stock without discarding, or discards from his meld, as the case may be; and play proceeds. All cards he melded in that turn are restored to his hand.

30. If, after a player goes out, another player has: too many cards, he pays for all of them; too few cards, he pays 10 for each missing card.

31. *Irregularities in discarding.* A discard is not final until the player releases it in such position that it touches the discard pile. A card exposed by a player in any other circumstances may be replaced in his hand without penalty.

32. If a player discards more than one card, and if attention is called to the irregularity before the next player in turn has ended his turn by discarding, the offender may retract either card; if the next player has taken either card, the offender must retract the other. If the next player has ended his turn by discarding, the offender may not retract either card and at his next turn may be subject to paragraph 28 if he has too few cards.

33. If a player discards without drawing, he may draw from the stock at any time before the next player in turn has drawn; after such time, the offender is subject to paragraph 28. In no case may a player meld after discarding.

34. *Looking back at discards.* A player who touches the discard pile so as to see previous discards may not take the top discard when next he draws (whether in his current turn, if he has not yet drawn, or in his next turn, if he has).

35. *Exposed card.* There must be a redeal by the same dealer, after a

proper shuffle and cut, if more than one card is exposed in dealing or if, before the deal ends, more than one card is found faced in the pack. After the deal is completed, no redeal may be called because of card exposure.

36. There is no penalty for exposure by a player of his own cards. If one card is exposed in the deal, the player to whom it is dealt must take it. If a player picks up and looks at any portion of another player's hand, the latter may choose either the hand that would have been his, or the offender's hand.

37. A card found faced in the stock, after the deal is completed, may be taken or rejected by the player whose turn it is to draw. If he rejects it, it is put in the middle of the stock (see paragraph 38) and play proceeds as if there had been no irregularity. If more than one card is faced at the top of the stock, the player's option applies only to the top such card; the next faced card is similarly available to the next player in turn, and so on. If more than one card is faced in the stock and the player in turn rejects the top faced card, his choice in drawing is between the topmost face-down card of the stock and the last discard.

38. Whenever in these rules it is provided (paragraphs 25 and 37) that a card be placed in the middle of the stock, "the middle" means the approximate middle of approximately ten or more cards. If there are fewer than ten cards in the stock, such card is placed, face up, in the approximate middle of the discard pile. [In Block Rummy, Gin Rummy and other variants, this is equivalent to making it a dead card.]

39. *Imperfect or incorrect pack.* A pack containing a card identifiable from its back must be replaced on demand of any player before the first card of any deal is dealt; after the deal begins, it stands as regular. If the pack contains an incorrect number of cards or a duplication of cards, or lacks any card essential to a correct pack, the deal is void if attention is called to the irregularity at any time before any cards are mixed for the next shuffle; but the results of previous deals with that pack are not affected.

40. *Invalid meld.* If a player lays down cards which are not in fact a set, they must be restored to his hand if discovered at any time before the cards have been mixed together; any card laid off on such a set remains on the table, but no card may be added to it unless three or more cards, which themselves form a valid set, have so been laid off.

41. If a player announces that he is out when he is not able to get rid of all his cards, he must show his full hand and lay down and lay off all he can. Play then proceeds as if no irregularity had occurred.

42. *Error in count.* An error in reckoning the points chargeable to a hand may not be corrected after that hand has been mixed with other cards. An error in recording an agreed count of a hand may be corrected at any time before settlement is made.

5

BLOCK RUMMY

Follow all the rules of basic Rummy, except:

The player who goes out must make a final discard; therefore his cards must constitute valid sets and still leave a card for discard. (If he was dealt seven cards, and has melded ◊10-9-8-7-6, leaving him with two cards, he cannot go out except by laying off. His two cards plus the card drawn might make a set, but he cannot meld it for want of a discard. So he would have been wiser to meld only four of his diamonds.)

After the stock is exhausted, the discard pile is not turned over. Play continues only so long as each successive player takes the top discard. When any discard is refused, play ends. All hands are shown, and the player with the low count wins the difference from each other hand. If two or more hands tie for low, they share the winnings equally.

QUEEN CITY RUM

Follow all the rules of basic Rummy except:

A player may not meld until he can go rummy.

When a player goes rummy he collects the value of his own hand (not the value of each other player's hand, and not double) from each other player.

COON-CAN, or DOUBLE RUM

Coon-can was the first name given to the game we now know as Rum or Rummy; it was also called Double Rum and, in spirit as in name, was an anglicization of Conquian. In Coon-can, the French-English 52-card pack replaced the Spanish 40-card pack, the rotation became clockwise in the English manner, and the joker was introduced as a wild card.

Follow all the rules of basic Rummy except:

Three to five play. Ten cards are dealt to each.

Shuffle together two full packs plus two jokers, making a pack of 106 cards.

Each joker is "wild"—it stands for any card its holder chooses to name. [There is no "trading" for jokers that have been melded.] In laying off on a sequence that includes a joker, one may change the designated value of a joker: If the meld ◊9-Joker-◊7 is on the table, a player may lay off ◊8 and thus designate the joker as either ◊10 or ◊6 (depending on the value chosen to be given it by any player who may subsequently lay off on that meld). In laying off on a group, one need only add a card of the same rank. (*Optional rule.* The designated value of the joker may be changed if it is at the end of a sequence, but not if it is in the interior of a sequence. In Coon-can, a joker may be moved only once and then it is placed crosswise to show that it may not be moved again.)

A joker left in the hand counts 15; an ace 11; face cards 10 each; other cards their index value.

B O A T H O U S E R U M

Follow all the rules of basic Rummy except:

A player in turn may draw the top card of the stock; or, before drawing that card, he may take the top card of the discard pile and then either the next card of the discard pile or the top card of the stock. In any event, he may discard only one card. Play does not end until a player can lay down his entire hand at one time.

An ace counts either high or low in a sequence, and sequences may go around the corner as in ♣2 ♣A ♣K.

In the settlement, a player pays only for the cards in his hand that do not form matched sets. The payment may be either one point for every unmatched card, or the index value of all unmatched cards (ace counting 11), as agreed.

O P T I O N A L R U M M Y R U L E S

Any of the following rules may be encountered in certain games or localities, for the reasons stated:

1. No one may go rummy; a player must meld in two or more turns to go out. (This prevents unduly large losses to a lucky hand that can go rummy before other players have had time to meld what they can. When any player makes one meld it is apparent that he is legally able to go out on his next turn, and other players are thereby warned to unload if they do not want to risk being caught with a large count.)

2. No calling of "rummy" when the player in turn overlooks the opportunity to lay off the top discard. (The optional "rummy" rule is seldom followed; too often a player chooses deliberately not to lay off a card, and he should have this freedom of choice. In some Rummy games, of course, a player is "forced" to lay off a card when able.)

3. A player must lay down his whole hand or none of it. This is the converse of optional rule No. 1 above. It tends to increase the scoring, but is not widely played.

P I F P A F

Pif Paf, pronounced peef-poff, is a combination of Rummy play and Poker betting. It originated (about 1940) in Brazil, where it was a major fad; but it did not take hold in the United States as the other South American importation, Canasta, did.

Follow the rules of Rummy, except:

Shuffle together two regular packs, making 104 cards. The game is best for four to seven players, though three or eight may play. In any case, each player receives nine cards.

No upcard is turned. The discard pile is started by the discard of the first active player, after he has drawn from the stock. A discard may be claimed out of turn by any player if it enables him to go out; if two or more claim the same card, it goes to the one nearest the left of the in-turn player.

No cards are melded until a player can lay down his whole hand (nine cards) with all cards matched. A group in rank (such as queens) must contain exactly three suits, neither more nor less, so that a group may have no more than six cards. Sequences are limited only by the end cards, king (high) and ace (low). If the stock is exhausted, no one having gone out, the discard pile is turned over without shuffling to form a new stock.

The game is played in the manner of Poker. Each player antes one chip. The dealer must then make a blind bet (without looking at his cards) of as many chips as there are players. Eldest hand (the player at dealer's left) may then, if he has not looked at his cards, double this blind bet, and if he does double, the player at his left (again without looking at his cards) may double eldest hand's bet; and so on. When a player does not choose to make a blind bet, he looks at his cards and then he, and each player in turn after him, after looking at his cards, must either put up the amount of the last blind bet or drop out of the play until the next deal.

When the turn comes around again to the last blind bettor, he may either raise his own previous bet, or may refuse to raise (in which case play begins). If the last blind bettor does raise, each player in turn thereafter may either call, or raise, or drop, until the highest previous bet has been exactly called by all players still in the pot. The limit for any player's total bet, including previous bets and including the amount by which he raises, is always twice the number of chips the last previous bettor has put into the pot. (For example: G, the dealer, bets 7 blind; A makes it 14; B looks at his hand and drops; C calls, putting in 14; D calls, putting in 14; E and F drop; G calls, putting in 7; A raises, putting in 14 more to make the total bet 28. B is out of it. C may raise 28 chips, putting in 42 to make his total contribution 56—twice the total contribution of B.)

The first player to go out wins the entire pot and deals next.

POINTERS ON RUMMY

Combinations. Two cards form a combination when the addition of a specific third card will form a matched set. There are three kinds of combinations, as shown in the diagram.

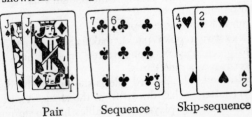

       Pair   Sequence   Skip-sequence

The skip-sequence is obviously inferior to the other two, since it can be filled only by one card, while the others can be filled by either of two. But what counts is the cards actually still available: a pair of jacks is worthless if the other two jacks are buried in the discard pile. If one of the cards needed to fill a pair or a sequence is *dead* (buried, or already melded) the combination is no better than a skip-sequence.

With no cards dead, a skip-sequence should be discarded before a two-place combination. A sequence is preferable to a pair, since the sequence can be extended to as many as thirteen cards, whereas a set by rank is limited to four cards.

A pair and a sequence interlock when they want a common card. In the example hand, the player has just drawn a four, filling a set, and he now has to break up a combination. The sevens and the club sequence interlock, since they both want the ♣7. The total spaces in the two combinations together is not two plus two, but three. Hence one of the two is the best candidate for release, since only one chance to fill is thereby abandoned. To give up a queen or a deuce would kill two chances.

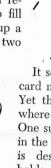

It seldom pays to pick up the discard merely to make a combination. Yet there are exceptional situations where such a course may "pay off." One such situation occurs very early in the game, when the player's hand is destitute of combinations. He holds, for example, the hand shown. The upcard was the ♠K, refused by the dealer, who drew and then discarded the ♡10. The player with this hand may very well pick up the ♡10. He thereby forms the most economical of double combinations—three cards with four places open. An added factor is that the ◇K looks like a safe discard.

Discarding. Keep track of all discards, to the best of your ability, and draw all possible inferences as what other players are holding. Discards picked up are the broadest tell-tales; almost invariably they indicate the filling of a set, and the only question is whether the set is a sequence or three of a kind. The answer is often readable from the player's ensuing discards. Also informative are the negative inferences—what discards each player refuses; what ranks are conspicuous by their absence from the discards.

A dead card is of course the safest discard; a card that may fill a set is wild and is held so long as safer discards are available. As among wild cards, the safest is one of different suit and adjacent rank to a previous discard of the next player: If the player at your left has discarded ◇7, your safest discard is the eight or six of one of the other three suits; your next-safest discard is ◇8, ◇6, or any seven.

Cards that fit with sets inferred to be held by other players should of course be saved. If stuck with such a *player* early, try to build a set around it; e.g., if you have to keep a ten because your left neighbor has previously picked up a ten, try to form a sequence. You may have to pick up a discard to do so, merely making a combination, but here is a situation in which the policy may pay. When you get a player late in the game, but before anyone has "cracked" (made the first meld), give consideration to "breaking the ice." If you lay down what matched sets you have, you may induce others to follow your example, and so gain opportunity to lay off your player.

Melding. The case against melding a matched set at first opportunity is that (a) you thereby give other players the chance to lay off on it; and (b) you show how near or how far you are from going out. What usually happens is that no one makes any meld until the stock is perhaps half gone; then someone "cracks" and all others hasten to do the same. The urgency (with three or more players, not with two) is that you cannot safely hold up your entire hand after one opponent has melded, because the chance to lay off may allow another opponent to go out.

You protect your own interests best by not "cracking" until you have good reason to believe another player is close to going out. This inference depends primarily on how many times he has taken the discard; another clue is his discard of combinations, tending to show that he has filled a set. But with a poor hand, and especially with one or more players, be quick to start the stampede. You limit your loss by "unloading," and may gain useful information from what the other players meld.

Block Rummy. The chief difference from Basic Rummy is that you must avoid above all being left with just two cards. Having to make a final discard, you cannot make a matched set, so must draw two players. Try to get down to three cards or one. Don't meld more than three cards in a set (unless you go out in that turn); if you have the fourth to three-of-a-kind, or additional cards in sequence, save them until you can lay them off without leaving yourself two non-player cards.

Because of the block feature, it becomes important when the stock gets low to unload high unmatched cards. But if you are stuck with cards you know your opponents want, cling to them and try to force a block, with no player going out.

Queen City Rum. Since the winner collects the count of his own hand, regardless of what the losers hold (matched or unmatched), the natural tendency is to save high cards. But the value of going out is enormously greater, on the average, than the value of having a high-count as against a low-count hand. Hence, if you find other players ditching low cards mechanically, save low cards.

Boathouse Rum. Owing to the greatly increased chances of filling sets, the abstract relative values of combinations are best forgotten. Reading the adverse hands by every available inference is the only safe guide, and your discarding should be based on what looks safest to let go rather than what looks best to keep.

Pif Paf. The paramount object is to form the hand so that it calls only one card to go out, since any such card can be claimed out of turn. Contrary to what one might think, the play does not continue very long on average before some hand goes out. Just as important as forming, say, two matched sets, is to be left with a double combination rather than with three disconnected cards. It therefore pays, much oftener than in basic Rummy, to pick up a discard merely to make a combination.

The limitation on a set by rank does not make it harder to form, in general, than a sequence. A combination in sequence calls four cards to fill (two duplicates of each next card); an odd pair likewise calls four cards. A completed sequence is easier to extend than three-of-a-kind— but going out with only two sets is rare. Certainly at the outset aim for three sets of three, discarding a duplicate card in a set by rank, or a fourth card in a sequence, rather than break up a two-card combination.

For example, suppose that your hand after the draw is as shown. If you save all the hearts, breaking a combination, you are left calling eight cards to reduce your hand to the desired situation (able to claim a discard out of turn to go out). But if you let go the ♡Q or ♡9, you are calling twelve cards for the same end. The point is that if you save the hearts, and draw the ♡K or ♡8, the five-card sequence is a white  elephant—you still have to get two more fillers to go out.

Many of the principles of Poker can be applied in the betting. But it is not so vital as in, say, Draw Poker, to feel assured that you have the best hand going in. The chief function of raises, even more than in Poker, is to freeze out some of the players who might otherwise "draw out" on you. It is true that if you have a good hand, you may wish to keep everybody in, so as to collect from more opponents when you win. But in Pif Paf your control of the play (such as it is) dwindles geometrically with each additional player who stays in. You may win by skill against one or two opponents, but with three or more the chance that lucky draws will put some player out ahead of you becomes too great to be worth the risk.

11

⌒ 5 0 0 R U M ⌒

This game is also called Pinochle Rum. In the embryo stage it was called Michigan Rum. The essential idea of this family is to give scoring value to melds in themselves, apart from their value in getting rid of cards from the hand. This idea has been extensively worked in a whole series of variants, which have also blossomed out with all manner of other special features. Best known of this group are, besides the aforementioned: Persian Rummy, Oklahoma, Canasta.

Number of players. 1. From two to eight may play. Three, four or five make the best game. Usually, each plays for himself, but four may play in two partnerships.

The pack. 2. A regular pack of 52 cards when four or fewer play; two packs shuffled together, when five or more play.

Rank of cards. 3. A (high or low), K, Q, J, 10, 9, 8, 7, 6, 5, 4, 3, 2, A (high or low).

Values of cards. 4. Ace counts 15 in all circumstances except when melded in a low sequence, 3-2-A; here the ace counts 1. Face cards count 10 each; other cards count their index value.

The shuffle and cut. 5. Draw for first deal; lowest card deals; ace ranks low in drawing. The dealer shuffles the pack and the player at his right cuts it.

The deal. 6. The dealer distributes cards one at a time face down, in clockwise rotation beginning with eldest hand (the player at his left). Each player receives: thirteen cards when two play; seven cards when three or more play.

7. The undealt remainder of the pack is placed face down in the center of the table, becoming the stock. The top card of the stock is turned face up and placed beside it; this upcard starts the discard pile.

8. The turn to deal rotates clockwise.

Object of play. 9. The object is twofold: (a) to score the point value of cards melded, and (b) to get rid of all cards in the hand. Cards may be melded in matched sets or may be laid off on sets previously melded by any player.

10. A matched set may comprise either:

(a) three or more cards of the same rank; or

(b) three or more cards of the same suit in sequence. An ace may be ranked high or low to make a sequence, in A-K-Q or 3-2-A.

The play. 11. Eldest hand plays first, and thereafter the turn to play

12

rotates clockwise. Each player must begin his turn with a draw and end it with a discard. After his draw and before the discard, he may, if able and willing, meld any number of cards.

12. In drawing, a player may always take the top card of the stock; but he may instead take any card in the discard pile, provided that he melds this card in the same turn. The card may be melded in a new matched set or may be laid off on a previous set. If he so draws a card from the discard pile, the player must also take all the cards above it in the pile. He may meld such cards in the same or any subsequent turn.

13. In melding, a player may (a) lay down one or more matched sets, each of three or more cards; and/or (b) lay off any number of cards on melds already on the table—opponents' melds as well as his own. Each player should keep all cards melded by himself segregated from the cards melded by other players. When a card laid off would fit with either of two melds, the player must state to which he chooses to attach it.

14. The player ends his turn by placing a card face up on the discard pile. This pile should be kept spread in an overlapping row, so that all cards may be read. (As a matter of etiquette, a player who draws from the discard pile should give all other players a reasonable time to examine all the cards he takes, before putting them in his hand. Correct procedure is to detach the card drawn, meld it, then spread all covering cards for inspection until all players have signified that they are satisfied.)

15. If any player goes out by getting rid of all cards from his hand, play ends. If a player can meld all his remaining cards, he may do so; he need not make a final discard.

16. If no player goes out by the time the stock is exhausted, play continues so long as each player in turn draws from the discard pile. It is not compulsory to draw if able. Play ends when first a player does not draw.

Scoring. 17. When play ends (whether or not any player goes out), each player computes his score as follows: He totals the values of all cards he has melded, and subtracts the values of all cards left in his hand. (Cards left in the hand count minus, whether or not matched in sets.) There is no bonus for going out.

18. The net score of each player for each deal is recorded on paper, in separate columns for each player. A running total is kept of each player's score. (The net of a deal, and therefore the running total, may be minus.) The first player to reach a total of plus 500 or more wins the game. All deals are played out; if two or more reach 500 in the same deal, the highest final total wins.

19. There is no bonus for winning a game (except by specific agreement). Each player collects from or pays to each other player, according to the difference of their final total scores.

Irregularities. Penalties and rectification are the same as in basic Rummy (paragraphs 21-42, pages 3-5) except as follows:

20. If a player takes any discard and does not show a valid melding use for it: if he has not added any discard to his hand, the discard pile is reconstructed by agreement of a majority of the players, there is no penalty, and play proceeds as if the irregularity had not occurred; if the offender has added any discard to his hand, he must expose his entire hand until the discard pile has been reconstructed.

POINTERS ON 500 RUM

Going out is a secondary consideration, unless opportunity offers to go out before an opponent has made any meld. Begin the game, at least, with the idea of getting as many cards into your hand as possible. Every meld depletes your hand of cards, and therefore of chances to make additional melds; try to get sizable batches from the discard pile in compensation.

Normally, all early discards are low, every player saving high cards on principle until forced to disgorge. Also, whenever possible players "salt" the discard by discarding from low combinations, and even from low sets. For example, suppose that after the draw you hold the hand shown.

The right discard is the ◇2! Precisely because your hand is so bad, you must break up your matched set to salt the discard pile. Actually, you have ironclad certainty that no one else can take the ◇2 for a meld, since you also have the ◇3, but the discard would be indicated even without this protection. The 6 points for the set of deuces is as nothing beside the chance to get a batch of cards by waiting two or three rounds and then reclaiming the ◇2.

If you happen to fill a low set by drawing from the stock, give consideration to breaking it up in order to salt the discard pile. The danger of so doing is proportional to the number of cards under your discard—the cards that may give another player opportunity to capture your "bait."

The normal course is never to discard an ace or a face card unless forced, or unless you are aiming to go out. But the deliberate discard of a dangerous card is sometimes an advisable defensive maneuver. Sometimes you have to "give to get." By giving your left neighbor a card you know he wants, you may "squeeze" out of his hand a card that you want (which you know he holds). In all such maneuvers, it is important to play to the score. Deliberately "feed" the player with the lowest score, if by so doing you keep dangerous cards out of the hands of the opponent with highest score.

Toward the end of a hand the question often arises whether to dig into the discard pile in order to make a meld, at cost of increasing your deadwood when one or two opponents are down to a few cards. Don't exercise a short-sighted economy here; it is a mistake to refuse a meld merely because it does not exceed the increase in your deadwood. There is a valuable equity in removing a batch of cards from reach of the other players (20 points at least), and the more cards you have the more difficult it becomes for the other players to avoid feeding you.

PARTNERSHIP 500 RUM

Follow the rules of 500 Rum, except:

Four play, two against two as partners. Partners sit opposite each other. They try to help each other form matched sets (as by discarding usable cards), but each player's melds are kept separate from his partner's. The scores of both partners are combined into a single net for the deal, and a single running total of deal scores.

PERSIAN RUMMY

Follow the rules of 500 Rum, except:

Four play, two against two as partners. Partners sit opposite each other.

Use a regular pack of 52 cards, plus four jokers. (Each regular pack includes two extra cards. A Persian Rummy pack thus can be formed from two regular packs, leaving one without jokers to be used in other games.)

Jokers are not wild; they form a separate rank and can be melded in groups of three or four, but not in sequences. Each joker counts 20. A group of four of a kind, if all four are melded at once, counts double. For example, four jokers melded at once count 160 instead of 80. Aces rank high, always counting 15. Thus A-K-Q is a valid sequence, but 3-2-A is not.

Unmelded cards taken from the discard pile are not added to the player's hand, but are left face up on the table, though they belong to the player who took them as though they were in his hand.

A game comprises two deals. The side having the higher total score after two deals receives a bonus of 50 for the game, and wins the difference of the final total scores. If a player goes out, play ends and his side receives a bonus of 25 points. When the stock is exhausted, each player in turn must continue the play if he can, by drawing from the discard pile either to lay off or to form a new matched set.

Pointers on play. Partners signal each other by discards: The discard of an ace calls for partner to discard a joker if he has one; the discard of a ten or face card calls for partner to discard an ace if he has one. If a player melds, whatever he then discards is not to be taken as a signal. In the closing stages of the game, when a player may have little choice of discard, there are no signals.

OKLAHOMA

Number of players. 1. From two to five may play. Three make the best game; next-best is four. Each plays for himself, except that four may play in two partnerships, partners sitting opposite each other.

The pack. 2. Shuffle together two regular packs of 52 cards, plus one joker, making 105 cards in all.

Rank of cards. 3. A (high or low), K, Q, J, 10, 9, 8, 7, 6, 5, 4, 3, 2, A (high or low).

4. The joker and all eight deuces are wild. A wild card may be desig-nated to be of any suit and rank, as the owner chooses.

Values of cards. 5. Each card has a point value, as follows:

CARD	IN A MELD	IN HAND
Joker	100	200
Ace	20	20
Queen of spades	50	100
K, Q, J, 10, 9, or 8 (except ♠Q)	10	10
7, 6, 5, 4, or 3	5	5
Deuce, designated higher than 7	10	20
Deuce, designated as 7 or lower	5	20

The draw. 6. The pack is spread face down. Each player draws a card, not one of the four at top or bottom. The player drawing the lowest card deals first and has choice of seats; next-lowest sits at dealer's left. In drawing, ace ranks high and joker is lowest of all.

The shuffle and cut. 7. The dealer shuffles the pack, and the player at his right must cut it, as in Contract Bridge (page 117).

The deal. 8. The dealer distributes cards one at a time face down, in clockwise rotation, beginning with eldest hand (the player at his left). Each player receives thirteen cards.

9. The undealt remainder of the pack is placed face down to form the stock. The top card of the stock is turned face up and placed beside it; this upcard starts the discard pile.

10. The turn to deal rotates clockwise.

Object of play. 11. The object is twofold: (a) to score points by meld-ing, and (b) to get rid of all cards in the hand. Cards may be melded in matched sets or may be laid off on the player's own previous melds.

12. A matched set may comprise either:

(a) three or four cards of the same rank, regardless of suits, as ◇5 ◇5 ♠5; or

(b) three or more cards of the same suit in sequence. An ace may be ranked either high or low to make a sequence, in A-K-Q or 3-2-A.

Wild cards. 13. Any number of wild cards may be included in one set. Deuces may be melded as such. When a deuce or the joker is melded with natural cards, the player must state the rank assigned to each wild card. [For example, if he melds ♠8 ♣2 ◇2, he must state whether he intends a group of eights, or a sequence 8-7-6 or 9-8-7 or 10-9-8. The statement can often be omitted because the wild card must be of a certain rank to make a valid set, as in melds of Q-Q-2, 10-Joker-8.] Such statement is binding for determination of what cards may later be added to the set.

14. When a player has melded the joker, he may later take it back in his hand in exchange for the natural card that it was stated to represent. For example, if the meld is ♣10-Joker-♣8, he may meld the ♣9 in place of the joker, which may then be used elsewhere. The joker may never be so captured from another player, and deuces once melded may never be recaptured.

The play. 15. The turn to play rotates clockwise. Each player must begin his turn with a draw and end it with a discard. After his draw and before the discard, he may, if able and willing, meld any number of cards.

16. In drawing, a player may always take the top card of the stock, and instead he may take the top card of the discard pile provided that he takes the entire discard pile and melds the top card in the same turn. This card may be melded in a new matched set or laid off on a previous meld. (In Oklahoma, the discard pile is called the "pack.")

17. To commence the play, eldest hand may take the upcard, if he wishes. If he refuses it, each other player in turn has option of taking it. Whoever takes the upcard plays first. If all refuse it, eldest hand draws from the stock, and play proceeds in turn.

18. All discards are placed face up in one pile, which should be kept squared up so that only the top card can be read.

19. The queen of spades may never be discarded so long as the player has any other card to discard. To go out, the player having a queen of spades must therefore either meld it or reserve it for his final discard.

20. A player may lay off cards only on his own previous melds. A group of four of a kind is closed: no additional cards may be laid off on it. [But a sequence may be extended to fourteen cards, with an ace at each end.]

21. If any player goes out by getting rid of all his cards, he wins the deal and play ends. If the last card of the stock is drawn, and the player discards without going out, the play ends without a winner.

Scoring. 22. When play ends, each player computes his score as follows: He totals the values of all cards he has melded, and subtracts the values of all cards left in his hand. (Cards left in the hand count minus, whether or not matched in sets.)

23. If a player won the deal by going out, he scores a bonus of 100 points.

24. The net score of each player for each deal is recorded on paper, in a separate column for each player. A running total is kept of each player's score. The first to reach a total of 1,000 or more points wins a game, and receives a bonus of 200 therefor. All deals are played out; if two or

more reach 1,000 in the same deal, the highest total wins. If two or more tie, they share the game bonus equally.

25. At the end of the game, a player who has gone out with concealed hand in any deal receives a bonus of 250 points for each such deal (this bonus cannot count toward winning the game). A concealed hand is one that goes out in one turn, at any turn after the player's first—the hand having previously melded not a single card.

Irregularities. Paragraphs 21 to 42 on pages 3-5 apply, and also:

26. If a player discards the spade queen, having any other available discard, he must retract it on demand of any other player if made before the next player in turn has drawn. (Only a player reduced to two cards may discard the spade queen, and he must show his other card, which must also be a spade queen.)

27. If a player fails to designate the rank of a wild card when he melds it, he may not later lay off on the set in which it was used, or trade for the joker in such set.

28. If a player takes the discard pile and cannot meld the top card, he must restore the discard pile and his turn ends without other draw, meld, or discard. If he has added any discard to his hand, he must show his entire hand until a majority of the other players restore the discard pile to their satisfaction.

POINTERS ON OKLAHOMA

Don't meld too early in the play; after four or five draws your hand may form other combinations that will use more cards.

Usually hold a pair rather than a two-card sequence, as there is a better chance to improve your pair.

As a general rule you take the discard pile when it will give you more points in melds than the point value of the unmeldable cards.

Save an odd queen or a high spade—♤K, ♤J or ♤10—even when it is unmatched with other cards. If you draw the ♤Q you cannot discard it, and a matching card will improve your chance of melding it.

When you take the discard pile, before mixing it with your hand count back to remember which cards each other player has thrown.

It is both ethical and proper to throw a card that will put the next player out, if there is a danger that otherwise another player will go out concealed.

Prefer to meld three of a kind rather than four of a kind, using the fourth card in another meld. Four of a kind is a closed meld and you cannot go out by adding to it if you are left with a single card later.

— CANASTA —

In 1949 and 1950, Canasta—a form of Rummy—became a fad game in the United States, perhaps the greatest of all time, exceeding Mah Jongg of the 1920s and Contract Bridge of the early '30s. From 1951 through 1953 it displaced Contract Bridge from its usual position as the most-played American card game. In a matter of months Canasta acquired nearly 20,000,000 players, and the sale of merchandise connected with Canasta was unprecedented. After 1953 the popularity of the game dropped almost as rapidly as it had risen, but several million persons, chiefly women, continued to play Canasta or one of its many variants. Canasta originated in Uruguay and achieved popularity in Argentina before reaching the United States. The name means basket in Spanish and probably derives from the fact that the double or triple pack requires the use of a tray or basket in the center of the table to hold the stock and discards. After about 1954 variants of Canasta such as Samba became more popular than the parent game (see pages 23-25). Even those who played the original Canasta generally abandoned some of the official rules, especially No. 24 (below); they prefer to rule that a natural pair is always required to take the discard pile and that no card may be laid off on a completed canasta.

Number of players. 1. From two to six may play, each for himself. The best game is four, in two partnerships. Six may play in partnerships of three on a side, partners sitting alternately (see page 24).

The pack. 2. Shuffle together two regular packs of 52, plus four jokers, making 108 cards in all. (For six-hand, see page 25.)

Rank of cards. 3. If cards are drawn to determine partnerships and deal, they rank: A (high), K, Q, J, 10, 9, 8, 7, 6, 5, 4, 3, 2. The suits rank: Spades (high), hearts, diamonds, clubs. Jokers are void in drawing, and a player drawing one must draw again. Highest card deals. Outside of the draw, the cards have no relative ranking.

Wild and Special cards. 4. The four jokers and all eight deuces are wild. A wild card may be designated to be of any rank, as the owner chooses. All treys (threespots) are special cards, the red treys being different from the black treys.

Values of cards. 5. Each card has a point value, as follows:

Joker	50
Deuce	20
Ace	20
Each K, Q, J, 10, 9, 8,	10

Each 7, 6, 5, 4	5
Black 3	5
Red 3	100

(When one side has all four red threes, they count 200 each.)

The shuffle and cut. 6. The dealer shuffles the pack, and the player at his right cuts it. Each packet of the cut must comprise at least four cards.

The deal. 7. The dealer distributes cards one at a time face down, in clockwise rotation, beginning with eldest hand (player at his left). Each player receives: fifteen cards, when two play; thirteen cards, when three play; eleven cards, when four or more play.

8. The undealt remainder of the pack is placed face down to form the stock. The top card of the stock is turned face up beside it; this *upcard* starts the discard pile (often called the *pack*).

9. The turn to deal rotates clockwise.

Object of play. 10. The object is twofold: (a) to score points by melding; and (b) to get rid of all the cards from the hand, by melding them so as to form at least one *canasta*, which is seven or more of a kind. Cards may be melded in matched sets or laid off on previous melds of the same player or partnership.

11. A matched set comprises three or more cards of the same rank. (Sequences are not melded in Canasta.) Wild cards may be used to fill sets and to increase them in size, subject to these limitations: Every set must include at least two *natural cards* (as ◇8, ♣8; jokers and deuces never count as natural cards), and may not include more than three wild cards; except that additional wild cards may be added to a completed canasta.

12. Red treys are never melded in sets; wild cards (jokers or deuces) may not be melded in sets apart from natural cards; black treys may be melded only when going out.

13. A set of seven or more cards is a canasta. A canasta that includes no wild cards is natural; one that contains any wild card is mixed.

Red Treys. 14. If the upcard is a red trey or a wild card, another card must be turned upon it from the stock, and the discard pile is frozen (explained in paragraph 23).

15. Red treys are bonus cards, not used for forming sets. Each player dealt a red trey must in his first turn place the trey face up on the table and draw a replacement from the top of the stock.

16. On drawing a red trey from the stock, a player must face it on the table and draw the next card of the stock.

17. When a player takes the discard pile and there is a red trey in it, he must face it on the table, but in this case he does not draw a replacement from the stock.

Order of play. 18. Eldest hand plays first, and thereafter the turn rotates clockwise. Each player must begin his turn with a draw and end it

20

with a discard. After his draw and before his discard, he may, if able and willing, meld any number of cards.

19. In drawing, a player may always take the top card of the stock; but he may instead take the top card of the discard pile, provided that he melds this card in the same turn. The card may be melded in a matched set or may be laid off on a previous meld by the same player or partnership. If he so takes the discard, the player must then take the entire discard pile into his hand. (Rules on taking the discard are given in paragraphs 23 to 25.)

Taking the discard. 20. The discard pile may not be taken (even to go out) when it is topped by a black trey or a wild card.

21. The first meld made by a side (individual or partnership) is its *initial meld*. Prior to the initial meld, the discard pile is *frozen* for that player or partnership.

22. The discard pile is *frozen* for both sides or all individual players when it contains a red trey or a wild card. (In such cases it is sometimes called a *prize pile*.)

23. When the discard pile is frozen, a player may take it only to meld the top card together with a natural pair from his hand. For example, if the top card is the ♤K, the pile may be taken only by showing a pair of kings from the hand.

24. When the discard pile is not frozen, it may be taken (a) to meld the top card with a natural pair from the hand, or with a natural card and a wild card; or (b) to lay off the top card. But there is one exception to (b): a player having only one card may not take a discard pile comprising only one card, unless forced (paragraph 34).

25. Having established his right to take the discard pile (by melding the top card), the player must take the entire pile, with the exception of its top card, into his hand. He may then meld any and all additional cards he pleases.

Minimum count. 26. The initial meld by a player or partnership must have a minimum count, according to the accumulated score of the side for all previous deals:

ACCUMULATED SCORE	MINIMUM COUNT
Minus	No minimum
0 to 1495	50
1500 to 2995	90
3000 or more	120

27. The count of the meld is the total point values of the cards (paragraph 5). If the initial meld is made in taking the discard pile, the top card thereof may be counted toward the minimum, but all other cards counting toward the minimum must come from the hand. (Other cards from the discard pile may then be added to the initial meld.)

28. Once a side has made its initial meld, there is no count require-

ment for additional melds by the same player or other members of the same partnership.

29. To go out in making an initial meld, a player must meld a canasta. (See also the optional rule in paragraph 31.)

Going out. 30. When a player goes out by getting rid of all cards from his hand, his side wins the bonus for going out, and play ends.

31. A player may go out only if the melds of his side, including his final meld, include at least one canasta. (*Optional rule:* A side needs two canastas to go out.) Failing this requirement, he must keep at least one card in his hand. All melds of the same rank made by a partnership are amalgamated, to build up canastas. (By custom one member collects all the melds of a partnership in front of himself.)

32. If a player may legally go out, and can meld all cards remaining in his hand, he may do so; he need not make a final discard.

33. If able to go out before or after drawing but before melding any card, a player may ask his partner "Shall I go out?" The partner addressed must answer "Yes" or "No" and the player is bound by the reply. But a player may go out without asking permission.

34. If the last card of the stock is drawn, no player having gone out, play continues so long as each successive player takes the discard. In this period a player is *forced* to take the discard if he can lay it off, and the exception noted in paragraph 24 does not apply; but the rule that a side must have at least one canasta to go out overrules all other considerations.

35. In the forcing period, as defined in the preceding paragraph, it is not compulsory to take the discard to meld a new set with cards from the hand.

36. If the last card of the stock is a red trey, the player drawing it may meld, but may not discard, and play ends after he has melded or declined to do so.

37. A player goes out with a concealed hand if he melds all his cards at one turn, having previously made no meld. He may not lay off a card. His melds must include at least one complete canasta, but he needs no minimum point value.

Scoring. 38. When play ends, each player or partnership determines its net score for the deal by taking all appropriate items of the following schedule:

(a)	For going out	100
(b)	For concealed hand	100
(c)	For each red trey (but see paragraph 39)	100
(d)	For each natural canasta	500
(e)	For each mixed canasta	300
(f)	Total values of all cards melded	. . .
(g)	Total	. . .
(h)	Total values of all cards remaining in the hand	. . .
(i)	Difference; net score, plus or minus	. . .

39. If no player goes out, item (a) is omitted. If one side gets all four of the red treys, item (c) becomes 200 each, or 800 altogether. If a side fails to make any meld at all, and the other side (or another player) goes out, the red treys of the losers count as minus instead of plus, and are therefore added to item (h) instead of item (g).

Irregularities. 40. *Deal out of turn.* If the wrong player deals the deal stands; but if attention is called to it in time, the first play is made by the player whose turn it would have been, and he deals next.

41. *New deal.* There must be a new deal by the same player if it is ascertained, before each player has had a turn to play, that a card is faced in dealing or found faced in the deck; or that the dealer departed in any respect from the rules of correct procedure in dealing; or that a player was dealt an incorrect number of cards. After this time limit, the deal and any incorrect hand stand as regular.

42. *Incorrect hand.* If a player has too many cards, he must rectify the error by discarding without drawing in each turn until his hand is correct. If a player discards without drawing, he may be required to take the top card of the stock if attention is called to the omission before the next player has drawn.

43. *Exposed cards.* If in partnership play a player exposes one or more cards from his hand, except to make a legal meld, all such cards must be left face up on the table and discarded in successive turns, except that the obligation to discard lapses for each such card that is included in a valid meld (including its use to take the discard pile). There is no penalty for card exposure in two-hand games.

44. *Insufficient count.* If for the initial meld of his side a player shows less than the required count, he must validate his meld if possible with additional cards. If he cannot do so, or does not do so before discarding, all the cards he has exposed from his hand are dealt with under paragraph 43. If he has incorrectly taken the discard, he must restore it to the pile before making his own discard from his exposed cards.

45. *Undeclared red trey.* If a player is dealt or draws a red trey, and fails to declare it before the play of the deal ends (provided he has had at least one turn to play), his side is penalized 500 points.

46. *Taking discard pile.* A player who takes the discard (with or without the rest of the pile) into his hand should be stopped at once and required to leave it on the table. But there is no penalty if he has already shown cards from his hand that entitle him to take the discard, or if the discard can be taken to add to a meld already on the table. Should any question arise as to his legal right to take the pile, through his taking it into his hand prematurely, the opponents may require him to replace the pile and instead draw from the stock, and they may decide what cards of his hand belong properly to the restored discard pile.

47. *Incorrect meld.* If a player makes a meld including more than three wild cards, or attempts to add a wild card to a meld already con-

taining three, he must if possible rectify the error by moving one or more wild cards to another meld already on the table, or by melding additional cards to which they can be moved. If he is unable to rectify the error, the surplus wild cards together with any additional cards improperly exposed are dealt with under paragraph 43.

48. *Asking permission.* If a player asks permission to go out, he must go out if his partner answers yes; and either opponent may require him to go out, or not to go out, if he shows or indicates any meld before receiving his partner's answer, or if the form of his question or of his partner's negative reply transmits any additional information.

49. *Illegal play.* If a player illegally mixes a discard with his hand, or melds when it is his partner's turn to play, paragraph 43 governs.

50. *Condonement.* There is no penalty for an irregularity if the next opponent in turn plays before attention is called to it; but cards illegally exposed, or an illegal meld that cannot be rectified, must be restored to the offender's hand. An insufficient meld stands as sufficient.

51. *Point penalties.* Additional to the penalties and rectifications prescribed in the foregoing paragraphs, the following point penalties may be deducted from the accumulated score of the offending side, but never affect the minimum initial meld it needs in the current deal:

For an illegal draw, 50; plus an additional 50 if the card has been added to the hand. A player who attempts to change his draw, or who touches the top discard and cannot legally take it, has made an illegal draw.

For drawing out of turn, 100; plus an additional 100 if the offender adds the card illegally drawn to his hand.

For inability to go out, when required to do so (paragraph 48), 100.

For melding out of turn, 100 if it was an opponent's turn; 200 if it was the offender's partner's turn.

Canasta customs. The following customs and terms apply to most Canasta games:

The partner who melds first keeps all the melds, and all the red treys, for his side. The other partner keeps score for his side.

Score is kept on a regular Bridge score pad, with "We" and "They" columns. After each hand is played, the score for that hand is entered, then the total of each side is written down.

When a game ends, each side reckons its total score to the nearest hundred, counting 50 or more points as 100. The winners then receive the difference between these net scores. Thus, if a side wins by 5,030 to 3,050, it wins the difference between 50 and 31, or 19 "points" net.

A complete canasta is shoved into a pile, with a red card on top if it is a natural canasta, a black card if it is a mixed canasta.

Three-Pack Canasta. Six play, in three partnerships of two each; each player sits between two opponents, one of each other team:

```
              B       C
      A                       A
              C       B
```

Three full packs and six jokers are shuffled together; back designs and colors need not be the same. Thirteen cards are dealt to each player. Game is 10,000, and when a side reaches 7,000 it needs 150 for its initial meld. Four red threes count only 100 each. Five red threes count 1,000; all six count 1,200. A side needs two canastas to go out. The rules otherwise are as in four-hand Canasta.

Two-Hand Canasta. When two play, each player draws two cards from the stock and discards only one. (A player who takes the discard pile may not also draw from the stock.) A player needs two canastas to go out.

POINTERS ON PLAY

The primary object is to amass big melds, NOT to go out. A player who makes small melds whenever possible, and who reduces his hand to six or fewer cards, is almost sure to lose.

When you need 50 for the initial meld, do not meld without taking the pack. When you need 90, expend no more than 4 cards from your hand for the initial meld; when you need 120, no more than 6 cards.

When an opponent makes an initial meld and the pack contains several cards, freeze the pack.

Do not wait for natural canastas. Pay no attention to the bonus for concealed hand.

Having made your initial meld, discard a black three if you have one, to increase partner's chance to take the pack.

Try to keep your score just under 1,500 or 3,000 instead of just above either figure, by withholding melds if necessary.

OTHER FORMS OF CANASTA
SAMBA

Samba follows the rules of Canasta except for the following:

Cards. Three decks of 52 cards each, plus six jokers, making 162 cards in all.

Deal. Each player receives 15 cards, regardless of the number of players.

Draw. A draw from the stock (instead of taking the discard pile) is two cards, but only one card is discarded to end the turn.

Sequence Meld. Three or more cards of the same suit and in sequence (ace high, fourspot low) are a valid meld. Such a meld may be increased by sequential cards up to a total of seven, when it becomes a *samba*, and is turned face down. No card may be added to a samba, and it may never contain a wild card. A samba ranks as a canasta for purpose of going out. The bonus for a samba is 1,500.

25

Wild Cards. Wild cards may be used only in melds of cards of the same rank, and no meld may ever contain more than two wild cards.

Adding to a Canasta. The discard pile may not be taken to add its top card to a completed canasta. Only natural (not wild) cards from the hand may be added to a canasta.

Duplicate Melds. A side may meld two or more sets of the same rank. Either partner in his turn may combine melds of like rank (to build toward a canasta).

Taking the Pack. The discard pile may be taken only (a) by melding its top card with a natural pair from the hand, or (b) when not frozen, by adding its top card to a meld on the table. (But note that a sequence meld may *not* be initiated by the top of the discard pile, plus cards from the hand; it must come wholly from the hand.)

Initial Meld. Requirements for initial meld—

Minus	15
0 to 1495	50
1500 to 2995	90
3000 to 6995	120
7000 or more	150

Game. Game is 10,000 points.

Going Out. A side must have at least two canastas to go out and also to count its red three plus. (A samba is a canasta.) The bonus for going out is 200. No bonus for "concealed hand."

Red Threes. If all six red threes are drawn by one side they count 1,000.

CHILE

Chile follows the rules of Canasta in general, but uses the three-deck Samba pack of 162 cards, and allows the Samba sequence meld.

URUGUAY

Uruguay follows the rules of Canasta except for the following:

Wild Cards. Three or more wild cards, up to seven, are a valid meld. A canasta of wild cards counts 2,000.

Taking the Pack. The discard pile may be taken only by matching its top card with a natural pair from the hand. (Or, as is commonly said, "the pack is always frozen.")

BOLIVIA

Bolivia follows the rules of Samba except for the following:

Wild Cards. From three to seven wild cards form a valid meld. A canasta of seven wild cards is a *bolivia,* counting 2,500.

Samba. The samba (seven cards in suit and sequence) is called an *escalera*.

Game. Game is 15,000. The initial meld requirement stays at 150 from 7,000 up.

Going Out. A side must have two canastas, including an escalera, to go out.

Red Threes. Red threes count plus for the side if it has completed two canastas of any description.

Black Threes. A black three left in the hand when any other player goes out counts 100 minus. A black three melded in going out counts only 5.

MEXICANA

Mexicana follows the rules of Canasta except for the following:

Cards. Three decks of 52 cards each, plus six jokers, making 162 cards in all.

Deal. Each player receives 13 cards.

Extra Draw. After a player makes his first meld, he immediately draws 13 extra cards from the stock. In partnership play, only the partner who makes the initial meld may make this draw.

Sevens. The discard pile may not be taken when topped by a seven. But sevens may be melded as usual, and a canasta of sevens counts 1,000.

Going Out. To go out, a side must have two canastas, plus as many red threes as it has canastas.

PENNIES FROM HEAVEN

There are many local variations called by this name. In general, they follow the rules of Canasta except as follows:

Players. Six, in two partnerships, partners sitting alternately.

Cards. Four decks of 52 cards, plus eight jokers, making 216 cards in all.

Deal. Each player receives 13 cards. A packet of 11 additional cards is dealt before him face down; he may pick up this packet only after he has completed his first canasta.

Sevens. No seven may be discarded until both sides have completed a canasta of sevens (which counts 1,500). No seven may be discarded in going out.

Red Threes. Each red three counts 100, but all eight red threes held by one side count 1,000.

Initial Meld. Requirements for initial meld—

Minus	15
0 to 495	50
500 to 995	90
1000 to 1495	120
1500 or more	150

Wild cards. Wild cards may be melded apart from natural cards, and a canasta of wild cards counts 1,000. But the discard pile may not be taken when topped by a wild card.

Going Out. To go out, a side must have at least four canastas—one of wild cards (1000), one of sevens (1500), one natural and one mixed in any ranks (800).

Game. Game is 20,000 points.

QUINELLA

Quinella follows the rules of Samba except for the following:

Cards. Four decks of 52 cards, plus four jokers, making 212 cards in all.

Deal. Each player receives 11 cards.

Sequences. A sequence of seven counts as a canasta, but is not closed—additional cards may be laid off on it, up to the total of eleven cards (ace to four).

Wild Cards. May be melded and built into canastas.

Discard Pile. May be taken to lay off the top card on a sequence already melded or on a group of wild cards, as well as with a natural or wild-card pair from hand to initiate a meld.

Going Out. A side must have two canastas to go out, but its red threes count plus after it has one canasta.

Initial Meld. Minimum requirement is 50 up to 3,000, then 90 up to 6,000, and 120 thereafter.

Scoring. A joker counts 30 (not 50). The bonus for a wild-card canasta is 2,000. A sequence canasta of less than 11 cards counts 2,000; of 11 cards, 3,000. As in Samba, game is 10,000.

(Note: Many different special rules are adopted in different localities.)

TAMPA

Tampa follows the rules of Samba except as follows:

Melds. Sequences may not be melded. But wild cards may be melded in groups apart from natural cards. A wild-card canasta counts 2,000.

Red Threes. A red three counts minus 200 against a side that has not melded when the other side goes out. Otherwise, a side with one to four red threes scores 100 plus for each, or 1,000 for five threes, or 1,200 for six.

Black Threes. A black three left in hand counts 200 minus, but counts only 5 when melded in going out.

Discard Pile. May be taken only by a natural pair (not wild) matching the top card. Thus it is always "frozen."

Initial Meld. Minimum requirement is 50 up to 3,000, then 90 up to 5,000, then 120 up to 7,000, and 150 thereafter. As in Samba, game is 10,000.

Going Out. To go out, a side must have two "red" canastas. Wild-card and natural (not mixed) canastas are "red."

HOLLYWOOD CANASTA

Hollywood Canasta follows the rules of Samba except as follows:

Wild Cards. May be melded in groups apart from natural cards. A canasta of wild cards counts 2,000.

Other Melds. Each group or sequence meld must commence with at least three natural cards. One wild card may be used in a sequence canasta, and two may be used in a group canasta. No canasta (group, sequence, or wild-card) may be extended beyond seven cards. A mixed sequence canasta counts 1,000, a pure sequence canasta, 1,500.

Discard Pile. When the top card is natural, the discard pile may be taken by a matching pair or by two cards in suit and sequence. When the top card is a two, it may be taken by a pair of twos; when it is a joker, by a pair of jokers. When the pile is not frozen, the top card may be taken to lay off on any minor meld (less than seven cards).

Red Threes. Count plus if the side has made initial meld.

CUT-THROAT CANASTA
for three players

All rules of Canasta apply except as modified by the following:

1. Three players participate, each receiving a hand of eleven cards.
2. In drawing from the stock, a player takes two cards and discards one.
3. Each player plays for himself ("cut-throat") until the discard pile is taken for the first time.
4. The player who first takes the discard pile becomes the LONE HAND. The other two join in partnership against the LONE HAND, combining their melds and otherwise aiding each other.
5. The initial meld requirement for a player depends on his own score.
6. A red three counts only for the owner, plus or minus depending upon whether his side has or has not made any meld. The base scores of two partners therefore differ if they have not drawn an equal number of red threes. All other scores made by a partnership are totaled, and each partner receives the total, plus or minus his own red threes.
7. If a player goes out before the discard pile has ever been taken, he becomes a LONE HAND and the other two score as a partnership.
8. A player who melds before the discard pile has been taken, without going out, does *not* thereby become a LONE HAND.
9. If no one goes out, play ends with the discard of the player who drew the last card of the stock. If the discard pile was never taken, each player scores for himself.
10. Game is 7,500.

⤙ CONTRACT RUMMY ⤚

In Contract Rummy, the specifications as to what a player must meld to go out restrict him much more than in other families. This specification is by no means standardized throughout the country; local groups write their own "contracts" as they please. Contract Rummy may be considered the generic name of the family; other associated names are Liverpool Rummy, Joker Rummy, Progressive Rummy, King Rummy. The family may stem from a game developed by Ruth Armson, called Zioncheck.

Number of players. 1. From three to eight may play, each for himself.

The pack. 2. When three or four play, shuffle together two regular packs of 52, plus one joker, making 105 cards. When five or more play, shuffle together three regular packs, plus two jokers, making 158 cards.

Rank of cards. 3. A (high or low), K, Q, J, 10, 9, 8, 7, 6, 5, 4, 3, 2, A (high or low).

Values of cards. 4. Each card has a point value, as follows: each ace, joker, and other wild cards if any, 15; each face card, 10; each other card, its index value.

Wild cards. 5. The joker is wild; it may be designated of any rank and suit to aid in filling a set. By prior agreement, the players may create additional wild cards, such as all the deuces. (It is usual to do so.)

The shuffle and cut. 6. In drawing for deal, ace ranks low and jokers are void. Low deals first. The dealer shuffles, but may be assisted by another player. The pack is cut by the player at dealer's right.

The deal. 7. A game comprises seven deals. The turn to deal rotates clockwise.

8. The dealer distributes cards one at a time face down, in clockwise rotation beginning with eldest hand (the player at his left). Each player receives: ten cards in each of Deals 1, 2, 3, 4; twelve cards in each of Deals 5, 6, 7.

9. The undealt remainder of the pack is placed face down to form the stock. The top card of the stock is turned face up beside it; this *upcard* starts the *discard pile*. The discard pile should be kept squared up and is not open to inspection.

Object of play. 10. The player strives to get rid of all his cards by melding them on the table. Cards may be melded in matched sets or laid off on any previous melds.

11. A matched set may be either of two kinds:

(a) *group,* comprising three or four cards of the same rank;

(b) *sequence,* three or more cards of the same suit in sequence. The ace, ranking high or low, may be used to form a sequence A-K-Q or 3-2-A. But sequences do not go "round the corner"; a set 2-A-K is not valid.

Basic contract. 12. For his first meld of a deal, a player must lay down the basic contract—two or more matched sets of specified kind—as follows:

> Deal 1: two groups
> Deal 2: one group and one sequence
> Deal 3: two sequences
> Deal 4: three groups
> Deal 5: two groups and one sequence
> Deal 6: one group and two sequences
> Deal 7: three sequences

13. In Deals 1 to 6 inclusive, each set of the basic contract is limited to three cards, no more. In Deal 7, all twelve cards must be matched, the whole hand being laid down at once. (*Alternative rule:* In Deal 1, six cards must be melded for the basic contract; in Deal 2, seven cards; and so on, increasing by one card each successive deal. When this method is followed, it is customary to make the length requirement of a sequence four cards.)

14. When two or more sequences are required, they may be in the same suit only if not connected. For example, ◇10-9-8 and ◇6-5-4 may be melded in Deal 3, but not ♣Q-J-10 and ♣9-8-7.

The play. 15. Eldest hand plays first, and thereafter the turn to play rotates clockwise. Each player must begin his turn with a draw and end it with a discard. After his draw but before the discard, he may, if willing and able, meld the basic contract or lay off additional cards on previous melds, his own or opponent's.

16. In drawing, the player may take the top card of the stock or the top card of the discard pile, as he pleases. If he does not want the discard, he must so indicate; each other player in rotation may then claim the discard. The first to claim it may take it; he then must take the top card of the stock also (as penalty for the play out of turn), but may not discard at that time. The turn then reverts to the rightful player, who draws the top of the stock in accordance with his stated intention.

17. In melding the basic contract, a player must lay down the required kind and number of sets, comprising no more than the specified number of cards. Thereafter he may meld no additional sets, but may lay off any number of cards in any subsequent turn. (*Alternative rule:* Additional sets may be melded, but in this case a player who goes out must make a final discard.) A sequence may be extended to fourteen cards, with an ace at each end.

18. All discards are placed face up in one pile, which should be kept squared up so that only the top card can be read.

19. When the joker is melded in a sequence, any player in turn (having melded the basic contract) may lay off the natural card which it represents and then take the joker in his hand, using it for any purpose he wishes. When any other wild card is melded in a sequence, it may be moved to either end (changing its rank but not suit) by a player who wishes to lay off the natural card it was stated to represent. But no wild card other than the joker, once melded, may be recaptured, and no wild card including the joker, melded in a group, may be moved or captured.

20. Play continues until some player goes out by getting rid of all his cards. If the stock is exhausted, the discard pile is turned over, without shuffling, to form a new stock.

Scoring. 21. When play of a deal ends, each player is charged with the total values of all cards remaining in his hand. The player having the lowest cumulative score after the seventh deal wins the game, and collects from each other player according to the differences of final totals.

Irregularities. [Paragraphs 21 to 42 on pages 3-5 apply, except for paragraph 40, which is replaced by the following.] 22. *Invalid meld.* If a player's first meld does not in every respect conform to the basic contract, he must restore the entire meld to his hand whenever the error is discovered, provided no part of his meld has been mixed for the next shuffle. Any card he has laid off remains on the table, but he may lay off no more cards until the turn after he has melded a correct basic contract.

Pointers on play. It is usually losing tactics to take the top discard out of turn, and a penalty card from the stock, in any deal—unless one's hand is largely composed of cards that can be laid off once the basic contract is down.

In the final deal it is especially unwise to take the top discard out of turn unless it is essential to a five-card sequence. For example, with ♡9-8-6-5 it would be proper to take ♡7.

Generally, the strategy of Basic Rummy (pages 9-10) is applicable to Contract Rummy.

CONTINENTAL RUM

In this game (and its variants) the group is eliminated as a valid set, only the sequence being allowed. Together with the rule that a player must meld his entire hand or nothing, this feature stamps Continental Rum as of the Contract Rummy family—the motif of which is to circumscribe narrowly the ways of going out.

Number of players. 1. From two to twelve may play. Best is six or more.

The pack. 2. Shuffle together two or more regular packs of 53 cards (the 52 cards plus a joker). With five or fewer players, use two packs; with six to eight players, three packs; nine to twelve players, four packs.

Rank of cards. 3. A (high or low), K, Q, J, 10, 9, 8, 7, 6, 5, 4, 3, 2, A (high or low).

Wild cards. Jokers are wild, together with any additional cards the players may agree upon (usually deuces). A wild card may be designated to be of any suit and rank, as the owner pleases.

The shuffle and cut. 4. Two or three players should coöperate in shuffling. The dealer has the right of final shuffle. He should take a batch of cards sufficient for the deal from the top of the pack, and have it cut by the player at his right.

The deal. 5. The dealer distributes cards in batches of three at a time face down, in clockwise rotation, beginning with eldest hand (the player at his left). Each player receives fifteen cards.

6. The undealt remainder of the pack is placed face down, forming the stock. The top card of the stock is turned face up beside it; this *upcard* starts the *discard pile*. The discard pile should be kept squared up and is not open to inspection.

7. The winner of a deal becomes the next dealer.

Object of play. 8. The player strives to form his entire hand into matched sets, so as to be able to lay it down and win the deal.

9. A valid matched set comprises three or more cards of the same suit in sequence. The ace may be used as high, in A-K-Q, or low, in 3-2-A. Two or more sequences in the same suit may be counted as separate sets, even though they connect. But there is no sequence "around-the-corner" as 2-A-K. [Groups of three or more of a kind do not count.]

The play. 10. Eldest hand plays first, and thereafter the turn to play rotates clockwise.

11. Each player must begin his turn with a draw and end it with a discard. After drawing but before discarding, he may lay down his whole hand and win the deal, provided every card is matched and the sets conform to paragraph 12.

12. To go out, the player must meld at least four sets, none of more than five cards, with no unmatched card. The consequence of this rule is that only three patterns are possible for a complete hand:

3-3-3-3-3
4-4-4-3
5-4-3-3

13. In drawing, the player may take the top card of the stock or the top card of the discard pile, as he pleases.

Scoring. 14. The winner of a deal collects from each other player: 1 chip for going out; 2 chips for each joker melded by the winner; 1 chip for each wild card other than jokers melded by the winner.

15. *Optional.* Besides the basic settlement of paragraph 14, many players agree on bonuses, such as:

To winner, for having drawn no card	10 chips per player
for having drawn only one card	7 chips per player
for melding no wild card	10 chips per player
(played only when there are wild cards additional to jokers)	
for all cards of same suit (which may include deuces of same suit, but no joker)	10 chips per player
To dealer, for lifting from the full pack exactly the number of cards needed to deal each player 15 cards	1 chip per player

Irregularities. [Paragraphs 21 to 42 on pages 3-5 apply, except for paragraph 40, which is replaced by the following.] 16. *Going down illegally.* If a player lays down a hand which does not conform to the requirements stated above, he must leave his hand face up on the table and play proceeds with his hand exposed. Any collections he has made are returned. Any other player who has exposed his hand may pick it up.

Pointers on play. In general the principles stated (pages 9-10) for basic Rummy are applicable to Continental Rum; keeping in mind that a combination can consist, in Continental Rum, only of two near cards of the same suit.

Best policy is to go out as soon as possible, and not play for extra bonuses; an exception may be found only when the special bonuses of paragraph 15 apply and a player has specifically two natural four- and two natural three-card sequences plus one deuce; in such case he may postpone going out in hope of catching a natural card to make up his hand. The player should know whether or not many of the cards that will fill his hand are already discarded and dead; if they are, he should go down.

Hold up for two or three rounds; any of eight cards will fill the hand for a bonus.	Go down—only the ◇7 will fill the hand for a bonus.

⟶ GIN RUMMY ⟵

The principal fad game, in the years 1941-46, of the United States, Gin Rummy (then called simply Gin) was devised in 1909 by Elwood T. Baker of Brooklyn, N. Y., a whist teacher; the name, suggested by Mr. Baker's son, played on the alcoholic affinity of rum and gin; the game was resurgent 1927-30, then dormant until 1940, then adopted by the motion-picture colony and the radio world, who gave it the publicity essential to a fad game. Gin Rummy is a two-hand game and is hardly worth playing, except by addicts, in any other form.

Number of players. 1. Two play. Three may participate in the same game, usually with one sitting out while the other two play. Four or more, in pairs up to almost any number, may play a partnership game, but this is done by playing separate two-hand games and combining scores.

The pack. 2. A regular pack of 52 cards. Two packs should be used, so that while one player deals the other shuffles for the next deal.

Rank of cards. 3. K (high), Q, J, 10, 9, 8, 7, 6, 5, 4, 3, 2, A.

Value of cards. 4. Face cards count 10 each; aces, 1; other cards their pip value.

The shuffle and cut. 5. One pack is shuffled and spread, and each player draws a card; if he draws one of the four cards at either end, he must draw again.

6. The player drawing the high card has choice of cards and seats, and whether or not he will deal first. If the cards drawn are otherwise of the same rank, the suits rank: spades (high), hearts, diamonds, clubs.

7. Either player may shuffle, the dealer having the right to shuffle last. Non-dealer must cut the pack.

The deal. 8. The dealer distributes the cards one at a time face down, alternately to his opponent and to himself until each has ten cards.

9. The undealt remainder of the pack is placed face down in the center of the table, becoming the *stock*. The top card of the stock is turned face up and placed beside it; this *upcard* starts the *discard pile*.

10. The winner of a hand deals the next hand. The winner of a game deals the first hand of the next game. He has choice of cards and seats.

Object of play. 11. To reduce one's count of deadwood to less than the count of the opponent, by forming matched sets consisting of three or four cards of the same rank or three or more cards of the same suit in sequence.

The play. 12. Non-dealer plays first, and the turn to play alternates thereafter.

13. In each turn, a player must draw either the upcard (top card of the discard pile) or the top card of the stock, and then must discard one card (which may not be an upcard he has drawn in the same turn) face up on the discard pile. It is optional with the players whether previous discards are open to inspection (see paragraph 43).

14. On the first play, if non-dealer does not wish to take the upcard he must so announce and dealer may have the first turn by drawing the upcard; if dealer does not wish the upcard, non-dealer draws the top card of the stock and play proceeds.

Knocking. 15. Each hand begins when a legal deal is completed and ends when either player knocks.

16. A player may knock in any turn, after drawing and before discarding, if the value of the unmatched cards in his hand (after he discards) will be 10 points or less. He need not knock when able to do so. Having knocked, he discards one card face down and spreads his hand, arranged into matched sets and unmatched cards. The opponent then spreads his hand, removes from it any unmatched sets, and lays off whatever cards he has that match the knocker's matched sets (but see paragraph 21).

17. The point values of the two players' unmatched cards are then compared, and the result of the hand is scored (see *Scoring,* below).

Drawn game. 18. Neither of the last two cards in the stock may be drawn; if the player who draws the fiftieth card discards without knocking, his opponent may not take the discard and the hand is a draw. The same dealer deals again.

Scoring. 19. If the knocker's count is less than his opponent's, the knocker wins the hand; the difference in counts is scored to his credit.

20. If the opponent ties or beats the knocker, he has undercut him; he wins the hand, and scores 25 points plus the difference in counts, if any, subject to paragraph 21.

21. If the knocker has a count of zero (has all ten of his cards matched in sets) he is *gin;* his opponent may not lay off and the knocker wins the hand even if the opponent also has a count of zero; and the knocker receives 25 points plus the difference in counts, if any.

22. A running total of each player's score is kept, with a line drawn under his score every time he wins a hand. [Example: A player wins the first hand by 11 points; he scores 11 and draws a line under it. The same player wins the next hand by 14 points; he writes down 25 and draws another line.]

Game. 23. The player first scoring 100 points or more wins the game. He adds to his score 100 points game bonus.

24. If the loser has not won a hand during that game, the winner adds an additional 100 points shutout bonus.

25. Each player then adds to his score 25 points for every hand he has won (called a *line* or *box* bonus).

26. The two players' total scores are then determined and the player with the higher score wins the difference between the two scores.

Irregularities. [Condensed, by permission, from the *Laws of Gin Rummy* by Walter L. Richard, C. E. Van Vleck and Lee Hazen.]

27. *New Deal.* A deal out of turn may be stopped at any time before the upcard is dealt; thereafter it stands as a correct deal.

28. There must be a new deal by the same dealer if it is found, before the completion of the deal, that the pack is imperfect or that a card is faced in the pack; or if a card is exposed in dealing, or if a player has looked at the face of a card.

29. Other occasions for a new deal are covered in laws governing other irregularities.

30. *Irregular hands.* If either player's hand is discovered to have an incorrect number of cards before that player has made his first draw, there must be a new deal.

31. After the first draw, if it is discovered that both players have incorrect hands, there must be a new deal. If one player's hand is incorrect and the other player's hand is correct, the player with the correct hand may decide either to have a new deal or to continue play. If play continues, the player with the incorrect hand must correct his hand by drawing without discarding, or by discarding without drawing, and may not knock until his next turn to play.

32. After a knock, a player with too few cards is charged 10 points for each card missing, and may not claim the undercut bonus; if the knocker's opponent has more than ten cards, the hand may not be corrected, the offender may not claim an undercut bonus, and can lose or tie but may not win the hand.

33. If the player who knocks has an incorrect number of cards, the penalty for an illegal knock applies.

34. *Imperfect pack.* When two packs are being used, a card from the other pack found in the stock is eliminated and play continues. If it is discovered, after the knock, that the pack is incomplete, the deal stands. Discovery that the pack is imperfect in any way has no bearing on any score that has been entered on the scoresheet.

35. *Premature play.* If non-dealer draws from the stock before dealer has refused the upcard, the draw stands without penalty as his first play. If a player draws from the stock before his opponent has discarded, the draw stands as his proper play.

36. *Illegally seeing a card.* If a player drawing in turn sees any card to which he is not entitled, every such card must be placed face up next to the discard pile. The offender may not knock until his next turn to play, unless he is gin. The non-offender has the sole right to take any of the exposed cards until first thereafter he draws from the stock; then

the offender has the same right until first thereafter he draws from the stock; when each player has drawn from the stock, the exposed cards are placed in the discard pile.

37. If a player drawing out of turn sees a card to which he is not entitled, the rule given in the preceding paragraph applies, except that the offender may never take such cards, but may draw only his opponent's discard or the top card of the stock in each turn.

38. *Exposed card.* A card found exposed in the stock, or in the other pack or away from the table, is shuffled into the stock and play continues. Accidental exposure of a card in a player's hand is not subject to penalty. An exposed card becomes a discard when the holder indicates intent to discard it; when his opponent has seen and can name such a card, the holder may not thereafter knock in that turn.

39. *Illegal knock.* If a player knocks with a count higher than 10, but his opponent has not exposed any cards before the error is discovered, the offender must leave his hand face up on the table until his opponent has completed his next play. However, if the knocker's hand is illegal only with respect to the count of his unmatched cards, his opponent may accept the illegal knock as legal.

40. If the knocker has more than 10 points, and the error is discovered after the opponent has exposed any of his own cards but before he has laid off any cards, the opponent may choose which of the following penalties to apply: To make the knocker play the rest of the hand with all his cards exposed; or to permit the offender to pick up his hand, in which event the offender may not score for any undercut or gin bonus in that hand.

41. If the knocker has an incorrect number of cards, his opponent may demand a new deal; or may require the offender to play with his hand exposed and to correct his hand on his next play or plays, either by drawing without discarding or by discarding without drawing.

42. If a player, after knocking, inadvertently discards a card which makes his knock illegal, he may replace that discard with a discard which makes his knock legal.

43. *Looking back at discards.* Players may agree in advance that looking back at discards will be permitted. In the absence of such agreement, a player who looks back at a covered discard loses his right to his next draw.

44. *Picking up wrong discards.* If a player inadvertently picks up the wrong discard, he may correct or he may be made to correct the error, if attention is called to it prior to his opponent's next discard.

POINTERS ON GIN RUMMY

A hand of Gin Rummy comes to an end, on average, after seven to ten draws. Winning policy is to knock as soon as possible. The only exception is that a player may be forced to wait for a lower count, or to refrain from knocking at all, when he may be undercut. But the player should be

deterred only by positive evidence that such is the case; vague appre-
hension or timidity can cost many points. Knocking at the earliest opportunity, even regardless of undercut hazards, will win much more than
waiting "a few more draws" to reduce the count or to try for gin.

Particularly foolish is waiting in the hope of getting a gin hand. The
occasional gin bonus so earned is worth far less than the points lost by
giving the opponent opportunity to reduce, or to knock first with a lower
count. The only occasion to wait deliberately for gin is an end-situation
where is it crystal clear that any lesser hand will be undercut.

The normal policy in discarding is to aim for a hand of two matched
sets, with four or less unmatched cards. For example, suppose that the
hand after a draw from the stock is:

To discard the deuce or ace, in order
to hold all the combinations, would
be poor policy. It would aim toward
a three-set hand, that is, the hand
would have to complete two additional sets to be able to knock. The
right discard is from the diamond
combination or the eights. The hand
will then be able to knock after filling only one additional set, by obtaining two additional cards that
total seven or less.

Because of the two-set target, the player must collect some low cards
—fourspot or lower. When such cards chance to be drawn, they should
be saved, except possibly in the rare cases where the player is forced
to aim for three matched sets. Even then, it is risky business letting the
opponent have an ace or deuce, especially after six or more draws.
Whether to pick up a low discard, merely because it is low, depends on
circumstance. Obviously the play is indicated when the hand already
has two matched sets. As a general rule, drawing from the stock is preferable when the hand needs to fill a set; yet many good players make it
a rule never to pass by the upcard if it is an ace or deuce. The idea in
this policy is that to the value of the low card in one's own hand is added
the value of keeping it out of the opponent's hand.

COMBINATIONS

The normal rule is to take the discard only to complete a set, never to
make a mere *combination*. (A combination is a pair of the same rank, or

two cards of a suit in sequence or skip-sequence.) Some exceptions arise: One has been noted above, the possible seizure of the upcard when it is an ace or deuce.

Another example is as follows. The non-dealer holds the hand shown. The upcard is the ♡8. The player may well take it and discard the ♡K. The argument here is: the hand is very poor in combinations; the ♡8 will improve it greatly with a *double* combination; the ♡K is a relatively safe blind discard; the non-dealer is due to make a blind discard anyhow. Every one of these conditions is necessary to justify taking the upcard. If, for example, the hand were held by the dealer and if the upcard were refused by the non-dealer, the dealer should not take it. With a poor hand, a player should aim primarily to avoid making dangerous discards, and the dealer should here let his opponent make the first discard, as a guide to his own play.

The question of what to discard usually narrows to a few cards. The player should save combinations (but not at the cost of letting go equally vital low cards), together with what low cards he needs for a two-set knock. Yet there is a good deal of art in choosing discards from two or three candidates. At the beginning of a deal, a few discards are perforce "blind." Thereafter, there is some clue to what cards are safe and what are not. The (relatively) safe discards are those of same rank, or in sequence, with cards already discarded or refused by the opponent. Also, a card of adjacent rank and different suit with the opponent's discard is fairly safe. Kings are safer than lower cards, as blind discards, since they can be used in only one possible sequence.

All possible inferences should be made as to what the opponent holds. When he takes a discard, the normal assumption is that he has filled a set. The cards that are dead or are in one's own hand may help to show whether the set is three of a kind or a sequence. The discards that the opponent does not take also show by elimination what he does not hold. One of the significant pointers is the non-appearance of any cards of a given high rank. The early discarding by both players is often a stream of face cards; when no jacks, say, have appeared within six draws, the player without jacks may infer that his opponent holds a pair. If the game goes to as many as a dozen draws, each player can infer precisely what the other holds.

Two constant purposes are served by all these inferences. First, the player wants to avoid "feeding" his opponent, and also to save cards that are "players" on the opponent's sets. Second, the player wants to know how near his opponent is to knocking. If, for example, the opponent has picked up two discards, the presumption is that he has filled two sets and needs only some low off cards to knock. The indicated policy is to ditch high combinations, both to "unload" and to avoid giving him a low card.

ILLUSTRATION OF GIN RUMMY SCORING

YOU	HE
13	49
30	50
55	
87	
118	
118	
75	
100	
293	
50	
243	

First hand. YOU knock with 6. HE has 19. You score 13.

Second hand. HE goes gin—knocks with 0. You have 24. He scores the 24 + 25 points gin bonus, 49 in all.

Third hand. HE knocks with 8. You have 9. He scores 1, giving him a total of 50.

Fourth hand. YOU knock with 10. HE has 27. You win 17 and your new total is 30.

Fifth hand. HE knocks with 4. YOU also have 4. You score 25, the undercut bonus. Now your score is 55.

Sixth hand. YOU knock with 7. HE has 39. You win 32 and your new total is 87.

Seventh hand. YOU go gin. HE has 6, so you score 6 + 25, adding 31 to your score, putting you over the 100 mark with a total of 118, and giving you game. You have five boxes, a total of 125 points at 25 each; he has two boxes, worth 50 to him; so you write down 75 more points for boxes. You add 100 for winning the game. Your grand total is 293; his is 50. So your winnings for the game are the difference in scores, or 243 points net.

VARIATIONS IN GIN RUMMY RULES

Many people play that after ten cards have been dealt to each player, the next card is not turned up but is merely dealt face down to the non-dealer, giving him an eleventh card in his hand. He makes the first discard to begin play.

Many people play that the opponent may lay off on gin; but even though he lays off enough to reduce his own count to zero, the knocker gets the gin bonus and wins the hand.

There are numerous variations in scoring. Some give only a 20-point bonus for gin, a 20-point bonus for each box, and a 10-point bonus for undercut. There are other scoring variations played in certain localities. However, in this book the bonus is 25 points in each case.

Many people play that the deal alternates, regardless of who wins each hand.

Some permit the ace to be either high or low in sequences (A-K-Q as well as A-2-3); but do not go as far in this respect as Round-the-Corner Gin, described later in this book.

There are countless other minor variations, most of which are not widely enough played to warrant description here.

SIMULTANEOUS GAMES

Hollywood Gin. One of the most popular forms of the game is for two players to play three games simultaneously.

The scoresheet is laid out with three double columns, one for each game. The first hand won by a player is entered only in Game 1; the second hand he wins is entered in Games 1 and 2; the third hand he wins, and all subsequent wins, are credited to him in Games 1, 2 and 3.

When either player reaches 100 or more points in any game, that game is ended and no more scores are applied to it, but scoring goes on in the other two games. So, if one player wins a shutout game, meaning that in Game 1 he reaches 100 before his opponent has scored, then the opponent's first score will apply to Game 2, since Game 1 is now closed.

Bonuses for undercut, gin, game, and shutout are awarded in the usual manner. Play continues until all three games have been completed.

GAME 1		GAME 2		GAME 3	
YOU	HE	YOU	HE	YOU	HE
17	26	8			
25					

Illustration of scoring: YOU win the first hand, scoring 17. This is entered to your credit in Game 1. YOU win the second hand, scoring 8. Now you have a score of 25 in Game 1 and a score of 8 in Game 2. HE wins the third hand, scoring 26. HE scores this in Game 1, so the score in that game is now 26 to 25 in his favor, but he scores nothing in Game 2, since this is the first hand he has won.

Continuous Games. Instead of playing three games at once, as in Hollywood Gin, some players like to play an unlimited series of games. When Game 1 is finished, Game 4 is begun automatically, and now each score still applies to three games. Thus, the winning score that ends Game 1 is the first score in Game 4; the winning score that ends Game 2 is the first score in Game 5, etc.

Some players go even further and make every winning score begin a new game if the player who wins that hand is already entitled to score in every game in progress. In this method, if a player happens to win a series of six or seven hands, but by margins that do not put him over the 100 mark in any game, there may be six or seven separate games in progress at the same time. This is unusual, of course, but when it does happen the scoresheet is likely to stretch out too far for one scorepad or sheet of paper.

When playing continuous games, any player may announce, just before a new hand is dealt, that he chooses to end the series. In this case all games in progress are ended but no new games are begun.

The basic principle of scoring in continuous games is this: Each winning score entitles a player to score in one game more than he did with his previous winning score.

PARTNERSHIP GIN RUMMY

Four or more players, in even numbers, may play partnership games.

When four play, all four draw cards from a spread deck and the two low play as partners against the two high (unless the partnerships were prearranged). Partners sit opposite each other, as they would in bridge, and each plays the first hand against the opponent at his right. Regular two-handed gin is played, the only difference being that game is not won until a side reaches a score of 125. The bonus for game remains 100.

After both hands have been finished, the partnership scores are combined and the side with the net plus score makes the only score for that hand. For example: Players A and B form a partnership against players C and D. A plays the first hand against C and wins by 16. B, playing against D, loses by 12. A and B together have a net plus of 4; on the scoresheet they score 4 points for the hand and will eventually get the box bonus for winning that hand.

If one hand results in a drawn score, it is not replayed; the result of the other hand will determine the score.

After both partners have completed the first hand, each turns and plays against the opponent at his left; after that hand, he plays again against the opponent at his right; and so on.

When one hand has been finished, the players announce the result to their partners. (This is very important, for the strategy of partnership play consists largely in trying to win every hand, no matter how narrow the margin, and collect the box bonus. If one partner has already won by 32, for instance, the other partner may risk a very doubtful knock and the danger of being undercut if he is quite sure his partner's score will still give his side an advantage and win the hand.)

A player who has finished may watch his partner. He may not advise him, except that if his partner's opponent knocks, he may call attention to the various ways of arranging his hand, what cards may be laid off, and any irregularity in knocking committed by the opponent.

When six play, there are three members on a team; when eight play, four members on a team, etc. In these cases, it is customary for all partners to sit on the same side of a long table. Each plays against the opponent opposite him, and does not change opponents throughout the game. Game is usually set at 150 for six players, 175 or 200 for eight players, 200 for ten players. In all cases the other scoring rules of two-handed play apply, including 100 as the game bonus. The other rules are the same as in four-handed play.

Simultaneous games (described in preceding pages) may be scored in partnership play.

GIN RUMMY FOR THREE PLAYERS

There are three popular ways by which three persons may play Gin Rummy. In two of these ways, only two play at a time, the third sitting out. In the other way, all three play at once.

Chouette. This method will be familiar to Backgammon players. All three players cut; high is "in the box"; next-highest is "captain" and plays two-handed against the man in the box; low sits out but scores along with the captain. The captain deals the first hand. When the captain wins a hand, he plays the next; when he loses a hand, he becomes the idle player and his partner becomes the captain. The man in the box plays through the entire game. When the game ends, he settles the total score with each of his opponents. If he has won the game, he remains in the box. If he has lost the game, the captain of the last hand becomes the man in the box; the idle player becomes the captain for the first deal of the next game.

The idle player may watch the captain and advise him on all plays, but in case of disagreement the captain has the final word.

Cutthroat. An individual score is kept for each player, but only two play at a time, following regular two-handed rules. The players drawing the two highest cards play the first hand, the lower of these two cards dealing first. After the first hand, the loser sits out while the other two play; if a hand ends in a draw, the player with the lower count stays in (but scores nothing) and if their counts are the same they cut cards to see who stays in.

At the end of each hand, the winning player scores in his column on the scoresheet, and the game ends when any player's score reaches 100. Each player's score is then calculated separately for box bonuses. The winning player adds 100 to his score for game bonus. Each player then settles with each other on the difference between their total scores. If any player has failed to score at all in that game, the winning player collects double from him for shutout.

The idle player may watch but may not at any time advise either of the active players.

Battle Royal. Each player receives ten cards, and in each turn may draw either of the two previous discards (unless one of them was taken by the opponent at his left, in which case he may draw only the card just discarded). At the start, if the player at the dealer's left refuses the upcard, the next player has a chance at it, and then the dealer if it is again refused.

An individual score is kept for each player, and each of his winning hands is scored in his column. Only one score may result from each hand. The game ends when a player reaches 200 points, but the bonus for winning the game remains 100.

When a player knocks, the player at his left puts down his matched sets and lays off on the knocker's hand, then announces the count of his unmatched cards but does not show them. The third player may now lay off on the hand of the knocker in its present form (for example, the knocker puts down ♡Q-J-10; the next player added ♡9; the third player may lay off ♡8). If the knocker has a lower count than either opponent, he wins the total of their unmatched cards.

If the second player undercuts the knocker, the third player may lay off on both opposing hands. If this enables the third player to undercut (tie or beat) the second player, that player may now lay off on the third player's hand (but may not lay off any more cards on the knocker's hand).

If the second player did not undercut the knocker, but the third player does, the second player may now lay off on the third player's hand; and this privilege continues so long as any player may undercut (tie or beat) his opponent. The knocker, of course, may never lay off a card.

The last player to undercut wins a 25-point undercut bonus plus the total of all unmatched cards in the other two players' hands.

If the knocker goes gin, he wins a 50-point bonus plus the total of his opponents' unmatched cards, and no laying off is permitted. If either opponent has not scored at all when the game ends, the winner collects double from him.

ROUND-THE-CORNER-GIN

The ace is either high or low in rank, and the ranking of cards is continuous, so that the ace may be used in the sequence K-A-2 (and the sequence extended, in either direction, as far as you wish). If you are stuck with an ace in your hand, it counts 15 points.

A player who goes gin receives a 20-point bonus. The opponent, however, may lay off on a gin hand, and if by so doing he reduces his own count to 0 he gets an undercut bonus of 20 points. This offsets the gin bonus and neither player scores for that hand.

A two-handed game ends when either player reaches 125; a four-handed game ends when either player reaches 150. Bonus for game is 100 in all cases.

The discards are open to inspection.

OKLAHOMA GIN

This game should not be confused with the game of "Oklahoma," which is a different type of game. In Oklahoma Gin, the rules are the same as in regular Gin Rummy except that the upcard determines how many points you will need to knock. If it is a face card or a ten, you need ten points as usual; but if it is, for example, a six, you may not knock unless your count is 6 or less; if it is an ace, you need a count of 1, or to go gin. (As some play, when the upcard is an ace you must go gin. You may not knock with any unmatched card.)

Many players score the hand double when the upcard is a spade. That is, the net score—including gin or undercut bonus—is doubled. The box bonus is not affected.

OPEN GIN, or DOUBLING GIN

In any turn, before he draws, a player may say, "I double." His opponent may say "I refuse," in which case the hand is over and the doubler wins—how much, will be explained later. Or the opponent may say "I accept" and then play continues normally; but when the hand ends, the score, whatever it is, will be multiplied by two.

When one player has already doubled, the sole right to double passes to his opponent. A second double, if accepted, would make the ultimate score worth four times its normal value.

Many players limit the doubling principle to one double and one redouble, to keep the score from increasing beyond all reason. Other players, who have more of the gambling instinct, let them run on without limit, so that the final score may be multiplied by eight, sixteen, thirty-two or even more. Players should decide (in advance) according to their own preference. But the basic rule is always this: The sole right to double lies with the player who did not double last.

The most convenient way to keep track of doubles is with a "doubling cube" of the type used in Backgammon. Doubling cubes look like big dice, but their faces are marked with the numbers 2, 4, 8, 16, 32 and 64. The face turned up shows the number by which the final score is to be multiplied.

After a player has doubled, the procedure is as follows:

If the double is refused, the doubler must immediately knock (without drawing). It does not matter what his unmatched count is; he may even have a hand without a matched set! Nevertheless he knocks and announces his unmatched count.

Now the opponent, who resigned, shows his matched and unmatched cards, with the privilege of laying off as usual. The doubler wins a 10-point bonus plus the difference in counts if his count is lower. If his count is not lower he still gets the 10-point bonus and wins the hand. For example: You double, your opponent resigns. You knock and have a count of 36. Your opponent has a count of 31. You score 10 points.

Another example: You double, your opponent resigns. Your count is 12, his is 26. You win the difference, 14, plus 10, a total of 24. But when a double is refused, you may not score a gin bonus.

If the game had previously been doubled once, and then your opponent refuses a redouble, your score including the 10-point bonus will be multiplied by two, since the game had already been doubled. In other words, an accepted double applies to any score from that time on.

If the double is accepted, the doubler draws as usual. Then he may either knock or not, as he pleases; but of course he may not knock unless his count is 10 or less. The basic principle here is that a double accepted does not affect the rules in any way but one: The final score will be precisely twice as much as it would have been without the double and acceptance.

When Doubling Gin is played, the game does not end until a player reaches 200. A double never affects anything but the score for that particular hand. It does not double the box bonus, and it does not increase the bonus for winning the game, the score for a shutout game, or the score for any hand played previously. But it does double the bonus for gin or undercut, since those are part of the score of the immediate hand.

Your use of doubles should not affect any other rules of the game you prefer to play. You may play simultaneous games, partnership, or any variation you prefer. In simultaneous games, however, this rule is necessary: The double affects only those games in which both players are entitled to score. Suppose Player A has won two hands. Player B has won only one. Therefore Player A is entitled to score in all three games, while Player B is entitled to score only in Games 1 and 2. Player A doubles, Player B resigns. Player A's count is 14, Player B's count is 31. In Games 1 and 2, Player A scores 17 + 10, or 27 in each game; but in Game 3 he scores only 17, the difference in counts. If Player B had had the lower count, Player A would have scored 10 each in Games 1 and 2, and there would have been no score in Game 3.

CAROUSEL

Two or more may play Carousel. When two play, a single deck of cards plus a joker is used. When three or more play, two decks plus two jokers are used, shuffled together. Jokers are wild, and a joker left in the hand counts 25. Other cards count as in Gin Rummy. Melds are as in Gin Rummy; in the two-deck game, three or four of a kind may not include duplicate cards.

There is no discarding. Each player is dealt ten cards and the player at the dealer's left has first play. In each turn, a player must draw from the stock; then must meld one or more cards. If he cannot (or does not wish to) meld, he must draw up to three more cards from the stock. After drawing any card, he may meld. After he melds, or after he has drawn his third additional card, the turn passes to his left.

A player may break up any meld on the table to create plays for his own cards, provided he leaves only legal melds on the table. Thus, from ◇8-7-6-5 he may draw the eight or five to form three of a kind with cards from his hand; or he may draw a five from that meld, and a five from another meld, to combine with one five from his hand; etc. But he could not draw a five from ◇7-6-5, for that would leave ◇7-6, which is not a meld.

In any turn, but before drawing, a player may knock if his unmatched count is 10 or less. All players then show their hands and the player with the lowest unmatched count is the winner, collecting the counts of all other players. If the knocker is not the winner he pays an additional 10 points. If two or more players tie for low, they divide the winnings. There is no laying off.

The bonus for going gin (all cards matched) is 25 points, scored only by the player who knocks. Game ends when one player reaches 150, and the bonus for game is 100. A player who is shut out pays double.

TUNK

Two to five play Tunk. Two or three players use a single deck; four or five players use a double deck. Deuces are wild. Melds are as in Gin Rummy, but a meld of three or four of a kind may not include duplicate cards; nor may a deuce be added to four of a kind.

Seven cards are dealt to each player and the next card turned to start the discard pile. Only the player at dealer's left, whose turn comes first, may take this upcard.

Play proceeds as in any Rummy game—draw, meld if you wish, discard. A player in turn, but without drawing, may knock ("tunk") if his unmatched count is 5 or less. He then puts his hand down as in Gin Rummy. Each other player then has one more turn to draw, meld and lay off on the tunker's hand (but not on any other hand), and discard. There is no laying off on the tunker's hand if all his cards are matched.

When there are not enough cards left in the stock to give each player a draw after a tunk, the hand is redealt and there is no score.

After a player has tunked and each other player has had his turn, the unmatched count of each player is charged against him on the scoresheet. When a player's count reaches 100, he is out of the game and the others continue play until only one—the winner—has failed to reach 100.

KNOCK RUMMY

Knock Rummy, also called Poker Rum, is the fastest-moving of all Rummy variants. A player may go down whenever he pleases; the object in forming sets is merely to reduce the deadwood charged against him. From this game was developed Gin Rummy, which is essentially the same with the limitation that the deadwood must be reduced to 10 or less.

Number of players. 1. From two to six may play. Best for two to five.

The pack. 2. A regular pack of 52 cards.

Rank of cards. 3. K (high), Q, J, 10, 9, 8, 7, 6, 5, 4, 3, 2, A.

Values of cards. 4. Face cards count 10 each; aces, 1; all other cards their index value.

The draw. 5. Each player lifts a packet of not less than four cards from a stacked pack and shows the bottom card. Low deals. Ties for low cut again, the suits having no relative ranking.

The shuffle and cut. 6. The dealer shuffles the pack and the player at his right cuts it.

The deal. 7. The dealer distributes cards one at a time face down, in clockwise rotation, beginning with eldest hand (player at his left). Each player receives: ten cards, when two play; seven cards, when three or four play; six cards, when five or more play.

8. The undealt remainder of the pack is placed face down in the center of the table, becoming the *stock*. The top card of the stock is turned face up and placed beside it; this *upcard* starts the *discard pile*.

9. When two play, the winner of a hand deals the next. When more than two play, the turn to deal rotates clockwise.

Object of play. 10. The object is to knock with a lower amount of deadwood than all other players. The deadwood is the total of cards not included in matched sets.

11. A matched set may comprise either: three or four cards of the same rank; or three or more cards of the same suit in sequence.

The play. 12. Eldest hand plays first, and thereafter the turn to play rotates clockwise. Each player must begin his turn with a draw and end it with a discard.

13. In drawing, the player may take the top card of the stock or the top card of the discard pile, as he pleases. He must end his turn by discarding one card, all discards being placed face up in one pile. The discard pile should be kept squared up and is not open to inspection.

14. After drawing and before discarding, a player may knock regardless of the contents of his hand. To knock is to lay the whole hand face up on the table, then discard one card, ending the play.

15. If the player who draws the last card of the stock discards without knocking, the deal is abandoned without score and the player at the left of the previous dealer deals next.

Scoring. 16. When any player knocks, each player lays down his hand arranged in matched sets as he pleases, and announces the total of his deadwood. The hand with lowest count wins the difference of the counts from each other player. If any other player ties the knocker, he wins instead of the knocker. If the knocker does not at least tie for lowest count, he pays a penalty of 10 points to the lowest hand (besides the settlement on difference of counts).

17. If the knocker goes rum, having no deadwood, he receives an additional 25 points from each other player, even from a player who also has a rum hand.

Irregularities. Paragraphs 21 to 39 on pages 3-5 govern all irregularities.

Pointers on play. The count of deadwood on which it is profitable to knock varies with the number of players in the game and how many turns they have had to draw.

Against one opponent, it is wise to knock if dealt any count of 50 or less. With two or three opponents, it is unwise to knock on the first turn with a count of more than 35. With four or five opponents, the minimum should be 25.

For each round of play (one draw by each player) these minimums should be reduced by 10 points in two-hand play; by 5 points in larger games; with the proviso that 10 points are enough for a knock at almost any stage of a two-hand game (but see Gin Rummy, page 34).

KALUKI

This is the same as basic Rummy, except as follows:

Two full packs are shuffled together, with four jokers, making 108 cards. Ace ranks either high or low, so that A-K-Q and 3-2-A are valid sequences but 2-A-K is not. Each player is dealt fifteen cards.

A player's first meld must comprise cards totaling 51 or more. Aces count 15, face cards 10, other cards their index value. Jokers are wild, and when melded count the same as the cards they are designated to represent. A joker in the hand counts 25.

A player may not draw the discard nor lay off until after he has made his initial meld, except that he may take the discard if he makes a correct meld in that turn. A melded joker may be captured ("traded") by any player in exchange for the natural card it represents.

The player who goes out scores all the points remaining in the other hands.

Pointers on play. More than half the time, a player finds enough in his original hand to make an initial meld of 51 or more. The meld should be made at once, so that the player can draw from the discard pile when he wishes. The great opportunities for melding, enhanced by laying off on the initial melds (two or three sets each), give strong chance to go out within a few rounds. With four or more players, it is a fact that some hands go out usually within six rounds. Consequently there can be no thought of holding up melds to avoid letting other players lay off on them. The chances are too great of being caught. Even jokers can rarely be hoarded with safety.

PANGUINGUE

Panguingue, called "Pan" for short, grew out of Conquian. It is the chief card game in many gambling clubs of the Pacific Coast and the southwestern United States.

Definitions. 1. The following terms are defined as used in Panguingue.

CONDITIONS. Certain melds for which the owner collects chips immediately.

BORROWING. Taking extra cards from one's previous melds to complete new melds.

FOOT. The bottom portion of the pack, set aside until needed.

FORCING. Making legal demand that a player pick up and meld the top card of the discard pile.

HEAD. The top portion of the pack, from which the hands are dealt and cards are drawn during the play.

NON-COMOQUERS. Aces and kings, so called from their special privilege in forming groups.

ROPE. A sequence.

SPREAD. A meld.

STRINGER. A sequence.

TOP, GOING ON. Paying a forfeit to drop out of a deal.

VALLE CARDS. Threes, fives, and sevens.

Number of players. 2. Any number up to about fifteen may play. In clubs, the usual limit is eight per table. For social play, six or seven make the best game.

The pack. 3. From five to eight regular packs, from which all eights, nines and tens have been discarded. The standard number of packs is eight, but in some places fewer are used.

Rank of cards. 4. The cards in each suit rank: K (high), Q, J, 7, 6, 5, 4, 3, 2, A. The jack and seven are in sequence.

The draw. 5. A portion of the pack is shuffled and spread face down. Each player draws a card. Lowest card is eldest hand for that deal (first to receive cards), and second-lowest becomes the first dealer. Players drawing equal cards, in contest for these two positions, must draw again.

6. Eldest hand chooses his seat, and the first dealer takes the place at his left. The other players may take places as they please.

Rotation. 7. The rotation of dealing and play is to the right, or counter-clockwise (not to the left, as is usual in most games). The winner of each deal becomes eldest hand for the next, and the player at his left deals.

The shuffle. 8. At the commencement of play, and occasionally thereafter, all eight packs should be shuffled together in convenient batches. Two or more players should assist in this shuffling. At other times, the duty of shuffling falls upon the player at dealer's left. He shuffles the cards used in the previous deal with a batch from the foot, leaving the head of the pack intact.

47

The deal. 9. The dealer distributes ten cards to each player, in batches of five cards at a time, beginning with eldest hand and continuing in rotation to the right. He then cuts the undealt stock into two parts. The head (top portion) is placed in the center of the table; the foot (bottom portion) is set aside, to be drawn upon should the head be exhausted.

10. The top card of the head is turned face up beside it to start the discard pile.

Dropping. 11. All settlements are made with chips. Immediately after the deal, each player in turn beginning with eldest hand declares whether he will play in the deal or drop. If he drops, he pays a forfeit of two chips. (Dropping is often called *going on top,* for the reason that the forfeits are by custom piled on the foot of the pack.) The forfeits go to the player who wins the deal (by going out).

12. The hands of players who drop are not returned to the stock, but are kept separate so that the cards will not get into play during that deal. By custom, such hands are placed crosswise under the foot of the pack.

Object of play. 13. The object is twofold: (a) to win chips by melding certain groups of cards called conditions; (b) to go out by melding all the cards in the hand.

Melds. 14. The two types of melds are sequences and groups. A sequence is three or more cards of the same suit, adjacent in rank, as ♡ J 7 6. A group is three or more cards of the same rank, subject to the provisions of paragraph 15.

15. Aces and kings (called non-comoquers) may be melded in groups regardless of suits. [For example, ◇A ◇A ♤A is a valid meld.] In all other ranks, however, the basic three cards of a meld must be either (a) all of the same suit, or (b) of three different suits. [For example, ♡J ♡J ♡J and ♡J ♤J ◇J are valid melds, but ♡J ♡J ◇J is not.]

Conditions. 16. Threes, fives, and sevens are valle cards; all other ranks are non-valle.

17. Certain types of melds are called conditions. On melding a condition, a player immediately collects chips from every active player, as follows:

    (a) A group of valle cards of different suits—1 chip.

    (b) A group of valle cards of the same suit—4 chips in spades, 2 chips in any other suit.

    (c) A group of non-valle cards of the same suit—2 chips in spades, 1 chip in any other suit.

    (d) A sequence A, 2, 3 or K, Q, J—2 chips in spades, 1 chip in any other suit.

Laying off. 18. A player may add cards to his own melds (never to those of another player) provided that he preserves the character of the original meld. A group in the same suit may be increased only by other cards of the same rank and suit. A group of three in different suits may be increased by cards of the same rank and of any suits whatsoever. [For example, though ♡J ♡J ♤J is not a valid meld, ♡J ♡J ♤J ◇J is correct, for it contains three different suits, and the extra ♡J can in effect be laid off on this basic group at the same time that it is melded.]

19. A player may borrow cards from his own melds of four or more, to make new melds, and may rearrange his melds with new cards from the hand to make additional melds, always provided that the resultant melds are valid. [For example, from ♤ J 7 6 5, either the jack or the five may be borrowed to complete a group. From ◇4 ◇4 ♧4 ♡4, a four of diamonds may be borrowed to complete a sequence. Having melded ♤ Q J 7, a player may later add ♤ K J 6 and rearrange the cards to make ♤ K Q J and ♤ J 7 6.]

20. For each extra card added to a condition, a player collects again the value of the condition, except that in case of type (b), a group of valle cards of the same suit, he collects only 2 chips in spades, 1 chip in any other suit.

21. If by rearranging his melds with added cards, a player makes a condition where there was none before, he collects for the condition. (Such a case is given at the end of paragraph 19.)

The play. 22. Each player in turn, beginning with eldest hand, draws one card, either the top of the discard pile or the top of the head of the pack. He then melds, if he can and will; he may not take the discard at all except to meld it. He then discards the card drawn, or a card from his hand. Before discarding he may meld any number of cards, in original melds or cards laid off on previous melds. (In some localities, the player may draw only from the pack, not from the discard pile.)

23. To go out a player must meld, in one or more turns, exactly eleven cards. In his final turn, he must therefore meld the card he drew, together with all cards remaining in his hand.

24. When a player can use the discard to lay off on his previous melds, he must do so on demand of any other active player. (Such demand is called forcing; its object is to reduce a player to one card in his hand, so that he cannot initiate a new meld.)

25. When a player has melded ten cards, having no card left in his hand, the player at his left may not discard any card he can use and thereby go out, unless such player has no safe card to discard.

26. When any player goes out, by melding his eleventh card, he wins the deal and play ceases.

Scoring. 27. The winner collects 1 chip from each other active player, plus the value of all the conditions he has melded. (Thus he collects for his conditions twice over.) An optional rule is that a player who has made no meld must pay the winner two chips.

Irregularities. [See Rummy, paragraphs 21-42, pages 3-5.] 28. *Wrong number of cards.* If a player finds that he has more or less than ten cards, before he has made his first draw, he may discard all his cards and demand a new hand from the top of the stock. If, after his first draw, a player's hand is found incorrect, he must discard his hand and retire from that deal, must return all collections he has made for conditions, but must continue to make due payments to others for conditions and winning.

29. *Foul meld.* If a player lays down any spread not conforming to the rules, he must make it valid on demand. If he cannot do so, he must return any collections made in consequence of the improper spread and legally proceed with his turn. If he has already discarded, he must then return all collections he has made on that hand, discard his hand, and retire from the play until the next deal, but must continue to make due payments to others for conditions and winning. However, if he has made the meld valid before attention is called to it, there is no penalty.

30. *Putting neighbor out.* If a player avoidably discards a card that his right-hand neighbor can lay off, when that player has no unmelded card left, and that player then goes out, the offender must pay the losses of all other active players to the winner.

CONQUIAN

Conquian is the ancestor of Panguingue, which has all but replaced it, and may be the ancestor of all the games we now know as the Rummy family. Its name was corrupted to Coon-can (page 6).

Number of players. 1. Two.

The pack. 2. A regular pack stripped to forty cards by discarding all kings, queens, and jacks. (Originally the game was played with the Spanish pack, which can be made from a regular pack by discarding the tens, nines, and eights. But discarding the face cards instead is simpler.)

Rank of cards. 3. 10 (high), 9, 8, 7, 6, 5, 4, 3, 2, A.

The shuffle and cut. 4. The dealer shuffles the pack and his opponent cuts it.

The deal. 5. The dealer gives cards two at a time, beginning with his opponent, until each has ten cards. The undealt remainder of the pack is placed face down to form the stock.

Object of play. 6. The player strives to go out by melding all his cards. To do so he must form them into matched sets.

7. A matched set is either (a) three or four cards of the same rank, or (b) three or more cards of the same suit in sequence.

8. A player may lay off additional cards on his own melded sets, and may borrow from a set of four or more to complete a new meld. [For example, having melded ♡ 9 8 7 6 he may later take the 9 or the 6 to complete another group.]

The play. 9. Dealer's opponent begins the play by turning over the top card of the stock. If he wishes to keep it, he may do so. If not, he passes, and dealer then has the option of taking the turn-up. If he also refuses it, he discards it face down and turns up the next card from the stock. The play continues in the same way by alternate turns: both players have option of taking the turn-up, first option going to the player that turned it, and when both refuse it, the one who had second option turns the new card.

10. At any time that a turn-up or discard is taken, the player discards one card from his hand face up beside the stock. His opponent then has choice of taking this card or of turning a new card from the stock. When a discard is not taken, it is turned face down.

11. A player may meld before refusing the turn-up (whether he has first or second option), or after taking a card—turn-up or discard—but before making his discard. At this time he may meld any number of cards, and may lay off additional cards on his own previous melds.

12. If a player can pick up a discard and add it to his melds, his opponent may demand that he do so. (Such demand is called forcing; its object is to reduce the player's opportunity to initiate new melds.)

13. To go out, a player must meld eleven cards. In his final turn, he must therefore meld the card he draws, together with all cards remaining in his hand, and make no discard. A player who goes out wins the deal, and play ceases.

Scoring. 14. Each deal is treated as a separate game. The winner collects a prefixed stake (say, one chip) from the loser. If neither player goes out by the time the stock is exhausted, the game is drawn; each antes the basic stake to form a pool that goes to the winner of the next game.

Irregularities. 15. *Turning more than one card.* If a player turns up and sees more than one card of the stock, his opponent has first right to any such card illegally seen, regardless of the normal procedure of the game.

16. *Other irregularities.* If a player makes an incorrect meld, fails to discard, or commits any other irregularity not covered in paragraph 15, he must correct it on demand of his opponent if the latter makes the demand before continuing play. If not corrected in time, an error stands as regular and play continues.

⟿ POKER ⟿

Poker is traditionally the national card game of the United States, but is known and played throughout the world and perhaps by more people than play any other card game. The modern game of Poker originated in the United States, probably in the early years of the nineteenth century; the first known reference to its present name is in the 1830's. Its origin, however, is ancient. The first game known to have been played on the same principles was a Persian game, As or As Nas; the principle of building structures—sequences, and cards of the same rank—was even more ancient in China, whence the game we know as Mah Jongg, and our modern Rummy games. The development was gradual, through a long line of European and English games that included Pochen (bluff) in Germany—whence, no doubt, our name for the game. The American game crystallized as Straight Poker, the basic principles of which govern all Poker games, and branched off into two main families, Draw Poker and Stud Poker, under which the most popular variants will be grouped in this book.

DRAW POKER (JACKPOTS)

Definitions. 1. The following terms are defined as used in Poker.

ACTIVE PLAYER. One who has not refused to put at least as many chips in the pot as any other player, and who has not discarded his hand.

ANTE. A chip or chips required to be put into the pot before the deal.

BANKER. The person (usually a player) who keeps the original stock of chips and sells them to (or redeems them from) the other players.

BET. Broadly, any chips put into the pot; usually applied, however, to the first bet in any betting interval.

BETTING INTERVAL. A period of time during which each active player in turn has the right to bet or to drop out.

BUG. The joker used as an ace or in a straight or flush.

BUY-IN. Same as *stack* or *takeout*.

CALL. To put in the pot exactly as many chips as will make one's total contribution as great as that of any other player. In any betting interval except the last, a player who calls is said to "play" or to "stay in." In the last betting interval, a player is said to "call" or to "see" a bet.

CHECK. A bet of nothing; theoretically, a bet so low that it is not worth putting in the pot.

CHIP. The token, usually a circular disk, that is the unit of currency for betting in a Poker game; also called a CHECK.

DRAW. A deal of additional cards to replace a discarded portion of a player's hand.

DROP. Discard one's hand, rather than put enough chips in the pot to remain an active player.

FOUL HAND. A hand not of exactly five cards. The holder is deemed to drop whenever it is discovered and cannot win a pot.

JACKPOTS. A Draw Poker game in which every player antes equally before the deal, and a pair of jacks or better is required to open.

OPEN. To make the first bet in the first betting interval in Draw Poker.

OPENERS. A hand strong enough to open (almost always, a pair of jacks or any better hand) in any Draw Poker game in which the rules so require.

PASS. To make no bet in turn. In some variants of Poker, this is equivalent to dropping.

POT. All the chips bet on the outcome of any one deal. An active player is said to be "in the pot."

RAISE. To bet more than is necessary to call; the amount by which a bet exceeds the amount necessary to call.

ROTATION. The progress of the turn to deal, the distribution of cards in the deal, and the right to bet, which move from player to player to the left (clockwise).

ROUND. In dealing, a round of cards is the service by dealer of one card to each active player; a round of deals is one deal by each player in the game; a round of betting is one turn to bet for each active player, so that a betting interval may comprise one or more rounds.

SHOWDOWN. Comparison of the full hands of all active players, to determine which wins the pot.

STACK, or TAKEOUT. The smallest number of chips a player may have issued to him by the banker. A player's supply of chips at any time is also termed his stack.

WILD CARD. A card—the joker, or a card of the regular pack—that may be designated by its holder as representing any other card.

Players. 2. Draw Poker may be played by any number of players from two to eight; six or seven make the best game.

The pack. 3. A regular 52-card pack is used. Traditionally, this should be the "standard" (2½-inch) size rather than the narrower "bridge size" (2¼ inches wide); but actually it makes no difference.

[In a great number of games the pack contains 53 cards, of which the fifty-third is the joker. This card is most often termed the bug, and the holder of it may designate it an ace, or, at his option, any other card that would give him a straight, flush, or straight flush (paragraph 16). For example, if holding A A 3 2 Joker, the player could call the joker an ace and hold three aces; if holding 9 8 6 5 Joker, he could call the joker a seven; if holding ◊ A J 7 5 Joker he could call the joker ◊K and have a flush, or call it an ace and have a pair of aces; if holding ◊ 10 9 8 7 Joker, he could call it ◊J and have a straight flush. In this book, the letter B will symbolize the joker so used. There are other Poker-playing groups who make the joker a wild card that may be designated by its holder to represent a card of any rank and suit, whether or not the player already holds such card.]

Rank of cards. 4. A (high), K, Q, J, 10, 9, 8, 7, 6, 5, 4, 3, 2; A (low) only in the sequence 5 4 3 2 A.

Seating. 5. Players take seats at random unless any player demands, before the game begins, that the seats of the respective players be determined as provided in the next paragraph.

6. When any player demands a reseating, the banker has first choice of seats. The first dealer (see paragraph 13) may either take the seat to left of the banker or may participate with the other players in having his position determined by chance. The dealer then shuffles the pack, has the cards cut by the player to his right, and deals one card face up to each player in rotation beginning with the player at his left. The player thus dealt the highest-ranking card sits at the right of the banker, the player with the next-highest card at the right of that player, and so on. If two players are dealt cards of the same rank, the card dealt first ranks higher than the other.

7. After the start of the game, no player may demand a reseating unless at least one hour has elapsed since the last reseating. A player entering the game after it begins must take any vacant seat. A player replacing another player must take the seat vacated by that player. Two players may exchange seats, after any showdown and before the next deal begins, provided no other player objects.

8. When there is no banker, the dealer has first choice of seats.

The shuffle and cut. 9. Any player on demand may shuffle the pack. The pack should be shuffled three times in all. The dealer has the right to shuffle last and should shuffle the pack at least once.

10. The dealer offers the shuffled pack to his right-hand opponent, who may cut it or not as he pleases. If this player does not cut, any other player may cut. If more than one player demands the right to cut, the one nearest the dealer's right hand shall cut. Except in case of an irregularity necessitating a new cut, the pack is cut only once.

11. The player who cuts divides the pack into two or three portions, none of which shall contain fewer than five cards, and completes the cut by placing the packet that was originally bottom-most on top. [If a card is exposed in cutting, the pack must be shuffled by the dealer and cut again. Irregularities requiring a new shuffle and cut are covered on page 65.]

12. If no player wishes to cut, the deal proceeds and the dealer may not shuffle again before dealing.

The deal. 13. At the start of the game any player shuffles a pack and deals the cards face up, one at a time to each player in rotation beginning with the player at his left, until a jack is turned up. The player to whom the jack falls is the first dealer. Thereafter, the turn to deal passes from each player to the player at his left. A player may not voluntarily pass his turn to deal.

14. The dealer distributes the cards from the top of the pack, face down, one card at a time to each player in clockwise rotation, beginning with the player at his left and ending with himself, until each player has five cards. He then places the undealt cards beside him, face down, for later use. [Exposure of a card in dealing, or failure to give a player a card due him, does not necessitate a new deal. Irregularities requiring a redeal or causing a misdeal are covered on page 65.]

Object of the game. 15. The object of the game is to win the pot by having the highest-ranking Poker hand at the showdown, or by making a bet that no other player calls.

Rank of hands. 16. Poker hands rank, from highest to lowest:

(a) *Straight flush*—five cards of the same suit in sequence. The highest straight flush is A, K, Q, J, 10 of the same suit, called a *royal flush*. The lowest straight flush is 5, 4, 3, 2, A of the same suit. As between two straight flushes, the one headed by the highest card wins. [When any card of the pack is designated as *wild*—see page 73—a straight flush loses to five of a kind, which is the highest possible hand.]

(b) *Four of a kind*—four cards of the same rank. This hand loses to a straight flush but beats any other hand. As between two hands each containing four of a kind, the four higher-ranking cards win. [When there are several wild cards, it is possible for two players to hold four of a kind of the same rank. In this case, the winning hand is the one with the higher-ranking fifth card.]

(c) *Full house*—three cards of one rank and two cards of another rank. As between two full houses, the one with the higher-ranking three of a kind is the winner. [When there are several wild cards, two players may have full houses in which the three-of-a-kind holdings are of the same rank; the higher of the pairs determines the winning hand.]

(d) *Flush*—five cards of the same suit. As between two flushes, the one containing the highest card wins. If the highest cards are of the same rank, the higher of the next-highest cards determines the winning hand, and so on; so that ♠ A K 4 3 2 beats ♡ A Q J 10 8, and ♠ J 9 8 6 4 beats ♡ J 9 8 6 3.

(e) *Straight*—five cards, in two or more suits, ranking consecutively; as 8 7 6 5 4. The ace is high in the straight A K Q J 10 and low in the straight 5 4 3 2 A. As between two straights, the one containing the highest card wins, so that 6 5 4 3 2 beats 5 4 3 2 A.

(f) *Three of a kind*—three cards of the same rank. As between two hands each containing three of a kind, the one with the higher-ranking

Royal flush

Straight flush

Four of a kind

Full house

Flush

Straight

Three of a kind

Two pair

Pair

King high

three of a kind wins. [When there are several wild cards, there may be two hands containing identical threes of a kind. In such cases, the highest-ranking unmatched card determines the winner. If these cards are of the same rank, the higher-ranking fifth card in each hand determines the winner.]

(g) *Two pairs*—two cards of one rank and two cards of another rank, with an unmatched fifth card. As between two hands each containing two pairs, the one with the highest pair wins. If the higher pairs are of the same rank, the one with the higher-ranking second pair wins. If these pairs too are of the same rank, the hand containing the higher of the unmatched cards is the winner.

(h) *One pair*—two cards of the same rank, with three unmatched cards. As between two hands containing pairs of the same rank, the highest unmatched card determines the winner; if these are the same, the higher of the second-highest unmatched cards, and if these are the same, the higher of the lowest unmatched cards. For example, 8 8 9 5 3 beats 8 8 9 5 2.

(i) *No pair*. This loses to any hand having a pair or any higher-ranking combination. As between two such hands, the one containing the highest card wins; if these two cards are tied, the next-highest card decides, and so on, so that A 8 7 4 3 loses to A 9 7 4 3 but wins from A 8 7 4 2.

Two hands that are identical, card for card, are tied, since the suits have no relative rank in Poker.

[There are some "extra hands" not included among the traditional Poker combinations listed above, but played at the option of the players in certain games. These extra hands are described on page 72.]

The betting. 17. Before the deal each player antes one chip of such value as the players may agree (or the dealer antes for all—see paragraph 21 of the Rules of Betting, page 62).

18. At the conclusion of the deal, all players look at their hands. Eldest hand (the player nearest the dealer's left) may open the betting if he has a pair of jacks or better; or he may pass, whether or not his hand is good enough to open. If he passes, each player in turn to his left has the same option, until someone opens.

19. All the chips bet go into the center of the table, forming the pot. Before putting any chips in the pot, a player in turn announces whether he is betting, calling or raising; and, if he is betting or raising, how much. A player may not raise by an amount less than the bet he calls, unless there is only one player besides himself in the pot.

20. If every player in turn, including the dealer, passes, there is a new deal by the next player in rotation and the ante is repeated. If any player opens, each player in turn after him (including players who passed on the first round) must either call, or raise, or drop.

The Draw. 21. When each player has exactly called the highest previous bet, without raising, or has dropped, the first betting interval ends. The dealer picks up the undealt portion of the pack, and each active player in turn to his left may discard one or more cards, whereupon the dealer gives him that number of cards, face down, from the top of the pack. A player need not draw unless he so chooses. [If he plays his original five cards without drawing he is said to "stand pat."]

22. If the dealer is an active player, he must announce how many cards, if any, he is drawing. At any time following the draw and before the first player in turn bets or checks in the final betting interval, any active player may ask any other active player how many cards he drew. The latter player must answer, but the questioner has no redress if the answer is incorrect. [It is considered unethical, however, to give an incorrect answer intentionally.]

23. The dealer may not serve the bottom card of the pack. If the pack exclusive of this card does not suffice for the draw, the dealer must assemble all cards previously discarded, plus the bottom card of the original pack; shuffle these cards; offer them for a cut; and continue dealing. The cut shall be as provided in paragraph 10 except that only an active player may cut. The opener's discards are excluded from the new pack if they have been put in the pot.

Second betting interval. 24. When all active players have had their turns to draw, the player who opened may either check or bet. If he checks, each active player in turn after him may either check or bet, until any player bets. If any player bets, each active player in turn after him (including players who checked originally) must either drop, or call, or raise. If the opener has dropped, the duty of checking or betting first falls to the active player nearest his left.

25. No player may check, bet, call, raise, or drop, except in his proper turn. A player in turn may drop even when he has the privilege of checking. At any time that a player discards his hand, or permits it to be mixed with any discard, he is deemed to drop and his hand may not be reclaimed.

The showdown. 26. When each player has either called the highest previous bet, without raising, or has dropped; or when every active player has checked; the full hand of every active player is placed face up on the table and the highest-ranking hand wins the pot. If two or more hands tie for highest rank, they divide the pot evenly, an odd chip going to the player who last bet or raised.

Showing openers. 27. The player who opens must prove that he held a legal hand of five cards including the strength required to open. If he is in the showdown he must show his entire hand face up. In any other case, before discarding his entire hand he must show his openers face up and his remaining cards, if any, face down.

Splitting openers. 28. The player who opened may split his openers (discard one or more cards essential to them) and he need not announce that he does so. He may put his discard in the pot, face down, for reference later. [For example, having opened with ♠Q ♡Q J 10 9, he may discard the ♠Q and draw one card. It is not customary for the opener to put his discard in the pot, since he can usually demonstrate to the other players' satisfaction that he held openers.]

False openers. 29. If it is ascertained at any time that a player opened without proper openers, or that his hand contains too many cards, his hand is foul and all chips he has bet are forfeited to the pot.

30. If false openers are discovered before the draw, any other player in turn to the offender's left (excluding those who passed in their first turns) may open and play continues; but any player except the offender may withdraw from the pot any chips he put in after the pot was falsely opened. If no one can open, the remainder of the pot remains for the next deal.

31. If false openers are discovered after every player but the offender has dropped, each other player may withdraw from the pot any chips he put in after the pot was falsely opened.

32. If false openers are discovered after the draw, and when any active player remains, play continues and the pot goes to the highest legal hand at the showdown, whether or not any player had openers. [If there is no legal hand qualified to win the pot, the pot remains and goes to the winner of the next pot.]

ADDITIONAL RULES OF BETTING

Chips. 1. The white chip is the lowest betting unit. Each red chip is worth five white chips; each blue chip is worth ten white chips; each yellow chip (optional) is worth twenty-five or one hundred white chips, as agreed. (Or any other relative values may be adopted.)

2. Each player must start the game with the same number of chips, this number (or minimum takeout) to be established by agreement among the players. [It should be no less than ten times the ante, in a game in which the dealer antes; five times the limit, in a game in which a maximum limit is established; one hundred white chips, in a table-stakes game.]

3. A player who has lost half or more of his minimum takeout may remain in the game by adding one-half the minimum takeout to it. Any player at any time may have additional chips issued to him in units of the minimum takeout.

The banker. 4. One person, who may be a player, is designated as the banker. He keeps the entire original stock of chips. At no time may any other player touch the banker's stock of chips or execute any transactions on behalf of the banker.

5. The banker may issue chips to the players only in the quantities established as the minimum takeouts, and only in exchange for vouchers

signed by the players. The banker may redeem chips from the players, when he needs them to replenish the banker's supply, by destroying their vouchers in exchange for the return of the chips or by issuing his own vouchers for them.

6. If the banker is a player, he issues chips from the bank to himself as to any other player and exchanges his own vouchers for them.

The kitty. 7. By agreement among the players, there may be established a kitty or pool which is to be the joint property of all players and is to be used to defray expenses, such as for cards, refreshments, etc. The kitty may be made up of (a) one white chip from every passed pot, in a game in which every player antes; (b) one white chip from every pot containing forty or more chips; and (c) chips paid by players as penalties for infractions of rules, if such penalties are adopted in the game.

Limits. 8. Originally betting in Poker was unlimited—"sky's the limit" —and a player was able to bet whatever he was willing to put into the pot (including a promissory note if his opponent was willing to accept it in lieu of cash). If a player was unable to call an opposing bet, and his note or "marker" was not acceptable to his opponent, by tradition he had twenty-four hours to raise the amount necessary to call. In that case the opposing hands were sealed separately and the existing pot was sealed and put in the care of some custodian until such time as the money necessary to call was available or until the twenty-four-hour period had elapsed. This method and tradition are now obsolete and a limit of some sort is established for every Poker game.

9. *Fixed Limit.* The limit may be fixed at ten times the amount of the usual opening bet in Straight or Draw Poker, and ten times the amount of the compulsory or usual first bet in Stud Poker; for example, if the usual first bet is one white chip, the limit for any bet or raise is one blue chip; if the usual first bet is one red chip, the limit is five blue chips, etc.

10. The most commonly played form of fixed-limit Poker game establishes (in Draw Poker) one unit as the uniform amount of every bet and raise before the draw, and two units after the draw; when a deal is passed out, these limits are doubled for the next pot and until the pot is won, making the limits two units before the draw and four units after the draw. This would be known as "one and two" limits. Whatever the limit, it is in the same proportion; so that it might be "twenty and forty" or "fifty and one hundred." In Stud Poker, the same principle is followed: one unit is the limit until the last betting interval, when the limit becomes two units. Every bet and raise is the limit. Sometimes (in Stud Poker) the limit is increased to two units whenever a player has an open pair; if so, it remains two units even if the player with the open pair drops and no active player has a pair showing. In some Stud Poker games the limit is "one-two-three-four"—that is, one unit on the first face-up card, two on the second, three on the third and four on the last.

11. *Pot limit* is a method of fixing the limit by the size of the pot: A

player may always raise by as many chips as there are in the pot at the time, including in the size of the pot the number of chips required for him to call. [For example, there are 30 chips in the pot; a player bets 10 chips; the next player may raise 50 chips, for after he has put in 10 chips to call there will be 50 chips in the pot. His total contribution to the pot will then be 60 chips. At this point there will be 100 chips in the pot, and the next active player in turn (not the one who bet originally) will need 60 chips to call; therefore he may raise 160 chips, putting in 220 chips altogether.] Pot limit is seldom played without an additional restriction on the betting—usually table stakes (paragraph 15).

12. *Doubling limit*—a player may double the bet of the last opponent who raised. [Thus, if the first bet is four, the next player may make it eight, and the next player may make it sixteen. If it now comes back to the player who originally bet four, he may make it thirty-two, but need put in only twenty-eight more chips, having previously put in four. Nevertheless, the next player may make it sixty-four, by adding fifty-six chips to his previous bet of eight.] The size of bets can mount so quickly in this game that it is customary to put on some invariable maximum limit, such as one hundred chips, beyond which the doubling cannot go.

13. *Previous bet limit,* or "bet the raise," is a method by which the most any player can raise is the largest number of chips a previous player has put into the pot at one time. [For example, the first player bets four; the second player may raise to eight; the third player may raise to sixteen. The player who originally bet four can now put in twelve chips to call and sixteen chips to raise, but the next player may raise by only twenty-eight chips, since that is the largest number that have so far been put into the pot at one time.]

14. In a different form of pot limit, a player's total bet, in any turn, including the amount necessary to call and the amount by which he raises, cannot exceed the size of the pot at the time. This and any other pot limit method is unpopular among players who like fast games, it being so often necessary to count the size of the pot before a bet can be made.

Table Stakes. 15. In any Poker game except those with low fixed limits, i.e., in any pot limit, doubling-up or no-limit game, a player who has not enough chips to call the preceding bets and who cannot obtain more chips may stay in for the showdown by betting all the chips he has left. If there are other players in the pot and they wish to continue betting, their bets above this amount go in a "side pot" in which the short player has no interest. Play continues normally until there is a showdown, when the player who was short competes on even terms for that part of the pot to which he contributed in full. When this principle is embodied in the fixing of the limits, the game is known as "Table Stakes."

16. In a table-stakes game the limit for each player is the number of chips he has on the table in front of him. He cannot bet more, nor can any player bet more against him.

A player who bets all the chips he has in front of him is said to "tap" himself; a player who bets as many chips as an opponent has in front of him is said to "tap" that opponent.

17. A player in a table stakes game may obtain additional chips from the banker, and add them to his stack on the table, at any time that he has dropped out of a pot in progress and at any time between a show-down and the beginning of the next deal. However, he may at no time reduce the number of chips he has in front of him, by cashing them in, or by removing them from his stack, except when he leaves the game.

18. A player who is tapped remains in the pot until the showdown, drawing cards on even terms with the other players, without needing to make further contributions to the pot. If he has the best hand at the showdown, he takes the main pot. He has no interest in any side pots.

19. Any bets that one or more players cannot meet in the main pot are put into a side pot. At the showdown, this side pot goes to the active player who has an interest in the side pot.

20. A player who drops loses his interest in all pots.

[For example: A has 40 chips, B 80, C 150 and D 200. A bets 20; B calls, putting up 20; and C raises 50, putting up 70 chips in all. This bet taps A. For this reason, C puts into the pot only 40 chips—20 to call A's bet, and 20 as a raise that A can call—and keeps 30 chips just outside the pot. D calls, putting 40 chips in the pot and 30 chips just out-side it. A calls, putting in his remaining 20 chips and tapping himself. B calls, putting in 20 chips to complete the main pot, which is now shoved in a heap and separated, plus 30 chips which will go into the side pot. There are now 90 chips in the side pot. In the next betting interval A is not concerned. B checks and C bets 50 chips. D calls for 50 chips. B calls for 10 chips, which are all he has left. Therefore, 10 chips each from C, D and B go into the first side pot, completing that pot, and a second side pot is made up of the 40 chips from C and 40 chips from D. At the showdown, the main pot will go to the highest of the four hands. The first side pot will go to the highest hand as among B, C and D only. The second side pot will go to the higher hand as between C and D.

If there had been still another betting interval, and C had bet his remaining 30 chips, for D to drop would have meant losing his interest in all three pots. A player who drops concedes a superior hand to the player whose bet he does not call; that player succeeds to all his rights.]

The ante. 21. Before each deal, in Draw Poker, an ante or initial con-tribution to begin the pot is made by one or more players, by either of the following methods:

(a) In Jackpots, each player at the table antes one white chip, unless the dealer antes for all by agreement; when the dealer alone antes, he puts in one red chip if there are five or fewer players in the game, one blue chip if there are more than five players in the game.

(b) Eldest hand (player at dealer's left) antes by betting one white chip, and the player at the left of eldest hand raises (called the "straddle") by putting in two white chips, constituting a one-chip raise. When this method is used, eldest hand may count his one-chip bet toward calling the two-chip straddle and any other higher bet made subsequently by another player, and the straddler may count his two-chip bet in the same way. If no player including eldest hand calls the two-chip bet, the straddler wins and takes the three chips. (See *Blind Opening*, page 71.)

[In a method known as the Block System, each pot is begun with twenty-five chips, of which the dealer puts in nineteen, constituting the ante; eldest hand makes a compulsory opening bet of two chips, and the player at his left a compulsory straddle of four chips. Before the draw, the limit for a raise is two chips; after the draw, the limit is the total number of chips it cost each player to stay in for the draw.]

22. In games of Stud Poker an ante is optional under method 21 (a), but customarily no ante is required.

Betting. 23. In each betting interval, the turn to bet begins with the player designated by the rules of the variant being played, and moves to each active player to the left. A player may neither pass nor bet until the active player nearest his right has put the correct number of chips into the pot or has discarded his hand.

24. In Draw Poker, the first in turn before the draw is eldest hand. The first in turn after the draw is the player who made the opening voluntary bet before the draw.

25. In Stud Poker, the first in turn in each betting interval is the player whose exposed cards are higher than those of any other player. If two or more players have identical high holdings, the one nearest dealer's left is first in turn. In the first betting interval, the higher player must make a bet of at least one chip or such other minimum as may be established by agreement. In any later betting interval, he may check.

26. Unless a higher bet has been made in that betting interval, an active player in turn may check, which means that he elects to remain an active player without actually betting in that turn. [In some variants of Poker, checking is specifically prohibited.]

27. Whenever only one active player remains, through every other player's having dropped, the active player wins the pot and there is a new deal by the next dealer in turn.

28. No two players may play in partnership, and there may be no agreement between two or more players to divide a pot.

Irregularities in betting. 29. Chips once put in the pot may not be withdrawn except:

(a) By a player who, after he has anted, is dealt out—see paragraph 7 on page 66;

(b) In Jackpots, when another player has opened without proper openers (see paragraph 32 on page 59);

(c) In Draw Poker, by the players who opened blind and straddled, in case of a misdeal—see paragraph 3 on page 65;

(d) In Stud Poker, when the dealer has failed to deal a player any card face down—see paragraph 25 on page 86.

30. *Installment or string bets.* A player's entire bet must be put in the pot at one time. Having put in any number of chips, he may not add to that number unless the original number was insufficient to call, in which case he may add exactly enough chips to call. If, however, he announced before putting in any chips that he was raising by a certain amount, and he puts in an amount insufficient for such a raise, he must on demand supply enough additional chips to equal the announced amount of his bet.

31. *Insufficient bet.* When a player in turn puts into the pot a number of chips insufficient to call, he must either add enough chips to call and may not raise; or he must drop and forfeit chips already put in the pot. When a player raises by less than the minimum permitted, he is deemed to have called and any additional chips he put into the pot are forfeited to it.

32. *Bet above limit.* If a player puts in the pot more chips than are permitted by the limit, it stands as a bet of the limit and additional chips are forfeited to the pot. An exception is made in Table Stakes, when a player's bet exceeds the number of chips an opponent has; in that event, the player may withdraw the excess and either bet it in a side pot, or, if there are no other players willing or able to meet that bet in the side pot, restore those chips to his stack.

33. *Announcement in turn of intention to pass or bet.* If a player in turn announces that he passes or drops, his announcement is binding on him whether or not he discards his hand. If a player in turn announces a bet but does not put any chips in the pot, the announcement is not binding on him; but if he puts any chips in the pot, he is bound by his announcement and must if able supply such additional chips as are necessary to bring his bet up to the announced amount. In any event, other players who rely upon an announcement of intention do so at their own risk and have no redress in case under these rules the announcement need not be made good. [In many circles it is considered unethical to announce any intention and then not make good on it.]

34. *Announcement out of turn of intention to pass or bet.* If a player out of turn announces his intention to pass or drop when his turn comes, but does not actually discard his hand; or to make a certain bet, but does not actually put any chips in the pot; his announcement is void and he may take any action he chooses when his turn comes. Any other player who acts in reliance upon the announcement does so at his own risk and has no redress. [As in the case of paragraph 33, above, failure to make good on such an announcement, and especially if the announcement was intentionally misleading, is in many circles considered unethical.]

35. *Bet out of turn.* If a player puts any chips in the pot out of turn, they remain there and the play reverts to the player whose turn it was. If any player to the offender's left puts chips in the pot, he has bet out of turn and is equally an offender. When the offender's turn comes, if the

chips he put in were insufficient to call, he may add enough chips to call; if the amount was exactly sufficient to call, he is deemed to have called; if the amount was more than enough to call, he is deemed to have raised by the amount of the excess but cannot add chips to increase the amount of his raise; if no player before him has bet, he is deemed to have bet the number of chips he put in. If the chips he put in were insufficient to call he may forfeit these chips and drop. He may never add chips to raise or to increase his raise.

36. *Pass out of turn.* It is not improper to pass or drop out of turn when only one other active player remains. When more than one other active player remains, the pass out of turn is among the most damaging of Poker improprieties, but there is no penalty therefor except by agreement of the players. [In a fixed limit game, the offender should as a penalty call the first bet in that betting interval, up to the limit established for the game at that time. In any other game, the offender should call a bet up to five per cent of the minimum takeout.] In any case the offender's hand is dead and he cannot win the pot.

IRREGULARITIES IN DRAW POKER
(See also Rules of Betting, paragraphs 29 to 36, page 63, and the rules governing false openers, paragraphs 29 to 32, page 59.)

Redeal. 1. Any player, unless he has intentionally seen the face of any card required to be dealt to him face down, may call for a new shuffle, cut, and deal by the same dealer if it is ascertained, before the dealer begins dealing the second round of cards, that:

(a) a card was exposed in cutting;

(b) the cut left fewer than five cards in either packet;

(c) two or more cards are faced in the pack;

(d) the pack is incorrect or imperfect in any way (see paragraphs 17-18).

(e) a player is dealing out of turn (see next paragraph).

2. If a player is dealing out of turn, and a redeal is called, the deal reverts to the proper player in turn. In a game in which every player antes, no one need ante again. Any other ante or straddle that has been put in the pot is forfeited to the pot. If no redeal or misdeal is called within the time limit provided, the deal stands as regular and the player at the left of the out-of-turn dealer will be the next dealer in turn.

Misdeal. 3. A misdeal—one due to the dealer's error—loses the deal, if attention is drawn to it by a player who has not intentionally seen any face-down card dealt to him. The deal passes to the next player in turn. Any ante made solely by the dealer is forfeited to the pot. If all players have anted equally, their antes remain in the pot and no one need ante again. An ante made solely by eldest hand, and any following straddle, may be withdrawn.

4. A misdeal may be called:

(a) by any player who has not intentionally seen any face-down card dealt to him, if before the dealer begins the second round of cards it is ascertained that the pack was not shuffled or was not offered for a cut;

(b) by any player to whom the dealer gives two face-up cards in Draw Poker or any other form of closed Poker, provided that player has not intentionally seen any face-down card dealt to him and has not contributed to the error (see paragraph 9); and provided he calls for the misdeal immediately;

(c) if the dealer gives too many cards to more than one player.

5. If the dealer stops dealing before giving every player enough cards, due solely to his omission to deal one or more rounds, it is not a misdeal and the dealer is required to complete the deal whenever the irregularity is discovered. [For example, if the dealer stops dealing after giving each player only four cards; or if the dealer gives the first five of seven players five cards each and the sixth and seventh players only four cards each, having stopped dealing after the fifth player on the last round.]

6. If the dealer deals too many hands, he shall determine which hand is dead, and that hand is discarded; but if any player has looked at any face-down card in any hand, he must keep that hand.

7. If the dealer deals too few hands, he must give his own hand to the first omitted player to his left. Any other player who has been omitted and who has anted may withdraw his ante.

Exposed card. 8. If the dealer exposes one or more cards from the undealt portion of the pack, after the deal is completed, those cards are dead and are placed among the discards. (See also Stud Poker, paragraph 25 on page 86.)

9. There is no penalty against any player for exposing any part of his hand, and he has no redress. A player who interferes with the deal and causes the dealer to expose a card may not call a misdeal.

10. Each player is responsible for his own hand and has no redress if another player causes a card in it to be exposed.

Irregularities in the draw. 11. *Wrong number of cards.* If the dealer gives a player more or less cards than he asks for in the draw, the error must be corrected if the player calls attention to it before he has looked at any of the cards. Unless a card has been served to the next active player in turn, the dealer must correct the error by supplying another card or restoring the excess to the top of the pack, as the case may be. If the next player has been served, the player may discard from his hand additional cards to accept an excess draw without going over a five-card hand; if he has already discarded and the draw is insufficient to restore his hand to five cards, his hand is foul. If the player has looked at any card of the draw and the entire draw would give him an incorrect number of cards, his hand is foul.

12. *Card exposed.* If any card is exposed in the draw, whether or not it was faced in the pack, the player must accept the first such card but

any additional exposed card to be dealt to him is dead and is placed among the discards. After the dealer has served all other active players, he serves additional cards due the player from the top of the pack.

13. *Draw out of turn.* If a player allows a player at his left to draw out of turn, he must play without drawing, or drop. If he has already discarded any card, his hand is foul.

14. A player may correct a slip of the tongue in stating the number of cards he wishes to draw, but only provided the dealer has not yet given him the number of cards he first requested.

15. If a player discards a number of cards that would make his hand incorrect after the dealer gives him as many cards as he asked for, his hand is foul.

Incorrect hand. 16. A hand having more or less than five cards (or any other number of cards designated as a player's hand in the Poker variant being played) is foul and cannot win the pot. If every other player has dropped, the pot remains and goes to the winner of the next pot.

[Players may agree that a hand with fewer than five cards is not foul, but may compete for the pot with the best Poker combination he can make with the cards he has.]

Incorrect pack. 17. If it is ascertained at any time before the pot has been taken in that the pack has too many cards, too few cards, or a duplication of cards, the deal is void and each player withdraws from the pot any chips he contributed to it, any other laws of the game to the contrary notwithstanding; but the results of pots previously taken in are not affected.

Imperfect pack. 18. If the pack contains any card that is torn, discolored or otherwise marked so as to be identifiable from its back, the pack must be replaced before the deal in progress or any later deal can be completed; but the play of the pot in progress is not affected if the deal has been completed.

Irregularities in the showdown. 19. *Hand misstated.* If a player in the showdown announces a hand he does not actually hold, his announcement is void if attention is called to the error at any time before the pot has been taken in by any player (including the player who miscalled his hand). ["The cards speak for themselves."]

20. *Designation of wild cards.* If in the showdown, a player orally designates the suit or rank of a wild card in his hand, or implies such designation by announcing a certain hand, he may not change that designation (*e.g.* an announcement of Joker-J-10-9-8 as "jack-high straight" fixes the joker as a seven). A player may always show his hand without announcement and need not designate the value of a wild card unless another active player demands that he do so.

21. *Concession of a pot.* A player who has discarded his hand after

another player's announcement of a higher hand may not later claim the pot even if the announcement is determined to have been incorrect.

POKER CUSTOMS

Any of the following customs, which in some cases are followed only in certain sections and in other cases are followed throughout the country, may be given the force of law if the players in any particular game so desire.

Time limit. Before the game begins, a time for quitting is established. It is almost essential to a harmonious game that such a time limit be established and that it be strictly adhered to. Losers in a game will always want to continue play, and if the winners accommodate them the quitting time will become later and later and the circle will eventually break up because so many of the players cannot stand such late hours.

When the quitting time approaches, any player may announce that he will "deal off." This means that his next turn to deal will be the first of a complete round of deals, one by each player. When the player at his right has dealt, the game ends.

Cards. It is possible to speed up the game by using two packs of cards, of contrasting back designs. While one player deals, the player at his left assembles and shuffles the pack for the next deal; the second player to the left of the present dealer assembles the discards to prepare the pack with which he will deal when his turn comes.

When there are eight players in a Draw Poker game, especially when it is a lively game in which five or six players stay in on nearly every pot, the dealer sometimes sits out—takes no cards himself, so that only seven play in each pot.

In home games, new cards are introduced only at the option of the host. If the cards are furnished by the players themselves—as by a kitty to which all contribute—or in a club or other public place where there is no host, new cards should be introduced upon the reasonable demand of any player. In a private club, the rule usually is that a player may have new cards introduced whenever he is willing to pay for them himself.

Roodles. In Draw Poker games among players whose usual game is not Jackpots, it is customary to have "a round of roodles" whenever a full house or higher hand shows up. This means that for one round of deals, everyone antes, Jackpots are played and the limit is doubled. If everyone antes customarily, then the ante in a round of roodles is doubled. Sometimes roodles are played only after four of a kind or a better hand is held.

Royalties. When a player holds four of a kind, each other player in the game—even those who are not in the pot—must pay him some pre-established amount such as one, two or five chips; if a player has a straight flush each other player pays him twice as much as for four of a kind; and in some cases, a royal flush is paid four times as much as four of a kind. These are also called premiums, bonuses, or penalties. A player does not qualify for royalties unless the pot is opened.

Chips and betting. No chips may be removed from the table at any time, except to redeem them with the banker. (This is almost a universal rule.)

In a Table Stakes game, a player may cash in any additional takeout he has obtained from the banker after the first, provided he does so in units of the minimum takeout. He may not cash in his original minimum takeout and he may not cash in any winnings until he leaves the game. The principle is that the total number of chips in play must never be less than it was at the start of the game.

When a player bets, he should stack his chips on the table between himself and the pot, and remove his hand so that the other players may quickly count them if they so wish. Then he pushes them into the pot. This is a good rule in the case of any bet requiring several chips. Even where this rule is in effect, however, it is customary for a player who is merely "chipping along" with one white chip to toss it into the pot.

A player who wants to stay in a pot and temporarily has not enough chips to do so customarily "goes light" or "shy" by pulling out of the pot toward himself as many chips as mark his debt to the pot. The excuse for this is that it avoids delay in the game which might be occasioned if the players waited until the banker issued more chips; in addition, some players feel that they create a better psychological impression by the implication that they expect to win the pot and then will not need to have more chips issued to them. Nevertheless this custom is frowned upon in nearly all games and is best prohibited by rule. Separation of any chips from the pot makes it more difficult to count; it is easy for honest confusion to arise as to which chips are the player's and which belong to the pot; and a minor sharper can almost always come out a few chips to the good if he is allowed to pull chips out of a pot.

In most games, and especially in games played socially in homes, an announced bet is taken at face value and the player must make good on it. It does not matter whether he has spoken in turn or out of turn. Failure to make good is treated as repudiation of a debt, and is considered unsportsmanlike.

Irregularities in the deal. In games not played "for blood," time will be saved and hard feelings avoided if minor irregularities in the deal are straightened out at the time, as follows:

If one player has six cards and another four, the player with the short hand draws a card face down from the hand with six cards.

If one or more players (not the entire table) have only four cards, the dealer gives each of them another card from the top of the pack.

If one or two players have six cards, and the other hands are correct, they offer their hands face down to the dealer, but before looking at the face of any of them, and he draws the excess cards and restores them to the top of the pack. But even where this type of adjustment is permitted, a player's hand is foul and must be discarded if it contains more than five cards and he has looked at any of them.

Ethics. In a social game a sharp distinction is drawn between a bantering line of conversation intended to mislead opponents and direct lying which other players in the game are almost sure to accept at face value.

Some degree of intentional deceit is as much a part of Poker as bluffing. Each player must judge, from the standards existing in the particular game, how far he can go. In most games, however, it is considered unethical to declare that one is "betting blind" when actually he has seen his hand; to answer a direct question as to how many cards he drew with an incorrect answer (in most cases he does not have to answer at all—see paragraph 22 on page 58); to announce that he cannot open when in fact he can (he need not open unless he wants to, but he should phrase his statement in some other way); to announce that he intends to drop or to bet when in fact he has no such intention; etc. Intentionally breaking the laws of the game is in some circles considered as bad as downright cheating.

The custom of betting blind arose in games where it is considered unsportsmanlike to check or make a low bet on a strong hand with the intention of raising any bet. There is no justification in the Poker spirit for calling sandbagging unsportsmanlike; there is no sense in taking any action blind; but there is no arguing with custom.

Such standards are not traditional in Poker, but in general players will find that their games are more pleasant and harmonious and that their Poker-playing circles will be less likely to break up if a strict code of ethics is adopted and followed.

OPTIONAL OPENING REQUIREMENTS

Acepots. All the requirements are the same as in Jackpots, except that a pair of aces or better is required to open. Even when there are eight in the game, this restriction causes too many hands to be passed out unless the joker, the bug or other wild cards are in use.

Four-flush to open. A player may open, as usual, with jacks or better; or he may open on any four-flush. The four-flush, if not improved, has no special value after the draw. [In some Draw Poker games, however, and in many Stud Poker games, a four-flush is played to beat a pair, but lose to two pairs.] The object of making a four-flush open is to speed up the game; it is more likely that someone will hold openers, and other players are supposedly encouraged to come in on low pairs on the assumption that the opener may not even have a pair. However, since it is losing play to open on a four-flush, this special rule has little effect on a game among good players, though a one-card draw to a straight flush is worth opening on and that opportunity might be lost if the four-flush rule were not in effect.

Any bobtail to open. Jacks or better, as usual, or any bobtail (four-flush or double-ended four-card sequence) suffices as openers. All the comments in the preceding paragraph apply as well to this game. It must be remembered that a one-end sequence such as A K Q J or an inside straight such as 9 8 6 5 does not fulfill the opening requirements.

Progressive Jackpots. If, jacks being required, the pot is not opened, for the next pot queens are required; then kings, aces (and in some games, up to two pair).

BLIND OPENING

This form of Draw Poker is known by many different names—Blind Tiger, Tiger, English Poker, Australian Poker, Pass and Out—and is played in many minor variants, but none is materially different from any other.

The laws of Draw Poker are followed except in the following respects, which concern principally the first betting interval and the showdown.

The blind. 1. Whether or not there was any ante before the deal, at the conclusion of the deal the player at dealer's left (called the *age,* or the *blind*), without looking at his hand, must make an opening bet of one chip.

The straddle. 2. The player at the left of the blind must *straddle* by betting two chips. In effect, he raises one chip. The player at his left may then straddle again, if he has not looked at his hand, betting four chips; or this player may look at his hand before taking action. (The advantage of straddling is to gain position; the last player to straddle becomes the last bettor in the betting interval after the draw. Unless this rule is followed, there is no purpose to straddling.) If the voluntary straddle of four chips is made, the next player, still blind, may straddle by betting eight, etc.; usually some limit is put upon the number of straddles permitted. A player who has looked at his hand may not straddle except in the case of the first straddler, who is forced to do so.

Betting. 3. After the last straddle, each player may look at his hand. In turn to the left of the last straddler, each player must either pass or bet. If he passes, he is out and may not come back in that pot. If he bets, the first player to bet must raise the last straddle by the amount of the limit —the limit is usually the amount by which the last straddler raised. Once any player has made this voluntary bet, each player in turn after him may either call, raise, or drop; the age counts his opening bet toward his call, and each straddler counts his previous bet toward his call. If all other players have dropped when it comes around again to the blind, he may call, raise, or drop, and so may each successive straddler.

4. If no one calls the amount of the last straddle, that player takes the pot, which includes the blind, his own chips, and any straddle up to his. If anyone calls, as soon as bets are equalized there is a draw and then a

second betting interval in accordance with paragraphs 21 to 25 on pages 62-63. The limit after the draw is usually the amount by which the last straddler raised.

[For example: G deals; A bets one blind; B straddles, betting two blind. C looks at his hand and drops. D plays, betting three. E and F drop. G plays, putting in three chips. A plays, putting in two chips. B raises, putting in two chips, one to call, and one to raise, since that is the limit before the draw. D, G and A all put in one chip each, calling. After the draw, D will bet first since he is at the left of the straddler. The limit after the draw will be one chip.]

5. *Optional rule.* There may be no more than two straddles, and the limit for a raise is always two chips before the draw and four chips after the draw, regardless of the number of straddles.

Rank of hands. 6. In addition to the hands listed in paragraph 16 on page 55, the following hands have value:

BIG CAT, or BIG TIGER: King high, eight low, no pair. Loses to a flush, beats any lower-ranking hand.

LITTLE CAT, or LITTLE TIGER: Eight high, three low, no pair. Ranks next below a big cat.

BIG DOG: Ace high, nine low, no pair. Ranks next below a little cat.

LITTLE DOG: Seven high, deuce low, no pair; ranks next below a big dog, beats a straight or any lower hand.

As between two cats or dogs of the same rank, ties are broken as between any two no-pair hands. (See paragraph 16 (h) on page 57.) That is, K Q 10 9 8 would beat K J 10 9 8; 7 6 4 3 2 would beat 7 5 4 3 2.

[The object of using cats and dogs is to increase the number of hands worth drawing to and so bring more players into the pot, enlivening the game. Such hands, and other special hands which are defined in the glossary, are encountered in any type of Poker game, but most often in blind opening games. Some few players rule that since a cat or dog beats a straight, a cat flush or dog flush beats a straight flush and becomes the highest-ranking hand.]

OPEN ON ANYTHING

In many Draw Poker games there are no requirements for openers; a player may make the first bet whenever he feels like it. This game may be played in either of two ways: Pass and out, or pass and back in. The former is also called "Bet or drop." Each player in turn, beginning at the dealer's left, must either make some bet or drop; if any bet has been made before him, he must of course at least call it. Usually the minimum bet is so low, however, that a player can afford to toss in his chip and stay in the pot, if no one has made a larger bet before him; for this reason, the privilege of "checking" came into being. In the "pass and back in" game, a player may pass on the first round and come in afterward if someone else bets, as in Jackpots.

WILD-CARD GAMES

In the following games all the laws of Draw Poker are followed except as stated.

Poker with the bug. The pack comprises 53 cards, including the joker, which serves as the *bug*. The bug may count as an ace, or as any card that will make up a straight or a flush. A player may open the pot on jacks or better, or on any bobtail (four-flush or double-ended four-card draw to a straight). In a flush, the bug ranks as the highest-ranking card not already in the player's hand. [For example, if a player holds A K 7 5 and the bug, he has an A K Q flush. Occasionally, players prefer to count the bug always as an ace, so that the foregoing would be a double-ace flush and would beat a flush comprising A K Q 8 7 in another player's hand; but this is not customary practice.] Five aces are the highest-ranking hand.

Joker Poker. In old books, the alternative name Mistigris is sometimes given to this game. The rules are the same as in Draw Poker, with jacks or better required to open, except that the joker is added to the pack as a fifty-third card and is fully wild—its holder may designate it as any card from the pack he does not actually hold in his other four cards. When a player holds four of a kind and the joker, he may designate the joker as a fifth card of the same rank and indeterminate suit, giving him five of a kind, the highest-ranking hand.

Deuces wild. (In England deuces are called freaks, and this game is called Freak-pots.) All the rules of Draw Poker are followed, with jacks or better required to open, except that each of the four deuces is fully wild. A player may designate any deuce in his hand as representing any card he does not actually hold among his other cards, and may also designate a deuce as a card of any given rank and indeterminate suit to make five of a kind, which is the highest-ranking hand.

Other wild cards. No wild card but the bug, the joker, or deuces is encountered in most serious games; but in many of the hilarious games described on pages 74 *et seq.* the dealer may arbitrarily designate any card, or rank or assortment of cards, as being wild. Wild cards so designated are fully wild, in accordance with the rules given above for the joker and for deuces.

Naturals and wild cards. It is optional to rule that as between two hands that would otherwise tie, the one containing the fewer wild cards is the higher-ranking Poker hand. (This means that in competition for low hand, as in High-low Poker, such a hand would lose; in competition for high, it would win.) The question of naturals vs. wild cards must be decided by agreement before the game, unless covered by house rules. In the absence of such agreement or rule, naturals and wild cards count the same.

FREAK DRAW POKER GAMES

Old-fashioned Poker was a game requiring patience and conservatism; everyone got to know what was a poor hand and what was a good hand, and would throw anything away if it did not fit the conventional requirements of a good hand. The effort to enliven the game took the course of creating many wild cards, and giving each player more than five cards to choose from, so that everyone would have what is a "good hand" under conventional standards. There are literally thousands of Poker variants that have been created and are being created daily with this end in view. Many of them are born in "dealer's choice" games, in which each dealer can state the rules of the Poker game that is to be played, what cards are wild, what will be the winning hand, etc. Nomenclature in this field is hopelessly confused because the dealer has the right to name as well as to define his game. Some of the principal variants are defined in the following pages.

SPIT IN THE OCEAN

The game now generally known as Spit in the Ocean is actually a large family of games embracing a common essential feature: Each player combines the cards dealt to him with one or more cards exposed on the table and made part of the hand of every player. This is not new; the old French games of Brelan and Ambigu embraced this principle of play. The names used below are most frequent in literature on the game.

Spit in the Ocean. Four cards are dealt face down to each player, and one card is turned up in the center. The exposed card and every other card of the same rank are wild. The exposed card forms the fifth card of every active player's hand. There is a betting interval; then each player may discard any number of cards from his hand and draw cards from the dealer to replace them, as in Draw Poker (paragraphs 21 to 23 on pages 57-58, except that a player may discard his entire hand if he wishes); then there is another betting interval and a showdown.

Spit in the Ocean is sometimes played with the center card part of each player's hand, as described above, but not wild. It is sometimes played with the center card not wild, but each card of the same rank in a player's hand wild.

Wild Widow. Four cards are dealt to each player, face down, and a fifth card is turned up on the table. All cards of the rank of this exposed card are wild. There is a betting interval, then a fifth card is dealt, face down, to each active player. There is another betting interval, and a showdown. The exposed card in the center is not counted as part of any player's hand; it merely marks the rank of wild cards. This game is also called Pig in the Poke.

Stormy Weather. The dealer gives each player four cards, one at a time, face down; and after each of the first three rounds of cards, he deals one card face down to the center of the table, so that there is widow of three cards there. There is a betting interval, beginning with the player at dealer's left and with nothing required to open; then each active player may discard any part of his hand and draw cards to replace it, up to the full four cards; paragraphs 21 to 23 on pages 57-58 apply. After the draw, the dealer turns up one card in the center of the table, and there is a betting interval; a second card, and another betting interval; the third card, and the final betting interval. Each active player may select one of the three cards in the center to be his fifth card in the showdown. This same game, without a draw and with the last turned card and others of its rank wild, has been called Procter and Gamble.

Cincinnati. The dealer gives five cards to each player, face down, and an extra hand of five cards in the center of the table, face down. The cards in the center are turned up one at a time, with a betting interval following the turn of each card; the active player at dealer's left bets first in each betting interval. After the final betting interval there is a showdown in which each player may select any five cards from among his hand and the five cards in the center. This game is also called Utah, or Lamebrains.

Lamebrain Pete, or Cincinnati Liz. This is the same game as Cincinnati except that the lowest exposed card and all other cards of the same rank are wild.

Tennessee. This is the same game as Cincinnati except that the five cards to be exposed on the table are not dealt as an extra hand but are turned up, one by one, from the top of the undealt portion of the pack.

Round the World. This is the same game as Cincinnati except that only four cards are dealt face down to each player and only four cards are dealt as a widow to the center of the table. In the showdown, each player selects his hand from the eight available cards.

Bedsprings. Five cards are dealt face down to each player, and two rows of five cards each to the center of the table. A card is turned up in the center and there is a betting interval; then another card in the same row, followed by a betting interval; and so on through that row, after which the cards of the other row are turned up one by one with a betting interval following the turn-up of each. After the tenth card has been turned up in the center, there is a final betting interval and a showdown in which each active player must select his hand from his five cards plus any two cards in line, one card of each row. Thus each player has seven cards from which to choose the best five.

Twin Beds. This is the same game as Bedsprings except that the cards are turned up one from each row alternately, and in the showdown a player may select his five-card hand from his own hand plus the five cards of either row, giving him ten cards in all to choose from. It is often played that the last card turned up and all other cards of the same rank are wild.

Southern Cross. Each player receives five cards face down, after which the dealer lays out nine cards in the center of the table, face down, in a cross of five cards crossed by four cards. These cards are turned up one at a time, with a betting interval following each turn-up. After the final betting interval, each active player may select a five-card Poker hand from his own five cards plus either five-card crossbar of the cards in the center. Sometimes it is played that the center card of the cross and all other cards of the same rank are wild.

X Marks the Spot. This is the same as Southern Cross, five cards being dealt face down to each player, except that only five cards are dealt to the center, in a three-by-two cross; these are turned up one by one, with a betting interval following each. The center card of the cross, and all other cards of the same rank, are wild. In the showdown, each active player may select his five-card hand from his own hand, plus all five of the cards in the center.

Criss-Cross. Five cards are dealt to each player, then five cards are laid out in the center in a three-by-two cross, face down. These cards are turned up one by one, with a betting interval following each turn-up. The center card is turned up last. It and all other cards of the same rank are wild. Each active player in the showdown may select his five-card Poker hand from his own five cards plus either arm of the cross, eight cards in all.

SHOTGUN

Shotgun is a combination of Draw Poker dealing and five-card Stud Poker betting. Each player receives three cards face down; here the deal is interrupted for a betting interval. Each player then receives another face-down card followed by another betting interval; then a fifth face-down card, and still another betting interval. There is then a draw, and a final betting interval as in Draw Poker.

Double-barrelled Shotgun is a Stud Poker variant and will be covered on page 89.

Mike. All cards are dealt face down. After each player has been dealt two cards, there is a betting interval; then a betting interval after each subsequent round of one card to each active player has been dealt. After the last card has been dealt, there is a final betting interval and a showdown. There is no draw, but it is customary to deal six, seven or eight cards to each player, depending on the rules stated by the dealer, and from these cards he selects any five for his Poker hand in the showdown.

TWO-CARD POKER

Two cards are dealt, face down, to each player; there is a betting interval, after which each active player may discard one or both of his cards and draw cards to replace them, or may stand pat. After the draw there is a final betting interval and then a showdown in which the highest two-card Poker combination wins (two-card flushes and straights not counting). [This game is most often played high-low—see Hurricane, page 93.]

THREE-CARD POKER, or MONTE

Three cards are dealt face-down to each player, and after a betting interval each player may discard one, two, or three cards and draw cards to replace them; or may stand pat. After the draw, there is a final betting interval and a showdown in which the highest three-card Poker combination wins the pot, straights and flushes not counting. (In one variation, the hands rank as follows: Three of a kind, pair, three cards of the same suit in sequence, three-card flush, three cards in sequence of any suit, then high card.) [This game is most often played high-low—see page 93.]

WHISKEY POKER

Each player receives five cards face down, and an extra hand of five cards is dealt face down in the center of the table to serve as the widow.

A pool may be formed by equal antes from all players before the deal, the pool going to the highest hand in the showdown; or the lowest hand in the showdown pays for the drinks (which was apparently the original purpose of this game, and the origin of its name).

Eldest hand plays first. He may pass, or knock, or exchange his hand for the widow. If he knocks, it means there will be a showdown when his turn comes next. If he exchanges, he lays his own hand face up on the table. If he passes, the next player in turn has the same privileges.

When any player exchanges his hand for the widow, the player in turn after him may discard one or all five of his cards (but no other number) and select cards from the new widow to replace them. The discarded cards are added to the widow. Once the widow has been taken, each player must either exchange or knock; he may no longer pass without knocking. (*Variant.* A player may pass once, but never twice in succession.)

If no one exchanges on the first round, the dealer turns the original widow face up and play continues. Whenever the play comes around to a player who has knocked, there is a showdown.

KNOCK POKER

Three to five players make the best game. Each antes one chip before the deal. Five cards are dealt to each player, face down, as in Draw Poker; the undealt cards are placed in the center to form the stock, and the play is as in Rummy. Eldest hand (player at the dealer's left) draws the top card of the stock and discards, and thereafter each player in turn has his choice between the top card of the stock and the top discard. The discard pile should be kept squared up and is not open to inspection.

Any player in turn, after drawing and before discarding, may knock. This means there will be a showdown when his turn comes again. The knocker then discards, and each player has one more turn, in which he may draw as usual; and then must either drop and pay the knocker a chip, or discard and stay in.

When the knocker's turn comes again, he does not draw but there is a showdown among all players who stayed in. If the knocker has the high hand, every player who stayed in pays him two chips. If any other player ties the knocker, they divide the winnings except that the knocker keeps chips paid to him by players who dropped out. If anyone beats the knocker, he gets the antes and the knocker pays two chips to every player who stayed in.

It is customary for bonuses to be paid (by every player, including those who may have dropped) as follows: two chips each for knocking on the first round and winning without drawing a card (in this case, the player who knocks passes his turn to draw to the player at his left); one chip each for knocking before drawing on the first round, then drawing the top card of the stock and winning; four chips each for winning with a royal flush, two chips each for winning with any other straight flush, and one chip each for winning with four of a kind.

Irregularities. On the first round, a hand with six cards may discard without drawing, and a hand with four cards may draw without discarding; thereafter, an irregular hand discovered at any time is foul. If such a hand is discovered before anyone has knocked, the holder pays two chips to the pot; if discovered after a knock but before the showdown, he pays two chips to the knocker; if discovered after the showdown, he pays two chips to the winner of the hand; and in no case can he collect.

If the knocker's hand is foul, he pays as for any losing hand.

If a player draws more than one card from the stock, his hand is foul; the cards he drew go on the top of the discard pile and the next player has his choice of them, as well as his right to draw from the stock if he wishes.

Pointers on play. The knocker accepts one disadvantage, in that every other player will have one more draw than he; but his compensating advantage is that he irrevocably wins the chips of players who drop out—the same advantage that makes Blackjack so profitable a game for the dealer —and has a chance to win the antes, in addition to which he pays no more when he loses than he collects when he wins. For this reason it pays to knock when it is probable that your hand is better than other players' hands are likely to be with one more draw than you have had.

In general, two pairs are enough for knocking on the first round, though in a game of five or more players the fourth and later players should have at least queens up. On the second round, you need three of a kind; and on the third round, a high straight or a flush.

A player who stays in instead of dropping when someone has knocked receives, in effect, three-to-one odds on the extra chip it may cost him to stay; he has a further advantage if there is any possibility at all that he may win the pot; and he will win, regardless of how weak his own hand is, if some other player can beat the knocker. This does not mean that it pays to stay in blindly, but too much conservatism is losing play.

STRAIGHT POKER

The rules of Draw Poker govern with one exception: There is no draw. Each player receives five cards face down; eldest hand (the player at dealer's left) must make an opening bet, there is a single betting interval, and a showdown.

This game is very widely played as a two-hand game; it is occasionally played by three or four players; and it is almost never played by larger groups. When played, it is usually by serious gamblers for high stakes; almost the only no-limit play still to be found is Straight Poker between two or three players. More than any other form of the game, Straight Poker is a game of bluff and psychology; as shown in Table 6 on page 111, A-K high figures to win against one opponent, and a pair of eights against two opponents, but since these are barely better than even chances it may be assumed when a player bets heavily that he has something even better, and the skill in the game is concerned with figuring out how much better he may be.

OLD POKER GAMES

Poker with the Buck. This, one of the earlier forms of Poker, is listed in many books as Straight Poker, or Bluff. There is a deal of five cards face down to each player, a betting interval and a showdown—no draw. Some token such as a penknife (originally a buckhorn-handled knife, whence the name) is called the buck. The first dealer antes one chip for each player and passes the buck along to the player at his left. That player will ante for the next deal and pass the buck, so that the obligation to ante is always marked by the buck. The winner of each pot deals the next. Betting begins with the player at the dealer's left; a player may pass and come back in if anyone bets. If no one bets, there is another ante by the player who has the buck, and the deal passes to the player at the previous dealer's left.

Originally, the game seems to have been limited to four players and a 20-card pack was used, the A, K, Q, J and 10 of each suit.

As, or As Nas. An ancient Persian game, this may be the ultimate ancestor of Poker. The pack consists of five cards (ace to ten, or the equivalent) in each suit, and as many suits as there are players: For example, four players use a 20-card pack. All the cards are dealt out, face down, five to each player. Each player, after looking at his hand, may make a bet or may drop; once a bet has been made, the betting process of calling, raising, or dropping is the same as in Poker, and in the showdown four of a kind is the highest hand, then three of a kind, then two pairs, then a single pair. There are no straights or flushes; if no one has a pair, then all hands must tie. Poker as originally played in the United States was almost identical to this game.

Gile, Gilet, Gillet or ***Trionfetti.*** This may be the most ancient European ancestor of Poker. Four play, and the 32-card Piquet pack is used, ace to seven in each suit. Each player antes equally to each of two pots. Three cards are dealt, face down, to each player. First there is betting and a showdown for the first pot, for which the highest hand is three of a kind (a *tricon*) and the next-highest a pair (a *ge*); if no pair or better is held, this pot is combined with the second, and there is a betting interval and then a showdown for *point;* in this showdown the highest hand is a *flux* or flush, three cards of the same suit; if there is no flush, or as between two flushes, the highest point wins, two aces counting 21, an ace and a face card counting 20½, an ace 11, a face card or ten 10, and other cards their index values; but if any player has two or more cards of the same suit, no player may count the cards of more than one suit in his hand.

Brelan, or ***Bouillotte.*** Four usually play, each for himself, with a 20-card pack including ace, king, queen, nine and eight of each suit. Each player is dealt three cards and the next card is turned up and is counted by each player as part of his hand. Rotation, and order of preference, are to the right, beginning with the dealer. The dealer makes a blind bet, which may be straddled by the players in order to his right. After the betting there is a showdown in which four of a kind (*brelan carré*) is the highest hand and *brelan* (three of a kind) is next-highest; the holder of the former receives a bonus of four chips from each player, and the holder of the latter a bonus of one chip from each player (if it is the winning hand). If no one has a brelan, the winner is determined by the *point:* All hands are shown, and the suit having the highest point-count in all four hands and the exposed card, counting ace as 11, face cards 10 each, and nine and eight their index values, is the winning suit; the active player having the highest point count in this suit wins the pot. In case of ties the dealer, and after him each player in order of preference to the right, wins. If two suits tie for point, the active player in order of preference may select one of them as the suit that wins. If no active player has a card of the suit that wins, the suit having the next-highest point in all thirteen cards becomes the suit that wins.

Ambigu. This old French game was played by two to seven players, with a 40-card pack—ace to ten in each suit with no face cards, ace ranking low. At the start, each player antes equally to the pool. Two cards are dealt to each player and each in turn may stand pat or may discard one or two cards and draw replacements; and may bet, as in Poker. If no one calls a bet in this interval, the lone bettor withdraws his bet and is paid a penalty equal to a player's ante by the last player who refused to call. If anyone calls the bet, betting proceeds as in Poker and all players who have passed after the bet, or who pass after the call, are out. When this betting interval ends, each active player receives two more cards and each in turn may now discard from his four cards and draw. There is now a betting interval, as in Poker, followed by a showdown. But if no one bets, everyone antes again and there is a new deal. In the showdown, the hands rank as follows: Four of a kind (*frezon*), high; three of a kind with a fourth card of a different suit; flush; three of a kind with a fourth card of the same suit as one of the three; sequence, or four-card straight; prime, or Dutch flush—four cards of different suits; point, or the highest point count of cards of the same suit in the same hand, each card counting its index value (ace counting 1). The highest-ranking hand wins the pot plus bonuses from all players, active and inactive, of one chip if he won on point; or, if he won with a higher-ranking hand, one extra chip for each combination he holds or can beat. For example, with three of a kind and the fourth card of another suit he would collect six chips, because he has two combinations—three of a kind and prime—and can beat four others, point, prime, sequence, and three of a kind without the prime.

Brag. This is the English representative of the Poker family. The full 52-card pack is used. There are three wild cards, the ace of diamonds, jack of clubs and nine of diamonds, ranking in that order and called *braggers* (in other forms of the game, all jacks and nines are braggers). The dealer alone antes, his ante being a blind opening bet. Three cards are dealt face down to each player, and there is a betting interval as in Poker, each player in turn having the privilege of dropping, calling or raising until the bets are equalized. If no one calls, each other player pays the dealer one chip. After the betting interval, if anyone has called, there is a showdown in which three of a kind and pairs are the only combinations of value, and in which natural cards beat combinations including wild cards. As between combinations including wild cards, and otherwise of equal rank, the one including the highest-ranking wild card wins. [There were several variants of Brag, most of them representing combinations of the basic game with other similar games.]

Commerce. The 52-card pack is used, and the dealer gives each player three cards, one at a time, in each round of dealing turning up one card in the center of the table to make a three-card widow. The dealer may exchange his hand for the widow; whether or not he does so, each player in turn may then exchange one card for a widow card until someone knocks. When any player knocks, play ends and there is a showdown in which the hands rank: three of a kind, pair, and point (as in Ambigu). [In later developments of the game, the highest hands were: three of a kind, then a three-card straight flush, then a three-card flush, then a pair, and finally point.]

Poch* or *Pochen was a gambling game for three to six players. Equal antes are first distributed to compartments of a layout labelled: ace, king, queen, jack, ten, marriage, sequence, poch. Five cards are dealt to each player, the next card turned for trump, and the holders of the trump ace, king, etc., collect at once from the layout. The only real competition comes with *poch*—the best pair, three of a kind, or four of a kind. There is a betting interval as in Poker. To open or stay, a player has to have at least a pair. After due betting, raising, etc. there is a showdown of all hands still left in, and the best takes the pot together with the chips on poch in the layout. (When a high trump is missing from the cards dealt, chips on that compartment of the layout stay and are increased by subsequent antes.) The hands are then played out as at Whist (except that player who cannot follow suit does not play at all to that trick) and the first to get rid of all his cards collects from each other player one chip per card in that player's hand.

Gleek, an ancient English game, was a three-hand game played with a 44-card pack—the 52-card pack with deuces and threes deleted. Each player was dealt twelve cards and the next was turned for trump; dealer collected a payment from each opponent if he turned an ace. The players then bid for the seven undealt cards; the high bidder exchanged seven discards for them, and his payment was divided by the other two players. There was then betting and raising, as in Poker, as to who had *ruff* —the longest suit, with the card-values counted to break ties (as in Piquet, to determine point); four aces, however, won ruff against any suit. Next there was payment to each player for mournival, gleek, and honors; *mournival* was four of a kind and *gleek* three of a kind, only aces, kings, queens and jacks counting; *honors* was the four highest trumps. Finally the cards were played, as at Whist, and a player winning in tricks more cards than his original twelve collected for each card over twelve so won.

⇌ STUD POKER ⇌

Definitions. 1. The definitions in paragraph 1 on page 52 apply, and in addition:

BOARD. The exposed cards of all active players. A player can "beat the board" when his cards, including his hole card, form a higher-ranking Poker combination than any other player has showing.

CINCH HAND. A hand that no other player can beat in the showdown, regardless of his hole card.

FOLD. Drop; turn one's cards all face down to signify that one drops.

HOLE CARD. A card dealt face down to a player, in accordance with the rules of the game.

Players. 2. Stud Poker may be played by any number of players from two to fourteen; seven to nine make the best game.

The pack. 3. A regular 52-card pack is used. [The use of any wild card, such as the joker, is rare in Stud Poker.]

Rank of cards. 4. A (high), K, Q, J, 10, 9, 8, 7, 6, 5, 4, 3, 2; A (low) only in the sequence 5 4 3 2 A.

Seating. 5. Players take seats at random. (By prior agreement of the players, paragraphs 5 to 8 on page 54 may apply).

The shuffle and cut. 6. Any player on demand may shuffle the pack, the dealer having the right to shuffle last.

7. The dealer offers the shuffled pack to his right-hand opponent, who may cut it or not as he pleases; if he does not cut, each other player in order to the right may cut. Except in the case of an irregularity requiring a new cut, the pack should be cut only once. Each packet into which the pack is cut should contain at least five cards.

8. If no player wishes to cut, the deal proceeds and the dealer may not shuffle again before dealing.

The deal. 9. The dealer deals one round of face-down cards and then one round of face-up cards, at which point he interrupts the deal for a betting interval. At the end of this betting interval he deals another round of face-up cards, one to each active player, and again pauses for a betting interval. This process continues until—

(a) each active player has received five cards, one face down and four face up, with a betting interval after each round of face-down cards is dealt and a showdown after the final betting interval; or

(b) in any betting interval a player makes a bet which no other player

83

calls, in which case the bettor wins the pot and there is a new deal by the next dealer in rotation.

10. During each betting interval the dealer should hold the undealt portion of the pack in his hand. If he does put it down on the table, he must make sure not to let it be mixed with any hand or discards.

Object of the game. 11. The object of the game is to win the pot by having the highest-ranking Poker hand at the showdown, or by making a bet that no other player calls.

Rank of hands. 12. The Poker hands rank, in the showdown, from highest to lowest as follows:

    (a) Straight flush
    (b) Four of a kind
    (c) Full house
    (d) Flush
    (e) Straight
    (f) Three of a kind
    (g) Two pairs
    (h) One pair
    (i) High card or cards, as between hands having no pair or better.

[The rank of hands is set forth in detail in paragraph 16 on pages 55-57. In some games, a four-flush is played to beat a pair but lose to two pairs.]

13. Incomplete hands of four or fewer exposed cards, for the purpose of establishing the first bettor in any betting interval, rank from highest to lowest as follows:

    (a) *Four of a kind;* as between two such hands, the four higher-ranking cards are high.

    (b) *Three of a kind;* as between two such hands, the higher-ranking three of a kind are high.

    (c) *Two pair;* as between two such hands, the highest pair determines the high hand, and if the highest pairs are the same, the higher of the two lower pairs.

    (d) *One pair;* as between two such hands, the higher pair is high; if two hands have the identical pair, the highest unmatched card determines the high hand, and if they are identical the higher of the two other cards.

    (e) *The highest card;* if two players tie for highest card, the next-highest card in their respective hands determine the high hand, and so on.

As between two holdings that are identical card for card, the one nearest the dealer's left is high for purposes of betting (but has no superiority over the other in the showdown).

[Flush and straight combinations of four or fewer cards have no higher rank, for determining the first bettor, than any other holdings including no pair; except when a fourflush is played to beat a pair, in which case a fourflush showing bets ahead of a pair.]

14. If through the dealer's or his own error a player has all his cards exposed, all are taken into consideration for establishing the first bettor; and if at the start of the final betting interval such player has a straight, flush, full house or straight flush showing, his hand outranks any combination of exposed cards that his hand would beat in a showdown.

The betting. The betting rules on pages 59 to 63 apply, and in addition:

15. In each betting interval the player with the highest exposed combination (as defined by paragraphs 13 and 14) has the privilege of betting first. In the first betting interval, this player must bet at least the minimum established for the game. In any subsequent betting interval, this player may check.

16. If in any betting interval every active player checks, the betting interval ends. Another round of cards is dealt, or there is a showdown, as the case may be. If in any betting interval any player bets, each active player in turn after him must at least call the highest previous bet or drop.

17. At the start of each betting interval the dealer must announce which player bets first, naming the combination which gives him the high exposed holding at that point (for example, "pair of eights bets" or "first ace bets"). The dealer should also announce, after the third and fourth face-up cards are dealt, any player's combination that, when combined with his hole card, may make a flush, a straight, a four-flush or a one-card draw to a flush or straight (announced by saying "possible flush" or "possible straight").

18. *Optional law.* In the final betting interval, a player may not check or call unless his full hand, including his hole card, will beat the exposed cards of the highest combination showing. Such player may, however, bet or raise. [This rule is designed to protect players against making pointless calls; at the same time, it eliminates some bluffing opportunities. Like other optional rules, it should not apply unless there has been prior agreement among the players in the game that it will.]

The showdown. 19. At the end of the final betting interval each active player turns up his hole card and the highest-ranking Poker hand wins the pot.

Irregularities. Paragraphs 29 to 36 of the rules of betting on pages 64-66 apply and in addition:

20. *Irregularities in dealing.* At any time before the dealer begins dealing the second round of cards, a player who has not looked at a card dealt face down to him may call for a new shuffle, cut and deal if it is ascertained that:

(a) the pack was not shuffled or cut;

(b) a card was exposed in cutting, or the cut left fewer than five cards in either packet;

(c) two or more cards are faced in the pack;

(d) the pack is incorrect or imperfect in any way; but paragraph 17 on page 67 applies;

(e) a player is dealing out of turn.

21. When there is a redeal, the same dealer deals again unless he was dealing out of turn, in which case the deal reverts to the proper player in turn. If only the out-of-turn dealer has anted, his ante remains in the pot and the in-turn dealer antes also.

22. If the dealer deals too many hands, he shall determine which hand is dead, and that hand is discarded; but a player who has looked at the hole card of any hand must keep that hand.

If the dealer deals too few hands, he must give his own hand to the first omitted player to his left. Any other player who has been omitted and who has anted may withdraw his ante.

23. If the dealer gives a player two face-down cards instead of one on the first round of dealing, he omits that player on the second round of dealing and (unless the rules of the game require two hole cards, as in Seven-card Stud) he turns up one of the cards. The player who received the two cards may not look at them and then turn up one of them. If the dealer gives a player more than two cards on the first round of dealing, that player may require a redeal if he does so before the second round of dealing has begun; if the error is not noted until later, his hand is dead.

24. If in dealing any round of face-up cards the dealer omits a player, he moves back the cards dealt later, so as to give each player the face-up card he would have had if no irregularity had occurred; except that if attention is not called to the irregularity before the first bet is made in the ensuing betting interval, the hand of the player who was omitted is dead.

25. *Exposed card.* If the dealer gives any player a hole card face up, the player must keep that card and instead receive his next card face down. The player has no redress, except to receive his next card down, unless the dealer repeatedly fails to correct the error until the player has four cards; at which point, if the dealer has never given him a face-down card, the player may if he wishes drop out, withdrawing from the pot all chips he has put in. If the player instead stays for his fifth card, and receives it also face up, he may withdraw his chips from the pot and the dealer must supply to the pot that number of chips; but if the player instead remains in the pot by checking or calling any bet, there is no penalty on the dealer.

26. A card found faced in the pack during any round of dealing must be dealt to the player to whom it falls. A card at the top of the pack exposed during a betting interval, either because it is faced in the pack or because it is prematurely dealt, is discarded. In dealing the next round of face-up cards, the dealer skips the player to whom such card would have fallen, and deals in rotation, ending with the last player who would have received the exposed card if it had not been exposed. In each subsequent round of cards, on demand of any player the dealer must begin the rotation with the player who would otherwise have received the top card.

[For example: A, B, C and D are active players. Each has three cards, one
face down and two face up. Thinking
the second betting interval has ended,
the dealer gives a face-up card to A and
a face-up card to B; then attention is
called to the fact that the betting interval has not ended. The cards given to
A and B are dead, and are placed face-
up at the bottom of the pack or are put
among the discards. The betting interval
ends, all four players staying in. The dealer gives face-up cards successively to
C, D, A, and B. During this betting interval, C drops. After this betting interval,
on demand of D, the top card of the pack is dealt to D, the next card to A and
the next card to B. However, if no player had demanded this the dealer would
have begun the final round by dealing first to A.]

27. *Impossible call.* If the player last to speak in the final betting interval calls a bet when his five cards, regardless of his hole card, cannot
possibly beat the four showing cards of the player whose bet he calls, his
call is void and the chips may be retracted provided any player calls
attention to his error before the hole card of any other active player
is shown.

28. If the dealer errs in calling the value of a hand or in designating
the high hand, no player has any redress; but if the first bet is made by
the player incorrectly designated by the dealer, it is not a bet out of turn.

29. The dealer does not have the option of dealing a player's first card
up and his second card down intentionally. A player may not turn up his
hole card and receive his next card face down; if he turns up his hole
card, he must play throughout with all his cards exposed.

SEVEN-CARD STUD

This game is also called Down the River, Seven-Toed Pete, Peek Poker,
and by other names.

Each player receives two cards face down (but dealt one at a time)
and then one card face up. The first betting interval comes at this point.
Three more rounds of face-up cards are then dealt, with a betting interval
after each, and a final round of face-down cards, with a final betting interval. Thus each player has four cards face up and three cards face down.
In the showdown, a player selects any five of these cards as his hand.

SEVEN-CARD STUD, ENGLISH STYLE

As Stud Poker is played in England, each player receives two cards
face down and one card face up, as in Seven-Card Stud. There is a betting
interval, then two more face-up cards are dealt, with a betting interval
after each. Each active player may then discard one card and draw a
replacement as in Draw Poker, the replacement being dealt face up or

face down according to the card discarded; there is then a fourth betting interval. Each player may then discard and draw one more card, as before, after which there is a final betting interval and a showdown. Each player has only five cards for the showdown.

A player may stand pat instead of drawing, but if he stands pat for the first draw he must remain pat for the second draw.

FREAK FIVE-CARD STUD GAMES

Joker Stud. This is regular Stud Poker played with a 53-card pack, with the joker as a wild card or with the joker as the bug. The game with the joker wild has the drawback that if the joker is dealt face up, the betting usually stops abruptly and the player who got the joker gets the pot. This is not true when the joker is used as the bug, and this is not a bad game.

Fourflush Beats a Pair. This is occasionally referred to as New York Stud. In the showdown, a fourflush beats a single pair but loses to two pairs or any higher hand. In the final betting interval, a player with a fourflush showing bets first as compared to a player with any single pair showing.

Betting variants. To encourage players to stay in on the first round, some play that if no one calls the first bet, everyone antes the amount of that bet for the next deal, and the limit for the next deal is doubled, except in a pot-limit game. Others play that if no one calls the first bet, everyone must pay the amount of the minimum bet to the high card; this, of course, encourages the player who is high to make more than the minimum first bet, since otherwise at least one player—the one last to speak—could play against him for no more than it would cost to drop.

Baseball. (This is most often played in Seven-card Stud—see page 87.) Five-card Stud is played with all nines wild; any three in the hole is wild; any player who is dealt a three face up must either drop or pay to the pot as many chips as are already in the pot, and in the latter case his facing three is wild; and any player who is dealt a four face up is immediately given an additional face-up card by the dealer. In the showdown a player with more than five cards selects any five to be his hand.

Take It or Leave It, or *Shove 'em Along.* After the hole cards have been dealt, the dealer deals the first face-up card and pauses; the player may either accept or reject this card. If he rejects it, he shoves it along to the second player and the dealer replaces it (he must keep the replacement). The player to whom the card is shoved may either accept or reject it, as did the first player. If no one accepts a card before it comes back to the first refuser, it is dead. When a player accepts a card, the dealer gives a face-up card to the next player in turn and the same process is repeated. Each time every player has the same number of face-up cards, there is a betting interval. [As some play, every time a player rejects a card he must pay a chip to the pot.]

Butcher Boy. All cards are dealt face up, one at a time. When a card of the same rank as a previously dealt card shows up, it is transferred to the player who was previously dealt that rank, giving him a pair. There is then a betting interval and the deal is resumed with a face-up card to the player from whom the card was transferred (or, if he has dropped, to the next active player in turn). The deal continues in this way, with a betting interval after the transfer of each card, and the pot goes to the first player to get four of a kind. (This game may be played only by very liberal bettors, since theoretically no one should stay against a better hand and when the first card is transferred everyone else should drop.)

Four of a kind. This is less a Poker game than a drinking bout. After the pack is shuffled and cut, the dealer turns up the top card. He then deals one card face up to each player in rotation, dealing continuously; when the first card of same rank as the first exposed card is dealt, the player to whom it is dealt orders a drink (any drink); when the second card of that rank shows up, the person to whom it is dealt pays for the drink; and when the third and last card of that rank shows up the person to whom it is dealt drinks the drink. The cards are then shuffled and cut for a new deal by the next player in rotation. Every player antes before each deal, and the entire pot goes to the last player on his feet.

Beat Your Neighbor. Each player is dealt five cards face down, but no one looks at any of his cards. The first player in turn turns up a card and there is a betting interval. At the end of this betting interval, the player at his left turns up his cards one by one until he has a higher-ranking Poker combination than the first player, at which point there is another betting interval. Play continues in this way until the last active player has gone through the process of turning up his cards. If any player turns up all five of his cards without beating his right-hand neighbor, he is out of the pot and the player at his left begins to turn up cards. When the turn comes back to any player, if he is still in the pot, he may turn up additional cards in an effort to beat his right-hand neighbor. The highest hand or Poker combination showing at the end wins the pot.

DOUBLE-BARRELED SHOTGUN

This game is also called Texas Tech. It begins like Shotgun (page 76); after each player has been dealt three cards face down, the deal is interrupted for a betting interval; one more face-down card is dealt to each active player, with another betting interval; and one more face-down card is dealt to each active player, after which each player may discard and draw as in Draw Poker. After the draw, each player turns up one card—any card he chooses—and there is a betting interval; then each successively turns up a second, a third, and a fourth card, with a betting interval after each, so that the hands at the end are as in Five-card Stud, with four cards up and one hole card.

PISTOL STUD

Regular Five-card Stud is played, except that there is a betting interval after the hole cards are dealt, and another after each round of face-up cards is dealt, making five betting intervals in all.

MEXICAN STUD

Flip, Peep-and-Turn are other names for this game.

The betting is as in regular Five-card Stud except that all cards are dealt face down. After receiving his first two cards, and then after receiving each other card dealt to him, each player turns up a card—either of his two hole cards that he chooses.

Rickey de Laet is the same game except that every player's hole card, and every other card of the same rank in his hand, is wild.

Shifting Sands is the same as Mexican Stud except that the first card that a player turns up, and every other card of the same rank in his hand at the showdown, is wild.

FREAK SEVEN-CARD STUD GAMES

Seven-card Flip. The first deal is four face-down cards to each player (one at a time), after which each player may turn up any two of his cards after examining them all. After this the game is the same as Seven-card Stud from the second betting interval on.

Kankakee. A joker is used, but is not shuffled in with the pack. It is placed in the center of the table, is fully wild, and is common to all hands. Seven-card Stud is played, except that after each player has been dealt his two original hole cards there is the first betting interval, the wild joker representing the first face-up card for each player and the player at dealer's left being the first bettor. Three more face-up cards and one final face-down card are then dealt to each active player, with a betting interval after each.

Baseball. Seven-card Stud is played with all nines and threes wild, except that when a three is dealt face up the player must either put up the size of the pot or drop. When a four is dealt face up, the dealer gives that player an additional hole card immediately.

Football. This is the same as Baseball except that all sixes and fours are wild, a four dealt face up requires the player to match the pot or drop, and a deuce dealt face up entitles the player to a free hole card, dealt immediately.

Heinz. Seven-card Stud is played with fives and sevens wild, but a player being dealt one of these cards face up must match the pot or drop.

Woolworth. This is a Seven-card Stud with fives and tens wild, but a

90

player dealt a five face up must pay five chips to the pot, or drop, and a player dealt a ten face up must pay ten chips to the pot, or drop.

Innumerable other wild-card variations are played, including (listed by George Coffin in "Fortune Poker"): *Dr. Pepper:* Seven-card Stud, with all tens, fours and deuces wild; *Four Forty-Four:* Eight-card Stud with four cards face down and one up, with a betting interval, then three more face-up cards, with a betting interval after each, and all fours wild. In *Four Forty-Two,* deuces are wild. In *Three Forty-Five,* three face-down cards are dealt and one up, then a betting interval, then three more face up with a betting interval after each, then an eighth card face down and a final betting interval. All fives are wild.

LOW HOLE CARD WILD

In this form of Seven-card Stud, the lowest-ranking of a player's three hole cards, and every other card of like rank in that player's hand, is wild. This, with the exception of Seven-card High-Low Stud (page 93), is probably the most popular form of Seven-card Stud. The appeal of the game lies partly in its uncertainty; having paired the lower of his first two hole cards, a player has a winning hand subject only to the danger that he will be dealt a still lower card for his seventh card (and third hole card), nullifying the value of the low cards previously dealt him.

SIX-CARD STUD

This is the same as Five-card Stud except that after the fourth face-up card is dealt, and the betting interval that follows it, a sixth card is dealt face down to each player and there is a final betting interval. In the showdown, each player may select five of his six cards to be his hand.

EIGHT-CARD STUD

There are many variations in the dealing of this game, the feature common to all being that each player ends with four cards face down and four cards face up. Two cards may be dealt face down and four face up, then two more face down, with a betting interval after each of the face-up cards and after each of the last two face-down cards; or three cards may be dealt face down and one face up, followed by the first betting interval, with three more face-up cards and one more face-down card and a betting interval after each; or the first four face down, a betting interval, and then four face up with a betting interval after each. In any case, each player in the showdown selects five of his eight cards.

⟳ LOW AND HIGH-LOW POKER ⟳

As early as 1903, and perhaps earlier, someone thought of increasing the action of a Poker pot by providing that the highest and lowest hands divide the pot. Probably it was a losing player who maintained that he never held a good hand, but in any case it was an inducement to players who felt themselves unlucky to continue play. In the 1920's, this idea gained currency; in the 1930's it came to rival old-fashioned Poker in popularity; and by the 1940's it was the principal form of the game in play. The inevitable consequence of this trend was that Low Poker, generally called Lowball, came to be played to the exclusion of the original Poker game in which the highest hand was the winner. Especially in California, where in 1911 Attorney General Harold Sigel Webb had ruled that all forms of closed Poker are predominantly games of skill and therefore beyond the reach of the anti-gambling laws, Lowball came to be the most popular Poker variant, occupying the attention of at least fifty per cent of those who played the game.

HIGH-LOW POKER

In High-Low Poker, the rules are precisely the same as in standard Draw or Stud Poker except that nothing is ever required to open; a player may always draw (in Draw Poker) as many cards as he wishes, even his entire hand; and in the showdown the highest and lowest hands split the pot, with any indivisible chip going to the high hand.

The definition of the lowest hand became confused in the years in which many freakish variants of High-Low or Low Poker were devised. Strictly, the lowest hand is that hand which would not, in a regular (High) Draw Poker game, win from any other hand in the showdown, according to the ranking in paragraph 16 on page 55. The lowest possible hand, therefore, is 7 5 4 3 2 in two or more suits.

Developments along these lines have been innumerable. They include:

Low Poker with the ace low. In many High-Low games, the ace ranks as the high card in determining the high hand, but as the low card in determining the low hand, so that the lowest possible hand is 6 4 3 2 A of two or more suits. This principle is carried all the way, so that if there is no hand lower than one pair, a pair of aces is the lowest possible pair and will win the low half of the pot against two deuces.

Low Poker with the bug. When High-Low Poker is played with the bug, in the low end of the game the bug is simply another ace; a player

92

may count the bug as part of a straight or flush in trying for high, but need not do so in trying for low. Many play that the bug is not only an additional ace but is an extra low card ranking between deuce and ace; for example, 5 3 2 A Bug is "double ace low," not a pair of aces; and in contention for the low hand of the pot it beats 6 4 3 2 A. Similarly, 6 4 3 A Bug would beat 6 4 3 2 A; 6 4 3 2 A and 6 4 3 2 Bug would tie.

Freak High-Low games. There is almost no variant of Poker that cannot be played high-low, but there are many variants—especially in Seven-card Stud—that are more often played high-low than otherwise. Among these are Double Barreled Shotgun; Take It or Leave It (called, in the high-low variant, Hilo-Picalo); and Baseball and the games related to it, in which there are many wild cards and certain penalty cards.

High-Low Five-card Stud. Regular five-card Stud is played, with each player entitled, before the last card is dealt, to turn up his hole card and receive one card face down. Another variant is for the last round to be dealt always face down, whereupon each player may turn up either of his hole cards, shuffling the cards on the table if he wishes but not removing them.

Two-card High-Low Poker, or Hurricane. In this game, two cards are dealt to each player, one at a time, face down; deuces are wild, and ace is either high or low. The highest possible hand is a pair of aces and the lowest possible hand is double-ace low, which may be either two aces, ace-deuce, or two deuces. Straights and flushes do not count. Usually the game is played with declarations (page 94) so that the same player may compete for both high and low. Sometimes there is a draw, in which after the first betting interval each player may discard and draw one or two cards, after which there is a final betting interval and a showdown with or without declarations.

Three-card Poker, or Monte. This is a three-card form of Hurricane (see above); three of a kind are high. When straight flushes and flushes count toward high, a straight flush beats three of a kind but a flush loses to three of a kind, beating a single pair. In the competition for low, straight flushes and flushes do not count, so that a player with 3-2-A of the same suit has a three-high hand.

HIGH-LOW SEVEN-CARD STUD

Regular Seven-card Stud is played, and in the showdown each player selects any five of his cards to be his high hand, and any five to be his low hand. The high and low hands split the pot, and a player may win both ways and take the entire pot. The game is usually played with no wild card and with the ace counting high only, so that the lowest possible hand is 7-5-4-3-2. Sometimes it is played with declarations (page 94).

Division of Side Money. When Seven-card High-Low Stud is played with table stakes (as it usually is), complications arise in the division of side pots. The rules governing the division of side money are as follows (based on the book "Oswald Jacoby on Poker"):

(a) No one without the highest or lowest hand in the showdown can share in a side pot. There is no separate comparison among players in the side pot.

(b) If a player without an interest in a side pot wins both high and low, all the active players in each side pot divide that side pot equally. If a player without an interest in a side pot wins one way, and a player in a side pot wins the other way, the latter receives that entire side pot. The main pot, of course, is always split between the high and low hands.

Suppose A and B are in the side pot, C and D are not. C wins both high and low; A and B split the side pot regardless of their hands (other players who may have been in that side pot, but have dropped, have relinquished their rights). Suppose A wins high, C wins low; A wins the entire side pot.

(c) Suppose A and B are in the side pot, C is not. A wins high, B and C tie for low. A wins two-thirds of the side pot, B wins one-third.

(d) Suppose A is in the side pot, B and C are not. C wins high, A and B tie for low. A wins half the side pot and the rest of the side pot is withdrawn by the players.

DECLARATIONS

When High-Low Poker is played with declarations, each active player must declare, before the showdown, whether he is trying for high, for low, or for both (which is possible when each hand is selected from more than five cards, or when there are several wild cards which players may designate in one way for high and in another way for low).

There are two principal methods of declaring:

Hidden declarations. Each player conceals in his hand a white chip if he is trying for low, a red chip if he is trying for high, and one of each if he is trying for both.

Contract Poker. Each player in turn, beginning with the last player who bet or raised, must openly declare high, low, or double (both).

Division of the pot. Whichever method is used, a player must win the way be declared or he has no share in the winnings. If a player declares both high and low, and wins high but not low, he loses.

In the showdown, each hand is compared only with the hands of other players who declare the same way. If there are four players, A, B and C declare for high and D declares for low, D automatically wins half the pot; the highest hand among A, B and C wins the other half, even though it may happen that D actually had the highest hand.

If all players declare the same way, the winning hand receives the entire pot.

If no one wins the way he declares, all the active players divide the pot equally. For example, A and B each declare both ways, C declares for high only, D declares for low only. A has the high hand, B the low hand; neither can win because neither won both ways. C cannot win because there was a higher hand, D cannot win because there was a lower hand. The players take one-fourth of the pot each.

LOWBALL

Lowball is five-card Draw Poker in which the entire pot goes to the lowest hand. The game is often played with the 53-card pack, including the bug, but seldom with any other wild card. Ace ranks low, and straights and flushes do not count; ace and bug in the same hand count as a pair of aces, not as double-ace low. The lowest possible hand, 5-4-3-2-A (whether in one or more suits), is called the bicycle, or wheel. Lowball is almost always played with a low fixed limit, which is twice as much after the draw as before.

California Lowball. The following rules are typical of those followed for Lowball games in the Poker clubs of California, where this game is most popular.

Only the dealer and the one or two players to his left ante; the total of their antes is the limit before the draw. [For example, if the limit before the draw is 2 chips, dealer antes 1 and the player at his left antes 1. If the limit is 3, dealer and the two players at his left ante 1 each. However, no more than three players ante; if the limit were 5, dealer would ante 1 and the other two players 2 each.] The limit after the draw is twice the limit before the draw.

The first turn to open is the player at the left of the last ante. The game is "pass and out" before the draw. The antes all count toward meeting the bets of other players.

After the draw it is permissible to check but a player who checks may not thereafter raise, but may only call. [In some clubs, a player who checks a seven-high or better loses all interest in additions to the pot; that is, if he calls a bet and loses, he loses everything; if he calls a bet and wins, the bettor withdraws his bet and the winner gets only the pot as it was when he checked.]

Five cards constitute a hand. More or less, hand is dead.

Card off table is dead.

Card faced in deck is dead.

If seven or under is faced by dealer before draw, player must accept it; eight or over, he may accept or reject it and receive another card (off the top of the pack, before the dealing to other players is resumed).

Card faced by dealer after draw is dead and player receives additional card after other players receive theirs. If dealer faces his own card he must take it.

Player must take number of cards he calls for. If he says "Give me two —no, I mean three" he still gets two. If it fouls his hand, hand is dead.

Draw up to five cards.

All players must keep cards at table level in sight. Hand held below table level is dead.

When players call for cards dealer "burns" (discards) top card face down and then fills players' requirements.

All called hands must be shown. Full five cards spread.

A hand thrown away cannot be retrieved if any card touches any other card or cards.

Player is responsible for his own hand. If fouled by another player, hand is dead.

If player makes insufficient bet he must add additional chips or forfeit that already bet. Money once in pot may not be removed.

No string bets. Player cannot go back to his stack in order to raise unless he has announced "Raise" clearly.

No husband and wife at same table.

All hands must be played out. No splitting pots unless an actual tie.

JACKS BACK

Regular Jackpots Draw Poker is played, but if no one opens the right to open goes around the table again for a Lowball (or similar) pot. The principal games played on this second round are:

Low Poker. Often this is not pure Lowball, for flushes and straights count and the lowest possible hand (ace being low) is 6-4-3-2-A; but some prefer to play Lowball as it is described in the preceding section.

Tens High. There is no minimum requirement for opening, and no difference from regular Draw Poker except that any hand containing jacks or better is foul in the showdown.

Best flush. Only "flushes" count in the showdown. If there is no true flush, the best fourflush wins; if there is no fourflush, the best three-card flush wins; and even two cards of the same suit have been known to win a pot, where no one had three cards in one suit. Cards of other suits do not count except for breaking ties between flushes.

In any Jacks Back game, the cards are thrown in and the deal passes if no one opens on the second round.

Hi-lo, or Kings Back. Draw Poker is played, the same as Jackpots except that kings or better are required to open the first time around; the second time around, if no one opened the first time, Lowball is played, pass and out, and if no one opens this time the dealer takes the ante.

BETTING VARIANTS IN POKER

Cold hands. Each player contributes to a pot, five cards are dealt to each player, face up, and the best hand showing takes the pot (there is no draw). Cold hands are often played to dispose of a few odd chips at the end of a session, and in such cases the players do not necessarily contribute equally to the pot.

Freezeout. Each player must drop out of the game when he loses his stack, until the last remaining player has won the complete stacks of all others. It is not necessary for everyone to begin with the same number of chips, but a player having fewer than others is at a disadvantage.

Pots to be won twice. Any Poker game is played; all bets go into the pot and remain there until any player has won two different hands, whereupon that player gets the entire pot. A player who has won once should have and display some sort of marker so that everyone can tell who has a leg on the pot.

Side bets; high spade. A side bet in Poker does not depend on who has the best Poker hand; such bets go in the pot. The most frequent side bet is on "high spade." (In fact, there are some variants of Poker in which the player with the best Poker hand and the player with the high spade divide the pot.) House rules frequently prohibit side bets.

Limit on raises. It is customary to limit the number of raises in each betting interval (for example, to three); or to limit the number of times any one player may raise in any betting interval (for example, twice, or three times); except that no such limit is customary when two players only remain in the final betting interval.

POKER PENALTIES PAID IN CHIPS

Adoption of the following penalties is optional, but they are the best cure for careless repetition of irregularities. They are summarized from The Laws of Poker in the book "Fortune Poker" by George S. Coffin.

Pass out of turn. 2 chips prior to the last betting interval, 5 chips on last betting interval.

Examining another player's discards. 3 chips. This includes examining the hand of the winner of a pot when he has not been called and has thrown in his hand without showing it.

Failure to show hand after calling the final bet. 10 chips.

Causing dealer to expose a card (by touching the card while it is being dealt). 2 chips.

Mixing pack and discards. 5 chips, if the offense necessitates reshuffling before the deal can continue.

Failure by dealer to announce number of cards drawn. 2 chips.

Prematurely exposing one's own cards. No penalty for first or accidental offense; 2 chips each for repeated or intentional offense.

Failure to turn down cards, when dropping. 2 chips.

Dealer's failure to give player a hole card. If a player receives all five cards face up, in Stud Poker, through the dealer's neglect to deal him a card down on demand, that player may withdraw his chips from the pot and drop out, and the dealer must supply that number of chips, up to a limit of 20 chips.

POINTERS ON POKER PLAY

In any form of Poker there are "three P's," like the three R's of school days, that control strategy: Percentage, Position, Players.

Percentages. The first principle, subject to very few exceptions, is: Don't play unless you think you have every other player beaten.

Reference to the tables of percentages (pages 109-113) will furnish a guide to the relative infrequency of the various Poker hands, and so the probability that any such hand will be the best hand dealt. These tables will also show that the best hand before the draw (in Draw Poker) or the best holding in the first cards dealt (in Stud Poker) stands to win, and that an inferior hand playing against the best hand will lose in the long run.

The advisability of staying in to draw to an inferior holding is often stated as follows: You count (roughly) the number of chips in the pot and compare it with the number of chips it will cost you to play; these are the odds you are offered by the pot. If these odds are greater than the odds against your drawing the winning hand, you play; if they are less, you drop.

For example: There are 10 chips in the pot. It will cost you 2 to play. The odds you are offered are 10 to 2, that is, 5 to 1. You hold (Draw Poker) a four-flush; if you draw one card to it, the odds are 38 to 9, which is slightly more than 4 to 1, that you will not fill. The odds offered by the pot are greater; therefore you should play—if there were assurance that your flush, if you filled it, would win the pot. There is the further factor, at times, that after you decide to stay some other player will raise and the odds offered by the pot will go down. So the percentages are modified by your position (which determines the danger that the pot will be raised after you); and by your appraisal of the other players and what they hold (by which you will judge the chances that a flush will be good enough to win the pot).

Position. The player who is last to bet invariably has an advantage. Skillful play consists largely in watching for opportunities to make your decision as late as possible; and dropping in all doubtful cases when other players will make their decisions after you.

At the start, the dealer in Draw Poker has the best seat; the player at his left has the worst and is said to be "under the guns."

The opener of a pot coincidentally accepts the worst position after the draw. For this reason it is best not to open a pot if it is probable that another player will do so.

A player should make no bet, raise, or call without considering how many players still have a chance to act, and what they may do. In general, do not play on a hand that is barely good enough, when someone after you may raise.

Bluffing. There are two purposes to bluffing: (1) To create constant doubt in the minds of opponents, so they cannot be sure you have a good hand when you bet and will call the bets you make legitimately on strong hands; (2) to win the pot because the bluff succeeds and all other players drop.

Bluffing pays dividends even when you show no profit therefrom, because it accomplishes purpose (1); but if in the long run you lose more than a very small amount by your bluffs, it is better not to bluff at all.

The primary question to ask yourself before making any bluff is: Is this precisely the way I would play the strong hand I pretend to have, if I really had it? If the answer is No, you will lose.

The amount of a bluffing bet is important. Too small a bet will seldom have the desired effect. A very large bet is too risky; if the player being bluffed happens to have made a big hand, you will be called and the loss will be all out of proportion to the possible gain. For example: There are 30 chips in the pot; you are playing table stakes and both you and the opponents have ample chips. You bet 100 chips. This is too much to risk to win 30 chips (the best you can do, for if you are called, you lose). Both Jacoby and Coffin, in their books on Poker, advise betting the size of the pot; in this case, 30 chips. This is a normal bet and should not in itself arouse suspicion; and if you have at least an even chance, in your estimation, of winning by your bluff, you have made a reasonable bet because you stand to win as much as you stand to lose.

Even when you have built up your bluffs skillfully, and choose your victims carefully, you will lose many of your bluffs—enough to get yourself the "advertising" that brings you calls on your good hands. If you can win half your bluffs, or nearly so, it is winning practice. If you lose substantially more than half your bluffs, quit bluffing.

When a player bluffs and wins, he should never show his hand, no matter how strong his impulse to gloat. There will be plenty of time to show his bluffing hands when he loses.

POINTERS ON DRAW POKER

Opening. Whether or not to open depends on several factors: How large the pot is, in proportion to the amount required to open; how conservative or free the other players are; how good the chance is—depending both on the habits of the other players, and on how many players are yet to speak—that the pot will be opened if you do not open. As previously stated, it is always better not to open if you are fairly sure someone else will, because the opener accepts the worst position after the draw.

In a four- or five-handed game, it is wise to open whenever you have jacks or better. Passing a better hand because it is composed of low cards is strictly a gamble for a killing, and the wisdom of this depends on your style of play.

With a very good hand—a pat high flush or full house, or three aces— the biggest profits often come from opening in any position, so as to reraise if another player raises; but if you do not customarily open in first or second positions, to do so only on good hands is a dead giveaway and probably no one will raise, bet against you, or call, so it is best to maintain your style of play and sandbag even with such a hand.

Two low pairs are the most dangerous hand for opening in an early position. Unless someone raises, it is likely that several others will play; and if someone raises, you are beaten. If several others play, the odds are that one of them will improve, ending with two pairs; and the chance of your improving your two low pairs is only about 1 in 12. It is usually best to pass this hand, in a seven-hand game, except in the last three positions; and to throw it away if someone else opens and two or three others have played before your turn comes again.

Staying in. The average winning hand in a six- to eight-hand Draw Poker game, with nothing wild, is jacks up or queens up—that is, two pairs that are slightly better than average. Unless the odds offered by the pot are better than the odds against your having at least this good a hand coming out, you should not play.

It is almost never worth while staying in on a single pair less than kings, and then only when there is virtual assurance that no one will raise before the draw. (Consult Table 6 on page 111 and you will see how slight is the chance of winning on a single pair that is not the highest. When jacks or better are required to open, you have not an even chance of being the highest hand going in unless you have at least kings.)

Two low pairs are not worth playing against more than two opponents, and then only when there is no danger that someone after you will raise. (The danger of a raise exists even from players who passed originally, unless you know them to be chronic openers.) Paradoxically, two low pairs are more often worth a raise than a call, as will be explained below under *Raising.*

Drawing. Table 8 on page 112 shows the chance of improving any given hand to which you may draw. Mathematically it is best to draw three cards to a pair and two cards to three of a kind. Special circumstances may render a different draw advisable, however.

An ace or king kicker should be kept whenever playing against one or two opponents, one of whom can be placed with two pairs. Usually this occurs only when you are last to draw and the opponent or opponents have drawn one card each. It is about as good to keep a king as an ace, though keeping a king is quite unusual in practice.

Calling. Calling is a losing game, in general.

When a one-card draw bets, and another one-card draw calls, triplets are seldom worth much. When a one-card draw bets and a one-card draw raises, triplets are worth nothing, and neither is a low straight. A low flush is doubtful. The only sound call is a high flush or full house, and the only sound raise is jacks full or better. (The foregoing applies to pat hands as well as to one-card draws.)

Every call is subject to scrutiny of players yet to speak, and whether or not they may have you beaten (regardless of what you may think of your chance to beat the player who bet). An example: A draws three, B three, C and D one each. All check to D, who bets. A raises. B holds three kings. If B thinks D is bluffing, he should call; he can probably beat A, and he disregards C, who would not have checked a strong hand with only one player, and a doubtful one, to speak after him. If C had filled any straight or flush he would have had to bet, it being from 12 to 30 to 1 (depending on the strength of C's pat hand) that he had D beaten. A player in A's position, in such a case, will often win this pot because he can read D's bluff and B is not keen enough to know when he has A, and not D, to contend with.

But another example: A opens and draws one, B three, C one, D one. A and B check; C bets, D raises, A calls. B has three kings; they are worthless and he must throw them away. If A is a good player, he has a low full; if he is a poor player, B still cannot put a large number of chips in the pot when C, behind him, may have a reraise.

Raising. The usual effect of a raise before the draw is to drive out players who might otherwise have stayed; therefore do not raise before the draw unless this is your purpose. (The exception is when you are in a late position and everyone who is likely to come in has already done so.)

With more than two players still to be heard from, or unless at least three players are already in, do not raise if your hand is so strong that it will probably win, without improvement, even if one or more players should improve.

With two pair, a hand that will usually win from one or two opponents but lose if three or more play, the hand next to the opener may profit by raising. In the same position, with a straight or a high three of a kind, it is wiser simply to stay in and let others come in.

Nevertheless, an immediate raise on less than queens up (in a low-limit game, tens or nines up) is a losing game for the average player. A raise when three players are already in should not be made with less than aces up and it is safer to have three of a kind.

The opener (or a player behind him who did not raise) should not reraise without three jacks or better. Against one opponent, the opener is unwise to reraise on any three of a kind; for a pat hand will beat him, and any weaker hand will probably not call after the draw. The opener can better simply call, draw one card to his three of a kind, and wait to raise after the draw if the opponent does not stand pat.

If the opener reraises, the player who raised originally should have an ace-high flush to raise again, which will be the third raise; and the fourth raise—that is, a second raise by the opener or a further raise by any other player—should not be made with less than a full house. Not even a third raise should be made without a high full house if it is against a player who drew one card, who probably would not have stayed in to draw to a straight or a flush, and who bets out or raises a bet.

A raise "on the come"—that is, on a hand that is worthless unless it fills, such as a one-card draw to a straight flush—is almost always bad. It cuts the odds offered by the pot, for seldom will all the other players meet the raise. Against one player it is a losing game because with even the most favorable draw the odds are two to one or more against filling, while the raise cannot get better than even money from a single opponent.

Draw Poker with the bug. Introduction of the bug (joker) as a fifth ace and as a wild card in straights and flushes increases the number of good hands. Consequently it requires slightly more to bet, raise, or call.

It is seldom wise to stay in (when someone else has opened) with less than aces, or to raise, when next to the opener, with less than queens up. With a low straight, it is usually as good or better to raise immediately, and take a chance on driving other players out, as to try to suck them in by just playing. Nevertheless, three aces will usually win a pot, and consequently a straight, a better hand, is dependable enough to permit a sandbagging policy if you prefer it.

A straight or flush including the bug is far more desirable than a natural straight or flush, because it reduces the danger of having a pat hand against you.

With the bug, an ace, and a face card of the same suit as the ace, a two-card draw is better than three cards to the bug-ace; but if the face card is of a different suit, it is better to discard it and draw three.

Having the bug with three cards of a suit, your chance of filling the flush is only slightly greater than when there is no bug in the pack (10 chances in 48 as against 9 in 47). It is seldom wise to play this hand when you would not play a four-flush in regular Draw Poker.

Draw Poker with the joker. When the joker is included as a fully wild card, it dominates the whole strategy of the game. The average winning hand goes up to three of a kind. The joker is almost always worth a play (unless the hand contains no pair or ace and the pot has been raised). The joker and a pair, or the joker and three cards in suit or sequence, or in near-sequence (as Joker-8-7-5), is worth a raise; for to the ten or more cards that will turn such a hand into a straight or flush, as the case may be, must be added nine cards that will give you three of a kind—a good enough hand to win most pots, when you and not another player holds the joker.

Open on anything. The fact that no minimum hand, such as jacks, is required to open a pot does not affect the probabilities of the deal. If a hand is not good enough to win a pot in a jacks-or-better game, it will not, except by accident, be good enough in a blind-opening game.

The one difference, in a blind-opening game, is that players who pass cannot come back in, so the danger of being sandbagged is removed. Therefore the dealer, after all others (except the blind and one straddler) have passed, has a good bet on a pair of tens; the hand figures to beat two opponents. The blind, after all but the straddler are out, has a good bet on any pair. See the table on page 111. Even weaker hands than these—a pair of eights and an ace-king high, respectively—have a slightly better-than-even chance of winning.)

Deuces wild. The average hand after the draw is three of a kind; three aces will win about fifty percent of the pots.

The basic requirement for staying in, in most cases, is to hold at least one deuce. A two-pair hand should be thrown away, and any single pair without a deuce (except aces, in the rare case in which they may be played against one opponent only) should be dropped, as should any other single pair.

As between a draw of two cards to two aces and a deuce, and a one-card draw to a possible straight flush, it is better to draw to the aces; the odds are against hitting the straight flush, and if you miss entirely you still have a fair hand with three aces; you have nothing if you draw to the straight flush and miss. But with a low pair, a deuce, and a straight-flush draw, it is better to draw to the straight flush.

Aces to open. The average hand to open is two pairs, tens or jacks up; the most usual opening hand, however, is a pair of aces. It is unwise to raise before the draw on less than queens up, or to play on less than two low pairs or a pair of aces; and if you play two low pairs and the opener draws one card, you should usually drop if you do not improve.

Four-flush, or any bobtail, to open. Despite the fact that the rules make it permissible, it is not wise to open on such hands. The exception is any one-card draw to a straight flush, even if it is open only at one end or in the middle.

Blind opening. Since a player cannot check and come back later in this game, you always know the number of active players still to speak after you. The blind and each straddler must be considered in the light of players who have not yet spoken, since they had to make their bets without knowledge of their cards. The hands on which you have a sufficiently better than even chance of being high before the draw are as follows:

Against six active opponents, aces; against four or five, kings; against two or three, tens; against one (for example, if you are the blind and all except the one straddler have dropped), any pair.

The strength required for raising and reraising is the same as in any other Draw Poker game having the same number of players.

The principal privilege offered by the game is that of straddling, because it improves the player's position; and unless it would drive the stakes entirely out of reason, a player should straddle when he can.

Introduction of cats and dogs means that, in an average game, someone will end with a pat hand about one time in three pots. Bobtail straights in the middle ranges—such as 9 8 7 6—should seldom be played; there are too many additional hands that will beat them. A four-flush is a good draw whenever it would be in any other Draw Poker game. The best draws to straights are those that also offer chances of making cats and dogs; for example, K Q 10 9, which will make a dog with an ace, a straight with a jack, or a cat with eight. Twelve out of forty-seven cards will fill this hand, so the odds against it are about three to one and it should be played whenever the pot offers substantially better than those odds.

POINTERS ON STUD POKER

Staying in. The "book" requirement for staying in a Stud Poker pot is that you should be able to beat any showing combination; and perhaps this is the ideal desideratum. From the practical standpoint, however, if any appreciable number of players followed this rule there would be no game of Stud Poker.

The average "conservative" player requires to play: a pair back to back; an ace in the hole; a king in the hole with the upcard no lower than eight; a queen or jack in the hole with the upcard no lower than ten.

The "beat the board" applies invariably in only one case (and this is one of the few cases in the realm of games in which it is possible to use the word "invariably"): Do not stay in against a pair showing unless you have a higher pair.

Seven-card Stud. Thought to be a loose game, in which luck should play a bigger part than in Five-card Stud, and therefore to enliven the game and lure the average player in, this actually is a game in which the exercise of skill can pay greater dividends than in the five-card game.

The average winning hand is an average three of a kind—eights or higher—unless the play is very wild and loose, in which case a medium-sized straight or flush is the average winning hand. The fact that the game is a free one, so that more players draw cards and the average winning hand goes up, does not in any way affect the advisability of conservative play. While the majority of pots will go to liberal players who stayed on possibilities and luckily filled, the conservative player will still win far more because he will not have a large number of losing pots to drain away his winnings.

To stay in on the first round you should have: A pair; three cards in sequence; three cards of the same suit; or two cards as high or higher than the highest card showing.

To stay in on any subsequent round—that is, when each player has received four or more cards—you should have either a better hand than any that can be seen or inferred, or a chance to draw a hand that will almost surely beat the hand of any other player, provided the odds against your drawing such hand are less than the odds offered by the pot.

DRAWING

Draw one—do not split two pairs unless you know an opponent has two higher pairs.

Draw one—split openers only to draw to a straight flush.

Draw one—but do not split openers to draw to a straight or flush.

DEUCES WILD

Deuces wild—draw two to the A-A-2 unless there have been several raises, in which case draw one to a royal flush.

Deuces wild—discard the six of hearts and draw one card to the straight flush, flush or straight possibility.

POKER WITH THE BUG

The joker is the bug—draw three cards to bug and ace.

The joker is the bug—draw two cards to bug, ace, jack.

105

POKER WITH THE BUG

The joker is the bug—usually draw one to the two pair.

The joker is the bug—usually draw two to the bug and pair.

Having opened, draw three. If another player opened, draw one.

Having opened, draw one. (In Blind Opening, against one opponent, draw three.)

OPENING

Open; the chance of a higher pair is reduced by the A-K holding.

Pass, unless dealer or next to dealer; someone else should open.

POINTERS ON LOW AND HIGH-LOW POKER

High-Low. In regular five-card high-low games, playing for high and playing for low are treated as independent problems. With a hand good enough to compete for high, you generally follow the principles stated earlier in this book, remembering that you are competing for only half the pot and that the odds you are offered on a poor draw are only half what they usually are, while the winning high hand will be about the same as in regular Draw or Stud Poker.

The best draw, of course, is a combination like 6-5-4-3, or 5-4-3-2, that can make either a straight or a nearly sure win for low.

In a seven-hand game, the average winning low hand is nine-high. Such a hand, pat, is worth a raise. It must be remembered one may lose heavily on a "cinch" hand in high-low Draw Poker, since someone may tie the hand and it will receive only one-fourth the pot, perhaps after having put in nearly one-third. Whereas there are only four perfect high hands (royal flushes), there are 1,020 perfect low lands.

Four cards, eight high, are worth drawing to.

The skill in the game consists largely in knowing when a hand you started out playing for high will actually turn out to be the low hand. Flushes and full houses have been known to win "low."

In high-low games with declarations, it is worth declaring for both high and low when you have better than a 50% chance of winning both ways; though it is distasteful for players to risk, say, a 90% chance to win high on a 60% chance to win low. Nevertheless it is profitable in the long run to do so.

High-low Seven-card Stud. The essential principle of this game is to play for low, not for high. High cards, and even a high pair, in the first three cards should be thrown away. Three of a kind should be played. The best three-card combinations are three low cards of the same suit or a possible straight. Such holdings offer possibilities of winning both ways. To play a combination that can win only one way risks total loss for half gain. A straight for high and eight for low has a better-than-even chance to win both ways and a far greater chance to win at least one way.

Lowball. Although a nine- or ten-high will win more than half the pots, such a hand is not worth opening on in an early position unless it offers also a good one-card draw to a seven-high or lower in case there are several raises. For example, 9-6-3-2-A, or even 10-7-3-2-A, which can be broken for a one-card draw; not 9-8-3-2-A, which cannot come out better than eight high even with a fortunate one-card draw. In no form of Poker is position more important than in Lowball. In late position, when no one has raised, even a "rough" (relatively poor) ten-high pat hand is worth staying in; in last position, when no one has raised, a pat nine-high is worth a raise.

With a one-card draw to an eight, the odds are two to one against

107

getting an eight-high hand, even money on having no worse than a ten.

With a one-card draw to a seven, the odds are three to one against getting a seven-high hand, two to one against an eight-high hand or better, even money on having no worse than ten.

While worse hands often win, about the lowest sound raise after the draw is 7-5 high.

A nine or a "smooth" ten should be played pat against one or two opponents who draw one each, but should usually (not always) be broken for a good one-card draw against a pat hand.

MISCELLANEOUS FREAK GAMES

Spit in the Ocean. The minimums for playing are, generally, a wild card in the hand; or a pair of aces; or any three of a kind; or a draw to a straight flush. The requirements in the many variants depend on the number of cards from which one may choose his hand, and the number of wild cards; in most of them, four of a kind is about as low a hand as you can hope to win on, and in some of them a high straight flush is doubtful, five of a kind being the only safe bet. A few minutes' observation will usually be necessary.

Pots to be won twice. The player who wins the first pot has about a two-thirds chance of being the eventual winner; the player who wins the second pot has almost as good a chance. Having won a pot, play boldly, raise freely, and take chances on draws that would be unwise in a regular game. Not having won a pot, be very conservative; your chance of winning the final pot is very poor and chips you put in, except when you have a strong chance of winning, are probably contributions to another player.

POKER PROBABILITIES

Tables of Poker probabilities serve the player in a general way only; they will hurt as much as they help if blind dependence is placed upon them. An opponent's play of his hand is a much better clue to its value than a table that says he is unlikely to have as good a hand as he represents.

Most of the following tables are expressed in percentages. Some readers more easily grasp the concept of "odds," expressed as "2 to 1," etc. Such odds are merely a way of expressing a fraction: If you have a ⅓ chance of winning, by subtracting the numerator 1 from the denominator 3 you find there is one chance for you, two chances against you, in other words odds of 2 to 1 against you; if you have a ⅔ chance, you find in the same manner that the odds are 2 to 1 in your favor. Percentages are merely fractions of which the denominator is always 100. If you read in a table that your chance is .40, it means ⁴⁰⁄₁₀₀; subtract 40 from 100 and you find that the odds are 60 to 40 against you, or 3 to 2.

Tables 6, 7, 9 and 10 are not exact (nor are similar tables in other books); the method by which they were calculated is not strictly correct. The correct method would entail so much time and effort that it has never been attempted, especially since the calculations given here and in other Poker books are close enough to serve all practical purposes.

TABLE 1
Possible Poker Hands in a 52-Card Pack

HAND		NUMBER	FREQUENCY
Straight flush		40	1 in 64,974
Four of a kind		624	1 in 4,165
Full house		3,744	1 in 694
Flush		5,108	1 in 509
Straight		10,200	1 in 255
Three of a kind		54,912	1 in 47
Two pairs		123,552	1 in 21
One pair		1,098,240	1 in 2½
No pair			
Ace high	502,860		
King high	335,580		
Queen high	213,180		
Jack high	127,500		
Ten high	70,380		
Nine high	34,680		
Eight high	14,280		
Seven high	4,080		
		1,302,540	1 in 2
		2,598,960	

Comment: The "average hand" is A-K high. These are the chances of being dealt such a hand in the first five cards.

TABLE 2
Possible Poker Hands in a 52-Card Pack Including the Joker Used as the "Bug"

HAND	NUMBER	FREQUENCY
Five of a kind	1	1 in 2,869,685
Straight flush	204	1 in 14,067
Four of a kind	828	1 in 3,466
Full house	4,368	1 in 657
Flush	7,804	1 in 368
Straight	20,532	1 in 140
Three of a kind	63,480	1 in 45
Two pair	138,600	1 in 21
One pair	1,154,560	1 in 2½
No pair	1,479,308	1 in 2
Total hands possible	2,869,685	

Comment: While inclusion of the bug greatly increases the number of straights and flushes, and makes aces up, three aces, aces full and four aces more frequent than when nothing is wild, so does the bug make it less likely that anyone will hold a pair or better. With the 52-card pack, about 50% of all hands are a pair or better; with the bug added, only 48% have a pair or better.

TABLE 3

Possible Poker Hands in a 53-Card Pack Including the Joker as a Wild Card

Five of a kind	13
Straight flush	204
Four of a kind	3,120
Full house	6,552
Flush	7,804
Straight	20,532
Three of a kind	137,280
Two pair	123,552
One pair	1,268,088
Less than one pair	1,302,540
Total	2,869,685

Comment: Note that three of a kind occur more frequently than two pair, and that the "average hand" is a low pair. Even against a single opponent it is unwise to bet less than sevens.

TABLE 4

Possible Poker Hands in a 52-Card Pack with Deuces Wild

	NUMBER OF DEUCES					
	NONE	ONE	TWO	THREE	FOUR	TOTAL
Five of a kind		48	288	288	48	672
Royal flush	4	80	240	160	....	484
Straight flush	32	576	2,232	1,232	....	4,072
Four of a kind	528	8,448	19,008	2,832	....	30,816
Full house	3,168	9,504	....	....	....	12,672
Flush	3,132	7,264	2,808	....	....	13,204
Straight	9,180	37,232	19,824	....	....	66,236
Three of a kind	42,240	253,440	59,376	....	....	355,056
Two pairs	95,040	....	....	....	....	95,040
One pair	760,320	461,728	....	....	....	1,222,048
No pair	798,660	....	....	....	....	798,660
Total	1,712,304	778,320	103,776	4,512	48	2,598,960

Comment: Note the greatly increased frequency of four of a kind; flushes and full houses should not be bet so strongly as in other games.

TABLE 5

Possible Poker Hands in a Stripped Pack of 40 Cards
(deuces, threes and fours removed)

Straight flush	28
Four of a kind	360
Full house	2,160
Flush	980
Straight	7,140
Three of a kind	23,040
Two pairs	51,840
One pair	322,560
Less than one pair	249,900
Total	658,008

Comment: Although a full house still beats a flush, it occurs more frequently, and the flush should not be bet so strongly as with a full pack.

TABLE 6

Chance of Being High in the First Five Cards (Draw or Stud) with the
52-Card Pack, Nothing Wild

	NUMBER OF OPPONENTS						
YOUR HAND	1	2	3	4	5	6	7
Three of a kind	.97	.94	.92	.89	.87	.84	.82
Two pair	.93	.86	.80	.74	.68	.63	.59
Pair of aces	.89	.79	.70	.62	.55	.49	.43
kings	.88	.78	.69	.61	.54	.48	.42
queens	.83	.68	.56	.46	.38	.32	.26
jacks	.79	.63	.50	.40	.32	.25	.20
tens	.76	.58	.44				
nines	.73	.53	.39				
eights	.70	.49					
sevens	.66	.43					
sixes	.63	.40					
fives	.60	.36					
fours	.57	.32					
threes	.53	.28					
twos	.50	.25					

Comment: The theoretical "break-even" point is 50% against one opponent, 33⅓% against two, 25% against three, 20% against four, etc.; and having any greater probability of winning, you should show a net profit in the long run. But this applies only in showdown, where there is no betting. Where players have the option of dropping, the pots you win will not return profits in direct proportion to the number of players.

Original holdings of a straight or higher have so nearly 100% chance of being high that the figures are not given.

111

TABLE 7

Draw Poker—Chance That an Opponent Improved
(Each Player Drew Three Cards)

			CHANCE THAT IT WAS DRAWN BY ANY ONE OF			
HAND	1 OPP'S.	2 OPP'S.	3 OPP'S.	4 OPP'S.	5 OPP'S.	6 OPP'S.
Two pairs	.16	.30	.41	.50	.58	.64
Three of a kind	.12	.24	.34	.43	.52	.59
Full house	.01	.03	.04	.05	.07	.08
Four of a kind	.003	.01	.01	.015	.02	.025
Chance of any improvement by any opponent	.29	.50	.65	.76	.83	.88

TABLE 8

Draw Poker—Chance of Improving in the Draw

Three cards to a pair—odds against making

Two pair	5¼ to 1
Three of a kind	8 to 1
Full house	97 to 1
Four of a kind	359 to 1
Aces up or better	6 to 1
Any improvement	2½ to 1

Two cards to a pair and ace kicker—odds against making

Aces up	7½ to 1
Any two pair	5 to 1
Three of a kind	12 to 1
Full house	119 to 1
Four of a kind	1,080 to 1
Aces up or better	4 to 1
Any improvement	3 to 1

Two cards to three of a kind—odds against making

Full house	15½ to 1
Four of a kind	22½ to 1
Any improvement	9 to 1

One card to three of a kind (with any fourth card)—odds against making

Full house	15 to 1
Four of a kind	46 to 1
Any improvement	11 to 1

One card to two pair—odds against making a full house, 11 to 1

One card to a fourflush—odds against making flush .... 38 to 9 (4 to 1)

One card to a possible straight—

HOLDING   ODDS AGAINST
Four-card sequence, K Q J 10 to 5 4 3 2........ 39 to 8 (5 to 1)
Inside straight (9 8 6 5, 8 7 6 4, etc.).............. 11 to 1
A K Q J or 4 3 2 A... 11 to 1

One card to a double-end straight flush (as ◇ 10 9 8 7)—odds against making
Straight flush ....22½ to 1
Another flush .... 5 to 1
Another straight .... 6½ to 1
Any improvement .... 2 to 1

One card to a single-chance straight flush (as ◇ A K Q J or ◇ J 9 8 7)—odds against making
Straight flush .... 46 to 1
Another flush .... 5 to 1
Another straight .... 14 to 1
Any improvement .... 3 to 1

Two cards to a three-card sequence in same suit (as ◇ 10 9 8)—odds against making
Straight or flush .... 11 to 1
Two pairs or better .... 7½ to 1

Four cards to an ace—odds against making
Pair of aces .... 3 to 1
Two pair (or better) .... 11 to 1
Aces up .... 14 to 1

TABLE 9

Stud Poker—Chance of Having the High Hole Card

			NUMBER OF OPPONENTS					
YOUR HOLE CARD	1	2	3	4	5	6	7	8
Ace	.94	.89	.83	.79	.74	.70	.66	.62
King	.86	.74	.63	.55	.47	.40	.35	.30
Queen	.78	.61	.48	.37	.29	.23	.18	.14
Jack	.70	.49	.34	.24	.17	.12	.08	.05

⟶ CONTRACT BRIDGE ⟵

Contract Bridge, its international success, its hold on the imaginations of millions who treat it more as a hobby and as a science than as a pastime, and its widespread use as a medium of intellectual competition, is one of the outstanding sociological phenomena of the 20th century. In 1960 it was estimated that more than fifty million people in all countries play Contract Bridge. Thousands of them travel continental distances at their own expense to compete for higher ranking among Bridge players. In the fashionable world, knowledge of at least the mechanics of Contract Bridge is deemed a social necessity, and proficiency at the game is a social asset. This condition has stemmed by gradual growth in the English-speaking world over hundreds of years and a long line of related card games known as "The Whist Family."

History. England was apparently the incubation point of the game in which an entire pack of cards is dealt equally among four players; one suit is designated as trump; the object of the game is to win tricks, and two play as partners against the other two, the partners being seated alternately. The earliest such game dates prior to 1529 (the first known reference); the names of games in this family run from Triumph through Trump, Slamm, Ruff and Honours, Whisk, Whist (the eponym), Bridge-Whist, Auction Bridge, Contract Bridge. Whist was so well known to Englishmen in the 17th century that Charles Cotton, in "The Compleat Gamester," did not bother to describe its mechanics. The international spread of the game, however, was occasioned by the tremendous success of Edmond Hoyle's "Short Treatise on Whist," published at the end of 1742; this book gave the word Hoyle as a common noun to the English language, was translated into all western tongues, and made of Whist a hobby game among millions. Whist eventually developed a literature of several hundred volumes, and the American Whist League in 1793 had 9,000 members who met in annual congresses that hundreds attended. The hold of the game on serious players in England was little less. Gambling variants of Whist (Boston, Cayenne) flourished. But in the meantime (1883) there had appeared a booklet describing a game, Biritch or Russian Whist, a combination of dummy Whist and the Russian game of Vint; and though this booklet made little stir on its appearance, it inspired a game that spread through the fashionable Riviera resorts and eventually emerged as Bridge, described in this book as Bridge-Whist. Once Bridge was introduced to the London clubs, Whist almost immediately ceased to exist except as a tournament game. Gradual development of Bridge produced Auction Bridge, perhaps the best game of the family; then Contract Bridge, differing only in the scoring (and therefore in its strategy) from Auction Bridge, as the result of experiments in new scoring methods that had begun in 1915. Plafond, a game on the same principle, was played in France as early as 1918. Harold S. Vanderbilt of New York, who among other Auction Bridge experts had experimented with the new game, worked out a scoring table (1925) that embraced the features of vulnerability and inflated bonuses for bidding and making slams. This scoring table, in its essentials, proved to have the necessary appeal to the millions of Auction Bridge players. In 1927, after one book (by Florence Irwin) had appeared on Contract Bridge, Ely Culbertson of New York set out to publicize this game by methods that are acknowledged to have borne the symptoms of genius. Culbertson succeeded in making Contract Bridge into an international fad and bringing his own name into international prominence. From its beginning in 1927, the literature of Contract Bridge had grown by 1960 to 9,000 volumes, 1,200 of which were published in one year (1932). There were at one time 6,000 professional Contract Bridge teachers in the United States (the estimated figure in 1959 was 4,000) and approximately two million books on Contract Bridge were sold, at prices ranging from 10c to $4.95, each year from 1955 through 1960. The American Contract Bridge League, organized in 1927, had 100,000 members in 1960, and these members played in several hundred tournaments for "master points," the rating system adopted by the League, through which a member receives a certain number of points for winning or placing high in each tournament, according to its importance. As many as 4,000 members of the League attended its largest tournament each year, travelling distances up to 3,000 miles and spending several hundred dollars each for the privilege, though no gambling was permitted and so no hope of monetary gain was involved. Meanwhile there were still several million Whist players and as many more who still played Auction Bridge in the United States, though the more serious players had turned to Contract Bridge. Persons outstanding in the promotion of games of the Whist family, in addition to Hoyle and Culbertson, included "Cavendish" (Henry Jones) of England, in Whist; Milton C. Work, in Auction Bridge; Charles H. Goren, who succeeded Culbertson (about 1949) as the principal authority on Contract Bridge.

Alone among card games, Contract Bridge is governed by an international code of laws, prepared and promulgated by the National Laws Commission (of the American Contract Bridge League) in the Western Hemisphere, by the Portland Club and the British Bridge League in the British Empire, and by the European Bridge League in the countries of its respective members. This code of laws, which describes the mechanics of the game as well as the treatment of irregularities, follows.

LAWS OF CONTRACT BRIDGE

Copyright 1948 by The National Laws Commission and published at $1.00 by The John C. Winston Company, Philadelphia. Reprinted by permission.

THE SCOPE OF THE LAWS

The Laws are designed to define correct procedure and to provide an adequate remedy in all cases where a player accidentally, carelessly or inadvertently disturbs the proper course of the game, or gains an unintentional but nevertheless unfair advantage. An offending player should be ready to pay a prescribed penalty graciously.

The Laws are not designed to prevent dishonorable practices and there are no penalties to cover intentional violations. In the absence of penalty, moral obligations are strongest. Ostracism is the ultimate remedy for intentional offenses.

The object of the Properties is twofold: to familiarize players with the customs and etiquette of the game, generally accepted over a long period of years; and to enlighten those who might otherwise fail to appreciate when or how they are improperly conveying information to their partners—often a far more reprehensible offense than a violation of a law.

When these principles are appreciated, arguments are avoided and the pleasure which the game offers is materially enhanced.

PART I—DEFINITIONS

THE PLAYERS—

PARTNER—The player with whom one plays as a SIDE against the other two. He occupies the opposite seat at the table.

OPPONENT—A player of the other side.

DECLARER—The player who for his side first bid the denomination named in the contract.

DUMMY—Declarer's partner.

CONTRACTOR—Declarer or dummy.

DEFENDER—An opponent of declarer.

HONOR—Any Ace, King, Queen, Jack or ten.

HAND—The cards originally dealt to a player or the remaining portion thereof.

ROTATION—The order of progression applying in the game, which is from player to player clockwise.

DENOMINATION—The suit or no-trump named in a bid.

ODD TRICK—A trick won by declarer in excess of six.

CALL—A comprehensive term applicable to a bid, a double, a redouble or a pass.

BID—An offer to contract to win at least a specified number of odd tricks in a specified denomination.

PASS—A call signifying that a player does not, on that occasion, elect to bid, double or redouble.

PLAY—To contribute a card to a trick, including the first card which is the LEAD.

TRUMP—Each card of the suit, if any, named in the contract.

FOLLOW SUIT—To play a card of the suit led.

REVOKE—To play a card of another suit when able to follow suit.

OVERTRICK—A trick won by declarer in excess of his contract.

UNDERTRICK—A trick by which declarer falls short of his contract.

SLAMS: Grand Slam—the winning of thirteen tricks by one side; Little Slam—the winning of twelve tricks by one side.

VULNERABLE—Having won a game toward rubber.

The meaning of the following terms is clarified in the laws: Pack, section 1; Deal, section 8; Contract, section 22-b; Sufficient Bid, Insufficient Bid, section 23; Double and Redouble, sections 24 and 25; Trick, section 47; Penalty Card, sections 67, 68 and 69; Game, section 94; Rubber, section 95.

PART II–THE DRAW, THE SHUFFLE, THE CUT, THE DEAL

The pack—rank of cards and suits. 1. Contract Bridge is played by four players with a pack of 52 cards, comprising 13 cards in each of 4 suits. The suits rank downwards in the order—Spades (♠), Hearts (♡), Diamonds (◇), Clubs (♣). The cards of each suit rank downwards in the order—Ace, King, Queen, Jack, 10, 9, 8 ,7, 6, 5, 4, 3, 2. When practicable, two packs with distinguishable backs are used.

*The draw.** 2. Before every rubber, each player draws a card from a shuffled pack spread face downwards on the table. A drawn card should not be exposed until all players have drawn. If a player exposes more than one card, or draws one of the four cards at either end of the pack, or draws a card from the other pack, he must draw again. In drawing, equal cards rank according to suit.

Partnerships. 3. The two players who draw the highest cards play as partners against the other two. The player with the highest card deals first and has the right to choose his seat and the pack with which he will deal. He may consult his partner but, having announced his decision, must abide by it. His partner sits opposite him. Thereafter, the opponents may, after consultation, determine their respective occupancy of the two remaining seats.

The shuffle. 4. The pack for each deal is prepared by the player on the

---

* If more than four persons desire to play, it is customary to follow the rules for Club Procedure (page 133) to determine which of them shall have the right to play.

left of its dealer, if practicable while the other pack is being dealt. Preparing a pack consists of collecting the cards, shuffling them, and placing the shuffled pack face downwards on the left of the next dealer. The cards should be shuffled thoroughly and in full view of all players, but without exposing the face of any card.

5. A properly prepared pack should not be disturbed until its dealer picks it up for his deal, at which time he is entitled to the final shuffle. No player may shuffle a pack other than its dealer and the player on his left.

The cut. 6. A pack must always be cut immediately before it is dealt. The dealer presents it to the player on his right, who lifts off a portion and places it on the table toward the dealer beside the bottom portion. Each portion must contain at least four cards. The dealer completes the cut by placing the bottom portion uppermost.

New shuffle—new cut. 7. Before the first card is dealt, any player may demand a new shuffle or a new cut. There must be a new shuffle and cut if a card is faced in cutting, or if there is a redeal. When there is a new shuffle, only the dealer may shuffle.

The deal. 8. The dealer must deal the cards face downwards, one at a time in rotation into four separate hands of 13 cards each, the first card to the player on his left and the last card to himself. If he deals two cards simultaneously or consecutively to the same player, he may rectify the error, provided he does so promptly and to the satisfaction of his opponents.

9. The dealer must not allow the face of any card to be seen while he is dealing. Until the deal is completed, no player may look at the face of any card, and no one but the dealer may touch any card except to correct or preclude an irregularity.

Changing the dealer. 10. The turn to deal passes in rotation unless there is a redeal, in which case the same dealer redeals.

Changing the pack. 11. The packs should be used alternately unless there is a redeal. The pack originally belonging to a side must be restored if reclaimed, but a deal may not be stopped to restore a pack. A pack containing a distinguishable damaged card must be replaced.

PART III—GENERAL LAWS COVERING IRREGULARITIES

Redeal. 12. There must be a redeal:

(a) If, before the last card is dealt, a redeal is demanded because a player is dealing out of turn or with an uncut pack.

(b) If it is ascertained before the last card is dealt that the cards have not been dealt correctly, or that a card is faced in the pack elsewhere.

(c) If it is ascertained before the first call is duly made that a playe has picked up another player's hand and seen a card in it.

(d) If it is ascertained before the cards have been mixed togethe that one player has picked up too many cards, another too few; or tha the pack, when the deal began, did not conform in every respect to th requirements of section 1.

(e) If the players have allowed their hands to be mixed togethe before finding a missing card, or in the belief that a redeal is in order.

There may not be a redeal except as provided above.

Missing card. 13. A missing card, when found, is deemed to belong t the deficient hand.

When clause (d) or (e) of section 12 applies, there must be a redeal

When neither clause applies, the deal stands, and, if the missing car was found in a trick, the defective trick law (section 80 or 81) applies The missing card may become a penalty card under section 26 or 67, o failure to have played it may constitute a revoke. It must be placed ir the deficient hand unless it becomes a penalty card or is found in a trick that stands as played.

Surplus card. 14. If a player has too many cards, there must be a redea unless he has omitted to play to a trick, in which case the defective trick law (section 80 or 81) applies.

Drawing attention to an irregularity. 15. When an irregularity is committed, any player (except dummy if he has looked at another player's hand) may draw attention to it and give or obtain information as to the law covering it. The fact that the offending side draws attention to its own irregularity does not in any way affect the rights of the opponents.

Enforcement of a penalty. 16. Either opponent individually (but not dummy) may select or enforce a penalty. If the opponents consult as to penalty selection or enforcement, or if either opponent waives the penalty; the right to penalize is cancelled, but the rectification provisions (if any) of the applicable section still apply.

17. After attention has been called to an irregularity, no player may call or play until all questions in regard to rectification and penalty enforcement have been determined.

18. The penalty provisions of the laws apply only after agreement on the fact that an irregularity has been committed, and after specific statement of the penalty to be applied.

19. All questions as to what course to follow must be settled by the players before the game continues. A penalty once paid or other action once taken stands, even though at some later time it is discovered to have been incorrect.

Improper remarks and gestures. 20. If by a remark or unmistakable gesture a player other than declarer: discloses his intentions or desires, or the nature of an unfaced hand, or the presence or absence of a card in an unfaced hand; or improperly suggests a lead, play, or line of play; or improperly directs attention to the cards on a trick to which his partner has yet to play:

(a) If the offense occurred before the auction closed, (penalty) either opponent may require the offending side to pass whenever it is its turn to call; and if the offending side become defenders, declarer may require or forbid the opening lead of a specified suit.

(b) If the offense occurred after the auction closed, (penalty) declarer or either defender, as the case may be, may require the offender's partner to withdraw any lead or play which may have been suggested by the improper remark or gesture, and to substitute a card which does not conform to the improper suggestion. This penalty may be exacted on any trick subsequent to the offense but only on one such trick. The offender's partner may not be required to withdraw his card from a trick to which an opponent has played after him. Before this penalty may be enforced, a majority of the players must agree as to what lead, play or line of play has been improperly suggested.

PART IV — THE AUCTION

Duration of auction. 21. The auction begins when the last card of a correct deal has been placed on the table. The dealer makes the first call, and thereafter each player calls in rotation. After the first call has been made, the auction continues until three players have passed in rotation. This closes the auction.

Procedure after auction is closed. 22. After the auction is closed:

(a) If no player has bid, the hands are abandoned and the turn to deal passes in rotation.

(b) If any player has bid, the last bid becomes the contract and the play begins.

Bids. 23. Each bid must name a number of odd tricks, from one to seven, and a denomination, and must supersede any previous bid by naming either a greater number of odd tricks or the same number in a higher denomination. A bid that supersedes the previous bid is sufficient; one that does not is insufficient. The denominations rank downwards in order: No Trump, Spades, Hearts, Diamonds, Clubs.

Doubles and redoubles. 24. A player may double only if the last preceding bid was made by an opponent and no call other than a pass has intervened. A player may redouble only if the last preceding call other than a pass was a double by an opponent.

25. All doubles and redoubles are nullified by a proper subsequent bid. If there is no subsequent bid, the scoring value of the contract is increased as provided in section 98.

Card exposed during the auction. 26. If during the auction a player faces a card on the table, or sees the face of a card belonging to his partner:

(a) If an Ace, King, Queen or Jack, or a lower card prematurely led, or more than one card;* (penalty) the owner's partner must pass when next it is his turn to call. Every such card must be left face up on the table until the auction closes; and if its owner is then a defender, it becomes a penalty card.

(b) If a single card, lower than a Jack and not prematurely led, there is no penalty.

IMPROPER CALLS†

Improper call prematurely overcalled in rotation. 27. If a player calls before the penalty for an improper call by his right-hand opponent has been enforced (see section 17,) the auction proceeds as though it had been a proper call; except that if the improper call was a bid of more than seven, or a double or redouble made when only a pass or bid could be a proper call, the auction proceeds as though the improper call had been a pass.

Changing a call. 28. If a player changes a call in any way and does so practically in the same breath, his last call stands. There is no penalty unless he has changed to an improper call, in which case the appropriate "improper calls" section applies.

29. If a player changes a call in any way, and does not do so practically in the same breath, the change of call is void, and:

(a) If the first call was improper, the appropriate "improper calls" section applies.

(b) If the first call was a proper call, either the offender must allow his first call to stand, in which case (penalty) his partner must pass when next it is his turn to call; or the offender must substitute any other proper call, in which case (penalty) his partner must pass whenever it is his turn to call.

Insufficient bid. 30. If a player makes an insufficient bid, he must substitute either a sufficient bid or a pass.‡ If he substitutes—

(a) The lowest sufficient bid in the same denomination, there is no penalty.

(b) Any other bid, (penalty) the offender's partner must pass whenever it is his turn to call.

---

* If two (or more) cards are faced or seen at different times, clause (a) applies to both of them even though one has been picked up as provided in clause (b).

† All possible improper calls are listed under this heading. Calls not recognized by nor dealt with in these laws are merely improper remarks. The auction proceeds as if an improper remark had not been made, unless the remark is sufficiently informative to warrant the imposition of a penalty under section 20(a).

‡ As provided in section 18, a player is entitled to select his substituted call after the applicable penalties have been stated. Any call he may have substituted previously is void, unless his left-hand opponent has overcalled it, in which case section 27 applies.

(c) A pass, (penalty) the offender's partner must pass whenever it is his turn to call; and if the offending side become the defenders, declarer may require or forbid the opening lead of a specified suit.

Call out of rotation. 31. A call out of rotation is void. The auction reverts to the player whose turn it is to call; and—

(a) If a player has passed out of rotation before any player has bid, or when it was the turn of the opponent on his right to call, (penalty) the offender must pass when next it is his turn to call.*

(b) If a player has made any call out of rotation other than a pass listed in (a), (penalty) the offender's partner must pass whenever it is his turn to call.†

32. A call is not out of rotation when made without waiting for the hight-hand opponent to pass, if he is required to pass because of a law infringement.

33. If a player, whose turn it was to call, calls before attention has been drawn to a call out of rotation by his left-hand opponent, the auction proceeds as though that opponent had not called.

Simultaneous calls. 34. A call made simultaneously with another player's proper call is deemed to be a subsequent call.

Naming bid incorrectly in doubling.‡ 35. If a player in doubling or redoubling names an incorrect number of tricks or a wrong denomination, he is deemed to have doubled or redoubled the bid as made.

Doubling when the only proper call is a pass or bid. 36. If a player doubles or redoubles a bid which his side has already doubled or redoubled, (penalty) he must substitute any proper call, and his partner must pass whenever it is his turn to call. In addition, if the offender elects to pass, either opponent may cancel all previous doubles and redoubles.

37. If a player doubles his partner's bid, redoubles an undoubled bid, or doubles or redoubles when there has been no bid, (penalty) the offender must substitute any proper call, and his partner must pass whenever it is his turn to call.

Bid, double or redouble when required to pass; bid of more than seven. 38. If a player bids more than seven, or bids, doubles or redoubles when required by law to pass; the offender is deemed to have passed, and (penalty) the offending side must pass whenever it is its turn to call, and if the offender becomes a defender, declarer may require or forbid the opening lead of a specified suit.

---

* Example: North (dealer) 1 Heart, South pass. The pass is void, and the auction reverts to East. After East has called, South must pass. Thereafter, North and South may in rotation make any proper call.

† Example: North (dealer) 1 Heart, South 1 Spade. The 1-Spade bid is void, and the auction reverts to East. After East has called, South may make any proper call. Thereafter, North must pass whenever it is his turn to call, but South may make any proper call whenever it is his turn to call.

‡ It is improper to state the number of tricks or the denomination in doubling.

Doubly improper call. 39. If a player makes a call subject to penalty under two or more "improper calls" sections, either section may be applied but not both.

Call after the auction is closed. 40. A call made after the auction is closed is cancelled. If it is a pass by a defender, or any call by a contractor, there is no penalty. If it is a bid, double or redouble by a defender, (penalty) declarer may require or forbid the other defender to lead a specified suit when first it is the latter's turn to lead.

REVIEWING THE AUCTION

41. A player who does not hear a call distinctly may forthwith require it to be repeated. There is no redress for a call based on a misunderstanding or on misinformation.

42. A player is entitled to have previous calls restated either when it is his turn to call, or after the auction closes but before the opening lead has been duly made. His request should be responded to only by an opponent. Dummy, or a player required by law to pass, should not ask to have calls restated, but may review the auction at an opponent's request and should correct errors in restatement.

43. After the opening lead, calls may not be restated, but declarer or a defender is entitled to be informed what the contract is and whether, but not by whom, it was doubled or redoubled.

PART V—THE PLAY

Commencement of play. 44. After the auction closes, the defender on declarer's left makes the opening lead. After the opening lead dummy spreads his hand in front of him on the table, face up and grouped in suits with the trumps on his right. Declarer plays both of the contractors' hands.

Dummy's rights. 45. Dummy should refrain from all comment and from taking any active part in the play, except that he may:

(a) Give or obtain information as to fact or law.

(b) Question players regarding revokes as provided in section 71.

(c) Draw attention to an irregularity, or try to prevent one apparently about to be committed.*

Dummy forfeits these rights if he looks at a card in another player's hand.

Dummy's limitations. 46. Dummy should not exchange hands with declarer, lean over to see a defender's cards, leave his seat to watch declarer play, or, on his own initiative, look at the face of a card in any other player's hand. If dummy, as a result of any such act, sees a card in any other player's hand, and thereafter:

---

* Example: He may warn declarer against leading from the wrong hand, but only when it is apparent that declarer is about to do so.

(a) Is the first to draw attention to a defender's irregularity, declarer may not enforce any penalty for the offense.

(b) Warns declarer not to lead from the wrong hand, (penalty) either defender may choose the hand from which declarer shall lead.

(c) Is the first to ask declarer if a play from his hand constitutes a revoke, and the revoke card is consequently withdrawn, (penalty) either defender may require declarer to substitute his highest or lowest correct card.

LEADS AND PLAYS

The sequence and procedure of play. 47. The leader to a trick may play any card in his hand. After a lead, each other hand in rotation plays a card, and the four cards so played constitute a trick.

48. In playing to a trick, each player must if possible follow suit. This obligation overrides all other requirements of the laws. If unable to follow suit, a player may play any card.

49. A trick containing a trump is won by the hand playing the highest trump. A trick that does not contain a trump is won by the hand playing the highest card of the suit led. The hand winning a trick leads to the next trick.

Played card. 50. A card in any hand is played when named as the one a player proposes to play; but a player may change his designation if he does so practically in the same breath.

51. A card in any unfaced hand is played when it touches the table face upwards after being detached from the remaining cards with apparent intent to play; a defender's card so detached is also played as soon as his partner sees its face.

52. A card in dummy or any other faced hand is played when touched unless for a purpose other than play either manifest or mentioned.

Taking back played card. 53. A played card may not be withdrawn except:

(a) To comply with a penalty.

(b) To correct a revoke.

(c) To correct the error of playing more than one card to a trick.

(d) To substitute another card after an opponent has corrected either a revoke or a failure to comply with a lead or play penalty.

Premature lead or play by a defender. 54. If a defender leads to the next trick before his partner has played to the current trick, or plays out of rotation before his partner has played, (penalty) declarer may require the offender's partner to play:

(a) His highest card of the suit led; or

(b) His lowest card of the suit led; or

(c) A card of another specified suit.

If declarer has played from both contractors' hands, a defender is not subject to penalty for playing before his partner.

Lead out of turn. 55. A lead out of turn may be treated as a correct lead. It must be so treated if the non-offending side plays a card before attention is drawn to the irregularity.*

56. If either defender requires declarer to retract his lead out of turn, the card wrongly led is replaced without penalty; and if declarer has led from the wrong hand, he must lead from the correct hand and (penalty), if he can, a card of the same suit. A defender's drawing attention to declarer's lead out of turn is equivalent to requiring its retraction.

57. If declarer requires a defender to retract his lead out of turn:

(a) If it was a contractor's turn to lead, declarer leads from the correct hand and the card led out of turn becomes a penalty card.

(b) If it was the other defender's turn to lead, (penalty) declarer may forbid the lead of that suit, in which case the card wrongly led is picked up; or may treat the card led out of turn as a penalty card, in which case any card may be led.

Simultaneous leads or plays. 58. A lead or play made simultaneously with another player's proper lead or play is deemed to be subsequent to it. If a defender leads or plays two or more cards simultaneously, he may play either card, and the other card becomes a penalty card.

Inability to lead or play as required. 59. If a player is unable to lead or play as required to comply with a penalty, either because he has no card of the required suit or because of his obligation to follow suit, he may play any correct card. The penalty is satisfied, except in the case of a penalty card, which must be played at the first legal opportunity.

Playing before penalty has been enforced. 60. If declarer plays from either hand before enforcing a lead or play penalty, he is deemed to waive the penalty.

61. If a defender plays to a contractor's lead out of turn after declarer has been required to retract it, the defender's card becomes a penalty card.

62. A play by a member of the offending side, before a penalty has been enforced, does not affect the right of the non-offending side to enforce a penalty.

EXPOSED CARDS

Declarer exposing cards. 63. Declarer is never subject to penalty for exposure of a card, and no card of declarer's ever becomes a penalty card.

64. If declarer plays more than one card he must designate which is his play, and must restore any other card to his hand.

65. If declarer exposes his hand after an opening lead by the wrong defender, and before dummy has spread any part of his hand, dummy becomes declarer.

---

* If, after an opening lead by the wrong defender, declarer exposes his hand, see section 65.

66. If declarer intentionally exposes his hand otherwise than as provided in the preceding section, it is treated as a claim or concession of tricks and section 88 applies.

Defender exposing cards. 67. If a defender faces a card on the table, or sees the face of a card belonging to his partner before he is entitled to see it in the normal course of play or penalty enforcement; any such card becomes a penalty card, except as otherwise provided in these laws.*

Disposition of a penalty card. 68. A penalty card must be left face upward on the table until played. A defender should not pick up a penalty card and restore it to his hand; but if he does so, and if declarer plays from his own hand or dummy before requiring that the card be faced on the table again, such card ceases to be a penalty card.

69. A penalty card must be played at the first opportunity, whether in leading, following suit, discarding or trumping. The play of a penalty card is always subject to the obligation to follow suit, or to comply with a lead or play penalty. If a defender can play two or more penalty cards, declarer may designate which one is to be played.

Defender improperly exposing his hand. 70. If a defender improperly exposes his remaining card or cards, declarer may treat the remaining cards of either defender as penalty cards. The hand of the other defender, if exposed, may be picked up.

THE REVOKE†

Inquiries regarding a revoke. 71. Any player, including dummy, may ask a player who has failed to follow suit whether he has a card of the suit led, and may demand that an opponent correct his revoke.

Correcting a revoke. 72. A player must correct his revoke—

(a) Made in any of the first eleven tricks, if aware of it before it becomes established.

(b) Made in the twelfth trick, if aware of it before the cards have been mixed together. There is no penalty for a revoke made in the twelfth trick and it never becomes established.

73. To correct a revoke, the offender withdraws the revoke card and follows suit with any card. A revoke card from a defender's unfaced hand becomes a penalty card; any other revoke card may be replaced without penalty. The non-offending side may withdraw any card it played after the revoke but before attention was drawn to it.

Acts that establish a revoke. 74. A revoke in any of the first eleven

---

* Exceptions to section 67: A card led out of turn may be treated as a correct lead (section 55) or may be picked up (section 57-b). An exposed card may not be treated as a penalty card if dummy improperly (section 46-a) draws attention to it, or to the irregularity that caused its exposure.

† The penalty provisions of the revoke law are subject to section 46 if dummy has forfeited his rights. A claim of revoke does not warrant inspection of turned tricks except as permitted in sections 78 and 79.

tricks becomes established when the offender or his partner leads or plays to a subsequent trick or signifies his intention of doing so by naming a card, by claiming or conceding a trick, or by exposing a hand.

Procedure when a revoke is established. 75. When a revoke is established, the revoke trick stands as played. It counts in transferring tricks as a trick won "after the revoke."

76. If a revoke becomes established, after play ceases two tricks are transferred to the non-offending side if the revoking side has won two or more tricks after the revoke. One trick only is transferred if the revoking side wins but one trick after the revoke. There is no penalty for an established revoke:

(a) If the revoking side wins no trick after the revoke.

(b) If it is a subsequent revoke in the same suit by the same player.

(c) If attention is first drawn to it after the cards have been mixed together.

(d) If it is made in failing to play any card faced on the table, including a card from dummy's hand or a penalty card.

TRICKS

Gathering and arranging tricks. 77. Each completed trick must be gathered and turned face down on the table by the side winning it. The cards of each turned trick should be kept together so that the trick can be readily identified. All the tricks taken by a side should be arranged together in front of declarer or of one defender in such manner that their number and sequence are apparent.

Inspecting tricks; mixing cards before a claim is settled. 78. Declarer or either defender may, until his side has led or played a card to the next trick, inspect a trick and inquire what card each hand has played to it. Except as above provided or to account for a surplus or missing card, turned tricks may be inspected before play ceases only with the other side's consent.

79. After play ceases, the tricks and unplayed cards may be inspected to settle a claim of a revoke or of honors, or the number of tricks won or lost. If, after such claim, an opponent so mixes the cards that the claim cannot be proved, it must be allowed.

Defective trick. 80. If a hand has played too many cards to a trick, or has omitted to play to it, and if attention is drawn to the irregularity before a player of each side has played to the next trick, the error must be rectified. A card withdrawn from a defective trick, if played from a defender's unfaced hand, becomes a penalty card.

81. If attention is drawn to a defective trick after a player of each side has played to the next trick, the defective trick stands as played, and:

(a) A hand with too few cards plays the hand out with fewer cards than the other hands, does not play to the final trick (or tricks), and if it wins a trick with its last card the lead passes in rotation.

(b) A hand with too many cards forthwith faces and adds to the defective trick (but without changing its ownership) a card it could properly have played to it.

Trick appropriated in error. 82. A trick appropriated by the wrong side must be restored on demand to the side that played the winning card, and, in any case, its scoring value must be credited to that side, subject to section 93.

FAILURE TO COMPLY WITH A LEAD OR PLAY PENALTY

83. If a player is able to lead or play a penalty card, or a card or suit specified by an opponent in conformity with an agreed penalty, but instead plays an incorrect card:

(a) The offender must correct his error if aware of it before he or his partner plays another card. If the incorrect card was played from a defender's unfaced hand, it becomes a penalty card. A card played from the hand on the offender's left may be withdrawn if it was played after the error and before attention was drawn to it.

(b) After the offender or his partner has played another card, the incorrect card may not be withdrawn. After play ceases (penalty), there is a transfer of tricks to the non-offending side as though the offense were an established revoke (section 76).

CLAIMS AND CONCESSIONS

Concession of trick which cannot be lost. 84. The concession of a trick which cannot be lost by any play of the cards is void if attention is called to the error before the cards have been mixed together.

Concession of trick which has been won. 85. If a player concedes a trick he has in fact won (as by claiming nine tricks when his side has already won ten, or conceding defeat of a contract his side has fulfilled), the concession is void. If the score has been entered it may be corrected as provided in section 93).

Defender claiming or conceding tricks. 86. A defender may show any or all of his remaining cards to declarer for the purpose of establishing a claim or concession. If a defender makes a claim or concession in any other manner, he may be liable to penalty under section 20.

87. A concession of tricks by a defender is not valid unless his partner accedes. This provision does not preclude the enforcement of a penalty for a defender's irregularity.

Declarer claiming or conceding tricks. 88. If declarer intentionally exposes his hand, specifically claims or concedes one or more of the remaining tricks, or suggests that play may be curtailed, it is deemed to be a claim by declarer; and—

(a) Play should cease; and declarer should place and leave his hand face upwards on the table and forthwith make an adequate statement of his intended line of play.

(b) At any time after declarer's claim a defender may face his hand and may suggest a play to his partner. Declarer may not enforce any penalty for an irregularity committed by a defender whose hand is so faced.

(c) Declarer's claim must be allowed if both defenders accede to it, or if either defender allows his hand to be mixed with other cards.

(d) Either defender may require that play continue, in which case the section 89 applies.

89. If either defender requires that play continue after declarer's claim, declarer must play on, leaving his hand face upwards on the table. Declarer may make no play inconsistent with any statement he may have made. Unless declarer has stated his intention to do so at the time of making his claim—

(a) He may not lead a trump while either defender has a trump.

(b) He may not finesse either in the suit led or in trumping the suit led.

If declarer attempts to make a play prohibited by this section, either defender may require him to withdraw it, provided neither defender has played a card after it.

PART VI—THE SCORE

Keeping score. 90. Each side has a trick score and a premium score. The scores of the respective sides for each rubber should be entered in two adjacent vertical columns, the trick points in descending order below a horizontal line separating the trick and premium scores, the premium points (i.e., all points other than trick points) in ascending order above this line. A scorer should enter scores made by his side in the left-hand column. Whenever a game is scored, a line should be drawn across the trick score of both sides and underneath all trick point entries made in that game, none of which carry over to the next game. Subsequent trick points should be entered only below lines so drawn. Lines drawn prematurely should be forthwith erased.

Recording the score. 91. When play ceases, all four players are equally responsible to see that the number of tricks won by each side is correctly determined, and that all scores are promptly and correctly entered in the score or scores, in accordance with the scoring table (section 98).

Scoring transferred tricks. 92. A transferred trick ranks for all scoring purposes as a trick won in play by the side receiving it.

Correcting the score. 93. A proven or admitted error in any score may be corrected at any time before the rubber score is agreed, except that: If each player keeping score has made an error in entering or failing to enter a part score, or in omitting to score a game or in awarding one; such an error may not be corrected after the last card of the second succeeding correct deal has been dealt, unless a majority of the players consent.

A game—the rubber. 94. A game is won by the side which first scores a total of 100 or more trick points for odd tricks bid and won.

95. A rubber ends when a side has won two games, and the winners of the final game add to their score: 500 points if their opponents have won one game, 700 points if their opponents have not won a game. At the end of the rubber the trick and premium points of each side are added. The side with the larger total score wins the rubber, irrespective of the number of games (if any) which it has won. The difference between the two totals represents the number of points won.

Effect of incorrect pack. 96. Scores made as a result of hands played with an incorrect pack are not affected by the discovery of the imperfection after the cards have been mixed together.

Scoring an unfinished rubber; player obliged to leave. 97. If for any reason a rubber is not finished, the score is computed as follows: If but one game has been completed, the winners of that game score 300 points; if but one side has a part score (or scores) in an unfinished game, that side scores 50 points; the trick and premium points of each side are added, and the side with the larger total score * wins the difference between the two totals.

THE PROPRIETIES

(1) It is reprehensible to profit by information gained as a result of an irregularity committed by one's own side for which no penalty, or a penalty incommensurate with the information gained, is prescribed.

(2) It is improper to infringe a law deliberately, as by making an insufficient bid, whether or not a penalty is prescribed.

(3) A player should refrain from—

    a. Varying the formulae used in calling;*

    b. Calling with special emphasis, inflection or intonation;

    c. Passing or doubling with exceptional haste or reluctance;

    d. Making a call with undue delay which may result in conveying improper information to partner;

---

* The recommended calling formulae are: "Pass" (avoid "I pass" or "no bid"); "1 heart" (avoid "I bid"); "1 no trump" (avoid "without" or "without a trump"); "double" (avoid stating the number of tricks or the denomination doubled); "6 spades" avoid "little slam").

Contract Bridge scoring table. 98.

	Odd Tricks Bid and Won in	Undoubled	Doubled
TRICK POINTS FOR CONTRACTORS	Clubs or Diamonds, each	20	40
	Hearts or Spades, each	30	60
	No Trump { first / each subsequent	40 / 30	80 / 60

Redoubling doubles the doubled points for Odd Tricks.
Vulnerability does not affect points for Odd Tricks.
100 Trick Points constitute a game.

	Overtricks	Not Vulnerable	Vulnerable
PREMIUM POINTS FOR CONTRACTORS	Undoubled, each	Trick Value	Trick Value
	Doubled, each	100	200
	Making Doubled or Redoubled Contract }	50	50
	Undertricks		
DEFENDERS	Undoubled, each	50	100
	Doubled { first / each subsequent	100 / 200	200 / 300

Redoubling doubles the doubled points for Overtricks and Undertricks,
but does not affect the points for making Doubled Contracts.

PREMIUM POINTS FOR HOLDERS	Honors in One Hand	{ 4 Trump Honors / 5 Trump Honors or 4 Aces at No-Trump	100 / 150
	Slams Bid and Won	{ Little, not vulnerable 500, vulnerable / Grand, " " 1000, "	750 / 1500
CONTRACTORS	Rubber Points	{ Two game / Three game	700 / 500

Unfinished Rubber—Winners of one game score 300 points. If but one
side has a part score in an unfinished game, it scores 50 points.

Doubling and Redoubling do not affect Honor, Slam, or Rubber points.
Vulnerability does not affect points for Honors.

e. Indicating in any way approval or disapproval of partner's call or play;

f. Giving by word, manner or gesture an indication of the nature of the hand held;

g. Making a remark or gesture or asking a question from which an inference may be drawn;

h. Giving unauthorized information as to an incident of the auction or play;

i. Volunteering information which should be given only in response to a question;

j. Requesting, except for his own benefit, a review of calls or a placing of cards played to a trick;

k. An unnecessary hesitation, remark or mannerism which may deceive the opponents;

l. Attracting attention to the score, except when necessary to do so for his own information;

m. Calling attention to the number of tricks needed to complete or defeat the contract or to the fact that it has already been fulfilled or defeated;

n. Playing a card with special emphasis;

o. Playing with undue delay when the play does not need consideration;

p. Preparing to gather a trick before all four hands have played to it;

q. Detaching a card from his hand before it is his turn to lead or play;

r. Failing to keep the tricks in correct order and distinct from one another, or allowing some to be placed on the opposite side of the table;

s. Watching the place in a player's hand from which he draws a card, and drawing any inference therefrom;

t. Making gratuitous comments during the play as to the auction, the adequacy of the contract or the nature of the hand.

(4) It is improper to attempt to conceal a revoke by revoking again, or to conceal a revoke card if a hand is not played out, but there is no obligation to call attention to an established revoke or other irregularity committed by self or partner.

(5) It is improper to play out of turn, carelessly or otherwise.

(6) While it is reprehensible to allow partner's hesitation, remark or manner to influence a call, lead or play, it is proper to draw inferences from an opponent's gratuitous hesitation, remark or manner, but such inferences are drawn at one's own risk.

(7) It is proper to warn partner against infringing a law of the game

(e. g., against revoking, or against calling, leading or playing out of turn).

(8) All four players are responsible to see that each hand plays a card, and but one, to each trick, and should forthwith correct such an irregularity.

(9) Declarer should play out all hands in which there is any doubt as to the eventual outcome.

(10) Bystanders or members not playing should refrain from making gratuitous remarks. They should not call attention to any irregularity or mistake, or speak on any question of fact or law except when requested to give an opinion.

(11) It is improper to employ, without explaining its meaning to the opponents, a convention in calling or an unusual convention in play, the significance of which may not be clear to them. When applied to a call, the term convention covers a call designed to convey an arbitrary or artificial meaning, or used by a player with the assurance that his partner will not accept it in its natural sense. Such a call is not subject to penalty as an improper remark. It is necessary that a convention so used should be fully understood by the other side, and players using convention calls should be ready to reply fully to a proper inquiry by an opponent as to their meaning or use. Should it be necessary to make such an inquiry during the auction, the partner of the player who has made the convention call should reply. The committee of any Association, Tournament or Club, or a group of persons playing Contract Bridge, may prohibit or restrict the use of conventions which are both generally unrecognized and sufficiently intricate to cause unreasonable delay.

RULES FOR CLUB PROCEDURE

The following rules, governing membership in new and existing tables, have proven satisfactory in club use over a long period of years:

Definitions. MEMBER—An applicant who has acquired the right to play at a table either immediately or in his turn.

COMPLETE TABLE—A Table with six members.

INCOMPLETE TABLE—A Table with four or five members.

Time limit on right to play. A. An applicant may not play in a rubber, unless he has become a member of a table before a card is duly drawn for the selection of players or partners.

Newly formed tables. B. If there are more than six applicants, the six highest-ranking ones become members. The four highest-ranking members play the first rubber. Those who have not played, ranked in their order of entry into the room, take precedence over those who have played. The latter rank equally, except that players leaving existing tables to join the new table rank lowest.*

---

* Precedence between those of equal rank is determined by drawing cards, the drawer of the higher-ranking card obtaining precedence.

Existing tables. C. An application establishes membership in a table either forthwith or (if the table is complete) as soon as a vacancy occurs, unless applications in excess of the number required to complete a table are made at the same time, in which case precedence between applicants is established as in the preceding rule.

D. After each rubber place must be made, by the member who has played the greatest number of consecutive rubbers at that table,* for any member who did not play the last rubber, except that a member who has left another existing table must draw cards for the right to play his first rubber with the member who would otherwise have played.

E. If a member breaks up a game by leaving three players at a table, he is not entitled to compete against them for entry at another table.

Membership limited to one table. F. No one can be a member of more than one table at the same time, unless a member consents, on request, to make a fourth at another table and announces his intention of returning to his former table as soon as his place can be filled. Failure to announce such intention results in loss of membership at his former table.

BRIDGE PROCEDURE AND ETIQUETTE
FOR BEGINNERS

The four players first draw cards for partners and to determine the first dealer. They have two packs of cards, one with a "blue" back design and the other with a "red" back design (any contrasting designs and colors will do, but the cards are traditionally spoken of as red and blue). One pack is spread face out across the table, as shown on page 583. Each player draws one card but keeps it face down until all players have drawn; then all show their cards.

The cards drawn are the ♣K, ♠10, ♡10, ♠3, respectively. The player who drew the highest card, the king, has the right to choose his seat and to choose the pack with which he will deal; he is the first dealer. He takes the seat at the table designated as North. The player with the next-highest card, the ♠10, which outranks the ♡10 because spades are a higher suit, must take the South seat opposite him, and North and South are partners. The other two players take the East and West seats, and either of them may take either of these seats he chooses. North, the first dealer because he drew the highest card, chooses to deal with the blue pack. Throughout the rubber, North and South will always deal with the blue cards, and East and West always with the red cards.

The shuffle. East takes the blue pack and shuffles it for North; the pack with which any player deals was always prepared for him by the player at his left. At the same time, South takes the red pack and shuffles it for the second deal of the game, which will be by East. The dealer has the right to shuffle the pack last, before it is cut, but few players avail themselves of this privilege in Bridge.

In shuffling, a player in a Bridge game should use the riffle shuffle; other forms of shuffling are not in accordance with Bridge etiquette.

---

* See the footnote to page 133.

Divide the pack, face down, into two piles of roughly the same size. Place them both on the table and bring together the corners only, so that they touch. Now hold down each portion with your fingers and bend up the corners with your thumbs. Slide the two portions a little closer together so that they will interlock by about one quarter of an inch. Let the cards riffle downward, by gradually releasing the pressure of your thumbs. They will fit together as though meshed, and the cards will be mixed. Now relax the pressure of your fingers on the cards, and slide the two portions of the pack together.

About three shuffles of this type will mix the cards adequately.

East and South having shuffled their packs, each puts the shuffled pack on the table at his right. The pack that South shuffled will remain there until East is ready to deal with it. The pack that East shuffled, however, must be dealt immediately, so North picks it up with his left hand, transfers it to his right hand, and puts it down on the table beside him.

The cut and deal. West, the player at North's right hand, cuts the blue pack by lifting off about half of it and putting it down on the table toward North. North completes the cut by taking up the bottom portion, the one remaining nearer to West, and putting it on top of the other portion. He then picks up the cut pack and begins to deal.

North deals the cards one at a time, face down, to the four players (including himself) in rotation, the first card going to East. In dealing, he holds the pack in one hand and with the other hand slides the cards off one by one, moving both his hands a few inches toward the player who is to receive the next card. It is not proper to remove each card with the thumb and forefinger and flip it or set it down on the table in front of the player.

When the entire pack has been dealt in this manner, each player has thirteen cards. Until this time, no player should touch or look at any card dealt to him. When the deal is complete, each player picks up his cards and looks at them, sorting them (usually) into suits.

The auction. North, as the dealer, is entitled to bid first. He may pass or bid. A pass is an expression of unwillingness to bid (or double, or redouble, which are legal calls only when there has previously been a bid). A bid is an offer to win a certain minimum number of tricks with a named suit as trump, or with no trump.

All bids are made in terms of "odd-tricks," an odd-trick being a trick won in excess of six. Thus, a side that wins seven tricks has won one odd-trick.

The form of a bid is as follows: "One spade"—an offer to win seven tricks with spades as trumps; "Two no trumps"—an offer to win eight tricks without a trump suit; etc. The highest possible bid is a bid of seven odd-tricks, because there are only thirteen tricks altogether, the first six tricks being known as the "book" and the additional seven tricks being the odd-tricks.

The turn to bid moves from player to player in clockwise rotation. Each successive bid must be sufficient to overcall the preceding bid; either it must name a greater number of odd-tricks, or it must name the same number of odd-tricks in a higher-ranking denomination. In bidding, no trump ranks highest, then spades, hearts, diamonds, clubs. Thus, a bid of two spades will overcall a bid of two hearts, but it would take a bid of three diamonds to overcall a bid of two hearts.

North, the first bidder in our game, passes. East passes, South passes, and West passes. All four players have passed, and this first deal is "passed out." All four players toss their hands into the center of the table, face down, and West gathers them in and begins to shuffle them for the time when South will deal. East shifts the shuffled red deck from his left to his right hand, North cuts it, and East deals another hand. When a hand is passed out, the deal passes to the next player in rotation.

This time it is East's first turn to bid. East passes, but South opens the bidding with a bid of one heart. West doubles. The effect of a double is to increase scoring values if the bid that is doubled becomes the contract. Once a bid is doubled, the side that made the bid may redouble, which further increases the scoring values. (A side may not double its own bid, nor may it redouble a bid that has not been doubled by an opponent.) A double does not affect the rank of a bid; in this case, the one-heart bid may still be overcalled by one spade, or by anything higher, the same as it could be if it were not doubled.

After West's double, North passes. East bids two diamonds. South passes and West bids two no trump. North passes and East bids three no trump. South and West both pass, but North doubles this bid. Then East, South and West pass.

This closes the auction. Once any bid has been made, the auction continues as long as any one is willing to make a higher bid, or to double the last bid, or to redouble a doubled bid; but when there are three consecutive passes the auction is closed and the last bid becomes the contract.

The bidding just described would be written, in Contract Bridge notation, as follows:

EAST	SOUTH	WEST	NORTH
Pass	1 ♡	Double	Pass
2 ◇	Pass	2 N T	Pass
3 N T	Pass	Pass	Double
Pass	Pass	Pass	

The play. Now the auction is ended. The contract is three no trump doubled and West is the declarer. This means that West will play both his own hand and his partner's hand, his partner's hand being called the dummy.

West is the declarer even though it was East who made the final bid of three no trump. The declarer is the player who first for his side bid the denomination named in the contract. Since West was the first mem-

ber of his side to bid no trump, so long as his side wins the contract at
no trump, West will be the declarer.

North makes the opening lead. The player at declarer's left always
leads to the first trick. North may lead any card in his hand; he does this
by placing it face up in the center of the table. As soon as North has led,
but not before, East spreads his hand on the table as dummy. If there
were a trump suit, he would put the trumps at his right, but this is a
no-trump contract and the suits may be put down in any order provided they are kept separate. From this point on, West as the declarer
will play both the dummy's cards and his own, but from each hand in
its proper turn.

The turn to play moves in clockwise rotation, and each player plays
one card; the lead to a trick and the cards of the other three players
constitute a completed trick.

Each player in turn must follow suit to the lead if he can; if he cannot
follow suit he may play any card. Each trick is won by the highest card
of the suit led, if it contains no trump; if there is a trump suit, a trick
containing a trump is won by the highest trump it contains. The winner
of each trick leads to the next trick and may lead any card.

One player for each side gathers in all the tricks won by his side,
stacking them face down in front of him. Declarer gathers the tricks for
his side; either of the opponents (the defenders) may gather in the
tricks for his side, but it is customary for the tricks to be taken in by
the partner of the defender who wins the first trick for his side.

The tricks are kept separate from each other, overlapping as shown in
the illustration, so that their number and the order in which they were
won is apparent. See the illustration on page 396.

Scoring. When all thirteen tricks have been played, the tricks taken by
the respective sides are counted and the result agreed upon. The score
for that deal is then determined in accordance with the Scoring Table
(page 131) and entered by the scorekeeper, or scorekeepers, on a
bridge scorepad.

Any player may keep score. It is best if at least one player on each
side keeps score. But regardless of how many players keep score, all four
players are equally responsible to see that the score for each deal is
correctly entered.

The bridge score is divided by a horizontal line, the trick score of each
side going below that line and the premium, or honor, score of each side
going above that line.

In the trick score can go only the values of odd-tricks bid and made
by declarer's side. If declarer bids three no trump and wins only eight
tricks, he has not fulfilled the contract and can score nothing in the trick
score, not even for the two odd-tricks he made. If he bid three no trump
and wins ten tricks, he scores in his trick score the value of the three
odd-tricks he both bid and made; the fourth odd-trick is an overtrick
and must be scored above the line.

When a side amasses 100 trick points, whether they are made in one or more deals, it wins a game. Both sides then start at a score of zero toward the next game.

When a side has won two games, it has won the rubber. In addition to its other scores, it receives a bonus of 700 points if its opponents have not won a game in that rubber, a bonus of 500 points if its opponents have won a game. All the scores of both sides are then totaled up, and the side with the greater number of points has won the rubber by the margin of the difference in scores. A pack is spread for another draw, and the players draw again for partners and seats and begin a new rubber (often, by agreement, the players pivot as explained on page 156, or play a match game in which partnerships do not change).

Premium points include, in addition to overtricks made by declarer, penalties for undertricks; slam bonuses; and honors.

When declarer fails to fulfill his contract, his opponents score the points prescribed by the scoring table for each trick by which he falls short.

When a side bids and makes a contract of six odd-tricks, it scores the premium for a little slam; if it bids and makes a contract of seven odd-tricks it scores the premium for a grand slam. These premiums are scored only when the slam is bid for and the contract is fulfilled. If the contract is not fulfilled, declarer scores nothing, even if the odd-tricks he did win were sufficient to make a game; or if, for example, he bid a grand slam and actually made only a little slam.

Vulnerability affects the premiums. A side becomes vulnerable when it has won a game toward the rubber. Vulnerability exposes it to greater undertrick penalties, but entitles it to greater premiums for slams and for overtricks when it fulfills a doubled or redoubled contract.

Honors are scored by the side holding them, whether they are in the hand of declarer, dummy, or either defender. When a player holds four trump honors (A, K, Q, J, 10) in his hand, his side receives 100 points; if he holds all five trump honors, or all four aces at a no-trump contract, his side receives 150 points. There is no bonus for holding this many honors in a suit that is not trump or for holding all four aces when the contract is not no trump.

Contract Bridge is a partnership game, and points earned or lost by one partner are scored equally for or against his side. At the end, settlement is made by each player individually on the basis of the entire score of his side.

ILLUSTRATION OF CONTRACT BRIDGE SCORING

Following is an illustration of the scoring of a rubber played between North-South on one side and East-West on the other. South keeps score; therefore he will record all North-South scores in the column marked

"We" and all East-West scores in the column marked "They." The letters
(a), (b), etc., are shown only for purposes of illustration, of course, and
would not appear on the actual score sheet.

WE	THEY
500 (g)	100 (d)
30 (f)	50 (d)
100 (e)	60 (b)
200 (e)	50 (a)
150 (c)	60 (b)
	120 (d)
40 (f)	
60 (g).	
1080	440

(a) South bids three no trump and wins only eight tricks. East-West
score for one undertrick, not vulnerable.

(b) East bids two spades and wins ten tricks. Though he has made
"four spades," he scores below the line only the two odd-tricks he bid for
and the other two go above the line and do not count toward game. If
he had bid four spades and won the same number of tricks, it would
have been game.

(c) North bids four hearts and wins eleven tricks. Technically, only
120 points are scored below the line, and 30 points above the line; but
since the 120-point score ends the game, and all the points will count
in the long run anyway, the scorekeeper saves trouble by writing the
entire 150 points below the line. Now a line is drawn across both sides
of the score sheet, for the first game has been won by North-South. The
60-point part-score of East-West will not help them toward making the
next game. However, the points will of course count in their final total.

(d) West bids three clubs, which North doubles. West plays the hand at three clubs doubled and wins ten tricks. The three odd-tricks he bid for, at their doubled value, give him 120 points below the line— enough to make game. He receives 50 points bonus for fulfilling the doubled contract, and 100 points for a doubled overtrick, not vulnerable. A line is drawn under the 120-point score, ending the second game.

(e) East bids four hearts, which South doubles, and East wins only nine tricks. Therefore East is down one, and North-South score 200 points for one undertrick, doubled and vulnerable. In addition, North held four honors in hearts, and his side scores 100 points therefor; honors are scored to the credit of the holders, whether declarer, dummy, or a defender.

(f) North bids one no trump and wins eight tricks. Forty points are scored below the line for the odd-trick bid and made, and 30 above the line for the overtrick. Every odd-trick made at no trump, except the first one, counts only 30. This applies whether it is scored below the line or above.

(g) South bids three diamonds and wins nine tricks, fulfilling the contract. This gives him 60 points below the line, and, when added to the 40 points North-South made on the preceding hand, brings the total up to 100, constituting a game. North-South score 500 points bonus for the rubber (the bonus is 500 points because East-West also won a game).

Now all the scores are totalled. North-South have a total of 1,080 points, East-West have 440. The difference is 640. North-South win a 6-point rubber, equivalent to 600 points. In bridge scoring, except in match games, remainders of less than 50 points count as nothing; remainders of 50 points or more count as a full 100. If the difference had been 650 points, North-South would have won a 7-point rubber. (In set matches, the exact score counts; see page 156.)

ILLUSTRATIONS OF IRREGULARITIES

All irregularities in Contract Bridge are covered by the Official Laws (pages 116-134); but there are several irregularities that are particularly frequent and that the average player may have difficulty in adjusting by following the bare language of the laws. These most frequent irregularities, and the remedies or penalties for them, are illustrated in the following paragraphs.

In all these illustrations South is declarer, North dummy, West and East the defenders, with West the proper opening leader.

Lead out of turn. West should make the opening lead, but East leads the ◇7. South may say to West, "Lead anything but a diamond." Or South may permit West to make any lead he pleases, but in this case ◇7 becomes a penalty card: East must place it face up on the table in front of him and leave it there. The first time he can legally lead or play it he must do so, subject only to his duty to follow suit.

In another case, North makes an opening lead, thinking that West has won the contract. But South is the actual declarer. North's card is put back in his hand. There is no penalty against the declaring side for exposing cards, since the information so given can be utilized only by the opponents.

Declarer leads from wrong hand. North (dummy) won the last trick, but South leads the ♠K from his own hand. West says, "The lead is in dummy." South replaces the ♠K in his own hand and must lead a spade from dummy. When South plays to that trick, he does not have to play the ♠K if he has another spade he prefers to play. (If dummy had not held a spade, South could have led any card from dummy.)

West could accept the out-of-turn lead of the ♠K, if he wished, by following to it at once, before either he or East made any remark about its irregularity.

Revoke corrected. South leads ◇6. West has some diamonds, but he plays ♣9. Dummy plays ◇K and East plays ◇3. At this juncture West says, "Wait, I have a diamond."

There is time for West to correct his revoke, because it is not established—neither West nor East has led or played to the next trick.

West must leave the ♣9 face up on the table as a penalty card. He may play any diamond he wishes, and he elects to play ◇A. Now declarer may retract his play of the ◇K from dummy and substitute a small diamond. But East may not change his card on the trick.

In another case, South revokes and notices his error in time for correction. He replaces the revoke card in his hand, without penalty, and follows suit with any card he chooses.

Revoke established. South leads ♠K. West has a spade, but plays ♡7. East wins the trick with the ♠A and leads a heart.

It is now too late for West to correct his revoke. East, a "member of the offending side," has led to the next trick and the revoke is established. Play proceeds normally, and let us suppose that East-West win one more trick.

South's contract was two spades, and when play is ended he has won eight tricks. But, as the revoke penalty, he may take two of East-West's tricks and transfer them to his pile. That gives him ten tricks in all. He scores 60 below the line for making two spades, and 60 above the line for two overtricks. Note that South does not get game for making ten tricks at spades. He bid only two spades, and that is all he can score toward game. Tricks transferred as the result of a revoke penalty are scored exactly as though won in play. If South, having bid two spades, had won ten tricks without the revoke, he could not have made game; therefore he cannot make game as a result of the revoke penalty.

Finally, take a case in which West revokes, and East, who wins the trick, establishes the revoke by leading to the next trick; play continues, but East-West do not win another trick.

After the play is completed, South may take only one trick as the revoke penalty—the trick on which the revoke occurred. He is not entitled to any trick the defenders won before the revoke occurred because obviously the revoke could have had nothing to do with how such tricks were won. The purpose of the laws is only to prevent a side from profiting from its breach of law.

Incorrect hand. West deals, and South becomes declarer at a six-spade contract. With only three tricks left to be played, it is discovered that dummy has four cards left and West has only two, East and South having three cards each. The entire deal is called off and West, after a proper shuffle and cut, must deal again. It does not matter that South could have made his contract easily no matter what card was taken from dummy and given to West.

In another case, with three tricks left to be played it is discovered that South, West and North have three cards each and East has only two. The missing card is found on the floor. The deal stands; the missing card is restored to East's hand. Suppose it is the ♠7 and on some previous trick East has failed to follow suit to a spade lead. East must pay the penalty for a revoke; the missing card is considered to have been in his hand all the time.

Still another case: West deals; South plays a game contract and apparently fulfills it, but before the cards are mixed together it is discovered that the pack contains two threes of diamonds and no four of diamonds. The result does not stand; the pack is replaced or corrected and West deals again. But all scores made previous to that deal stand.

Claim by declarer, disputed by a defender. With five cards left in each hand, South spreads his hand and says, "I have the rest." West says, "You'd better play it out."

South must leave his hand face up on the table and continue play. Unless he announced his intention to do so in making his claim, he may not make any play whose success depends on finding a certain card in the hand of one of the defenders rather than in the hand of the other.

POINTERS ON CONTRACT BRIDGE

Contract Bridge is too complex a game to be reduced to a few simple rules and formulas; there are thousands of textbooks on the subject and none of them comes close to exhausting the strategy of the game. The beginner's best course is to pick up the basic approach to Contract Bridge strategy from books, but to acquire most of his understanding of the game from practice in actual play.

Contract Bridge strategy falls naturally into two parts, bidding and play. The play is subject to individual analysis. It is almost necessary, in bidding, to have some understanding with one's partner as to the conventional meaning of the various bids. To this end innumerable systems have been devised. The most popular is the Goren System.

Outline of The Goren System of Bidding*

GOREN POINT-COUNT TABLE

High-Card Points	*Quick Tricks*
Ace = 4 pts.	A-K = 2
King = 3 pts.	A-Q = 1½
Queen = 2 pts.	A or K-Q = 1
Jack = 1 pt.	K-x = ½

High-card points (usually called simply *points*) are counted for nearly every bid. To them are often added distributional points, described below. Quick tricks are counted only for opening bids on borderline hands and, often, when considering a double of an opponent's bid.

Game and Slam Requirements. 26 pts. will normally produce a game. 33 pts. will normally produce a small slam. 37 pts. will normally produce a grand slam.

DISTRIBUTIONAL POINTS
In addition to High-Card Points

The Opening Bidder Counts For Original Bids

Void Suit = 3 pts.
Singleton = 2 pts.
Doubleton = 1 pt.
Add 1 pt. for all 4 aces.
Deduct 1 pt. for an aceless hand.

Deduct 1 pt. for each unguarded honor (examples: Q-x, J-x, singleton K, Q, or J).

The Responder Counts When Raising Partner's Suit

Void Suit = 5 pts.
Singleton = 3 pts.
Doubleton = 1 pt.
Promote honors in partner's bid suit by 1 pt. (unless these honors already total 4 pts.).
Deduct 1 pt. from total distributional points if hand contains only three trumps or if hand has 4-3-3-3 distribution.

For Rebids. After partner has raised opening bidder's suit:
  Add 1 additional pt. for the fifth card in the trump suit.
  Add 2 additional pts. for the sixth and each subsequent trump.

MINIMUM BIDDABLE SUITS

For an Opening Bid
4-Card Suits—must contain 4 high-card points (example—K-J-x-x, A-x-x-x)
5-Card Suits
Any 5-Card Suit (x-x-x-x-x)

For a Response or Rebid
Q-10-x-x or better (example— Q-10-x-x, K-x-x-x, A-x-x-x)
Any 5-Card Suit (x-x-x-x-x)

* Authorized outline of the Goren System of Bidding as condensed from *Goren's Point Count System Made Easy, Contract Bridge Complete,* and *Contract Bridge in a Nutshell,* all published by Doubleday & Co., New York, and from *Point Count Bidding* and *Contract Bridge for Beginners,* both published by Simon and Schuster, New York; all by Charles H. Goren.

REBIDDABLE SUITS

4-Card Suits	No 4-card suit is rebiddable
5-Card Suits	Must be Q-J-9-x-x or better
6-Card Suits	Any 6-card suit is rebiddable (x-x-x-x-x-x)

OPENING BID REQUIREMENTS

One of a suit

  (a) 14-pt. hands must be opened.

  (b) 13-pt. hands may be opened if a good rebid is available (a rebiddable suit or a second biddable suit).

  (c) All openings must contain two quick tricks.

  (d) A third-position opening is permitted with 11 pts. if hand contains a good suit.

Two of a suit
(*forcing to game*)

  (a) 25 pts. with a good 5-card suit (1 pt. less with a second good 5-card suit).

  (b) 23 pts. with a good 6-card suit.

  (c) 21 pts. with a good 7-card suit.

Three, four, or five of a suit (*preëmptive bids*)

Preëmptive bids show less than 10 pts. in high cards and the ability to win within two tricks of the contract vulnerable and within three tricks not vulnerable. They should usually be based on a good 7-card or longer suit.

One No-Trump

16 to 18 pts. (in no-trump bidding only high-card points are counted) and 4-3-3-3, 4-4-3-2 or 5-3-3-2 distribution with Q-x or better in any doubleton.

Two No-Trump

22 to 24 pts. and all suits stopped (J-x-x-x; Q-x-x; K-x; or better).

Three No-Trump

25 to 27 pts. and all suits stopped.

Choice of Suits. Generally speaking, bid your longest suit first. With two 5-card suits bid the higher-ranking first. With two or more 4-card suits, bid the suit immediately lower in rank to your short suit (doubleton, singleton, or void).

RESPONSES

General Principles. Any bid of a new suit by the responding hand is forcing on the opening bidder for one round. Thus, each time the responder bids a new suit the opener must bid again. If responder should jump, his bid is forcing to game.

With less than 10 pts., responder should prefer to raise partner if partner has opened in a major suit, and to bid a new suit himself at the one level in preference to raising a minor-suit opening bid. With 11 or 12 pts., responder can make two bids but should not force to game. With 13 pts. or more he should see that the bidding is not dropped before a game contract is reached, if a convenient contract can be found. With 19 pts. he should make a strong effort to reach a slam.

Responses to Suit-bids of One. Raise. To raise partner's suit responder must have adequate trump support. This consists of J-10-x, Q-x-x, x-x-x-x, or better for a non-rebid suit; and Q-x, K-x, A-x, or x-x-x for a rebid suit.

Raise partner's suit to two with 7 to 10 pts. and adequate trump support.

Raise to three with 13 to 16 pts. and at least four trumps. Raise to four with no more than 9 high-card points plus at least five trumps and a short suit (singleton or void).

Bid of a new suit. At one level requires 6 pts. or more. This response may be made on anything ranging from a weak hand, where responder is just trying to keep the bidding open, to a very powerful one when he is not sure where the hand should be played.

At two level requires 10 pts. or more.

Jump in a new suit requires 19 pts. or more (the jump shift is reserved for hands where a slam is very likely. Responder should hold either a strong suit or strong support for opener's suit).

No-trump responses (made on balanced hands). One no-trump requires 6 to 10 pts. in high cards (this bid is often made on an unbalanced hand if responder's suit is lower in rank than the opening bidder's and responder lacks the 10 pts. required to take the bidding into the two level).

Two no-trump requires 13 to 15 pts. in high cards, all unbid suits stopped, and a balanced hand.

Three no-trump requires 16 to 18 pts. in high cards, all unbid suits stopped, and 4-3-3-3 distribution.

Responses to Suit-bids of Two. An opening bid of two in a suit is unconditionally forcing to game and responder may not pass until game is reached. With 6 pts. or less he bids two no-trump regardless of his distribution. With 7 pts. and one quick trick, he may show a new suit or raise the opener's suit. With 8 or 9 high-card points and a balanced hand, responder bids three no-trump.

Responses to Preëmptive Bids. Since the opener has overbid his hand by two or three tricks, aces, kings and potential ruffing values are the key factors to be considered when responder is contemplating a raise. One or two trumps constitutes sufficient support.

Responses to a One No-Trump Bid. Balanced hands. Raise to 2 N T with 8 or 9 pts., or with 7 pts. and a good 5-card suit. Raise to 3 N T with 10 to 14 pts. Raise to 4 N T with 15 or 16 pts. Raise to 6 N T with 17 or 18 pts. Raise to 7 N T with 21 pts.

Unbalanced hands. With less than 8 pts. plus a 5-card suit, bid two diamonds, two hearts, or two spades. (Do not bid two clubs on a 5-card club suit.) With 8 pts. or more and a 4-card major suit, bid two clubs. (This is an artificial bid asking opener to show a 4-card major if he has one. See section on rebids by opening one no-trump bidder.) With 10 pts. and a good suit, bid three of that suit. With a 6-card major suit and less than 10 pts. in high cards, jump to game in the suit.

Responses to a Two No-Trump Opening. Balanced hands. Raise to 3 N T with 4 to 8 pts. Raise to 4 N T with 9 or 10 pts. Raise to 6 N T with 11 or 12 pts. Raise to 7 N T with 15 pts.

Unbalanced hands. With a 5-card major suit headed by an honor, plus 4 pts., bid the suit at the three level. Show any 6-card major suit.

Responses to a Three No-Trump Opening. Show any 5-card suit if the hand contains 5 pts. in high cards. Raise to 4 N T with 7 pts. Raise to 6 N T with 8 or 9 pts. Raise to 7 N T with 12 pts.

REBIDS

Rebids by Opening Bidder. The opener's rebid is frequently the most important call of the auction, as he now has the opportunity to reveal the exact strength of his opening bid and therefore whether game or slam is in contemplation. His opening is valued according to the following table:

13 to 16 pts.	Minimum hand
16 to 19 pts.	Good hand
19 to 21 pts.	Very good hand

13 to 16 pts. *Minimum hand.* If partner has made a limit response (one no-trump or a single raise) opener should pass, as game is impossible. If partner bids a new suit at the one level, opener may make a single raise with good trump support, rebid one no-trump with a balanced hand, or, with an unbalanced hand, rebid his own suit or a new suit (if he does not go past the level of two in the suit of his original bid).

16 to 19 pts. *Good hand.* If partner has made a limit response (one no-trump or a single raise) opener should bid again, as game is possible if responder has maximum values. If responder has bid a new suit, opener may make a jump raise with four trumps, or jump in his own suit if he has a 6-card suit, or bid a new suit.

19 to 21 pts. *Very good hand.* If partner has made a limit response (one no-trump or a single raise) opener may jump to game in either denomination, according to his distribution. If responder has bid a new suit, opener may make a jump raise to game with four trumps, or jump to game in his own suit if it is solid. With a balanced hand and 19 or 20 pts., opener should jump to two no-trump. With 21 pts. he should jump to three no-trump. With 22 pts. and up he should jump in a new suit (forcing to game and suggesting a slam).

Rebids by Opening No-Trump Bidder. Two-club convention. When the responder bids two clubs, the opening bidder must show a 4-card biddable major suit if he has one:

With four spades, he bids two spades;
With four hearts, he bids two hearts;
With four cards in each major, he bids two spades;
With no 4-card major suit, he bids two diamonds.

Opening no-trump bidder must pass: When responder raises to two no-trump and opener has a minimum (16 pts.); when responder bids two diamonds, two hearts, or two spades, and opener has only 16 or 17 points and no good fit for responder's suit; when responder bids three no-trump, four spades, or four hearts.

DEFENSIVE BIDDING

Overcalls. An overcall is a defensive bid (made after the other side has opened the bidding). Prospects for game are not as good as they are for the opening bidder, in view of the announced adverse strength, and safety becomes a prime consideration. Overcalls are therefore based not on a specified number of points but rather on a good suit. Generally speaking the over-caller should employ the same standards as a preëmptor; he should be able to win in his own hand within two tricks of his bid if vulnerable and within three tricks not vulnerable.

One No-Trump Overcall. An overcall of one no-trump is similar to a one no-trump opening bid and shows 16 to 18 pts. with a balanced hand and the opening bidder's suit well stopped.

Jump Overcall. Any jump overcall, whether it is a single, double or triple jump, is preëmptive in nature and shows a hand weak in high cards but with a good suit that will produce within three tricks of the bid if not vulnerable and within two tricks vulnerable.

Takeout Doubles (also called *negative* or *informatory* doubles). When a defender doubles and all the following conditions are present: (a) his partner has made no bid; (b) the double was made at the doubler's first opportunity; (c) the double is of one, two or three of a suit—it is intended for a takeout and asks partner to bid his best (longest) suit. This defensive bid is employed on either of two types of hand: (1) a hand of opening-bid strength where the doubler has no good or long suit of his own but has good support for any of the unbid suits; and (2) where the doubler has a good suit and so much high-card strength that he fears a mere overcall might be passed out and a possible game missed.

Overcall in Opponent's Suit (cue-bid). The immediate cue-bid (example: opponent opens one heart; defender bids two hearts) is the strongest of all defensive bids. It is unconditionally forcing to game and shows approximately the equivalent of an opening forcing bid. It normally announces first-round control of the opening bid suit and is usually based on a void with very fine support in all unbid suits.

Action by Partner of Overcaller. The overcaller's bid is based on a good suit; therefore less than normal trump support is required to raise (Q-x or x-x-x). A raise should be preferred by the partner to bidding a suit of his own, particularly if the overcaller has bid a major. The partner of the overcaller should not bid for the sole purpose of keeping the bidding open. A single raise of a one-no-trump response should be made only in an effort to reach game. If appropriate values are held, a leap to game is in order, since a jump raise is not forcing.

Action by Partner of Takeout Doubler. In this situation, the weaker the hand the more important it is to bid. The only holding that would justify a pass would be one that contained four defensive tricks, three in the trump suit. The response should be made in the longest suit, though preference is normally given to a major over a minor.

Since the partner of a doubler may be responding on nothing, it is a good policy for the doubler to subsequently underbid, while doubler's partner should overbid. If doubler's partner has better than an average hand, game is very probable (and doubler's partner should so indicate by jumping in his best suit, even if it is only four cards in length).

Action by Partner of the Opening Bidder (when the opening bid has been overcalled or doubled). When the opener's bid has been overcalled, the responder is no longer under obligation to keep the bidding open; so a bid of one no-trump or a raise should be based on a hand of at least average strength. Over a takeout double, the responder has only one way to show a good hand—a redouble. This bid does not promise support for opener's suit but merely announces a better-than-average holding. Any other bid, while not indicative of weakness, shows only mediocre high-card strength.

SLAM BIDDING

When the two partners have been able to determine that they have the assets for a slam (33 pts. between the combined hands plus an adequate trump suit) the only thing that remains is to make certain that the opponents are unable to cash two quick tricks. Various control-asking and control-showing bids have been employed through the years, but only three have stood the test of time—Blackwood, Gerber, and cue-bids (individual ace-showing).

Blackwood Convention. After a trump suit has been agreed upon, a bid of four no-trump asks partner to show his total number of aces. A response of five clubs shows either no aces or all four aces; five diamonds shows one ace; five hearts shows two aces; five spades shows three aces. After aces have been shown, the four no-trump bidder may ask for kings by now bidding five no-trump. The responder to the five no-trump bid now shows kings as he showed the number of aces in response to the four no-trump bid: by bidding six clubs if he has no king, six diamonds if he has one king, etc., but six no-trump if he has all four kings.

Gerber Convention. This convention is similar to Blackwood in that it asks for the number of aces. Its advantage lies in the fact that it initiates the response at a lower level. A sudden burst into four clubs is Gerber and asks partner to show the number of his aces. If he bids four diamonds, he shows no aces; four hearts, one ace, etc. If the asking hand desires information about kings he bids five clubs and now a response of five diamonds denies holding a king, five hearts shows one king, and so on.

Cue-bidding (individual ace-showing). The Blackwood and Gerber conventions are designed to cover only a small number of potential slam hands. Many slams depend on possession of a specific ace, rather than a wholesale number of aces. Cue-bids are employed in such cases. *For example:* Opener bids two spades, responder bids three spades, opener now bids four clubs; the four-club bid shows the ace of clubs and invites responder to show an ace if he has one.

BIDDING CONVENTIONS

A convention, in the Bridge sense, is an understanding between partners that a given call will have some definite meaning. (For example, that an opening bid of one no trump will show a hand containing 16 to 18 points, rather than some other number.) Bidding conventions are not unethical provided a partnership has no better way of understanding their meaning than have its opponents: Unless it may reasonably be assumed that the opponents will properly understand the call as well as one's partner, the conventional meaning should be explained to them in advance.

The principal conventions in general use, other than the takeout double, cue-bids, and slam tries described in the preceding pages, are:

Forcing bids. A bid that is conventionally forcing requires partner to keep the bidding open; that is, to make sure the player who made the forcing bid gets another chance to bid. For example:

SOUTH	WEST	NORTH	EAST	SOUTH	WEST	NORTH	EAST
1 ◇	Pass	2 ♡	Pass	1 ◇	Pass	2 ♡	2 ♠

To keep the bidding open, South must now bid; for if South passes, a pass by West will close the auction and North will not have another chance to bid.

South need not bid to keep the bidding open; for even if South and West both pass, North will have another chance to bid.

It must be kept in mind that the word "forcing" applies only to Bridge convention, never to Bridge law. A player may always legally pass if he wishes to. However, to pass a forcing bid will have a bad effect on partnership confidence.

The following are the forcing bids almost universally observed:

An opening two-bid in a suit—forcing to game. Both partners must make sure the bidding is kept open until a game contract is reached. Even when the two-bid is enough to complete the game, the partner must respond at least once.

A jump response or rebid in a new suit—forcing to game, as explained in the preceding paragraph.

A jump response in no trump or in partner's suit—forcing to game, but may be passed if the contract reached will produce game (when combined with a part-score previously made).

A response in a suit to partner's opening bid—forcing for one round. That is, the opening bidder must keep the bidding open, but thereafter either partner may pass (unless a game-forcing bid is made). This one-round-forcing bid loses its forcing character when, with a previous part-score, the contract reached will suffice for game.

A rebid in a new suit. Any subsequent bid in a new suit by the responding hand (but not by the opening hand) is forcing for one-round; and a jump rebid by the responding hand is a force to game. There are exceptions to both these principles.

The last three are not forcing when the bidder passed originally.

Two-club Convention. A small group of players use an opening bid of two clubs as an artificial game-forcing bid (artificial, in the sense that the two-club bidder does not necessarily have any strength in the club suit). If the partner's hand is so weak that he cannot make any other bid, he must respond two diamonds, regardless of his actual holding in the diamond suit.

When the two-club convention is used, opening two-bids in spades, hearts, and diamonds may be given either of two meanings: (a) very strong hands, but not strong enough to demand unequivocally that a game contract be reached; or (b) weaker hands, including a strong suit of six or more cards but with only about 6 to 12 points—fewer than are needed for an opening one-bid.

Fishbein Convention. Over an opponent's preëmptive bid (three or four in a suit), an immediate bid of the next-higher suit, as three hearts over three diamonds or four clubs over three spades, is *artificial*, requiring partner to take out in his best suit as though he were responding to a takeout double. A double of a preëmptive bid is for penalties and a no-trump overcall indicates the bidder's willingness to play at no-trump.

Unusual No-trump. A no-trump overcall of two or more which common sense tells us could not have a natural meaning is a request to partner to bid his best minor suit. The no-trump bidder usually has at least five diamonds and five clubs. When the opponents have bid two suits, the unusual no-trump shows length in the other two suits, whether major or minor suits.

OTHER BIDDING SYSTEMS

Vanderbilt Club Convention. First of the bidding systems was that proposed by Harold S. Vanderbilt, wherein an opening bid of one club is artificial and forcing, showing at least 3½ quick tricks; a one-diamond response by partner shows that he has less than 2 quick tricks, and any other response by partner promises at least 2 quick tricks.

Culbertson System, or Approach-Forcing System. In its time, about 1930 to 1948, this was the most popular of all systems and the Goren System grew from it; both the Culbertson and Goren Systems have been called "standard American bidding."

Roth-Stone System. First published in 1945 by Alvin Roth and Tobias Stone of New York, this system advises: 1, "sound" (strong) opening bids and overcalls. 2, an opening major-suit bid shows at least a five-card suit. 3, a one no-trump response to a major-suit bid is forcing for one round.

Kaplan-Sheinwold System. The product of Edgar Kaplan and Alfred Sheinwold of New York, this system employs a weak opening one-notrump bid (12 to 14 points, whether or not vulnerable). Five-card major suits and forcing one-notrump responses are used, as in the Roth-Stone System, but opening suit-bids are made on weaker hands. Jump raises of minor suits are weak, single raises are strong.

LEADING AND PLAYING CONVENTIONS

The four cards of each trick are played consecutively by *leader, second hand, third hand, fourth hand.*

In leading, one should select the highest card in sequence of the suit led, as K from K-Q or K-Q-J; except that from a suit of three or more cards headed by A-K, the king and not the ace is led. From a short suit (three cards or less) the highest is usually led; from a longer suit not including a sequence of honors, the fourth-highest card is usually led. There are exceptions, as shown in the table of leads on page 152.

"Second hand low"—that is, second hand should play a low card—is an ancient maxim of Whist-family games, but there are many exceptions and each case should be judged individually.

"Third hand high" is an equally time-honored principle, and there are fewer exceptions to it.

In playing to a trick (as distinguished from leading) one should select the lowest of equal cards; thus, whereas from Q-J the queen would be led, the jack would be played in a later position.

Falsecarding. The defenders should usually play conventionally. When a defender falsecards (plays unconventionally) it should be because he calculates the advantage of deceiving declarer to outweigh the risk of loss from deceiving his partner.

Declarer, however, cannot lose by falsecarding, since he has no active partner to deceive.

Rule of eleven. When a player leads his fourth-highest card of a suit, his partner (and, of course, declarer as well) by subtracting the index number of the card from 11 can know the number of higher cards in the other three hands. For example, West leads ♢5. East then knows that the South, East and North hands together contain exactly six diamonds higher than the ♢5. If East holds two of these cards, and sees three in dummy, he knows that declarer holds only one diamond higher than the five.

CONVENTIONAL LEADS

(Condensed, by permission, from Culbertson's Summary,
by Ely Culbertson)

HOLDING IN SUIT	LEAD AT SUIT BIDS	LEAD AT NO-TRUMP
A-K-Q alone or with others	K, then Q	K, then Q
A-K-J-x-x-x-x	K, then A	*A, then K
A-K-J-x-x or A-K-x-x(-x)	K, then A	Fourth best
A-Q-J-x-x	A	Q
A-Q-10-9	A†	10
A-Q-x-x(-x)	A	Fourth best
A-J-10-x	A†	J
A-10-9-x	A	10
A-x-x-x-(-x)	A	Fourth best
A-K-x	K	K
A-K alone	A	K†
K-Q-J alone or with others	K, then J	K, then Q
K-Q-10 alone or with others	K	K
K-Q-x-x(-x-x)	K	Fourth best
K-Q alone	K	K
K-J-10 alone or with others	J	J
K-10-9-x	10	10
Q-J-10 or Q-J-9 alone or with others	Q	Q
Q-J-x or Q-J	Q	Q
Q-J-8-x (four or more)	Q	Fourth best
Q-10-9 alone or with others	10	10
J-10-9 or J-10-8 alone or with others	J	J
J-10-x or J-10	J	J
J-10-x-x or more	J	Fourth best
10-9-8 or 10-9-7, alone or with others	10	10
10-9-x-x(-x)	10	Fourth best
K-J-x-x(-x-x)	Fourth best	Fourth best
Any other four-card or longer suit not listed above	Fourth best	Fourth best

---

* The lead of the ace of an unbid suit at a no-trump contract requests partner to follow suit with his highest card of the suit led, even the king or queen, unless dummy reveals that the play of such a card would sacrifice an eventual trick.

† Usually not a good lead at this contract.

LEADS IN PARTNER'S BID SUIT

HOLDING IN SUIT	LEAD AT SUIT BIDS	LEAD AT NO-TRUMP
A-x, K-x, Q-x, J-x, 10-x *or any other doubleton*	High card	High card
J-10-x, 10-x-x or x-x-x	Highest	Highest
A-J-x, A-x-x, K-J-x, K-x-x, Q-10-x, Q-x-x, J-x-x	Highest	Lowest
Q-J-x(-x)	Q	Q
A-x-x-x *or better*	A	Fourth best
K-Q-x(-x)	K	K
Any other 4 or more cards	Fourth best	Fourth best

PERCENTAGE TABLES

for Contract Bridge and other games in which a 52-card pack is dealt into four 13-card hands

The following tables are expressed in percentages; see the preamble to the tables of Poker probabilities on page 108.

TABLE 1

Distributions of the cards of a suit among the hands of the four players; and distributions of the four suits in the thirteen cards held by one player.

DISTRIBUTION	PERCENTAGE		DISTRIBUTION	PERCENTAGE	
4-4-3-2	21.55	%	7-3-3-0	0.26	%
4-3-3-3	10.53	%	7-5-1-0	0.11	%
4-4-4-1	3.	%	7-6-0-0	0.005	%
5-3-3-2	15.5	%	8-2-2-1	0.2	%
5-4-3-1	13.	%	8-3-1-1	0.12	%
5-4-2-2	10.6	%	8-3-2-0	0.1	%
5-5-2-1	3.17	%	8-4-1-0	0.04	%
5-4-4-0	1.24	%	8-5-0-0	0.003	%
5-5-3-0	0.9	%	9-2-1-1	0.02	%
6-3-2-2	5.6	%	9-3-1-0	0.01	%
6-4-2-1	4.7	%	9-2-2-0	0.008	%
6-3-3-1	3.5	%	9-4-0-0	0.0009	%
6-4-3-0	1.3	%	10-2-1-0	0.001	%
6-5-1-1	0.7	%	10-1-1-1	0.0004	%
6-5-2-0	0.65	%	10-3-0-0	0.0001	%
6-6-1-0	0.07	%	11-1-1-0	0.00002	%
7-3-2-1	1.9	%	11-2-0-0	0.00001	%
7-2-2-2	0.5	%	12-1-0-0	0.0000003	%
7-4-1-1	0.4	%	13-0-0-0	0.0000000006299	%
7-4-2-0	0.36	%			

This table gives *a priori* probabilities only. For example, it should not be assumed that when the combined hands hold eight cards of a suit divided 4-4, there is a 21.55% chance that the five outstanding cards of

153

that suit will divide 3-2, because that is the percentage of probability that a 4-4-3-2 distribution will be dealt; while if the combined eight cards are divided 5-3, there is only a 15.5% expectancy of a 3-2 break. Consult Table 4, regardless of the way a given suit holding is divided between the partnership hands.

TABLE 2

Chances that the combined hands of a partnership will hold a suit-length of:

AT LEAST	PERCENTAGE	AT LEAST	PERCENTAGE
7 cards	100. %	11 cards	1.6 %
8 cards	84. %	12 cards	0.16 %
9 cards	39. %	13 cards	0.006%
10 cards	8.7 %		

TABLE 3

The chances that you will be dealt the following holdings in high cards are:

HOLDING	PERCENTAGE	HOLDING	PERCENTAGE
All four aces	0.26 % (1 in 385)	No ace	30. %
Three aces	4. %	No face card	0.36 % (1 in 275)
Two aces	21. %	No honor-card	0.054% (1 in 1828)
One ace	44. %	(ten or higher)	

A hand with no card higher than a nine is called a Yarborough, because the Earl of Yarborough bet all comers that in any given hand they would hold at least one ten or better card; the earl gave odds of 1,000 to 1, whereas proper odds were 1827 to 1.

TABLE 4

The chances that the opponents' cards in a suit will be divided in a given way (neither opponent's hand being known):

YOUR COMBINED HOLDING IN SUIT	OPPONENTS HOLD	OPPONENT'S CARDS IN SUIT WILL BREAK		
11 cards	2 cards	1-1	52	%
		2-0	48	%
10 cards	2 cards	2-1	78	%
		3-0	22	%
9 cards	4 cards	3-1	49.7	%
		2-2	40.7	%
		4-0	9.6	%
8 cards	5 cards	3-2	68	%
		4-1	28	%
		5-0	4	%

YOUR COMBINED HOLDING IN SUIT	OPPONENTS HOLD	OPPONENT'S CARDS IN SUIT WILL BREAK	
7 cards	6 cards	4-2	48.4 %
		3-3	35.5 %
		5-1	14.5 %
		6-0	1.5 %
6 cards	7 cards	4-3	62 %
		5-2	30.5 %
		6-1	6.8 %
		7-0	0.5 %
5 cards	8 cards	5-3	47 %
		4-4	32.8 %
		6-2	17 %
		7-1	2.9 %
		8-0	0.2 %
4 cards	9 cards	5-4	59 %
		6-3	31.4 %
		7-2	8.6 %
		8-1	1 %
		9.0	0.04%

TABLE 5

The chance that an opponent's honor will be guarded is:

		ONE OUTSTANDING HONOR WILL BE		
YOUR COMBINED HOLDING	UNGUARDED	GUARDED ONCE ONLY	GUARDED ONLY TWICE	GUARDED THREE TIMES OR MORE
11 cards	52.0%	48%		
10 cards	26.0%	52%	22%	
9 cards	12.0%	41%	37%	10%
8 cards	5.0%	27%	41%	27%
7 cards	2.0%	16%	36%	46%
6 cards	1.0%	9%	27%	64%
5 cards	0.4%	4%	18%	78%
4 cards	0.1%	2%	10%	87%

PARTY BRIDGE

Four, five or six players make one Bridge game; eight players make two tables. Twelve or more players in even fours may play Progressive Bridge, the most popular form of Bridge-playing in parties. Serious players may play Duplicate Bridge, if the number available is precisely four, eight, twelve, or any greater number of players in even pairs.

Duties of the host or hostess. The hostess (or host) should make all decisions as to what form of Bridge is to be played. She should tell her guests where to play, and with whom, and should decide the rules to be followed. She should consider the probable desires of her guests but should not consult them; for any disagreement among them would put her in an uncomfortable position.

The host or hostess should play in the game, when possible; it is embarrassing to guests when the host or hostess insists on deferring places at the table to them. An exception is found when there are exactly seven players available. Unless they will be satisfied to play some game other than Bridge, the best solution is to persuade them to play a six-hand Bridge game.

When there are eight players, the four best should be put at one table and the other four at the other, but the reason for the grouping should not be stated.

Set and semi-set matches. If a husband and wife must play at the same table, the hostess may suggest a set match, in which the husband and wife are permanently partners. With only four players, the carried couple will remain partners throughout, and there is this slight deviation from the usual scoring method: Instead of figuring the score of each rubber to the nearest 100 points, the entire score is carried over from each rubber to the next.

When husband and wife play in a cut-in game, it may be "semi-set": When husband and wife are both in the game, they are always partners. When either is cut out, partnerships are determined as usual.

Set and semi-set matches should not be suggested when the married couple are patently superior, or patently inferior, to the players against whom they would be pitted.

Pivot Bridge. When one player in the game is far superior, or far inferior, to the others, pivot play should be suggested; this permits each player to play an equal number of times as the partner of each other. The schedules are as follows.

Four players. Before the first rubber, cut for partners and seats as usual. Considering that each player has a number, change at the end of each rubber, as follows.

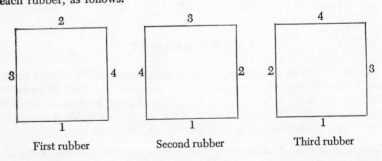

First rubber   Second rubber   Third rubber

Five players. Before the first rubber, cut for partners and to establish precedence, the player cutting the highest card being No. 1, the player cutting the lowest card being No. 5. Change partners as follows:

156

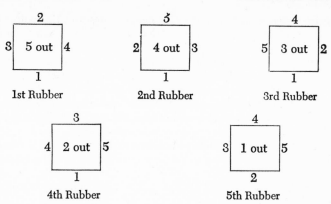

2	3	4
3| 5 out |4	2| 4 out |3	5| 3 out |2
1	1	1
1st Rubber	2nd Rubber	3rd Rubber

3	4
4| 2 out |5	3| 1 out |5
1	2
4th Rubber	5th Rubber

Double rubbers. On the completion of the schedule, players cut to begin the schedule anew; or, if they know in advance that they will have time, they may play double rubbers, in which a partnership remains together until two rubbers have been completed.

PROGRESSIVE BRIDGE

Twelve or more, in even fours, may play. Place the tables in as nearly circular arrangement as possible.

Each table should have its number conspicuously placed on it, and should be provided with at least two score-pads and pencils, and with two unopened packs of cards.

Prepare the tally cards in advance. Some tally cards have the "table and couple numbers" printed on them; others must be properly marked with pen or pencil. Two separate piles of tally cards should be made (of different-colored tallies); each pile should contain one tally for each table and couple number; thus, a card marked "Table 1—Couple 1" in each pile. As the guests arrive, each lady draws a card from one pile, and each gentleman from the other pile, so that (if there are equal numbers of ladies and gentlemen) the game will begin with a mixed couple as partners at each table.

When all guests are seated, make a clear announcement of the rules of the game (a specimen announcement is given below).

A prize must be provided for the highest score and a "booby" prize for the lowest score; at mixed parties, there should be two prizes for each, one for the ladies and one for the gentlemen; at unmixed parties there should be a prize for the second-highest score, but no second booby prize. Special prizes may be offered for the first slam bid and made, the most slams, the highest score in any round, etc.

The Progressive Bridge Laws (next page) say that each player must subtract his opponents' score from his own after each round is completed. This is the only logical way to determine the winner, but it is usually unpopular. Since it is the duty of the hostess to please her guests, it is usually wiser for the hostess to let each player score all the points she makes.

But whatever the scoring system, insist that each player enter her opponents' score for each round on her tally card, as well as her own. At the end of the game, add up the "My Score" totals on all the cards, and the "Opponents' Score" totals on all the cards; unless these totals are the same, there is an error in addition or in entering a score on one of the tallies. When the prizes are valuable, it is worth while checking to see where the error occurred, to make sure the prize is not given to the wrong person because of a scoring error.

When it appears that all tables but one have finished, walk to that table so that the progression may be called just as soon as the last deal is finished and while those players are adding and entering their scores.

Urge the guests to call you when there is any irregularity for which a penalty is demanded. When angry arguments arise, it is no crime for the hostess to make compromises so that each side gets the full score it would have had if the irregularity had never occurred.

There may be exactly as many rounds as there is time for. About twenty minutes before she wants the game to end, the hostess may say, when calling the progression, "This will be the last round. At the end of this round, add up your scores, write your names on your tallies, and bring them to me."

The following is a specimen announcement that the hostess may make before the game begins, with such changes as the circumstances require:

"For this first round, the two ladies draw for deal; high deals. After the first round, the visiting lady—the one who has just come to the table—will deal.

"You will play four deals in each round, one by each player. If a hand is passed out, it is not dealt over—each side simply scores zero for that deal.

"On the first deal, neither side is vulnerable; on the next two deals, the dealer's side is vulnerable and the other side is not; on the last deal, both sides are vulnerable.

"After the fourth deal, add up your scores, but wait till I call the progression. Then the couple with the high score at each table will move to the next table and change partners, except at Table 1, where the couple with the high score will remain and not change partners, and the losing couple will go to Table (the table with the highest number).

"You get 500 points extra for game in one hand, vulnerable; 300 points extra for game in one hand, not vulnerable; and 50 points extra when you bid and make a contract which is not game.

"Doubling and redoubling are permitted, but no one may score more than 1,000 points in a single hand, except by bidding and making a slam.

"Please call me if there is anything you do not understand."

Before planning or starting the game, the hostess should carefully read the Laws of Progressive Bridge and be sure that she understands them.

THE LAWS OF PROGRESSIVE BRIDGE

(Copyright, 1935, by National Laws Commission. Reprinted by permission.)

Arrangement of tables. 1. The game is played by two or more tables of four players each. The tables are numbered consecutively from Table No. 1 to the highest number.

Comment: It is customary to provide each table with two decks of cards having different backs. The tables should be numbered conspicuously for the convenience of the players, and each one should be provided with one or more pencils and a score pad showing contract scoring.

Tally cards. 2. Prior to the beginning of play, the game director or committee prepares individual tally cards, one for each player. Each tally card bears a table number and designates a position (North, South, East, or West) at the table.

The tally cards may be drawn at random by the players or assigned by the game director, as he prefers. When play is called each player takes the position assigned by his tally card.

Comment: At mixed parties is is customary to arrange the tallies and seat assignments so that a gentleman will always have a lady as a partner and vice versa. This is accomplished by having tallies of two different kinds or colors, one for the ladies and the other for the gentlemen.

A round. 3. A round consists of four deals, one by each player. When all tables are through play, the game director gives a signal and the players move to their positions for the next round according to the type of progression used.

Comment: Each round should take about 20 minutes and the average session of play is from 6 to 7 rounds.

A deal passed out. 4. Only four hands are dealt at each table, one by each player. If a deal is passed out (that is, if all four players pass at their first opportunity to declare), the deal passes to the left and both sides score zero for that deal.

Method of progression. 5. At the conclusion of each round, the winning pair at Table No. 1 remain and the losing pair move to the last table.

At all tables except Table No. 1, the losers remain and the winners move up one table toward Table No. 1.

Comment: The above is the standard method of progression, but this may be waived or altered to suit the wishes of the game director or the players. Special tallies may be arranged or obtained, assigning positions for each round in such a way as to give each player as wide a variety of partners as possible.

Selection of partners. 6. At mixed parties, it is customary but not essential for a gentleman to play with a lady partner and vice versa. If the standard method of progression is used, the visiting lady at each table becomes partner of the gentleman who remains.

If the players are all of the same sex, the four players at each table draw cards to determine partners at the start of each round. The two new arrivals at each table draw first, and the one drawing higher has choice of seats and is the first dealer. The one drawing lower sits at the left of the first dealer. The two players who remain at the table from the preceding round then draw, the higher becomes the partner of the dealer. Thus all players change partners after each round.

Comment: Since the chief function of progressive bridge is social, it is preferable to change partners at each round. However, if for some reason a pair contest is desired, the same partnerships may be retained throughout by simply progressing as described in Law No. 5 without changing partners at the next table. Another method is to have the original N-S pairs remain in the same positions throughout the game, and to have the E-W pairs progress one table at a time until they reach Table No. 1, and then go to the last table. In this case, the progression is followed automatically, regardless of which pair wins at each table.

Draw for deal. 7. Unless the dealer is already determined under Law No. 6, the four players at a table draw for first deal. The player who draws highest is the first dealer and may select either deck.

Progressive Bridge scoring—Comment: With the exceptions specifically mentioned below, the scoring for Progressive Bridge is exactly the same as for Rubber Bridge:

Each deal is scored and recorded separately, and no trick points are carried over from one deal to the next.

Game is 100 points for tricks bid and made in one deal. The game premium is 300 points, if not vulnerable, and 500 points if vulnerable, and it is allowed only when game is bid and made in one deal.

A premium of 50 points is scored for making any contract less than game. This premium is in addition to the value of the tricks made. Premiums for a small and grand slam are allowed only if bid for.

Scoring limits. 8. A side may not score more than 1,000 points in a single deal, except in the case of a slam contract fulfilled.

Comment: It is not correct to prohibit doubles or redoubles. The limitation of penalties avoids the necessity of this restriction.

Vulnerability. 9. The first deal of each round shall be played and scored as if neither side were vulnerable.

The second and third deals of each round shall be played and scored as if the dealer's side were vulnerable and the other side not vulnerable.

The fourth deal of each round shall be played and scored as if both sides were vulnerable.

Comment: This is the most desirable method of determining vulnerability in Progressive Bridge, but if preferred all deals may be played as though neither side were vulnerable, or all deals as though both sides were vulnerable. In any event, the method should be announced before play starts.

Recording the score. 10. One of the four players at each table is appointed to record the score. He enters the result of each deal on the score pad separately and, at the end of the round, totals all the points made by each side.

He enters on the individual tally of each player the points made by that player's side and also the points made by the opponents.

Comment: Correctly designed tallies provide spaces to record both "My Score" and "Opponent's Score." It is important that both be entered on the tally, for otherwise the record would be meaningless. [But most players prefer to count only the scores they make themselves, regardless of their opponent's score.]

Computing total scores. 11. At the conclusion of the game, each player totals his score. He also totals the scores of his opponents, as recorded on his tally, and subtracts his opponents' total from his own. The difference, plus or minus as the case may be, is recorded in the space provided at the bottom of his tally.

Comment: Let us suppose that a player scores 2,460 points, and the opponents score 1,520 points against him. This makes his net score +940 for the entire session. On the other hand, if a player scores only 1,650 points, and the opponents score 1,940 points against him, then his net score for the session is —290 points. Do not make the mistake of recording only plus scores, for that method gives false results, and is likely to lead to improper doubling and redoubling.

Determining the winner. 12. The player with the largest plus score is the winner. Other players with plus scores rank in descending order followed by the players with minus scores, the one with the largest minus being last.

Comment: The method of awarding prizes is left to the discretion of the game director. At mixed parties it is usual to award one or more prizes to the highest ladies and one or more prizes to the highest gentlemen.

PROGRESSIVE RUBBER BRIDGE

Progressive Rubber Bridge follows the methods of progression and change of partners described in the preceding laws, but the scoring is somewhat different.

Under this arrangement it is preferable to play 6 or 8 deals to a round, or to fix the length of a round by a definite time limit—say 30 minutes. If the length of a round is determined by a time limit, any deal which has been started before time is up may be completed, but no new hand may be dealt.

Rubber scoring is used. [See the scoring instructions on pages 129-131.] As many rubbers as possible are completed during the time allotted. A rubber completed in two games carries a bonus of 700 points. A three-game rubber carries a bonus of 500 points. If a side has won one game toward o rubber and the other side has not won a game, 300 points are allowed for the single game won. If a rubber is unfinished and one side has made one or more part-score contracts in an unfinished game, but the other side has made no part-score in that game, the side with the part-score(s) adds 50 points to its score.

Vulnerability is determined by the state of the score and not according to Law No. 9 in the Progressive Code. A side is vulnerable when it has won a game and remains vulnerable until the conclusion of that rubber. However, vulnerability lapses at the conclusion of a round and a new rubber is started at the beginning of each new round.

At the end of a round each player enters on his tally only his net gain or loss—not his total score. At the end of the session these net gains and losses are totalled and the player's final score, plus or minus as the case may be, is entered at the bottom of this tally.

[If each side is permitted to enter all the points it has scored, without subtracting its opponents' score; and if each side has scored a game toward an unfinished rubber, then each side adds 300 points to its score; and if each side has a part-score in an unfinished game of an unfinished rubber, then each side adds 50 points to its score.]

DUPLICATE CONTRACT BRIDGE

The controlling principle of Duplicate Bridge is that each partnership, or pair, compares its scores only against the scores of pairs that held the same cards in the same deal. Each deal, having been bid and played, is preserved in its original form so that it may be played by other players and the scores compared. This is intended to eliminate the luck of the deal from Contract Bridge, and to a large extent it does so.

Number of players. Four players in two partnerships may play Replay Duplicate. Eight or more players may play a pair game, an individual game, or a team-of-four match.

Equipment. A set of duplicate boards, or trays, and one pack of cards for each board. Each tray has four pockets, corresponding to the compass points, for holding the hands of the respective players. The face of each tray is marked with an arrow pointing toward one pocket, and with an indication of the dealer and vulnerability. There should be at least 16 boards to a set, numbered consecutively, with dealer and vulnerability as follows:

DEALER	VULNERABILITY
N–1, 5, 9, 13	Neither–1, 8, 11, 14
E–2, 6, 10, 14	N-S only–2, 5, 12, 15
S–3, 7, 11, 15	E-W only–3, 6, 9, 16
W–4, 8, 12, 16	Both–4, 7, 10, 13

Boards numbered 17 to 32, if used, correspond to boards 1 to 16 respectively except in their identifying numbers.

Shuffle and deal. Any player, in the presence of an opponent or of the tournament director, prepares a board by shuffling the pack of cards and dealing it, one card at a time face down, into four packets, each of which he inserts in a pocket of the duplicate board.

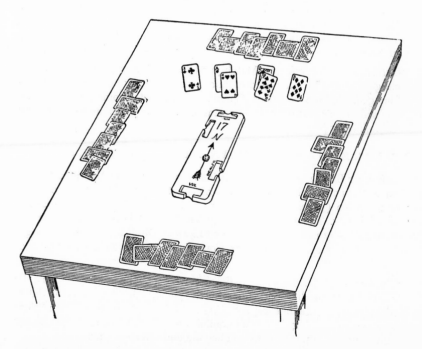

The auction. The arrow on the board is pointed in the direction of the room designated as North. Each player takes the hand from the pocket nearest him, and counts his cards to make sure he has thirteen. The player designated as dealer calls first, and the auction proceeds as described on page 135 until the contract is determined. There is no redeal when a hand is passed out.

The play. The opening lead, exposure of dummy, and subsequent play are as in Rubber Bridge, except: After a trick is completed, each player retains possession of his card and places it face down on the table directly in front of him, pointed lengthwise toward the partners who won the trick. Declarer plays dummy's cards by naming or touching them, and dummy turns them and keeps them in front of him.

Scoring. The score of each board is independent of the scores of the other boards, and trick points scored on one board cannot count toward game on a subsequent board. No rubber premium is scored. Instead the following premiums are scored:

	DEALER'S SIDE	
	VULNERABLE	NOT VULNERABLE
For bidding and making a game contract	500	300
For making a contract of less than game	50	50

If match-point scoring is used to determine the winner of the game, there is no premium for holding honors in one hand.

In other respects the scoring of each board follows the schedule shown on page 131.

Determining the winner. Match-point scoring is always used in individual games, is most often used in pair games, and may be used in team-of-four games or replay games. Cumulative (or "total point") scoring may be used in pair and team-of-four games. These methods are explained on the following pages.

IRREGULARITIES IN DUPLICATE BRIDGE

Rubber Bridge and Duplicate Bridge are governed by the same laws so far as the nature of the two games makes it possible. The Laws of Contract Bridge (pages 116-134) govern in Duplicate Bridge except as provided below. The following description and the laws of the game are condensed, by permission, from The Laws of Duplicate Contract Bridge, © 1949 by the National Laws Commission of the American Contract Bridge League.

Tournament Director. One person, who may be a player, must be appointed to conduct and supervise the game or tournament. His duties include: listing the entries; selecting suitable movements and conditions of play; maintaining discipline; administering the laws; assessing penalties and assigning adjusted scores; collecting and tabulating results.

Drawing attention to an irregularity. The Director must be summoned as soon as attention is drawn to an irregularity. Players do not have the right to assess or waive penalties on their own initiative.

Adjusted score. The Director may assign an adjusted score when the laws provide no penalty which will fully indemnify a non-offending contestant for an opponent's irregularity, or when no rectification can be made that will permit normal play of the board; but may not assign an adjusted score on the ground that the penalty provided by the laws is unduly severe or unduly advantageous to the non-offending side. An adjusted score may be assigned by altering the total-point score on the board, or by the assignment of zero or more match-points. Penalty points amy be assessed against the offending side, indemnity points given to the non-offending side; these need not balance.

Bidding and playing conventions. A player may make any call or play (including an intentionally misleading call such as a "psychic" bid) except that he may not make a call or play based on a partnership understanding unless the opposing pair may reasonably be expected to understand its meaning, or unless his side has announced its use before either member has looked at his hand. If the Director decides that a pair has been damaged through its opponents' failure to make such announcement, he may assign an adjusted score.

The Director, on a player's request, may require the player who made a call or play to leave the table and his partner to explain its meaning.

The Director (or other authority) may forbid the use of such conventions as might place other contestants at a disadvantage or take too long to explain.

Dummy's rights. In addition to the rights stated on page 24, dummy may: notify the Director of any matter that may affect the legal rights of his side; keep count of the tricks won and lost; draw attention to another player's card played to the preceding trick and pointed in the wrong direction. He may play the cards of the dummy hand as directed by declarer; if he places in the played position a card that declarer did not name, the error may be corrected before a card has been led to the next trick and a defender may withdraw a card played after the error but before attention was drawn to it. If dummy (in the Director's opinion) suggests a play, the Director may require or forbid declarer to play that card or its equivalent.

Error in play from dummy. Declarer may change his designation of a card to be played from dummy if he does so practically in the same breath, or if he designated a card that is not there.

Improper information. If a player receives improper information about a board, he should notify the Director; who shall require that the board be played and scored normally if that seems feasible, and otherwise shall assign an adjusted score. Examples of improper information: Looking at the wrong hand; seeing another player's card before the auction begins; overhearing calls or remarks; partner's improper remark or gesture.

Revoke time limits. A revoke made in the twelfth trick must be corrected if discovered before all four hands have been returned to the board. An established revoke is not subject to penalty if attention is first drawn to it after the round has ended and the board has been moved. In all other respects the provisions stated on page 126 apply.

Claims and concessions. The concession of a trick which cannot be lost by any play of the cards is void, provided the error is brought to an opponent's attention before the round has ended and the board has been moved. The concession of a trick the player has in fact won is void, provided the error is brought to the Director's attention within 30 minutes after the end of the session.

If a claim or concession is disputed, the Director must be summoned and no action should be taken without him. The Director determines the result on the board, awarding any doubtful trick to the claimant's opponents.

Wrong number of cards. If the Director decides that one or more pockets of the board contained an incorrect number of cards, he should correct it if possible, and should then require that the board be played normally unless a player gained information of sufficient importance to warrant assigning an adjusted score.

Interchanged cards. If the cards or hands in a board become interchanged during a session, the Director rates separately each group that played identical boards as follows: Each score receives 1 match-point for each lower score in the same group, ½ match-point for each identical score in the same group, and ½ match-point for each pair in the other group(s).

Disciplinary penalties. For an error in procedure (failure to count cards, playing the wrong board, etc.) which requires an adjusted score for any contestant, the Director may assess a penalty against the offender (10% of the maximum match-point score on one board is recommended.) A similar indemnity may be awarded to a contestant who is required to take an adjusted score through no fault of his own. The Director may increase the penalties for flagrant or repeated violations. In total-point play, 100 total points are equivalent to 1 match-point.

Appeals. If there is a tournament or club committee in charge, appeal may be made to it from any ruling of the Director on a question of disputed fact or an exercise or discretionary power. Appeals from the Director's ruling on points of law may be made only to the National Laws Commission, 33 West 60th St., New York 23, N. Y.

REPLAY DUPLICATE—FOR FOUR PLAYERS

Replay Duplicate is a contest between two pairs. It is played in two sessions, called the *original play* and the *replay*.

The players take places, one being designated North. The boards are shuffled, and are played with the arrows pointing North. Any number of boards is feasible.

A separate score slip is kept for each board. At the close of the session the boards and score slips are laid aside where they will be undisturbed.

At some later time, the same four players take the same relative positions about the table. The boards are replayed with the arrows pointing East. Again a separate score slip is kept for each board.

The scoring may be by match points or total points. If the former method is used, each deal is treated as a separate match. The pair having the better net score on a deal is credited with 1 point. The final scores are the totals of these match points.

If total-point scoring is employed, the two slips for each deal are compared, and the pair having the net plus score is credited with that amount. The net scores for all deals, so determined, are totaled, and the pair having the larger total wins the difference.

The game tends to become a test of memory rather than of bridge skill. To check this tendency the following measures are recommended:

1. Do not play the boards in consecutive order. Choose the tray to be played next at random from the stack.

2. Avoid comment of any sort about the deal after its original play.

3. Allow at least a week to elapse between the original play and the replay.

It is sometimes desired to make the game a test of skill in the play alone. The bidding during the original play is then recorded, and for the replay this bidding is read to fix the contract and declarer.

INDIVIDUAL CONTESTS—FOR EIGHT OR TWELVE PLAYERS

In an individual game, each player plays once with every other as partner, and twice against every other as opponent.

The initial seating of the players in games for two or three tables is shown below:

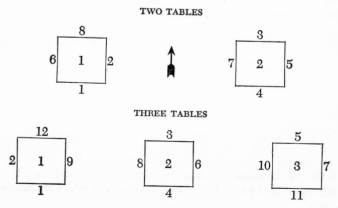

TWO TABLES

THREE TABLES

The game may be conducted without guide cards, thus:

1. Allow the players to take places at random. Reserve the North posi‧tion at Table 1 for the supervisor; this player is "anchor," retaining his seat throughout the game.

2. From this schedule inform each player of his number, and tell him who is the player of the next-lower number.

3. Announce that after each round, all players but the anchor will progress, each player taking the seat vacated by the player of next-lower number. (Player 1 follows Player 7 or 11 respectively.)

A new set of boards is played in each round. They are played at all tables, being circulated at convenience. The eight-player game requires seven rounds, with a total of 14, 21, or 28 boards. The twelve-player game requires eleven rounds, and the only feasible number of boards is 33.

The scoring of individual contests is by match-points.

TEAM-OF-FOUR CONTEST—FOR EIGHT PLAYERS

The team-of-four match between two teams has long been recognized as the most accurate test of Bridge skill known. Two tables are provided, in different rooms if possible. One pair of Team 1 sit N-S at Table 1, and the other pair sits E-W at Table 2. The members of Team 2 take the remaining positions, its E-W pair playing at Table 1 and its N-S pair at Table 2.

The number of boards to be played should be a multiple of 4. From one to one and one-half hours are usually required for the play of twelve boards. The first fourth of the boards are placed on Table 1 and the second fourth on Table 2. These boards are shuffled, dealt, played and scored.

The two tables then exchange boards, each replaying the ones played at the other table. Care must be taken to see that in every case the arrow points toward the North player.

When the boards have been replayed, the two pairs of Team 2 ex‧change places, retaining the same partners but playing against the other pair of opponents. The remaining boards are divided equally between the two tables, to be shuffled, dealt, played, scored, exchanged and replayed as explained above.

When all the boards have been replayed, the team whose members, considering all boards and all scores, have a net plus score, is the winner.

MITCHELL PAIR GAMES—FOR THREE OR MORE TABLES

The Mitchell game is the simplest and most popular of the Duplicate pair movements.

One way of the room is arbitrarily designed at the North-South direc‧tion, regardless of the actual compass direction. The tables are numbered and arranged in numerical order with Table No. 1 at the North end of the room. With players of average speed about 24 boards can be played in three hours.

The entire number of boards to be played is equally divided into as many set as there are tables. The method of distriubtion depends upon whether the number of tables is odd or even. With an odd number of tables, one set is placed on each table, beginning with Table 1, which receives the lowest numbered set of boards, the next set on Table 2, and so on.

Each pair of players takes as its pair number the number of the table at which it starts play. At Table 4, for example, would be North-South pair 4 and East-West pair 4. These numbers are retained throughout the contest.

When the signal to commence play is given the boards at each table are bid, played, and scored.

When the play of the original set of boards at each table has been completed the tournament director gives the signal to progress. The North-South pairs remain stationary. The East-West pairs move to the next higher numbered table. The boards are moved to the next lower numbered table. This progression is continued until each East-West pair has played against each North-South pair, and each pair has played each set of boards.

Distribution of boards and progression for an even number of tables. The sets of boards are distributed regularly until half of them have been placed on the tables. *The next set is placed on a stand or chair,* known as the relay stand. Following this, each of the remaining tables receives its regular quota of boards, except the last table, *which receives none.* The pairs at this table play, simultaneously with Table 1, the boards which have been allotted to Table 1, passing the boards back and forth between the two tables. The first and last tables share the same boards throughout the contest.

The relay stand is always placed *exactly half way between the first and last tables.* The players at the lower numbered table next to the relay table shuffle the relay boards. These boards, however, are not played in the first round.

The North-South pairs do not progress. The East-West pairs progress to the next higher numbered table in the same manner as for an odd number of tables. The boards are passed to the next lower numbered table, except that from the higher numbered table above the relay stand the boards are passed to the relay stand. The lower numbered table next the relay stand secures its trays from the relay stand, taking the set of boards that was not in play during the preceding round. The boards that were played simultaneously by the first and last tables are passed to the next-to-last table.

Incomplete table. If an odd number of pairs enter the game so that one table is incomplete, the odd pair is seated E-W at the highest-numbered table, assuming that table number for its pair number. This pair does not play the first round, but at the completion of the round moves to Table 1 and enters the regular progression. Each E-W pair in its proper turn sits out one round when it comes to the last, or incomplete, table. In distributing the trays and and arranging the progression, the odd pair (or half table) is considered a regularly constituted table; for example, 5½ tables would require the arrangement for 6 tables and 8½ tables would require the arrangement for 9 tables.

Comparing scores. In the Mitchell game all N-S pairs play the same hands, and all E-W pairs play the same hands. Therefore each pair can compare scores only with others in its own direction, and there are really two separate contests—one for N-S pairs, and one for E-W pairs. There will be one pair of winners in each group, and they should receive equal prizes or honors.

Match-point scoring for the Mitchell game. Match-point scoring is the most popular method for duplicate play. In this method all scores made by N-S pairs on a given deal are tabulated in a vertical column for purposes of comparison. Each score receives one match-point for each other N-S score it beats and ½ match-point for each N-S score it ties. For example, in a section of 9 tables, there would be 9 scores; the highest score would have beaten 8 others and would therefore receive 8 match points; the second highest score would have beaten 7 others and would receive 7 points, etc. The E-W scores are similarly tabulated and compared among themselves.

Each board is rated separately, and when all have been rated the total number of match-points awarded to each pair is computed. The match-point figure on each board represents the number of pairs beaten on that board, and the match-point total represents the total number of pairs beaten on all boards. The pair having the greatest number of match-points in each group is the winner in that group.

The simplest method of recording scores is to provide a traveling score slip for each board, which remains with the board throughout the game, and on which all results for the board are recorded.

A traveling score slip is folded, in such a way that its face cannot be seen, and tucked in one of the pockets of each board. After the play of that board is completed at each table, the North player unfolds the traveling score slip, enters the score (plus or minus) of his pair on the line corresponding to his pair number, and returns the slip to the board.

Howell movement. The Howell movement is one in which each pair plays one set of boards against each other pair. The movement is somewhat complicated and in order to direct the movement of the players and the boards Howell movement guide cards are necessary. These may be obtained in sets for any number of tables from three to thirty, a different set of guide cards being required for every number of tables.

AUCTION BRIDGE

There is no difference between Auction Bridge and Contract Bridge except in the scoring. However, this profoundly affects the strategy of the respective games. The scoring in Auction Bridge is as follows (taken from the 1926 revision of the Auction Bridge Laws, the latest revision; and copyright, 1926, by the Whist Club, New York).

Scoring. Provided declarer has won at least the number of odd-tricks named in his contract, declarer's side scores for each odd-trick won:

	UNDOUBLED	DOUBLED	REDOUBLED
With no trump	10	20	40
With spades trump	9	18	36
With hearts trump	8	16	32
With diamonds trump	7	14	28
With clubs trump	6	12	24

Game and Rubber. When a side scores, in one or more hands, 30 points or more for odd-tricks, it has won a game and both sides start fresh on the next game. When a side has won two games it wins the rubber and adds to its score 250 points.

Doubles and Redoubles. If a doubled contract is fulfilled, declarer's side scores 50 points bonus plus 50 points for each odd-trick in excess of his contract. If a redoubled contract is fulfilled, declarer's side scores 100 points bonus plus 100 points for each odd-trick in excess of his contract. These bonuses are additional to the score for odd-tricks, but do not count toward game.

Undertricks. For every trick by which declarer falls short of his contract, his opponents score 50 points; if the contract is doubled, 100 points; if it is redoubled, 200 points.

Honors. The side which holds the majority of the trump honors (A, K, Q, J, 10), or of the aces at no-trump, scores:

For 3 honors (or aces)	30
For 4 honors (or aces), divided	40
For 5 honors, divided	50
For 4 trump honors in one hand	80
For 4 trump honors in one hand, 5th in partner's hand	90
For 4 aces in one hand at no-trump	100
For 5 honors in one hand	100

Slams. A side which wins twelve of the thirteen tricks, regardless of the contract, scores 50 points for small slam. A side which wins all thirteen tricks, regardless of the contract, scores 100 points for grand slam. Even if set one at a seven-bid, declarer scores 50 for small slam.

Points for overtricks, undertricks, honors and slams do not count toward game. Only odd-tricks count toward game, and only when declarer fulfils his contract.

CONTRACT AND AUCTION BRIDGE VARIANTS

Four-deal Bridge, also called Chicago or Short Bridge. In a cut-in game, a player who is "cut out" often has a long wait till the rubber ends and he can get back in. Playing Four-deal Bridge, no player ever has to wait more than 15 or 20 minutes. The game is often called "Chicago" because it originated in the Standard Club of Chicago, Ill.

A round consists of four deals, one by each player in turn. Vulnerability is automatic, as follows:

First deal: Neither side vulnerable.

Second and third deals: Dealer's side vulnerable, opponents not vulnerable (even if they previously made game).

Fourth deal: Both sides vulnerable.

A passed-out deal is redealt by the same dealer. There is a bonus of 300 for making game when not vulnerable and 500 when vulnerable. A part-score carries over as in rubber bridge and can help to make game in the next deal or deals, but is cancelled by any game. There is a bonus of 100 for making a part-score on the fourth deal. After four deals have been played, the scores are totaled and entered on the back score, as in rubber bridge, and there is a new cut for partners, seats, and deal.

More points are usually scored in Four-deal Bridge than in the same number of deals at rubber-bridge—estimates vary from 15% to 50% more. This is chiefly because at least one side is vulnerable in three deals out of four.

The strategy of the game, as described above, causes fourth hand, not vulnerable (on the second and third deals), to bid on almost any border-line hand, so that there can be no redeal that might bring a vulnerable game or slam to his opponents.

Because of the artificiality of the bidding this strategy often causes, and for some other reasons, players may wish to adopt the rules used at the Cavendish Club of New York: On the second and third deals the dealer's side is *not vulnerable* and the opponents are vulnerable.

Gentlemen's Agreement. Regular Contract Bridge is played except that no contract that will not produce game is played unless it is doubled.

Summer Bridge. In games outdoors, when the wind may blow over the cards, it is usually agreed that exposure of a card during the deal does not require a redeal.

Goulash. Regular Contract or Auction Bridge is played, except that when a deal is passed out (or, as some play in Contract Bridge, when the contract if fulfilled will not produce a game) there is a redeal by the same dealer in the following manner: Each player arrranges his cards into suits, the order of the cards in each suit being as he pleases. The four hands are stacked, face down, the eldest hand at the bottom, then dealer's partner's hand, and so on with dealer's hand on top. This pack is not shuffled but is cut;

then the same dealer redeals it in three rounds of five, five and three cards at a time. (This almost always produces very freakish distributions.) Bidding and play then proceed normally. Mayonnaise and Hollandaise are other names for this procedure. In the extension known as Passing Goulashes, after the completion of the goulash deal each player passes three cards to his partner; then, after seeing the cards passed to him, passes two cards to his partner; and finally, in the same way, passes one card. The bidding then begins.

Contract Whist. The preliminaries and auction are as usual, but there is no dummy. Each player holds and plays his own cards. Contract Bridge scoring is used.

Plafond. The French game Plafond was the first successful variant along the lines that grew into Contract Bridge; it was played, also, in other continental countries and in England, but never to any extent in America. The Auction Bridge scoring table was used, except that only odd-tricks bid and made counted toward game, overtricks going in the premium score at 50 per trick; premiums for undertricks, slams and honors were twice as much as in Auction Bridge, and the rubber bonus was 400.

Nullo, Antibridge. These are devices that have been proposed to reduce the luck of the deal by giging a player with a bad hand a chance to bid and score as declarer. *Nullo* is a denomination ranking above spades and below no-trump; a nullo contract is played without a trump suit and is scored the same as no-trump except that every trick the declarer *loses* counts *for* him and every trick he wins counts against him. Therefore if a player bids 3 nullos and wins four tricks he makes his contract, and game, for the nine tricks won by his opponents count for him. *Antibridge* extends the same principle to trump contracts, but a *minus* or *negative* bid ranks next-higher than the regular or positive bid: Minus 4 hearts ranks above 4 hearts but below 4 spades and is a bid to win no more than three tricks with hearts trumps.

Spanish Bridge. In Spain, a bid of nullos is permitted; in the auction it ranks between spades and no-trump; in the scoring, it is the same as no-trump.

Reverse Bridge. A player may make any bid *reversed:* If his bid becomes the contract, the rank of the cards will be reversed, the deuce being the highest card of each suit, the three next-highest, etc., the ace lowest. A reverse bid ranks next under a natural bid of the same denomination; two no-trump reversed overcalls two spades but may be overcalled by a natural bid of two no-trump. A reversed contract scores the same as a natural contract of the same denomination.

Five-suit Bridge. For a year or two (1938-39) there were manufactured 65-card packs of playing cards including a fifth suit, which in the United States was green in color and marked with an eagle; in England blue in color and marked with a crown, being called the *royal* suit. When Contract Bridge is played with this pack: Eagles rank higher than spades but below no-trump. Sixteen cards are dealt to each player and the last card is turned face up as the *kitty*. Bidding is as in Contract Bridge, but declarer's book is eight tricks, each trick over eight being an odd-trick. When the opening lead has been made and dummy goes down, declarer may exchange any card in his hand or dummy for the kitty; the exchanged card remains face up in a corner of the table. It takes 120 points to make game, no trump counting 40 per trick, eagles 30, spades or hearts 25, diamonds or clubs 20. A six-bid (all but two tricks) is a small slam, a seven-bid (all but one trick) a grand slam, and these score as in Contract Bridge; an eight-bid is a super-slam, for which the bonus is 1,500 not vulnerable, 2,000 vulnerable. Five aces in one hand, at no-trump, count 300. The name Quintract was applied to this game.

Percentage Bridge. The invention of George H. Rodger, Percentage Bridge is played with a 60-card pack, five suits of twelve cards each (there being no deuces), the fifth suit being the percentage suit.

Each player receives fifteen cards, and declarer's book is seven tricks. Bids for odd-tricks mean tricks over seven.

The percentage suit has a point value for each card, as well as a regular function as a fifth suit. The ace, king, queen and jack of percentage count 12 each, the other cards their pip value, the total of the suit being 100.

Each odd-trick counts 100 points in the trick score. Each bid must be expressed in terms of points, counting 100 for each odd-trick plus the number of points in percentage cards contracted to be won. Thus, a bid of 320 diamonds is a contract to win, with diamonds as trumps, three odd-tricks plus 20 points in percentage cards. Every bid must contract for at least 10 percentage points, so a bid of 300 no trump would be a contract to win two odd-tricks at no trump plus all 100 of the percentage points. Percentage may be bid like any other suit.

In scoring percentage points, figure to the nearest ten—thus, 15 percentage points count only 10, but 16 percentage points count 20.

The rank of bids is by the total number of points; 260 clubs overcalls 250 no trump.

A total of 450 points below the line is needed to make game. If declarer makes his contract, he scores the amount of his contract below the line; above the line he scores 100 for each overtrick if undoubled, 200 if doubled and 400 if redoubled; nothing extra for additional percentage points.

The rubber bonus is 1,000. The bonus for a small slam (610 to 700 bid and made) is 500; for a middle slam (710 to 800) is 1,000; for a grand slam (810 to 900) is 2,000. Honors do not count.

If declarer makes enough odd-tricks for his contract but fails in percentage points, he scores nothing and the defenders get a bonus of 150 above the line; if he fails in tricks alone, he scores nothing and the defenders get 200 for each undertrick; if he fails in both tricks and percentage points, the defenders get 250 for each undertrick. These values are doubled if the contract is doubled, and quadrupled if the contract is redoubled. There is no vulnerability.

Super Contract Bridge. Capt. John M. Ellicott, U.S.N. Ret., devised this Contract Bridge variant. It is played with a 53-card pack that includes the joker. Each player receives thirteen cards, the last card being placed face up on the table; after the opening lead is made and dummy goes down, declarer may exchange any card in his hand or dummy for this card, showing the card he exchanges for it.

The joker may be named as the highest-ranking card of any suit (including trump) at the time it is played, but it may not be named as a card of any suit to which the holder has previously failed to follow. If used as a trump, the joker counts as a trump honor; and six trump honors, or five aces at no trump, in one hand earn a bonus of 300. Naming the joker as part of a suit to which the holder previously failed to follow counts as a revoke.

Pirate Bridge. R. F. Foster devised this game, the earliest of the efforts to avoid prefixed partnerships. After a bid, another player in turn could *accept*, thus constituting himself the bidder's partner. Acceptance could be made after a pass or double, but not after a previous acceptance of the same bid. A new suffcient bid began the whole process over again. If no one accepted, the high bidder could select any partner who did not double. The opponent nearest declarer's left made the opening lead and the dummy was put opposite declarer, so that play was as in any Bridge game.

Cutthroat Contract. S. B. Fishburne invented this game of variable partnerships, taking a name more often applied to three-hand Bridge. But four play, and partnerships are determined in the auction.

The bidding proceeds as in Contract Bridge, except: The player who makes the opening bid must have at least three honor-tricks or 13 high-card points (4-3-2-1 count), and must have at least four cards in the suit he bids (he may, however, bid no-trump); and there can be no doubles until a bid has been followed by three consecutive passes. If the final bid is not a game contract, there is a new deal by the next dealer in turn. Most players prefer the rule that when the bidding is opened, the next player *must* bid *at least* four no-trump (unless, of course, the opening bid was higher than four no-trump, in which case the next player may pass). Other players make the obligatory second bid, or overcall, three no-trump instead of four.

The high bidder is declarer, and upon the close of the auction he selects one of the other three players as his partner. That player must sit opposite declarer, and if necessary exchanges seats with the player who was there. He then accepts or rejects partnership with declarer; if he accepts he scores with declarer and may redouble an opposing double, and if he rejects he scores with the defenders and may not redouble. After he accepts or rejects, declarer's lefthand opponent may double or pass, whereupon the auction continues (with only doubles, redoubles and passes permitted) until it closes again. The opening lead is then made and the play proceeds.

Each player has a separate column on the scoresheet, and at the end of the game each settles individually with each other. Honors are scored only by the player holding them. The first player to win two games wins the rubber, the bonus being 700 if neither defender is vulnerable and 500 if either of them is; if dummy accepted and is not vulnerable, he gets a game bonus of 300. Each opponent of declarer scores undertricks individually, at vulnerable rates if declarer is vulnerable, or if declarer selected a vulnerable dummy and the selection was accepted; otherwise undertricks are scored at nonvulnerable rates.

Some special penalties are necessary: 50 points to each other player for a pass out of turn, 300 for a bid or double out of turn, but none for an insufficient bid; 300 for making an opening bid without the required values. But in the latter case, if the offender becomes declarer and announces his error before the partner he selects has either accepted or rejected, there is no penalty; and if dummy is the offender, declarer may void the entire deal but the penalty applies against dummy.

Elective Contract. This game designed to eliminate prefixed partnerships in Contract Bridge was published by F. Dudley Courtenay and Leonard Gracy. After the first round of bidding, any player upon making a bid could elect one of the other three players as his partner; if that player accepted, he moved if necessary to the seat opposite the bidder and the auction proceeded from the bidder's left, with the partnerships fixed thereafter. If the elected player rejected, it cancelled the election, the auction proceeded, and if there were three passes the declarer could elect any other player as before, not necessarily the one he elected previously. A new bid, however, would begin the entire process again. If the final dummy rejected he scored with the defenders, though his was the dummy hand. There were no rubbers; game bonus was 300 points not vulnerable and 500 vulnerable.

Bridge Whist. Better known, in its day, simply as Bridge, the game of Bridge-Whist superseded Whist as the favorite club game in about 1896, but was itself superseded by Auction Bridge and is now obsolete.

Four played, two against two as partners, as in every Whist-family game. The dealer could make (name) the trump, or no-trump; or could pass ("bridge") this privilege to his partner, who then had to make the trump. Eldest hand could double or pass; if he passed, his partner could double; if either doubled, dealer could redouble, and if he did not redouble, his partner could; if either redoubled, their opponents could double again, in the manner described above, and so the doubles could go on indefinitely, increasing the scoring value of tricks by geometric progression to whatever limit, if any, was placed on the value of a trick.

Eldest hand, if he did not wish to double, said, "May I lead?" and his partner replied either "Pray do," or "No, I double." When eldest hand finally led, dealer's partner became dummy as in Auction or Contract Bridge; but whichever side won the odd-trick scored all its odd-tricks toward game.

The values of odd-tricks were:

If trumps were	♠	♣	♢	♡	N T
Each odd-trick counted	2	4	6	8	12

These odd-trick values were multiplied by 2, cumulatively, for each double. The first side to score 30 in odd-tricks won a game; the first side to win two games won the rubber and scored a bonus of 100. Only odd-tricks counted toward game; other scores went in the honor column: A little slam counted 20, a grand slam 40. A side with three trump honors, or with chicane (a hand without a trump), scored twice the trick value; four trump honors scored four times the trick value if divided, eight times if in one hand and nine times if partner held the fifth honor; five trump honors in one hand scored ten times the trick value. At no-trump, three aces scored 30, four aces divided 40, four aces in one hand 100.

Royal Auction. When Auction Bridge was first played, the scoring was the same as in Bridge Whist, dealer was compelled to make some bid, and there was *numerical overcalling* (that is, a bid of three spades, worth 6 points in odd-tricks, could be overcalled by one heart, worth 8 points). The 2-point spade suit became almost meaningless and was used only for artificial bids. To overcome this, spades were given a double valuation: one could bid spades, or *royal spades* (called royals, or, colloquially, "lilies"); and whichever won the contract, the same suit would be trump but royal spades counted 9 points per odd-trick. This valuation was retained in later revisions of the scoring table. [In America, numerical overcalling was abandoned in 1915, but in Great Britain it was retained in the official laws (of the Portland Club) as long as Auction Bridge was played.]

THREE-HAND BRIDGE GAMES

Three-hand Bridge, or Cutthroat Bridge. Three play; four hands are dealt as usual, and the one opposite dealer will become the dummy of the highest bidder. The auction proceeds among the three players until a bid, double or redouble is followed by two consecutive passes. The player at declarer's left leads, the extra hand is spread as dummy opposite declarer, and play proceeds. The game is equally adaptable to Auction and Contract Bridge scoring. A separate score is kept for each player, and declarer individually, or each defender individually, scores the points earned by his side. The first player to win two games wins the rubber; in Contract Bridge scoring, the premium is 700 if neither defender has a game, 500 if either of them has.

Special irregularities include: A double out of turn may be cancelled by the player who is doubled, and thereafter neither opponent may double him at any contract; there is no penalty for any other improper call during the auction, but after the auction closes the regular Contract Bridge penalties apply.

In a variant known as Exchange Dummy, declarer may elect (before seeing the dummy) to put down his own hand as dummy and play with the extra hand as his own hand.

In one popular variant, each player in turn takes the dummy and plays a contract of two no-trump redoubled. There is no bidding.

Towie. Towie, developed by J. Leonard Replogle, has been the most successful of the three-hand Contract Bridge variants; but actually it is more often played by four, five, or even as many as seven contestants, though only three play at one time. Four hands are dealt, as in Contract Bridge, after which the dealer turns up six cards of the hand opposite him, which will be the dummy. The auction proceeds as in three-hand Bridge. When the contract is less than game, there is a goulash (page 172) after which dealer must shuffle dummy's hand before exposing any of its cards. Otherwise, the player at declarer's left leads; the remainder of the dummy is turned up, and declarer puts it between his two opponents; and play proceeds as in Contract Bridge.

The differences from present Contract Bridge scoring are: Each odd-trick at no trump counts 35. Each overtrick counts 50 (100 if doubled, 200 if redoubled). The premium for fulfilling a doubled contract is 50 if not vulnerable, 100 if vulnerable, and these premiums become 100 and 200 respectively if the contract is redoubled. Undertricks, if doubled, count 100 for the first, 200 each for the second, third, and fourth, and 400 for each additional, if not vulnerable; 200 for the first, 400 for each additional, if vulnerable; and these values are multiplied by 2 if the contract is redoubled. For winning his first game, a player receives a 500-point bonus; for winning the rubber, an additional 1,000. Undoubled undertricks are 50 each if not vulnerable; if vulnerable, 100 for the first and 200 for each additional.

If declarer fulfills his contract, he scores the points in his column; if declarer is defeated, each other player, including all inactive players, scores the undertrick penalties. Honors are scored only by the player who holds them.

If an opponent of dealer turns up any card in dummy, he must pay dealer 100 for each opponent, including himself; but other players are not affected. If dealer violates the proper procedure in turning up dummy's cards, each other player scores 100; except that a card of dummy's exposed during the deal (up to six such cards) is not penalized and does not require a redeal. There must be a redeal if dealer exposes more than six cards in dummy.

A call out of turn is void and the offender must pass throughout the remainder of the auction. It may be condoned only by both active opponents.

An insufficient bid must be made sufficient and the offender must pass thereafter. It may be condoned only by both active opponents.

The penalty for an established revoke is two tricks for the first revoke and one trick for each subsequent revoke by the same player; but only tricks won after the revoke are available for transfer.

Triangle Contract. George S. Coffin introduced Triangle Contract in 1932, but it has been replaced by Trio, which follows.

Trio (Contract Bridge for Three), introduced by George S. Coffin. The three players are designated as South, North, and East, seated in those compass positions. South and North are partners against East and the dummy, which is in the West position. Four hands are dealt. After the deal the entire dummy hand is faced and is seen by all players during the bidding. Only the three active players bid. South always bids first, then North, then East, and so on in rotation. Any player may become declarer, though East always plays the dummy. The player (which may be dummy) at declarer's left makes the opening lead and play proceeds as in Bridge. Score is kept as in Contract Bridge, with East and dummy constituting one side and North-South the other. Hence, East wins or loses doubly, North and South each singly. After each rubber the North player moves into the seat at his right and becomes South, and the previous South player becomes East.

Stanley Three-hand Bridge, introduced by Enos Stanley. Three play; four hands are dealt and the dummy is concealed until the bidding ends. The three players bid in rotation. Book is three tricks, not six: That is, a player need win only four tricks to make a one-bid, seven tricks to make a four-bid, nine tricks to make a small slam and ten for a grand slam. Scoring for odd tricks is as in Contract Bridge: three no-trump bid and six tricks won scores 100 trick points and makes game. The high bidder becomes declarer and plays the dummy, which is placed opposite him as in regular Bridge. But every trick won by the dummy counts for the opponents, not for declarer.

TWO-HAND BRIDGE GAMES

Double Dummy. Two players sit in adjoining seats at a card table; four hands are dealt, each player having a dummy opposite him. The players bid without looking at their dummies, until a pass following a bid, double, or redouble closes the auction. Then each player exposes his dummy, the hand at declarer's left leads, and the play continues with the location of all cards known to both players.

Honeymoon Bridge. This name is applied to several two-hand Bridge variants:

1. The same as Double Dummy, except that neither player exposes his dummy to his opponent; the player against declarer makes the opening lead from his own hand, then each player places his dummy in a rack so that he can see it but his opponent cannot. Each trick consists of four cards, one played from each hand in turn as in Contract or Auction Bridge.

2. (Also called Draw Bridge, or Strip Bridge.) The players sit opposite each other. Each is dealt thirteen cards, one at a time, and the remaining cards form a stock, placed face down between the two players. Nondealer leads, and thirteen tricks of two cards each are played, the winner of each trick leading to the next; after each trick, each player draws a card from the top of the stock, the winner drawing first. The first thirteen tricks do not count. When the stock is exhausted, the auction begins, the dealer bidding first. The auction closes when a bid, double, or redouble is passed by the opponent; then declarer's opponent leads and the last thirteen tricks are played, the result of them determining the score at the contract reached.

3. The same as described in the preceding paragraph (2), except that the stock is placed on the table face up, so that a player may judge whether he wishes to win the trick and draw first, or lose it and take a chance on the second card from the top of the stock. The stock should always be kept squared up: a safe, but more troublesome, method, is to keep the stock face down but turn up its top card before each trick.

Chinese Bridge, or Semi-exposed Dummy. This is the same as Double Dummy, except that after the deal each player takes his dummy and lays out six of its cards in a row face down, then six more cards face up, one on each of the face-down cards, then one face-up on the table. The bidding and play proceed; in the play, each time a player plays one of the face-up cards in his dummy, he turns up the face-down card, if any, below it.

Single Dummy. This is the same as Double Dummy except that one dummy is turned face up before the auction begins. Each player, in bidding, must specify whether he bids "with the dummy" or "without" (which means that if he becomes declarer he will take the closed dummy). A player may bid "with" and then on a later round bid "without." When the auction closes, each player's dummy goes opposite him, the closed dummy is turned up, and play proceeds.

WHIST

Four play, two against two as partners. The cards are dealt in clockwise rotation, one at a time, beginning with eldest hand, face down except for the last card, which is turned face up; this is the trump card, fixes trump, and becomes part of the dealer's hand just before he plays to the first trick.

The object is to win tricks, each odd-trick counting one point.

In England, there were originally Short Whist and Long Whist: In Short Whist, the game was won by the first side to amass 5 points; in Long Whist, game was 10 points. Game later was fixed at 5 points. Honors count (only the ace, king, queen, and jack): 2 points for three honors, 4 points for all four. The value of a game is the difference between the winners' and losers' total score in that game. The first side to win two games wins the rubber, the margin of victory being expressed in rubber points: 1 rubber point if the losers have 3 or 4 points, 2 rubber points if they have 1 or 2 points, 3 rubber points if they have no point.

In the United States, honors are not scored, game is 7 points, and there are no rubber points.

IRREGULARITIES IN WHIST

New Deal. There must be a new deal by the same dealer:

(a) If any card except the last is faced in the pack.

(b) If, during the deal or during the play of the hand, the pack is proven incorrect or imperfect, but any prior score made with that pack shall stand.

If, during the deal, a card is exposed, the side not in fault may demand a new deal, provided neither of that side has touched a card. If a new deal does not take place, the exposed card is not liable to be called.

Anyone dealing out of turn, or with his adversaries' pack, may be stopped before the trump card is turned; after which the deal is valid, and the packs, if changed, so remain.

Misdealing. It is a misdeal:

(a) If the dealer omits to have the pack cut, and his adversaries discover the error before the trump card is turned and before looking at any of their cards.

(b) If he deals a card incorrectly and fails to correct the error before dealing another.

(c) If he counts the cards on the table or in the remainder of the pack.

(d) If, having a perfect pack, he does not deal to each player the proper number of cards and the error is discovered before all have played to the first trick.

(e) If he looks at the trump card before the deal is completed.

(f) If he places the trump card face downward upon his own or any other player's cards.

A misdeal loses the deal unless during the deal either of the adversaries touches a card, or in any other manner interrupts the dealer.

The Trump Card. The dealer must leave the trump card face upward on the table until it is his turn to play to the first trick; if it is left on the table until after the second trick has been turned and quitted, it is liable to be called. After it has been lawfully taken up it must not be named, and any player naming it is liable to have his highest or his lowest trump called by either adversary. A player may, however, ask what the trump suit is.

Irregularities in the Hands. If, at any time, after all have played to the first trick (the pack being perfect), a player is found to have either more or less than his correct number of cards, and his adversaries have their right number, the latter, upon the discovery of such surplus or deficiency, may consult and shall have the choice:

I. To have a new deal; or,

II. To have the hand played out; in which case the surplus or missing cards are not taken into account.

If either of the adversaries also has more or less than his correct number, there must be a new deal.

If any player has a surplus card by reason of an omission to play a trick, his adversaries can exercise the foregoing privilege only after he has played to the trick following the one in which the omission occurred.

Cards Liable to Be Called. The following cards are liable to be called by either adversary:

(a) Every card faced upon the table otherwise than in the regular course of play, but not including a card led out of turn.

(b) Every card thrown with the one led or played to the current trick. The player must indicate the one led or played.

(c) Every card so held by a player that his partner sees any portion of its face.

(d) All the cards in a hand lowered or shown by a player so that his partner sees more than one card of it.

(e) Every card named by the player holding it.

All cards liable to be called must be placed and left face upward on the table. A player must lead or play them when they are called, providing he can do so without revoking. The call may be repeated at each trick until the card is played. A player can not be prevented from leading or playing a card liable to be called; if he can get rid of it in the course of play, no penalty remains.

If a player leads a card better than any of his adversaries hold of the suit, and then leads one or more other cards without waiting for his partner to play, the latter may be called upon by either adversary to take the first trick, and the other cards thus improperly played are liable to be called; it makes no difference whether he plays them one after the other or throws them all on the table together. After the first card is played the others are liable to be called.

A player having a card liable to be called must not play another until the adversaries have stated whether or not they wish to call the card liable to the penalty. If he plays another card without awaiting the decision of the adversaries, such other card also is liable to be called.

Leading Out of Turn. If any player leads out of turn, a suit may be called from him or his partner the first time it is the turn of either of them to lead. The penalty can be enforced only by the adversary on the right of the player from whom a suit can rightfully be called.

If a player so called on to lead a suit has none of it, or if all have played to the false lead, no penalty can be enforced. If all have not played to the trick, the cards erroneously played to such false lead are not liable to be called, and must be taken back.

Playing Out of Turn. If the third hand plays before the second, the fourth hand may also play before the second.

If the third hand has not played, and the fourth hand plays before the second, the latter may be called upon by the third hand to play his highest or lowest card of the suit led; or, if he has none, to trump or not to trump the trick.

Abandoned Hands. If all four players throw their cards on the table, face upward, no further play of that hand is permitted. The result of the hand, as then claimed or admitted, is established; provided, that if a revoke is discovered, the revoke penalty attaches.

Revoking. A revoke is a renounce in error not corrected in time. A player renounces in error when, holding one or more of the cards of the suit led, he plays a card of a different suit.

A renounce in error may be corrected by the player making it, before the trick in which it occurs has been turned and quitted, unless either he or his partner, whether in his right turn or otherwise, has led or played to the following trick, or unless his partner has asked whether or not he has any of the suit renounced.

If a player corrects his mistake in time to save a revoke, the card improperly played by him is liable to be called. Any player or players who have played after him may withdraw their cards and substitute others; the cards so withdrawn are not liable to be called.

The penalty for revoking is the transfer of two tricks from the revoking side to their adversaries. It can be enforced for as many revokes as occur during the hand. The revoking side cannot win the game in that hand. If both sides revoke, neither side can win the game in that hand.

The revoking player and his partner may require the hand in which the revoke has been made to be played out, and score all points made by them up to score of six.

At the end of a hand, the claimants of a revoke may search all the tricks. If the tricks have been mixed, the claim may be urged and proved, if possible; but no proof is necessary and the revoke is established if, after it has been claimed, the accused player or his partner mixes the cards before they have been examined to the satisfaction of the adversaries.

The revoke can be claimed at any time before the cards have been presented and cut for the following deal, but not thereafter.

Miscellaneous. Any one, during the play of a trick, and before the play of a trick, and before the cards have been touched for the purpose of gathering them together, may demand that the players draw their cards.

If any one, prior to his partner playing, calls attention in any manner to the trick or to the score, the adversary last to play to the trick may require the offender's partner to play his highest or lowest of the suit led; or, if he has none, to trump or not to trump the trick.

If any player says, "I can win the rest," "The rest are ours," "We have the game," or words to that effect, his partner's cards must be laid upon the table, and are liable to be called.

When a trick has been turned and quitted, it must not again be seen until after the hand has been played. A violation of this law subjects the offender's side to the same penalty as in case of a lead out of turn.

If a player is lawfully called upon to play the highest or lowest of a suit, or to trump or not to trump a trick, or to lead a suit, and unnecessarily fails to comply, he is liable to the same penalty as if he had revoked.

In all cases where a penalty has been incurred, the offender must await the decision of the adversaries. If either of them, with or without his partner's consent, demands a penalty to which they are entitled, such decision is final. If the wrong adversary demands a penalty, or wrong penalty is demanded, none can be enforced.

WHIST VARIANTS

Bid Whist. No trump is turned. Eldest hand bids first; each bid is expressed in points, one for each odd-trick or honor (ace, king, queen and jack only) the bidder contracts to score. Honors score for the side that holds them originally. Each player has only one turn to bid, and may either bid or pass; a bid must be higher than the preceding bid. The high bidder names the trump, then leads any card. If his side makes the bid, it scores whatever it makes and the opponents score for any honors they hold. If the bidder's side fails to make its bid, the opponents score their odd-tricks and honors, plus the number of tricks by which the bidder fell short of his contract. Every deal is a separate game. The highest possible bid is 11 (seven odd-tricks and four honors) and in many games honors are not counted.

Setback Bid Whist. This is Bid Whist in which the bidding side, when it does not fulfill its contract, is set back by the amount of its bid; while its opponents always score whatever they make.

Auction Bid Whist. Bid Whist is played, except that the auction continues until a bid is followed by three passes.

Other Bid Whist variations. Some count honors, but the bidder's side may not count them unless it wins the odd trick. Others score honors for the side that wins them in tricks, not for the side that holds them. In some games, neither side can score unless it wins the odd-trick.

Norwegian Whist. All cards are dealt face down, and every hand is played at no trump. Each player in turn, beginning with eldest hand, must bid or pass until a bid is made; any bid fixes the play. The possible bids are *grand*, which means the play will be to win tricks; or *nullo*, which means the play will be to lose tricks. If all four players pass, the hand is played at nullo and eldest hand leads; if anyone bids, the player at his left leads first at nullo, the player at his right first at grand. At grand, the bidder's side scores 4 for each odd-trick it wins; it opponents score 8 for each odd-trick they win. At nullo, either side scores 4 for each odd-trick its opponents win (some score only 2 per trick at nullo). Game is 50. Irregularities are governed by the Whist laws, except: A bid out of turn costs the offending side 20 points, which are deducted from its score, and the offender is barred from the bidding. The penalty for a revoke is three tricks, transferred to or from the offenders at the option of their opponents.

Scotch Whist is not a genuine member of the Whist family; it is described on page 247.

Solo Whist (referred to also as Whist de Gand). This is a game of variable partnerships. In the deal, the last card is turned for trump. Each player in turn, beginning with eldest hand, may bid or pass; the possible bids, from lowest rank to highest, are:

Proposal: To win eight tricks, with a partner; worth 5 points.

Solo: To win five tricks, without a partner; 10 points.

Misère: To win no trick, at no trump, without a partner; 15 points.

Abundance: To win nine tricks, without a partner, naming a trump suit other than the turn-up; 20 points.

Abundance in Trumps: To win nine tricks, without a partner, accepting the turn-up as trump; 30 points.

Spread: To win no trick, at no trump, without a partner and with all one's cards exposed; 30 points.

Slam: To win all the tricks, without a partner; the bidder to name the trump and to lead first; 40 points.

Each bid overcalls any lower one. When a player bids "I propose," each player in turn after him may say "I accept" (unless he or an intervening player makes a higher bid); and unless the proposal and acceptance are overcalled, these two players become partners. The bidding continues until a bid or acceptance has been followed by three consecutive passes; having passed in one turn, a player must pass in each subsequent turn, except that eldest hand may accept a proposal by dealer.

If all pass, or if "I propose" is followed by three passes, a *grand* is played. This is a no-trump contract at which the winner of the last trick loses 10 points to each other player.

At any other bid, each loser pays to each winner the value of the bid plus 1 point for each trick over the bid (if it was made) or short of it (if it was beaten).

Eldest hand always leads first, except when another player bids slam.

Boston. The favorite Whist game of the early 19th century, among players who liked to bet on the result, was Boston or one of its variants. Four play, each for himself. Two packs are used, to be dealt alternately; they are shuffled before the game begins, and not thereafter. The tricks are kept stacked separately, and are so gathered for the next deal with that pack; if a deal is not played, each player arranges his cards into suits and the hands are stacked as in a goulash deal at Contract Bridge. Thirteen cards are dealt to each player, and a card is then cut from the still pack; this card denotes *first preference* (for a trump), and the suit of the same color is second preference, called *color*. Each player in turn, beginning with eldest hand, may pass, or may bid and continue to do so as long as in each turn he is willing to overcall the preceding bid. Having passed, a player in turn may bid a misère or spread, but nothing else. The bids, ranking from lowest to highest are:

Boston, to win five tricks; *six; seven; little misère,* to lose all the tricks after each player has discarded one card face down; *eight; nine; grand misère,* to lose all thirteen tricks; *ten; eleven; little spread,* to lose all the tricks with one's cards exposed, after each player has discarded one card face down; *twelve; grand spread,* to lose all thirteen tricks with one's hand exposed; *grand slam,* to win all thirteen tricks. All bids except the misères and spreads are to win that number of tricks. An exposed hand is exposed before the first lead, which is always made by eldest hand.

In bidding, a player may merely name a number of tricks; if unopposed, he may name either the turn-up or color as trump. He may be overcalled by the same number of tricks in color, and this in turn may be overcalled by the same number of tricks in first preference. [For example: a heart is turned; eldest hand says "Six"; second hand says "I keep," meaning he bids six with diamonds trumps; the next two players pass and eldest hand says "I keep over," meaning he bids six with hearts trumps. In each case the bid was sufficient to overcall, as would have been any higher-ranking bid by any player.]

The cards are played as in Whist. Boston scoring was most complex, and various schedules were followed; in some cases additional points were scored for overtricks, but the American preference was for limiting the bidder to the point value of his bid, however many tricks he won; others scored one additional point for each overtrick. One schedule is:

		LOSS IF DEFEATED	
			EACH
BID	SCORE IF MADE	1ST TRICK	OTHER TRICK
5	12	10	10
6	15	15	10
7	18	20	10
8	23	25	10
9	32	35	10
10	42	45	15
11	63	70	15
12	106	120	15
13	166	180	20
Little Misère	20	20	0
Grand Misère	40	40	0
Little Spread	80	80	0
Grand Spread	160	160	0

When all four players passed, some played a grand, or *misère partout,* in which there was no trump, the play was to lose tricks, and the player (or players) winning the most tricks paid each other player one point for each trick difference in their results.

Boston de Fontainebleau. This was a variant of Boston in which no card was turned for trump; each player in bidding named his trump suit or his contract. The bids ranked, from lowest to highest: Five, or Boston; six; little misère; seven; Piccolissimo (a bid to win exactly one trick, at no trump, after each player has discarded one card face down); eight; grand misère; nine; little spread; ten; grand spread; eleven; twelve; slam (to win thirteen tricks); spread slam (to win thirteen tricks with one's hand exposed). In bids of the same number, the suits ranked no trump (high), diamonds, hearts, clubs, spades. Each bid had to overcall the previous one, there being no privilege of keeping or keeping over as in Boston. Once having passed, a player could not reënter the bidding. Before the opening lead, the bidder could call for a partner, provided he had bid to win tricks and if any player accepted him, they became partners at a contract three tricks higher than the bid.

A pool was invariably formed before the deal, the players contributing equally; this pool went to the winning player or side, and in case of a grand it went to the player or players winning the least number of tricks. If the bidder or bidding side was defeated, it had to match the amount of the pool, which then remained for the next deal.

Russian Boston was similar to Boston de Fontainebleau, with some additional scores: 10 points for *carte blanche* (in this case, a hand void of trumps); honors (ace, king, queen and jack of trumps) counted as overtricks if the bidder made his contract, four overtricks if he held all four of them, two overtricks if he held three of them.

French Boston was similar to Boston. The ◊J was the highest trump except when a diamond was turned as trump, in which case the ♡J was the highest trump. The scoring values of bids varied with the trump suit, and the schedule influenced the early Bridge scoring.

Cayenne. Four play, in partnerships, and receive thirteen cards each as in Whist, except that all are dealt face down. The trump card is cut from the still pack and is called cayenne. Dealer may select any suit as trump, or may name grand (no trump) or nullo (no trump, in which a side scores its opponents' odd-tricks). If dealer does not make the decision, his partner must. The play is at Whist; in trump play, honors (ace, king, queen, jack and ten of the trump suit) count as well as odd-tricks, 1 point for having the majority, plus 1 point each for the difference from the opponent's number of honors, so that three honors count 2, four honors 4, five honors 6. After the play, each side multiplies its points by the value of the trump suit. If cayenne is trump, the score is multiplied by 4; if the same color as cayenne is trump, by 3; if cayenne is red and clubs are trump, or if cayenne is black and hearts are trump, by 2; if the fourth suit is trump, the actual score is not increased. At grand or nullo, the odd-trick result is multiplied by 8. Winning thirteen tricks, or slam, counts 6; twelve tricks, or little slam, 4. The first side to score 40 adds an 8-point bonus.

Dummy, and Mort (the French word for dummy) are three-hand Whist variants; four hands are dealt, a trump turned, the dummy then exposed, after which the play proceeds as in Whist. The game must be played in sets of three deals, one by each player, who takes the dummy when he deals; for having the dummy is an advantage. The dummy is dealt opposite the dealer, who plays the cards of both hands but each in proper turn.

Vint. The Russian game Vint may have suggested certain aspects of Bridge, but it is a Whist game, with no exposed dummy. The bidding is as in Auction Bridge, the suits ranking: no trump (high), hearts, diamonds, clubs, spades. The values of odd-tricks depend on the bid; if it was a one-bid, each odd-trick counts 10 for the side winning it, a two-bid, 20, and so on, so that at a seven-bid each odd-trick counts 70. Odd-tricks count toward game, which is 500 and is won by the first side to reach that total, even in the middle of a hand; the winner of a game receives a premium of 1,000. Other premiums are: for a little slam, 1,000 if not bid, 6,000 if bid; for a grand slam, 2,000 if not bid, 7,000 if a little slam was bid, 12,000 if a grand slam was bid; for having the majority of the five trump honors, 10 times the odd-trick value for each honor held; for having the majority of the aces at no trump (or for having two aces and winning the odd-trick), 25 times the odd-trick value; for *coronet* (any three cards in sequence) 500, plus 500 more for each other card in sequence with the three, and double these values for coronet in trumps, or for any coronet at no trump.

Preference is a name given in one games compendium for a three-hand Vint variant.

⤙ TRUMPS ⤚

One of the most prolific families of games is based on this pattern: each player receives five cards; a card is turned to fix the trump suit; the object of play is to win at least one trick, or at least three tricks. When this pattern originated is unknown; a score of such games, differing only in superficial features, flourished in the 17th century and probably much earlier. The simplest was perhaps Triomphe, Triumph, or Trumps, described in Cotton's Compleat Gamester (1674) as French-Ruff. This game has given its named to the family, but may or may not be the ultimate ancestor. Cotton also describes Five Cards (now called Spoil Five), Lanterloo (now called Loo), and the now obsolete Beast.

The family may be conveniently divided in two branches, according to the terms of the play. In Trumps, a player must win a majority of the tricks to collect from the pool. Other ancient games of this type are La Mouche, Man d'Auvergne, Beast, Maw (?), and Spoil Five. Probably of later origin is Ecarté. The addition of bidding for the right to name the trump produced Napoleon and Euchre. The other branch comprises games in which a player collects if he wins any trick, and usually pays a forfeit if he wins none: Lanterloo, Mistigri, Pamphilius, Kontraspiel, and Rams.

Several members of the Trumps family have achieved such popularity as to become "national games." R. F. Foster accords this status to Spoil Five in Ireland and Loo in England, in the 18th century; and in the 19th century, Ecarté in France, Napoleon in England, Euchre in the United States. We may add that Five Hundred, a "long" game based on Euchre, was a serious rival to Auction Bridge in the United States at the beginning of the 20th century.

SPOIL FIVE

This game is also known as Five Cards and Five Fingers. It probably originated in Ireland. Early sources state that it was based on an earlier game, Maw, but we have no record of the rules of Maw.

Number of players. 1. From two to ten may play. The game is best for five to seven.

The pack. 2. A regular pack of 52 cards.

Rank of cards. 3. The highest trump is the five; second is the jack; third is the ♡A, whatever the trump suit. The cards from ten to two rank, in the black suits, in the reverse of the normal order. This fact may be remembered from the expression "highest in red; lowest in black."

In the trump suit the rank is:
Hearts: ♡5 (high), J, A, K, Q, 10, 9, 8, 7, 6, 4, 3, 2.
Diamonds: ◇5 (high), ◇J, ♡A, ◇A, K, Q, 10, 9, 8, 7, 6, 4, 3, 2.
Clubs or Spades: 5 (high), J, ♡A, A, K, Q, 2, 3, 4, 6, 7, 8, 9, 10.

In plain suits the rank is:
Hearts or Diamonds: K (high), Q, J, 10, 9, 8, 7, 6, 5, 4, 3, 2, (◇A).
Clubs or Spades: K (high), Q, J, A, 2, 3, 4, 5, 6, 7, 8, 9, 10.

The pool. 4. To begin a game, each player antes one chip. So long as this pool is not won, each successive dealer adds one chip to it. After it is won, all players ante again to form a new pool.

The deal. 5. Each player receives five cards, dealt in batches of 3-2 or 2-3; the dealer may choose either order, but whichever he starts he must adhere to. After all hands are dealt, the next card of the pack is turned up to fix the trump suit.

Robbing. 6. If the trump card is an ace, dealer may take it in exchange for any card in his hand, provided that he does so before the opening lead. The custom is for dealer to put his discard face down under the pack, leaving the ace in sight; the discard signifies the exchange.

7. A player to whom the ace of trumps is dealt may take the trump card in exchange for any card in his hand. This exchange must be made in the player's first turn to play, and is signified by passing a discard face down to the dealer, who puts it under the pack.

8. When the trump card is so taken or robbed, there is no compulsion to play it on the current trick.

The play. 9. Eldest hand (player at left of the dealer) makes the opening lead. He may lead any card. Except as provided in paragraph 10, a lead requires each other hand either to follow suit or to trump: even though able to follow to a plain-suit lead, a player may trump if he wishes. If unable to follow suit, a hand may play any card. A trick is won by the highest trump, or, if it contains no trump, by the highest card of the suit led. The winner of a trick leads to the next.

10. The three highest trumps, the five, jack, and ♡A, have the privilege of reneging when an inferior trump is led. That is, when a player holds any one of these as his only trump, and a lower trump is led, he may discard instead of following suit. But there is no reneging on the lead of a superior trump: when the five is led, no renege is legal, and when the jack is led the five may renege but not the ♡A.

Object of play. 11. Each player strives to win three tricks, or better, all five; if he cannot do so, his object is to prevent any other player from doing so. When no player has won three tricks, the deal is spoiled.

12. On winning the third of three tricks, a player may throw in his

hand and claim the pool. If he does not do so, but plays on, he is said to jink it; he must win all five tricks, else the deal is spoiled.

Settlement. 13. The winner of three tricks takes the pool. The winner of five tricks collects the pool and also an additional chip from each other player. When the deal is spoiled, the pool is left to be won in a later deal.

Irregularities. 14. *Foul hand.* If a player is dealt the wrong number of cards, he may demand a redeal before the opening lead. If at any later time a player is found to have too few or too many cards, his hand is foul and must at once be discarded; he cannot win the current deal.

15. *Misplay.* A player is barred from winning the current pool (in the current or any later deal, though he must ante in his turn as dealer) if he:

    (a) robs the trump card when he does not hold the ace of trumps;

    (b) leads or plays out of turn;

    (c) fails to follow suit or trump when able to follow suit, or reneges on the lead of a superior trump;

    (d) exposes any card in his hand after another player has won two tricks.

FORTY-FIVE

This variant of Spoil Five eliminates the spoil; points are scored in every deal. It is played by two, four, or six players, in two partnerships. Partners sit alternately. The side that wins three or four tricks scores 5 points, or 10 points for winning all five. The side first to reach a total of 45 wins a game.

AUCTION FORTY-FIVES

This elaboration of Forty-Five is described as it is now played in Canada.

Number of players. 1. Four or six, in two partnerships. Partners sit alternately.

The pack. 2. The pack and rank of cards are as in Spoil Five, paragraphs 2 and 3. But in drawing cards for partnerships, the cards in all suits rank in the Whist order, from ace (high) to deuce. The two or three drawing highest cards are partners against the others.

The deal. 3. Each player receives five cards, dealt in batches of 3-2 or 2-3; the dealer may choose either order, but whichever he starts he must adhere to.

Bidding. 4. Eldest hand (player at left of the dealer) declares first. Each player in turn must pass or make a bid higher than any previous bid. All bids are made in multiples of 5, up to 30, no suit being specified. The dealer in his turn may hold, that is, offer to play at the preceding highest bid, which his offer thereby supersedes. When dealer holds, each other player who did not pass may in turn bid higher; the bidding continues until all players but one have passed.

Drawing. 5. The high bidder (or dealer, if he held and was not overcalled) names the trump suit. Each player then discards as many cards as he pleases from his hand, and dealer serves each in turn with an equal number of cards to restore his hand to five. (In some localities, the dealer in a six-hand game is permitted to replace his own discards by robbing the pack—looking at all remaining cards and picking out what he likes.)

The play. 6. The opening lead is made by the player at the left of the one who named the trump. All other rules of play are as in Spoil Five, paragraphs 9 and 10.

Scoring. 7. Each trick counts 5, and the highest trump in play counts 5. After the play, each side counts what it has taken. If the bidder's side has taken at least the amount of its bid, it scores all that it won. If the bidder's side fails, the amount of the bid is deducted from its score. The opposing side in either case scores what it won in tricks.

8. If a side bids and makes 30 (all the points) it scores 60 instead of 30.

9. The side that first reaches a total of 120 points wins a game. A side that has 100 or more points is not allowed to bid less than 20.

Irregularities. 10. *New deal.* There must be a new deal by the same dealer if he fails to adhere to his chosen order of dealing, or if a card is exposed during the deal, or if any player receives more or less than five cards.

11. *Wrong number of cards.* If any hand is found to be incorrect, after the first bid but before the opening lead, it must be rectified. A short hand must draw additional cards from the stock; a long hand must have excess cards drawn from it and discarded by the right-hand opponent.

12. *Foul hand.* If any hand is found to be incorrect after the opening lead, it is foul and must be immediately discarded. The offender's side may not score in that deal, and, if it made the high bid, the bid is scored as lost.

13. *Exposed card.* If, after the opening lead, a player exposes illegally any of the three highest trumps, his hand is foul (see paragraph 12). If he exposes any lower card, he must leave it face up on the table and play it at the first legal opportunity thereafter.

LOO

Originally this game was called Lanterloo, after the French *lanterlu,* the refrain of a 17th-century popular song. Several variants developed, and each was itself played under different rules in different localities. The principal variants depend on how many cards are dealt to each hand (three-card or five-card), whether the pool is divided or is won by a single hand (division or full), and whether the payment for loo is fixed or variable (limited or unlimited). First described below is Three-Card Division Loo, perhaps the most-played game.

Number of players. 1. From five to eight; fewer make a dull game; more can play, but then the game becomes unwieldy.

The pack. 2. A regular pack of 52 cards.

Rank of cards. 3. The cards in each suit rank: A (high), K, Q, J, 10, 9, 8, 7, 6, 5, 4, 3, 2.

The pool. 4. The dealer antes three chips to start a pool. If it comprises only his ante, the pool is a single (also called *bold stand*, or *force*). All payments for loo and forfeits for irregularities go into the pool, and when it is so increased it is a *double*.

The deal. 5. Each player receives three cards, dealt one at a time in clockwise rotation, beginning with an extra hand placed between the dealer and eldest hand (player at his left). The extra hand is called the *miss* (or dumby, or dummy, or widow). In some localities, no miss is dealt when the pool is single.

6. When the pool is double, the next card of the pack, after the hands are dealt, is turned up to fix the trump suit for the deal. When the pool is single, the turn of trump is deferred as explained in paragraph 9.

The play, single pool. 7. No player may drop out of the deal in a single pool. Eldest hand may, if he wishes, discard his original hand and take the miss instead. (In some localities, each player in turn has option of taking the miss if it has not been taken before him.)

8. Eldest hand makes the opening lead. Where the rule is to defer the turn-up of trump, he may lead any card. After any lead, each other hand must follow suit if able; must trump if able when void of a plain suit led; and in any case must head the trick if able, by playing a card that could win the trick. A trick is won by the highest trump, or, if it contains no trump, by the highest card of the suit led. The winner of a trick leads to the next. (These rules must be followed so far as they can be without knowledge of what the trump suit will prove to be.)

9. So long as every hand follows suit to every lead, no card is turned for trump. But as soon as any hand fails to follow, the trick is completed and then a trump card is turned. The trump suit must be taken into account in determining the ownership of all tricks. On this account, cards are not thrown into the center, but as played are kept face up in front of the owners.

10. If the rule is to turn the trump card before the opening lead, all rules of play are as in double pool, paragraph 14.

The play, double pool. 11. Each player in turn after the deal, beginning with eldest hand, must declare whether he will play or drop out for that deal. (Dealer is responsible for requiring these declarations, and must not look at his own hand until all other players have declared.) Any player who stays may take the miss in exchange for his own hand, if it has not been taken before him.

12. If only one player stays, he wins the pool without play. The dealer may thus take the pool if all others pass (drop). If only one player stands, ahead of the dealer, the latter must stand, but he may play either for himself or to defend the pool. In playing for himself, he may not take the miss; in defending the pool, he must do so. His action thus is tantamount to a declaration.

13. After the dealer has declared, a player holding three trumps (flush) may show it and take the pool without play. In this case, all other players who stayed in the deal are looed. If two or more players have flushes, the one nearest the left of the dealer wins. When no flush is declared, the hands are played out. (In some localities, flush is not counted and all deals are played out.)

14. The opening lead is made by the active player nearest the left of the dealer. He and all subsequent leaders must lead a trump if he has two trumps (or, in some localities, if he has any trump); must lead the trump ace if he has it, or the king if the ace was turned for trump, or a trump known to be the highest in play through the previous fall of higher-ranking trumps. After any lead, each other hand must follow suit if able; must trump if able when void of a plain suit led; and in any case must head the trick if able, by playing a card that could win the trick. A trick is won by the highest trump, or, if it contains no trump, by the highest card of the suit led. The winner of a trick leads to the next.

Settlement. 15. *Single pool.* One chip is paid out of the pool for each trick won. Each player who failed to win a trick is looed and must pay a forfeit of three chips to the next pool.

15. *Double pool.* One-third of the pool is paid out for each trick won. Each player who stayed in and did not win a trick is looed and must pay three chips to the next pool. (The pool can return to single only when every player who stayed in a double took a trick.) When dealer defends the pool, he neither pays nor collects, the only settlement being made by his lone opponent.

Irregularities. 16. *Revoke.* Any error in failing to follow the rules of play may be corrected if the next hand has not played after the offender. If the error is discovered at a later time, before the cards are gathered for the next deal, it is a revoke. The offender must pay six chips to the next pool, and all other players who participated in the deal divide the current pool equally, regardless of what may have been the outcome of the actual play. If the pool does not divide evenly, odd chips are left in the next pool.

17. *Forfeits.* An offender must pay three chips into the current pool for:

(a) Misdealing, as by exposing a card or dealing the wrong number of cards; and a new deal by the same dealer is then compulsory;

(b) Turning a trump, in a single pool, before any player has refused a suit; and the card turned is then void;

(c) Declaring out of turn, in a double pool; and the declaration is void;

(d) Looking at his hand, as dealer in a double pool, before all other players have declared;

(e) Leading or playing out of turn;

(f) Failing to pay for loo before the turn-up of trump in the next deal.

LOO VARIATIONS

Unlimited Loo. The name Limited Loo is given to any variant where the payment for loo is fixed. In Unlimited Loo—one of the deadliest gambling games ever devised—this payment is equal to the number of chips currently in the pool.

Irish Loo. There is no distinction between single and double pools. No extra hand is dealt. The trump card is turned before the opening lead. Before the play, each player in turn must pass or stand. All players who stand may better their hands by drawing cards from the stock in exchange for discards. If all others pass, the dealer wins the pool, and if only one ahead of him stands, he may play for himself or to defend the pool. The rules of play are as at double pool in Loo, paragraph 14.

Five-card Loo. This is the same as Irish Loo with five cards dealt to each hand instead of three. All antes, payments for loo, and forfeits, are in multiples of five, so that the pool can be distributed equally for the five tricks won.

Pam-Loo. This Five-card Loo variant is the Loo game most frequently referred to in literature of the 18th century (and the references are copious). Pam, the jack of clubs, is always the highest trump, and may be used as a wild card to complete a flush or blaze. A flush is five cards of the same suit; a blaze is five face cards. These hands win the pool without play, the precedence being: pam-flush and pam-blaze (equal), natural trump flush, natural plain-suit flush, natural blaze (lowest). Between equal hands, the one nearest the left of the dealer wins.

In friendly games, it became the custom for a player leading a high trump to say "Pam, be civil"—a plea to the holder of pam to let the trick go, since pam is always sure of a trick. The formal rules presently took cognizance of the social odium attached to ignoring this plea, by providing (a) that the holder of pam could always renege on a trump lead; (b) "Pam, be civil!" could properly be uttered only on lead of the ace of trumps; (c) the holder of pam was bound to honor a proper plea.

NAPOLEON

Better known as Nap, this is the folk-game of England, having supplanted Loo, which it relegated to obsolescence early in the 19th century.

Number of players. 1. From two to six may play.

The pack. 2. A regular pack of 52 cards.

Rank of cards. 3. The cards in each suit rank: A (high), K, Q, J, 10, 9, 8, 7, 6, 5, 4, 3, 2.

The deal. 4. Each player receives five cards, dealt one at a time.

Bidding. 5. There is one round of bidding. Each player in turn, beginning with eldest hand (player at left of the dealer), must pass or make a bid higher than any preceding bid. Each bid is the number of tricks, out of five, that the bidder will contract to win if allowed to name the trump suit. A bid of five is nap. If all others pass, the dealer must bid. The usual rule is that dealer in this position may bid one, but the least any other player may bid is two. No suit is named in making a bid.

The play. 6. The high bidder names the trump suit and leads first. He may lead any card. After any lead, each other hand must follow suit if able; if unable, the hand may play any card. A trick is won by the highest trump, or, if it contains no trump, by the highest card of the suit led. The winner of a trick leads to the next.

Object of play. 7. The high bidder tries to win at least the number of tricks he has bid. All other players combine against him to defeat this object. The moment the issue is settled—the bidder makes his minimum, or the opponents take their "book" to defeat him—play ends and all cards left in the hands are faced on the table (to be examined for possible revoke).

Scoring. 8. If he makes his bid, the bidder collects from each player as many chips as the bid. If the bid is defeated, the bidder pays this number to each opponent. A bid of nap, however, wins 10 from each opponent if it is made, though it pays only 5 if defeated.

Irregularities. 9. *Misdeal* does not lose the deal; the cards are shuffled and redealt by the same player.

10. *Wrong number of cards.* If a player is dealt the wrong number of cards, he may demand a new deal before he bids or passes, but if the error is not noticed until later, he must play on with the incorrect hand. A short hand cannot win one or more final tricks; if it wins a trick with its last card, the turn to lead passes to the left. If the bidder's hand is correct and an opponent's incorrect, the bidder does not pay if he loses but collects if he wins. If the bidder's hand is incorrect and all others correct, the bidder does not collect if he wins but pays if he loses.

11. *Play out of turn.* The bidder incurs no penalty for leading or playing out of turn, but the error must be corrected on demand if made before the trick is gathered: otherwise it stands as regular. If an opponent leads or plays out of turn, he must pay three chips to the bidder and collect nothing if the bid is defeated.

12. *Revoke* is failure to follow suit when able. If a revoke is noticed

and claimed before settlement for the deal, the play is void. If it was the bidder who revoked, he must pay all opponents as though he had lost; if it was an opponent, he must pay the bidder the full amount due him for winning, while the other opponents pay nothing.

NAP VARIANTS

Sir Garnet, or Widow Nap. An extra hand is dealt. A player who bids nap may pick up this widow, then choose the best five cards of the ten for his hand.

Peep. A widow of one card is dealt. Before declaring in his turn, a player may peep privately at the widow card, paying one chip to the pool for the privilege. The high bidder takes the widow and discards one card. Settlement is as usual, but a player who bids and makes nap takes the pool in addition to his other winnings.

Nap Pool. A pool is formed by an ante of two chips from every player. So long as it is not won, each successive dealer antes two more chips. Additional rules may be invoked to swell the pool: peep may be allowed; forfeits assessed for irregularities; a player who bids nap and fails must double the amount in the pool. The pool is won by the first to bid and make nap.

Purchase Nap, or Ecarte Nap. This is an extension of Nap Pool. After the deal, before the bidding, each player in turn may discard as many cards as he pleases and draw an equal number from the stock, paying into the pool one chip for each card drawn.

Special bids. A bid of nap (but only if this bid is made) may be overcalled by Wellington, and that by Blücher. These also are bids to win all five tricks, and collect only 10 if made, but Wellington pays 10 if lost, and Blücher pays 20. (*Variant rule:* Wellington collects 20 or pays 10; Blücher callects 30 or pays 15.)

A bid of misère offers to avoid taking any tricks, the hand being played without a trump suit. It overcalls a bid of three, and may be overcalled by a bid of four. It scores as a bid of three.

ECARTE

This game is little-played outside of European gaming rooms. Though it is two-hand, the casino rules permit the participation of spectators in the betting. A player may cover all the bets offered against him, in which case he may bar comment or advice as to his own play; or he may permit spectators to back him in whole or part, whereupon he is bound to listen to their advice, though he may disregard it if he wishes.

Number of players. 1. Only two actually play, though any number may be concerned in the betting.

The pack. 2. A pack of 32 cards, made by discarding from a full pack all cards lower than sevens. In practice, two such packs are used alternately.

Rank of cards. 3. The cards in each suit rank: K (high), Q, J, A, 10, 9, 8, 7.

The shuffle and cut. 4. The dealer shuffles his own pack and offers it to his opponent for a cut. His opponent may shuffle once, in which case the dealer must shuffle again. The cut must leave at least two cards in each packet.

The deal. 5. Each player receives five cards. The turn to deal alternates; to determine first dealer, each draws a card from a pack shuffled by his opponent, and high deals first. The dealer may deal a batch of three to each, beginning with his opponent, then a batch of two, or he may deal two, then three. But he must continue to follow the order he first adopts, except that he may change by giving oral notice prior to the cut at the beginning of a new game.

6. The eleventh card of the pack is turned face up for trump. If it is a king, the dealer scores 1 point immediately. (This gives him the game if he already has 4 points.)

Drawing. 7. If satisfied with his original hand, the non-dealer may require play to begin at once, by saying "I play" or "I stand." Or, he may seek to better his hand, saying "I propose." Dealer may then refuse, insisting on play of the original hands, or may accept.

8. On acceptance of proposal, the non-dealer must discard from one to five cards. The dealer serves him an equal number of cards from the pack. The dealer may then discard and draw, but he may keep his original five cards if he wishes.

9. Repeated proposals may be made by the non-dealer, and additional cards are dealt to replace discards so long as the dealer accepts each proposal. Play begins when either player stands. When the pack nears exhaustion without a stand, the non-dealer is entitled to draw first, and dealer may take what is left, but neither may discard more cards than remain available to him in the pack. With the pack exhausted, the hands must be played.

The play. 10. The non-dealer leads first. He may lead any card. Prior to the first lead, either player holding the king of trumps may show it and score 1 point. Non-dealer, if the king is not in sight, must give warning "I play" before leading, so as to give dealer a chance to declare the king.

11. The leader to any trick must announce the suit orally; if he fails to do so, his opponent may not be penalized for revoke in that trick. The second player to a trick must follow suit if able and must win the trick if able. Thus, he must play higher, if he can, in following suit, and trump if he cannot follow to a plain-suit lead. A trick is won by the higher trump or the higher card of the suit led. The winner of a trick leads to the next.

Object of play. 12. To win at least three tricks; thereafter to win all five (*vole*).

Scoring. 13. If the original hands were played without drawing, the player who stood scores 1 point for taking three or four tricks, or 2 points for vole. If he takes less than three, his opponent scores 2 points.

14. If any cards were drawn after the original deal, either player wins 1 for three or four tricks or 2 for vole.

15. The player who first reaches a total of 5 points wins a game. The usual method of scoring is to provide each player with four chips, which he transfers from one pile to another as he wins points.

Irregularities. 16. *Exposed card.* If a player sees more than one card in drawing for deal, the lower-ranking card counts.

17. If a player looks back at his discard or at his opponent's tricks, he must play on with his hand exposed. (He may look at his own tricks.)

18. *Misdeal.* If the wrong player deals, his opponent may demand a redeal before the trump is turned and before seeing a card dealt to him; after this, but before he has made any declaration or play, the opponent may have the dealt cards put aside, and they will stand as the next deal unless the current deal ends the game.

19. If one or more cards are exposed in dealing (except the eleventh card) and neither player has seen his hand, there must be a redeal; if only dealer has seen his hand, non-dealer may require a redeal if the exposed card is his; if both have looked at their hands, the deal stands.

20. If the dealer gives the wrong number of cards to either player: Before the trump is turned, the error may be corrected, by reëstablishing the correct order of the cards. After the trump is turned, but before non-dealer has seen his hand, the latter may either require a redeal or permit the incorrect hand to be corrected by discarding or by drawing an additional card or cards (but not the trump card).

21. When non-dealer requires a new deal, he may at his option be the dealer, with his own pack, the misdeal thus losing the deal.

22. *Incorrect hand.* When, having more than five cards, a player makes any declaration, draws cards, or plays, he loses 1 point and may not score for the king; but neither player may ever score more than 2 points plus the point for the king (if he has it) in any hand.

23. *False claim of king.* If a player claims the point for king without holding it, his opponent may withdraw all cards he has played to previous tricks and cause the play to be recommenced.

24. *Irregularities in the draw.* If a player discards more cards than he draws, he may increase his discard to accept the additional cards. If dealer gives non-dealer the wrong number of cards, non-dealer may discard, or draw additional cards, to make his hand correct. But if in any other case a player has more than five cards after the draw, he may not score for the king; he may not score for winning three or four tricks; and he may score only 1 point for vole.

25. *Revoke.* When a player fails to follow suit or win a trick, though able to do so, the cards are withdrawn from the tricks and replayed, and the offender may not score for winning three or four tricks, and may score only 1 point for vole.

26. *Incorrect pack.* Discovery that the pack is incorrect voids the current deal but any previous deal or a draw for dealer with that pack stands.

Pointers on Ecarte play. The play of the cards is almost entirely mechanical, with little scope for art. Practically the entire game is a matter of when to stand and when to propose. This has been reduced to a matter of mathematics, in the so-called *jeux de règle*. All hands deemed worth playing are summarized in the table below. The rank of plain cards needed depends on the number of trumps in the hand; the rank of the trumps is largely immaterial. Although K-Q-J is much pleasanter to hold than 9-8-7, the latter also is a proper stand if the spots on the two side cards total 17 or more. Where the table shows only four cards, the hand is a proper stand whatever the fifth card.

TRUMPS	2ND SUIT	3RD SUIT	4TH SUIT
None	K Q	K	Q
"	K J	K J	Q
"	K A	K	K
"	Q J	K	K
"	Q J	Q J	K
One	K Q 7		
"	K 8 7	K	
"	K Q	Q	7
"	K A	K 7	
"	K A	K	7
"	K 7	K	A
"	K	K	9 8
"	Q J A	J	
"	Q J	K 7	
"	Q J	Q A	
"	Q J	J	J
Two	K 7	9	
"	Q 10	8	
"	Q	Q	7
"	Q	J	A
"	J 10	10	
"	J	J	J
"	A 10	A	
Three	8 7		
"	9	8	

Any hand of four or five trumps is a *jeux de règle*.

From three or more trumps lead a trump; having the trump king, lead it. In all other cases, the correct card to lead is italicized in the table above.

There is some scope for judgment in whether to propose, even having a playable hand, in the hope of getting cards to make vole. The decision should take account of whether the trump king has yet appeared, and how many cards if any the opponent previously drew.

The rule-of-thumb in discarding is to keep only trumps and kings. If only two cards can be discarded under this rule, the hand is likely to be a regulation stand.

EUCHRE

The term bower indubitably comes from the German *Bauer* (one of several terms for a jack), but all efforts to find a German origin for Euchre have come to naught. As stated by the American Hoyle of 1864: "The game is unknown in Germany, except in those parts where it has been introduced by wandering Americans. . . . As it has been traced to the counties of Lancaster, Berks, and Lehigh, in Pennsylvania, where it first made its appearance about forty years since, it is not difficult to conjecture how it arose." The conjecture is that the Pennsylvania Dutch endeavored to play Ecarté by imperfect hearsay, giving it their own pronunciation and eventually their own rules. Certain it is that Pennsylvania is the area from which Euchre spread throughout the country to become one of the leading games.

Number of players. 1. From two to seven may play. Different variants are adapted to different numbers of players. First-described below is the four-hand game, in two partnerships.

The pack. 2. A pack of 32 cards, made by discarding from a full pack all cards below the sevens.

Rank of cards. 3. The jack is the highest trump; it is called *right bower*. The *left bower* is the jack of the other suit of same color as the trump; it ranks as the second-best trump. The suit of the left bower is called *next*, while the two suits of opposite color are *cross* suits. The rank of the cards is:

Trumps: J (right bower, high), J (left bower), A, K, Q, 10, 9, 8, 7.
Next: A (high), K, Q, 10, 9, 8, 7.
Cross: A (high), K, Q, J, 10, 9, 8, 7.

Drawing for partnerships. 4. The pack is spread face down and each player draws a card. The lowest card has choice of seats and deals first; the two lowest are partners against the other two. In drawing only, the cards rank as in cross suits except that ace is low, below the seven. Players drawing equal cards must draw again.

Shuffle and cut. 5. Dealer has the right to shuffle last. The pack must be cut by the player at his right, leaving at least four cards in each packet of the cut. Usually, two packs are used alternately, one being shuffled by dealer's partner while the other is dealt.

The deal. 6. Each player receives five cards, dealt in batches of 3-2 or 2-3. The dealer may choose either order, but whichever he chooses he must adhere to. After all hands are dealt, the next card of the stock is turned up to propose the trump suit.

Making. 7. The turn-up proposes the trump suit, but its acceptance depends on one or two rounds of *making*. Eldest hand (player at left of the dealer) speaks first. He must say either "Pass" or "I order it up." The latter statement accepts the turn-up suit. If he passes, dealer's partner must say either "Pass" or "I assist," the latter meaning acceptance. If the first two players pass, the third must either pass or order it up.

If the first three players pass, dealer signifies a pass by *turning it down,* that is, placing the turn-up face down under the pack. He usually signifies acceptance of the turn-up by discarding one card face down from his hand (see paragraph 10).

8. If dealer turns it down, there is one more round of declaring. Each in turn, beginning with eldest hand, must either pass or make it by naming a suit other than that rejected (provided, of course, that all players ahead of him have passed). If all four players pass in the second round, the cards are thrown in and the next dealer deals.

9. The hand that makes the trump (whether by ordering it up, assisting, accepting, or naming a new suit) has the right to declare "I play alone." The partner then discards his hand and does not participate in the play.

10. If the turn-up is accepted, by him or another plaper, dealer has the right to take the turn-up into his hand in exchange for a discard, provided that he makes the discard before the opening lead. By custom the turn-up is left on the pack until the dealer chooses to play it.

The play. 11. When the maker plays alone, the opening lead is made by the player at his left; otherwise it is made by the eldest hand, regardless of who is the maker.

12. The leader to any trick may lead any card. Each other hand must follow suit if able; if unable, the hand may play any card. A trick is won by the highest trump, or, if it contains no trump, by the highest card of the suit led. The winner of a trick leads to the next.

Object of play. 13. The object is to win three tricks, or all five tricks. The latter is called *march.* If the maker's side fails to win three tricks, it is *euchred.*

Scoring. 14. Only the side that wins a majority of the tricks scores. The side that made the trump, playing in partnership, scores 1 point for winning three or four tricks, 2 points for march. The maker playing alone scores 1 point for three or four tricks, 4 points for march. (Of course this score benefits the partner of the lone player also, since they go to a joint account.) If the making side is euchred, the other side scores 2 points.

15. The side first to reach a total of 5 points wins a game. (By agreement the game is sometimes fixed at 7 or 10 points.) The score is by custom kept by small cards not used in the pack, as a three and a four.

16. (*Optional rule.*) The side first to win two games is credited with 2 rubber points, plus the difference between the total rubber points awarded to each side separately as follows: 3 points for a game in which the losers scored nothing; 2 for a game in which the losers scored 1 or 2; 1 for a game in which the losers scored 3 or 4. When rubbers are played, settlement is made according to the rubber points only.

Irregularities. 17. *New deal.* There must be a new deal by the same dealer if a card is exposed in dealing, or if a card is found faced in the pack, or if the pack is found to be imperfect (in the last case, scores of previous deals stand).

18. *False declaration.* If a player says "I order it up" or "I assist," using the term proper only to an opponent, there is no penalty; he is deemed to have accepted the turn-up. If a turn-up is turned down, and if a player then names the same suit for trump, his declaration is void and his side may not make the trump.

19. *Declaration out of turn.* If a player makes any declaration out of turn (except a pass), his side may not make the trump.

20. *Wrong number of cards.* If, before the first trick is quitted, any hand is found to have the wrong number of cards, there must be a new deal; if the error is discovered at a later time, play continues and the side with the incorrect hand may not score for that deal.

21. *Lead out of turn.* If a player leads out of turn, and the trick is gathered before the error is noticed, it stands as regular. If the error is noticed at a previous time, the erroneous lead becomes an exposed card and other cards played to the trick are retracted without penalty; when the offending side next gains the lead, the opponent at right of the leader may name the suit to be led. A lone player may not be so penalized for a lead out of turn, but may be required to retract it.

22. *Exposed card.* If a player exposes a card from his hand, except in properly leading or playing it, such card must be left face up on the table and played at first legal opportunity. But there is no penalty against a lone player for exposing cards.

23. *Illegal information.* If a player looks at the cards of any quitted trick, or improperly gives information to his partner about the quitted tricks, previous play, or his own hand or intentions, the opponent at right of the leader may name the suit to be led at the next time the offending side gains the lead.

24. *Revoke* is failure to follow suit to a lead when able. A player may correct his revoke before the trick is gathered; otherwise it stands established. For established revoke, the opponents of the offender may score

2 points or require 2 points to be deducted from the revoking side (the penalty being 4 points in case of a lone player).

Pointers on Euchre play. At 0-0 score, eldest hand and his partner have little interest in ordering it up, for if it is turned down their side will have first chance to name a new suit. The only occasion for ordering it up (thereby assuring the dealer at least one trump) is a hand of three fairly sure tricks, including at least two trumps.

The partner of the dealer may well assist on any two trumps and one side ace or king, or even less strength. But if the turn-up is a bower or ace, he should give consideration to playing alone: if he cannot assist and play alone, he should usually pass so as to allow dealer to play alone.

The dealer should usually accept the turn-up, for he thereby gains a trump and forestalls two undesirable events: a make by the opponents; a call of lone hand by an opponent, which would deprive dealer of his great advantage of playing last to the opening lead. But the dealer may well turn it down when he is better prepared for another suit as trump, especially a cross suit, e. g., when he has a black bower and the turn-up is red.

Normal requirements for accepting the turn-up give way to urgencies of the score in certain situations. The commonest of these is: one side is *at the bridge*, having 4 points, while the other side has 1 or 2 points. The latter side could win the game by calling alone and winning a march; the side at the bridge usually accepts the turn-up regardless of its cards, for at worst it suffers euchre, but 2 points do not give the opponents the game. Another common situation arises when one side has 3 points. The other side must then be conservative, for if it makes the trump the first side needs to win only three tricks to go game, whereas if the first side makes the trump it needs all five tricks for game.

In the play it must be remembered that each player holds only five cards, in which four suits can be represented: For everyone to follow twice to the same suit is almost unheard of. The first time a suit is led, you may as well play your highest card unless someone before you has already played a higher. It is never compulsory to lead a trump, but with two trumps, including one high one, and two cards of a side suit, including one high one, a trump lead often pays.

SET-BACK EUCHRE

This is a variation in scoring. Only the maker's side scores; when it is euchred, 2 points are deducted from its score. The traditional way of keeping score is to give each side (or each player, in non-partnership play) five chips. For each point he wins, a player puts one chip in the center pool; for each euchre he suffers, he takes out two chips. The first to get rid of all his chips wins a game. Set-back, like regular Euchre, is a game of bidding to the score, but the list of emergency situations is somewhat different. For example, when any player is at the bridge, another player will usually make the trump if he can speak first, regardless of his own score. At worst, he is set back 2, but the game is kept alive for at least one more deal.

Penalty Euchre or Euchre Loo is a form of Set-back suitable to four or five players. An extra hand or widow of five cards is dealt. Each player in turn has the right to discard his original hand face down and take either the widow or the hand discarded by a player ahead of him. The turn-up fixes the trump for the deal, and the dealer may not take it. Eldest hand makes the opening lead and each player gathers his own tricks. Every player has twelve chips at the outset, and the first to get rid of his chips wins a game. Each player puts one chip in the center pool for each trick he wins; if he wins no trick, he receives one chip from each other player who did win a trick.

THREE-HAND EUCHRE

This form is also called Cutthroat Euchre. Each plays for himself. There is of course no assisting. The maker of trump plays alone against the other two in temporary partnership. The maker scores 1 point for winning three or four tricks, 2 for march; or, each opponent scores 2 for euchre. All other rules are the same as in four-hand Euchre, except as to irregularities. On page 203, paragraphs 17, 20, 24 apply; paragraphs 21, 22, 23 apply only to opponents of the maker; the other paragraphs never apply.

Blind Euchre is a variant best for three-hand play. A widow of two cards is dealt. To accept the turn-up, a player must take the widow, then discard any two cards face down, and play against the others in temporary partnership. If none takes the widow, the deal is abandoned without score.

TWO-HAND EUCHRE

The pack comprises 24 cards, made by discarding the sevens and eights from the regular Euchre pack of 32. The rules follow the fourhand game, with the modifications obviously necessary. The maker scores 2 for march; the only applicable rule on irregularities is paragraph 24, page 203.

RAILROAD EUCHRE

Euchre was at one time much-played by commuters en route to and from their offices. Many features were introduced to speed up the tempo of the scoring, not only to complete games faster but also to pile up larger differences of score in a few games. All such features are called collectively Railroad Euchre. Any or all of the following may be added to the regular game.

The joker is added to the pack. It always ranks as the highest trump, above the right bower. If a joker is turned up, hearts are trumps.

Exchange. A lone player has the right to discard one card face down, and to receive in exchange one card from his partner's hand, chosen by the partner without consultation or exposure of his hand. This exchange is additional to dealer's vested right to take the turn-up. If dealer declares alone, he takes the exchange card from his partner before committing himself as to the turn-up, so that if the card received does not suit him he can discard it for the turn-up. If dealer's partner declares alone, dealer is entitled to give him the turn-up.

Where exchange is allowed, it may be agreed that the maker can try for an increased score by foregoing it. (Dealer, to earn this chance, must also refrain from taking the turn-up.) The pat-hand maker scores 1 point for winning three or four tricks, 5 for march; euchre costs 3 points.

Opposing alone. Either opponent of a player who has declared alone may declare that he will oppose alone. Where the lone maker is allowed exchange (preceding paragraph), the lone opposer has the same right. The euchre of a lone maker by a lone opposer counts 4 points. If the pat-hand rule is adopted (preceding paragraph), opposing a lone pat hand alone is not permitted.

Laps. When a side goes over the total of 5 points in winning a game, the excess is carried over to the next game. The effect of this rule is to preserve the incentive to playing alone, whatever the score.

Slam. A game counts double if the losers fail to score a point; a single game can therefore be a rubber.

Jambone. A lone player may expose his whole hand, and allow the opponents (without consultation) to name the card he must play to each trick. If the jambone player wins march, he scores 8 points. Opposing jambone alone is not permitted.

Jamboree. If the maker of trump holds the five highest trumps (without help of the turn-up), he scores 16 points (which includes the score for march). This rule is interpreted by some players to mean the actual five top-ranking trumps, beginning with the joker if used or the right bower, if it is not; other players take it to mean the five highest trumps in play, regardless of what they happen to be. In either case, the rule is about as useful as royalties for a royal flush in Poker.

AUCTION EUCHRE

Number of players. 1. Five to seven may play.

The pack. 2. With five players, the regular Euchre pack of 32 (see page 201). With six players, add the sixes to the pack, making 36 cards. With seven players, use a full pack of 52 cards. The joker may be added to the pack by agreement.

Rank of cards. 3. The jack of the trump suit is right bower; the left bower is the jack of the other suit of same color as the trump. The suit of the left bower is *next;* the suits of opposite color are *cross suits.* The rank of the cards, so far as the pack extends, is as follows:

Trumps: Joker (high), J (right bower), J (left bower), A, K, Q, 10, 9, 8, 7, 6, 5, 4, 3, 2.

Next: A (high), K, Q, 10, 9, 8, 7, 6, 5, 4, 3, 2.

Cross: A (high), K, Q, J, 10, 9, 8, 7, 6, 5, 4, 3, 2.

Drawing for position. 4. The pack is spread face down and each player draws a card. The lowest has choice of seats and deals first; the next-lowest sits at his left, and so on. In drawing only, the cards rank as in cross suits except that the ace is low, below the deuce. Players drawing equal cards must draw again.

Shuffle and cut. 5. Dealer has the right to shuffle last. The pack must be cut by the player at his right, leaving at least four cards in each packet of the cut.

The deal. 6. Each player receives: five cards, dealt in batches of 3-2 or 2-3, when there are five or six players; seven cards, dealt in batches of 4-3 or 3-4, when there are seven players.

7. After the first round of the deal, a widow is dealt to the center of the table: two cards when there are five or six players; three cards (or all that remain) when there are seven.

Bidding. 8. There is one round of bidding. Each player in turn, beginning with eldest hand (player at left of the dealer), must pass or make a bid higher than any preceding bid. All bids are made in numbers alone, no suit being specified. The obligations of the bids are explained below.

9. *Five-hand.* Bid of 3: to win three tricks, with aid of the widow and one partner. Bid of 4 or 5: to win this number of tricks, with aid of the widow and two partners. Bid of eight: to win five tricks, playing alone with help of the widow. Bid of 15: to win five tricks, playing alone and without using the widow.

10. *Six-hand.* Bid of 3, 4, or 5: to win this number of tricks, with aid of the widow and partners. Bid of 8: to win five tricks, playing alone, with aid of the widow. Bid of 15: to win five tricks, playing alone and without using the widow.

11. *Seven-hand.* Bid of 4 or 5: to win this number of tricks, with aid of the widow and one partner. Bid of 6 or 7: to win this number of tricks, with aid of the widow and two partners. Bid of 10: to win seven tricks, playing alone, with aid of the widow. Bid of 20: to win seven tricks, playing alone and without using the widow.

12. If his bid permits, the high bidder takes the widow into his hand and then discards an equal number of cards face down. He then names the trump suit. If entitled to partners, he chooses them before the opening lead.

Partners. 13. *Six-hand.* There are two partnerships of three each, partners sitting alternately. When the high bid commits the maker to play alone, the other two partners place their hands face down on the table and stay out of the play.

14. *Five-hand and seven-hand.* There are no fixed partnerships, but when the bid permits, the maker of trump chooses one or two partners for that deal. He may choose any he will, regardless of the positions at the table, so that all players of a partnership might play consecutively to the trick. The players not in partnership with the high bidder combine in temporary partnership against his side.

The play. 15. When the trump maker plays alone, the opening lead is made by the player at his left; otherwise it is made by eldest hand, regardless of who is the maker.

16. The leader to any trick may lead any card. Each other hand must follow suit if able; if unable, a hand may play any card. A trick is won by the highest trump, or, if it contains no trump, by the highest card of the suit led. The winner of a trick leads to the next.

Scoring. 17. The amount of the bid is credited to the maker if his side wins at least that number of tricks, or to the opponents if he fails. Nothing is earned by taking extra tricks beyond what are necessary to make or defeat the bid. In five-hand and seven-hand play, a score earned by a partnership is credited in full to each member separately.

18. Each deal is treated as a separate game, settlement being made at once by chips taken from a common pool. At the end of a session, the partnerships in six-hand pay and collect according to the difference of chips won; in five-hand and seven-hand, the total of chips won is divided by the number of players to determine the average winning, and each player collects or pays according as his own stack is above or below the average.

CALL-ACE EUCHRE

This is a method of determining the temporary partnerships in a game of four, five, or six players where there are no fixed partnerships. The trump suit is decided by making, as in the four-hand partnership game (page 202). The maker names any suit (trump or plain), and the holder of the highest card in that suit becomes his partner. Since not all the cards of the pack are in play, the partner may not know that he is such until a late or the last trick. But in any case he must say nothing to reveal that he is the partner, after he discovers the fact. He may and should help the maker by suitable choice of leads and plays, so helping the maker to infer his identity. (The same strictures of course apply also to the opponents of the maker; "talking across the table" by either side is unethical.)

When the maker himself holds the highest card of the named suit, he is deemed a lone player. The maker may deliberately play alone, either by announcing his intention and calling no suit for partnership, or by naming a suit of which he holds the ace. For march, a lone player scores as many points as there are players in the game. Made by a partnership, march counts 2 in four-hand; 3 if there are more players.

HASENPFEFFER

Like the parent game, this variant of Euchre was probably invented by the Pennsylvania Dutch. It may have been named after the rabbit dish hasenpfeffer, or more likely, after the German expression *Hase im Pfeffer,* used like the American "in a pickle," for the player to whom the joker is dealt is apt to find it not an unmixed blessing.

Number of players. 1. Four, in two partnerships. Partners sit opposite each other.

The pack. 2. A pack of 25 cards, made by discarding all cards below the nines from the full pack and adding the joker.

Rank of cards. 3. The joker is always the highest trump. Second-best is the jack of trumps, right bower; third-best is the jack of the other suit of same color as the trump, left bower. The rank in trumps is thus: Joker (high), J (right bower), J (left bower), A, K, Q, 10, 9. In plain suits, the rank is: A (high), K, Q, (J), 10, 9.

The deal. 4. Each player receives six cards, dealt in batches of three at a time, beginning with eldest hand (player at left of the dealer). The last card of the pack is placed face down on the table as the widow.

Bidding. 5. There is one round of bidding. Each player in turn, beginning with eldest hand, must pass or make a bid higher than any preceding bid. All bids are made in numbers from one to six, without specifying a suit.

6. If all four players pass, the player holding the joker must show it and make a bid of three, which stands. Should no player have the joker (it being the widow card), the deal is abandoned without score.

7. The high bidder takes the widow into his hand, names the trump suit, and discards one card face down.

The play. 8. The trump maker leads first. He may lead any card. After any lead, each other hand must follow suit if able; if unable to follow suit, a hand may play any card. A trick is won by the highest trump, or, if it contains no trump, by the highest card of the suit led. The winner of a trick leads to the next.

Scoring. 9. If the side that made the trump wins at least the number of tricks bid, it scores one point for every trick taken. If it fails to make the bid, the amount of the bid is deducted from its score (the side is *set back*). In either case, the other side scores one point for each trick it has taken.

10. The side that first reaches a total of 10 points wins a game. If both sides reach 10 in the same deal, the side that made trump wins.

Irregularities. Follow the rules for Euchre, paragraphs 17-24, page 203.

Pointers on Hasenpfeffer play. A holding of three cards in a suit will probably win a trick through length, if nothing else, as trumps. Count each joker, or bower or trump ace (if adequately guarded), as an additional trick, and count each side ace a trick. It is proper to base a bid on the expectation that partner will furnish one trick. A typical minimum hand for a bid of three is three trumps (of any ranks) and a side ace. Bold bidding is likely to pay better than conservative bidding.

If long (three or more cards) or notably strong in trumps, the bidder should open the suit. But with no side tricks to protect, the opening lead of a low side card may turn out better. The play involves much guessing, but the partner of the maker should usually try to show as quickly as possible where his tricks, if any, lie. The opponents should try to force the lead into the hand of the maker or his right-hand opponent, rather than into either of the other two hands.

DOUBLE HASENPFEFFER

Three, four, or six may play, using a Pinochle pack of 48 cards; the right bower is the highest trump. With four or six, there are two partnerships, partners sitting alternately. The whole pack is dealt out, without a widow. The lowest bid permitted is for half the number of tricks, and dealer must bid at least this number if the other players pass. The trump maker may play alone, in which case he may discard one or two cards face down and receive an equal number from his partner or partners, selected by them but without any consultation between partners. The discard is made before seeing partner's cards, and the cards received are not shown.

A lone player who fails is set back by as many points as there are cards per hand; if he wins, he scores twice as much as he makes. If dealer bids the minimum and fails, he is set back only half the minimum. The player or side first to reach a total of 62 points wins a game.

FIVE HUNDRED

Five Hundred is based on Euchre, but gives much greater scope for skill because the entire pack is in play and each hand is ten cards. It was devised to meet a widespread demand for a game intermediate in difficulty between Euchre and Whist. The rules were first copyrighted by the United States Playing Card Company in 1904. Five Hundred was an instant success, and it remained the foremost social game for a decade, until supplanted by Auction and Contract Bridge.

Number of players. 1. From two to six may play. Different variants are adapted to different numbers of players. First described below is the three-hand game; each plays for himself.

The pack. 2. A pack of 33 cards, made by discarding all cards below the sevens from a full pack and adding the joker. [For other numbers of players, the number of cards in the pack varies accordingly; and a 62-card pack is manufactured especially for the six-hand game.]

Rank of cards. 3. The joker is always the highest trump. Second-best is the jack of trumps, right bower; third-best is the jack of the other suit of same color as the trump, left bower. The rank in trumps is: Joker (high), J (right bower), J (left bower), A, K, Q, 10, 9, 8, 7. In each plain suit the rank is: A (high), K, Q, (J), 10, 9, 8, 7.

4. The bidding denominations rank: no trump (high), hearts, diamonds, clubs, spades.

Drawing. 5. Cards may be drawn from a pack spread face down, for first deal. Lowest card is the first dealer. In drawing for deal only, ace ranks low, below the two, and the joker is the lowest card of the pack.

Shuffle and cut. 6. Dealer has the right to shuffle last. The pack is cut by the player at his right; the cut must leave at least four cards in each packet.

The deal. 7. Each player receives ten cards, dealt in clockwise rotation, beginning with eldest hand (the player at left of the dealer), in batches of 3-4-3. After the first round of the deal, a widow of three cards is dealt face down in the center of the table.

Bidding. 8. There is one round of bidding. Each player, beginning with eldest hand, must pass or make a bid higher than any preceding bid. Each bid must name a number of tricks, from six to ten, together with an intended denomination, no trump or a suit [as, "Six spades"]. To overcall a previous bid, a player must bid more tricks, or the same number of tricks in a higher-ranking denomination.

9. The high bid becomes the contract, and the two other players combine in temporary partnership against the contractor.

10. If all players pass, the deal is abandoned without a score. (*Optional rule:* A passed deal is played at no trump, each player for himself. Eldest hand leads first. Each trick won counts 10 points. As there is no contract, there is no setting back.)

The play. 11. The contractor takes the widow into his hand and then discards any three cards face down. He then makes the opening lead.

12. The leader at any time may lead any card. Each other hand must follow suit if able; if unable, the hand may play any card. A trick is won by the highest trump, or, if it contains no trump, by the highest card of the suit led. The winner of a trick leads to the next.

13. At no trump, the joker wins any trick to which it is played; when the joker is led, the leader must specify the suit that it calls for. The joker may be played on a lead by another hand only when the owner is void of the suit led.

Scoring. 14. If the contractor makes his bid, he scores according to one of the following tables:

AVONDALE SCHEDULE (Recommended)

TRICKS	6	7	8	9	10
♠	40	140	240	340	440
♣	60	160	260	360	460
◊	80	180	280	380	480
♡	100	200	300	400	500
No Trump	120	220	320	420	520

Copyright, 1906, by The United States Playing Card Co.

ORIGINAL SCHEDULE

IF TRUMPS ARE	6 TRICKS	7 TRICKS	8 TRICKS	9 TRICKS	10 TRICKS
Spades	40	80	120	160	200
Clubs	60	120	180	240	300
Diamonds	80	160	240	320	400
Hearts	100	200	300	400	500
No Trump	120	240	360	480	600

INVERTED SCHEDULE

IF TRUMPS ARE	6 TRICKS	7 TRICKS	8 TRICKS	9 TRICKS	10 TRICKS
Clubs	40	80	120	160	200
Spades	60	120	180	240	300
Hearts	80	160	240	320	400
Diamonds	100	200	300	400	500
No Trump	120	240	360	480	600

15. There is no credit for extra tricks over the contract, except that if the contractor wins all ten tricks he scores a minimum of 250 (more, if his bid was for more).

16. If the contractor fails to make the contract, the value of his bid is deducted from his score. It is possible for a player to be set back until he has a minus score; he is then said to be *in the hole* (from the common practice of drawing a ring around a minus score).

17. Whether the contract is made or defeated, each opponent of the contractor scores 10 for each trick he himself has taken.

18. The player first to reach a total of plus 500 points wins a game. If two or more players could reach 500 in the same deal, the contractor wins against an opponent; as between opponents, the first to reach 500 in the course of play wins, and the deal is not played out unless the contractor could also reach 500 by making his bid.

[An optional alternative is to require 1,000 or 1,500 for game. The scoring is speeded up by awarding points for cards won in tricks: 1 for each ace, 10 for each face card or ten, the pip value for each lower card, nothing for the joker. These points of course do not reckon in the question of whether the contractor makes his bid. He scores them only if he makes; the opponents always score them.]

Nullo. 10. By agreement the players may allow an additional declaration, nullo. This is a bid to win no tricks, at no trump. Its value is 250, so that it ranks higher than eight spades, lower than eight clubs (Avondale schedule). If the nullo contractor fails, each opponent scores 10 for each trick taken by the contractor, and the latter is set back 250.

Irregularities. 20. *New Deal.* There must be a new deal by the same dealer if a card is found exposed in the pack; if the dealer gives the wrong number of cards to any hand; or if, before the last card is dealt, attention is called to the fact that the cut was omitted or that the dealer departed in any way from the prescribed method of dealing (as by dealing batches 3-3-4 or 4-3-3, or laying out the widow at any time but after the first round).

21. *Bid out of turn.* In three-hand play, there is no penalty for a pass or bid out of turn; the call is void, and the player may make any legal call in his proper turn. In partnership play, a bid (not a pass) out of turn is void and that side may make no further bid (though a bid made previously by partner of the offender is not cancelled).

22. *Wrong number of cards.* If, during the bidding, two hands (excluding the widow) are found to have the wrong number of cards, there must be a new deal by the same dealer. If the widow and one hand are incorrect, they must be rectified; another player draws out the excess cards and gives them to the short hand; and the player whose hand was incorrect is barred from bidding.

If, during the play, the contractor and an opponent are found to have incorrect hands, or if there is one incorrect hand due to an incorrect pack, there must be a new deal by the same dealer. If two opponents have incorrect hands, the contractor's being correct, the bid is deemed to have been made and the opponents may not score. The contractor may continue play in an effort to win all the tricks, and he is deemed to win all the final tricks to which the short hand cannot play. If the opponents' hands are correct, the contractor's hand and his discard incorrect, the bid is lost, but the deal is played out to determine how many tricks are to be credited to each opponent.

23. *Exposed card.* A card is deemed exposed if it is dropped face up on the table, held so that a partner sees its face, or named by the owner as being in his hand. An exposed card must be left face up on the table and played at first legal opportunity thereafter. But there is no penalty against a contractor playing alone for exposing cards, except in case of a corrected revoke (paragraph 25).

24. *Lead or play out of turn.* A lead out of turn must be retracted on demand of an opponent, and cards played to it may be retracted without penalty. The card led in error is treated as an exposed card; the bidder may require the partner of the offender to lead a named suit, or not to lead the suit of the exposed card.

If a player plays out of turn, not as leader, his card is deemed exposed.

If an error in leading or playing out of turn is not noticed until the trick is gathered, it stands as regular.

25. *Revoke.* Failure to follow suit to a lead when able is a revoke. A revoke may be corrected at any time before the next ensuing lead, otherwise it stands as established. When a revoke is corrected, the incorrect card is deemed exposed, including a case where it belongs to a contractor playing alone. If an established revoke is claimed and proved before the cut for the next deal, and the revoking hand was on the contracting side, the contract is scored as lost; if the revoking hand was an opponent, the contract is scored as made, and the opponents score nothing.

26. *Illegal information.* If a player gives information illegally to his partner, or looks at a trick after it is gathered and quitted, or if the contractor's discards are looked at by him after the opening lead, or by another player at any time: the opponent at the right of the leader may name the suit to be led on the next occasion the offender or his partner gains the lead.

27. *Error in score.* A proved error in recording scores must be corrected on demand made before the first bid (not pass) of the next deal after that to which the error pertains. In any other case, recorded scores may not be changed.

Pointers on Five Hundred play. The normal minimum trump length for any bid is five cards, or four including two or three of the highest trumps. A rough method of determining how many tricks a hand will take is to count one trick for each trump in excess of three, and one trick for each side ace and king.

The widow may properly be counted on to improve the pattern of the hand, as by adding a trump or an extra card to a long side suit. Specifically, when you hold four cards of a suit, it is about 5 to 3 that the widow will furnish at least one more card, and when you have a five-card length, the chance is about 5 to 4. But to count on the widow to furnish specific high cards, valuable because of their rank, is a losing proposition. Reckoning as "places open" the missing high cards, any one of which would justify your bid, your chances of finding one such card in the widow are approximately as follows:

> 1 place open, odds are 7 to 1 against
> 2 places open, odds are 3 to 1 against
> 3 places open, odds are 9 to 5 against
> 4 places open, odds are 6 to 5 against
> 5 places open, odds are 5 to 4 in favor

When you need one of five or more specific cards, you probably have not enough to outbid the other players anyhow.

With great trump strength and little else, bid the maximum value of the hand, and even stretch it if necessary to shut out an overcall. For example:

The rule-of-thumb count shows six tricks; yet to bid six spades, the lowest bid, is probably futile. Bid at least seven; many experienced players will bid eight without a qualm, since another spade or diamond from the widow will give good chances of making.

With general strength rather than excess trumps, be conservative. There is less chance of an overcall, and more prospect of setting back an overcaller.

The rule-of-thumb count shows eight tricks, but obviously the hand stands to lose at least the right bower and two side aces unless it is very lucky. There is no urgency to bid more than seven, and the hand might well pass a seven-bid ahead of it, content to defend.

Discarding is a relatively easy problem: you discard what you can spare. Vital to save are: trumps, all cards in side suits of four or more, necessary guards to side kings and possibly side queens.

The contractor should almost always open trumps, in order at least to pull two trumps for one. After pulling all or most of the adverse trumps, he should try to establish any side suit of four or more cards. Lacking a long side suit, he should try to manage the play so as to make the most of his side cards, by throwing the lead to the left-hand opponent.

The bid of no trump is usually reserved for a hand of general strength but lacking in bowers. The joker is essential if the hand does not have all four suits stopped, and even with stoppers the hand may be wrecked by the joker held by an opponent. The greatest comfort to a no-trumper is a long solid or nearly solid suit, such as A-K-Q-8-7. The opening lead gives the contractor the essential advantage of starting on his long suit before the opponents can attack his stoppers in their long suits.

The nullo bid—to lose all the tricks—obviously requires an extraordinary hand. The holding of some high cards, even aces and even the joker, is not necessarily fatal; what counts is the number of small cards in each suit. The holding of K-J-9-7 can never be forced to take a trick (against adverse leads), and A-Q-10-8 is reasonably safe. An important point is that the nullo contractor must lead first, and therefore must have at least one suit that is reasonably safe even after he has opened it.

FOUR-HAND FIVE HUNDRED

The four-hand game is played with fixed partnerships, partners sitting opposite. The pack is 42 cards, made by discarding the twos, threes, and black fours from a 52-card pack. The joker may be added if desired; usually it is not. Each player receives ten cards and the balance goes to the widow. If one side's score reaches minus 500, its opponents win the game. All other rules are as in the three-hand game, except that two always play against two.

TWO-HAND FIVE HUNDRED

The pack and the deal are the same as in the three-hand game, except that the hand at dealer's left is dealt face down on the table and is dead. With these ten cards out of play, the bidding is largely guesswork. Not to be left "at home" by a bold opponent, a player is bound to be forward in bidding and to speculate on buying just what he needs from the widow. If one player's score reaches minus 500, the other wins the game.

The two-hand game may also be played with a 24-card pack, ninespot low; the widow is four cards, no extra hand is dealt, and the rules otherwise are as in three-hand.

FIVE-HAND FIVE HUNDRED

Five players use the regular 52-card pack, usually with the joker added, so that each player receives ten cards and there is a three-card widow as in three-hand.

After the bidding, the high bidder may select any other player to be his partner; if he bid for eight or more tricks, he may name any two partners. (Some play that the high bidder selects his partner by naming a card, as in Call-Ace Euchre, page 208.)

SIX-HAND FIVE HUNDRED

For six players there is available a 62-card pack that includes spot cards numbered 11 and 12 in each suit and 13 in each of two suits; the joker may be added, making a 63-card pack and permitting a deal of ten cards to each player and three to the widow. There are two sides of three partners each, the partners being seated alternately so that each has an opponent on his right and left.

— STOPS —

Stops is the generic name for a whole family of games, grouped together because of certain similarities rather than because of any known blood relationship. The common essential feature of such games is that the play stops, temporarily or finally, when a card specified to be played next is not available.

History. In the 17th century, European society was seized by a gambling fever that led to the invention of a myriad simple card games designed for the rapid redistribution of wealth. We know the names of many of these games; the rules of few. A much-exploited plan seems to have been a layout on which the bettors placed stakes, which were then collected by the persons who chanced to be dealt the corresponding cards. One of the few survivors is Matrimony.

The terms on which the stakes of the layout could be collected were in many cases made more complex, perhaps to heighten the suspense, and this may have been the origin of the "stops" principle, as exemplified in Pope Joan. Not a few of the old-time fashionable games were *potpourris* of various ideas, ending with stops play; examples are the German Pochen (or French Poque) and the Italian Stoppa.

In the course of time, the stops idea became of interest in itself, and was exploited apart from a layout and betting. The game Comet is called "the new game" in a 1768 book, and its invention is said to have been inspired by the return of Halley's comet in 1759. Only Matrimony and Pope Joan are mentioned in Bohn's Handbook of Games (1850). In the latter part of the century we find first mention of Newmarket, Snip Snap Snorem, Enflé. Fan Tan and Eights appear to have developed later.

MICHIGAN

In England this game is called Newmarket. Other variant names are Stops, Boodle, Saratoga, Chicago.

Number of players. 1. From three to about eight may play. A large number —five or more—makes a faster and more hilarious game than a small number.

The pack. 2. A regular pack of 52 cards.

Rank of cards. 3. The cards in each suit rank: A (high), K, Q, J, 10, 9, 8, 7, 6, 5, 4, 3, 2.

The layout. 4. In the center of the table is placed a layout of "boodle" or "money" cards, taken from another pack. These are one ace, king, queen and jack, of different suits, as: ♡A, ◇K, ♤Q, ♧J. Prior to the deal, the layout is "dressed" by all the players. Each player is provided with Poker chips, and he must distribute a prefixed number on the boodle cards. Since the deal is an advantage, the dealer must put out twice as many chips as the quota for the other players. The usual rule is that a player must put one chip on each card, the dealer, two chips. An alternative rule is that each player may distribute the quota of four or eight chips as he pleases.

The deal. 5. First dealer is determined by lot, as by dealing cards around until the first jack appears. Thereafter, the turn to deal rotates clockwise. In fairness, a session of Michigan should be terminated only at a time when all players have dealt an equal number of times.

6. The dealer distributes the whole pack, one card at a time, as far as it will go. (It is permissible for some hands to have one more card than other hands.) One more hand is dealt than the number of players; the extra hand or widow is dealt at the immediate left of the dealer. The cards are dealt in clockwise rotation, the first card to this hand.

The widow. 7. The extra hand belongs to the dealer. After looking at his own hand, he may, if he wishes, discard it face down and take up the widow instead. If he does not take the widow, he is bound to sell it to the highest bidder. Chips paid for the widow go to the dealer, and the buyer discards his own hand face down. If none takes or buys the widow, it is set aside, still face down.

The play. 8. Eldest hand (player at left of the dealer) makes the first lead. He may choose any suit, but must lead the lowest card he holds in that suit.

9. The played cards are not stacked together in tricks; each card as played is placed face up in front of the owner. The player must announce orally the rank of his card in playing it, and, if it is a lead, also the suit. This oral announcement is necessary to keep the game from bogging down, since the turn to play does not rotate but skips about in accordance with the chance of the deal.

10. After any lead or play, the holder of the next-higher card of the same suit must play it. [For example, if eldest hand leads and announces "five of clubs," the six of clubs must then be played if possible.]

11. The upward sequence of plays is stopped sooner or later, because it reaches the ace, or because the next card wanted is in the discarded hand or was previously played. The player of a card that proves to be a stop makes a new lead. (He should give reasonable time to ascertain that it is really a stop; the custom is to say "Stop!" and then wait a few seconds before leading.)

12. Each new lead must be in a different suit from the last series of plays, and the leader must always lead the lowest card he holds in the

suit he chooses. If unable to change suit, the player must pass, and the turn to lead rotates to the left until it reaches a player who can change suit. If none can change suit, play ends. (Some play that the last player may then lead his lowest remaining card of the same suit.)

13. On playing a card corresponding to any of the four boodle or money cards, a player at once takes all the chips on that card. Chips that are not won during a deal remain on the boodle cards (together with subsequent antes) until eventually won.

14. The first player to get rid of all his cards wins the deal, and play ends immediately.

Settlement. 15. The winner of a deal collects one chip from every other player for each card remaining in his hand. (An optional rule is that he collects two chips for each unplayed boodle card.)

Irregularities. 16. *Misdeal.* Exposure of a card in the deal does not require a redeal. An incorrect hand discovered before there has been any play must be corrected (a short hand drawing the excess from a hand with too many cards), but after that it stands.

17. *Error in play.* A player who violates a rule of play may not win the hand or collect by playing a boodle card, and must pay each other player one chip; if he goes out first, the others continue play. If the offender fails to play a card lower than the boodle card of the same suit, and that boodle card is not played during that deal, the offender must pay the holder of the card the number of chips on it.

18. *Condonement.* The error of leading the same suit as that previously stopped may be condoned only by agreement of all other players.

Pointers on Michigan play. One's original hand is best retained if it contains a boodle card or a better-than-average number of face cards and aces. The purpose in taking or buying the widow is not only to get rid of a poor hand but also to have advance knowledge of the stops created by the discarded hand. The amount that should be invested for this purpose depends on many factors, but generally should not exceed as many chips as there are players.

The natural choice in leading is the longest suit in the hand, and this is generally sound policy. But a suit containing a boodle card should usually be led at every opportunity.

Keep track of all the stops—the cards in the discarded hand (if you have taken the widow) and the leads. Having gained a stop with only a few cards left, try to hold the lead by playing sure-stop cards first, reserving doubtful cards to the last.

BOODLE

Follow all the rules of Michigan except:

The pack is dealt in equal hands to the players, leaving three or more cards for a widow.

PLAYERS	CARDS PER HAND	WIDOW
3	15	7
4	12	4
5	9	7
6	8	4
7	7	3
8	6	4

There is no exchange of one's original hand for the widow, which remains out of play to create stops. The dealer announces the number of chips that each player must put on the layout; the dealer is not required to place more, as he has no advantage. The player is free to distribute the chips as he will. (The variant in which equal amounts were required to be placed on each boodle card was called Saratoga, and this developed into Michigan.)

MATRIMONY

This is a betting game of pure chance. Any number up to twenty-six may play. In the center of the table is a layout with five divisions:

Matrimony (any king and queen)
Intrigue (any queen and jack)
Confederacy (any king and jack)
Pair (two cards of the same rank)
Best (highest diamond)

The dealer announces the number of chips he will bet; it may not be less than a minimum established by agreement before the game begins. He distributes them as he pleases on the layout. Every other player must then distribute a quota of chips as he pleases, one less than the number placed by the dealer. Then the dealer distributes a round of cards face down, one to each player, and a round face up.

Each player in turn to left of the dealer turns up his face-down card, and the first who shows the requisite combination collects the chips from matrimony, intrigue, confederacy, pair. When any such combination fails to be dealt, the chips on the corresponding part of the layout remain there, increased by whatever the players contribute subsequently.

According to the earliest sources, a player whose turned-up card was the ace of diamonds took all chips in the layout. The ace of diamonds as a face-down card had no value except as part of a pair. Later sources state that best is won by (a) the ace of diamonds, (b) any other ace, the first turned, if the ace of diamonds is not turned, (c) the highest diamond shown after all the cards are turned face up.

POPE JOAN

Follow all the rules of Michigan except:

Discard the eight of diamonds from the pack. The layout has eight compartments, as follows:

Pope (nine of diamonds)
Matrimony (king and queen of trumps)
Intrigue (queen and jack of trumps)
Ace (of trumps)
King (of trumps)
Queen (of trumps)
Jack (of trumps)
Game (see text)

Many different practices exist as to the cards in the layout, and the manner of placing bets on them. The usual rule is that only the dealer antes, *e.g.*, one chip to Pope, two to matrimony, three to intrigue, etc. Or, the dealer must ante a prefixed number of chips, which he may distribute as he pleases. But modern practice tends to the rule that all players (including dealer) must ante one chip on each compartment of the layout.

The deal is as in Michigan, except that the last card of the pack is turned for trump, and the widow is set aside as a dead hand to form stops. The stakes on compartments of the layout are won when the corresponding cards are played; matrimony and intrigue may be taken only by a player who plays both of the named cards. The chips on game go to the first player to get rid of his cards. A player left with the nine of diamonds (Pope), when another wins, is exempt from payment of chips for cards left in the hand.

SPINADO

Follow all the rules of Michigan except:

Discard the eight of diamonds from the pack. (Some players also discard all the deuces.) The king is the highest-ranking card in each suit, the ace lowest. Deal a widow, but this widow is always left face down to form stops.

The layout comprises only three parts:
Matrimony (king and queen of diamonds)
Intrigue (queen and jack of diamonds)
Game (see text)

A player collects from matrimony or intrigue only on playing both named cards. The chips on game go to the player who first gets rid of all his cards, plus payment for cards left in the other hands. The ace of diamonds is called spinado, and it may be played next by the owner after he has played regularly. When played, spinado creates a stop, even though the owner has the next in sequence with the previous card he played.

Additional rules sometimes encountered are: The winner of a deal does not ante for the next. On playing the king of diamonds, a player collects two chips from each other player; on playing any other king, he collects one chip. On playing the ace of diamonds, a player may then lead a card that wins a pool, even though it is not the lowest of the suit in his hand.

COMET

Number of players. 1. From two to five may play.

The pack. 2. From two regular packs discard all the aces. Put all the remaining black cards in one pack, all the red cards in another; then exchange the ♣8 and ◇9. These nines are the comets. Use the two packs alternately.

Rank of cards. 3. The cards rank K (high), Q, J, 10, 9, 8, 7, 6, 5, 4, 3, 2. Suits are ignored.

The deal. 4. The dealer distributes the cards in batches of two or three at a time, in clockwise rotation beginning with eldest hand (the player at his left). The whole pack is not dealt out; some cards at the end of the deal are set aside face down (to create stops). Follow this schedule:

NUMBER OF PLAYERS	EACH PLAYER RECEIVES	CARDS PER BATCH	DEAD CARDS
2	18	3	12
3	12	3	12
4	10	2	8
5	9	3	3

The play. 5. Eldest hand begins the play by leading any card he wishes. He continues to play additional cards in upward sequence so long as he can. When he stops, for lack of the next rank required, the turn passes to his left-hand neighbor. Each player in turn thus continues playing cards in upward sequence so long as he can.

6. All kings are stop cards. On playing a king, a player may immediately commence a new sequence, beginning with any rank he pleases.

7. If unable to play at all in his turn, for lack of the required rank, a player must pass, and the turn goes to the left. If all the players pass in succession, the one who played last begins a new sequence with a card of any rank.

8. All cards as played are put in one pile, face up, in the center of the table. This pile should be kept squared up so that only the top card is readable.

9. To expedite the play, the rank of each card should be announced orally as it is played, and when a player must end his turn he should state "without queen" (or whatever rank is next required).

10. A player may, if he wishes, play any three or four nines simultaneously, or four cards of any other rank simultaneously (when this rank is called for). These are the only exceptions to the general rule that a player may play only one card of a rank at a time.

11. The off-color nine (as ♣9 in the red pack) is the comet. It is a wild card, and may be played by the holder at any time in his turn. When played, the comet creates a stop, and the player may begin a new sequence. It is not compulsory to play the comet when able; the holder may pass when he lacks a card of the next rank required.

Scoring. 12. On playing the comet, the holder immediately collects 2 chips from each other player. (*Optional rule:* The value of the comet is increased by 2 for each successive deal in which it is found among the dead cards. After a payoff for the comet at any increased value, it reverts to the base value 2 for the next deal.)

13. The player who first gets rid of all his cards wins the deal. Each loser pays the winner chips in amount of the numerical value of the cards left in his hand: face cards count 10 each, other cards their index value; the comet counts its current value, but for being caught with the comet in his hand, the loser has to pay double for all cards in his hand.

14. If the winner plays the comet as his last card, he collects quadruple if it was played as a natural nine, or double if it was played for any other rank. The quadruple or double applies both to the bonus for playing the comet and the collection for winning.

15. A player makes *opera* when he goes out on his first turn. (An optional rule is to allow double collection for opera. Early rules allowed only eldest hand to collect for opera, but this windfall should be extended to all players, except that in a two-hand game there should be no payments at all if both players can make opera.)

Irregularities. 16. *Illegal pass.* If a player passes when able to play a card other than the comet, he may not thereafter play any card of the rank refused.

17. *Play out of turn.* No penalty, but cards played out of turn must be retracted and the turn reverts to the rightful player. But if after a play out of turn and call of "without" the player at the left has duly played a card, the play stands as regular.

18. *Wrong rank.* If a player plays a card of wrong rank, he must on demand retract his plays to the point of error and replay correctly. But if he has called "without" and the next player has played any card, the plays stand as regular.

Pointers on Comet play. The ideal hand would be one having exactly one card or four cards of each rank. Such a hand makes opera, whatever may be the rank required at its first turn to play.

With any choice in early play, strive to get rid of unwanted duplicates, reducing the hand to the ideal pattern.

Having the comet, save it even at considerable risk for your last turn, but not for your last card unless the odds are heavily in your favor. The great value of the comet is to provide a stop; plan to use it as such in a turn when you hope to get rid of all your remaining cards.

COMMIT

Follow all the rules of Comet, except:

From three to seven may play. Use one regular pack of 52 cards, discarding the $\diamond$8. Deal the pack as far as it will go evenly, setting aside the extra cards left over as a dead hand. (With three players, put six cards in the dead hand.) Before the deal, a pool is formed by equal antes from all players, and the winner takes the pool. The ◇9 is the comet; it may be played only when the holder would otherwise have to say "without," and it calls for continuation either with the ◇10 or with any card of the next-higher rank (above that rank for which the comet was substituted). The comet has the fixed value of 2 chips, and each king counts 1 chip. When the comet or any king is played, the player at once collects its value from every other player. When play ends, losers pay the winner only for kings or comet left in their hands, paying 2 chips or 1, respectively.

FAN TAN

It has been recommended that this game be called Sevens or Parliament (as actually in some localities), but the name Fan Tan is almost universally known. The name is doubly ambiguous: There is a gambling game Fan Tan, widely played in China with soy beans. (An indeterminate number of beans is taken from a pot; the players bet on whether the remainder, after division of the beans by 4, will be 0, 1, 2, or 3; and the beans are then counted.) An ancestor of Sevens was called Fan Tan, and was itself probably an offspring of Play or Pay. The game of Fan Tan described here is sometimes called Card Dominoes.

Number of players. 1. From three to eight may play.

The pack. 2. A regular pack of 52 cards.

Rank of cards. 3. The cards in each suit rank: K (high), Q, J, 10, 9, 8, 7, 6, 5, 4, 3, 2, A.

The deal. 4. The cards are distributed one at a time in rotation clockwise, beginning with eldest hand (player at left of the dealer). The whole pack is dealt; it does not matter if some players receive one more card than others. (*Optional rule:* Each hand with the fewer number of cards antes 2 chips.)

The pool. 5. Prior to the deal, each player antes 1 chip, and this pool, increased by payments during the play, goes to the winner.

The play. 6. All sevens are set cards, and are always playable. The sevens as played are placed in a row in the center of the table; the eights must be played in a row above and the sixes in a row below. Each eight may be built up in suit until the pile reaches the king; sixes are built down in suit to aces.

7. Eldest hand has first turn to play. Until a seven is played, no other card is playable. Once a seven is set, the cards in suit and sequence both ways are playable.

8. Each hand in turn must play one card if able. If unable, he must say "pass" and pay 1 chip to the pool.

9. The player first to get rid of all his cards wins the deal and the pool.

Irregularities. 10. *Illegal pass.* If a player passes when able to play, he must pay 3 chips to the pool (additional to the chip for passing); if he passed when able to play a seven, he must in addition pay 5 chips each to the holders of the six and eight of the same suit.

PLAY OR PAY

Follow all the rules of Fan Tan except:

There are no set cards. Eldest hand may lead any card. The only card playable at any time is the next-higher in sequence and suit with the one previously played. Each suit must thus be built up in one pile to thirteen cards, the rank being circular (ace ranks above the king as well as below the two). The player who plays the thirteenth card of a suit gains a stop, and may lead any card of another suit.

FIVE OR NINE, also called DOMINO WHIST

Follow all the rules of Fan Tan except:

A set card may be either five or nine. Eldest hand, or the first after him who is not obliged to pass, may begin with either a five or a nine, and the first card played fixes the set rank for that deal. In any case, the set cards must be built up and down in suit to the limits of king and ace respectively.

EIGHTS

Other names by which this game is known are Crazy Eights, Crazy Jacks, etc. (according to the rank chosen to be wild), and Swedish

Rummy. It offers more scope for skill than any other Stops game, since there is much wider choice in the play.

Number of players. 1. Two, three or four may play. (Five or more may play with a double pack.) Four-hand may be played in two partnerships, or each for himself. But the best game is two-hand.

The pack. 2. A regular pack of 52 cards.

The deal. 3. Each player receives: seven cards, with two players; five cards, with three or more players. The rest of the pack is placed face down to form the stock. The top card of the stock is turned face up and placed beside it to form the starter.

The play. 4. Eldest hand (player at left of the dealer) has first turn. He must place on the starter a card that matches it either in suit or in rank. Each in turn must thus play one card on the starter pile, matching the last-played.

5. If unable to play in turn, a player must draw cards one by one from the top of the stock until he is able and willing to play or until he exhausts the stock. After the stock is exhausted, a hand must play in turn if it can; when it cannot, the turn passes to the left.

6. All eights are wild. An eight may be played regardless of the last previous card, and regardless of whether the hand is able to play a natural card at that time. In playing an eight, the owner must name a suit, and the next card played must be of that suit (or another eight). No limitation as to rank may be made in playing an eight.

7. The player first to get rid of all his cards wins the deal. In four-hand partnership, both players of a side must get rid of their hands in order to win. If the stock is exhausted and no hand can play, the game ends as a block.

Scoring. 8. The winner of a deal collects for all cards remaining in the other hands: 50 for each eight, 10 for each face card, 1 for each ace, the index value for each other card. If the deal ends in a block, the player or side with lowest count collects the difference of counts.

9. Each deal may be treated as a separate game. In two-hand play, it is usual to keep score on paper; the first to reach a total of 100 or more wins a game. He collects the difference of final totals, plus a game bonus of 100.

Irregularities. 10. *Misdeal.* Any player may require a new deal, before he has played or drawn from the stock, if a card is exposed in dealing; or if a hand has the wrong number of cards; or if the pack is incorrect or imperfect; or if the pack was not properly shuffled, or was not offered for a cut.

11. *Incorrect hand.* If a player has the wrong number of cards and a redeal is not required as provided in paragraph 10: he must draw from the stock without playing, to make the number of his cards correct, if he had too few cards; he must show a card that he could legally play, or

draw from the stock until he can show a card, then pass in turn, if he had too many cards.

12. *Failure to play when required to do so.* If a player does not play when able to do so, after the stock is exhausted, he must do so on demand of any other player; and he cannot win. Hands must be shown, when play is blocked, so that each player may satisfy himself that no opponent could have played.

Pointers on Eights play. If you are dealt an eight, try to save it for your last or next to last play. As a rule, dig into the stock rather than play it at any earlier stage.

To have more cards in your hand than your opponent is not necessarily a disadvantage, and it may grow to be a decisive advantage. The big killings come when a player is forced to take the rest of a sizeable stock in search of a card that isn't there.

If you succeed in your aim of making your opponent take the rest of a sizeable stock, you risk that he may corner a suit and hoist you by your own petard. However unequally the stock is divided, and if the disturbing element of the eights be eliminated, the player with the more cards can play them in an order that at worst limits his loss to a few points. In practice, an expert against a tyro will win nine deals out of ten by the simple process of taking the entire stock at his first turn!

SNIP, SNAP, SNOREM

Snip, Snap, Snorem is better-known in the English books as Earl of Coventry. It is described as a juvenile game, in which the leader to a series of plays is supposed to improvise a line in iambic tetrameter, and each following player is supposed to utter a line that rhymes and scans.

Number of players. 1. Four to eight may play.

The pack. 2. A regular pack of 52 cards.

The deal. 3. The pack is dealt out one card at a time, so far as it will go. It does not matter if some players receive one more card than others.

The pool. 4. All players are supplied with equal numbers of chips. Prior to the deal, each player antes 1 chip to form a pool, which, increased by payments during the play, goes to the winner. (*Optional rule:* Players having one less card than others ante 2 chips.)

The play. 5. Eldest hand (player at left of the dealer) leads any card. Following any lead, each player in succession is called upon to play another card of the same rank, if able, until all four of the rank are played. If unable to play, a player passes.

6. Whenever two consecutive hands play, the first of the two is snipped if he was the leader, or snapped if he played the second card of the rank, or snored if he played the third card of the rank. For being snipped, a

player pays 1 chip to the pool; for being snapped, 2 chips; for being snored, 3 chips. Any who plays after a pass by his right-hand opponent escapes payment.

7. If unable to play in turn, a player passes. (There is no forfeit, since the player is penalized by loss of the opportunity to get rid of a card.)

8. On playing the fourth card of a rank, a player makes a new lead, of any rank he pleases.

9. The player who first gets rid of all his cards wins the deal. Each loser pays 1 chip to the pool for each card remaining in his hand, and the winner takes the pool.

JIG

Follow all the rules of Snip, Snap, Snorem, except:

Each lead or play calls next for the next-higher card of the same suit. There is a stop whenever four cards in sequence have been played, or the next card required is dead. After a stop, the last hand to play starts a new sequence, playing any card. The sequence of rank is circular, the ace being in sequence with the king below and two above.

ENFLE

This game is also called Rolling Stone; in Germany, Schwellen.

Number of players. 1. From four to six may play, each for himself.

The pack. 2. From a regular pack of 52 cards discard low ranks to reduce the pack to a total of eight times the number of players. With four players, discard all sixes and lower cards; with five, all fours and lower cards; with six players, the deuces.

Rank of cards. 3. The cards in each suit (so far as they go) rank: A (high), K, Q, J, 10, 9, 8, 7, 6, 5, 4, 3.

The deal. 4. The whole pack is distributed in equal hands of eight cards.

The play. 5. Eldest hand (player at the left of the dealer) may lead any card. A lead calls upon each other hand to follow suit if able.

6. If all hands follow suit to the lead, it is won by the highest card. The winner leads to the next trick; he may lead any card in his hand. Complete tricks are discarded face down in a common pile.

7. The first hand in succession after the lead that fails to follow suit must pick up the cards already played to the trick, add them to his hand, and make a new lead. No other course is possible to a hand that is void of the suit led. But a hand may refuse to follow, even though able, and pick up the cards, thereupon leading any suit including the one refused.

8. The player first to get rid of all his cards wins the deal.

Scoring. 9. The usual method is to distribute equal stacks of chips to all players before the first deal. Prior to each deal, every player antes one chip to a pool, which is taken by the winner.

⇀ ALL FOURS ↼

In the several All Fours games, special scoring value is attached to four cards of the trump suit—the ace, jack, ten, and deuce. Some variants give points for other cards also, but the "all fours" feature persists in all members of this closely-related family.

History. All Fours apparently originated in Kent, and was "much played" there at least as early at the 17th Century. Developing in bourgeois circles at a time when the fashionable world was absorbed in fast gambling games, All Fours remained an English game; even today its descendants are scarcely known in continental Europe. It spread to America, probably taken there by very early waves of immigration, and was one of the principal card games of colonial times. By the beginning of the 19th century, it was the foremost American card game, and so remained for nearly a hundred years. (Though Poker dates from about 1830, not until the end of the century did it reach its present ascendancy.)

The original All Fours was known in America under a variety of names, as Seven-Up, Old Sledge, High-Low-Jack. A two-hand variant was named, after its place of origin, California Jack. All Fours presently gave way to a more elaborate offspring, Pitch, which probably developed in the New England states. This member of the family remains the best-known today.

Cinch, the best of the All Fours games as regards skill, is believed to have originated in Denver about 1885. It was espoused by many leading Pitch players, aroused considerable enthusiasm, and led to the formation of a Cinch League. For about ten years Cinch flourished as a major game, but now is little known.

SEVEN-UP

Number of players. 1. Two or three may play, each for himself, or four in two partnerships.

The pack. 2. A regular pack of 52 cards.

Rank of cards. 3. The cards in each suit rank: A (high), K, Q, J, 10, 9, 8, 7, 6, 5, 4, 3, 2.

The deal. 4. The players draw and high deals first; thereafter the deal rotates from player to player clockwise. The dealer shuffles the pack and must offer it to the opponent at his right for a cut; if that player refuses to cut, the cards are dealt as shuffled. Each player receives six cards, dealt in batches of three at a time, face down, beginning with eldest hand (player at left of the dealer). The next card of the pack is turned face up for trump. When there are more than two players, only the dealer and eldest hand may look at their hands until the turn-up is accepted or rejected.

Deciding the trump. 5. Eldest hand must first *stand* or *beg*. To stand means that he accepts the turn-up for trump, whereupon all players pick up their hands and the play begins. To beg means that eldest hand passes the decision to the dealer.

6. After a beg, dealer may either insist on the suit of the turn-up or agree to a different trump suit. To insist on the original turn-up he says "Take it;" eldest hand thereupon scores 1 point for gift, and play begins. To agree on a different trump, the dealer *refuses gift*. It is a rule that dealer must refuse gift if eldest hand lacks only 1 point for game.

7. When gift is refused, the dealer gives a batch of three more cards to each player. This is called *running the cards*. The original turn-up being discarded, another is faced from the stock; if it chances to be of the same suit as the first, it must be discarded, and the dealer must give out three more cards; and so on until a new suit is turned up. If the pack is exhausted without the turn of a new suit, the deal is abandoned and the same player deals again. If, after the cards are run, the turn-up proves to be of a new suit, that suit becomes trump, and the play begins.

The play. 8. If any additional cards have been dealt, each player discards enough from his hand to reduce it to six cards. All discards are set aside face down.

9. Eldest hand makes the opening lead. He may lead any card. After any lead, a hand unable to follow suit may play any card, plain or trump. If able to follow suit, the hand must either do so or (to a plain-suit lead) play a trump. The privilege of trumping thus supersedes the duty to follow suit. A trick is won by the highest trump, or, if it contains no trump, by the highest card of the suit led. The winner of a trick leads to the next.

Object of play. 10. Each player strives to win what he can of the 4 points available through play.

Scoring. 11. If the original turn-up is a jack, dealer scores 1 point at once. If the cards are run, and the jack of any suit is turned up for trump, dealer scores 1. (No score for turning up the jack of the rejected trump suit.)

12. For each of the following, won in play, the player or side scores 1 point:

High is the highest trump in play. It is scored by the owner.

Low is the lowest trump in play. It is scored by the player to whom it was dealt.

Jack is the jack of trumps. It is scored by the player who wins it in a trick.

Game is the total point-value of the cards won in play. The high cards count as follows (lower cards have no value):

Each ace	4
Each king	3
Each queen	2
Each jack	1
Each ten	10

13. The 1 point for game, in two-hand or four-hand play, goes to the side having won a majority of the points in the tricks. In a three-hand game, the player having a plurality of the points wins game; if the dealer ties for high count with another player, the latter wins game; if the two other than the dealer tie for high, game is not scored.

14. High and low are always scored, and if only one trump was in play, it scores 2 points as both high and low. Jack is not scored if the jack of trumps did not chance to be dealt.

15. The player or side first to reach a total of 7 points wins a game. The dealer may win the game point by turn of a jack. If, after the play, two players could reach or pass a total of 7, the points are counted in order: high, low, jack, game, and the first to reach 7 by this count wins the game.

Irregularities. 16. *Misdeal.* There must be a redeal by the same dealer if a card is exposed in the original deal; or if the pack was not shuffled or was not offered for a cut. A redeal may be demanded by a player who has not looked at his hand, before eldest hand has stood or begged. Exposure of a card when the cards are run cannot cause a redeal; but if a player's card is then exposed through no fault of his own, he may have it replaced from the top of the pack after all other players have received their cards.

17. *Revoke.* A revoke (failure to follow suit or trump, when able to follow suit) may be corrected before the lead to the next trick, but each player in turn after the revoker may withdraw his card and substitute another. If not corrected in time, the revoke trick stands, and from the offender's score are deducted 2 points if the jack was in play; 1 point if the jack was not in play. (In two-hand play, the non-offender may decide either to deduct such points from the offender's score or to add them to his own.)

18. *Exposed card.* In partnership play only, a player's card exposed except by a legal play (including a card withdrawn to correct a revoke) must be left face up on the table and must be played on demand of either opponent, provided such play is legal.

CALIFORNIA JACK

This game is also known as California Loo. A variant in which the stock is kept face down (eliminating the chief opportunity for skill) is called Shasta Sam. The All Fours rules apply as regards the preliminaries and irregularities.

Number of players. 1. Two.

The pack. 2. A regular pack of 52 cards.

Rank of cards. 3. The cards in each suit rank: A (high), K, Q, J, 10, 9, 8, 7, 6, 5, 4, 3, 2.

The deal. 4. Each player receives six cards, dealt one at a time. The rest of the pack is placed face up on the table to form the stock.

5. (In early times, the top card of the stock fixed the trump suit; or, when the players cut for deal, the higher card cut fixed the trump.) One extra card is dealt to fix the trump, then this card is buried approximately in the middle of the stock.

The play. 6. The opponent of the dealer makes the opening lead. He may lead any card. After any lead, the other hand must follow suit if able; if unable, he may play any card. (The All Fours privilege of trumping a plain lead, even when able to follow suit, has been eliminated in modern play.) A trick is won by the higher trump, or, if it contains no trump, by the higher card of the suit led. The winner of a trick leads to the next.

7. The winner of a trick, before leading, takes the top card of the stock, and his opponent takes the next below it. The stock should at all times be kept squared up so that only one card at a time is readable.

8. After the stock is exhausted, the six cards remaining in each hand are played out in tricks and play ends.

Scoring. 9. Each player is credited with what he wins in tricks, 1 point for each of the following:

> *High,* the ace of trumps.
> *Low,* the deuce of trumps.
> *Jack,* the jack of trumps.
> *Game,* 41 or more points for high cards, counting
> each ace 4, king 3, queen 2, jack 1, and ten 10.

10. The player first to reach a total of 7 points wins a game. The points are counted in the given order, and the first to reach 7 wins in a case where both could otherwise reach that total. Furthermore, when a player wins his seventh point in play, he may immediately claim the game, and if his claim is correct, the deal is not played out. If the claim proves to be incorrect (as it might be a miscount of game points), the opponent wins the game forthwith.

ALL FIVES

Follow the rules of California Jack except as to scoring. The points to be won in tricks are:

Ace of trumps	4
King of trumps	3
Queen of trumps	2
Jack of trumps	1
Ten of trumps	10
Five of trumps	5
Game	1

The point for game is settled as in California Jack, the high trumps counting toward it although they also score in themselves. The points are scored at once, as the cards are won, on a Cribbage board. The player first to reach a total of 61 wins a game.

AUCTION PITCH

This game, an elaboration of the earlier Pitch, is today the best-known member of the All Fours family. It is also known as Set-back. The All Fours rules apply as regards preliminaries and irregularities.

Number of players. 1. From two to seven may play. The best game is four, each playing for himself.

The pack. 2. A regular pack of 52 cards.

Rank of cards. 3. The cards in each suit rank: A (high), K, Q, J, 10, 9, 8, 7, 6, 5, 4, 3, 2.

The deal. 4. Each player receives six cards, dealt in batches of three at a time.

Bidding. 5. Eldest hand (player at left of dealer) declares first. There is only one round of bidding. Each player in turn must pass or make a bid higher than any previous bid. The only possible bids are one, two, three, and four. No trump suit is named in making a bid. A player may indicate that he bids four by making an opening lead.

The play. 6. The high bidder indicates the trump suit by making an opening lead of that suit. Even if he intended another suit for trump, the suit of his first lead (called the pitch) becomes trump.

7. If unable to follow suit to a lead, a hand may play any card. If able to follow suit, the player must do so or (to a plain-suit lead) play a trump. The privilege of trumping thus supersedes the duty to follow suit. A trick is won by the highest trump, or, if it contains no trump, by the highest card of the suit led. The winner of a trick leads to the next, and may lead any card.

Scoring. 8. For winning any of the following in tricks (regardless of to whom the cards were dealt), a player scores 1 point:

High, the highest trump in play.

Low, the lowest trump in play.

Jack, the jack of trumps.

Game, a plurality of points for high cards: ace 4, king 3, queen 2, jack 1, ten 10.

9. If the jack was not dealt out, there is no score for it. Game is not scored if two or more players tie for high count.

10. If the pitcher (high bidder) wins at least as many points as he bid, he scores all the points he takes; if he wins less than his bid, the amount of his bid is subtracted from his total score. A player may thus be "set back" or "in the hole." In any case, opponents of the pitcher score individually whatever points they take in tricks.

11. The player who first reaches a total of 7 points wins a game. (In some circles, 10 points are required for game.) If two or more players could reach 7 in the same deal, pitcher scores ahead of opponents; among opponents, the points are counted in order: high, low, jack, game. The first to reach 7 by this count wins the game. A common method of scoring is to provide each player with seven chips; each time he wins a point he puts one chip in a common pool. The number of chips left in front of a player shows how many points he needs for game. Chips so used for scoring should be kept separate from chips used for settlement, as in paragraph 12.

12. Each game is settled immediately in chips. The usual method is: the winner collects from each loser one chip, plus one chip for each time the loser was set back, plus one chip if the loser ended the game in the hole.

Irregularities. 13. *Misdeal.* Any irregularity in dealing that is the fault of the dealer is a misdeal, and loses him the deal. (The deal is an advantage.) Exposing an ace, jack, or deuce (or joker, if used) in dealing is a misdeal, but the dealer may correct his error (by giving another card instead, and discarding the exposed card) if he exposes any one other card.

14. *Improper bid.* An insufficient bid ranks as a pass; a bid out of turn is void and the offender must pass in turn.

15. *Revoke.* A revoke (failure to follow suit or trump, when able to follow suit) is established as soon as made, and play continues. The offender cannot score, and is set back by the amount of the bid (whether he is pitcher or opponent), and each other player, including the pitcher, scores what he makes.

16. *Pitch out of turn.* If a player pitches during the auction and when it is not his turn, a player who has missed his turn to bid may bid four; otherwise the out-of-turn pitch stands as a bid of four.

17. When the wrong player pitches, the correct pitcher may let the play stand and immediately name the trump, and must then lead a trump at his first opportunity; or the correct pitcher may require the lead to be withdrawn and may require the offender, at his first proper turn to play, to trump or not to trump or to follow suit with his highest or lowest card.

18. *Exposed card.* Any card exposed during the play, except as a play in turn to a trick, must be left face up on the table and played at the first

legal opportunity. A card exposed (but not led) during the auction may be picked up without penalty.

PITCH VARIATIONS

Smudge. This name is applied to different ways of rewarding a player for taking all four points in a deal.

(a) If the pitcher bid 4 and made it, he wins the game forthwith, unless he was in the hole, in which case his score becomes plus 4.

(b) Any player who takes all 4 points wins the game forthwith.

(c) Any player taking all 4 points scores 8, so that he wins the game if his score was no worse than—1.

Holding. Dealer has the right to "hold"—become the pitcher by bidding the same as the highest previous bid. Formerly prevalent, this rule is now obsolete.

Bunch. In a two-hand game where holding is allowed (see above), the dealer may have an additional privilege: he may propose bunch. His opponent must then either allow the dealer to win the bid at 2 or "bunch" the cards for a new deal.

Joker Pitch. The joker is added to the pack. It is always a trump, ranking below the deuce but never counting as low, which can only be a natural card. The joker makes a fifth point in play, counting 1 to the player who wins it in a trick. In precedence, the joker is scored after the jack, before game. In Joker Pitch, it is usual to require 10 points to win a game.

Pitch. American players gradually abandoned the All Fours features of turning a card for trump, begging, and running the cards. The rule became to let eldest hand name the trump suit. This variant was called Blind All Fours, or Pitch, from the requirement that eldest hand must pitch (first lead) a trump.

The idea of letting other players compete for right to name the trump was incorporated in a later variant called Commercial Pitch, or Sell Out. Here, the first bid was made by the player at left of eldest hand. The latter, in his turn, could either hold the right to pitch at a bid equal to the highest before him, or sell out by letting the high bidder pitch. If eldest hand pitched, the high bidder immediately scored the amount of his bid; if eldest hand sold out, he himself scored this amount. Obviously, eldest hand had a great advantage, since he could score merely by selling out; the only occasion to hold was virtual certainty of winning more than the bid in play. The whole scheme necessitated additional rules, e. g., no player was allowed to bid enough to give eldest hand the game, should he sell out—which meant that none could bid when eldest hand needed only one point. This unsatisfactory variant, revamped, became Auction Pitch.

Pedro. The impulse to enliven All Fours play by additional cards of value found expression in All Fives (page 232) and also in Pedro (in which the trump five counts 5 points toward game) and its variants. The term pedro has come to mean the five of trumps, just as pam, a term in Loo, has come to mean the jack of clubs.

Pedro Sancho. Follow the rules of Auction Pitch, except: The dealer has the right to pitch at a bid equal to the highest before him. The counting cards are:

High, highest trump in play	1
Low, lowest trump in play	1
Jack, jack of trumps	1
Game, the ten of trumps	1
Pedro, the five of trumps	5
Sancho, the nine of trumps	9

As there are (maximum) 18 points to be won in each deal, game is usually fixed at 100. The cards are scored in the order shown, for "counting out."

Dom Pedro, or Snoozer. Follow the rules of Pedro Sancho, with the addition of two more counting cards: the three, counting 3; and the joker (called snoozer), counting 15. Snoozer is always a trump, ranking below the deuce but never counting as low. In precedence, the trump three scores between game and pedro, while snoozer counts last.

CINCH

An elaboration of Pedro called Double Pedro or High Five was given the official name Cinch by players and writers who espoused it enthusiastically during the period after 1885. It undoubtedly offers more scope for skill than any other game of the All Fours family, but is now little played.

Number of players. 1. Four, in two partnerships. Though it can be played by any number from two to seven, each for himself, the partnership game is far superior.

The pack. 2. A regular pack of 52 cards.

Rank of cards. 3. The cards in each suit rank: A (high), K, Q, J, 10, 9, 8, 7, 6, 5, 4, 3, 2. The five of trumps is called *right pedro.* The five of the other suit of same color as the trump is *left pedro;* it also is a trump, and it ranks below right pedro, above the trump four.

The deal. 4. A pack is spread and players draw cards (as in Bridge) for partnerships, seats and first deal. Each player may shuffle, the dealer last. The player at dealer's right must cut, leaving at least four cards in each packet. Each hand receives nine cards, dealt in batches of three at a time. The turn to deal passes from player to player in clockwise rotation.

Object of play. 5. Each side strives to score by winning certain trump cards in tricks:

Ace (high)	1
Jack (jack)	1
Ten (game)	1
Five (right pedro)	5
Five (left pedro)	5
Two (low)	1
	——
	14

The bidding. 6. Eldest hand (player at dealer's left) declares first. There is only one round of bidding. Each player in turn must pass or make a bid higher than any preceding bid. The possible bids are from one to fourteen. No suit is named in bidding.

7. The highest bidder names the trump suit, without any consultation with his partner.

8. Should the first three players pass, the dealer must name a trump suit, but he does not thereby assume a contract; the deal is played out and each side scores whatever it takes.

The discard. 9. After the trump suit is named, each player discards from his hand all the cards that are not trumps. (It is permissible but foolish to retain a plain card; it is illegal to discard a trump.) The discards are set aside face down.

10. The dealer distributes cards from the top of the pack to restore each other hand in turn, beginning with eldest, to six cards. To restore his own hand, dealer *robs the pack*. That is, he fans the pack so that all cards are visible only to himself, and picks out all the remaining trumps. If there are not enough trumps to give him six trumps, he fills out his hand with whatever plain cards he chooses. If there are more than enough trumps remaining, he must place the extra trumps face up on the table.

11. Every player including dealer must in his turn state distinctly how many cards he needs to draw. Until the opening lead has been made, any player may ask another how many cards he drew, and the dealer must answer this question at any time it is asked if he failed to announce the number voluntarily.

The play. 12. The player who named the trump suit makes the opening lead. He may lead any card. After any lead, a player unable to follow suit may play any card; if able to follow suit, he must either do so or trump. The privilege of trumping thus supersedes the duty to follow suit. A trick is won by the highest trump, or, if it contains no trump, by the highest card of the suit led. The winner of a trick leads to the next.

Scoring. 13. At the end of the play, each side counts what points it has won in tricks. If the bidder's side has won at least the amount of the bid, the side having the higher total scores the difference. [For example:

bidders win 9, opponents 5, bidders score 4. Or, bidders win 6, opponents 8, opponents score 2.] If the bidding side failed to make its bid, the opponents score what they took in tricks plus the amount of the bid. [For example: Bidders win 5, having bid 8; opponents score 17, the total of 9 (which they won) plus 8 (the bid).]

14. If the dealer named the trump after three passes, each side scores whatever it wins in tricks.

15. The side that first reaches a total of 51 points wins a game. (Often the score is kept on a Cribbage board, in which case game is usually fixed at 61 points.)

Irregularities. 16. *Redeal.* There must be a redeal by the same dealer if demanded by his opponents (who may consult) when any card is exposed before the deal is completed; or if the pack is imperfect, or incorrect, or was not properly shuffled or cut; or if the wrong person is dealing; or if it is discovered at any time that two players were dealt incorrect hands. The dealer may decide to redeal if any one of his opponents causes a card to be exposed during the deal. His opponents may not call a redeal if either of them has intentionally looked at a card dealt to him.

17. *Bid out of turn.* A bid out of turn is void, but both members of the offending side must pass thereafter.

18. *Incorrect hand.* An incorrect hand discovered before a bid has been made requires a new deal by the next dealer in turn, and the current deal is void. Thereafter: A hand with too few cards plays on without penalty, and may draw from the discard to make his hand correct; a hand with too many cards may be corrected, before the discard, by the dealer's drawing the excess, face down, and putting it on the bottom of the pack; if a hand has too many cards after play begins, the holder's side may not score.

19. *Exposed card.* A card illegally exposed must remain face up on the table and must be played (if it legally can be) on demand of either opponent.

20. *Lead out of turn.* A card led out of turn is treated as an exposed card; and, if it was the offender's partner's turn to lead, either opponent may require the partner to lead a plain suit (if he has one).

21. *Play out of turn.* If a player plays before his partner, the intervening opponent not having played, the trick belongs to the non-offending side; but the player of the winning card leads to the next trick.

22. *Revoke.* A revoke may be corrected at any time before the trick is turned, unless a member of the offending side has played to the next trick; when a revoke is corrected, a member of the non-offending side may withdraw a card played after the revoke card. The penalty for a revoke discovered too late for correction is that the offending side may not score in that deal; but their opponents score only what they make, plus the contract if the bidder's side revoked.

23. *Illegal information.* If a player gives his partner illegal advice or information as to his hand, his intentions or desires, either opponent on any one subsequent trick may require the offender's partner to play his highest, or to play his lowest, card of the suit led; but a player may ask his partner if any play constitutes a revoke.

Pointers on Cinch play. The most you can win by making the trump is 14 points. The least that you can lose if you are defeated is 15. Hence you can never gain by deliberate overbidding.

The first consideration in bidding is whether you can reasonably expect to win one or both pedros. You need either a pedro guarded by some additional trumps, or trump length and strength that will probably catch a pedro dealt to the opponents. For example, Q-9-5-4 is worth a bid of five, for the likelihood that you can save your pedro; A-K-Q is worth a bid of at least six, for the likelihood that you can catch a pedro.

Trump length and strength is a much better basis for bidding than possession of the lower-ranking "counters." For example: A-K-J-8-7 is worth a bid of eleven, and A-K-Q-6 is worth twelve. The pedros, and also the deuce, are better out of your hand than in, when you have four or five trumps higher than the five.

Low bids are best used in a conventional system of bidding, to convey information to partner that you have certain "counters." For example: as first bidder, bid five when you have any pedro; six when you have an ace with two or more cards of the suit; seven when you have an ace-king.

There are fourteen trumps in play (very rarely must the dealer discard a trump). All plain cards are entirely negligible as regards rank. Therefore, always begin the play by fixing firmly in mind the number of cards each hand drew.

The game takes its name from the tactic of cinching a trick—that is, playing on it a trump higher than five so as to prevent the opponents from winning it with a pedro. As a rule-of-thumb, the third player to a trick (partner of the leader) is expected so to cinch a trick if he can.

RAZZLE DAZZLE

This name is usually given to Cinch when it is played by more than four players. It is also called Auction Cinch. With five or six, follow all the rules of Cinch, except:

Deal only six cards to each hand. The bidding is as usual, except that each player bids for himself. The high bidder names the trump, and the discard and draw follows as in Cinch. The bidder then names any trump card not in his hand; the holder of this card becomes his partner, and the two play against all the rest. Partners keep their seats, so that through the chance of the deal they may play consecutively. If the bidding partnership make their contract, each partner scores separately the full amount due. Opponents of this pair score individually whatever they win in tricks, plus the amount of the bid if the contract is not made.

⤚ HEARTS ⤙

Hearts is so-called because the object of play is to avoid winning hearts in tricks. In most variants, there are other counting cards also, and additional objectives. Among non-partnership games, Hearts is most like Whist in the opportunity and need for skillful play.

History. All the characteristics of modern Hearts are found in an 18th century game called Reverse. Its reported Spanish origin is borne out by the terms *quinola* and *espagnolette*; chief object was to avoid taking great quinola, the jack of hearts, and little quinola, the queen of hearts. There were other counting cards at various times, but from the outset large bonuses were given for (a) taking no tricks, or (b) taking all the tricks. The name of the game came from the latter feature, called the *reverse* or *reversis* because it was the reverve of the usual object of play.

Some time between 1850 and the end of the century, Reverse gave way to the very simple basic Hearts—simple as to rules, but difficult as Whist to play well. This austere game has been greatly popularized during the past fifty years by the addition of certain features that add to the variety and also tend to make the game easier to play *at*.

Number of players. 1. From three to six may play, each for himself. The best game is four-hand. Two may play Draw Hearts, and six or more are better advised to play the variant of Black Lady or Cancellation Hearts.

The pack. 2. A regular pack of 52 cards. If necessary to make the number of cards a multiple of the number of players, discard low cards in this order of preference: ♣2, ♢2, ♣3, ♠2.

Rank of cards. 3. The cards in each suit rank: A (high), K, Q, J, 10, 9, 8, 7, 6, 5, 4, 3, 2. Hearts are colloquially called "trumps," but there is never a suit having the trump privilege of winning other suits.

The deal. 4. The cards are distributed one at a time in clockwise rotation, beginning with eldest hand (player at left of the dealer), until the whole pack is dealt. All players should receive equal hands.

The play. 5. Eldest hand leads first. He may lead any card. After any lead, each other hand must follow suit if able; if unable, a hand may play any card. A trick is won by the highest card of the suit led. The winner of a trick leads to the next.

Object of play. 6. In general, the object is to avoid taking hearts in tricks. But (according to the method of scoring used) it may be advantageous to win all thirteen hearts.

Scoring. 7. Any of three methods may be used. The sweepstake method produces a stragegy of play radically different from that required with the other two (and with other Hearts games); perhaps on that account it is the most prevalent.

(a) *Sweepstake.* For every heart he won, each player puts one chip in the pool. If one player alone was *clear*—took no hearts—he wins the pool. If two or more players were clear, they divide the pool, leaving any odd chip in the next pool. If every player was *painted*—took one or more hearts—the pool remains as part of the next pool, forming a *jackpot*. The pool also becomes a jackpot if one player takes all thirteen hearts.

(b) *Cumulative scoring.* The hearts won by a player are charged against him on a scoresheet. A running total is kept for each player. Whenever a session of play ends (at a prefixed time or after a fixed number of deals), there is a general settlement. The average score is determined—the total of all scores divided by the number of players. Each player with a score higher than average contributes chips in the amount of his excess; each player below average takes out chips accordingly. [For example: The final scores in a four-hand game are 132, 95, 63, and 41. The total is 331, and the average 83 (approximately). The first two players pay 49 and 12 respectively; the second two collect 20 and 41 respectively. (The last is 42 better than average, but takes the loss on "breakage" as he is the biggest winner.)]

(c) *Howell settlement.* For each heart he has taken, the player puts in the pool as many chips as there are players in the game other than himself. For example, in a four-hand game, each heart costs three chips. Then each player withdraws from the pot a number of chips equal to thirteen less the number of hearts he took. [For example: After a deal in a four-hand game the hearts are distributed 6, 4, 2, and 1. The payments are respectively 18, 12, 6, and 3. The first player then withdraws 7, leaving him a loser by 11; the second player takes 9, losing 4 net; the third takes 11, winning 5 net; the fourth takes 12, winning 9 net.]

Irregularities. 8. *Misdeal.* It is a misdeal if a card is exposed in dealing, except through the fault of the player to whom it is dealt (in which case that player must accept the card) or if a player has an incorrect number of cards. A misdeal is void and loses the deal to the next player in turn. No misdeal may be claimed after the first trick is completed.

9. *Revoke.* If a player fails to follow suit when able, and does not correct his error before the trick has been turned and quitted, play is abandoned and the offender is charged all the minus points on that deal. If more than one player revoke, each is charged all the minus points. A revoke may be claimed at any time before the cards are mixed together so that it cannot be proved.

10. *Play out of turn.* There is no penalty for a lead or play out of turn, but if every player thereafter plays to it, the lead and the trick stand as regular. Any player who has not played to the trick may demand retraction of a lead or play out of turn, but a card once played may not be withdrawn except on such demand.

11. *Incorrect hand.* A player with too many cards must take the last trick. A player with too few cards must take every trick to which he cannot play, but the player of the card that would otherwise have won the trick leads to the next trick, if any.

Pointers on Hearts play. From short suits, as A-J-3, play the high cards first, so as to save the low card for eventual exit. A short suit without a low card, as Q-10-9, should usually be led out as fast as possible, so that it cannot be used by the other players to force the hand in the lead after its exit cards in other suits are gone. With such a holding in hearts, or any long suit lacking low cards, the only hope to avoid being painted is of course to discard some or all of these cards.

High cards in the hand are not dangerous if adequately quarded. For example, A-J-8-4-2 is reasonably safe from ever having to win a dangerous trick. But be cautious of using any long suit for repeated exit, unless it has a monopoly of the lowest cards. Generally try to reserve long suits to underplay leads by other hands.

It is of course imperative to keep track of all the cards played, of what suits have been refused by what players, and to plumb every source of interference as to the unseen hands. If able to do this, use the knowledge so gained to anticipate what each player may be expected to do if he is forced in the lead. It often develops that some players can be counted on to help, other to hinder, one's own plans.

In Howell or cumulative scoring, take a few hearts when necessary to insure against winning a greater number—especially, to avoid being stuck in the lead without exit. For example, with a handful of danger suits, including A-2 in hearts, exit first by cashing the ♡A and then leading the ♡2.

In sweepstake scoring, estimate at the outset your chance of taking no hearts. Remember that taking one is as fatal as taking twelve. If you seem predestined to be painted, as by having no low hearts or several danger suits, try to paint everybody and force a jackpot. With a handful of high cards, give thought to trying to take all the hearts, for the same purpose. But this campaign is usually difficult, and usually takes the forced coöperation of at least one other player who has a dangerous hand.

HEARTS VARIATIONS

Heartsette. No cards are stripped from the pack. The cards are dealt so far as they will go evenly, and the extra cards are placed face down to form a widow. The widow is added to the first trick and goes to the winner thereof.

Spot Hearts. Cumulative scoring is used, and the hearts are charged against the players according to their rank: ace 14, king 13, queen 12, jack 11, other cards their index value.

Joker Hearts. The joker is added to a pack as a heart ranking between the jack and ten. It wins any trick to which it is played unless the trick also contains one of the four higher hearts. Hence, the joker can never be got rid of by discard on a plain suit lead. If the scoring is as in Spot Hearts, the joker counts 20. This variant is most appropriate to three-hand play, each player receiving seventeen cards.

Domino Hearts. Only six cards are dealt to each player, the rest of the pack forming the stock. The rules of play are as usual, except that a player unable to follow suit must draw cards from the top of the stock until he can follow. After the stock is exhausted, a hand unable to follow suit may discard. Each player drops out of the deal when his cards are exhausted, and if he wins a trick with his last card the turn to lead passes to the first active player at his left. When only one player has any cards left, he must add them to his tricks. Each heart is charged as 1 point, and a game is won by the player with the lowest total when another player reaches 31.

Draw Hearts. This is a variant for two players. Each receives thirteen cards, and the rest of the pack is placed face down to form the stock. The rules of play are as in Hearts, but the winner of a trick draws the top card of the stock and his opponent draws the next, so that the hands are maintained at thirteen cards. After the stock is exhausted, the hands are played out without drawing. The player who takes the lesser number of hearts wins by the difference.

Auction Hearts. The auction principle can be applied to any of the Hearts variants, but is most appropriate to "straight" Hearts with sweep-stake scoring. There is one round of bidding. Each player in turn, beginning with eldest hand, must pass or make a bid higher than any preceding bid. A bid is the number of chips the player is willing to pay for the right to name "trumps," i.e., the suit whose cards shall count against the winners thereof. The high bidder names the trump and makes the opening lead. His payment for the privilege is added to the pool formed at the end of the deal by payments for trumps won in tricks. When the pool becomes a jackpot, the same player retains his right to name the trump, without additional payment, until the pool is won.

BLACK LADY

Black Lady is essentially Hearts with the addition of the queen of spades as a minus card, counting thirteen. This feature may have been suggested by Polignac or a similar game. The passing of cards prior to the play, however, goes right back to the ancestral game Reverse. Black

Lady and its elaborations have completely overshadowed the original Hearts in popularity.

Number of players. 1. From three to seven may play (but see the next paragraph). By far the best game is four-hand, each for himself.

The pack. 2. A regular pack of 52 cards. If necessary to make the number of cards a multiple of the number of players, discard low cards in this order of preference: ♣2, ♢2, ♣3, ♠2. If eight or more play, use a double pack.

Rank of cards. 3. The cards in each suit rank: A (high), K, Q, J, 10, 9, 8, 7, 6, 5, 4, 3, 2.

The deal. 4. The cards are distributed one at a time in clockwise rotation, beginning with eldest hand (player at left of the dealer), until the whole pack is dealt. All players should receive equal hands.

The pass. 5. After looking at his hand, each player passes any three cards face down to the player at his left. (Alternative rule: The cards are passed alternately left and right from deal to deal.) The player must pass before looking at the cards received from his righthand neighbor.

The play. 6. Eldest hand leads first. He may lead any card. After any lead, each other hand must follow suit if able; if unable, the hand may play any card. A trick is won by the highest card of the suit led. The winner of a trick leads to the next.

Object of play. 7. Each player strives either (a) to avoid taking any hearts or the ♠Q (called *Black Lady, Black Maria, Calamity Jane,* etc.); or (b) to win all these cards.

Scoring. 8. Each heart taken in a trick counts minus 1, and the ♠Q counts minus 13, except that if one player takes all fourteen counting cards no one scores for that deal. A running total is kept of each player's score. Settlement may be made as in *Cumulative scoring* under Hearts, page 241, or a game may be deemed won by the player with the best score (least minus) when another player reaches minus 100.

Irregularities. (Paragraphs 8 to 11 on pages 241-242 apply, and also): 9. In clubs, and also in many home games, it is usually a rule that the player having the ♠Q must get rid of it at first opportunity, by discard or by playing it under the ace or king. Where this rule is agreed, a violation of it costs the offender 26 points, no other hand scoring in that deal.

BLACK LADY VARIATIONS

Cancellation Hearts. This is a variant for six or more players, recommended when the mood is hilarious rather than studious. Two regular packs are shuffled together and are dealt out one at a time as far as they will go evenly. The extra cards at the end of the deal are placed face down to form a widow, which is added to the first trick and goes to the winner thereof. All rules of play are as in Black Lady, but duplicate cards (as both aces of spades) played to the same trick cancel each other and neither can win the trick. It is thus possible for the two of spades to win both queens, all other cards being likewise paired. If all cards played of the suit led are paired, the trick is held in abeyance and must be taken by the next hand to win a trick. The leader of a trick so held in abeyance leads again.

Omnibus Hearts. This variant is rapidly becoming the most popular of Hearts games. It is so called because it includes all the features found in different members of the family. The use of the $\diamond 10$ as a plus card may have been borrowed from Catch the Ten or from the All Fours family.

Follow all the rules of Black Lady, except:

The $\diamond 10$ scores 10 plus to the player winning it in a trick. If a player takes all fifteen counting cards ($\diamond 10$, $\spadesuit Q$, and thirteen hearts), he scores 26 plus for the deal; all other players score nothing. (The $\diamond 8$ or $\diamond J$ is sometimes used instead of the $\diamond 10$ to count +10.)

Discard Hearts is the same game as Black Lady, with the passing of three cards either to the left or to the right.

Slippery Anne is the same game as Black Lady.

Greek Hearts is Black Lady, with three cards passed each time but always to the right, with the $\diamond J$ counting +10, and with the added rule that the first lead of the game may not be a heart. There is no evidence that this game is played in Greece or even that any Greek ever played it.

SLOBBERHANNES

Number of players. 1. Four, five or six.

The pack. 2. For four players, a pack of 32 cards, made by discarding all cards below the sevens from a full pack. For five or six players, a pack of 30 cards—the pack of 32 with the black sevens discarded.

The deal. 3. The entire pack is dealt out, one card at a time. Each player receives: eight cards, with four players; six cards, with five players; five cards, with six players.

The play. 4. Eldest hand (player at left of the dealer) makes the opening lead. He may lead any card. After any lead, each other hand must follow suit if able. A trick is won by the highest card of the suit led. (There is no trump suit.) The winner of a trick leads to the next.

Scoring. 5. The object of play is to avoid winning the first trick, the last trick, any trick containing the $\clubsuit Q$. Each such trick counts minus 1, but if one player takes all three he loses an extra point, 4 in all.

6. Equal stacks of chips are distributed to the players at the outset. For each minus point a player pays one chip into a pool. At the end of the session, the pool is divided equally among all the players. To limit the supply of chips needed, the pool may be distributed equally after, say, every fourth deal.

(*Variant.* The first and last tricks cost one chip each; the ♣Q costs two less than the number of players in the game. If one player takes all three minus points, he collects instead of pays: as many chips as there are players. The pool is thus always kept at a multiple of the number of players and so can be distributed equally.)

POLIGNAC

Also called Four Jacks, Stay Away, or Quatre Valets, this game is almost identical with Slobberhannes. Follow its rules except:

The only minus points are the jacks. The ♠J (polignac) costs two chips, each other jack one chip. Before the opening lead, any player may announce capot, *i. e.*, that he will try to win all the tricks. If he succeeds, each other player must pay five chips to the pool. If he fails, the capot player must pay five chips. In either case, additional payment must be made for all jacks. (When settlement is made through a pool that is common property, the payment for a successful capot should instead be one chip from each other player, paid directly to the capot player.)

LIFT SMOKE

In the *American Hoyle* (1864) of Dick & Fitzgerald, this game is called Sift Smoke. In all later sources, it is called Lift Smoke. The difference is probably due to a typographical error, but we have been unable to ascertain whose is the error.

Number of players. 1. From four to six may play.

The pack. 2. A regular pack of 52 cards.

Rank of cards. 3. The cards in each suit rank: A (high), K, Q, J, 10, 9, 8, 7, 6, 5, 4, 3, 2.

The pool. 4. Prior to the deal, all players ante equally to form a pool, which goes to the winner of the deal.

The deal. 5. The dealer distributes cards one at a time in clockwise rotation, beginning with the eldest hand (player at his left), until each hand has as many cards as there are players in the game.

6. The last card dealt, which belongs to the dealer, is turned face up, and it fixes the trump suit for that deal. The rest of the pack is placed face down in the center of the table to form the *stock*.

The play. 7. Eldest hand may lead any card. A lead requires each other hand to follow suit if able; if unable, a hand may play any card. A trick is won by the highest trump, or, if it contains no trump, by the highest card of the suit led. The winner of a trick leads to the next.

8. The winner of a trick draws the top card of the stock. No other player draws from the stock. When a player's cards are exhausted, he retires from the deal and the others continue play. The last player to have any cards left wins the deal. If there are two or more survivors, all of whom play their last card to the same trick, the winner thereof is deemed the survivor.

CATCH THE TEN

This game is also called Scotch Whist.

Number of players. 1. From two to about seven may play. The best game is four-hand, in two partnerships.

The pack. 2. A pack of 36 cards, made by discarding all cards below the sixes from a full pack. (With five or seven players, discard also the ♣6.)

Rank of cards. 3. In the trump suit the cards rank: J (high), A, K, Q, 10, 9, 8, 7, 6. In each plain suit the rank is A (high), K, Q, J, 10, 9, 8, 7, 6.

The deal. 4. The whole pack is dealt out, one card at a time, all players receiving the same number of cards. The last card of the pack, which goes to the dealer, is exposed to fix the trump suit for that deal.

The play. 5. Eldest hand (player at left of the dealer) makes the opening lead. He may lead any card. Any lead requires each other hand to follow suit if able; if unable, a hand may play any card. A trick is won by the highest trump, or if it contains no trump, by the highest card of the suit led. The winner of a trick leads to the next.

Object of play. 6. There are two objects: (a) to win high trumps in tricks; (b) to win as many tricks as possible. The values of the trumps are:

Jack	11
Ace	4
King	3
Queen	2
Ten	10

Scoring. 7. At the end of the play, each side or player scores what it has won in high trumps. Also, the side or each individual player that has gathered more cards in tricks than were contained in its original hands scores 1 point for each excess card. [For example, in a five-hand game, each player receives seven cards; a player who wins two tricks (ten cards) scores 3 points. In partnership play, all tricks taken by a side are compared with the total of all partnership hands together. For example, in a six-hand game of two partnerships, each player receives six cards and a side eighteen; the side wins 1 point for each card taken in excess of eighteen.]

8. A running total score is kept for each side or player. The first to reach 41 points wins a game. If both sides or more than one player could otherwise reach 41 in the same deal, the points are counted in order: 10, cards, A, K, Q, J; the first to reach 41 wins.

OH HELL

In "family journals" this game is sometimes called Oh Pshaw or Blackout. Its origin is a latter-day mystery. It began to be played in New York clubs in 1931, and was said to have been introduced from England. It has spread rapidly.

Number of players. 1. Any number from three to seven may play. The best game is four-hand, each for himself.

The pack. 2. A regular pack of 52 cards.

The shuffle and cut. 3. Before each deal the pack is shuffled and cut as in Contract Bridge.

4. The cards are dealt one at a time. The deal and the rotation of the turn to deal are as in Contract Bridge, except as provided in the next paragraphs.

The deal. 5. In the first deal of a game, each player receives one card; in the second deal, two cards; and so on. In three-hand play, the number of deals per game is usually limited by agreement to fifteen. With more players, there are as many deals as the pack will allow, in view of the increasing number of cards per deal.

6. After each deal, the next card of the pack is turned to determine the trump suit for that deal. In four-hand, the thirteenth deal is played without a trump suit. With any other number of players, all deals may be played with a trump suit, but it is usual to agree to play the last deal at no trump.

Bidding. 7. Beginning with eldest hand (player at left of the dealer), each in turn must make a bid of zero (often expressed by "pass"), one, or more tricks, up to the number in that deal. The bid is the exact number of tricks that the player will undertake to win.

8. A scorekeeper is appointed; he must record all the bids on paper, and any player is entitled to be informed at any time how much each player has bid.

(*Optional rule.* Some players agree that the dealer, who bids last, may not make the deal "even," i.e., bid exactly the number of tricks that would fall to him if all previous bids were fulfilled. A less "rugged" rule is that the compulsion on the dealer to make the deal "over" or "under" does not come into force until each player in the game has dealt once; the number of cards per hand is then sufficient to give the player some leeway. When the dealer must not make it even, the scorekeeper has the additional duty of informing the dealer what is the forbidden number of tricks.)

The play. 9. Eldest hand (player at left of the dealer) makes the opening lead. He may lead any card. After any lead, each other hand must follow suit if able; if unable, a hand may play any card. A trick is won by the highest trump, or, if it contains no trump, by the highest card of the suit led. The winner of a trick leads to the next.

Scoring. 10. Each player who has bid one or more, and who makes exactly what he has bid, scores the amount of the bid plus 10 points. Each player who has bid zero and taken no trick scores 5 plus the number of tricks in that deal. Each player who has taken either more or less tricks than his bid scores nothing.

(*Alternative rules.* Some players prefer to allow a flat 10 for a bid of zero, some only 5.)

11. The scorekeeper records all points earned and keeps a running total of each player's score. At the end of the game, the player with the highest total wins.

Irregularities. 12. *Bid out of turn.* A player may change his bid, if he does so before the player at his left bids. In all other cases, a first bid or any bid out of turn stands (but if the bid was out of turn, the turn reverts to the rightful player).

13. *Play out of turn.* If a player leads or plays out of turn, he must retract the card on demand, leave it face up on the table, and play it at his first legal opportunity thereafter.

14. *Exposed card.* If a player exposes a card from his hand, other than in his turn to play, he must place it face up on the table and play it at his first legal opportunity thereafter.

15. *Revoke.* A revoke (failure to follow suit when able) may be corrected before the lead to the next trick, and any cards played to the trick after the revoke may be retracted without penalty. If a revoke is not corrected in time, there must be a redeal of the same number of cards by the same dealer and 10 points are deducted from the score of the offender.

16. *Information.* A player is always entitled to know how much any other player has bid and how many tricks he has won. [Except for legitimate inquiry in these matters, a player should refrain from giving any intimation of whether he expects himself or another player to "go bust".]

⟶ CRIBBAGE ⟵

Cribbage, originally spelled Cribbidge, is believed to have been invented by Sir John Suckling (1609-1642). It may have been based on an older game, Noddy. A reference by Gayton to "Noddy-boards" in 1654 implies that a board was used for scoring. In Cribbage, the jack was originally called *Noddy*, now *His Nobs*.

Number of players. 1. Two, but variants have been devised for three or four.

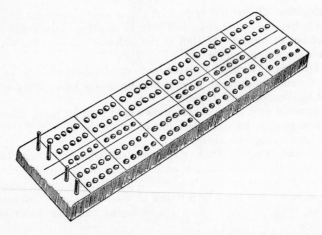

Cribbage board. 2. Score is kept on a so-called *Cribbage board* (see illustration). Each player has two pegs, which advance along two parallel rows of thirty holes each. Starting from "game holes" at the end of the board, the pegs are advanced down the outer row, then back the inner row; the distance between them always shows the player's last score, and the forward peg marks his cumulative total. The game of 61 is called *once around,* and 121 is *twice around.* Scoring is called *pegging;* sometimes this term is restricted to mean scoring by play, apart from the count of hands.

[The Cribbage board is a useful adjunct for scoring any game in which the increments are not large but are frequent.]

The pack. 3. A regular pack of 52 cards.

Rank of cards. 4. The cards rank: K (high), Q, J, 10, 9, 8, 7, 6, 5, 4

3, 2, A. Suits are largely ignored; in most of the play, the cards represent numbers only: ace is 1, face cards 10 each, other cards their index value.

The deal. 5. Each player receives six cards, dealt one at a time.

The crib. 6. Each player *lays away* any two cards from his hand, face down. The four cards so laid away form the *crib,* an extra hand that always belongs to the dealer.

The starter. 7. After the crib is laid away, the non-dealer cuts the remaining pack; there must be at least four cards in each packet. The dealer draws off the top card of the lower packet, and places it face up on the reunited pack. This card is the *starter.* If it chances to be a jack, the dealer at once pegs 2 points for *his heels.*

The play. 8. Each player retains his hand intact, placing the cards as played face up in a pile in front of himself.

9. Non-dealer leads first. He may lead any card. He announces its value orally [as, "Ten" if it is a queen]. Dealer then plays a card, and announces the total of both cards together [as, "eighteen" if he has played an eight after a queen]. Play continues by alternate turns, each player announcing the new total, until one in turn is unable to play without carrying the total over 31. This player must say "Go."

10. *Go.* A player must not call *go* if he has any playable card. After a proper call of *go,* the opponent must continue to play if he can (and thus may play twice in succession). In any event, the opponent of the player who called go pegs 1 for it, or 2 if he plays additional cards to make the total exactly 31. If 31 is reached by alternate plays, it is a go for the last to play, and he pegs 2.

11. The player who calls go, or suffers a go because his opponent makes 31, must lead for a new series of plays. The count toward 31 starts again from zero. There may be one, two, or three "goes" in a deal. The player who plays the last card pegs 1 for it, or 2 if he makes 31.

12. *Combinations in play.* Scores in addition to go may be earned in play by making any of the following combinations:

Fifteen: For making the count exactly 15, peg 2.

Pair: For playing a card of the same rank as that previously played, peg 2; or if this is the third card of the same rank played in succession, peg 6; or if it is the fourth card, peg 12. (Cards pair by rank, not by value: a king and queen are not a pair, although each counts 10.)

Run: For playing the third or a later card of three or more played in succession that are in sequence, peg the number of cards in the *run.* [*For example,* if the cards played are 7, 8, 9, the second player pegs 2 for fifteen and the first then pegs 3 for run.] A run is valid even if the cards are not played in strict sequence, so long as no foreign card intervenes. [*For example,* 8, 6, 9, 7 pegs for run, but 7, 8, 4, 9 is not a run, because the four intervenes.]

13. When a player adds one or more cards to a series after a call of go by his opponent, he is entitled to peg for any pair or run he makes. He may peg two or three times by extending the same run. But pairs and runs do not carry over from one series of plays to another, i.e., the last card played after a go does not pair with the next lead.

Showing. 14. The hands being played out, they are *shown*, i.e., counted and scored. The order of precedence in showing is: non-dealer first, then dealer's hand, finally dealer's crib. The starter is construed to be a fifth card belonging to each hand and to the crib.

15. The following combinations in the hand or crib score as indicated:

Fifteen: Each combination of cards that totals 15 scores 2.

Run: Each run of three or more scores the number of cards in the run.

Flush: Four cards of the same suit in the hand, without the starter, score 4; five cards of the same suit (with the starter) in hand or crib score 5. (No count for four-flush in the crib.)

His nobs: Jack of the same suit as the starter scores 1.

16. Each group of cards, differing from all others by at least one member, counts separately from all others. [Thus, *pair royal* (three of a kind) scores 6, since it contains three combinations of pairs, and *double pair royal* (four of a kind) scores 12. A hand of 8-8-9-10-J scores, besides 2 for pair, 8 for two runs of four, since either 8 can be used to make the run.] But a run of four or more may not be construed as several runs of three, for purpose of increasing the score. [*For example,* 8-9-10-J scores 4 as a single run, not 6 as a run of 8-9-10 and another of 9-10-J.]

[Accurate showing is facilitated by remembering certain constant values. Exclusive of fifteens, a *double run* (as K-K-Q-J) scores 8; a *triple run* (as K-K-K-Q-J) scores 15; a *quadruple run* (as K-K-Q-Q-J) scores 16, a *double run of four* (as K-K-Q-J-10) scores 10. The highest possible hand is J-5-5-5-5 where the jack is not the starter (as starter, it would score 2 to the dealer, but this is pegged previous to showing). It counts 8 for J-5 fifteens, 8 for fifteens in fives alone, 12 for double pair royal, and 1 for his nobs, a total of 29. The highest hands that can be made without fives are the following, each worth 24: 6-6-6-6-3; 9-8-8-7-7; 9-3-3-3-3; 7-4-4-4-4; 7-7-7-7-A. No hand can be constructed to count 19, 25, 26, or 27. "I have nineteen" is a time-honored way of saying "I have no score."]

17. Each player must count his hand aloud, for verification by his opponent. An optional rule is that if a player overlooks a score, claiming less than his due, the opponent may call "Muggins!" and himself score the points overlooked.

Game. 18. All points are pegged as soon as earned, the hands being shown in order of precedence (paragraph 14). The player first to reach a total of 61 or 121 (once around or twice around, as agreed) wins a game. Thus, a player may "peg out" during the play and win, even though his opponent, if allowed to show, might have amassed a greater total.

19. When the game is 121, the loser is *lurched* and loses a double game if he fails to reach 61. If lurch is played in once around, the loser must reach 31 to escape double loss.

Irregularities. 20. *Redeal.* Either player may demand a redeal by the same player if the cards are not dealt one at a time, if either hand receives the wrong number of cards, if a card is found faced in the pack, or if a card is exposed in dealing.

21. *Wrong number of cards.* If at any time the crib and one hand are found to have an incorrect number of cards, there must be a new deal; if either player had the correct number of cards, he pegs 2. If the crib alone is found incorrect, non-dealer pegs 2 and the crib is corrected by drawing out excess cards face down or dealing extra cards from the pack. If one hand alone is incorrect, the other and the crib being correct, the opponent of the incorrect hand may peg 2 and require its rectification, or may demand a new deal.

22. *Erroneous count.* An error in announcing the total of cards played in a series may be corrected by either player before another card is played; if the error is not noticed until later, the total stands as announced.

23. An error in showing a hand must be corrected on demand. If muggins is allowed, the call is not valid if made before the player who under-counted his hand has actually pegged his score.

24. *Illegal go.* A player who calls go or stops playing after a go when in fact he could play again may not correct his error after his opponent has next played; the cards he should have played are dead and may not be played at all (but they remain in the hand for showing); and the opponent of the offender pegs 2.

25. *Error in pegging.* If a player pegs less than the amount to which he is entitled, he may not correct his error after he has played the next card or (in case of showing) after the cut for the next deal. If a player pegs more than his due, the error must be corrected on demand if made before the cut for the next deal, and the opponent pegs 2.

Pointers on Cribbage play. As non-dealer, try to give the crib *balking* cards—least likely to develop a score. *Wide* cards (separated by two or more in rank) are preferable to *near* cards (as 8-9 or 8-10), which may become a run. As dealer, lay away what you can spare and at the same time (a) retain maximum score in hand and crib together, or (b) retain maximum chance for improvement, or both.

The best chance for improvement (through the starter) is to save a run. For example, with Q-9-8-4-3-2 save the run above all else. As dealer, lay away 9-8 to help the crib toward a run; as non-dealer, give Q-9 or Q-8 to balk. With a high-scoring hand, save the maximum count even if you have to help your opponent's crib. For example, with 8-7-7-6-4-4 give him the fours, a score of 2 against your 12. Then the turn of an 8, 7 or 6 will add 12 or 8 to your score, not more than 2 to his. To try to balk by giving him 8-6 would be poor policy.

253

As there are sixteen *tenth* cards (face cards and tens), you should never give a five to your opponent's crib except to save a natural big hand. But give a five to your own crib if you can spare it, since face cards are frequently given to balk.

The safest opening lead is a four, since dealer can neither make 15 nor exceed it. The worst lead is obviously a five. Bad to lead are aces, twos, and threes; very low cards should be saved for eking out a go. Sixes, sevens, eights and nines are dangerous, as they may allow dealer to make 15, but such leads are better than very low cards, and are positively desirable when you have other intermediate cards to back up the lead. The lead of a tenth card is much better than its reputation; it is particularly good from two or three tenth cards, for if dealer makes pair or plays any high card your second tenth card will probably win a go.

In the play, give thought to whether you wish to play *on* or *off*, i.e., cards that will or will not build toward a run, pair royal, etc. The decision depends upon what you have to back up your play: play on when, if your opponent scores, you can retort with a score, as by extending a run. Play off when you have no near cards.

The average value of a hand is 7 points; of the crib, 5. The average amount pegged during play is between 4 and 5, with 1 point always assured to the dealer (he always wins one go, if only by last card). These averages become important in the "home stretch." Remember that non-dealer shows first. If you are dealer in what may be the last hand of a game, strive to prevent your opponent from pegging in play. Play off, even though you thereby preclude pegging yourself. If his hand is big enough to put him out, you were always helpless, but if another deal is required, you have gained first count.

CRIBBAGE VARIATIONS

Five-card Cribbage. In Cribbage as originally devised, each player received only five cards. Two were laid away to the crib, so that each hand (with starter) comprised four cards, the crib five. Game was 61. Most modern players prefer the six-card game, twice around.

Three-hand Cribbage. Each player receives five cards and one card is dealt to the crib. Each player lays away one card. Eldest hand cuts the pack for the starter and leads first. When any player calls go, the other two must play in turn so long as they can, and the point for go is pegged by the last to play. The precedence in showing is: eldest hand first, then player at his left, then dealer's hand, and finally dealer's crib.

Four-hand Cribbage. This is played in two partnerships. Each player receives five cards, and lays one away to the crib. Eldest hand cuts the pack for the starter and leads first. When any player calls go, the others must play in turn so long as they can, and the point for go is pegged by the side last to play. Eldest hand's side shows first, then dealer and his partner, finally dealer's crib. The game is twice around, 121 points.

⟜ CASINO ⟜

Casino, often incorrectly spelled Cassino, probably dates back at least to the 17th century. One of the first references to it in English is found in *Hoyle's Games,* edited by Charles Jones, London, 1808. But several very similar games are described in earlier French and German manuals, as Papillon and Callabra.

Number of players. 1. Two, three or four; it is best for two, next best for four in two partnerships.

The pack. 2. A regular pack of 52 cards.

Count of cards. 3. An ace counts 1; other cards up to tens count their index value; face cards have no numerical count.

The deal. 4. To begin a deal, the dealer gives two cards face down to his opponent, turns two face up on the table, then gives, face down, two to himself; then a second round of two cards at a time like the first. He sets the pack aside and play begins. After these hands are played out, the dealer gives four cards to each player, two at a time, but gives none to the table. These new hands are played out—and so on. Six times successively the same dealer deals hands of four cards each, until the pack is exhausted, but gives cards to the table only at the outset. (When there are more than two players, each receives four cards in each round, but none to the table after the first round.) In serving the last cards of the pack, the dealer must announce "Last."

5. The turn to deal alternates, or passes in clockwise rotation.

The play. 6. Beginning with non-dealer (or eldest hand, the player at dealer's left), each player in turn must play one card from his hand until the hands are played out. The card played may be used to *trail, take in, build, duplicate* or *increase a build.*

7. *Trailing.* If unable or unwilling to make any other play, the player lays a card face up on the table.

8. *Taking in.* All cards on the table are open to capture, provided the player has a suitable card in his hand. A face card may be captured only by another of the same kind, as a queen by a queen. Cards so captured are *taken in:* the player puts them face down in a pile near himself. Lower cards may be taken in by pairing, and also by *building.*

9. *Building.* Two or more cards whose numerical total is ten or less may be taken in by a card equal to their total. [*For example,* a six and a three may be taken by a nine; a five, four and ace by a ten.]

10. A player may lay a card from his hand on a card or cards on the

table, making a *build* of two or more cards that he intends to take in at his next turn. [*For example*, a four from the hand may be laid on a three on the table, provided that the player has a seven in his hand.] Also, having a pair of the same rank in his hand, with a third card of the rank on the table, a player may build a pair, intending to take it in with his other card. [*For example*, the player has two tens; he lays one of them on a ten on the table, intending to take them in with the third ten.]

11. On making any build that is so left to be taken, the player must state the rank necessary to take it, and this statement is binding. For example, a player lays a five on a five and says "Building fives"; the opponent may not take in the build with a ten.

12. Any build left on the table may be taken in by an opponent (or partner) of the builder, with the specified card.

13. A player may not trail in a turn in which a build made by him remains to be taken in. (*Alternative rule.* He must take in something or duplicate the build, at his next turn.)

14. Face cards may not be built in any way; they may be taken in only by pairing. (*Alternative rule.* Face cards may be built in pairs or triplets.)

15. *Duplicating a build.* Any build may be duplicated to the extent of the cards available. [*For example*, if the cards on the table are 5, 4, 3, 6, all may be taken by a nine. Or, 5, 4, 9 may be taken by a nine. Having played a six from his hand on a four to make ten, a player may at his next turn take in his build together with a seven and three on the table, or may play a seven on a three and consolidate the two builds, still keeping the necessary ten in his hand.] But a player is not at any time required to take in cards except to comply with paragraph 13.

16. *Increasing a build.* A card may be added to a build, raising the rank of the card necessary to take it in, provided (a) that the build is single, not duplicated in any way; (2) the added card comes from the hand, not from the table. These conditions being met, a player may increase either his own or the opponent's build. [*For example:* Six has been built; a player holds an ace and a seven; he may add his ace to the build, making it seven. But: Six has been built; a player holds an ace and a ten and there is a three on the table; he may not add both the ace and the three to the build to increase it to ten.]

17. After the pack is exhausted and the last hands are played out, all cards remaining on the table belong to the player who was last to take in.

Scoring. 18. Each player (or side) counts the points he has won by cards taken in. The points to be counted are:

Cards, majority of the 52 cards	3
Spades, majority of the 13 spades	1
Big Casino, the ◇10	2
Little Casino, the ♤2	1
Aces, each counting 1	4
	11

19. If each player took in twenty-six cards, there is no score for *cards*.

20. A running total is kept for each player, and the first to reach 21 points wins a game. The margin of victory is the difference in totals; there is no bonus for game. If both might reach 21 in the same deal, the points are counted in order of precedence given in paragraph 18, *cards* first, and the first to reach 21 wins. If the outcome depends on the count of aces, these are scored in order: ♠A (first), ♣A, ♡A, ◇A. (*Alternative rule.* Each deal is a game.)

21. *Sweeps (optional).* Each time a player takes in all cards on the table, he scores one point for a sweep. To indicate this, he faces a card among his cards taken in. In counting out for game, sweeps rank in precedence behind aces.

22. *Overs (optional).* For each card taken in excess of thirty, a player (or side) scores one point. In counting out for game, overs rank in precedence behind sweeps. *Spade overs* are spades taken in excess of eight; if spade overs are scored, they count one point each and rank in precedence behind card overs.

23. *Double and Quadruple Game (optional).* If a player (or side) reaches 21 in two deals, his score is doubled (before deduction of his opponent's score); if he reaches 21 in one deal—possible only when sweeps and/or overs are scored—his score is quadrupled.

Irregularities. 24. *Misdeal.* In case a redeal is required, non-dealer may decide who shall deal next (in four-hand play, either opponent decides; in three-hand play, a misdeal loses the deal). There must be a redeal if the shuffle or cut was omitted, provided the opponent calls it before making any play. There must be a redeal at any time the pack is discovered to be incorrect.

25. *Exposed cards.* A card exposed in dealing or faced in the pack goes to the table and the dealer plays with a short hand; except that on the first round of dealing, before all four cards have been dealt to the table, the card exposed stands as dealt to the table.

26. *Incorrect hand.* If dealer gives an opponent too many cards, the opponent may face a card on the table and dealer plays the next round with a short hand. If a hand has too many cards by reason of failure to play in turn, it must trail in each subsequent turn during that round. If a hand has too few cards due to playing more than one card in a turn, it plays on with a short hand.

27. If there are too few cards to complete the deal, but the pack is correct, dealer plays the last round with a short hand.

28. *Cards exposed illegally.* In partnership play only, a card named or exposed except by a legal play in turn must be left on the table as though the player had trailed with it; he and his partner may never take it in.

29. In two- and three-hand play a player must trail with a card he exposes prematurely, or with which he tries to take in cards to which he is not entitled.

30. *Illegal play.* An illegal play must be corrected on demand made before an opponent plays thereafter.

31. *Improper build.* If a player makes a build and cannot take it in when required (either because he announced a build for which he has not the appropriate card, or because the build does not fit his announcement), his opponent may add one point to his own score or subtract one point from the offender's score.

[In two-hand play when every deal constitutes a game, any of the following irregularities forfeits the game: Incorrect number of cards dealt by dealer on any round but the first; incorrect hand not due to dealer's error; illegally taking in cards; improper build; looking back at cards previously taken in; failure by dealer to announce last. In other games, the last two irregularities (looking back, and failing to announce last) are not customarily penalized.]

Pointers on Casino play. Good players keep count of the cards and spades each player has taken in. In general, play to win as many cards as possible until the points for cards are settled.

Playing from a pair, prefer to take in with a spade, to trail with a non-spade.

The "cash points" ($\Diamond$10, $\spadesuit$2 and the aces) should be remembered; likewise the highest spot cards, tens, nines and eights. Most players do not make a great effort to remember all other cards, but try to know the opponent's last four cards by keeping track of cards unpaired because of building. For example, a four and three are taken in by a seven; the ranks 3, 4, 7 are unpaired. If later a four and two are taken by a six, the previous four is paired but the unpaired cards now are 2, 3, 6, 7. When the final hands are dealt, all unpaired cards not paired by the table or by your own hand will be in the opponent's hand.

Dealer must take a chance on building or trailing with his low cards, hoping to take them in; non-dealer (or eldest hand) should hold such cards to his last play or plays, unless he can safely build them or take them in, for he will play first on the next round and will have the best chance to take in.

When there are several cards on the table, it is often possible to figure out an opponent's hand by plays he failed to make. This should be done systematically: "If he had a ten he would have done this, if he had a nine he would have done that," and so on.

ROYAL CASINO

Follow all the rules of Casino except:

Kings count 13, queens 12, jacks 11, aces 1 or 14, and all these cards may be used to take in builds and may be built in triplets and quadruplets. (*Optional rule.* Little Casino counts 2 or 15, Big Casino 10 or 16, at the pleasure of the owner.) If a player takes in all cards remaining on the table, he scores 1 for *sweep,* but this score ranks last in order of precedence when the cards taken in are counted. A sweep is noted by turning one card face up among the cards taken in. The award of cards finally remaining on the table, to the player last to take in, does not count as a sweep.

[Royal Casino is the variant most popular today, especially in juvenile and family games. The right of face cards to take builds is a relatively recent innovation, but the counting of sweeps—which, strange to say, is unknown to many adult Casino players—goes right back to earliest times.]

CASINO VARIATIONS

Spade Casino. The count for majority of spades is replaced by a point count for each spade taken in: the two and jack count 2 each, all others count 1 each. The number of points at stake in each deal is thus increased (exclusive of sweeps) to 24. Game is usually fixed at 61, because of the custom of scoring on a Cribbage board.

Draw Casino. Four cards are dealt to each player and four to the table; the rest of the pack is placed face down to form the stock. After each play, the player draws the top card of the stock to restore his hand to four cards. After the stock is exhausted, the remaining cards are played out without drawing.

SCOPA

Scopa, or Scoop, is also called Italian Casino.

Number of players. 1. Two, four or six; best as a four-hand partnership game. Six also play in two partnerships of three.

The pack. 2. The pack has 40 cards, K, Q, J, 7, 6, 5, 4, 3, 2, A of each suit.

3. Each king counts 10, each queen 9, each jack 8, each ace 1, each other card its numerical value.

The deal. 4. Three cards are dealt face down to each player and four cards face up to the table, as in Casino; when the original hands have been played out, three more cards are dealt to each player but none to the table; and so on until the pack is exhausted. The rotation in dealing is counter-clockwise.

The play. 5. Each player in counter-clockwise rotation, beginning with eldest hand (the player at dealer's right), must play one card.

6. A player in turn may take in one card from the table with a card of the same rank played from his hand; or may take in two or more cards from the table whose sum equals the count of the card played from his hand. (A build may not be duplicated as at Casino.) When a player has a choice between taking a single card or a combination of cards from

the table, he must take the single card. Cards taken in are placed face down before the player who took them.

7. Cards remaining on the table after the last card has been played go to the player who last took in any cards.

Scoring. 8. A player *scoops* the table when he takes in every card on it. (It does not necessarily count as a scoop when a player receives the cards remaining on the table at the end.)

9. After play ceases, each player (or side) scores:

> 1 point for most cards won
> 1 point for most diamonds won
> 1 point for winning the $\Diamond$7
> 1 point for *settanta* (see below)
> 1 point for each scoop

10. Settanta is scored for the highest-counting four cards, one of each of the four suits, taken in by a player (or side). Such a group of four cards is called a *primiera* (see page 340). For the purpose of determining the highest-ranking primiera, each seven counts 21, each six 18, each ace 16, each five 15, each four 14, each three 13, each two 12, and each face card 10. The four sevens thus constitute the highest possible primiera, but it is not required that the primiera be four of a kind or even that it include a pair, so long as every suit is represented.

Game. 11. The first side to score 11 points wins the game. A player (or side) may declare himself out during play, and if he has 11 points he wins; if he has not 11 points the other side wins. If both sides reach 11 or more points, the first to claim game is the winner.

SCOPONE

Scopone is a form of Scopa, played by four players in two partnerships. The entire pack of 40 cards is dealt out, ten cards to each player, none to the table. Each player in rotation, beginning with eldest hand, plays one card until all are played; taking in and scoring are as in Scopa, and game is 15 points.

⇒ PIQUET ⇐

In the list of games known to Gargantua, Rabelais (1535) mentions Piquet, La Ronflé, and le Cent. The latter two are believed to have been virtually identical with Piquet. Le Cent, which is frequently alluded to in Elizabethan literature as Saunt or Sant, may have originated in Spain as Cientos. Piquet is sometimes written Picquet or Picket. For nearly five hundred years it has been one of the most popular two-hand card games in France and England, and is known the world over, though in the United States and elsewhere it is little played outside of card clubs. An indication of the universality of Piquet is that French, English, German and other manuals have for many generations alluded to the features of Piquet in explaining other games, and the pack of 32 cards, though used in scores of other games, is almost invariably called "the Piquet pack."

Legend has it that Piquet was invented by Etienne de Vignolles ("La Hire"), a French general who fought with Joan of Arc and made an effort to rescue her after her capture by the British.

Number of players. 1. Two, but variants have been devised for three and four players.

The pack. 2. A pack of 32 cards, made by discarding all cards below the sevens from a full pack.

Rank of cards. 3. The cards in each suit rank: A (high), K, Q, J, 10, 9, 8, 7.

The deal. 4. Each player receives twelve cards, dealt two at a time. The remaining eight cards are spread face down on the table in a fan, forming the *talon* or *stock*.

Discarding. 5. Non-dealer (called *majeur* in French, corresponding to the English *eldest hand*) begins by discarding face down any number of cards from one to five; he must discard at least one. He takes an equal number of cards from the top of the stock. If he leaves any of the first five, he may look at them without showing them to the dealer.

6. The dealer (*mineur*) may discard up to as many cards as are left in the stock. He is not obliged to discard any. He restores his hand by drawing an equal number from the stock. If he leaves any in the stock, he may either set them aside face down or turn them face up for both players to see.

7. A player may look back at his discards at any time. But all discards and any cards left in the stock by dealer must be kept out of play during that deal.

8. *Carte blanche* is a hand without a face card—king, queen, or jack. Either player dealt such a hand originally may score 10 for it. Non-dealer should announce carte blanche on picking up his hand; dealer may wait to announce carte blanche until non-dealer has discarded. The whole hand must be exposed to prove carte blanche.

Declaring. 9. Each hand being restored to twelve cards, they are compared for the scoring of *point, sequence, triplets* or *quartets.* In respect to each, non-dealer must first make an announcement, as "No point" or "Point of five." If he claims no score, dealer announces and scores any combination he holds in this category. If non-dealer claims a score, dealer replies "Good" or, if he has a combination that might be superior, elicits further information to determine the fact.

10. Only one player may score in each category. When both players have combinations in the same category, only the superior one (as explained below) scores.

11. *Point.* The best holding in any suit scores 1 point for each card. For example, if non-dealer's longest suit is five spades, while dealer's longest is four hearts, non-dealer scores 5. The longer of two unequal suits is superior. Non-dealer commences by announcing his greatest length, as "five." Having an equal length, dealer asks "How much?" As between equal lengths, that which has the greatest point value is superior; the point value is the sum of the separate cards, counting ace 11, each face card 10, lower cards their index value. Non-dealer announces the value of his suit, and dealer responds "Good" or "Equal" or "No good"; in the last case he must state the value of his superior suit. If the values as well as lengths are equal, neither player scores for *point.*

12. *Sequence.* A sequence of three cards of the same suit (*tierce*), as ◇J 10 9, scores 3; a sequence of four (*quart*) scores 4; a sequence of five (*quint*) or more scores 10 plus the number of cards. As between unequal lengths, the longer sequence is superior. Non-dealer first declares length, as "Four" or "Quart." Dealer responds "Good" or "Not good" or "Equal." In the last case, non-dealer must then state the rank of the highest card in his sequence. As between equal lengths, the higher rank is superior; if the ranks also are equal, neither player scores for sequence.

The player entitled to score for superior sequence may also score any additional sequences he holds. He announces merely the length of such additional sequences.

13. *Trios and quartets.* Three cards of the same rank (*trio*), as three aces, score 3 points; four cards of the same rank (*quatorze*) score 14; provided, in all cases, that the rank is not below ten. A quartet is superior to a trio; as between two quartets or trios the higher rank is superior. Non-dealer announces his best set, as "Three kings" and dealer responds "Good" or "Not good." There can be no equality. (In accordance with paragraph 15 a player might refrain from announcing the rank of his set, saying merely "Trio." In practice, this nicety is disregarded, because the identity of the set could almost invariably be inferred by the opponent.)

A player entitled to score for quartet or trio may score all additional sets he holds (of rank ten or higher).

14. Non-dealer is not obliged to claim a score for point, sequence, or set: he may say "No point" even though he must of necessity have at least three cards in some suit. He usually refrains from announcing, e.g., three or four kings, when it is evident that the dealer has four aces. (Even though entitled to score them under a superior set, a player will sometimes sink—refrain from announcing—three jacks or tens, in order to avoid confessing weakness by which his opponent might profit in the play.)

15. Formerly it was the rule that every combination entitled to score must be proved by being exposed to the opponent. Modern practice is to leave proof (except of carte blanche) to the play, since all the cards are eventually exposed. Prior to play, the player is required to divulge no more about his hand than is necessary to establish the superiority of his combination when it is not immediately good.

The play. 16. The declarations ended, non-dealer makes the opening lead. He may lead any card. After each lead, the second hand must follow suit if able; if unable, the hand may play any card. A trick is won by the higher card of the suit led. (There is no trump suit.) The winner of a trick leads to the next.

Object of play. 17. The objects in play are to score points for leads and plays; to win a majority of the tricks; to win last trick; to win all the tricks.

Counting. 18. Each player keeps track of the points he wins during a deal, by announcing orally his new total each time he scores. After the declaring, each player by custom announces "I start with—," the total he has earned in combinations.

19. During the play, each player counts 1 for every lead he makes of a card higher than nine, and 1 for each adverse lead that he wins with a card higher than nine. (The exclusion of the lower cards is traditional, but has largely disappeared in modern practice: the player counts 1 for his every lead and 1 for every adverse lead that he captures.)

Pic and repic. 20. If a player scores 30 or more in combinations alone, his opponent having no score, he wins a bonus of 60 points for *repic*. [For example, a hand of eight diamonds, with all four aces, would score 8 for point, 18 for sequence, 14 for quartet, a total of 40, earning the repic bonus to make 100.]

21. If a player reaches 30 points, with the aid of any point counted in play, while his opponent still has zero score, he wins a bonus of 30 points for *pic*. [For example, a hand of eight diamonds with three aces would score 29 in combinations; held by non-dealer, this hand would make pic by the opening lead; if the hand were held by dealer, non-dealer would escape pic by his opening lead.]

(*Note*. In the French rules, a player must jump in oral counting, as from "Twenty-nine" to "Sixty-two" or "Ninety-two," in order to score pic or repic. Should he utter the words "Thirty-two" he would lose claim to the bonus. The English rules have eliminated this and other ritualistic provisions of French Piquet.)

Tricks and capot. 22. The player who wins the last trick scores 1 extra point for it, unless he wins *capot*, the bonus for which includes the extra point.

23. The player who wins the majority of tricks scores 10, or, if he makes *capot* by winning all the tricks, 40. If the tricks are divided six and six, there is no score for tricks.

Scoring. 24. After the play, the total points won by each player during the deal are recorded on paper. The winner of a game may be decided by any of the three following methods:

Piquet au cent. The player first to reach a total score of 100 wins a game. Settlement is made on the difference of final scores, doubled if the loser failed to reach 50 points. The last deal of a game is played out; there is no "counting out" during the play.

Rubicon Piquet. This variant has so far replaced Piquet au cent that today "Piquet" means Rubicon Piquet. A game comprises six deals, the players dealing alternately after drawing cards to decide the first dealer. The player with the higher final score wins, and thereby earns a game bonus of 100. To this is added, if both players have reached 100, the difference of final scores; but if the loser has failed to reach 100 (even though the winner has also failed), the winner adds the sum of both scores to his game bonus.

Club Piquet. In many clubs the Rubicon game has been shortened to four deals. The scores earned in the first and last deals are doubled.

Irregularities. 25. *Redeal.* There must be a new deal by the same dealer if a card is exposed in dealing. If either player receives the wrong number of cards, non-dealer may require the error to be corrected or may demand a redeal.

26. *Error in discard.* After having touched the stock, a player may not alter his discard in any way, as by adding or retracting cards. If he has discarded more cards than are available to him in the stock, he must take all he can and play with a short hand.

27. *Error in drawing.* If a player draws too many cards from the stock, he may return the excess if he has looked at none of them. If non-dealer draws more than five cards and sees any of them, he loses the game forthwith. When non-dealer draws less than five, he must so announce; if he fails to do so, dealer may draw all that are left even though he has previously discarded only three cards or less. If dealer draws and sees any card from the stock before non-dealer has completed his draw, dealer loses the game forthwith.

28. *Error in declaring.* If a player says "Good" or otherwise concedes an adverse claim, he may not retract his concession even though he holds a superior combination in that category. If a player makes any misstatement in claiming a score for a combination, he may correct his error before he has played any card, and any due change is then made in scoring that category; should a player fail to correct a misstatement before playing a card, he scores zero for the deal, while the opponent may show and score all valid combinations of his original hand together with 23 points for tricks (1 for each lead, 1 for last, 10 for majority).

29. *Wrong number of cards.* If at any time after the opening lead one hand alone is found to have too many or too few cards, play continues: a hand with too many cards scores nothing for the play; a hand with too few cards scores as usual but cannot take the last trick—the opponent scores 1 for each final trick for which the offender has no card. If at any time both hands are found to have the wrong number of cards, the deal is void and there must be a redeal by the same dealer.

30. *Revoke.* The cards played after the revoke are retracted, the revoke is corrected, and play continues; there is no penalty.

Pointers on Piquet play. Non-dealer should usually try for point, keeping his longest suit intact and drawing his full five cards. A long strong suit, together with the opening lead, is also the best prospect to win majority of tricks. Aces should of course be saved, but kings and lower cards are frequently discarded when not supported by aces and when there is little prospect of making a quartet. For example:

Discard all the spades and hearts. Giving up these stoppers is a trifling matter, since the hand has the opening lead. Any diamond drawn will probably win point; the ◇K would make point, probably sequence also, and at least seven solid tricks. Against these considerations, saving the ♡Q in the hope of making a quartet would be poor policy.

Dealer, drawing fewer cards, has less chance to win point, and needs the equivalent of an ace more than non-dealer to win a majority of tricks. He should discard primarily to try for sequence or quartet, and to hold stoppers in his short suits, unless he happens to be dealt a long strong hand that justifies trying for point. For example, with the foregoing hand dealer should discard the ◇ 10 9 7. Though this gives up point, and a chance for a sequence of four, it preserves the chance for a quartet of queens and—more important—holds general protection that may win majority.

The best play is often to lead one's own long suit at every opportunity, seeking to knock out any adverse stoppers and cash some long cards. But an exception often arises, as when it is evident that the opponent is going to make his suit first and one's own long suit will have to be discarded on it. It may then be better to lead from a short but strong holding that is going to be saved intact anyhow, as K-Q-J. Another possible reason to refrain from leading one's long suit is that the opponent holds a tenace, as A-Q, and that the prospect of making long cards does not outweigh the sure loss of trick by leading into the tenace.

Most of the time you have enough information about the adverse hand to calculate exactly what is the best line of play. Whatever is not in your hand and discard is in his hand and discard; the declarations will usually show within a card or two exactly what his discards were.

PIQUET VARIATIONS

Piquet Normand. This is a variant for three players. Each receives ten cards, leaving only two for a widow. The dealer only may take the widow in exchange for two discards. Declaring is as in two-hand play, only one hand being eligible to score in any category. Any player who counts 20 before either of the others counts a point jumps to 90 or 60 for repic or pic. The 10 points for tricks go to the player winning a plurality; if two players tie for plurality, each scores 5. Capot counts 40 as usual. A pool formed by equal antes is won by the player first to reach a total of 100 points.

Piquet Voleur. This is a variant for four players, in two partnerships. The whole pack is dealt, each player receiving eight cards. Declarations are made in turn to the left, and the side entitled to score in any category (as sequences) may score all the combinations held by both partners in that category. A side reaching 20 before the other scores a point jumps to 90 or 60 for repic or pic. A game may be scored by any of the three methods used in two-hand.

IMPERIAL

Imperial is one of many games of the Piquet type that flourished in France prior to the Revolution, and has survived practically unchanged.

Number of players. 1. Two.

The pack. 2. A pack of 32 cards, made by discarding all cards below the sevens from a full pack.

Rank of cards. 3. The cards in each suit rank: K (high), Q, J, A, 10, 9, 8, 7.

4. In trumps only, the K, Q, J, A, and 7 are *honors.*

Chips. 5. For scoring purposes, a common pool of chips is placed on the table. Ten white and eight red chips are sufficient. A red chip is worth six whites. Each player keeps track of his score by drawing the appropriate number of chips from the pool. He must keep his stack in sight so that both players can see the state of the score at all times.

The deal. 6. Each player receives twelve cards, dealt in batches of two or three at a time. The dealer may choose either method, but must adhere to the one he starts.

7. The next card of the pack is turned face up, to fix the trump suit for that deal. If the turn-up is an honor, dealer scores 1 white chip at once.

Declaring. 8. Non-dealer declares first. He exposes any *imperials* (paragraph 11) he holds and takes chips for them. Then he announces his *point* (paragraph 13) and makes the opening lead.

9. Before playing to the opening lead, dealer exposes any imperials he holds and takes chips for them. Then he states whether non-dealer's point is "Good" or "Not good." There is no tie, for dealer must have a higher point to score it. Only one player may score for point, and the suit that scores must be exposed to the opponent. (Dealer may understate his point, when he can still win by omitting one or two of the lowest cards. Thus he may conceal the fact that his long suit is actually longer. But the cards concealed must be those at the bottom in rank.)

10. The order of declaring, as above, must be observed strictly. A player loses claim to his imperials if he refers to point first, or loses the point if he fails to announce it before leading or playing to the opening lead.

11. *Imperials* are certain combinations of cards, as follows:

Carte blanche is a hand without a face card (king, queen, or jack). It wins 2 red chips. (*Optional rule.* When a carte blanche is shown, only this and the other imperials are scored; no *point* is scored and the deal is not played out.)

Sequence is K-Q-J-A of any suit (with or without additional cards in sequence). It wins 1 red chip. (*Optional rule.* A sequence in trumps wins 2 reds.)

Quartet is four cards of the same rank, other than nines and eights. It wins 1 red chip.

12. The dealer, but not his opponent, may construe the turned trump card as part of his hand, for purpose of making sequence and quartet.

13. *Point* is the numerical total of the best suit in the hand, counting ace 11, each face card 10, lower cards their index value. For example, non-dealer holding ◇ K J A 8 7 announces "Point of forty-six." The player with the higher point wins 1 white chip.

The play. 14. Non-dealer may lead any card for the opening lead. The second player to any lead must follow suit if able; must trump if able when void of a plain suit led; and in any case must win the trick if he can. A trick is won by the higher trump, or, if it contains no trump, by the higher card of the suit led. The winner of a trick leads to the next.

15. The cards are not thrown in the center and gathered in tricks; each player keeps his own cards in a pile in front of himself.

Object of play. 16. The objects are: to win trump honors; to win as many tricks as possible.

Scoring. 17. If one player has captured all four of the highest trump honors (K, Q, J, A), he wins 1 red chip for *imperial tombée.* (Modern players eliminate the imperial tombée, which is rare anyway, in order to liven the scoring.)

18. For each trump honor captured in tricks the player wins 1 white chip. If imperial tombée is allowed, both players are construed to score simultaneously for honors at the end of play; if it is eliminated, each honor is scored at the time it is won.

20. Each time a player collects six or more white chips, he returns six whites to the pool and takes a red. Whenever a player takes a red (in exchange for whites or in direct payment of *capot,* etc.) his opponent must return to the pool all white chips he has at the moment. For determination of when whites must be so forfeited, scores must be settled in strict order:

1. Honor turned for trump
2. Imperials in hand
3. Point
4. Imperial tombée (if allowed)
5. Honors won in tricks
6. Majority of tricks

Honors may score simultaneously or consecutively (see paragraph 18). But imperials in hand are construed to score simultaneously, though non-dealer speaks first. Hence the dealer need not return his white chips to the pool, non-dealer having shown an imperial, if he himself has an imperial.

21. The player first to win five red chips wins a game, and the deal then in progress is abandoned.

Irregularities. 22. *Revoke* is failure to follow suit to a lead when able, or failure to trump a plain lead when able, or failure to win a trick when able. A revoke is established if not corrected before the next lead, and an established revoke may be claimed before the cards are mixed for the next deal. The hands must be replayed from the trick on which the revoke (now corrected) occurred, and the revoker may not score for tricks or for honors taken thereafter, while his opponent collects all due chips earned in the replay.

Other irregularities are settled by analogy with the rules for Piquet (page 261).

～ BEZIQUE ～

Bézique is said to be of Scandinavian origin, but its name and earliest popularity (about 1860) are rather associated with France. It is much played in England and France, especially its latest variant Six-pack Bézique. The basic game is described first.

Number of players. 1. Bézique is a game for two, though there are adaptations for three and four players.

The pack. 2. 64 cards, comprising two each of the A, K, Q, J, 10, 9, 8, 7 in each of four suits.

The shuffle and cut. 3. Each player cuts a portion of a shuffled pack and shows the bottom card; low deals first. Non-dealer shuffles, then the dealer. Non-dealer cuts about half the pack, and dealer completes the cut.

The deal. 4. Dealer gives eight cards to each player, three, two and three at a time, beginning with his opponent. He turns the next card, which fixes the trump suit. The undealt cards, or stock, go in the center of the table partly covering the exposed trump card. (*Optional rule.* No trump card is turned; the suit of the first marriage declared is trump.)

5. The turn to deal alternates.

Objects of the game. 6. The objects are two: To show and score for certain declarations; and to win in tricks aces and tens, called *brisques.*

Early play. 7. Non-dealer leads first; thereafter the winner of each trick leads to the next. Any card may be led, and any card played to a lead; such two cards constitute a trick. A trick is won by the higher trump, or, if it contains no trump, by the higher card of the suit led; of identical cards, the one led is the winner.

8. After winning a trick, and making any declaration in accordance with paragraph 9, the winner draws the top card of the stock and his opponent the next card, restoring each hand to eight cards.

Declarations. 9. After winning a trick and before drawing from the stock, a player may show any one of the following combinations face up on the table and score for it immediately:

Marriage (K, Q of the same suit),

in trumps	40
in any other suit	20
Sequence (A, K, Q, J, 10 of trumps)	250
Bézique (♠Q and ◇J)	40
Double bézique	500

Any four aces	100
Any four kings	80
Any four queens	60
Any four jacks	40
Trump 7	10

If dealer turns a seven as trump, he scores 10; thereafter either player may (upon winning a trick) exchange a trump seven for the trump card and score 10.

10. A player may declare and show more than one declaration in a turn, but may score for only one of them at that time, scoring any other of them (or a new declaration) the next time he wins a trick.

11. A card may not be used twice in the same declaration, but may be used in different declarations. The K, Q of trumps may be declared as 40, and the A, J, 10 added at a later turn to score 250; but if the entire sequence is declared at once, the K, Q may no longer be declared as 40. Bézique may be declared as 40 and a second bézique added for 500, but if double bézique is declared at once it counts only 500.

12. A declared card may be led or played as though it were in the player's hand.

Final play. 13. When only two cards remain in the stock, there may be no more declaring; the winner of the next trick takes the face-down card and the loser takes the exposed trump. Play continues, and a player must follow suit to the card led, if able, and must win the trick if able, subject to his duty to follow suit.

Scoring. 14. In addition to the scores for declarations, the winner of each brisque in tricks scores 10 for it, and the last trick scores 10.

15. The first player to reach a score of 1,500 wins the game; if both players reach 1,500 on the same deal, the higher score wins the game. (Or each deal may be played as a separate game.)

Irregularities. 16. *Misdeal.* There must be a redeal by the same dealer if it is discovered, before the first trick is completed, that the wrong player dealt; or that the rules of the shuffle, cut or deal were not observed; or that a player has the wrong number of cards; or that a card is faced in the stock. There must be a redeal if it is discovered at any time that each player has too many cards or that the pack is incorrect.

17. *Incorrect hand.* A hand with too few cards must play on and cannot win the last trick; a hand with too many cards does not draw from the stock until his hand is correct, and on each occasion that he does not draw for this reason, his opponent may look at the two top cards of the stock and select either. In the final play, a hand found to have too many cards is dead; all remaining tricks, and last trick, go to the opponent.

18. *Exposed card.* Non-dealer may demand a redeal if one of his cards is exposed in dealing; there is no penalty for card exposure at any other time. A card found faced in the stock is shuffled into the stock (unless a redeal is required, as provided in paragraph 16).

19. *Illegal draw.* If a player, in drawing, sees a card he is not entitled to see, his opponent when next drawing may look at the two top cards of the stock and select either.

20. *Lead out of turn.* A player may permit his opponent's lead out of turn to stand, or (before playing to it) may require that it be retracted.

21. *Stock incorrect.* If three cards remain in the stock at the end, the exposed trump is dead.

22. *Error in declaring.* A score incorrectly claimed for a declaration stands after the opponent has led or played to the next trick.

23. *Revoke.* If a player fails to play according to law in the final play, the revoke trick and all cards unplayed at that time belong to his opponent, who scores for last trick.

24. *Play of too many cards.* If a player leads or plays more than one card at a time, he may select one card and there is no penalty.

THREE-HAND BEZIQUE

A 96-card pack is used (three 32-card packs shuffled together). The player to dealer's left leads to the first trick, and thereafter the winner of each trick leads to the next; all three play to each trick, in clockwise rotation. Only the winner of the trick may declare. Triple bézique counts 1,500; a player having counted 500 for double bézique may add the third and count 1,500, provided all cards for this declaration are on the table, unplayed.

FOUR-HAND BEZIQUE

A 128-card pack is used (four 32-card packs shuffled together). Each may play for himself, or two against two as partners, who face each other across the table. All four play, to each trick, in clockwise rotation.

In the partnership game, the winner of each trick may declare, or may pass the privilege to his partner (whereupon if his partner cannot declare, the winner of the trick cannot declare). Partners may not consult on which shall declare. A player may put down cards from his own hand to form declarations in combination with cards previously declared by his partner and still exposed on the table, but he may not declare any combination his partner could not legally declare. [That is, if one partner has declared a sequence the other partner may not add a trump king to the queen in the sequence and score for a marriage.]

After the last card of the stock has been drawn, each player in turn must beat the highest card previously played to a trick, if able, even if it was his partner's.

Double bézique counts 500 and triple bézique 1,500 only if all the cards come from the hand of the same player.

Game is usually set at 2,000 points.

R U B I C O N   B E Z I Q U E

Follow all the rules of Bézique, except:

The pack is 128 cards (two full Bézique packs shuffled together). Nine cards are dealt to each player, three at a time. No trump is turned, the trump suit being fixed by the first marriage declared; and there is no count for the seven of trumps.

In addition to the declarations in Bézique (paragraph 9), the following declarations count:

Non-trump sequence ("back door")	150
Triple bézique	1500
Quadruple bézique	4500
Carte blanche	50

Carte blanche is a hand originally dealt without a face card (it may contain an ace). The holder shows it and scores for it; thereafter, in each successive turn in which he does not draw a face card, he may show the card drawn and score 50 again. Once he draws a face card he may no longer score for carte blanche.

Single, double, triple and quadruple bézique may be scored singly and then the entire score for the new combination counted as it is declared, provided all the cards required for each combination are showing on the table, unplayed, at the time it is declared.

When any card of a declaration is played from the table, the entire declaration may be scored in a later turn by restoring that card or its equivalent. [For example: A player declares four queens, scoring 60. He plays one of the queens, the ◇Q. Subsequently, upon winning a trick, he adds a ◇Q or any other queen and scores 60 again.]

Last trick counts 50. Brisques do not count unless necessary to break a tie, or in case of a rubicon.

Each deal is a game; there is a bonus of 500 for winning the game. It is a rubicon if the loser's score is under 1,000; the winner then receives all his own points, plus all the loser's points, plus all the brisques (320), plus 1,000 instead of 500 for game.

SIX-PACK BEZIQUE

Also called Chinese Bézique, this is the most popular development of Rubicon Bézique. Six 32-card packs are shuffled together, making a 192-card pack. Both players shuffle, non-dealer cuts, then dealer lifts off a portion of the pack and non-dealer guesses how many cards he lifted off: If dealer lifted exactly 24 cards he scores 250; non-dealer, if he guessed correctly, scores 150. Twelve cards are dealt to each player, three at a time.

The rules are as in Rubicon Bézique, except that brisques never count, so the played cards are left piled in a heap on the table. The cards required for bézique vary with the trump suit:

♠Q and ♢J if spades are trumps
♢Q and ♠J if diamonds are trumps
♡Q and ♣J if hearts are trumps
♣Q and ♡J if clubs are trumps

Four tens of trumps may be declared and count 900; four aces of trumps count 1,000, four kings of trumps 800, four queens of trumps 600, four jacks of trumps 400. Carte blanche counts 250.

The same suit may not become trump in two successive deals; a marriage of the previous trump suit may be declared first in any deal, but then counts only 20 and does not fix the trump suit.

Each deal is a game; the bonus for game is 1,000; the loser is rubiconed if his score is less than 3,000, whereupon the winner scores the totals of both players plus 1,000 for game.

EIGHT-PACK BEZIQUE

This is the same as Six-pack Bézique, but played with eight 32-card packs shuffled together, 256 cards in all; fifteen cards are dealt to each player, three at a time; the dealer receives his 250-point bonus if he lifts off exactly 30 cards for dealing. In addition to the declarations in Six-pack Bézique, there is a score of 2,000 for five aces of trumps, 1,800 for five tens of trumps, 1,600 for five kings of trumps, 1,200 for five queens of trumps, and 800 for five jacks of trumps. Quintuple bézique counts 9,000. The loser is rubiconed if his score is less than 5,000.

POLISH BEZIQUE

Regular Bézique is played, except that a player may remove from the tricks he wins all face cards, aces, and the ten of trumps, and may use these to form melds; but such cards form separate melds. They may not be combined with cards in the hand, or with cards melded from the hand. Brisques among them still score at the end.

CINQ CENTS (FIVE HUNDRED)

This is an obsolete variant of Bézique, played with the Piquet pack of 32 cards. Cards won in tricks count as in Pinochle: ace 11, ten 10, king 4, queen 3, jack 2. Melds count as in Bézique, there being of course no double bézique, and except that a sequence (A-K-Q-J-10) in a plain suit has a melding value of 120. A player may declare himself out as in two-hand Pinochle. If no one declares out and both players reach 500 on the same deal, game becomes 600 (unless one player has reached 600 while the other has reached 500, in which case it becomes 700), and so on by increments of 100. In this game, bézique (♠Q-♢J) is called binage, and Foster believed that it was from mispronunciation of this term that the name Pinochle developed.

POINTERS ON BEZIQUE PLAY

The game Bézique is well named: The strategy is dominated by the 500-point meld of double bézique. Never, so long as any hope remains of making this meld (though there is only one chance in sixteen or more of making it) does one play a queen of spades or jack of diamonds.

The melds are generally more important than they are in two-hand Pinochle, which is essentially the same game (whereupon the Bézique student may profit from reading the pointers on two-hand Pinochle, page 289). In Bézique there are only 160 points to be scored by cards, and with the 64-card pack there are more opportunities for melding. Therefore possible melding cards should be held on the chance that fitting cards will be drawn, but once a melding combination is completed in the hand the trick should be won, even if it means sacrificing trump length in the final play, to get the meld down and release the cards for play on lost tricks.

In Rubicon Bézique and its derivatives (Six-pack and Eight-pack Bézique) a player who can make the trump should do so, even if it means sacrificing an ace of the suit that will be trump. With four or more packs in play, a duplicate of the lost card will probably be drawn eventually. The danger is always great that the opponent will make his own long suit trump and so dominate the melding and play throughout the deal.

SIXTY-SIX

Once the most popular two-hand card game in Germany, Sixty-Six is related to Bézique; it probably preceded Bézique.

Number of players. 1. Two. But variants for three and four have also been devised.

The pack. 2. A pack of 24 cards, made by discarding all cards below the nines from a full pack.

Rank of cards. 3. The cards in each suit rank: A (high), 10, K, Q, J, 9.

The deal. 4. The players cut for deal; high deals. The dealer shuffles the pack and non-dealer cuts it. Each player receives six cards, dealt in batches of three at a time. The rest of the pack is placed face down to form the *stock*. The top card is turned over, and placed face up under the stock. This is the *trump card;* it fixes the trump suit for the deal.

The play. 5. Non-dealer makes the opening lead. During the early play, before the stock is exhausted or closed (paragraph 8), the second player to a trick may play any card—he need not follow suit. A trick is won by the higher trump or by the higher card of the suit led. The winner of a trick draws the top card of the stock, and his opponent takes the next card. Then the winner leads to the next trick.

6. *Trump card.* In his turn to play, and provided that he has won at least one trick, a player having the nine of trumps may exchange it for the trump card. But this privilege may not be exercised if the last face-down card of the stock happens to be the nine; the player drawing it must keep it, while his opponent gets the trump card.

7. *Marriages.* In his turn to lead, and provided that he has won at least one trick, a player having a *marriage* may meld and score it. A marriage is a king and queen of the same suit. A trump marriage scores 40, a plain marriage 20. Having shown the marriage, the player must then lead one of the cards. The non-dealer may show a marriage when he wishes to lead one of the cards for the opening lead, but he is not credited with the score until he wins a trick. (Some play that a marriage may be shown and scored at any time that it brings the player's score to 66 or over.)

8. *Closing.* A player, in his turn to lead, may close, bringing into effect the rules of later play before the stock is exhausted. Closure is signified by turning the trump card face down. Marriages may still be melded after the closure.

9. After the stock is exhausted, or after either player closes, the six cards remaining in each hand are played out. At this time, the second player to a trick must follow suit if able; if unable, the hand may play any card.

Object of play. 10. The object is to be the first to reach a total of 66 points in the deal. The points that can be scored are: (a) marriages; (b) counting cards won in tricks; (c) winning last trick, which counts 10 points; but this is not scored if, due to closure, the stock is not exhausted.

11. The cards won in tricks count as follows:

Each ace	11
Each ten	10
Each king	4
Each queen	3
Each jack	2
(No count for nines.)	

Scoring. 12. A player may at any time (in or out of his turn to play) claim that he has reached 66. The claim ends the play. If it is found to be correct, the claimant scores 1 game point if the loser has taken 33 points or more; 2 game points if the loser has less than 33 (*schneider*); or 3 game points if the loser has won not a single trick (*schwarz*). If the claim is found erroneous, the opponent scores 2 game points.

13. If play ends without a claim, the scores are determined, and if one player has 66 or more, the other less, the winner scores as in paragraph 12. If both have 66 or more, or both have 65, there is no score for the deal, but the winner of the next deal is credited with 1 additional game point.

14. The player first to reach a total of 7 *game points* wins a game.

Irregularities. 1. *Redeal.* The same dealer must deal again, if non-dealer so requires before playing to the first trick, when a card is exposed in dealing or in the stock, or if either player has too few cards, or if the pack was not properly shuffled, cut and dealt.

2. There must be a redeal by the same dealer if the pack is incorrect or if, before the first trick is completed, it is ascertained that a player has too many cards.

3. *Incorrect hand.* Unless a redeal is required, a hand with too few cards draws from the stock, a hand with too many cards refrains from drawing, until the hand is correct; but if the stock is exhausted or closed, the incorrect hand loses the game (3 game points).

4. *Revoke.* A player who does not follow suit when able, after the stock is exhausted or closed, loses the game (3 game points).

5. *Stock incorrect.* If the stock has three cards at the end, the last (trump) card is dead.

THREE-HAND SIXTY-SIX

Dealer takes no cards, and scores as many game points as are won on his deal by either of the players. If neither scores 66, or both score 66 or more but fail to announce it, dealer scores 1 game point and active players nothing. Game is 7 game points. A dealer cannot score enough to win game. His seventh point must be won when he is an active player.

FOUR-HAND SIXTY-SIX

Use the 32-card pack (A, 10, K, Q, J, 9, 8, 7 of each suit).

Eight cards are dealt to each player—three, then two, then three, in rotation to the left, beginning with eldest hand. Last card is turned for trump and belongs to dealer.

Eldest hand leads, and each succeeding player in turn must not only follow suit, but must win the trick if possible. Having no card of the suit led, a player must trump or overtrump if he can.

Scoring is the same as in the two-hand game, except that there are no marriages. A side counting 66 or more, but less than 100, scores 1 game point; over 100 and less than 130, 2 points; if it takes every trick (130), 3 points. If each side has 65, neither scores, and 1 game point is added to the score of the winners of next hand.

Game is 7 game points. In some localities the ten of trumps counts 1 game point for the side winning it in addition to its value as a scoring card. If one side has 6 game points and wins the ten of trumps on a trick, that side scores game immediately.

MARRIAGE

This is another version of Bézique, identical with Sixty-Six except:

L'amour may also be melded: this is the ace and ten of the same suit, counting 60 in trumps and 30 in a plain suit. For winning the last six tricks, a player scores 20, additional to the 10 for last. Every deal is played out, there being no fixed objective as in Sixty-Six. The player with the higher score for the deal scores 1, 2, or 4 game points, according to the score of the loser (2 for schneider, 4 for schwarz).

JASS

Number of players. 1. Two. But variants for three or four have been devised.

The pack. 2. A pack of 36 cards, made by discarding all cards below the sixes from a full pack.

Rank of cards. 3. In the trump suit the cards rank: J (high), 9, A, K, Q, 10, 8, 7, 6. (The nine is called *nell*, obviously a corruption of *manille* or *menel* meaning the lowest card when elevated to high rank.) In each plain suit the cards rank: A (high), K, Q, J, 10, 9, 8, 7, 6.

The deal. 4. Each player receives nine cards, dealt in batches of three at a time. The rest of the pack is placed face down to form the *stock*. The top card is turned over and placed under the stock; this is the trump card: it fixes the trump suit for the deal.

The play. 5. Non-dealer makes the opening lead. Until the stock is exhausted, the second player to a trick may play any card—he need not follow suit. A trick is won by the higher trump or the higher card of the suit led. The winner of a trick draws the top card of the stock; the opponent then draws the next card. The winner then leads to the next trick.

6. In his turn to lead, a player may meld any one (no more) of the following combinations:

Four jacks	200
Four aces, kings, or queens	100
Five cards of any suit in sequence	100
Four cards of any suit in sequence	50
Three cards of any suit in sequence	20
King and queen of trumps	20

For sequences, the rank A, K, Q, J, 10, 9, 8, 7, 6 obtains in the trump suit as well as in other suits.

7. After the stock is exhausted, the final nine tricks are played out. At this time, there may be no more melding. The second player to a trick must follow suit if able, and must win the trick in any way possible, if able, except that the jack of trumps may be withheld when the hand is void of a plain suit led and has no other trump.

Scoring. 8. At the end of play, each player is credited with what he won in tricks as follows:

Jack of trumps	20
Nine of trumps	14

Each ace	11
Each king	4
Each queen	3
Each jack (other than jack of trumps)	2
(No count for lower cards.)	

9. A running total score is kept for each player, and the first to reach 1,000 (or any other agreed amount) wins a game.

Irregularities. See Klaberjass, page 280.

FOUR-HAND JASS

Each plays for himself. The entire pack is dealt, nine cards to each player; the last card is turned to fix the trumps, but is part of the dealer's hand; except that the holder of the six of trumps may exchange it for the turned card, if he does so before playing to the first trick. Eldest hand (player at dealer's left) leads first, and each trick consists of four cards, one from each player in rotation; the winner of each trick leads to the next. A player may meld only in his turn and before playing to the first trick. Each player must follow suit to the lead if able, and must if able play a card that would win the trick over any played before; except that if his only trump is the jack, he need not trump a plain-suit lead with it. Scoring is as in two-hand Jass.

THREE-HAND JASS

The deal and play are the same as in four-hand Jass. The fourth hand is a widow, for which a player may exchange his hand, dealer having precedence, then eldest hand. If dealer exchanges, another player with the trump six may still exchange it for the turned trump card. A player may not exchange the trump six for the trump card and also exchange his hand for the widow.

KLABERJASS

Well-known in central Europe, Klaberjass reached the United States early in this century via the immigrant colonies along the Eastern seaboard. In the writings of Damon Runyon and others, the game is frequently mentioned, as Klob, Clob, Klab, Kalaber, and, often, Kalabriàs (which is a different game). The name Klaberjass means "jack of clubs," which originally was always the highest trump.

Number of players. 1. Two active players.

The pack. 2. A pack of 32 cards, made by discarding all cards below the sevens from a full pack.

Rank of cards. 3. In the trump suit the cards rank: J (high), 9, A, 10, K, Q, 8, 7. The jack is called *jass* or *jasz*, and the nine is called *menel*. In plain suits the rank is: A (high), 10, K, Q, J, 9, 8, 7.

The deal. 4. Each player receives six cards, dealt in batches of three at a time. The next card of the pack is turned face up and placed partly underneath it. This is the *trump card;* it proposes the trump suit for that deal.

Bidding. 5. Non-dealer declares first: he may *pass, take,* or *schmeiss.* To take is to accept the turned card for trump. To schmeiss is to propose that the cards be thrown in and redealt.

6. If non-dealer calls schmeiss, dealer may accede (saying "Yes"), in which case the deal is abandoned; or may refuse by saying "Take it." This refusal makes non-dealer the *maker* of trump, just as though he had *taken* voluntarily.

7. If non-dealer passes, dealer may pass, take, or schmeiss. Non-dealer may accept or refuse a schmeiss.

8. If both players pass in the first round, non-dealer may then pass again, or schmeiss, or name a suit for trump other than that rejected. After a schmeiss dealer may accept, or may refuse, and in the latter case non-dealer must name a new trump suit. If non-dealer passes a second time, dealer may name a new trump suit, or he may pass again; in the latter case the deal is abandoned without score.

9. Whoever takes, or is refused schmeiss, or names a new trump suit, is the maker of the trump.

Second deal. 10. The trump suit being decided, the dealer gives a batch of three more cards to each hand. By custom he then turns the bottom card of the pack face up, putting it on top. (The custom probably arose from the fact that non-dealer often sights the bottom card; formal exposure equalizes matters by letting the dealer see it too.)

Sequence. 11. Before the opening lead, a player may declare and score for a sequence of three or more cards in the same suit. For this purpose alone, the rank of every suit including trumps is: A (high), K, Q, J, 10, 9, 8, 7. A sequence of three counts 20, of four or more, 50.

12. Only one player may score for sequences. Non-dealer, holding one or more sequences, should say "Twenty," or "Fifty," the value of his best sequence. If dealer has no equal sequence, he says "Good." With a higher sequence, he shows it. With a sequence of equal length he asks the highest card in non-dealer's sequence, and so on.

13. A sequence worth 50 outranks one worth 20; as between sequences of equal length, the higher in rank takes precedence; as between two equal in length and rank, a trump sequence beats a plain sequence, or non-dealer wins if both are plain. The player entitled to score his best sequence may also score any additional sequences he holds. Sequences that score must be exposed face up after the first trick is complete; the cards may then be taken back into the hand.

14. If non-dealer makes the opening lead without declaring a sequence, he loses the right to do so. Having no sequence, he should properly say

"I lead" or other cautionary words before leading; if he does give notice, dealer must at once expose any sequence he wishes to score; if non-dealer fails to give notice, dealer may declare even after opening lead, but before he plays to the trick.

The play. 15. Non-dealer makes the opening lead. He may lead any card. After any lead, the second player must follow suit if able, and if void of a plain suit led must trump if able. On a trump lead the second player must "go over" if able—play a higher trump. A trick is won by the higher trump, or by the higher card of the suit led. The winner of a trick leads to the next.

16. *Dix.* When the turned card is made the trump, either player holding the seven of trumps (called dix) may exchange it for the trump card before playing to the first trick. The exchange is not compulsory, and has no scoring value, but may be advantageous by giving his hand a more valuable trump.

17. *Bella.* If one player has both the king and queen of trumps, he may score 20 by saying "Bella" at the time he plays the second of the two cards. There is no score without the announcement. It is not compulsory to score bella—the trump maker omits doing so when he sees that he must go bete.

Object of play. 18. Each player strives to win the counting cards in tricks, and to win *stich*, the last trick, which counts 10. The counting cards are:

Jass (jack of trumps)	20
Menel (nine of trumps)	14
Each ace	11
Each ten	10
Each king	4
Each queen	3
Each jack (except jass)	2
(No count for lower cards.)	

Scoring. 19. At the end of play, each player totals what he has made in sequences, bella, stich, and counting cards taken in tricks. If the trump maker has the higher total, each player scores his total. If the totals are equal, only the opponent of the maker scores. If the maker has the lower score, he is bete and the opponent scores the sum of the two totals.

20. The player first to reach a total of 500 points wins a game. Except by agreement, there is no "counting out" during a deal. If both players reach 500 in the same deal, it is played out, and the higher total wins.

Irregularities. 21. *Exposed card.* If a card that would go to non-dealer is exposed in dealing, that player may accept it or may demand a new deal before making any bid. If dealer exposed a card dealt to himself he must accept it. If a card is found faced in the pack, during the deal, either player if he has not looked at his cards may demand a redeal. If a player exposes one of his own cards after his first bid, he has no redress.

22. *Wrong number of cards.* If too many or too few cards are dealt to either hand, non-dealer, if he has not made his first bid, may decide whether there shall be a redeal or the error shall be corrected. In any other case the error must be corrected: a short hand draws additional cards from the top of the stock; a long hand is placed face down, and the opponent draws out each excess card and buries it in the stock without looking at it.

23. *False declaration.* If a player asks "how high?" or otherwise obtains unwarranted information about an adverse sequence when he himself has none or the superiority of the other has already been established, or otherwise causes his opponent to give information about his hand that the opponent could correctly have withheld, the offender loses the deal, and his opponent scores all the points for sequences, bella, stich, and counting cards.

24. *Revoke.* A revoke is failure to follow suit when able, or to trump when able, or to go over a trump lead when able. A revoke may be corrected without penalty before the next lead. In any other case, the opponent scores all the points for sequences, bella, stich, and counting cards.

25. *Turned cards.* If the dealer, after serving the three additional cards to each hand, omits turning the bottom card of the pack face up, non-dealer may decide whether or not this card shall be exposed at all. If a player erroneously exchanges a seven for the exposed bottom card or for the trump card when it was rejected, the opponent may require retraction ˚of the seven if he does so before playing to the next trick; otherwise the exchange stands as regular.

Pointers on Klaberjass play. The total points at stake per deal averages 110. The trump maker to avoid bete must on average win 60 points. As he has nine cards in the play, six in the bidding, the normal requirement for making the trump is a hand that can probably win 40 points. The typical hand contains jass, an ace, and a ten.

Trump length is not so vital as strength. Having jass, even alone, many experienced players will take on a hand worth only about 35. Lacking both jass and menel, be conservative, for either of these cards held by or dealt to your opponent may put you bete. With strong side cards and little in trumps, or with a sequence, let your opponent take or name a trump.

Normally, do not schmeiss on the first round as non-dealer. If dealer is strong enough to take, he will refuse, and will then collect all your points as well as his own. But the schmeiss gives scope for a certain amount of bluffing, or rather, psychological jockeying. With a borderline hand for a take, but even less prospect at any other trump, you may try an unorthodox schmeiss for the purpose of preventing dealer from naming a new trump on the second round. If he is a natural pessimist, or is bowed down by your previous good luck in drawing strong cards, he may leap at the chance to abandon the deal.

As dealer, after your opponent passes, use the schmeiss as a straight-forward device to deprive him of the chance to name a new trump. The typical hand for this schmeiss is too weak for a regular take—say about a 30-point prospect—but is better prepared to accept the turned suit than another.

Much the same considerations apply to non-dealer, after two passes. Schmeiss in this position to avoid letting dealer name his own trump, if you have a borderline hand for a make of your own. Or, schmeiss occasionally as an outright bluff in a desperate situation.

Do not count on the draw (the three extra cards) to furnish you specific high cards; your opponent has as good a chance to improve as you. If you do not start off with at least three cards that count 10 or more, keep on passing unless you choose to schmeiss as a bluff. But the draw has good prospect of giving you an extra card in any named suit. Therefore do not hesitate to value the blank menel or a blank ten as you would a guarded card. Even if you do not draw a guard, the menel or ten may still be high in its suit.

BELOTTE or BELOTE

The popular French game of Belotte is a two-hand game almost identical in its mechanics with Klaberjass. There are these differences: The highest-ranking melds are four of a kind, counting 200 for four jacks and 100 for four nines, aces, tens, kings or queens, the groups ranking in that order. A five-card sequence is worth 50, a four-card sequence 40, a three-card sequence 20. The player having the highest-ranking group scores all groups in his hand; the player having the highest-ranking sequence scores all sequences in his hand. Thus, both players may score for melds, each in a different classification. If the maker does not score more points than his opponent, he loses his own points but the opponent does not score the combined totals of both players. The bid equivalent to schmeiss is called *valse* (waltz). Modern variations of Belotte have incorporated the factors of bidding and doubling, copied from Bridge.

CLABBER

This is a game similar to Klaberjass and Belotte, playable by two, three or four. Pairs may play as partners. In a three-hand game, nine cards are dealt to each player; in a four-hand game, eight cards, dealer's last card being turned for trump.

Each player in turn, beginning with eldest hand, may either accept the first trump or pass; if all pass in the first round, each player in turn has the right to name the trump suit. The bid of schmeiss is not used. If all players pass twice each, there is a new deal. If any player names a trump, he becomes the maker and must outscore the other players combined (or, in a partnership game, his side must outscore the other side). The player at dealer's left always leads to the next trick.

ALSOS

Alsós is a popular Hungarian game, almost identical with Klaberjass, but more often played by three than by two. Almost all the Klaberjass rules apply: The 32-card pack is used; the deal is six cards to each player, after which a trump card and the bottom card are turned. In the first round of bidding, each player in turn may accept the turned trump or pass. If all pass, three more cards are dealt to each. On the second round of bidding, each may bid or pass, and the rank in bidding is no-trump (high), clubs, hearts, diamonds, spades; a previous bid to name the trump may thus be overcalled.

Sequences score 20 for three cards, 50 for four cards, 100 for five or more cards. Four of a kind count 80, and the rank is J, 9, A, 10, K, Q, 8, 7 in the trump suit, A, 10, K, Q, J, 9, 8, 7 at no trump, this being the rank of cards in trump and plain suits respectively. Bela (K-Q of trump) scores as played. These combinations are claimed and scored as in Klaberjass.

The bidder may increase his score by selecting any of the following "games" or declarations:

Cassa—to win the game (majority of points) including a bela; also called *bela cassa.*

Tous les trois (all three)—to win J 9 7 of trumps.

Csalad (the family)—to win A K Q of trumps.

All the trumps—to win A K Q J 10 9 of trumps.

Forty-four—to win all four aces.

Ultimo—to win the last trick with the trump 7.

Absolute—to win 82 points at a trump, 62 at no trump.

One hundred—to win 100 points at a trump, 80 at no trump.

Two hundred—to win 200 at a trump, 180 at no trump (but melds may be included).

Uhu—to win the next-to-last trick with the ◇A (or, if diamonds are trumps, with the ♡A).

Volat—to win all nine tricks.

Bettli—to win no trick.

An opponent of the bidder may double his declaration.

The count of cards won in tricks, and the rules of play, are as in Klaberjass.

Felsos. Alsós is "the jack game," so-called because the alsó, in Hungarian, is the jack, and the jack is the highest card. Felsös for the same reason is "the queen game," otherwise similar to Alsós.

Kalabrias, the name by which Klaberjass is often erroneously called, is an ancestor of Alsós (and perhaps of Klaberjass), but is a game for three active players. Usually there are four players at the table. Kalaber is a two-hand form of this game. Both have been supplanted by Alsós.

⟶ PINOCHLE ⟵

There are several games called Pinochle, and several related games not bearing its name. All these games are usually grouped in games literature as "the Bézique family," but only the Pinochle division of this family is widely popular in the United States. The principal forms of Pinochle are for two, three, and four players. The essential characteristics are: use of a 48-card pack; rank of the tenspot next below the ace and above the king; a primary object of melding (German: announcing) certain combinations of cards whose point-values are the same in all forms of the game; an object in play of winning counting cards in tricks.

History. Little is known of the history of any basic card game; less is known of the history of Pinochle than of most, and the etymology of its name is among the most doubtful. By various spellings—Pea-knuckle, Binocle, Pinocle, Penuchle—it has appeared in games books since about 1864. Legends about its origin are many but untrustworthy; one of the most persistent makes it a German game, but it is unknown there. Two-hand Pinochle is virtually Bézique by a different name; three-hand Auction Pinochle was almost surely constructed in the United States, by Central European immigrants, German- or Yiddish-speaking, as a medley of Pinochle, Tarok, and Skat. Partnership Pinochle grew out of one or the other or both, and the outstanding thing about this variant is the manner in which it has become one of the most popular family games of rural America, especially in the mid-West. In the 1940s and '50s Double-pack Pinochle became the most popular member of the family and Auction Pinochle (three-hand) declined in popularity.

The laws of the Pinochle games, on the following pages, are copyright 1951, 1949 and are reprinted by permission.

LAWS OF TWO-HAND PINOCHLE
(48-card Pack) *

The pack. 1. 48 cards, two each of A, K, Q, J, 10 and 9 in each of four suits, spades, hearts, diamonds and clubs.

Rank of cards. 2. A (high), 10, K, Q, J, 9.

The draw. 3. Each player lifts a portion of the pack, taking no more than half the cards remaining. Each then shows the bottom card of the portion he cut. Lower card determines the first dealer.

The shuffle and cut. 4. Both players may shuffle, dealer having the right to shuffle last. Non-dealer cuts the pack by lifting off no fewer than

---
* These laws also apply to the game with the 64-card pack, with the exceptions noted on page 290.

five nor more than forty-three cards. Dealer closes the cut by placing the remainder of the pack on top of the portion cut by non-dealer.

The deal. 5. The winner of each hand deals the next, if each hand is played as a separate game. When the game of 1,000 points is played, the deal alternates. Dealer gives twelve cards to each player, three at a time, beginning with his opponent.

The trump card and stock. 6. Dealer turns up the twenty-fifth card of the pack (next card after completing the deal) as the trump card. Every other card of same suit as the trump card is also a trump during that hand.

The undealt balance of the pack is left face down on the table, becoming the stock. The trump card is placed face up partly underneath the stock. If the trump card is a nine, dealer scores 10 immediately.

First lead. 7. The first lead is made by non-dealer.

Objects of the play. 8. The objects of the play are to score points by melding, by winning cards that count in tricks, and by taking last trick.

Early play. 9. The period from the first lead until the lead to the thirteenth trick is called early play. During this period, the following rules apply:

The card led, and the card then played by opponent of the leader, constitute a trick. Both the leader and opponent may play any cards they wish. There is no obligation to follow suit or to trump. A trick containing a trump is won by the higher trump; one containing no trump is won by the higher card of the suit led. If two cards identical in suit and rank are played to the same trick, the leader wins it. Each player gathers the tricks won by himself, and the winner of a trick leads to the next.

After a trick is won, and before the next lead, the winner draws the top card of the stock, and his opponent draws the next. Each hand is thus restored to twelve cards before the next lead.

Melds. 10. Any of the following combinations melded during the early play scores as indicated.

SEQUENCES	
A-K-Q-J-10 of trumps (flush)	150
K-Q of trumps (royal marriage)	40
K-Q of any other suit (marriage)	20
GROUPS	
♠A—♡A—◇A—♣A (100 aces)	100
♠K—♡K—◇K—♣K (80 kings)	80
♠Q—♡Q—◇Q—♣Q (60 queens)	60
♠J–♡J–◇J–♣J (40 jacks)	40
SPECIAL	
♠Q—◇J (pinochle)	40
9 of trumps (dix, pronounced deece)	10

Restrictions on melding. 11. (a) A player may meld only after having won a trick, and before drawing from the stock.

(b) A dix may be exchanged for the trump card, scoring also 10 as a meld. This exchange, or the meld of the second dix, may be made at the same time as another meld.

(c) With exception of the dix, a player may in one turn meld only one of the combinations listed in Section 10. Double combinations, such as double pinochle, are barred, but may be melded on two different turns as two melds.

(d) All melded cards must be left face up on the table until the end of the early play, or until played.

(e) For each additional meld, at least one card must be taken from the hand and placed on the table.

(f) A card already on the table may be used as part of a new meld under a different heading. A royal marriage on the table may be used as part of a flush by addition of A-10-J, but if all five cards are melded at once they score only for flush, not for marriage in addition. In all other cases, no card on the table may be used in another meld under the same heading. Duplicate melds require complete duplication of cards.

(g) If the addition of cards from the hand completes more than one additional meld, only one of them may be counted.*

(h) Cards on the table are still part of the player's hand and may be played at any time.

Later play. 12. The winner of the twelfth trick must expose the card he draws from the stock. His opponent then takes the last card (the trump card or the dix exchanged for it). Each player picks up from the table all cards remaining from his melds. The ensuing period, from the lead to the thirteenth trick to the final trick, is called later play. During this period the following rules obtain:

The leader may lead any card. His opponent must follow suit if able, and if the lead is a trump he must win if able. If void of the suit led, opponent must play a trump if able. If two cards identical in suit and rank are played to the same trick, the leader wins it. Otherwise, the trick is won by the higher trump, or, if the trick contains no trump, by the higher card of the suit led. The winner of a trick leads to the next.

Scoring. 13. At the end of play, each player counts the points he has won in tricks† as follows:

---

* For example, with 80 kings and 40 jacks on the table, addition of the ♠Q scores for pinochle but not for the marriage also. Another example: with three marriages in different suits on the table, addition of a marriage in the fourth suit would complete a "round trip"—kings, queens, and marriage. But only one score can be claimed; it would therefore be foolish to meld the marriage. The king should be melded alone for score of 80, and later the queen for score of 60, if opportunity offers.

† In practice it is customary for the winner of last trick alone to count, his opponent being credited with the difference from 250.

Each ace	11
Each ten	10
Each king	4
Each queen	3
Each jack	2
Last trick	10

Nines have no scoring value when won in tricks.

The total of points won in tricks is taken to the higher ten when the final digit is 7, 8 or 9, and to the lower ten when it is less; the total for both players together therefore may be 250 or 240.

Each player's score for the deal is the points won in tricks plus the points scored by melding.

The game. 14. The player who first reaches a total of 1,000 points, his opponent having less than 1,000, wins a game. If both reach 1,000 in the same deal, game becomes 1,250; and if both reach 1,250 in the same deal, game becomes 1,500; and so on by increments of 250.

(*Alternative method:* Each deal may be treated as a separate game; see page 288.)

Declaring out. 15. A player may at any time declare out, that is, claim that he has reached a total required to win a game. Play then ceases, and if the claim is found to be correct, the claimant wins the game even though his opponent is found to have more points. If the claim is incorrect, the claimant loses the game forthwith.

Irregularities. 16. *Exposed cards.* If dealer exposes a card going to himself, he must accept it; neither player may demand a new deal.

If dealer exposes a card going to his opponent, the latter may accept it or may demand a new deal by the same dealer.

If more than one card of the stock is exposed in turning the trump card, all are shuffled in the stock and opponent of dealer then cuts a card to be the trump card.

If after play has begun a card is found faced in the stock, the stock except for the trump card is shuffled and play continues.

There is no penalty for a player's exposure of any card belonging to his hand.

17. *Wrong number of cards.* If the wrong number of cards is dealt to either hand, either player may demand a new deal by the same dealer before playing to the first trick. In all other cases, play continues and the error is rectified as below.

If, after play has begun, a player is found to have too many or too few cards, he must draw a sufficient number of cards from the stock, or omit drawing any card a sufficient number of turns, to restore his hand to twelve cards. During the time that his hand is incorrect he may not meld. (If each deal is treated as a separate game, a player whose hand is incorrect, and who has played any card, loses the game forthwith.)

18. *Stock incorrect.* If at any time it is found that the number of cards

in the stock is odd when it should be even, both hands being correct, and the pack being correct, play continues. When only two cards remain in the stock, the player whose turn it is to draw may elect to take the trump card or the other. If he takes the trump card, the other is then exposed. The rejected card is in either case dead and does not count for either player.

19. *Incorrect draw.* If a player draws from the stock out of turn, his opponent may let the draw stand, or may appropriate the card incorrectly drawn and require the offender to expose the card he then draws.

If a player draws more than one card at a turn, the cards illegally drawn must be exposed and then replaced on top of the stock.

20. *Lead out of turn.* If a player leads out of turn, his opponent may allow the lead to stand as regular or may require it to be withdrawn without penalty.

21. *Revoke.* A player revokes if in the later play he fails, when able, to follow suit to a lead, to trump, or to win a trump lead. A player may correct a revoke before he has played to the next trick, and if his opponent has led to the next trick, such lead may be retracted after correction of the revoke.

If a revoke stands uncorrected, the offender may score nothing for points taken in tricks in that deal, but play continues to determine his opponent's score. (If each deal is treated as a separate game, a player who revokes and fails to make correction loses the game forthwith.)

22. *Error in scoring.* An error in entering a score, or in announcing the value of a meld, must be corrected on demand of either player if he has not played to the next trick; otherwise the score stands as recorded.

VARIATIONS IN LAWS

Any one of the following customs will be found prevalent in some localities or among some players.

Special melds. Many players count 300 for double pinochle (two jacks of diamonds and two queens of spades) if melded at the same time. Some count 80 for the meld "grand pinochle" (♠K-Q ◊J) if melded at the same time, whether or not spades are trumps.

Game. Many play that each deal is a separate game. The winner of each hand then deals the next. Some play that the game counts double when spades are trumps. A revoke, or having too many cards (after the holder has made any play), loses the game forthwith.

Declaring out. Many play that a claim to be out must be consummated by thereafter winning a trick; some play that the trick must be won on a lead from the claimant's own hand. In either case, the opponent may likewise declare himself out before the prior claim is consummated, in which case the winner will be whichever first wins the trick as required. If neither does so, and both have passed the game mark at the end of the play, the game continues for the next-higher score in accordance with paragraph 14 of the laws.

Doubling. When each deal is a separate game, doubling may be played, as in Backgammon (page 390): A player may double after winning a trick and drawing, but before leading to the next trick; his opponent may resign the game at its current value, or accept and play on at doubled value. A double may be proposed only by a player who did not double last in that deal.

POINTERS ON TWO-HAND PINOCHLE

It is desirable except in unusual circumstances to play for melds rather than to win counting cards during the early play. The score by melds does not necessarily run materially higher than the score by cards, but it is far more influenced by choice of plays. While several draws from the stock remain, one should hold on to cards that may be built into melds by fortunate draws from the stock.

During this period, it is better to let tricks go by, throwing worthless cards on them—even when by winning the trick the opponent can meld—than to win tricks with cards that may become melds. However, 40 jacks is a meld hardly worth saving for; the trump jack and diamond jack should be saved, and the others may be tossed on the opponent's leads when one is pressed for a play. A plain-suit ten may always be used to win a trick, but often should be saved until a meld is ready. Marriages of plain suits should be melded as soon as possible, to make the cards in them available for play (unless there seems to be hope of making 60 queens or 80 kings).

The odds are about 5 to 1 against getting a particular card in three draws; about 3 to 1 against getting it in four draws; assuming you do not hold and have not seen the duplicate of that card.

In leading, a long plain suit is most likely to embarrass the opponent, after it has been led two or three times. The ten of a plain suit is a lead very likely to win the trick, since the opponent will seldom sacrifice a trump or the chance for 100 aces to win it. This lead becomes futile when the opponent has melded 100 aces, for then he can put an ace to no better use than to win a ten.

It is well to hold trumps as long as possible, to build up a strong hand for the later play, especially with the purpose of winning last trick. Toward the end of the early play, however, it will be necessary to lead one or several trumps if there is danger that the opponent has made a flush. Seldom will any other lead surely prevent his winning the trick and melding his flush.

Every melding occasion calls for a review of the number of melding opportunities that will remain; ordinarily the less valuable melds should be made first, but not if there is danger that the higher melds will be lost thereby (as, a trump marriage for 40 points should not be melded separately if the A-J-10 are also held and the chance to meld them may be lost if delayed).

In the later play it is advantageous to know all one's opponent's cards, and experienced players remember them nearly every time. The play, usually, is for last trick; the hand with the longer trumps should conserve them, forcing the opponent to trump plain-suit leads, unless analysis indicates that last can be won even if the opponent's trumps are drawn.

64-CARD PINOCHLE, OR GOULASH

Two-hand Pinochle is often played with a 64-card pack, duplicates of the ace to the seven in each of the four suits. (In New York this game is often called Goulash because it is played with two Klaberjass packs shuffled together "in a goulash.") The rules of play are precisely as in 48-card two-hand Pinochle, except: Each player's hand consists of sixteen cards, dealt four at a time. The seven of trumps is the dix, counting 10 points and being exchangeable for the trump card; the nine of trumps has no scoring or melding value. Game is usually set at 1,500 because scoring opportunities are greater, though the count by cards is still 250 points per deal, the nines, eights and sevens having no count; but there are more cards in the hand with which to form melds, and more rounds of play in which to make them.

THREE-HAND PINOCHLE

Three may play the game described as two-hand Pinochle on page 284. The 48-card pack is used, each player is dealt twelve cards, and eldest hand (player at the left of the dealer) has the first play. Each trick consists of three cards, one from each player; only the winner of the trick may meld. There are only twelve cards in the stock, including the trump card (or dix), so melding opportunities are few, and 500 points makes a better game than 1,000. (When this game is played with the 64-card pack, the last card of the stock—that is, the trump card or dix exchanged for it—is not drawn but becomes a dead card.)

AUCTION PINOCHLE

In the principal three-hand form of Pinochle, only forty-five of the forty-eight cards are dealt to the players, fifteen to each, leaving a three-card widow. Players bid for the widow and the right to name the trump. In the East, the game is usually played by four players, the dealer sitting out each time; each deal constitutes a separate game, settlement being made immediately, usually in chips. In the West, only three play, all being active on each deal, and a game consists of 1,000 points. The eastern form of the game is described first.

LAWS OF AUCTION PINOCHLE
(Copyright 1951, 1949, and reprinted by permission.)

Definitions. The following terms are defined in the laws: active, inactive, Sec. 7; bete—single bete, Sec. 13; double bete, Sec. 21d; Bidder, Sec. 9; contract, Sec. 9; made contract, Sec. 21; opponent, Sec. 9; play over, Sec. 17; trick, Sec. 17; turn, Sec. 7; widow, Sec. 8.

Number of players. 1. The game of Auction Pinochle is played by three, four, or five players, of whom only three are active players at any one time.

The pack. 2. 48 cards, two each of A, K, Q, J, 10 and 9 in each of four suits, spades, hearts, diamonds and clubs.

Rank of cards. 3. A (high), 10, K, Q, J, 9.

The draw. 4. Each player lifts a portion of the pack, taking no more than half the cards remaining. The last player to cut must leave the bottom card on the table. When all have cut, each shows the bottom card of the portion he cut. Lowest card determines the first dealer, next-lowest sits at dealer's left, and so on. If two players draw cards of equal rank they cut again.

The shuffle. 5. Dealer shuffles the pack and places it on the table, face down, at his right.

The cut. 6. The player at dealer's right lifts no fewer than five nor more than forty-three cards from the top of the pack. Dealer picks up the remainder of the pack. The player who cut then places his portion face down on the table and dealer places his portion on top of it, completing the cut.

Order of the game. 7. Each player's turn, in dealing, bidding and playing, comes to him in rotation, which is to the left. There are three active players, who receive cards in the deal. When there are four players, dealer receives no cards; when there are five players, dealer and the player second from his left receive no cards. These players are inactive and may give neither advice nor information to the active players.

The deal. 8. Dealer deals three cards to each active player in turn, beginning with the player at his left; then deals three cards to the center of the table; then deals the remaining cards three at a time* to each active player in turn until each has fifteen cards. All cards are dealt face down. The three cards dealt to the center are termed the widow.

Bidding. 9. Each active player in turn, beginning with the player at dealer's left, must make a bid or must pass. A bid is expressed in points only, in multiples of 10 points. The player at dealer's left must bid 300† or more. Each successive bid must be higher than the last preceding bid. Having passed, a player may not thereafter bid. When two players have passed the auction is closed. The highest bid becomes the contract. The player who made the highest bid becomes the Bidder. The other two players jointly are the Bidder's opponents.

Looking at the widow. 10. (a) If the contract is 300, the Bidder may decline to expose the widow, and pay a forfeit to the kitty. The forfeit is the amount he would pay to one opponent upon conceding a single bete at a 300 bid (Section 21c). The deal then passes to the next player in turn.

(b) In any other case, the Bidder then turns the three cards of the widow so that all players may see them, after which he takes them into his hand.

Melding. 11. Only the Bidder may meld. Melding consists in announcing or showing certain combinations of cards which have value in points. At the request of any player, Bidder must show his melds. The following combinations have values as melds:

SEQUENCES

A-K-Q-J-10 of trumps (flush)	150
K-Q of trumps (royal marriage)	40
K-Q of any other suit (marriage)	20

GROUPS

♠A—♡A—◇A—♣A (100 aces)	100
♠K—♡K—◇K—♣K (80 kings)	80
♠Q—♡Q—◇Q—♣Q (60 queens)	60
♠J—♡J—◇J—♣J (40 jacks)	40

SPECIAL

♠Q—◇J (pinochle)	40
9 of trumps (dix, pronounced deece)	10

A card which is part of a meld under one heading may be counted as part of a meld under another heading but may not be counted as part of another meld under the same heading.

Burying. 12. After melding, and preferably before picking up any cards he shows upon the table, the Bidder must bury, or lay away, face down,

---

* It is customary, and equally proper, for the dealer to deal the cards 4-4-4-3, 4-4-4, 4-4-4, 3-3-3; or 3-3-3-1, 3-3-3-1, 3-3-3-1, 3-3-3, 3-3-3.

† See also optional laws, page 298. Some permit bids of 250, or of 200.

any three cards which he has not melded,* to reduce the number of the cards in his hand to fifteen. The cards laid away will count to the credit of Bidder after the cards are played.

Concession. 13. (a) The Bidder may concede defeat (single bete) after looking at the widow but before leading a card. A concession offered by the Bidder may not be withdrawn if either opponent has thereafter exposed any card or if both opponents have discarded their hands.

(b) Either opponent may propose that the Bidder's contract be conceded to him, and if the other opponent agrees the contract is made; but the other opponent may decline to concede.

First lead. 14. The Bidder always leads to the first trick. He may lead any card.

Announcement of trump. 15. Before leading to the first trick the Bidder must name the suit which will be trump. The Bidder may change his meld, the cards he buries and the trump suit as often as he wishes before he leads to the first trick, but not thereafter. If the Bidder names the trump and both opponents concede, he may not then change the trump.

Objects of play. 16. The objects of play are to win tricks containing cards which have scoring values; and to win the last trick. The scoring values of cards taken in tricks won,† and of the last trick, are:

Each ace	11
Each ten	10
Each king	4
Each queen	3
Each jack	2
Last trick	10

The nines have no scoring value when taken in tricks.

The play. 17. The card led to a trick and the two cards played in turn by the other two players constitute a trick. Any trick containing a trump is won by the highest trump. Any trick not containing a trump is won by the highest card of the suit led. Of two cards of identical suit and rank played to the same trick, the one played first is the higher. The winner of each trick leads to the next, and may lead any card.

Each player must follow suit to the card led if able. If void of the suit led, he must play a trump if able. If able neither to follow suit nor to trump, he may play any card.

If the card led is a trump, each player must, if able, play a higher

---

* If any of these cards is a trump, it is not necessary to announce that fact.

† Some players count aces and tens 10 each, kings and queens 5 each, jacks and nines 0. Other players count aces, tens and kings 10 each, queens, jacks and nines 0. In any case, including last trick, the total of points in play is 250.

trump than any previously played to the trick. This is called playing over. (He need not overtrump in playing to a plain-suit lead that the player before him has trumped.)

Result of play. 18. The Bidder gathers all tricks he wins into a pile, face down, at the bottom of which are the cards he buried. Either opponent similarly gathers in all tricks won by his side. When the last trick has been completed the two sides ascertain and agree on the number of points they have respectively taken in.

Means of settlement. 19. Settlement may be made with chips at the end of the play of each deal, or a score may be kept of the respective points won and lost by the players in the game.

The kitty. 20. A separate score, or a separate pile of chips, is maintained for an imaginary extra player called the kitty, who solely receives payment when a bid of 300 is conceded without exposure of the widow, who receives payment the same as an opponent when the contract is bete, and who pays the same as an opponent when the contract is 350 or more.* The kitty is the joint property of all players in the game. If the kitty has a deficit, they must supply it equally. When the game ends, or when a player leaves the game, each player takes his proportionate share of the kitty.

Settlement. 21. (a) In settlement, the Bidder pays to or collects from every other player, active or inactive and including the kitty as provided in section 20.

(b) If the point value of the Bidder's melds plus the points he wins in play equal or exceed the amount of his bid, or if the opponents concede, the Bidder's contract is made and he collects from each other player:

UNITS (OR CHIPS)*

BID	BASIC VALUE	VALUE IF SPADES ARE TRUMP
300-340	3	6
350-390	5	10
400-440	10	20
450-490	15	30
500-540	20	40
550-590	25	50
600-640	30	60
650 or more	35	70

(c) If the Bidder conceded after looking at the widow but before leading to the first trick, he pays to each other player the basic unit value of his bid, regardless of what suit he named as trump.

(d) If the Bidder led to the first trick and the sum of the point values of his melds plus his tricks do not at least equal the amount of his bid, the Bidder is double bete and pays to each other player: twice the basic

---

* See also optional schedules, Sections 44-45 and page 299.

unit value if spades were not trump; four times the basic unit value if spades were trump.

Scoring. 22. (a) When chips are used, each player pays or collects the value of his contract at its determination.

(b) When a score is kept, each player has added to his score any units he has won in each deal, and has subtracted from his score any units he has lost in each deal. One player is designated as scorekeeper, but every player is equally responsible for the correctness of the score. The totals of those players who are plus must equal the totals of those players who are minus at the end of every deal.

Irregularities. 23. *Misdeal.* There must be a new deal by the same dealer:

(a) If the pack was not properly shuffled or was not cut, and if a player calls attention to the fact before the widow has been dealt;

(b) If, in dealing, the dealer exposes more than one card of any player's hand;

(c) If any card of the widow is exposed in dealing;

(d) If at any time before the cards are shuffled for the next deal the pack is found to be incorrect (that is, not precisely as defined in Section 2). Scores made with the same pack in previous deals are not affected.

24. *Exposure of the widow.* (a) If a player sees a card in the widow before the auction closes, he may not make another bid.

(b) If at any time before the auction closes a player handles the widow and in so doing exposes a card, there must be a new deal by the next dealer in turn, and (penalty) the offender must pay to each other player, including the kitty and every inactive player, the unit value of the highest bid last made prior to his offense.

25. *Incorrect hand.* If any player has too few cards and another player, or the widow, has too many:

(a) If it is discovered before the widow has been properly exposed by the Bidder, the hand with too few cards draws the excess, face down, from the player or widow having too many.

(b) If it is discovered at any time after the widow has been properly exposed by the Bidder, and if the Bidder's hand contains the correct number of cards, the Bidder's contract is made; if the Bidder's hand contains an incorrect number of cards, he is single or double bete, depending on whether or not he has led to the first trick.

(c) If the widow has too few cards, there must be another deal by the same dealer.

26. *Illegal card exposure.* If a player drops, or names, or otherwise exposes his possession of any card, except in leading or playing it:

(a) If the player is or becomes the Bidder, there is no penalty.

(b) If that player is or becomes an opponent, (penalty) on the first lead or play at which he could legally play that card the Bidder may either require or forbid him to play it.

27. *Exposure of more than one card.* If the opponents of the Bidder, or either of them, expose more than one card after the first lead has been made, the Bidder's contract is made.

28. *Bid out of turn.* A bid out of turn is void without penalty; but the other two players (or either of them, if the other has passed) may treat it as a correct bid by bidding or passing over it.

29. *Insufficient bid.* If a bid out of turn is not high enough to overcall the last preceding bid:

(a) If the offender has previously passed, the bid is void without penalty.

(b) If the offender has not previously passed, he is deemed to have passed; but the other two players (or either of them, if the other has passed) may treat it as a correct bid by bidding or passing over it.

30. *Impossible bid.* If a player bids less than 300, more than 650,* or any figure not expressed in multiples of 10 points, his bid is void.

31. *Played card.* A card is played when its holder places it upon the table with apparent intent to play, or when he names it as the one he intends to play. A card once played may not be withdrawn, except to correct an irregularity when permitted by these laws.

32. *Improper burying.* If, after the Bidder leads, it is ascertained that he buried a card he melded, or buried too many or too few cards and as a result has an incorrect number of cards in his hand,† he is double bete.

33. *Information as to the auction and meld.* (a) Until an opponent has played to the first trick, the opponents may ask or state the number and nature of the cards melded by the Bidder, the point value of the meld, the amount of the bid and the number of points the Bidder needs to win in cards.

(b) After either opponent has played to the first trick, any player may ask what the trump suit is; but if any opponent names the trump suit except in response to such a question, or if an opponent asks or gives any information as to the amount of the bid, the nature or value of the meld, or the number of points either side has taken or needs, play ceases and the Bidder's contract is made.

(c) A player has no redress if he acts on incorrect information given in response to a question, or if he does not know what suit is trump.

34. *Looking at turned card.* (a) The Bidder may turn and look at the cards he buries, at any time before he leads or plays to the second trick. If he does so thereafter, he is double bete.

(b) Any player may turn and look at a trick until his side has played to the next trick. If the Bidder turns and looks at a trick thereafter, he is double bete; if an opponent does so, the contract is made.

35. *Trick appropriated in error.* A trick taken in by the side not winning it may be claimed and must be restored at any time before it is

---

* While it is possible to fulfill a higher contract than 670 no such bid is logically possible in practice.

† See Section 25(b).

covered by cards taken in on a subsequent trick; unless so claimed and restored it remains the property of the side that took it in.

36. *Revoke.* A player revokes, if, when able to play as required by law, he:

(a) fails to follow suit;

(b) fails to play over on the lead of a trump;

(c) fails to play a trump when he has no card of the suit led;

(d) fails to play an exposed card when directed by Bidder to play it.

The Bidder may correct a revoke at any time before he has led or played to the next trick; there is no penalty. An opponent may correct a revoke at any time before he or his partner has led or played to the next trick; play continues and if the Bidder does not make his contract the deal is void and he neither pays nor collects. A player may withdraw a card played after an opponent's revoke and before it was corrected.

Unless a revoke is corrected in time, play ceases and if the offender is the Bidder, he is double bete; if he is an opponent, the contract is made.

If both sides revoke, the penalty applies to the offense to which attention is first called; if attention to both revokes is drawn simultaneously, the penalty applies to the offense which was committed first.

37. *Lead out of turn.* (a) If the Bidder leads when it was an opponent's turn to lead, there is no penalty; the opponent whose lead it was may choose to treat the lead as a correct one, or may require that the card be withdrawn unless either opponent has played to it.

(b) If an opponent leads when it is not his turn to lead, the offense is treated as a revoke under Section 36.

38. *Claim or concession.* If at any time after the first lead is made:

(a) The Bidder concedes that he is bete, or an opponent exposes or throws in his cards or expressly concedes that the contract is made, play ceases and the concession is binding.

(b) An opponent suggests concession, as by saying to his partner, "Shall we give it to him?", the concession is not valid and play must continue unless said partner agrees.

(c) The Bidder claims that the contract is made, or an opponent claims that the Bidder is bete, play ceases and all unplayed cards are taken by the side which did not make the claim.

39. *Error in count of meld.* (a) If, after the Bidder leads to the first trick, he is found to lack a card essential to a meld he announced but did not show, he is double bete.

(b) If an incorrect point value was agreed upon for the Bidder's meld, correction may be made at any time before settlement is completed.*

40. If an inactive player is first to call attention to an irregularity by the Bidder, no penalty may be exacted for such irregularity.

---

* Example: The contract is 350. Bidder shows ♠ A K Q J 10 9 and ◇ K Q J. The agreed value is 210; Bidder plays and takes in 134. Before paying, he recalls that his melds as shown actually totalled 220. The contract is made subject to Section 41 (Settlement).

41. *Error in settlement.* (a) Chips paid and collected as a result of an erroneous agreement on the result of a bid, or on its unit value, are not returned.

(b) A score entered by a scorekeeper based on an erroneous agreement by all active players as to the result of a bid, or its unit value, may not be corrected after the cards have been mixed for the next shuffle.

(c) A score incorrectly entered by the scorekeeper—that is, not entered in accordance with the agreed result or value of the bid—may be corrected whenever it is discovered.

Optional laws. The following variants do not conflict with the spirit of the game and any of them may be adopted by agreement.

42. The compulsory first bid by the player at dealer's left may be set at 200, or at 250, instead of at 300. Sections 9, 10(a) and 30 must then be revised accordingly; the basic unit value of a bid of 200-240 is 1, and of 250-290 is 2.

43. The compulsory first bid may be omitted entirely, so that all three players may pass in the first round. Sections 9, 10 and 30 must then be revised as follows: Delete the third sentence of Section 9; substitute for the sixth sentence: "If all three players pass in the first round, the deal passes to the next player in turn. When any player has bid and any two players have passed, the auction is closed." Delete Section 10(a) and delete the words "(b) In any other case" from Section 10(b). From Section 30, delete "less than 300."

44. *Alternate Section 20.* The kitty collects singly on contracts below 350, and pays or collects twice (or four times, if agreed) the basic value of the contract at 350 or more; these payments do not vary, no matter what suit is trump and no matter whether a bete is single or double.

45. *Alternate Section 21(a).* Some players prefer to settle on the following or a similar schedule:°

BID	BASIC VALUE	VALUE IF SPADES ARE TRUMP	VALUE IF HEARTS ARE TRUMP
300-340	1	2	3
350-390	2	4	6
400-440	4	8	12
450-490	6	12	18
500-540	8	16	24
550-590	10	20	30
600-640	12	24	36
650	14	28	42

° There are several other methods of settlement in use. In many, a bid of 450 to 490 pays 20 if not in spades, 40 if in spades; a bid of 500 to 540 pays 40 if not in spades, 80 if in spades, etc., doubling each time a higher series of 50 points is reached; but this method tends to bring the value of an unusual score out of all proportion to the values that might be expected. In other games, the unit value of a bid is increased with every additional 10 points bid. In still other games where the basic value of 300 is 3, 350 is 7, 400 is 17, 450 is 27, 500 is 37, and so on.

46. *Settling on the average.* When a score is kept with pencil and paper, settlement may be made "on the average." This is an especially good method when some players may have large "plus" scores and others may have "minus" scores, being in the hole, as it is often called.

In this method, you add up all of the plus scores, then subtract the total of all the minus scores, if any, then divide the result by all the players in the game. Each player pays any amount by which his score is less than the average, and collects any amount by which his score is more than the average. For illustration, see page 321.

VARIATIONS IN LAWS

Any of the following customs will be found prevalent in some localities or among some players.

Kitty. Some use the kitty as a jackpot pool in the old-fashioned tradition: It collects the same as a player when the Bidder is bete, and the entire pool goes to the first player to bid and make a bid of 400 or higher. In some games where this custom is followed, a 350 bid takes half the kitty.

290 or 320. In some games where the minimum bid is 250, the third bidder after two passes may bid 290, but not 250 to 280; or he may bid 320 or more, but not 300 or 310.

Bonus payments. "In the mitt" is an expression applying to 100 aces received in the deal; in some games a one-chip bonus is paid to a successful bidder for this holding. "Graduated aces" means that the bonus increases with the bid, being 1 chip at 300, 2 chips at 350, 3 chips at 400, and so on.

In various games, bonuses are paid to the Bidder for melding a round trip, for melding double pinochle, and—a sort of booby prize—for holding all eight nines. In the last case, the payment applies whether or not any nines were found in the widow.

In some games the Bidder collects double if he makes his contract without looking at the widow (which however is added to his tricks).

Playing over. In some games it is obligatory to play over in every suit, not only in trumps. It is not usual, in such games, to score spades double.

AUCTION PINOCHLE FOR 1,000 POINTS
(The club game)

The mechanics of Auction Pinochle as played in the western clubs follows the description given on pages 291-294 except in the scoring, and except that there are seldom more than three players in the same game. There is no kitty.

The minimum bid is 100 (in some games it is fixed at 200) and the first player may pass if he wishes. When all three pass, there is a new deal by the next dealer in rotation.

Only the high bidder melds; he names the trump and leads first. If he makes his bid, he scores the exact amount bid; spades do not count double. If he does not make his bid, the amount bid is deducted from his score, so it is possible to have a minus score.

Each of the opponents gathers in his own tricks and scores independently for them. For this reason, every hand is played out, even though the Bidder may already have made, or lost, his contract.

The first player to reach 1,000 wins the game. The Bidder's points are counted first, so he wins if he and either or both opponents reach 1,000 on the same deal. If the two opponents reach 1,000 on the same deal, the points of eldest hand (player at the Bidder's left) are counted first.

Irregularities. The laws on pages 295-298 apply so far as they are applicable, but exceptions are necessary: If an opponent of the Bidder revokes, or leads out of turn, or exposes two cards, or has an incorrect hand, the bid is made and the offender may not score but the other opponent may. The Bidder may not condone any irregularity (such as a lead out of turn) that would otherwise give him his bid, unless the non-offending opponent also condones it. In the case of any such irregularity play continues to determine the score of the other opponent.

Ethics. Each player is expected to play to his own best advantage, but where there is choice of plays an opponent of the Bidder is expected to play first to defeat the contract. An opponent may, however, permit the Bidder to make a bid that will not give him game, if an alternative play might give the other opponent game.

AUCTION PINOCHLE FOR 1,000 POINTS
(The home game)

Three play, as in the game described in the preceding paragraphs; but while the high bidder names the trump and leads first, each player melds what he can. The Bidder scores his meld whether or not he wins a trick (the cards he buries counting as his first trick); if an opponent fails to take a trick, his meld does not count. If the Bidder makes his bid, he scores everything he makes; he is not limited to the amount of his bid.

The Bidder's points are counted first; but if both his opponents reach 1,000 on the same hand, and the Bidder does not, game becomes 1,250, and in the same manner may be increased to 1,500, and 1,750, and so on.

POINTERS ON AUCTION PINOCHLE

The following advice applies to Auction Pinochle as described on pages 291-299. When the game is played for 1,000 points, the strategy is in some respects different; but in general the following will be equally applicable to all forms of the game.

Bidding. Conservatism should be the keynote of bidding; the average player loses because he overbids. In general, expect the widow to add about 30 points playing strength to the value of a hand, but nothing to its melding value. In other words, bid the sum of the melds you actually have, plus the points you estimate you will win in the play, plus 30 points.

An exception is found when you have four or more "places open" to increase your meld; in that case the estimated melding value of the hand should include only the points that will be added by the least valuable card you may buy.

In estimating the playing value of a hand, in a suit of four or fewer cards every card except an ace should be counted as lost (a natural exception being made for solid holdings such as A-A-10); in a suit of five or six cards, four cards should be counted as lost, less any ace or A-10 held in the suit. It should be estimated that on your losing cards the opponents will pile every possible counting card. (This is an intentionally pessimistic approach to playing valuation, providing a safety factor for times when suits will break unexpectedly badly.)

As it stands, this hand melds 70. Buying the ♠10 will make it 180; the ♡10 or ♣A, 170; the ◇K or ◇J, 150. Therefore, estimated meld 150. Since the hand cannot be expected to win 150 points in play, it is not worth a bid where the minimum is 300. It is worth a minimum bid where the minimum is 250.

As between a reasonably sure bid at any level, and a merely probable bid at the next-higher level, the lower-level bid should be preferred. The higher-level bid may then be made if you are pushed to it; and the opponents will be wary of competitive bidding against you when they learn that you often have something in reserve.

Percentages. Following are the chances of finding a given card in a three-card widow dealt from the 48-card Pinochle pack.

PLACES OPEN	CHANCES	APPROXIMATE ODDS
1	961 out of 5456	5-1 against
2	1802 out of 5456	2-1 against
3	2531 out of 5456	even
4	3156 out of 5456	3-2 for
5	3685 out of 5456	2-1 for

When you already have one card of the suit and rank desired, the chance of finding the card is only half as great as shown in the table. For example, if you have ♠ Q Q ♢ J, the odds are 10 to 1 against making double pinochle.

Following are the suit-breaks you may expect in your long suits:

YOU HOLD IN SUIT	OPPONENTS HOLD	OPPONENTS' CARDS WILL BE DIVIDED	
10 cards	2 cards	1-1	52%
		2-0	48%
9 cards	3 cards	2-1	78%
		3-0	22%
8 cards	4 cards	3-1	50%
		2-2	40%
		4-0	10%
7 cards	5 cards	3-2	67%
		4-1	29%
		5-0	4%
6 cards	6 cards	4-2	48%
		3-3	34%
		5-1	15%
		6-0	3%
5 cards	7 cards	4-3	61%
		5-2	31%
		6-1	7%
		7-0 less than	1%
4 cards	8 cards	5-3	47%
		4-4	32%
		6-2	18%
		7-1	3%
		8-0 less than	1%

It should be noted that when the opponents hold an odd number of cards, the most even possible division is most probable; when they hold an even number of cards, the next most even division is most probable, except when they have only two cards of the suit.

Conclusions drawn from this table should always be modified by information derived from the bidding. High opposing bids, if not justified by melding strength known to be outstanding, are usually based on playing strength; playing strength usually means long suits; long suits in one opposing hand warn of bad suit-breaks.

Burying. The Bidder should usually bury such cards as will (a) give him as much of a two-suited hand as possible, (b) void at least one of the other suits, and shorten both as much as is permitted by the melded cards that must be held, (c) score safely in the discard any ten or other scoring card that is likely to be lost if held.

Occasionally it is necessary to retain a loser that might be buried; this happens when the Bidder's hand is deficient in trump length and he has some such holding as A-10-9 in a side suit. To bury both ten and nine would leave him with a blank ace, which he would have to cash at once to avoid having it dropped by a lead of the opposing ace. The opponents could then force him to trump leads of the suit. By retaining A-9 and burying only the ten, he can defer to at least the third round of the suit any necessity for trumping. This may lose a few points in the play but make up for it by saving the last trick. In a desperate case, the entire A-10-9 suit may be held in the hand; if the lefthand opponent can be induced to lead the suit, both the ace and ten will win tricks. This expedient, however, is more a stratagem than sound technique, for if the opponents play perfectly (which should usually be assumed) both the ten and the nine will be lost to them.

Play. The object of the Bidder's play is usually to maintain his control (usually, this means his trump length) so as to win the last trick. To this end he leads his longest side suit to force out the opponents' trumps without wasting his own. A second reason to force out opposing trumps in this manner is that an opponent cannot smear on his partner's winning trick if under the rules he must trump.

When a long side suit is led, the losing cards are led early if possible. All other things being equal, the play of a card that was melded is preferred to the play of a card that was not; the opponents know about the melded cards, and cannot be sure other cards were not buried.

The opponents' strategy is the converse of the Bidder's. They begin with the knowledge of what melded cards are in the Bidder's hand; they infer his long side suit and his shortest suit. Most often they lead the shortest suit at every opportunity, forcing out the Bidder's trumps. They play their low cards on the Bidder's tricks and smear their high ones on partner's tricks.

Certain conventions have grown out of the obvious advisability of some defensive plays. "An ace calls for an ace"—if the Bidder's lefthand opponent leads an ace, his partner is expected to play the other ace on the trick if he has it. A low lead into the Bidder calls for a low card—the leader's partner must trust that the leader has discovered the Bidder's void suit. The Bidder's righthand opponent should usually lead a trump through a weak trump suit; his lefthand opponent should lead a trump only when the opponents control all other suits and the Bidder can gain most by trumping them.

Concession. Mathematically, it pays to play a spade hand (rather than concede) when there is at least a 50-50 chance of making it; it pays to play any other hand unless the odds are 2 to 1 or more against making it. For example, if making a bid depends on finding four opposing trumps divided 2-2, the hand should be played even though the odds are 3 to 2 that it will not be made. In the long run it will be more profitable to collect singly twice and pay doubly three times than to pay singly five times. But when double betes pay a kitty as well as the other players, no hand should be played without approximately an even chance to make it, and a spade hand should not be played unless there is nearly a 2-to-1 chance that it will be made.

PARTNERSHIP PINOCHLE

The Partnership Pinochle games are played by four, two against two as partners (and there are double-pack variants for six and eight players). Many minor variations on the rules are possible, and are practiced sectionally; the influence of the Euchre and All Fours games has been felt in some of them. The rules of the basic game are given first; they are copyright 1949 and are reprinted by permission.

LAWS OF PARTNERSHIP PINOCHLE

Number of players. 1. The game of Partnership Pinochle is played by four players, in two partnerships.

The pack. 2. 48 cards, two each of A, K, Q, J, 10 and 9 in each of four suits, spades, hearts, diamonds and clubs.

Rank of cards. 3. A (high), 10, K, Q, J, 9.

The draw. 4. The pack is spread face down on the table and each player draws a card, but not one of the four cards at either end of the pack. The players drawing the two highest cards play as partners against the other two. If two players draw equal cards, both must draw again to determine which is higher. Highest card determines the first dealer. Partners sit opposite each other, each having an opponent at his left and right.

The shuffle. 5. Dealer shuffles the pack and places it on the table, face down, at his right.

The cut. 6. The player at dealer's right lifts no fewer than five nor more than forty-three cards from the top of the pack. Dealer picks up the remainder of the pack. The player who cut then places his portion face down on the table and dealer places his portion on top of it, completing the cut.

Order of the game. 7. Each player's turn, in dealing, melding and playing, comes to him in rotation, which is to the left (clockwise).

The deal. 8. Dealer deals three cards at a time to each player in turn, beginning with the player at his left, each player thus receiving twelve cards. Dealer must turn face up the last card of the last batch dealt to himself, the original bottom card of the pack. This turned card is the trump card.

The trump card. 9. If the trump card is a nine, dealer keeps it and his side scores 10 points. If it is any other card, the first player in rotation to the left who holds a nine may claim the trump card in exchange for the nine. (It is not compulsory to exchange, but in announcing that he is not exchanging a player should not reveal that he holds a nine; nor may he reclaim his prerogative if another player then claims the trump card.)

Every other card of the same suit as the trump card is also a trump for that deal.

Melding. 10. Each player places face up on the table any melds he may hold, as follows:

SEQUENCES

A-K-Q-J-10 of trumps (flush)	150
Double flush	1500
K-Q of trumps (royal marriage)	40
K-Q of any other suit (marriage)	20

GROUPS

♠A—♡A—◇A—♣A (100 aces)	100
All eight aces	1000
♠K—♡K—◇K—♣K (80 kings)	80
All eight kings	800
♠Q—♡Q—◇Q—♣Q (60 queens)	60
All eight queens	600
♠J—♡J—◇J—♣J (40 jacks)	40
All eight jacks	400

SPECIAL

♠Q—◇J (pinochle)	40
Double pinochle	300
9 of trumps (dix, pronounced deece)	10

A card that is part of a meld under one heading may be counted as part of a meld under another heading, but may not be counted as part of another meld under the same heading.

A dix surrendered in exchange for the trump card is scored by the player to whom it was dealt.

A memorandum is made of the total points melded by each side, but its total is not credited to a side unless and until it wins a trick.

First lead. 11. After the melds are shown and totalled, each player replaces his melded cards in his hand and the play begins. The first lead is made by the player at dealer's left.

Objects of the play. 12. The objects of the play are to win tricks containing cards of scoring value, and to win last trick. The scoring values of cards taken in tricks won, and of the last trick, are:

Each ace	10
Each ten	10
Each king	5
Each queen	5
Last trick	10

Jacks and nines have no scoring value when taken in tricks.* The total of points to be divided in play is 250.

---

* Some players prefer the traditional Pinochle count (paragraph 16 on page 293); others prefer an even more simplified count in which aces, ten and kings count 10 each, queens, jacks and nines 0.

The play. 13. The card led to a trick and the three cards played in turn by the other players constitute a trick. All the tricks won by a side are gathered by one partner. A trick containing a trump is won by the highest trump. A trick not containing a trump is won by the highest card played of the suit led. Of two cards of identical suit and rank played to the same trick, the one played first is the higher. The winner of each trick leads to the next, and may lead any card.

Each player must follow suit to the card led if able. If void of the suit led he must play a trump if able. If void of both the suit led and of trumps, he may play any card.

If the card led is a trump, each player must, if able, play a higher trump than any previously played to the trick. This is called playing over.

Scoring. 14. Two scores are kept, one for each side, and all points scored by either partner on one side are entered together. At the end of play of a deal, the points for cards won in tricks, last trick, and melds (provided that the side has won a trick) are entered for each side.

The side that first reaches a total of 1,000 points, the other side having less than 1,000, wins a game. If both sides reach 1,000 in the same deal, game becomes 1,250; and if both sides reach 1,250 in the same deal, game becomes 1,500; and so on by increments of 250.

Declaring out. 15. A player may at any time declare out, that is, claim that his side has reached the total required to win a game. Play then ceases, and if the claim is found to be correct, the claiming side wins the game even though the other side be found to have more points. If the claim is found incorrect, the claiming side loses the game forthwith.*

Irregularities. 16. *Misdeal.* There must be a new deal by the same dealer:

(a) if the pack was not properly shuffled or was not cut, and if a player calls attention to the fact before looking at his hand and before the last card is dealt;

(b) if more than one card, other than the trump card, is exposed in dealing;

(c) upon demand of an opponent, if dealer neglects to turn up his last card and its identity cannot then be determined. Lacking such demand, a trump card may be drawn by an opponent from dealer's hand, held face down, before melding begins.

17. *Wrong number of cards.* If one player has too many cards and another too few, and—

---

* When it is desirable to determine the margin as well as the fact of victory (that is, when it is significant whether a side wins by 1,060 to 800 or by 1,060 to 940) a side that incorrectly declares out is deemed to have lost the game by the difference between its actual score and 1,000 for its opponents, unless the opponents in fact have more than 1,000. All cards remaining unplayed at the time of the claim, and last trick, go to the claimant's opponents if the claim was incorrect, but are not scored if the claim was correct.

(a) the error is discovered before either of these two players has looked at his hand, the player with too few cards draws the extra cards from the hand with too many;

(b) the error is discovered after one of the players has looked at his hand, all players meld, and then the player with too few cards draws the extra cards from the unmelded cards of the player with too many; the card drawn may then be used by the former in melding, and he may change his meld;

(c) the error is discovered after the first lead, play continues; the last trick or tricks comprise only three cards each after the short hand is exhausted, and excess cards remaining in the long hand after the twelfth trick are dead; a side that held an incorrect hand may not score for points won in tricks or for last trick, but may score its melds if it won a trick.

18. *Incorrect pack.* If at any time the pack be found incorrect (not in accordance with Section 2), play ceases and no points for cards or melds score in that deal, but the results of previous deals are not affected.

19. *Exposed card.* A card dropped face up on the table, named by a player as being in his hand, or otherwise exposed except in melding and correct leading and playing, is an exposed card. An exposed card must be left face up on the table and must be played at first legal opportunity. If the card is still unplayed at the first turn thereafter of the partner of the owner to lead, either opponent may name the suit which he must lead.

20. *Lead or play out of turn.* If a player leads or plays out of turn, the card so played becomes an exposed card and is dealt with under Section 19.

21. *Revoke.* A player revokes if he fails, when able, to follow suit to a lead, trump, or play over on a trump lead. A side that revokes may score nothing for points taken in tricks, or last trick, in that deal, but does not necessarily lose its melds.

(The revoke penalty is by agreement sometimes applied to the exposure of a card and to leads and plays out of turn.)

22. *Played card.* A card is played when its holder places it upon the table with apparent intent to play, or when he names it as the one he intends to play. A card once played may not be withdrawn, except in correction of a lead or play out of turn.

23. *Information as to cards played.* (a) Until his side has played to the next trick, a player may require all four cards of a trick to be turned face up and the holder of each to be indicated.

(b) Except as provided in paragraph 23(a) above, no player may ask or give information about any cards previously played. If a player gives information to his partner in violation of this law, his side incurs the penalty for revoke, Section 21.

24. *Trick appropriated in error.* A trick taken in by the side not winning it may be claimed and must be restored at any time before it is

covered by cards taken in a subsequent trick; unless so claimed and restored it remains the property of the side that took it in.

25. *Error in count.* A player is entitled to the full value of any melds he shows on the table, even if he announces their value incorrectly. A side is entitled to all the points actually in its tricks, even though less is claimed by reason of miscounting. Erroneous announcements as to the value of melds and trick-points must be corrected on demand of any player if made before the score of the deal has been agreed upon by both sides and entered on the score sheet (or settled in chips).

26. *Error in entering score.* A score incorrectly entered by the score-keeper—that is, not entered in accordance with the agreed result or value; or an arithmetical error in adding scores, must be corrected on demand of any player if made before the winner of a game is agreed upon.

POINTERS ON PARTNERSHIP PINOCHLE

Preliminary analysis consists of figuring out the other hands from what they did not meld; and this process continues throughout the play. For example, one opponent melds 80 kings, the other melds 40 jacks; partner is marked with both queens of spades through the failure of either opponent to use it in a meld. The fall of any king during the play marks the player as lacking the queen of its suit, if he did not meld a marriage. This analysis is entirely accurate because it is never worth while sinking a meld for deceptive purposes.

When there is no bidding, it is often impossible to know which side, if either, has control of the trumps. The safest lead by eldest hand is usually his longest suit, for its establishment may be vital to force out two opposing trumps at a time if they have the best trumps. Even with the top trumps it is seldom wise to draw them at once unless the remainder of one's hand is readily establishable, or unless it can be assumed that partner controls the other suits.

Melded cards should be played in preference to unmelded cards unless there is specific reason to show partner length in the suit. Obviously, counting cards are played on partner's tricks and worthless cards on the opponents' tricks.

PARTNERSHIP AUCTION PINOCHLE

The laws of Partnership Pinochle are followed, except as follows:

No trump card is turned. Each player in turn, beginning with eldest hand, has one bid; the minimum bid is 100, bids must be in multiples of 10 points, and each bid must be higher than the previous bid. The high bidder names the trump, then everyone melds; the high bidder leads to the first trick.

If the bidding side makes its bid it scores whatever it makes; if it falls short, it is set back by the amount of its bid. Its opponents always score whatever they make, except that if they do not win a trick they can score nothing for their melds. The bidding side cannot score for its melds, even if they equal the amount of the bid, unless it wins a trick. The trick won need not contain any counting cards.

Game is 1,000, and the score of the bidding side is counted first. There is no claiming out during the play.

In counting cards, the simplified count of 10 each for an ace, ten, king, and last trick, with no count for other cards, is used about as often as the count described in paragraph 12 of the Partnership Pinochle laws.

If all four players pass, the deal passes to the next player in turn.

Irregularities. See Partnership Pinochle; also:

Bid out of turn. The bid is void and the auction reverts to the proper player. The offending side must pass thereafter. However, the bid out of turn stands as regular if the opponents wish.

Insufficient bid. Any sufficient bid must be substituted, and the offender's partner must pass.

Pass out of turn. The offending side must both pass thereafter.

Revoke. In addition to the revoke penalty of Partnership Pinochle (paragraph 21), if the revoke was made by the bidding side it cannot make its bid; if by its opponents, the bidding side cannot be set back. In the former case, however, the bidding side is not set back if its melds sufficed for its bid and it won a trick prior to the revoke trick; in the latter case, the bidding side must make its bid to score it. The revoke trick and all cards left in the hands at the time of the revoke, together with last trick, go to the non-offending side.

VARIATIONS ON PARTNERSHIP AUCTION PINOCHLE

Going over. Some play that the dealer may take the contract at the amount of the highest preceding bid, "without going over."

Continuous bidding. The procedure is the same as in regular Partnership Auction Pinochle except that each player may continue to bid in turn as long as he will bid higher than the preceding bid; except that a player who has passed may not enter the auction again. When three players have passed the auction is closed.

Partnership Auction Pinochle with a Widow. Only eleven cards are dealt to each player, in rounds of three, three, three, and two. The remaining four cards form a widow, which goes to the highest bidder. He takes the widow into his hand, then discards any four cards face down; he then names the trump and melding and play proceeds as usual. The Bidder's discard counts for him but does not represent a trick; his side must still win a trick to count its meld. (Optional rule: Instead of discarding, the Bidder looks at the four cards of the widow, keeps one for himself, gives one to his partner, and gives one each to his opponents; he does not show the widow or the cards he so distributes.)

DOUBLE-PACK PINOCHLE

The most popular form of Partnership Pinochle, this game arose in the 1930's and produced two innovations: A double pack, with no nines or lower cards; and bidding in which a player can tell his partner something about his hand.*

Number of Players. 1. Four, two against two as partners.

The Pack. 2. 80 cards, four each of A, 10, K, Q, J (ranking in that order) in each suit. The pack is made by mixing together two regular 48-card Pinochle packs, discarding all nines.

The Draw. 3. Each player draws a card from the pack. The two highest are partners against the two lowest, and the highest deals. There is no rank of suits, and if two or more players draw cards of the same rank they draw again to determine the order among themselves only. High card deals. [Example: A draws an ace, B and C draw kings, D draws a jack. B and C draw again; the higher will be A's partner, the lower D's partner. A deals.]

The Deal. 4. Dealer shuffles the pack and offers it to his righthand opponent, who cuts it approximately in half. The entire pack is dealt, four or five cards at a time, giving each player twenty cards. The turn to deal passes to the left.

The Bidding. 5. Beginning with the player at dealer's left, each player in turn may make a bid, announce a meld, or pass. Having once passed, a player may not reënter the auction.

6. The minimum bid is 500. Bids are made in multiples of 10 and each bid must be higher than any previous bid. [*Note:* It is customary to drop the extra zero at the end of every score and bid, for example, 50 instead of 500, 51 instead of 510, etc.]

7. Before any player has bid, each player in turn may announce the amount of his meld, without giving any other information as to the nature of his hand, as by announcing 100, 400 (or 10, 40), etc. He may announce more or less than the actual amount.

8. In making a bid, a player may state that it is based on a flush or on a long suit and may also announce a meld, as by bidding 500 and announcing a flush and 100 meld. He may not name a particular suit, or say he has two long suits, or give any information as to the playing strength of his hand. If a player announces a flush or long suit before any bid has been made, he is deemed to have bid 500. If a player announces a meld in points after a bid has been made, he is deemed to have overcalled the previous bid by 10 points for each 100 points or fraction of 100 points that he announces. [*Example:* Last bid was 500; if next player announces 100 meld he has bid 510, if he announces 140 meld he has bid 520.] NOTE: In some games only bids and passes are permitted, no announcements.

---

* These rules are based on those prepared by Richard Setian of Philadelphia.

9. If all four players pass (or announce melds) but no one bids, the hands are thrown in and the next dealer deals.

Melding. 10. The high bidder names the trump suit; once named, it cannot be changed. Each player then melds, scoring as follows:

SEQUENCES

A-K-Q-J-10 of trumps (flush) 150
K-Q of trumps (royal marriage) 40
K-Q of any other suit (marriage) 20
(No extra score for duplicated sequence; double flush counts only 300.)

GROUPS

Four aces (one of each suit) 100
Double aces (two of each suit) 1000
Triple aces (three of each suit) 1500
Four kings (one of each suit) 80
Double kings (two of each suit) 800
Triple kings (three of each suit) 1200
Four queens (one of each suit) 60
Double queens (two of each suit) 600
Triple queens (three of each suit) 900
Four jacks (one of each suit) 40
Double jacks (two of each suit) 400
Triple jacks (three of each suit) 600
(A quadruple group counts simply as two doubles; sixteen aces count 2000.)

PINOCHLES

Pinochle ($\spadesuit$Q & $\diamondsuit$J) 40
Double pinochle 300
Triple pinochle 450
Quadruple pinochle 3000

11. A card that is part of a meld under one heading may be counted as part of a meld under another heading but may not be counted as part of another meld under the same heading.

12. A side's melds do not count unless that side later wins a scoring trick. A worthless trick, such as four jacks, does not make the meld count.

The Play. 13. The high bidder leads. He may lead any card. Each player after him in turn must follow suit if able. If a trump is led he must play over if able. If he cannot follow suit he must trump if able. Of duplicate cards played to the same trick, the one played first ranks higher. The winner of each trick leads to the next.

Scoring. 14. Cards won in tricks may be scored in either of two ways, to be agreed upon before the game begins: (a) aces, tens and kings 10 each; or (b) aces and tens 10 each, kings and queens 5 each. Other cards count nothing. Last trick counts 20. Total to be won in cards is 500.

15. If the bidding side, in melds and cards, makes at least the amount of its bid, it scores all it makes; if it makes less than its bid, the whole

amount of the bid is subtracted from its score. Its opponents always score whatever they made.

16. Game is 3,550, and the score of the bidding side is counted first.

Irregularities. 17. *Misdeal.* There must be a new deal by the same dealer: (a) If the pack was not properly shuffled or was not cut and if a player calls attention to the fact before looking at any card dealt to him and before the last card is dealt. (b) If more than one card is exposed in dealing. (c) As provided in the paragraphs on *Wrong Number of Cards* and *Illegal Information.*

18. *Wrong Number of Cards.* If one player has too many cards and another too few: (a) If the error is discovered before either player has looked at his hand, the player with too few cards draws the excess from the player with too many. (b) If either player has looked at his hand, any player may require a new deal; or, by mutual agreement, after all players meld, the player with too few cards draws the excess from the player with too many and may then change his meld. (c) If the error is discovered after the first lead, it is a misdeal.

19. *Illegal Information.* If a player during the bidding gives unauthorized information, as by naming a suit or saying that he has two long suits, the opponents may claim a misdeal. (They may consult before deciding, but may not show or describe their hands.)

20. *Incorrect Bid.* A bid in turn may not be changed. A bid out of turn counts as a pass. An insufficient bid in turn must be replaced by a sufficient bid or a pass, if attention is drawn to it before the next player bids or passes; after that it stands without penalty.

21. *Incorrect Meld.* (a) If a claimed meld does not contain the proper cards, and the error is discovered before the first lead, the player may correct it by substituting correct cards, or withdraw it. (b) After the first lead, all claimed and undisputed scores stand and no correction may be made for a meld later found to have been erroneous; but this does not prevent correction of an error in writing down an agreed score.

22. *Lead or Play Out of Turn.* If a player leads or plays out of turn, and the opponent at his left plays before attention is drawn to the error, it stands as regular without penalty. If attention is drawn to the error in time, the card is withdrawn without penalty and the turn reverts to the rightful player.

23. *Revoke.* (a) A player revokes if he fails, when able, to follow suit, trump, or play over on a trump lead, as required by law. A revoke may be corrected before the revoker or his partner has played to the next trick, and if it is corrected the opponents may withdraw and replace cards they have played in the interval; a card played by the revoker's partner may be changed only to avoid a second revoke.

(b) A revoke not corrected in time becomes established. Play ceases. Neither side scores for points taken in cards. The amount of the bid is subtracted from the score of the revoking side (regardless of which side made the high bid). The opposing side scores its melds, whether or not it won a point in play.

(c) The tricks taken in should be stacked so that their order is apparent. They may be examined when a revoke is claimed, and if an opponent of the claimant has mixed them so that the fact cannot be clearly established, the claim must be allowed.

WIPE-OFF

This is Double-pack Pinochle with the proviso that a side must score 200 or more points in cards to count either its meld or its cards.

THREE-HAND DOUBLE-PACK PINOCHLE

There are two methods of dealing:

(a) 25 cards to each player and 5 to a widow; the high bidder must announce the trump *before* seeing the widow.

(b) 26 cards to each player and 2 to a widow; the high bidder may announce the trump *after* seeing the widow.

Game is 4,550. The minimum bid is 500, and if the first two pass, dealer must bid 500. There are no announcements of melds or suits in the bidding. Each player melds, and must win a scoring trick to make his meld count. The high bidder gets the widow cards and must discard that many cards before picking up his meld; his discard counts for him, but he must still win a trick to score his meld. Any irregularity in discarding is a revoke.

The high bidder may concede defeat before leading, in which case each opponent scores his meld plus 100, while the bidder is set back the amount of his bid.

SIX-HAND TRIPLE-PACK PINOCHLE

Six play in two partnerships of three each; each player has an opponent at his right and left. Three regular Pinochle packs, without the nines, are mixed together, making a pack of 120 cards. Each player is dealt 20 cards, and the rules of Double-pack Pinochle apply, except that game is 4,550, the minimum bid is 750, and the last trick counts 30.

Contract Pinochle. Four play, in two partnerships, using the 48-card pack, as in regular Partnership Auction Pinochle. The rules of the auction, however, are as in Contract Bridge: The dealer bids first and the auction continues until a bid is followed by three consecutive passes. Each bid must name a number of points (in multiples of 10 points) and a trump suit, the minimum bid being 100; there is no rank of suits, so that 110 spades is required to overcall 100 hearts, and there is no no-trump bid. A player in turn may double an opponent's bid, or redouble when an opponent has doubled.

Only the successful bidder and his partner may meld; they may combine their melds. The high bidder may then call for his partner to put down a card that can be used in a combined meld, and so long as the partner has the card called for, he may continue to call for one card at a time in the same way. When the partner does not have the card, the high bidder's turn to call ends, and his partner then has the same right.

The highest bidder leads to the first trick. If the bid is made, the bidding side scores it; if it is not made, the opponents score it. Only one side may score in each hand, and points above the contract do not count. The bid is scored at twice or four times its value if it was respectively doubled or redoubled (and some double it again if spades are trumps). The meld counts whether or not the bidding side wins a trick. Game is 3,000.

Irregularities. In the auction, the laws of Contract Bridge apply; in the play, the laws of Partnership Pinochle, except that the penalty for a revoke is that the revoke trick and all subsequent tricks go to the non-offending side.

Radio Pinochle. This is a form of Partnership Auction Pinochle in which, before the auction begins, each player may "broadcast" to his partner information as to the melds in his hand. The information is given by statements conforming to a formula agreed upon by players.

Firehouse Pinochle. Probably taking its name from its popularity with firemen sitting around waiting for an alarm, this form of Partnership Auction Pinochle has the following special rules: The minimum bid is 200. The high bidder must fix the trump suit by melding a marriage (or flush) in it; if he has more than one marriage he selects the trump from among them, but obviously without at least one marriage he cannot bid. Eldest hand bids first, and a player may continue to bid in turn until he has once passed. Eldest hand always leads first. Game is 1,000, and the score of the bidding side is counted first. Out of this game grew Check Pinochle, described next.

CHECK PINOCHLE

The pack. 1. The pack of 48 cards is used. Each player receives twelve cards, dealt three at a time.

Bidding. 2. The right to name the trump is determined by bidding. Each player, beginning with eldest hand, must bid or pass. The lowest bid allowed is 200, and all bids must be in multiples of 10. If the first three players pass, the dealer must bid 200; he may bid more if he holds a marriage. Under all other circumstances, no player may bid at any time if he does not hold a marriage. A player may continue to bid in turn so long as he is overcalled, but once he passes he must pass for the rest of the auction. The highest bidder names the trump suit.

Check awards. 3. After the bidding, each player melds if he can. Each player collects from one of his opponents:

For melding: round trip, 5 checks; flush, 2 checks; 100 aces, 2 checks; 80 kings, 60 queens, or 40 jacks, 1 check; double pinochle, 2 checks.

For making contract: 200-240, 2 checks; 250-290, 4 checks; 300-340, 7 checks; 350-390, 10 checks; and 5 checks more for each series of 50 points.

For defeating opponents' contract: twice the number of checks for making contract.

For slam (winning all 12 tricks): 5 checks.

For winning game: 10 checks, plus 1 check for each 100 points (or fraction thereof) by which winners' score exceeds losers'; plus 5 checks if losers have a net minus score.

The play. 4. Each player picks up his melds and the play begins. The high bidder makes the first lead. Thereafter the rules of play are as in Partnership Pinochle (see page 304).

Scoring. 5. The points won in tricks by each side are counted as follows:

Each ace	10
Each 10	10
Each king	5
Each queen	5
Last trick	10

Jacks and nines have no scoring value when won in tricks.

6. Trick points won by opponents of the high bidder are at once entered in their score. The bidder's side also scores all it makes, provided that the total of its trick points and melds is at least equal to its contract. If this total is less than the contract, the side scores nothing for tricks or melds, and the amount of the bid is subtracted from its score.

Game. 7. The side that first reaches a total of 1,000 points wins a game. The score of the bidder's side is counted first; that side wins if both sides reach 1,000 in the same deal.

Irregularities. 8. *Misdeal.* There must be a new deal by the same dealer if a card is exposed in dealing, or if at any time it is found that one player has too many cards and another too few. A deal out of turn is void if discovered before the auction has begun; after that it stands as a regular deal in turn.

9. *Incorrect hand.* If one hand has too few cards, the others being correct, and if the missing cards are found, they are restored to the short hand, play continues, and that hand is answerable for revoke as though the cards had been in the hand continuously.

10. *Exposed card.* A card exposed illegally must be left face up on the table and played at first legal opportunity; or, an opponent may call a suit to be led in the first turn of the offending side. If a player has choice of lead or play from more than one such exposed card, the opponent at his left may designate the card to be played. If a card is exposed before the end of the auction, the partner of the offender is barred from further bidding.

11. *Bid out of turn.* A bid out of turn is void, and partner of the offender is barred from bidding, except that the dealer's obligation to open the auction if the others pass still stands.

12. *Pass out of turn.* The pass is void, but both partners of the offending side are barred from bidding thereafter except that dealer's obligation to open the auction still stands.

13. *Bidding without a marriage.* If a player bids without a marriage in his hand, the opponents after consultation may elect: (a) to abandon the deal; or (b) to assume the contract at the highest or lowest bid they made during the auction; or (c) require the offending side to assume the contract at the highest bid it made during the auction.

14. *Revoke.* A revoke is defined as in Partnership Pinochle (paragraph 21 on page 307). The penalty for an established revoke is that play ceases as soon as the revoke is discovered, the previous tricks stand, but all remaining unplayed cards go to the opponents of the offending side. A revoke becomes established when a member of the offending side leads or plays to the next trick; until then the revoke may be corrected, the revoke card is subject to penalty under paragraph 10, and a member of the non-offending side may change a play he made after the revoke.

It is the custom of Check Pinochle players to apply the Contract Bridge laws when they are applicable and the laws above are not.

Pointers on play. Serious players of Check Pinochle have developed a code of bidding conventions. Some of these conventions are:

OPENING (FIRST) BIDS

TO SHOW	BID
Flush	250 or 270
100 Aces	260 or 280
Round house	290
Flush and 100 aces	360 or 410
A meld of 100	220

(Where alternative bids are given, the higher bid is made to show additional playing strength in the hand.)

Any free bid 10 points below the next-higher scoring mark (as 240, 290, 340) is forcing. Its usual meaning is that the bidder can support any suit, or can support any suit his partner is likely to bid, and so wants his partner to make the final bid and name the trump.

RESPONSES (WHEN PARTNER HAS BID)

TO SHOW	BID
A fair hand	10 more than partner
(40–50 supporting points)	260 over 200 to 220
100 aces	310 over 250
Flush	270, 300, 320, 350

A bid of 220 over partner's 200 denies strength but shows a desire to name the trump suit.

Every bid must, of course, be qualified by an "if possible." When partner has bid 200 and the intervening opponent 210, a bid of 220 is merely a competitive bid designed to keep the bid for one's own side. A jump to 230 would be equivalent to a bid of 220 when there is no opposing bid.

⟶ SCHAFKOPF ⟵

Tradition has it that Schafkopf (Sheepshead) originated among the Wends who settled in the Erzebirge (mountains of Bohemia and Saxony). Historical record attests that Wendish Schafkopf was the inspiration for the game Skat (q.v.), early in the 19th century. Many variations of Schafkopf have been noted, some of them having more in common with Tarok, Ombre, Solo, etc., than with each other. Three variants are described below. The first two are believed to be respectively "ancient Schafkopf" and the (later?) Wendish version. The third is the modern game played in the United States, and the rules of Walter L. Zarse are followed.

"ANCIENT" SCHAFKOPF

Number of players. 1. Four, in two partnerships.

The pack. 2. A pack of 32 cards, made by discarding all cards below the sevens from a full pack.

Rank of cards. 3. The four jacks are always the four highest trumps; whatever the trump suit, they rank: ♣J (high), ♠J, ♡J, ◇J. Then follow (high to low), the cards of the trump suit: A, K, Q, 10, 9, 8, 7.

4. In plain suits the rank is: A (high), K, Q, 10, 9, 8, 7.

The deal. 5. Each player receives eight cards, dealt in batches of four at a time.

Declaring. 6. Beginning with eldest hand (player at left of the dealer), each player in turn must declare whether he has a suit of five or more cards (including all jacks as cards of his longest suit). The longest or highest-counting such suit becomes the trump. As between suits of equal length, comparison is made by counting the ace 11, each face card 10, other cards their index value.

7. If no player holds a suit of five or more cards, the holder of the ♣J must name a suit to be trump.

The play. 8. Eldest hand makes the opening lead. He may lead any card. (In some localities, he was obliged to lead a trump.) After any lead, each other hand must follow suit if able; if unable, the hand may play any card. A trick is won by the highest trump, or, if it contains no trump, by the highest card of the suit led. The winner of a trick leads to the next.

Object of play. 9. Each side strives to win in tricks the cards that have counting value, as follows:

Each ace	11
Each ten	10
Each king	4
Each queen	3
Each jack	2

The total of points at stake in the pack is 120.

Scoring. 10. The side that takes 61 or more points in tricks wins the game. If the side that made the trump wins 61 to 90 points, it wins a single game; 91 or more points, a double game; all the tricks, triple game. Opponents of the maker win twice as much: double game for 61-90, quadruple for 91 or more; sextuple for all the tricks. Each deal is a separate game, and is settled at once.

WENDISH SCHAFKOPF

Follow all the rules of Schafkopf except:

Diamonds are always trumps; hence there is no declaring. All queens and jacks are permanent trumps, and the trump suit is ranked: ♣Q, ♠Q, ♡Q, ♢Q, ♣J, ♠J, ♡J, ♢J, ♢A, K, 10, 9, 8, 7. Partnerships are not fixed: the two players who hold the ♣Q (called Spadille or *die Alte*) and the ♠Q (Basto or *die Baste*) become partners. Neither may reveal his identity to the other except by the fall of the cards. If one player is dealt both the ♠Q and ♣Q, he must announce the fact and name some suit other than diamonds; the player holding the ace of this suit becomes his partner. Either partnership wins a single game for taking 61-90 points, double game (*schneider*) for 91 or more, quadruple game for winning all the tricks (*schwarz*).

MODERN SCHAFKOPF

Wendish Schafkopf was adapted to play for other numbers of players than four. In the three-hand cutthroat game, a widow was dealt, and whoever took the widow assumed a contract. This is the characteristic feature of the modern game, of which the three-hand variant is described below.

See also Yukon, page 495, a simple version played by children.

Number of players. 1. Three active players; four may participate, the dealer giving himself no cards but sharing the winnings and losses of the Opponents.

The pack. 2. A pack of 32 cards, made by discarding all cards below the sevens from a full pack.

Rank of cards. 3. The permanent trump suit of fourteen cards is ranked: ♣Q (high), ♠Q, ♡Q, ♢Q, ♣J, ♠J, ♡J, ♢J, ♢A, 10, K, 9, 8, 7. The cards of each plain suit rank: A (high), 10, K, 9, 8, 7.

The deal. 4. Each player receives ten cards, dealt in batches of 3-4-3. After the first round of the deal, two cards are dealt face down on the table to form a widow (*skat* or *scat*).

5. The three active players are called, in rotation to the left, forehand (left of dealer), middlehand, and endhand.

The play. 6. Any player in his turn, beginning with forehand, may pick up the widow if it has not been taken before him. Whoever takes the widow becomes the Player, and the other two combine against him in temporary partnership as the Opponents.

7. The Player discards any two cards face down; these cards belong to him at the end of the play.

8. Forehand makes the opening lead. He may lead any card. After any lead, each other hand must follow suit if able; if unable, the hand may play any card. A trick is won by the highest trump, or, if it contains no trump, by the highest card of the suit led. The winner of a trick leads to the next.

9. If all three players pass, the widow is set aside but belongs to the winner of the last trick. The game is *least*; the rules of play are as in paragraph 8.

Object of play. 10. When any takes the widow, both sides strive to win the cards of counting value, as follows:

Each ace	11
Each ten	10
Each king	4
Each queen	3
Each jack	2

The total of counting cards in the pack is 120.

Scoring. 11. The Player alone scores, plus if he takes a majority of the 120 points, minus if he fails. For taking 61-90, he scores 2 game points; for 91 or more (*schneider*), 4 game points; for all the tricks (*schwarz*), 6. He loses 2 game points if he takes only 31-60, or 4 if he takes less than 31, or 6 if he wins no trick.

12. In the game *least*, the object of each player is to take as few points as possible. If every player takes a trick, the one gathering the fewest points scores 2 game points. When two players tie for least, the one who did not win the last trick as between them scores 2 points. If each player gathers 40, the dealer scores the 2. If one player takes no tricks, he scores 4 game points, except that if all the tricks are taken by one player, this player loses 4, while the others score nothing.

⤖ SKAT ⤖

In 1811, some players at a Tarok Club in Altenburg (capital of the German Duchy of Saxe-Altenburg) became interested in Wendish Schafkopf. The chief enthusiast was Advocate F. F. Hempel. A new game was gradually evolved, combining features of Schafkopf and Tarok; it was christened Scat, the regular term for the widow in Tarok and other games (from Italian *scartare*, to discard, or *scatola*, a place of safe-keeping). First mention of the game in print occurred in the Osterländer Blättern, 1818. Seventy years later, it had become so popular that a congress was convened at Altenburg (August 7, 1886) to codify its rules, and more than a thousand players attended. The German spelling, Skat, was adopted.

German immigrants brought the game to the United States, and an American Skat League was founded at St. Louis, Mo., in January, 1898. This league still flourishes, and the description of Skat below follows its official rules.

Number of players. 1. Three active players, but four or five frequently participate. The dealer then gives no cards to himself or (in five-hand) to the third player at his left.

The pack. 2. A pack of 32 cards, made by discarding all cards below the sevens from a full pack.

Rank of cards. 3. The four jacks are always trumps, ranking: ♣J (high), ♠J, ♡J, ◇J. After them follow the cards of the trump suit, ranking: A (high), 10, K, Q, 9, 8, 7. The cards in each plain suit rank: A (high), 10, K, Q, 9, 8, 7.

4. The suits rank: clubs (high), spades, hearts, diamonds.

The deal. 5. Each active player receives ten cards, dealt in batches of 3-4-3. After the first round of the deal, a skat (widow) of two cards is dealt face down on the table.

6. The players in rotation to the left are called forehand (left of dealer), middlehand, and endhand. (German, *Vorhand, Mittelhand, Hinterhand.*)

Bidding. 7. Forehand has the vested right to name the game. The bidding is therefore begun by middlehand, who must pass or bid. If he bids, forehand can retain his right by making the same bid—expressed by "I stay" or "Stand" or "Yes." Middlehand may raise the bid if forehand stays, and so on until one of the two passes. The survivor then settles with endhand in the same way, having the right to supersede a bid by endhand with a bid for the same amount himself.

7. Each bid is made in terms of points alone, no game being specified. But each bid must be for a number of points that is possible in some game. The lowest bid is 10. (The theoretic maximum is 204, but bids of as much as 100 are rare.) Modern custom is to bid only in even numbers.

8. If neither middlehand nor endhand makes a bid, forehand must name a game, but in this case he has the added choice of naming least (Ramsch).

The games. 9. Whoever earns the right to name the game becomes the Player. He must name one of the fifteen possible games—one in which it is possible for him to make his bid. The base values of the games are as follows:

TRUMPS	◇	♡	♤	♧	JACKS TRUMPS		NO TRUMPS	
Tournee	5	6	7	8	Tournee grand	12	Simple null	20
Solo	9	10	11	12	Gucki grand	16	Open null	40
					Solo grand	20		
					Open grand	24		
					Least	10		

[The base values 1 to 4 were assigned to a game, *frage*, that has been eliminated from modern Skat.]

10. *Tournee.* If he names tournee, the Player looks at the top card of the skat without showing it. He may accept it as the trump suit, in which case he exposes it, picks up both skat cards without showing the second, and discards any two cards face down. If the top skat card does not satisfy the Player (*passt mir nicht*), he may turn the second face up, and it fixes the trump. The game is then second turn. The Player picks up both skat cards, without showing the first, and discards any two cards face down.

If either skat card is a jack, the Player has choice of accepting its suit as trump or declaring jacks trumps (*grand*). The game grand tournee can thus arise only by chance.

11. *Solo.* If he names solo, the Player names the trump—a suit or jacks —and sets the skat aside without using it. The Player has the right to try for increased score by predicting that he will win all the tricks (*schwarz*) or more than 90 points (*schneider*). Having made such announcement, he loses his game if he does not fulfill it.

12. *Gucki grand.* On naming this game (also called *guckser*), the Player picks up both skat cards without showing either, then discards any two cards face down. Jacks are trumps.

13. *Null.* When the game is null, there are no trumps. Every suit ranks: A (high), K, Q, J, 10, 9, 8, 7. The skat is set aside, and the Player loses his game if he wins a single trick. Alone among the games, null base values are invariable, so that the Player may not declare simple null if he has bid more than 20, or open null if he has bid more than 40.

14. *Open.* In open grand and open null, jacks are trumps and the Player exposes his whole hand for inspection by the Opponents before the

opening lead. The skat is set aside. To win open grand, the Player must take all the tricks; to win open null, no trick.

15. *Least.* The skat is set aside; jacks are trumps; the object of play is to take as few points as possible. This game may be declared only by forehand when neither other player bids.

The play. 16. Forehand makes the opening lead. He may lead any card. After any lead, each other hand must follow suit if able; if unable, the hand may play any card. A trick is won by the highest trump, or, if it contains no trump, by the highest card of the suit led. The winner of a trick leads to the next.

17. At the end of the play, the skat or the Player's discard is added to the Player's tricks, in any trump game except least. At the latter game, the skat goes to the winner of the last trick. In null games, the skat is ignored.

Object of play. 18. In all games except null and least, both sides try to win as many points as possible in tricks. The cards that count when won in tricks are:

Each ace	11
Each ten	10
Each king	4
Each queen	3
Each jack	2

The total of points in the pack is 120.

19. In null, the Player undertakes to win not a single trick. In least, each plays for himself and tries to win as few points as possible.

Scoring. 20. The player loses his game if:

(a) At null, he wins any trick.

(b) At open grand, he loses any trick.

(c) At tournee, solo, or gucki, he takes less than 61 in tricks. The Opponents win schneider if they take 90 or more points, schwarz if they take all the tricks.

(d) At solo, he fails to fulfill prediction that he will take schneider or schwarz.

(e) The value of his game (explained in next paragraph) proves to be less than his bid. In this case, the Player is said to have overbid.

21. The value of a game (other than null and least) is determined by multiplying its base value (paragraph 9) by the sum of all due multipliers. The multipliers arise from (a) matadors and (b) the outcome of the play, as explained below.

22. Matadors are trumps in unbroken sequence from the ♣J down. The Player is said to be *with* or *without* matadors, according as he does or does not hold the ♣J. [For example, if his trumps are headed by ♣J, ♠J, ♢J, he is "with two"; if his highest trump is the ♢J he is "without three." The commonest way that an overbid comes about is that the Player has bid "without," then finds a jack in the skat that reduces this

number.] The total of multipliers for matadors is the number that the Player is with or without, in hand and skat together.

23. To the matadors, add the appropriate item from the following table:

Game (Player makes 61-90) 1
Schneider made, not predicted (91 by Player; 90 by
    Opponents) 2
Schneider made, not predicted (by either side) 3
Schneider predicted and made by Player 3
Schneider predicted, schwarz made, by Player 4
Schwarz predicted and made by Player 5

[Examples of computing the value of a game: (a) The Player names gucki, takes 80 in tricks, has ♣J ♡J in trumps; the base value 16 is multiplied by 2 (the sum of 1 for matadors, 1 for "game"); the value is 32. (b) The Player, having three matadors, names club solo and predicts schneider, but takes only 90 in tricks. He loses the value of his game, base 12 multiplied by sum of 3 and 3, or 72.]

24. If the Player wins his game, its value is added to his score; if he loses, the value is deducted. But if he loses in a gucki grand or second turn tournee, the value of his game is doubled. When the Player is found to have overbid, the value of his game is that multiple of the base value next-higher than his bid. [For example, the Player has bid 30 and named spade solo, expecting to be "without two" but finding a jack in the skat that makes him "without one." He takes 76 points in tricks, thus failing to make schneider, which could save him. His game is worth only 22. He is charged with 33, the multiple of base value 11 next above his bid.]

25. *Least.* The player who takes the fewest points in tricks scores 10, or 20 if he has taken not a single trick. If each player takes 40 in tricks, forehand is deemed the winner (because he named the game) and scores 10. If two players tie for low, the one who did not take the last trick as between them wins the 10, except that if one player takes all the tricks he loses 30 while the others score nothing.

Settlement. 26. Score is kept with pencil and paper, a running total being recorded for each player. Four or five players may participate at one table; settlement must be made at any time that a player withdraws from the game. The scores at that time are totalled and divided by the number of players to determine the average score; each player then collects or pays according as he is above or below average. For example:

PLAYERS	SCORES	NET
A	213	82
B	157	26
C	118	−13
D	94	−37
E	71	−58
5)	653	
average	131	approximately

PROCEDURE AND IRREGULARITIES IN SKAT

(Excerpts from the Official Rules of the North American
Skat League, copyright 1945 and reprinted by permission)

Dealing. Section 1. The cards after they have been properly shuffled by
the dealer, must be cut once (by the player to his right, taking off three
or more, so as to leave at least 3 cards in each packet), and dealt in the
following order: 3-skat-4-3. The full deck of 32 cards must be taken up
and dealt.

Section 2. If all cards are dealt, and bidding has commenced, the game
must be played, even if the dealing was done out of turn; in such case the
next deal must be made by the one who should have dealt before and
then proceed as if no misdeal had been made, omitting, however, the
one who had dealt out of his turn; thus each player deals but once during
one round.

Section 3. In case a card is served face up, a new deal must be made.

Section 4. A dealer misdealing, and also, when turning a card face up,
must deal again. If in the course of a game it develops that cards had
been misdealt, i.e., that one or more players had either too many or not
enough cards, then the Player loses the game if he did not have the right
number of cards, even if the same thing occurred with one of the opponents. But if the Player had the right number of cards and one or both
of the opponents had too many or not enough, then the Player wins, even
if he would have lost the game otherwise. Each player should make sure
before beginning the game that he has 10 cards, neither more nor less.
(The dealer is no longer fined 10 points for misdealing.)

Section 5. The dealer has the right, and it is his duty, to call attention
to any error in the play.

Overbidding. If the player has overbid his game and one of the opponents makes an error, he wins the value of the game, being the amount
he might have lost had no error occurred and the same value shall be
charged against the opponent making such error. Both scored within a
circle.

The skat. Section 1. If before a game is announced, it is discovered
that one or both of the skat cards are in the hand or amongst the cards of
any participant, the dealer shall draw out of the hand of the person having the skat cards, or any of them, sufficient cards to leave said player 10
cards, after which the bidding shall proceed as if no mistake had been
made, but the player causing this proceeding shall be fined 25 points and
is forbidden to participate in the bidding and denied the opportunity to
play any game during this particular deal.

Section 2. If any player by mistake has looked at either of the skat
cards, he shall be barred from playing and fined 10 points. If he exposed
one or both skat cards, and he who plays a Tournee must turn the top
card (second turn is barred), or he can play any other play.

Section 3. A dealer looking at the skat during play is charged with 100 points (encircled). Reason for penalty entered in "Remarks" column.

Section 4. If a player, when turning, accidentally sees both cards without having announced second turn, he shall be compelled to turn the top card and loses the right to play Second Turn or Grand.

Section 5. The skat must not be looked at by any participant before the end of the game, except by the Player when playing a game with the aid of the skat. The two skat cards, except when the player plays a hand with the aid of the skat cards, shall remain with the dealer until the end of the game—and then turned face up on the table.

Section 6. If the player who plays a Solo looks at the skat, he loses his game, but opponents may insist on his continuing for the purpose of increasing his loss.

Section 7. If either opponent examines the skat, the Player wins. He has the same privilege as in Section 6 and the one who looks at the skat loses the number of points the Player wins.

Section 8. Whoever discards more or less than two cards loses his game.

Tricks. *Section 1.* All participants must keep their respective tricks in the order in which the cards were played so that each trick can be traced at the end of the game.

Section 2. The player has the privilege to throw his game after the first trick and claim schneider. He loses this privilege after two cards of the second trick are on the table.

Section 3. Participants have the privilege to examine the last trick made. This must, however, be done before the next card is played.

Section 4. Examining tricks taken, except the last, or recounting is not permitted. Should this be done the opposing side may claim the game.

Section 5. If a player throws down his cards and declares his game won, he cannot claim another trick.

Schneider and schwarz. *Section 1.* In order to win game the Player must have at least 61; to make schneider he must have at least 91; to make schwarz he must take every trick.

Section 2. The Player to be out of schneider must have at least 31 points, the opponents 30.

Section 3. Schneider or schwarz cannot be announced in any game in which the aid of the skat was required.

Section 4. A player announcing a Solo has the privilege before a card is played of increasing the Solo or announcing Grand, schneider or schwarz.

Revokes and misplays. *Section 1.* If the Player misleads or neglects to follow suit, he loses the game, even though he already has 61 or more points. Any one of the opponents, however, has the privilege to have such error corrected and proceed with the game to its end for the purpose of increasing the Player's loss. If, then, one of the opponents makes one of these errors, the Player wins his game, and the full value scored by the Player is charged, within a circle, against the opponent making the error.

Section 2. If either of the opponents leads wrongly, plays out of turn or neglects to follow suit, the error must immediately be corrected if possible. The play then must proceed to the end. If the Player then makes one of the errors above mentioned, he loses the game and the first error is fully condoned. If the game proceeds at the insistence of either of the opponents, and again one of the opponents makes one of the errors referred to above, all previous errors are condoned. The Player must get 61 or more points to enable him to get a bona fide game. [The meaning of this section is that no player can win a bona fide hand on a misplay by an opponent. In such case the hand must be played to the end to determine if the player could win his hand, or had a possible chance had the misplay by an opponent not occurred. The Skatmeister must be called to decide if the Player had a possible chance to win, and if so, he may so rule. He must okay the play if won. If the Skatmeister rules that the Player could not win, he then, nevertheless, receives credit for points, within a circle. The one making the error also loses the full value of the hand, within a circle.]

Section 3. If, during the progress of the game, the Player places his cards upon the table or exposes them, this shall be construed as his claiming the remaining tricks, and if he fails to make them all, he loses the full value of the game unless he already has 61.

Section 4. If, during the progress of the game, any one of the opponents places his cards upon the table or exposes them, this shall be construed as his declaring thereby to have defeated the Player's game, all the remaining cards belong to the Player, and should this make 61 or more points for the Player, he wins and the opponent who erred shall be charged with the full value of the game within a circle.

Section 5. Three-handed Tables. In a three-handed table the first card only, if played out of turn by the person who believes himself the one to lead, shall not be considered a misplay; nor shall any participant who may play out of turn on the last trick be in any manner penalized.

POINTERS ON SKAT

Solo bids. The minimum trump length normally required for a suit bid is five cards. A conservative rule is that for a solo bid the hand should have eight cards that are trumps, aces, or tens. But many experienced players will bid with a count of seven, or six. Of course, "shaded" bids should have compensation in extra top strength in trumps or a favorable pattern (as two long suits). Typical hands for club solo bids are:

♤ J ♡ J	♣ J	♣ J
♣ A Q 9	♣ 10 K Q 9	♣ A 10 Q 8 7
♤ A 7	♤ 10 Q 7	♤ ——
♡ 10 K	♡ A 7	♡ 10 8 7
◇ A	◇ ——	◇ K
CONSERVATIVE	SHADED	RISKY HAND

Gucki bids. The normal requirement for gucki is about an ace less than for solo, a count of seven (conservative) or six (practical). The advantages that may accrue from taking the skat, when you can pick your own trump, are (a) the chance to improve the pattern of the hand; (b) the opportunity to lay away a ten otherwise difficult to save; (c) the chance of buying an extra trump; (d) the chance of buying an ace or other helpful card. These advantages are given in order of likelihood, with (d) such a poor fourth that it should hardly enter into the bidding at all. The following tables show why.

CHANCES OF BUYING ONE CARD IN THE SKAT

TO FIND	PROBABILITY FOR	PERCENTAGE FOR	APPROXIMATE ODDS
Any one card	1/11	9%	10-1 against
Either of 2 cards	41/231	18%	5-1 against
Any one of 3 cards	20/77	26%	3-1 against
Any one of 4 cards	26/77	34%	2-1 against
Any one of 5 cards	95/231	41%	3-2 against
Any one of 6 cards	37/77	48%	even
Any one of 7 cards	6/11	55%	6-5 for
Any one of 8 cards	20/33	60%	3-2 for
Any one of 9 cards	153/231	66%	2-1 for

CHANCES OF BUYING TWO CARDS IN THE SKAT

OUT OF	PROBABILITY FOR (OUT OF 231)	PERCENTAGE FOR	ODDS AGAINST (APPROXIMATE)
2	1	½%	230-1
3	3	1½%	76-1
4	6	2½%	38-1
5	10	4 %	22-1
6	15	6½%	14-1
7	22	9 %	10-1
8	28	12 %	7-1
9	36	15½%	5-1

Tournee bids. In tournee the trump suit is fixed by the chance of the turn. The hand for this bid is therefore one that lacks any long suit, is therefore prepared equally to play any of two or three suits as trump, and has too much general strength to abandon without a fight. Any suitable hand will almost surely have two or more jacks, or the ♣J alone, together with at least two aces and a third suit having at least a ten.

Grand. A common rule for weighing whether a hand warrants a bid of grand is: count each jack and ace as one; the position of forehand as one; at least 5 of the 9 points are needed for a grand. What this says practically is that you need at least two jacks unless you have four aces. The occasion for naming grand is usually (a) a lucky monopoly of the jacks, or (b) one or two powerful suits, with enough side aces and jacks to stop the adverse long suits. Forehand, having the opening lead, can start his long suit at once before his stoppers are attacked; this is precisely the equivalent of an extra ace.

Null and open bids. These require such extraordinary hands that the player can scarcely fail to recognize them when they arise. For a simple null it is better not to be forehand, because it is easier to underplay an adverse lead than to exit on one's own lead.

Discarding. Usually there is little problem in discarding at gucki or tournee: you discard useless small cards. But a plain ten not accompanied by the ace is always a problem; sometimes it is best laid away, sometimes it is best saved as a stopper, even at the risk of being lost. The chance of saving it in play rests almost wholly upon leads of the suit by the Opponents. Hence the first consideration is how many times they are going to get in the lead. A hand so weak in top cards that it is going to lose the lead four or five times can better save a 10-x than one that is going to lose the lead only two or three times—in direct contravention of the common reaction of the tyro, to try to rescue a weak bid by burying a ten.

When no question of saving tens is involved, the normal discard is small cards from short suits, in order to limit the number of points the opponents can win on straight leads of these suits.

Plan of the Player. An old Skat maxim is: *Fordern ist die Seele des Spiels* (leading trumps is the soul of the play). Correct policy by the Player is usually to lead trumps as soon as he gains the lead, pulling two trumps for one.

As in three-hand Pinochle, the policy of the Opponents is to try to smear (discard) to each other the aces and tens that they could not otherwise win against the Player's trumps. To forestall a smear by one Opponent on the other's trump tricks, the Player should give up tricks to adverse trump stoppers on early rounds rather than later. For example, suppose the Player has ♣ J ♣ A 10 Q 9 in trumps at a club solo. He should plan to lead the suit from the bottom up, not the top down. Almost surely he must lose two trump tricks; he wants to let the Opponents make their jacks without gathering any side aces or tens.

The Player should not overlook the opportunity to get rid of unwanted small cards by discarding them on a suit of which he is void, instead of trumping. Look at the example labelled "risky hand" on page 324. Normal expectation is that the Player can win a solo club game only through one circumstance—the Opponents lead a spade before touching diamonds, and on a trick that does not contain both ace and ten the Player discards the ◇K. By sacrificing 15 points at most, he captures all the rest of the points in spades and diamonds—provided that no smears occur. Since he cannot expect to save anything in hearts with this play, he loses 30 in hearts besides 15 in spades, plus perhaps 10 in trumps, and takes about 65.

Opponents' play. The general principles of play by the Opponents are: to let the lead come from the righthand Opponent rather than the lefthand; righthand Opponent to lead by preference a suit to which the Player must follow, lefthand Opponent to lead by preference a suit of which the Player is void; to try to smear aces and tens to each other, if these cards otherwise would go to the Player.

The principal "headache" that falls on lefthand Opponent is what new suit to open when he is forced in the lead early. The ideal solution is to have an ace-ten, and lead the ten, thereby showing the fellow Opponent the ace. Next-best is to have a long side suit headed by ace alone; lead the ace, to give partner a chance to throw the ten, if he has it. If the Player has the guarded ten, partner may capture it by trumping.

RAUBER SKAT

In the variant "robber" Skat the rules as to the use of the skat are liberalized. The high bidder may pick up the skat in any game but least (also called *reject*). Foregoing this privilege is called handplay, and when handplay is elected one multiplier is added to whatever item applies in the table in paragraph 23, page 321. If he chooses instead to take skat, the high bidder may defer naming his game until he has seen the skat cards. The base values of the games are as follows:

TRUMPS	$\diamond$	$\heartsuit$	$\spadesuit$	$\clubsuit$	JACKS TRUMPS		NO TRUMPS	
	9	10	11	12	Grand	20	Simple null	23
					Reject	10	Open null	46

The null values are invariable. The Player may play any handplay game open, in which case its base value (whatever the suit or if jacks are trumps) is 59. If the Player loses in a handplay game, he loses singly; in a game where he has taken the skat, he loses doubly.

FROG

In German this game is Tapp or württembergischer Tarok; in French, Solo or *Sans Prendre;* in English, Solo, Heart Solo, Slough, Sluff, or Frog. It has even been called Rana, after the frog genus. But the name Frog is derived (by ear) from the German *frage* (I ask), the lowest game that can be bid in Skat and similar games.

Number of players. 1. Three active players, but four or five may participate, in which case the dealer gives no cards to himself (nor to the second player at his left, in five-hand).

The pack. 2. A pack of 36 cards, made by discarding all cards below the sixes from a full pack.

Rank of cards. 3. The cards in each suit rank: A (high), K, Q, J, 10, 9, 8, 7, 6.

The deal. 4. Each player receives eleven cards, dealt in batches of 4-3-4. After the first round of the deal, a widow of three cards is dealt face down on the table.

Bidding. 5. There is one round of bidding. Each player in turn beginning with eldest hand (player at left of dealer) must pass or make a bid higher than any preceding bid.

6. There are three possible bids, which rank: grand (high), chico, frog. At *grand,* hearts are trumps; the widow is set aside, but is added to the bidder's tricks at the end of the play. At *chico,* the bidder names any suit but hearts as trumps; the widow is set aside but belongs finally to the bidder. In *frog,* hearts are trumps; the bidder picks up the widow and then discards any three cards face down. His discards are added to his tricks after the play.

The play. 7. Eldest hand makes the opening lead. He may lead any card. After any lead each other hand must follow suit if able; if unable, the hand may play any card. A trick is won by the highest trump, or, if it contains no trump, by the highest card of the suit led. The winner of a trick leads to the next.

Object of play. 8. The other two players combine in temporary partnership against the high bidder. Each side tries to win counting cards in tricks.

9. The value of cards won in tricks is:

Each ace	11
Each ten	10
Each king	4
Each queen	3
Each jack	2

(Lower cards count nothing.)

Scoring. 10. The bidder collects from or pays to both opponents equally, according to what he himself wins in tricks over or under 60 points. The basic value of frog being agreed, chico counts twice as much, and grand four times as much. If the points in play are divided 60-60, there is no settlement for the deal.

Irregularities. 11. Follow the rules for Skat, pages 322 *et seq*.

SIX-BID SOLO

Players in the western United States developed this game early in the present century by elaboration of Heart Solo or Frog. Follow all the rules of Frog except:

There are six possible bids, ranking from low to high as follows:

(a) *Simple solo.* The bidder names any suit but hearts as trumps, and must win 60 points or more in tricks.

(b) *Heart solo*. Hearts are trumps. The bidder must win 60 points or more in tricks.

(c) *Misère*. There is no trump suit. The bidder must win not a single counting card (but he need not lose all the tricks to make his game).

(d) *Guarantee solo*. The bidder names any suit trumps; if he names hearts, he must win 74 points or more in tricks; if he names another suit, he must win 80 or more.

(e) *Spread misère*. Same as misère, except that the opening lead is made by the player at left of the bidder, and the latter spreads his whole hand face up on the table just prior to playing to the first trick.

(f) *Call solo*. The bidder names any card not in his hand, and the holder of that card must give it to him in exchange for any card the bidder chooses to let go. (If the called card is in the widow, there is no exchange.) The bidder then names any suit trumps, and he must win all 120 points in tricks (not necessarily every trick).

The widow cards are never picked up, and in misère they are not added to the bidder's tricks. Settlement for simple solo and heart solo is as in Frog—the bidder collects or pays for every point he wins over or under 60, at 2 per point in simple solo, 3 per point in heart solo. All the other games have a fixed value, which the bidder collects or pays according as he makes or fails to make the contract:

Misère	30
Guarantee solo	40
Spread misère	60
Call solo, hearts trumps	100
Call solo, another suit trumps	150

⇀ OMBRE ↼

No other card game held so long a tenure in the fashionable world as Ombre (or Hombre or l'Hombre). It probably originated in Spain, some time prior to the 15th century, and may be as old as Tarok. It spread throughout Europe, and remained a leading game for five hundred years; during at least two hundred of those years (17th and 18th centuries) it was undisputed favorite. Even as late as the 1880s, a standard European "Hoyle" devoted fifty pages to Ombre, only fifteen to Whist.

Ombre was originally played with the Spanish pack of forty cards, which can be made from the modern pack by discarding all tens, nines and eights. It was originally played only three-hand, two players combining in temporary partnership against ombre (i. e., the man, the high bidder). Later it was adapted for play by two, four, or more players, and to use of the fifty-two-card pack. A four-hand variant, Quadrille, became especially popular in France and England.

Among terms peculiar to the game are: spadill or spadille (♠A, always the highest trump), basto (♣A, always the third-best trump), manill or manille (the second-best trump, the card that in a plain suit would rank lowest), ponto (the trump ace when a red suit is trumps); also matador, respect, forcee, codill or codille, gano, chicane, rocambole, consolation; also the "hazards": charivary, chicoree, contentment, degout, discord, estrapade, fanatique, guinguette, mirliro, triomphante, and yeux.

Many of the features of this complex game—which may have died, like the dinosaur, from the sheer weight of its efflorescences—are preserved in current games, such as Skat, Frog, and Solo.

SOLO (OMBRE)

The game here described is a simplification of Ombre that became popular a hundred years ago and has outlasted the parent. Although the list of allowable bids has varied widely from time to time and place to place, Solo has never acquired an alternative name, and we have to call it Solo (Ombre) to distinguish it from variants of Tarok, Skat, and Whist, also called Solo.

Number of players. 1. Four players participate; each plays for himself, but there are temporary partnerships during the play.

The pack. 2. A pack of 32 cards, made by discarding all cards below the sevens from a full pack.

Rank of cards. 3. The ♣Q (called *spadille*) is always the highest trump. The second-best is the 7 of the trump suit (called *manille,* the same word as *menel* in Klaberjass). The third-best is the ♠Q (called *basto*). The whole ranking of trumps is as follows:

Spades or clubs: ♣ Q, 7, ♠ Q, A, K, J, 10, 9, 8.
Hearts or diamonds: ♣ Q, 7, ♠ Q, A, K, Q, J, 10, 9, 8.
The rank in each plain suit is: A (high), K, (Q), J, 10, 9, 8, 7.

4. The club suit has a privileged status. Any bid for clubs as trumps is in color; a bid for another suit is in suit. There is no relative rank among spades, hearts, and diamonds.

The deal. 5. Each player receives eight cards, dealt in batches of 3-2-3. (Modern practice is to deal cards one at a time.)

Bidding. 6. The six possible bids, in order from low to high, are as follows:

Frog in suit	2
Frog in color	4
Solo in suit	4
Solo in color	8
Tout in suit	16
Tout in color	32

7. At *frog,* the high bidder names the trump suit. He also names an ace not in his hand, and the holder of that ace becomes his partner, but must say nothing to reveal his identity before duly playing the ace. At *solo,* the bidder names the trump suit and plays alone against the other three. At *tout,* the bidder names the trump suit, plays alone, and must win all the tricks.

8. Eldest hand (player at left of the dealer) bids first and settles with the player at his left. The two players may bid against each other until one passes. Then the survivor settles with the next player, and so on. A player who has once passed may not reënter the bidding.

9. The high bidder is not committed to play the game named in his winning bid; he may choose that or any higher-ranking game. When he chooses a game in color, clubs are trumps; when the game is in suit, the bidder names a suit other than clubs. If the game is frog, he names an ace to fix his partner. (Should the bidder himself hold all four aces, he may name a king.)

10. A player holding both spadille and basto (the black queens) is not permitted to pass before at least a solo in suit has been bid, either by himself or an opposing bidder. This compulsion is called *forcee.*

11. If all four players pass without a bid, the holder of spadille (♣Q) must expose it and play a frog, in suit or color as he pleases.

The play. 12. Eldest hand makes the opening lead. He may lead any card. After any lead, each other hand must follow suit if able; if unable, the hand may play any card. A trick is won by the highest trump, or, if it contains no trump, by the highest card of the suit led. The winner of a trick leads to the next.

Object of play. 13. At frog or solo, the bidder (with the aid of his partner, in frog) makes his game if he wins five tricks. At tout, the bidder must win all eight tricks.

Scoring. 14. The base values of the games are given in paragraph 6. At frog, the bidder and his partner each win or lose the base value from each opponent. At solo or tout, the bidder wins from or loses to each other player.

15. Each deal is a separate game and may be settled at once. Or, score may be kept on paper, with losses entered as minus quantities, and settlement made when a session ends.

Irregularities. 16. *Revoke.* If a player fails to follow suit when able, and fails to correct the error before the trick is gathered, his side loses at once and he must pay the loss for every member.

17. *Play out of turn.* If an opponent of the bidder at solo or tout, or any player at frog, leads or plays out of turn, or exposes a card other than by legal play, his side loses at once and he must pay the loss for every member.

(*Variant rule.* To mitigate these severe penalties, it may be agreed that for any such irregularity a player must pay a forfeit into a pool, which is divided equally among the four players at the end of the session.)

CALABRASELLA

The *Westminster Papers* (Vol. III, 1870) called Calabrasella "the Italian national game." Henry Jones ("Cavendish") made an effort to popularize it in England, with little success. The name suggests that it originated in Calabria, a province in the toe of Italy; folk etymology would trace to the same source the games of Callabra and Kalabriàs. But the use of the Spanish pack makes a Spanish origin seem equally likely, and Calabrasella is in principle much like Ombre.

Number of players. 1. Three active players but four may participate, the dealer giving himself no cards.

The pack. 2. A pack of 40 cards, made by discarding all tens, nines, and eights from a full pack.

Rank of cards. 3. The cards in each suit rank: 3 (high), 2, A, K, Q, J, 7, 6, 5, 4.

The deal. 4. Each player receives twelve cards, dealt two at a time. The remaining four cards are placed face down on the table to form the widow (*scat*).

Bidding. 5. Beginning with eldest hand (player at left of the dealer), each in turn must either pass or elect to play. If any elects to play, he becomes the Player, there is no further bidding, and the play begins. If all pass, the deal is abandoned and the next dealer deals.

The play. 6. The Player names the three of any suit that is not in his hand; the holder of the named card must give it to the Player in exchange for any card the Player chooses to give up; this card is not shown to the third player. If the named card chances to be in the widow, the Player may not call for another card instead. If the Player was dealt all four threespots, he may call for a two.

7. The Player next discards face down one, two, three or four cards. He must discard at least one. He turns the widow face up for all to see, and selects the ones he pleases to replace his discards. The four remaining cards—widow and discard—are set aside and belong at the end of the play to the winner of the last trick.

8. The two Opponents combine in temporary partnership against the Player. The Opponent at his left makes the opening lead. He may lead any card. After any lead, each other hand must follow suit if able; if unable, a hand may play any card. A trick is won by the highest card of the suit led. (There is no trump suit.) The winner of a trick leads to the next.

Object of play. 9. Each side strives to win counting cards in tricks, and to win last trick, which counts 3 points. The counting cards are:

Each ace   3
Each 3, 2, K, Q and J   1

Each suit contains 8 points, and the whole pack, with the 3 for last trick, 35 points.

Scoring. 10. Each side totals its points at the end of the play. The Player collects from or pays to each Opponent, according to the difference of the totals. For example, the Player wins 22 points; he collects 9 points (22-13) from each Opponent. But if one side wins all 35 points in the pack, the losers pay 70 each. In a four-hand game the dealer settles as an Opponent, but may give no advice.

11. Each deal is a separate game and is settled at once, as by chips.

Irregularities. 12. *Looking at the widow.* If, before any player has declared "I play," a player intentionally looks at any card of the widow, he must pay each other player 35 points. If an Opponent looks at any card of the widow before the Player has discarded, the card must be turned face up and the Player may discard accordingly. If the Player looks at any card of the widow before discarding, he may not exchange any cards with the widow; the whole widow must be turned face up, then set aside.

13. *Exposed card.* If an Opponent illegally exposes any card from his hand to his partner (as by leading or playing out of turn), the Player may halt the play, claim all the remaining tricks and the widow, and score 3 for last; the Opponents score only for cards won prior to the offense.

14. *Revoke.* A revoke by failure to follow suit when able may be corrected without penalty before the lead to the next trick. If not corrected in time, a revoke stands established; at the end of play, 9 points are deducted from the score of the revoking side and added to the score of the other side.

Pointers on Calabrasella play. A player experienced in other three-hand games, such as Skat and Auction Pinochle, is likely to underrate the strength necessary to take the widow. For lack of a trump suit, the Player is defenseless against the cashing of an adverse solid suit. In fact, few hands dealt would merit playing but for the opportunity to strengthen the hand by obtaining a three and exchanging discards for the widow. Even these props are not enough to bolster an average hand (*e.g.*, one card for each rank) to a probable winner (as has been erroneously maintained). The initial hand should be about two deuces better than average.

But the chances of "picking up something in the play" are greater than in any other two-against-one game when the opposition is weak. Calabrasella is comparable to Whist in the possible squeezes and throw-ins that can occur. This fact is bound to weigh in the bidding.

⇌ TAROK ⇌

Probably the most ancient card game still played is Tarok (also Tarock, Taroky, Tarocchini). Once played throughout Europe, it is still a leading game in Central Europe, notably Czechoslovakia. It requires a special pack, originally of 78 cards, and many examples of the pack have survived from 15th-century Italy and France; this is called the tarot pack.

Though there have been many local variations in Tarok play, the basic rules appear to have been remarkably stable. The rules given below, for the variant most-played today, are taken from a German encyclopedia, which also says:

"Little is known for certain of the history of this ancient game. According to one version, it originated in Portugal and derived its name, as well as the names of the principal cards (Skus, Mond, Pagat), from certain notorious highwaymen and gamesters. Another version holds that Tarok is of French origin. A third version, which seems the most likely, is that about 1400 the Prince of Pisa, Francesco Fibbio, developed Tarok from the ancient Italian game Trappola. Trappola is the oldest card game known in Germany. It required only thirty-two cards. In the course of time the pack was enlarged to seventy-eight cards for Tarock."

Number of players. 1. Three. But four may participate; the dealer then gives himself no cards, but shares in the winnings and losses of the Opponents.

The pack. 2. A pack of 54 cards made by discarding 24 suit cards from the full tarot pack. As manufactured today, the Tarok pack comprises:

(a) 22 trump cards. One of them (the Skus, or Skis, herein called the joker) may bear a picture or simply the number XXII. The other 21 trumps are numbered from XXI to I. The two extreme cards, XXI (Mond) and I (Pagat), have special value and may have special markings.

(b) 32 plain cards, eight in each of four suits here called spades, hearts, diamonds, clubs. In each suit there are four face cards, herein called king, queen, cavalier, and jack. [The full tarot pack also has ten cards in each suit numbered from ace (as one) to ten, but only four of each suit are used in Tarok.]

Rank of cards. 3. The trumps rank: Joker (high), XXI, XX, and so on in order to I.

In each red suit the cards rank: K (high), Q, C (cavalier), J, A, 2, 3, 4.
In each black suit the cards rank: K (high), Q, C, J, 10, 9, 8, 7.

Counters. 4. Nineteen cards of the pack are counters, having point values as follows:

Joker	5
XXI	5
I	5
Each king	5
Each queen	4
Each cavalier	3
Each jack	2

The thirty-five cards that have no point value are herein called nulls.

Trick values. 5. The foregoing values given for the counters are not absolute, but determine trick values as follows (but see paragraph 19):

(a) A trick comprising three nulls counts 1;

(b) A trick comprising one counter and two nulls counts the value of the counter;

(c) A trick comprising two counters and one null counts 1 less than the total of the counters;

(d) A trick comprising three counters counts 2 less than their total.

The deal. 6. The rotation of dealing and playing is to the right, counter-clockwise (instead of to the left, as in most modern games). The three active players are called forehand (at right of dealer), middlehand, and endhand (who is the dealer when no more than three players are at the table).

7. Each player receives sixteen cards, dealt in batches of eight cards at a time. After the first round of the deal, six cards are dealt face down upon the table to form a widow (called the scat or skat in Europe).

Bidding. 8. Forehand declares first, and the bidding continues until a winning bidder is determined. A player who once passes may not bid thereafter. There are only two possible bids: threesome (after the German *Dreier*) and solo.

9. A bid of solo always overcalls a bid of threesome. Furthermore, solo by forehand has precedence over solo by either other player, and solo by middlehand supersedes solo by endhand. If forehand's bid of threesome is overcalled, or middlehand's bid of threesome is overcalled by endhand, the threesome bidder can in each case bid solo and thereby overcall the opposing bidder.

10. If all three players pass without a bid, the deal is abandoned without a score. (*Variant rule:* Forehand in such case scores 25 points. This is actually the prevalent rule in Germany. Since forehand actually calls "Tapp" or "Trapper" instead of passing, the variant is called Tapp-Tarok.)

11. The winning bidder becomes the Player; the other two combine in temporary partnership as the Opponents.

The play. 12. If the winning bid was threesome, the Player picks up the top three cards of the widow and puts them into his hand, then discards any three cards face down. At the end of the play, the discards belong to the Player and the three untouched cards of the widow belong to the Opponents.

13. The Player may not discard a king. He may discard a trump, but must announce the fact if he does so. (Local rules differ as to whether he must show the trump so that the Opponents will know its rank, or merely announce that he has laid away a trump. Of course the situation is very rare.)

14. *Optional rule.* After seeing the widow cards, the Player may elect to play for *game* or for *consolation.* For game, he tries to win 36 or more points in play; for consolation, he tries to avoid winning more than 35.

15. *Variant.* If the top three cards of the widow do not suit the Player, he may expose them on the table and instead take the bottom three. If he then plays, the game counts double. He may similarly reject the bottom three cards, spreading them face up, and reclaim the top three which he rejected. He must then play, the game counting triple. In any case, the Player discards three cards face down; these cards belong to him, while the other three go to the Opponents. In this variant, a bid of threesome can be twice overcalled by the same bid, these overcalls being offers to play the double or triple game. In some localities yet another overcall is allowed, committing the bidder to play at quadruple value.

16. If the winning bid is solo, the widow is set aside, and at the end of the play is added to the tricks of the Opponents.

17. Forehand invariably makes the opening lead, regardless of who is the Player. He may lead any card. After any lead, each other hand must follow suit if able, a trump on a trump, a suit on a suit. If unable to follow suit to a plain lead, a hand must trump if able. If unable either to follow suit or trump, a hand may play any card. A trick is won by the highest trump, or, if it contains no trump, by the highest card of the suit led. The winner of a trick leads to the next.

Melds. 18. Before the opening lead, but after the Player (in a threesome) has discarded, any hand holding a meld must declare it. There are two possible melds: the three trump counters: joker, XXI, and I; and the four kings. Each meld counts 50 in a threesome, 100 in a solo. If each deal is settled as a separate game, melds are settled as soon as they are shown; any meld collects its value from both other players.

Scoring. 19. The Player wins his game if he gathers 36 or more points in tricks, together with his discard; or, if the game was consolation, he takes no more than 35. (Note: This rule derives from former times when the point count of the counters was absolute. With a total of 71 points in counters, 36 is a bare majority. Under the modern rule of paragraph 5— an effort to reconcile the addition of points for tricks with the old constants—the number of points countable per deal varies, and often is 75 or more. In many localities it is therefore the rule that the Player wins only if he gathers a majority of the points in play.)

20. If the Player wins his game, he scores double the number of points he took over 35, plus 50 for threesome or 100 for solo. For example, if he took 48 points, he scores 76 or 126, as the case may be.

21. If the Player fails to make his game, each Opponent scores the value of the bid (threesome 50, solo 100) plus double the number of all points taken by the two Opponents over 35.

22. The score may be kept on paper. In this case, a meld is credited to the holder regardless of the outcome of the play; the Player alone scores if he wins; each Opponent scores if the Player loses. When a session ends, each player settles with every other according to the difference of scores. Or, each deal may be treated as a separate game and settled at once. In this case, melds are paid for as soon as declared; the Player collects from or pays to both Opponents.

Ultimo. 23. If the player wins the last trick with the trump I (Pagat), he scores a bonus equal to the value of the game (threesome 50, solo 100).

24. The Player may, before the opening lead, announce ultimo, *i.e.*, that he will try to win the last trick with the trump I. If he succeeds, he scores a bonus of twice the game-value; if he fails, he loses this amount. Success or failure of ultimo has no effect on winning or losing the game (taking more than 35 points in tricks). If ultimo is announced, and the Player loses his trump I on an earlier trick, he is nevertheless credited with its 5 points if he wins last trick; if he plays the trump I unnecessarily, the 5 points go to the Opponents regardless of who captured the Pagat.

25. After announcement of ultimo, either Opponent may announce contra-ultimo, *i.e.*, that he will try to win Pagat from the Player. (*Note.* Old rules state that he must capture it on the last trick. This is manifestly absurd, since the Player could almost invariably avoid quadruple loss at cost of double loss, by throwing Pagat at some earlier time.) If he succeeds, the Opponents win a bonus of quadruple the game-value; if he fails, the Player collects this amount. (*Note.* The only feasible rule is to allow the Player double bonus for saving Pagat at all, or quadruple if he wins the last trick with it.)

TRESETTE

This is a popular Italian game; but the rotation (counter-clockwise), the 40-card pack and the rank of cards will be strange to Americans.

Number of players. 1. Four, as partners, two against two; partners sit opposite each other.

The pack. 2. 40 cards—the 52-card pack with tens, nines and eights deleted.

Rank of cards. 3. 3 (high), 2, A, K, J, Q, 7, 6, 5, 4. (Note that the jack ranks above the queen.)

The deal. 4. Ten cards are dealt to each player, five at a time.

Rotation. 5. The rotation in dealing and play is counter-clockwise.

Objects of the game. 6. The objects are: to meld certain combinations of cards, and to win counting cards in tricks.

Melding. 7. A player on looking at his hand says (the equivalent of) "Good play" if he holds any of the following combinations: Three or four of a kind, provided the rank of the cards is three, two, or ace; and *nap*, which is A-2-3 of the same suit (any suit). Provided he has made the announcement, a player may then, upon winning a trick, announce what the combination was—as, "three aces," or "nap" (he need not specify the suit).

The play. 8. Eldest hand leads, and each player in turn after him must follow suit if able; if not able he may play any card. The highest card of the suit led wins each trick, which consists of one card from each player. The winner of a trick leads to the next.

9. Upon leading, a player may call upon his partner to "play his best" or to "play the ace" of the suit led.

10. A player may announce, upon playing to the lead of another player, how many cards he has in the suit led.

11. A player may announce, upon leading or playing, that there is another (unspecified) suit in which he is void, or has only one or two cards.

Scoring. 12. Upon conclusion of play, each side scores:

For each meld, 1 point for each card in the combination.

For each ace won in tricks, 1 point.

For each three, two, or face card won in tricks (in effect), ⅓ point; that is, for each three such cards won, the side scores 1 point, though it scores nothing for an odd one or two of them.

For winning the last trick, 1 point.

13. The first side to reach 31 points and claim the game wins it. The claim may be made during the play of a hand. If the claim is not justified by the score, the other side wins the game.

MEDIATORE

This is a form of Tresette in which there is no melding. Each player contributes 5 chips to a pool before the deal. Partnerships are not fixed, but are determined by the bidding. Nine cards are dealt to each player, and the remaining four are set aside as the widow.

Eldest hand may elect to be Mediator (which is an undertaking to win 6 of the 11 possible points), or may pass; if he passes, the right to become Mediator moves to the player at his right, and so on in rotation. When a player becomes Mediator, he may elect to play alone; or he may call for a specified card and the holder of that card becomes his partner.

The Mediator then takes the widow into his hand and discards four cards. If he called for a card and it is in the widow, he must play alone.

When the Mediator plays alone, he must match the pool, putting in 20 chips; when he has a partner, that partner identifies himself and they put in 10 chips each.

Playing and scoring (except for melds) are as in Tresette. The Mediator's discard counts as a trick for him. If the Mediator, or his side, wins the majority of the 11 possible points they take the pool; if he does not, there is no penalty; the pool remains and there is another deal without additional contributions from the players. But a player who becomes Mediator must always match the pool, so on the next deal there will be 40 chips in the pool for the Mediator (and his partner, if any) to match.

PRIMIERA

This ancient game is popular with Italian-Americans. The 40-card pack is used—K, Q, J, 7, 6, 5, 4, 3, 2, A. Four play, and each antes to form a pot. Four cards are dealt to each player; the rotation is counterclockwise throughout. The object is to make any of the following combinations:

Primiera—one card of each suit; highest ranking.

Flush—four cards of one suit; next-highest.

Fifty-five—ace, seven, six of one suit.

As between combinations of the same class, rank is determined by the point-values of the cards: Each seven counts 21, six 18, ace 16, five 15, four 14, three 13, two 12, face cards 10 each.

Each player in turn, beginning with eldest hand (the player to dealer's right), may discard any number of cards and be dealt replacements from the stock. This process continues until any player knocks, whereupon there is a showdown and the highest-ranking hand wins the pot. If hands are otherwise tied, eldest hand has precedence, and after him each player in rotation to his right. If no one knocks when the pack is exhausted, the discards are shuffled and play continues.

⇌ CHESS ⇌

There is no other game so esteemed, so profound and so venerable as Chess; in the realm of play it stands alone in dignity. The one challenger for preëminence produced by the pack of playing cards—Auction or Contract Bridge—rivals Chess only in profundity, not in antiquity. The more ancient games, dice and the track games (such as Pachisi and Backgammon) played with dice, approach Chess as little in profundity as in prestige. The mechanics of Chess is simple for anyone capable of playing the game enjoyably; the ultimate science of the game is unfathomable, whence, no doubt, its inexhaustible appeal even to its best-informed students, and its infinite vitality.

Chess is a board game for two players.

History. See under Pachisi, page 399.

Definitions. 1. The following terms are defined as used in Chess.

ATTACK. In the name of an opening, a White choice of moves.

BACKWARD PAWN. One that is subject to attack from an enemy pawn if advanced, especially if the advance is difficult to enforce without loss.

CASTLING. A certain compound move of the king and one rook, conventionally denoted by O-O or O-O-O. (See paragraph 21.)

CENTER. The central squares, specifically d5, d4, e5, and e4.

CHECK. A threat to capture the enemy king.

CHECKMATE. The situation of a king threatened with capture, when no parry of the threat is possible.

COUNTER. In the name of an opening, a Black choice of moves.

DEFENSE. In the name of an opening, a Black choice of moves.

DEVELOPMENT. The initial phase of a game, particularly the moving of other pieces off the first rank and castling so as to "unite the rooks."

DIAGONAL. A line of squares parallel to a diagonal of the board.

DISCOVERED CHECK. One delivered by a queen, rook, or bishop by moving a piece off its line of attack.

DOUBLE CHECK. Check by each of two pieces simultaneously.

DOUBLE PAWN. Two pawns of the same color on the same file.

DOUBLE JUMP. The advance of a pawn from the second rank to the fourth.

END-GAME. The phase of a game in which, usually, the dominating object is to queen a pawn; sometimes applied to the rest of a game after the original queens are exchanged.

en passant (abbreviated *e. p.;* French, "in passing"). A form of pawn capture. (See paragraph 19.)

EXCHANGE. Capture and counter-capture, especially of like pieces. TO WIN THE EXCHANGE—to capture a more valuable piece in return for a lesser, especially to win a rook for a bishop or knight.

FIANCHETTO. The development of a bishop at N2 (see Notation, paragraph 35.)

FILE. A line of squares perpendicular to the sides at which the players are seated.

FORK. Simultaneous attack on two pieces or squares.

GAMBIT. The offer of a pawn, sometimes a minor piece, especially in the opening. The offer is made in the expectation of gaining equivalent positional advantage for the sacrificed piece.

HALF-OPEN FILE. One from which the player's own pawn has disappeared, but not the enemy pawn.

HOLE. A third-rank square in front of an unmoved pawn, liable to occupation by the enemy because the pawns on both adjacent files have advanced or disappeared; more generally, any square in one's own half of the board on which an enemy piece can settle without being dislodged by a pawn attack.

IN PASSING. See *en passant.*

INTERPOSE. Move a piece on the line to avert a check from an enemy queen, rook, or bishop.

ISOLATED PAWN. One that cannot be defended by another pawn because the pawns on both adjacent files have disappeared.

J'adoube (French, "I adjust"). The conventional phrase used when a player wishes to touch a piece without being legally committed to move it or capture it.

MAJOR PIECE. A queen or rook.

MATE. Checkmate.

MID-GAME. The phase of a game after the opening and before the end-game.

MINOR PIECE. A bishop or knight.

OPENING. The initial phase of a game, usually considered to last until both players have completed their development; a specific series of early moves, such as "the Catalan Opening."

OPEN FILE. One not obstructed by a pawn of either color.

PASSED PAWN. One that can advance without opposition from enemy pawns, there being none on the same file or either adjacent file.

PERPETUAL CHECK. An endless series of checks from which a king cannot escape (or which cannot be averted without loss of the game); one form of drawn game.

PIECE. This term is often restricted to pieces other than pawns.

PIN. The partial or complete paralysis of a piece by a queen, rook, or bishop, through the fact that a move of the pinned piece off the line would expose the king to check or a valuable piece to capture.

PROMOTION. The replacement of a pawn that has reached the eighth rank by a queen or other piece.

QUEENING. Promotion.

RANK. A line of squares parallel to the sides of the board at which the players are seated.

RAPID TRANSIT. Chessplay under the time limit of a few seconds per move.

SMOTHERED MATE. Checkmate by a knight, the king being largely or wholly shut in by pieces of his own color.

STALEMATE. A position in which the player to move can make no legal move, but is not in check; this is an automatic drawn game.

FIG. 1. The chessboard.   FIG. 2. Initial position of the pieces.

The board. 2. The chessboard is a large square composed of 64 small squares. The small squares are colored alternately light and dark. The two players sit at opposite sides of the board, which is so turned that each player finds a light square in the corner at his right hand.

3. A column of squares extending from one player's side of the board to the other's is called a file. A row of squares at right angles to a file is called a rank. The term diagonal is self-explanatory.

4. In printed diagrams, common usage is to place the White side of the board at the bottom.

The pieces. 5. Each player commences with sixteen pieces, which are arranged on the two ranks nearest himself, as shown in Fig. 2. The pieces are of six different kinds, as follows:

Pawn (each player has eight pawns, all on the second rank)
Rook (two rooks, in the corners)
Knight (two knights, next to the rooks)
Bishop (two bishops, next to the knights)
Queen (one queen, in the center)
King (one king, in the center)

6. The placement of queen and king is usually expressed as "Queen on her own color." That is, White's queen goes on the light square, of the

two in the center of the first rank, and Black's queen goes on the dark square. Both queens therefore stand on the same file.

Object of play. 7. To win the game, a player must capture the enemy king. The capture is never actually made; play ends forthwith if a king is checkmated, that is, threatened with capture and unable to escape.

8. When a move is made that directly attacks a king, the player by custom draws attention to the fact by saying "Check!" (There is no legal obligation to give this warning.) The player whose king is attacked must parry the attack if able; if instead he makes a move that leaves his king in check, such a move is void and must be retracted. Similarly, a move that exposes one's own king to check is illegal and must be retracted.

9. The majority of games end by resignation of one player, before his king is checkmated. Sometimes this is because checkmate is imminent and the player can find no way to avert it; sometimes one player gains such advantage in material or position that his opponent concedes further struggle to be useless.

The moves. 10. Each of the six kinds of pieces has powers peculiar to itself. "The moves" are as follows.

11. King may move to any adjacent square, on the file, rank, or diagonal. Once in a game the king may combine with the rook in a compound move castling, explained below.

12. Rook may move any distance along an open file or rank.

13. Bishop may move any distance along an open diagonal. Each bishop is forever chained to squares of the same color as that on which it is initially posted. Note that each player begins with a "white" and a "black" bishop.

14. Queen combines the powers of rook and bishop. She may move any distance along an open file, rank, or diagonal.

15. Knight makes a leaping move, which may be described as from one corner to the corner diagonally opposite in a rectangle of three squares by two. Other pieces standing within the rectangle do not obstruct the move, which is not along a line but point-to-point. At most, the knight has a choice of eight moves, as shown in Fig. 3.

16. Pawn moves forward along the file, never backward. From its initial post on the second rank, the pawn has the option of moving up one square or two squares (double jump); after having left the second rank, it may advance only one square at a time. The pawn also has other peculiarities described in paragraphs 18, 19, 20.

Capture. 17. Any piece but a pawn can capture an enemy piece standing on a square that it can reach by its regular move. A captured piece is removed from the board, and the captor takes its place on the same square.

18. The pawn does not attack and cannot capture an enemy on the same file. It may capture on an adjacent square, diagonally forward.

19. Under certain circumstances, a White pawn (for example) may capture a Black pawn in passing. (More common in books of all lan-

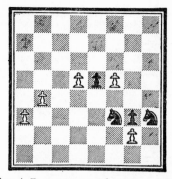

Fig. 3. Knight move. The Black knight can capture any of the White pawns.

Fig. 4. Pawn moves. The White QRP has advanced one square; the QNP has made a double jump. The pawns on the KN file block but do not attack each other, but the White pawn can capture either Black knight. If the Black KP has just made a double jump, it can be captured in passing by the White QP or KBP.

guages is the French *en passant,* abbreviated to *e. p.*) This rule was made to prevent a pawn from escaping entirely the attack of an enemy pawn on an adjacent file, through the double jump privilege. Suppose that a Black pawn has made a double jump, and now stands adjacent to a White pawn on the same rank. Had the Black pawn advanced only one square, it would have been susceptible of capture. Under the *e. p.* rule, it may still be captured, despite the double jump. White may move his pawn to the square jumped over by the Black pawn and remove the latter from the board. But he must do so at once, if at all; having permitted the Black pawn to get by, White may not later capture it *e. p.*

Promotion. 20. A pawn that reaches the enemy first rank must be removed from the board and replaced by another piece of the same color. This promotion is usually called queening, since the usual choice is to replace the pawn by a queen, the most powerful piece. But the player may choose rook, bishop, or knight, if he wishes, and sometimes there is advantage in such underpromotion.

Castling. 21. The move castling is a move of king and one rook. It is legal only if (a) neither king nor that rook has moved during the game; and (b) the squares on the rank between king and rook are vacant, and neither of the two nearest the king is under enemy attack; and (c) the king is not in check. Castling is executed by moving the king two squares toward the rook along the first rank, then moving the rook to the square passed over by the king. As shown in Fig. 5, the player may castle with either rook. In English the two modes are traditionally called castling king's side and queen's side.

345

Fig. 5. Castling. The White king can castle with either rook, if neither piece has yet moved. The Black bishop does not prevent 0-0 or 0-0-0, since the squares it attacks are not moved over by the king in either case. The Black kings and rooks show the position after castling on queen's side (left) and king's side (right).

Fig. 6. Stalemate positions. At top, the Black queen stalemates the White queen and king; with Black to move, the game is drawn. At lower right, the Black queen stalemates the White king. At lower left, the White king stalemates the Black king, which is locked in by his own pawn.

The play. 22. By custom the players are called White and Black. White invariably makes the first move, and thereafter the players move alternately.

23. In offhand play, unlimited time is allowed for deliberation—whence the reputation of Chess as a slow game. But all tournament games (and many offhand club games) are played under a strict time limit, the overstepping of which forfeits the game. The standard international rule is that a player must make 30 moves in the first two hours of his own time, 45 moves in the first three hours, and so on by increments of 15 moves per hour. Time is kept separately for each player. Shorter limits are applied in some contests; so-called rapid transit Chess allows only ten seconds deliberation per move.

Drawn games. 24. A player is stalemated if he has no legal move, but his king is not in check. A stalemate is an automatic drawn game. A draw also results if the pieces remaining on the board are insufficient to force checkmate, *e. g.*, a White king and two knights against the lone Black king. A game may be abandoned as drawn because both players consider their winning chances nil—or too hazardous to plumb.

25. Under certain circumstances, a draw may be claimed. Commonest is perpetual check—a player demonstrates that he can check the enemy king without cessation, and states that he intends to do so. Another situation is the recurrent position—if the same position of all pieces occurs three times in a game, with the same player to move on each occasion, this player may claim a draw. Seldom applicable is the fifty-move rule—if during fifty consecutive moves no capture has been made and no pawn

has moved, either player may claim a draw, but the claim is denied if the opponent can demonstrate a forced win. A few endings that are known to be wins require more than fifty moves to force actual checkmate.

Irregularities. [Most of the Chess-playing countries are members of a league, the Federation International des Echecs (F. I. D. E.), which has promulgated standard rules for play and tournament procedure. The chief provisions of the code are as follows.]

26. *Touch and move.* If a player touches one of his own men, he must move it if he can legally do so. If he touches an adverse man, he must if legal capture it. If a player touches several men, his opponent may choose which is to be moved or which is to be captured, provided that a legal move is available.

27. *Adjusting.* A player may touch his own pieces in order to adjust them, provided that he gives verbal notice of his intention, as by saying "I adjust." A player must not touch an adverse piece for purpose of adjusting, but may request his opponent to adjust.

28. *Completed move.* A completed move, if legal, may not be retracted. A simple move is completed when the player removes his hand from the piece; a capturing move is completed when the adverse piece is taken from the board and the player removes his hand from the capturing piece; a promoting move is completed when the pawn is taken from the board and the player removes his hand from the piece that replaces it.

29. *Illegal move.* If a player makes an illegal move, and his opponent draws attention to the fact before touching any of his own men, the illegal move must be retracted, and the player must if possible make a legal move with the same piece, or, if the illegal move was a capture, must if possible make a legal capture of the same piece.

30. *Erroneous position.* If during play it is proved that an illegal move was made and not retracted, or that the number or position of the men was altered illegally, the position just prior to the illegal move or alteration must be restored, and the game continued from that point.

If during play or immediately afterward it is proved that the pieces were initially placed on the board incorrectly, or the board was turned wrong, the game is annulled.

31. *Erroneous checkmate.* An erroneous announcement of checkmate, on the move or in several moves, is void without penalty and the game must be continued.

32. *Deportment.* A player may not take advice from spectators, nor refer to or have at the table any written notes other than the record of the game. A player should not comment on any of the moves of his opponent, nor in any way annoy or distract his opponent. A player forfeits the game if he willfully upsets the board or disarranges the men, refuses to comply with a legal requirement, arrives more than an hour late for commencement or resumption of play, or exceeds the time limit.

Descriptive notation. **33.** Chess books in English generally use a de-

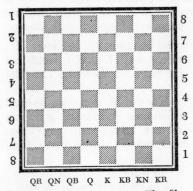

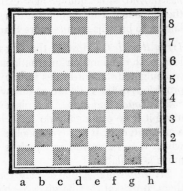

QR QN QB Q K KB KN KR   a b c d e f g h

FIG. 7. Descriptive notation. The files have the same names for both players, but the rows are numbered differently for each.

FIG. 8. Algebraic notation. Files and rows are designated alike for both players.

scriptive notation for the moves that descends from Hoyle. The pieces are abbreviated to initials: K, Q, B, R, P. Older books use Kt for knight, but this is being supplanted by N. Many problem books use S (from German *Springer*).

34. Each file is designated by the first-rank piece that originally stands on it, as K-file, Q-file. For the other pieces, K or Q needs to be prefixed according as the file is on the king's half or the queen's half of the board, as QB-file, KR-file. The ranks are designated by numbers 1 to 8, going upward in each case away from the player whose piece moves. Each rank thus has a dual designation: White starts with his pieces on his ranks 1 and 2, but these are Black's ranks 8 and 7.

35. A square is identified by its file and rank, in that order. Because of the ambiguity in rank, the color of reference must be named, as White's KN5. The color is omitted in recording moves, since the reference is always to the color of the moving piece.

36. A move is written: initial of the piece moved, then the square moved to (if non-capturing), joined by a hyphen, as P-K4. Additional information is given when necessary to avoid ambiguity, as N-KB3, KN-N5, R(2)-K1. For a capturing move, the hyphen is replaced by the symbol x, read "takes," and instead of the square moved to is written (when sufficient) the initial of the piece captured, as PxP, BxN.

37. Other symbols used are:

O-O	Castles king's-side
O-O-O	Castles queen's-side
ch or +	Check
!	Read "Best"; marks a good move
?	Read "Query"; marks a bad move
!?	Used in sense of "Is this a good move?"
±	White has the better game
∓	Black has the better game

38. Moves are numbered consecutively, each move comprising one by White and one by Black. An example of linear writing: 1 P-K4, P-K4; 2 N-KB3, N-QB3; 3 B-N5, P-QR3. In old books a fractional form is used, White moves being above the line and Black below, as

$$\frac{1 \text{ P-K4}; 2 \text{ N-KB3}; 3 \text{ B-N5}}{\text{P-K4}; \quad \text{N-QB3} \quad \text{P-QR3}}$$

In columnar form, it is usual to put the White moves in one column and the Black in another, as

1 P-K4	P-K4
2 N-KB3	N-QB3
3 B-N5	P-QR3

39. When a series of moves is begun by a Black move, a dash is placed after the ordinal number to represent the omitted White move, as 19 —, Q-R5.

Algebraic notation. 40. A more condensed notation is used in Germany and other countries, and in all problem books whatever the language. Each file and rank has an invariant designation, as shown in Fig. 8. A square is designated by its file and rank, in that order, as f5 (in the descriptive notation this is "White's KB5" or "Black's KB4"). Pieces are designated by their initials, the knight usually being S. A move is indicated by the square moved from and the square moved to, joined by a hyphen. The initial of the moving piece is prefixed (though actually not necessary) except when the moving piece is a pawn. The moves of the example under the preceding section would be written:

1 e2-e4	e7-e5
2 Sg1-f3	Sb8-c6
3 Bf1-b5	a7-a6

41. In linear writing, the notation is further abbreviated by omitting the first square; only the initial of the piece (except pawn) is prefixed to the square moved to. The same moves would be written linearly: 1 e4, e5; 2 Sf3, Sc6; 3 Bb5, a6.

42. A capture is indicated by a colon (:), written in place of the hyphen or after the move. A continuation of the above game might be:

4 Bb5:c6	d7:c6
5 d2-d4	e5:d4

In linear form this becomes: 4 Bc6:, d7:c6 (written in full, else there would be ambiguity); 5 d4, d4: (here there is no ambiguity in the shorter form).

43. Other symbols used are

O-O	Castles with h-rook
O-O-O	Castles with a-rook
!	Best; a good move
?	Doubtful; a bad move
+ or †	Check
++ or †† or #	Checkmate

POINTERS ON CHESS PLAY

Values of the pieces. The relative values of the pieces have been determined theoretically on the basis of the number of squares each commands from a central square in an open board. The theoretic scale corresponds closely with practical experience, but it must never be forgotten that the actual fighting power of a piece depends on the particular position. A piece cannot exert its maximum strength at all times; sometimes a piece may be worse than useless—a fatal obstruction to its own friends.

The relative fighting powers of the pieces other than the king are in ratio of:

Queen	9
Rook	5
Bishop	3
Knight	3
Pawn	1

The knight and bishop are approximately equal. One or the other may be a stronger piece to have in a given position, but the position more often favors the bishop. Two bishops have united power somewhat greater than a knight and bishop, and markedly greater than two knights.

Material superiority. The two players commence with the same number and kind of pieces. In the course of exchanges (captures and counter-captures), a vital consideration is to maintain at least equality of force. To lose a single pawn (more than the opponent) may be fatal; many a game has been won by this material superiority. To lose the exchange, by which is usually meant losing a rook for a knight or bishop, is a severe blow. Even the minor exchange (involving knight and bishop) may be a decisive aspect of the battle.

But this matter of material equality cannot be treated apart from positional advantages. Though loss of a single pawn spells potential loss, many a game has been won by deliberate sacrifice of pawns and other pieces. The point is that positional considerations are, after all, paramount. The possession of a larger army is no salvation if the enemy can mobilize a stronger detachment in a decisive local engagement.

To illustrate the danger of material inferiority, let us suppose that White wins a Black pawn in the opening. Now if White can force the "swap" for all other pieces, one for one, leaving himself with king and pawn against the Black king, and if he can then queen the pawn, he has an easy win.

The greater danger of material inferiority is that the enemy can use his greater fighting power to increase his advantage, both material and positional. For example, a White king and bishop cannot win against the lone Black king. But now add a couple of pawns to each side, and Black should resign, for White will win the Black pawns and emerge with overwhelming preponderance.

Minimum endings. End-play can be understood only in the light of the minimum material superiority required to administer a checkmate by force.

> K+Q vs. K is a win.
>
> K+R vs. K is a win.
>
> K+B vs. K is a draw.
>
> K+N vs. K is a draw.

(Because of their manifest superiority, the queen and rook are called major pieces, the bishop and knight minor.)

> K+B+B vs. K is a win.
>
> K+B+N vs. K is a win (long and difficult).
>
> K+N+N vs. K is a draw.
>
> K+N+N vs. K+P is sometimes a win.

The reason why a king faced by two knights may lose if "accompanied by an officious friend" is that the knights can stalemate the king; if the pawn can be restrained until this stage, its forced move gives the stronger party time to turn the stalemate into a checkmate.

> K+Q vs. K+R is a win.
>
> K+Q vs. K+R+B or N is a draw.
>
> K+Q vs. K+B+B is usually a draw.
>
> K+Q vs. K+B+N is usually a win.
>
> K+Q vs. K+N+N is usually a win.
>
> K+R+B vs. K+R is usually a draw.
>
> K+R vs. K+B or N is usually a draw.

Fig. 9. Queen vs. rook. White can win, by forcing the Black king to the edge of the board and then giving mate, despite all defense the rook can attempt.

Fig. 10. Single pawn endings. (Each group of three is a separate diagram.) At upper left, Black to move is a draw by stalemate; White to move wins. Upper center, either to move, Black can draw by forcing eventual stalemate. Lower left, either to move, drawn game. Lower right, White to move, Black wins; Black to move, drawn game.

The ending K+P vs. K is a race to queen the pawn. If the lone king can never get in front of the pawn, or capture it, he naturally loses. If he once stands on the square immediately ahead of the pawn on the file, he can draw. The stronger party should try to exclude him from this square by moving his king ahead of the pawn, eventually forcing the lone king off the file. But this process cannot work in case of a RP; a useful fact to remember is that if the lone king can reach the square B8 ahead of the RP he can draw.

The endings, two pawns against one, three pawns against two, etc., are in general wins for the stronger party. His extra pawn can usually be developed into a passed pawn (unopposed by any adverse pawn on the same file or on either adjacent file). To stop the passed pawn, the enemy king has to abandon the protection of his own pawns, which then fall prey to the stronger party. The addition of minor pieces to the position (e.g., K+N+P+P vs. K+N+P) usually does not enable the weaker party to draw, but the addition of major pieces alone (e.g., K+Q+P+P vs. K+Q+P often does so. A one-pawn superiority is least advantageous when only "heavy" pieces remain on the board, for these pieces most effectively attack the bases of pawn chains and also restrain the kings from taking offensive action.

Positional advantage. It has been noted that "material equality cannot be discussed apart from positional advantages." In the following paragraphs are listed some of the most frequent such advantages, achieved as stepping stones to victory.

Command of the center. The four central squares (d5, d4, e5, e4), and to a lesser extent the "half-center" (c5, c4, f5, f4), are of crucial importance. Pieces posted in the center have their maximum range. The center

Fig. 11. Command of center. After 1 P-K4, P-K3; 2 P-Q4, P-Q4; 3 N-QB3, PxP; 4 NxP, White has greater command of the center. His QP is more advanced than the Black KP; this difference can often be developed into a decisive advantage.

Fig. 12. The outpost knight. The knight cramps Black's pieces. If Black drives it away by P-KB3 he seriously weakens his KP and the squares near his king. If he plays BxN, the pawn recaptures and is equally unpleasant to Black.

is normally the avenue through which the pieces must advance to make contact with the enemy. Any superiority in command of the center is a distinct advantage, often decisive. For example, if a piece or pawn can be posted on the enemy fourth rank, and maintained there, while the enemy is excluded from one's own fourth rank, the advanced piece tends to split the enemy into two wings and hamper communication between them.

Outpost knight. The queen, rook and bishops can attack the enemy from a distance, through open lines. But the knight has to be brought close to the enemy to press on him at all. Hence the knight has most to gain by finding an advanced post (especially in the center). The so-called outpost knight on the enemy fourth or third rank is a particular "thorn in his side" because its attack on surrounding squares cannot be obstructed.

Open files. A file is open when no pawn of either color stands on it; a file is half-open for a player when his own pawn has disappeared from it. Now, a rook can rarely be brought to bear on the enemy forces except through an open or half-open file. As has been said, a rook "gravitates" to an open file, where it may attack enemy pieces, guard a friendly outpost, or spring forward to an advanced post and attack the enemy along the rank. So serious are these threats that a player must usually oppose his own rook to an enemy rook on an open file, neutralizing its power if only by the threat of exchange. In early play (e.g., where no more than one file is open), command of an open file that the opponent cannot so neutralize is likely to be a potent weapon.

Diagonals of one color. The bishops are able to sally forth very early and attack the enemy directly. Such attack is normally neutralized by enemy pawns and minor pieces standing on the bishop's diagonals. If the pawn's advances are such as to leave a diagonal clear, such an open diagonal "beckons" to a bishop as an open file beckons to a rook. A bishop that reaches right through the enemy lines to the eight rank gives powerful support to an advanced knight or to the queen. Hence a constant defensive preoccupation is to avoid becoming weak on diagonals of one color—when the enemy has a bishop of that color left.

Pawn skeleton. Pawns must advance to liberate the bishops, queen and rooks. Often they must be used to break the enemy front line of pawns and so create avenues of infiltration for the other pieces. Yet every pawn advance is in a sense weakening, for it abandons the direct guard of squares in one's home territory. Pawn advances, being irrevocable, have to be precisely calculated, not only for the immediate effects but for the long-range possibilities. The premature advance of a pawn may let an enemy outpost settle on a central square, or open a deadly avenue for the enemy king should the play turn into a king-and-pawn ending. The player must take care of the pawn skeleton; an organic weakness in it may prove decisive. For example, a doubled pawn (two pawns of the same color on the same file) is a potential weakness that can usually be capitalized in end-play and often in mid-game. Enforcing a structural

FIG. 13. Pawn formations. On the two center files, the White pawns are in the aggressive phalanx formation, while the Black pawns are in a defensive chain. The unmoved White pawns on the king's side offer solider protection to the castled king than do Black's pawns; Black's advance P-KN3 has left holes at his KB3 and KR3 where White pieces may settle, but the pawn at N3 may give needed support for an aggressive advance P-KB4.

FIG. 14. Local superiority. Black won by a combination commencing 19—BxRP ch; 20 KxB, Q-R5 ch; 21 K-N1, BxP. This sacrifice of two pieces is based on the fact that Black can attack the denuded king with queen and rook quickly (e.g., 22 KxB, Q-N4 ch; 23 K-R2, R-Q4 followed by R-R4 mate), while the White pieces, unwisely massed on the queen's side, cannot move to the defense fast enough.

weakness in the enemy pawn skeleton is often as good as winning a pawn outright.

Local superiority. Every advantage, material or positional, can be interpreted to have accrued from the concentration of superior force in a local engagement. This interpretation covers the simple advance of an unopposed piece to a good post, the forced withdrawal of a piece when attacked by a less valuable piece, as well as the massing of more attackers than defenders against an assailed piece. The player must continually assure himself that he has left no piece "loose" (attacked but not guarded), that none of his pieces is in danger of being trapped or overwhelmed, that he can bring up as many defenders as the opponent can bring up attackers, that he can sufficiently neutralize the enemy's occupation of dominating posts.

Mobility. The opportunity to concentrate a superior force in a local skirmish (total forces being equal) can in turn be interpreted as invariably due to superior mobility. Certainly a player whose lines of interior communication are cut or hampered, say by an enemy outpost in the center, finds defense difficult and often inadequate. Modern analysis has discovered many refined methods of exercising restraint upon the enemy, compelling his pieces to take inferior posts, holding back pawn moves that would liberate him. Some notable victories have been won, not by checkmate or gain of material, but simply by a kind of suffocation of the entire adverse army.

Tactics. In pursuit of a more remote objective, the player is often able to exert momentary threats, easily met, but limiting the opponent's choice of replies. For example, after the opening 1 P-K4, P-K4, White's strongest continuation is considered to be 2 N-KB3. The attack on Black's KP is easily met, yet Black does not have so wide a choice of moves as he does after another continuation, e.g., 2 N-QB3. White's objective is to develop his pieces; the momentary attack on the pawn is a tactical accident, as it were; but the continual exertion of tactical threats has been called the soul of Chess play.

Pin. A piece is said to be pinned when it cannot vacate a line without exposing its own king to check. For example: 1 P-Q4, P-Q4; 2 P-QB4, P-K3; 3 N-QB3, B-N5. The Black bishop pins the White knight, which now cannot legally move. The same term is used when a piece is paralyzed, not legally, but practically. For example, suppose that the above game continues: 4 N-KB3, N-KB3; 5 B-KN5. Now the Black KN is said to be pinned; although it may be moved legally, to do so is practically undesirable since it would lose the queen for a bishop.

FIG. 15. Pins. White's QN is absolutely pinned, since to move it would be illegal. Black's KN is dynamically pinned, since to move it would cost Black his queen.

FIG. 16. Discovered check. Black has foolishly moved N(from K5)-B3. (Correct is 4—Q-K2; 5 QxN, P-Q3 recovering the piece.) White moves N-B6, discovering check from the queen while the knight attacks and wins the Black queen.

The effect of a pin is to reduce or destroy the mobility of a piece, including its power to guard fellow pieces. Beginners are prone to make ludicrous mistakes through overlooking that guard by a pinned piece is usually no guard at all. A direct danger to the pinned piece occurs when it can be attacked by a less valuable piece, or when more attackers than defenders can be brought to bear upon it. The pin precludes the normal remedy for such assaults—withdrawal. For example: 1 P-K4, P-K3; 2 P-K4, P-Q4; 3N-QB3, N-KB3; 4 B-KN5. Now Black must reckon with the possible advance 5 P-K5, threatening to win the knight for a pawn.

Discovered check. Checks of every sort must be watched carefully. A check is not dangerous in itself, but may become dangerous because of the limitation of choice in reply. Intrinsically menacing is a discovered check —administered by moving a piece off the line of a queen, rook, or bishop, and so unmasking its attack on the enemy king. The chief danger is that the unmasking piece can do vital damage—capture an enemy, spring to a post in the enemy camp where it would otherwise be lost—and the enemy is powerless to capture the marauder because he first has to meet the check. For example: 1 P-K4, P-K4; 2 N-KB3, N-KB3; 3NxP, NxP; 4 Q-K2, KN-B3??; 5 N-B6 ch. Though the check can be met by interposition at K2, Black is helpless to save his queen.

Double check. A discovered check becomes a double check when the masking piece, also, delivers a check. The only legal reply to a double check is to move the king. An obvious hazard is that if the king happens at the moment to be immobile, he is checkmated.

Fork. A fork is a simultaneous attack on two points. For example: 1 P-K4, P-K4; 2 N-KB3, N-QB3; 3 B-N5, P-QR3; 4 B-R4, P-QN4; 5 B-N3, N-B3; 6 O-O, P-Q3; 7 P-B3. Now 7 NxP is a mistake for then 8 B-Q5 forks both knights, and since both are unguarded, White wins a minor piece for his pawn.

FIG. 17. Fork. Black has erroneously played NxKP. White wins a piece by B-Q5, forking the two unprotected knights.

FIG. 18. Fork. White can ignore the attack on his KB, for if Black plays NxB White recovers the piece by the fork Q-R4 ch.

One "prong" of a fork is often an attack on the king; potential checks have to be examined continually to see if they allow dangerous forks. For example: 1 P-K4, P-K4; 2 N-KB3, P-KB3(?). This way of protecting the KP is intrinsically undesirable because it deprives the Black KN of his best square. But more, it opens the way for a diagonal check on the Black king. Can this fact be capitalized? The answer is yes, for 3 NxP is sound. If 3—PxN, then 4 Q-R5 ch forces the king to move, after which he speedily succumbs to a mating attack. Or, if Black plays 4 P-KN3, then 5 QxKP ch forks the king and rook, winning a superiority of material at once.

A fork is often utilized to supply potential, rather than actual, guard. For example: 1 P-K4, P-K4; 2 N-KB3, N-QB3; 3 B-B4, B-B4; 4 P-QN4, BxP; 5 P-QB3, B-B4; 6 O-O, P-Q3; 7 P-Q4, PxP; 8 PxP, B-N3; 9 N-B3, N-R4(?) White can disregard this time-wasting attack on his bishop, utilizing the time to make another developing move, for if 10 NxB then 11 Q-R4 ch recovers the piece by a fork.

Simultaneous attack on two different squares can also be initiated by two different pieces in consequence of a single move; attack is unmasked from a queen, rook, or bishop, while the masking piece attacks elsewhere. Like discovered checks, such batteries (to borrow a term from the realm of Chess problems) must be watched continually.

Opening principles. A great deal of analysis has been made of the opening. Space permits us only to identify the principal variations.

Two purposes have to be served in the opening: (a) To develop the pieces (knights, bishops, queen) to their most effective preliminary posts, without undue loss of time; (b) to maintain at least equality in command of the vital central squares. The ideal formula for this purpose is to move each center pawn (K and Q pawns) once, each minor piece once, the queen once, and castle, uniting the rooks. However, this ideal process must often be interrupted to meet specific threats of the opponent. The same piece may have to move several times in the opening; center pawn advances may prove more effective if deferred until they have the support of developed pieces. Nevertheless, the fact remains that the player cannot afford to waste time in development, unless an equal waste of time is incurred by his opponent.

To allow the emergence of the other pieces, one center pawn or the other must be moved to the fourth rank. Both players can advance to the fourth rank at once, if they choose; the early battle is likely to focus on the effort to move up the other center pawn to the fourth, without disadvantage or with positive advantage. Opening variations fall into two general classes, according to which pawn is first moved to the fourth, the KP or the QP.

King's-pawn openings. After 1 P-K4, P-K4; 2 N-KB3, N-QB3, the chief continuations are:

> 3 B-N5 (Ruy Lopez or Spanish Opening), to which the standard replies are 3——P-QR3 (Morphy Defense), 3——N-KB3 (Berlin Defense), 3——P-Q3 (Steinitz Defense).
>
> 3 B-B4, B-B4, after which may follow 4 N-B3, N-B3 (Guioco Piano), or 4 P-QN4 (Evans Gambit), or 4 O-O, N-B3, 5 P-Q4 (Max Lange Attack).
>
> 3 B-B4, N-B3 (Two Knights Defense), which may develop into a Guioco Piano, etc., or diverge with 4 N-N5 (Prussian Attack).
>
> 3 N-B3, N-B3 (Four Knights Game), which may continue 4 B-N5, B-N5 (Double Ruy Lopez).
>
> 3 P-Q4 (Scotch Game), which may develop 3——PxP, 4 NxP or 4 B-B4 (Scotch Gambit).
>
> 3 P-B3 (Ponziani Attack).

After 1 P-K4, P-K4; 2 N-KB3, Black may avoid the regular reply (N-QB3) and try an irregular defense:

> 2——P-Q3 (Philidor's Defense).
>
> 2——N-KB3 (Petroff Defense or Russian Opening).

After 1 P-K4, P-K4, White may steer away from the foregoing openings with:

> 2 B-B4 (King's Bishop Opening), and Black may reply 2——B-B4 (Classical Defense) or 2——N-KB3 (Berlin Defense).
>
> 2 P-Q4 (Center Game), which may lead to 2——PxP; 3 P-QB3 (Danish Gambit).
>
> 2 N-QB3 (Vienna Game), which may continue 2——N-QB3, 3 P-B4 (Vienna Gambit).
>
> 2 P-KB4 (King's Gambit). Black may refuse the pawn by 2——B-B4 (King's Gambit Declined) or 2——P-Q4 (Falkbeer Counter Gambit). If Black accepts the gambit by 2——PxP, White may continue 3 B-B4 (Bishop's Gambit) or 3 N-QB3 (Pernau Gambit) or 3 N-KB3 (Knight's Gambit). The last leads into many much-analyzed variations (Allgaier, Cunningham, Kieseritzky, Muzio).

After 1 P-K4, Black may forsake the regular reply (P-K4) for an irregular defense:

> 1——P-K3 (French Defense), with the usual continuation 2 P-Q4, P-Q4.
>
> 1——P-QB4 (Sicilian Defense), of which the most popular line is 2 N-KB3, N-QB3 (or P-Q3); 3 P-Q4.
>
> 1——P-QB3 (Caro-Kann Defense), which leads to 2 P-Q4, P-Q4.
>
> 1——P-Q4 (Center Counter Gambit), with usual play 2 PxP, QxP.
>
> 1——N-KB3 (Alekhine's Defense), with the characteristic continuation 2 P-K5, N-Q4; 3 P-QB4, N-N3; 4 P-Q4.
>
> 1——N-QB3 (Nimzowitsch Defense), with usual play 2 P-Q4, P-Q4.
>
> 1——P-KN3 (King's Fianchetto), the idea of which is to move 2——B-N2 and later advance the center pawns to attack whatever formation White adopts.

Queen's-pawn openings. After 1 P-Q4, P-Q4; 2 P-QB4 (Queen's Gambit), many systems of defense have been tried and analyzed. The characteristic differences between them, as a rule, arise late in the opening (after six to a dozen moves). The chief early options are:

> 2——PxP (Gambit Accepted), and now a major divergence depends on whether White plans to move his KP one or two steps, as 3 N-KB3, N-KB3; 4 P-K3, or 3 N-QB3, N-KB3; 4 P-K4.
>
> 2——P-K3; 3 N-QB3, N-KB3 (Orthodox Defense). White may continue with an old line 4 B-B4 or with 4 B-N5 (Pillsbury Attack). After the latter usually follows 4——QN-Q2, 5 P-K3, and two of the many defenses are then 5——B-K2, 6 N-B3, O-O, 7 B-Q3, PxP, 8 BxP, N-Q4 (Capablanca Defense), and 5——P-B3, 6 N-B3, Q-R4 (Cambridge Springs Defense).

2——P-K3; 3 N-QB3, P-QB4 (Tarrasch Defense).

2——P-QB3 (Slav Defense).

2——P-K4 (Albin Counter Gambit), a risky and probably unsound line.

After 1 P-Q4, Black may defer decision as to his center pawns with 1——N-KB3, and after 2 P-QB4 may follow:

2——P-K3, the idea of which is to play 3 N-KB3, P-QN3 (Queen's Indian or West Indian Defense) or 3 N-QB3, B-N5 (Nimzo-Indian Defense).

2——P-KN3 (King's Indian or East Indian Defense), which may develop 3 N-KB3, B-N2 or 3 N-QB3, P-Q4 (Gruenfeld Defense).

2——P-Q3 (Tchigorin's Defense) with the idea 3 N-KB3, N-QB3; 4 N-B3, P-K4.

2——P-K4 (Budapest Defense) with the idea 3 PxP, N-N5.

After 1 P-Q4, P-Q4, White may reserve the option of transposing into the Queen's Gambit (P-QB4) or another line with:

2 P-K3 (Stonewall), which allows the characteristic formation 2——P-KB4, 3 N-QB3, P-K3.

2 N-KB3, N-KB3; 3 P-K3 (Colle System), and 3——P-QB4; 4 P-B3 leads into a kind of Queen's Gambit with colors reversed.

2 N-KB3, N-KB3; 3 P-KN3 (Catalan Opening), which White follows up with B-N2 and P-QB4 soon.

After 1 P-Q4, Black may try an irregular defense (instead of P-Q4 or N-KB3) with

1——P-KB4 (Dutch Defense).

1——P-QB4 (Benoni Counter Gambit), the characteristic position of which is reached by 2 P-Q5.

Irregular openings. Most of the openings other than 1 P-K4 or 1-PQ4 are attempts to reach variations of the Queen's Pawn openings favorable to White, through transposition of moves. This is especially true of:

1 P-QB4 (English Opening), which can be diverted into different channels by 1——P-K4 (From Gambit).

1 N-KB3 (Zukertort Opening), which may lead to 1——P-Q4; 2 P-QB4 (Reti System), or 1——N-KB3, 2 P-QN3 (Nimzowitsch Attack).

The following are the commonest of other irregular first moves by White:

1 P-KB4 (Bird's Opening).

1 P-K3 (Van't Kruys Opening).

1 P-QN4 (Polish Opening, Orang-utan Opening).

1 P-QB3 (Saragossa Opening).

1 P-KB3 (Krazy Kat).

CHESS VARIANTS

Chess at odds. Chess does not lend itself readily to any system of handicapping, whereby a weaker player can compete on even terms against a stronger. Odds-chess is encountered in off-hand play, but never in tournament competition. The following are the commonest ways of giving odds, in order of magnitude from least to greatest:

The draw. A draw counts as a win for the odds-receiver.

Pawn and move. The odds-giver takes Black and removes his KBP; White begins with two moves in succession, but he may not move beyond his fourth rank.

Knight. The odds-giver removes his QN, usually taking White.

Rook. The odds-giver removes his QR; he usually takes White and also posts his QRP (otherwise protected) on R3.

Rook and Knight. The odds-giver removes his QR and KN, usually taking White.

Queen. The odds-giver removes his Q, taking White.

Capped pawn. The odds-giver must give mate with his unpromoted KBP; any other outcome is a loss for him.

Battle Chess. This is an old-time method of "getting out of book play." A screen is placed across the center of the board, between the two players, and each then disposes his army as he sees fit, subject to these rules: There must be one pawn on each file, none on the first rank; no piece may be placed beyond the third rank; the two bishops must be placed on squares of opposite color. With all dispositions made, the screen is lifted, and the players proceed to play Chess under the regular rules.

Kriegspiel. This is a method of playing Chess under conditions more nearly like those of warfare, where a combatant does not know all about the disposition of the enemy forces. It requires three Chess sets and the services of a referee. Each player has a board and men, which he arranges out of sight of his opponent. The referee keeps track of the actual disposition of all White and Black pieces on his own board. The referee is a go-between, announcing to each player when the other has made a move. For a non-capturing and non-checking move, the referee merely says "White has moved" or "Black has moved." When White makes a capture, the referee announces "White captures on (name of square)"; or he may simply remove the Black piece from Black's board, also informing White that his last move was a capture. When a move gives check, the referee announces the fact to both players, together with the direction of the check, i.e., on the file, on the rank, on the long or short diagonal, or by a knight.

On his own board, each player must maintain his own forces in accordance with his actual moves and with directions of the referee. But he may distribute the enemy pieces as he fancies them to be. He has several sources of inference as to their position. He may try long-range sweeps with his queen, rooks, and bishops, in order to detect the presence of adverse obstructions. To any "try" that is an impossible move the referee says "No." A hazard in this method of exploration is that if any try is possible, it stands as the player's move. Another oft-tried method is to march the king ahead of his own defenders, in order to detect the squares guarded by the enemy.

To shorten the process of discovering pawn captures, a player at his turn to move may ask "Any?" meaning "Can any of my pawns make a capture?" To answer affirmatively, the referee says "Try," whereupon the player must try at least one pawn capture. He may continue trying until he has found it, or he may make another move instead. When a pawn capture is of another pawn en passant, the fact is announced. This is the sole case in which the referee divulges what piece has been captured.

It is usual for the two players to be in the same room, so that each may hear what passes between the referee and his opponent. A count of the unsuccessful "tries" when capture by a pawn is possible may show the number of pawns the player has left; repeated noes from the referee may indicate that a player is trying several different impossible moves, and therefore that he has one or two long-range pieces in open action.

Giveaway Chess. The object in this game is to get rid of all one's pieces. The king has no privileged status, being captured like any other piece. The sole rules are that, when able to capture, a player must do so; he may make his own choice among possible captures; a pawn advanced to the eighth rank must promote to a queen. A stalemate is reached if the player in turn to move can make no move, but has one or more pieces remaining on the board; this is an automatic draw.

Four-hand Chess. It is believed that the immediate ancestor of Chess was a four-hand partnership game. A form of this game is still sometimes played, on a board extended on each side by two or three additional rows of eight squares each. Each of the four players has pieces of distinctive color, which he sets up in the recess on his side. The turn to move rotates clockwise, and players sitting opposite combine as partners. Their pieces do not attack and check each other, but combine as a single army. However, when one king is checkmated, the pieces of his color are entirely out of play: they may neither move nor be captured. The partner continues play alone against two opponents, having only one turn to their two. If he can raise the checkmate, he can regain the help of his partner. A side wins only by checkmating both enemy kings.

All moves including castling are as in regular Chess, except for certain pawn peculiarities. There is no initial double-jump, and no en passant capture. Pawns of different but allied color do not block each other; when they meet on a file, either may jump over the other. On reaching the 14th rank (farthest from the owner), a pawn does not promote, but simply reverses its movement and returns along the file to its home side of the

board. A pawn promotes in the rare event it reaches an enemy first rank
(by repeated captures).

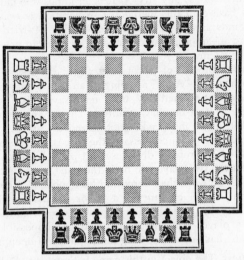

FIG. 19. Four-hand Chess. Blue and Black are partners against White and Red.
The players move in turn clockwise.

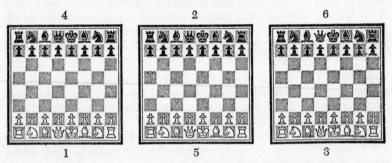

FIG. 20. Team Chess. All White players are a team against the Black. Players
move in rotation of the numbers.

Team Chess. This is a way of playing four-hand, six-hand, or eight-hand
Chess without special boards. A pair have an ordinary board and pieces.
The boards are set side by side, and all the White men are set up on one
side, all the Black on the other. All players of one color form a team. The
individuals move in rotation such that the same interval on every board
separates a White move from its Black reply.

The pieces may roam across all the boards alike, for these form a
single arena. The rules are as in Four-hand Chess; a side wins only by
checkmating all of the enemy kings.

⚊ CHECKERS ⚊

Checkers, or Draughts, is known in every modern language but English by some variant of *dama* (woman), since in earliest times it was rated scornfully as "Chess for women." But these names may have originated as puns on *damm* (dam, dike), for the variant prevalent in middle-Europe during the 15th century was called *Dammspiel*, with clear reference to the dike-formation of the pieces. In the 16th century, Dammspiel was largely supplanted by a variant said to have come from Spain, and this variant has persisted in England as Draughts, in America as Checkers. The first scientific study of the game was published in 1668 by Peter Mallet, a French mathematician. A host of English analysts, beginning with Joshua Sturges in 1800, demonstrated that Draughts is fully as profound as Chess.

In Europe during the 18th century, the so-called "Spanish game" largely gave way to "Polish Checkers"—invented in Paris about 1732 and dubbed Polish merely because its first advocate was a Pole. Variants of the "Polish" game today reign supreme in France, Germany, even Spain, where the "Spanish game" is all but forgotten. There are also other national variants, notably "Turkish Draughts," which is closely akin to the original Dammspiel.

Checkers is a board game for two players.

Definitions. 1. The following terms are used in Checkers. This list does not include many particularized names explained in the text, such as the names of openings, types of shots, etc.

BLOCK. A position in which all the pieces of one color are immobilized.

COOK. An improvement or deviation from published analysis, especially when reserved by a tournament competitor to spring as a surprise upon his opponents.

CRAMP. The restraint exerted by some pieces upon enemy pieces (usually in a corner), when the latter cannot advance without loss or disadvantageous exchanges.

CUT. An exchange of pieces, especially when the captures are completed in different systems.

DOUBLE-CORNER. A pair of squares, 1 and 5 or 28 and 32.

EXCHANGE. A capture and counter-capture of pieces of opposite color.

HUFF OR BLOW. The (now obsolete) rule that if a player fails to capture when able, making a simple move instead, the opponent may either enforce the capture or remove from the board the piece that should have captured.

KING ROW. The first rank, on which single men are crowned, either 1-2-3-4 or 29-30-31-32.

MAN OFF. Simplify the position by exchanges.

MOVE, THE. Advantage in frontal opposition of the pieces, in the sense that a player having "the move" can force an enemy piece or pieces to retreat (see section *The Move,* page 376).

PERPETUAL DRAW. A draw achieved by repetition of the same series of moves, deviation from which is impossible or fatal to the opponent.

RESTRICTION PLAY. Competition in which the first two or three moves are fixed by the chance selection from an admitted list of sound openings.

SHOT. A forced series of exchanges, especially when it results in advantage to the player that forces it.

SINGLE-CORNER. Square 4 or square 29.

SQUEEZE. Attack on an enemy piece, especially when it is thereby forced to advance.

STAR MOVE (or STARRED MOVE). The only correct move to win or to hold the draw, indicated by an asterisk.

STEAL (A PIECE). Win a piece that is isolated from its fellows, so that it can neither be defended nor advanced in safety.

STROKE. A series of exchanges (and moves), especially when it results in advantage to one player. (This term is sometimes used as synonymous with *shot,* but is usually reserved for more extended operations, especially when non-capturing moves intervene between exchanges.)

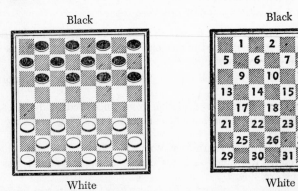

Black   Black

White   White

FIG. 1. Initial position of the pieces.   FIG. 2. Notation of the Checkerboard.

The board. 2. The checkerboard is identical with the chessboard: a large square composed of 64 small squares, colored alternately light and dark. The two players sit at opposite sides of the board, which is so turned that each player finds a light square in the corner at his right hand.

3. The pieces are placed, and move solely upon, the dark squares. The formation near the player's right hand is called a double corner, that near his left is a single corner.

4. In printed diagrams, the colors of the board are reversed, so that the pieces may be printed on white spaces. There is no uniformity of procedure in placing the Black and White sides. In problem diagrams, where there is a stipulation as "Black to move and win," the color named is usually fixed at the bottom, but even here the practice is not universal.

The pieces. 5. Each player commences with twelve pieces, which are arranged on the three ranks nearest himself, as shown in Fig. 1. All the pieces are alike in physical structure and bestowed powers; they are single men.

Object of play. 6. A player wins when his opponent, in turn to move, can make no move. This can happen in either of two ways: (a) the player has lost all his men by capture; or (b) all his remaining pieces are immobilized.

The play. 7. The two players move alternately, Black invariably moving first to begin a game. There are two kinds of moves, capturing and non-capturing.

8. The non-capturing move is to an adjacent vacant square (along a diagonal, since the pieces move wholly on the black squares). A single man may move only forward, and therefore has choice of no more than two simple moves.

9. The capturing move is a jump. If a piece (say Black) stands adjacent to an enemy (White), and the square just beyond this enemy on the same line is vacant, it (Black) jumps over the enemy to the vacant square. The man so jumped (White) is then removed from the board. If the jumping piece lands on a square from which it can jump another enemy, it must do so in the same turn, continuing to make captures until it runs out of victims. In any such series, the jumping piece may zig-zag at will, changing direction in successive captures; but a single man captures only forward.

10. If able to make a jump, the player must do so in preference to a simple move. (Formerly, the "huff or blow" rule provided that if a player should make a simple move, when able to jump, the opponent could then remove from the board the piece that should have jumped, or demand retraction of the simple move and completion of the jump. The present rule is that all jumps must be completed; a simple move, when the player can jump, is illegal and must be retracted.)

11. The player may make his own choice, where alternatives exist, as to what piece to move in jumping, and what direction to go in a series of jumps. (This freedom of choice is the chief feature in which the British-American game differs from other national variants.)

12. On reaching the last rank, farthest away from the owner, a single man is crowned, becoming a king. Its promotion is marked by plac-

ing another checker on top of it, the two then being moved as a unit. A player is required by rule to crown the enemy men reaching his side of the board.

13. A king may move in any (diagonal) direction, forward or backward. As to simple moves and jumps, the same rules apply to it as to a single man. If a single man reaches the king row by a jump, it must stop to be crowned: it may not continue capturing (as a king) in the same turn.

Irregularities. [The Standard Laws of Checkers, drafted in 1852, have remained in force virtually unchanged. In 1938 the American Checker Association amplified it with some regulations on tournament procedure, and also changed the "huff or blow" provision. The chief rules are as follows.]

14. *Touch and move.* If the in-turn player touches one of his own playable pieces, he must move it. If any part of a playable piece is moved over an angle of the square on which it is stationed, the play must be completed in that direction.

15. *Adjusting.* Touching an unplayable piece does not constitute a move, and such piece, if displaced, must be put back. A player may touch his own pieces for purposes of arranging, if he gives verbal notice of his intention, and may request the opponent to adjust his (opponent's) pieces, but should not touch the adverse pieces for any purpose except capture.

16. *Time limit.* If the in-turn player does not move previously, the referee calls "Time" at the end of five minutes, or one minute if the player must jump and has only one way to jump. The player must move within a minute after the call of "Time," else he forfeits the game.

17. *Leaving the table.* After the first move (or selection of the opening by ballot), neither player may leave the table without permission of the referee, and he then must be accompanied either by his opponent or by a person appointed by the referee. (The purpose of this rule is to prevent a player from consulting books during the course of a game.)

18. *Drawn games.* A game is declared drawn when neither player can force a win. A player may ask the referee for a "count of moves." If the referee accedes, the opponent must then demonstrate a win or must show an increased advantage within forty more of his own moves, failing which the game is declared drawn.

19. *Matches.* A match between two players always comprises an even number of games, each player having the Black side the same number of times.

Notation. 20. For purposes of recording games and positions, the dark squares of the board (left white in printed diagrams) are numbered from 1 to 32, as shown in Fig. 2 (page 364). A move is denoted by the number of the square on which the piece originally stands, followed by the number of the square on which it comes to rest, joined by a hyphen, *e.g.,*

11-15, 22-18, 15-22, 25-18. Capturing moves are written in the same way as simple moves. The moves are not labelled as to color; until a king is crowned, the color of the moving piece is evident from the move, for Black pieces move up and White pieces down. In tabular form, the moves are arranged in columns, to be read downward, not across.

21. The only additional symbol regularly used is the star (°). This marks a move as essential (according to analysis) to complete a win or hold a draw.

Restriction play. 22. Offhand games are played in "go as you please" style—each player may make what opening moves he prefers. This style was long ago found impracticable for serious competition. Experts can force the "scientific draw" almost at will, by adhering to the strongest openings and the best "book" moves. In a world championship match between Wyllie and Martin, the same game, move for move, was played thirty-seven times, neither competitor being willing to risk a deviation from the safest line. To revitalize tournaments, restriction play was introduced.

23. Black has choice of seven opening moves, and White has choice of seven replies. Thus there are 49 two-move combinations, of which two are barred because they lose a White piece without compensation (9-14, 21-17 and 10-14, 21-17). In the two-move restriction, one of the 47 playable combinations is selected by chance, and the competitors in a match must commence each game with this opening. (The match comprises an even number of games, with each player taking the Black side the same number of times.) Four of the 47 openings are particularly weak for White, and were formerly barred, but today are usually included in the balloting.

24. In American competition, even the two-move restriction has been found insufficient, so that championship events now use a three-move restriction. The list of three-move combinations established as playable now numbers about 150.

POINTERS ON CHECKERS PLAY

Openings. Certain opening moves and early formations have acquired traditional names, as follows:

Alma: 11-15, 23-19, 8-11, 22-17, 3-8.

Ayrshire Lassie: 11-15, 24-20.

Black Doctor: 11-15, 23-19, 8-11, 22-17, 9-13, 17-14, 10-17, 19-10, 7-14.

Boston: 11-15, 22-17, 9-13, 17-14.

Bristol: 11-16.

Bristol Cross: 11-16, 23-18.

Centre: 11-15, 23-19, 8-11, 22-17, 15-18.

Cross: 11-15, 23-18.

Defiance: 11-15, 23-19, 9-14, 27-23.

Denny: 10-14.

Double Corner: 9-14.

Douglas: 11-15, 22-17, 8-11, 17-13, 4-8, 25-22.

Dundee: 12-16.

Dyke: 11-15, 22-17.

Edinburgh: 9-13.

Fife: 11-15, 23-19, 9-14, 22-17, 5-9.

Glasgow: 11-15, 23-19, 8-11, 22-17, 11-16.

Kelso: 10-15.

Kelso Cross: 10-15, 23-18.

Laird and Lady: 11-15, 23-19, 8-11, 22-17, 9-13, 17-14, 10-17, 21-14.

Maid of the Mill: 11-15, 22-17, 8-11, 17-13, 15-18.

Nailor: 11-15, 23-19, 8-11, 26-23.

Old Fourteenth: 11-15, 23-19, 8-11, 22-17, 4-8.

Orthodox: 11-15, 23-19.

Paisley: 11-16, 24-19.

Pioneer: 11-15, 22-17, 8-11, 25-22.

Second Double Corner: 11-15, 24-19.

Single Corner: 11-15, 22-18.

Souter: 11-15, 23-19, 9-14, 22-17, 6-9.

Switcher: 11-15, 21-17.

Tillicoultry: 11-15, 23-19, 8-11, 22-18.

Wagram: 11-15, 22-17, 9-13, 24-20.

Waterloo: 11-15, 23-18, 8-11, 18-14.

Whilter: 11-15, 23-19, 9-14, 22-17, 7-11.

Whilter Exchange: 11-15, 23-19, 7-11, 22-18.

White Doctor: 11-16, 22-18, 10-14, 25-22, 8-11, 24-20, 16-19, 23-16, 14-23, 26-19.

White Dyke: 11-15, 22-17, 8-11, 17-14.

Will-o'-the-Wisp: 11-15, 23-19, 9-13.

The following tabulation gives the 47 two-move openings and the principal continuations from each.

9-13, 21-17, 5-9, 25-21, 9-14, 29-25 (a), 6-9, 23-18. (a) Better 30-25.

9-13, 22-17, 13-22, 25-18, 6-9, 18-14 (a), 10-17, 21-14, 9-18, 23-14, 12-16. (a) Better 29-25, 11-15.

9-13, 22-18, 6-9, 25-22 (a), 1-6, 24-20, 10-15, 28-24, 7-10, 29-25, 3-7. (a) Or 18-14, 9-18, 23-14, 10-17, 21-14, 12-16, 24-20, 16-19, 25-22.

9-13, 23-18, 12-16, 18-14 (a), 10-17, 21-14, 6-10, 27-23, 10-17, 24-19, 8-12, 25-21. (a) Or 24-20, 16-19, 18-15, 11-18, 22-15, 5-9, 25-22, 9-14, 30-25.

9-13, 23-19, 11-15 (a), 22-18, 15-22, 25-18, 10-14 (b), 18-9, 5-14, 27-23, 8-11, 29-25, 6-10. (a) Or 11-16, 26-23, 16-20, 30-26. (b) Or 7-11, 19-15.

9-13, 24-19, 11-15, 28-24, 6-9, 23-18 (a), 1-6, 18-11, 7-23, 27-18, 12-16, 26-23, 16-20. (a) Or 22-18, 15-22, 25-18, 8-11 (b), 18-14, 9-18. 23-14, 10-17, 21-14, 11-16, 26-23. (b) Or 9-14, 18-9, 5-14, 24-20, 8-11, 29-25, 11-15, 19-16.

9-13, 24-20, 11-15 (a), 22-17 (b), 13-22, 25-11, 8-15, 21-17 (c), 5-9, 17-13, 9-14. (a) Or 5-9, 22-18, 10-14, 25-22, 7-10, 27-24, 3-7. (b) Or 23-18, 8-11, 27-23, 6-9, 32-27. (c) Or 29-25, 10-14, 25-22, 7-11, 22-18.

9-14, 22-17, 11-15 (a), 25-22, 15-19, 24-15, 10-19, 23-16, 12-19, 17-10, 6-15, 21-17. (a) Or 11-16, 25-22, 16-20, 17-13, 8-11, 22-18, 4-8, 18-9, 5-14, 29-25.

9-14, 22-18, 5-9, 24-20 (a), 11-16, 20-11, 8-22, 25-18, 4-8, 28-24, 8-11, 29-25, 10-15, 25-22, 7-10, 24-20, 3-7, 27-24, 1-5, 32-28, 9-13. (a) Or 24-19, 11-15, 18-11, 8-24, 28-19, 4-8, 26-22, 8-11, 27-24.

9-14, 23-18 (formerly barred), 14-23, 27-18, 12-16 (a), 18-14, 10-17, 21-14, 6-9, 14-10, 7-14, 22-18, 14-23, 26-12, 11-15, 25-22, 9-14, 29-25, 8-11, 24-19, 15-24, 28-19, 11-16. (a) Or 5-9, 26-23.

9-14, 23-19, 11-16 (a), 26-23 (b), 6-9, 24-20, 9-13, 20-11, 8-24, 28-19, 14-17. (a) Or 5-9, 27-23, 11-15, 22-18, 15-22, 25-18, 7-11, 26-22, 11-15, 18-11, 8-15, 24-20, 15-24, 28-19, 4-8, 30-26. (b) Or 27-23, 16-20, 32-27, 5-9, 22-17, 8-11, 19-16, 12-19, 24-8, 4-11, 17-13, 1-5, 25-22, 14-17.

9-14, 24-19, 11-15 (a), 22-18 (b), 15-24, 18-9, 5-14, 28-19, 8-11, 25-22, 11-15. (a) Or 5-9, 22-18. (b) Or 27-24, 8-11, 22-18.

9-14, 24-20, 5-9 (a), 22-18 (b), 10-15, 28-24. (a) Or 11-15, 22-17, 8-11, 28-24, 4-8, 23-19, 15-18, 26-23. (b) Or 22-17, 11-15, 17-13, 1-5, 28-24, 8-11, 23-19.

10-14, 22-17, 7-10, 17-13, 3-7, 24-20 (a), 14-18, 23-14, 9-18. (a) Or 25-22, 14-17, 21-14, 9-25, 29-22, 11-15, 23-18, 5-9, 18-11, 8-15, 26-23, 9-14, 23-18.

10-14, 22-18, 11-16 (a), 24-19 (b), 7-10, 25-22, 16-20, 18-15, 9-13, 29-25, 3-7, 22-18, 7-11, 18-9, 5-14, 26-22. (a) Or 11-15, 18-11, 8-15, 24-20, 4-8, 28-24, 8-11, 23-19, 7-10, 25-22. (b) Or 24-20, 16-19, 23-16, 12-19.

10-14, 23-18 (formerly barred), 14-23, 26-19 (a), 6-10, 27-23, 11-15, 30-26. (a) Or 27-18, 12-16, 32-27, 16-20, 26-23, 6-10 (b), 30-26. (b) Or 11-15, 18-11, 8-15, 22-18.

10-14, 23-19, 14-18 (a), 22-15, 11-18, 21-17, 8-11, 17-14 (b), 4-8, 24-20, 11-15. (a) Or 11-16, 22-17, 16-23, 17-10, 7-14, 26-19, 8-11, 25-22. (b) Or 17-13, 9-14, 26-23, 11-16.

10-14, 24-19, 7-10 (a), 22-18, 11-16, 26-22, 8-11, 28-24, 16-20, 22-17, 4-8, 30-26. (a) Or 6-10, 27-24, 9-13, 22-18, 11-15.

10-14, 24-20, 11-15 (a), 22-18, 15-22, 25-18 (b), 6-10, 26-22, 8-11,

27-24, 3-8, 24-19, 1-6, 30-25*. (a) Or 14-18, 22-15, 11-18, 23-14, 9-18, 21-17, 6-9, 17-13, 1-6, 25-22. (b) Or 26-10, 6-15, 25-22, 8-11, 30-26.

10-15, 21-17, 11-16, 17-13 (a), 16-20, 22-18, 15-22, 25-18, 8-11, 29-25 (b), 9-14, 18-9, 5-14, 25-22, 14-17, 24-19, 4-8, 22-18, 11-16, 28-24. (a) Or 23-18, 16-20. (b) Or 24-19, 11-16, 29-25, 7-10, 25-21, 9-14, 18-9, 5-14, 26-22.

10-15, 22-17, 11-16 (a), 17-14 (b), 9-18, 23-14, 16-20, 26-23, 15-18, 25-22, 18-25, 29-22, 8-11. (a) Or 9-13, 23-19, 13-22, 19-10, 6-15, 26-17. (b) Or 23-19, 16-23, 26-10, 6-15, 17-13, 9-14, 25-22, 12-16, 27-23, 8-12, 24-19.

10-15, 22-18, 15-22, 25-18, 11-15 (a), 18-11, 8-15, 29-25 (b), 9-14, 25-22, 14-18, 23-14, 15-19, 24-15, 6-10. (a) Or 9-13, 18-14, 11-15, 24-19. (b) Or 26-22, 4-8, 24-19, 15-24, 28-19, 8-11, 22-18, 6-10, 29-25.

10-15, 23-18, 7-10 (a), 27-23, 3-7, 24-20, 9-14, 18-9, 5-14, 22-18 (or 22-17). (a) Or 9-13, 24-20, 12-16, 21-17, 16-19, 17-14.

10-15, 23-19, 7-10, 22-17 (a), 11-16, 26-23, 8-11, 17-14. (a) Or 26-23, 9-14, 22-18.

10-15, 24-19, 15-24, 28-19, 6-10 (a), 22-18 (b), 11-15. (a) Or 9-14, 22-18. (b) Or 22-17, 9-14, 25-22, 11-15.

10-15, 24-20, 7-10, 28-24 (a), 3-7, 23-19, 9-14, 26-23. (a) Or 23-18, 3-7, 27-23, 9-13, 32-27, 5-9.

11-15, 21-17, 9-13, 25-21, 6-9 (a), 23-18 (b), 8-11, 27-23, 9-14. (a) Or 8-11, 30-25, 4-8, 24-19, 15-24, 28-19, 11-15, 17-14. (b) Or 30-25, 8-11, 17-14, 10-17, 21-14, 9-18, 23-14, 11-16.

11-15, 22-17, 9-14, 25-22, 15-19 (a). (a) Or 8-11, 17-13, 11-16, 24-19, 15-24, 28-19, 4-8, 22-18, 8-11, 18-9, 5-14, 29-25, 16-20, 25-22, 11-16.

11-15, 22-18, 15-22, 25-18, 12-16, 29-25 (a), 9-13, 18-14, 10-17, 21-14, 16-20, 23-18. (a) Or 18-14, 9-18, 23-14, 10-17, 21-14, 6-9, 26-23, 9-18, 23-14, 8-11, 29-25, 4-8, 25-21, 8-12, 27-23.

11-15, 23-18, 8-11, 27-23, 4-8, 23-19 (a), 10-14, 19-10, 14-23, 26-19, 7-14. (a) Or 32-27, 15-19, 23-16, 12-19, 24-15, 10-19, 22-17.

11-15, 23-19, 8-11, 22-17 (a), 3-8, 25-22, 11-16, 26-23, 7-11, 31-26, 9-14, 29-25. (a) Or 27-23, 9-14.

11-15, 24-19, 15-24, 28-19, 9-14 (a), 22-18, 7-11, 18-9, 5-14, 26-22, 11-15, 27-24, 8-11. (a) Or 8-11, 22-18, 11-16, 18-14, 9-18, 23-14, 16-23, 27-18, 10-17, 21-14, 12-16, 26-23, 4-8, 31-27, 8-12, 27-24, 6-9, 25-21, 16-20, 32-27.

11-15, 24-20, 15-19 (a), 23-16, 12-19, 22-18, 10-14 (b), 18-15, 19-23, 26-19, 7-11, 15-10. (a) Or 8-11, 28-24, 4-8, 23-19. (b) Or 9-14, 18-9, 5-14, 25-22, 10-15, 22-18, 14-23, 27-11, 8-15, 32-27.

11-16, 21-17, 16-19 (a), 24-15, 10-19, 23-16, 12-19, 17-14, 9-18, 22-15, 7-10. (a) Or 16-20, 17-13, 8-11, 22-18, 9-14.

11-16, 22-17, 16-19 (a). (a) Or 16-20, 17-13, 8-11, 25-22, 4-8, 22-18, 9-14.

11-16, 22-18, 8-11, 25-22 (a), 16-20, 29-25. (a) Or 18-14, 9-18, 23-14, 10-17, 21-14, 4-8, 24-19, 16-23, 27-18.

11-16, 23-18, 16-20, 24-19, 10-14, 26-23, 8-11, 22-17, 7-10, 30-26, 11-16, 26-22, 9-13, 18-9, 5-14, 22-18.

11-16, 23-19 (formerly barred), 16-23, 26-19, 8-11, 27-23, 9-14, 22-18, 4-8.

11-16, 24-19, 8-11, 22-18, 10-14 (a), 26-22, 16-20, 22-17, 7-10, 30-26, 11-16, 26-22, 9-13, 18-9, 5-14, 22-18. (a) Or 4-8, 18-14.

11-16, 24-20, 16-19 (this forms the Bristol, as does the trunk line given for 11-15, 24-20).

12-16, 21-17, 16-19 (a), 23-16, 11-20, 25-21, 9-13. (a) Or 16-20, 17-13, 11-15, 23-18. (b) Or 9-13, 25-21, 16-19, 23-16, 11-20, 17-14.

12-16, 22-17, 16-19 (a), 24-15, 10-19, 23-16, 11-20. (a) Or 8-12, 17-14.

12-16, 22-18, 16-19 (a). (a) Or 8-12, 24-19, 10-14, 26-22, 16-20, 22-17.

12-16, 23-18, 16-20, 24-19 (a), 11-15. (a) Or 26-23, 8-12, 22-17.

12-16, 23-19 (formerly barred), 16-23, 27-18, 11-16, 22-17.

12-16, 24-19, 16-20, 22-18 (a), 11-15, 18-11, 8-24, 28-19. (a) Or 28-24, 10-14, 22-17, 7-10, 32-28.

12-16, 24-20, 8-12, 28-24 (a), 3-8, 23-18 (b), 16-19, 24-15, 10-19, 18-15. (a) Or 22-18, 3-8. (b) Or 22-17, 16-19, 24-15, 10-19, 23-16, 12-19, 25-22.

Elementary shots. The loss of a piece (not compensated by a counter-capture) usually means loss of the game. It is true there are piece-down drawing positions, even wins, and that a piece is sometimes sacrificed with expectation of regaining it eventually. Examples of early sacrifices are seen in both the Black Doctor and White Doctor openings. But piece-down draws depend upon very special formations. It remains generally true that loss of a piece spells defeat.

The game abounds with possible shots and strokes leading to the gain of material, or to a winning position with equal pieces (often through gaining the first king). Besides examining the strategical merits of a contemplated move, the player always has to check whether it sets up a winning shot for his opponent. A beginner can scarcely get through a dozen moves without making this kind of mistake: 11-15, 22-17, 12-16 (?), 24-19, 15-24, 28-12; White wins a piece and the game. The accompanying diagrams show the principal formations that allow two-for-one shots.

Black

White

Fig. 3. White wins by 24-19.

Black

White

Fig. 4. White wins by 27-24.

Black

White

Fig. 5. White wins by 26-23.

Black

White

Fig. 6. White wins by 26-22.

Black

White

Fig. 7. White wins by 27-24.

Black

White

Fig. 8. White wins by 28-24.

Many shots depend on the rule that jumping is compulsory. If therefore a player attacks an adverse piece, he commits itself to capture it if the opponent does not defend; the opponent thus has a "tempo" (to use a Chess term) to attack elsewhere, perhaps with greater force. This point is brought out in Fig. 9. Black can win the man on 16 by 8-12, but to do so will be fatal, as White can move 22-17, winning two-for-one.

Black

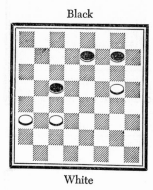

White

Fig. 9. Example of the tempo.

Black

White

Fig. 10. White wins by 31-26, 22-31, 32-28, 31-24, 28-3.

Another way of gaining a tempo is illustrated in Fig. 10, the "in and out shot." A piece is sacrificed to force an adverse man to the king row, and the new king is committed to make a capture next move. Most of the long strokes depend on a key capture, the compulsion to make which deprives the victim of time to make a vital defensive move. This point is illustrated by the "slip shot," Fig. 11. After White's third move (23-14) Black is a piece up, and would be glad to stay out of trouble by 27-31, but the forced jump precludes this move.

Getting an early king, back of the enemy single men, is often a decisive advantage. This is the point of the stroke known as the "Goosewalk," Fig. 12. Nevertheless, the king must often be circumspect in attacking from the rear. The sort of thing that can happen is epitomized by this simple problem: White man on 22, kings on 13, 10; Black kings on 2, 29, 30. White wins by 13-9, 29-25 (he cannot avoid attacking the man from 25 or 26), 9-5, 25-18, 10-6. After the exchanges, the remaining Black king is trapped.

Besides the simple shots, which can be calculated easily enough over the board, there are many strokes not so easy to foresee. A stroke may lead to the gain of material, but more often it brings a superior or decisive position, the forces being equal. Only a position-judgment nurtured by study and experience can steer the player through the shoals. As a matter of fact, the expert player has to rely largely upon memory; he has learned by rote a large number of completely-analyzed stroke positions. A few of them are shown in the accompanying diagrams.

Black

White

FIG. 11. White to move and win.

Black

White

FIG. 14. Black to move and win.

Black

White

FIG. 12. The "Goosewalk"
Black to move and win.

Black

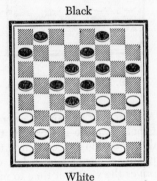

White

FIG. 13. The "Big Stroke"
White to move and win.

FIG. 11

White wins by 27-23, 20-27, 18-15, 11-18, 23-14, 9-18, 32-14.

The "Goosewalk" or "Farmer"

The position is reached by: 11-15, 22-18, 15-22, 25-18, 8-11, 29-25, 4-8, 25-22, 10-15, 24-20, 12-16, 27-24. (White's last move threatens 24-19, but it is a mistake. Correct is 21-17.)

Black wins by: 15-19, 24-15, 16-19, 23-16, 9-14, 18-9, 11-25. Next move Black captures the man on 9. Pieces remain even but Black gets a king, which cannot be prevented from emerging, while White is shut out from the king row.

The "Big Stroke."

The position is reached by: 11-15, 23-19, 8-11, 22-17, 4-8, 17-13, 15-18, 24-20, 11-15, 28-24, 8-11, 26-23, 9-14, 31-26, 6-9, 13-6, 2-9, 26-22, 9-13. (Black's last move loses. Correct is 1-6.)

White wins by: 20-16, 11-20, 22-17, 13-22, 21-17, 14-21, 23-14, 10-17, 25-2. Pieces remain even, but the Black king row is open while White's is still closed. However Black plays, White will have a king to run down the Black single men.

Black

White

FIG. 15. White to move and win.

Black

White

FIG. 16. Black to move and win.

Black

White

FIG. 17. Black to move and draw.

Black

White

FIG. 18. White to move and win.

The position in Fig. 14 is reached by 10-14, 23-19, 11-16, 26-23, 9-13, 24-20. (White's last move looks good, but is a blunder. Correct is 22-17.)

Black wins by: 14-17, 21-14, 6-10, 20-11, 10-26, 31-22, 8-31, and Black is two pieces ahead.

The position in Fig. 15 is reached by: 9-14, 22-17, 11-15, 25-22, 8-11, 29-25, 11-16, 23-18, 14-23, 27-11, 16-19, 24-15, 10-19, 22-18, 7-16, 25-22, 3-7, 18-15, 5-9, 22-18, 9-13, 17-14, 4-8, 31-27, 16-20, 14-9, 12-16, 26-22, 7-11. (Black's last move is a mistake; 1-5 will draw.)

White wins by: 21-17, 1-5, 17-14, 19-23, 14-10*, 5-14, 18-9*, 11-25, 30-21*, 6-15, 27-4. White is a piece ahead.

A lock is an end position in which two or more pieces are held at bay by a lesser number of enemies, particularly through the blocking of kings

375

by their own advanced single men. The next three examples show strokes that culminate in double-corner and single-corner locks.

The position in Fig. 16 may arise from the Bristol opening.

Black wins by: 16-20, 32-27 (nothing else is any better), 11-16, 10-6, 3-7, 6-1, 16-19, 24-15, 7-10, 15-6, 12-16. Four White pieces are locked in the double corner by one Black piece.

In order to appreciate the position in Fig. 17, which can arise from several openings, try forcing a Black man to the king row. It will speedily be seen that Black will have to sacrifice a piece that he never recovers, or let the White king out to run wild.

Black draws by: 7-11, 8-4 (the alternative 32-27 would win if Black should foolishly play 28-32, for then 8-4 and White wins two-for-one, but after 32-27 White moves 17-21 and crowns at leisure), 15-18, 22-8, 17-22, 26-17, 13-22, 32-27, 22-26, 30-23, 28-32, 27-24, 32-27, 23-18, 27-20, 18-15, 20-16, 15-10, 16-11. Black guards square 7 to prevent 10-7, whereby at the sacrifice of one man White could break the lock.

In Fig. 18 White wins by: 11-16, 24-28, 31-27, 23-32, 16-23.

Two of the commonest shots that can occur with kings on the board are shown in Figs. 19 and 20.

Black

White

Fig. 19. The "side shot"
White wins by 15-11, 8-15, 10-26.

Black

White

Fig. 20. The "breaches"
White wins by 19-15.

The move. Of fundamental importance in all of end-play is the move, which is equivalent to what Chess players call the opposition. In Fig. 21, Black to move finds the move against him, and the fact costs him the game. He has to retreat to the edge of the board, and the White king, following him, eventually traps him. If the turn to move were White's, the move would likewise be against him, but he can draw since he can reach the double corner: 24-28, 16-19, 28-32, 19-24, 32-28 and Black can make no headway.

Black

White

Fig. 21. Black to move loses.

Black

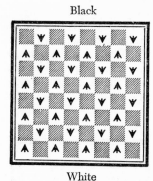

White

Fig. 22. The Black and White "systems" of files.

The general rule for calculating which player has the move is based on systems of squares, illustrated in Fig. 22. The Black system comprises the squares in the four columns terminating in 1, 2, 3, and 4. The White system comprises the columns terminating in 29, 30, 31, 32.

If the pieces on each side are equal, count the number of pieces of both colors in either system; if the number is odd, the player in turn to move has the move: if the number is even, the player in turn finds the move against him.

Exceptions to the foregoing rule can occur through locks. The simplest case is shown in Fig. 23. White starts with the move against him.
The play is: 28-24, 4-8, 24-19, 8-11, 19-23, 11-16 (if the Black single man heads for 18, White will force a cut by 26-22 and gain the move; or if Black goes to 19, the cut by 27-23 wins), 23-27, 16-20, 27-32, 20-24, 30-26, 29-25, 26-31, 24-28 (forced, else White will win the man by 32-28), 31-26. Now, in effect, White has gained the move, without exchange, for the double-corner lock leaves him with the move against the Black king.

Black

White

Fig. 23. White to move and win.

Black

White

Fig. 24. Exchange in the same system.

377

As was seen in the foregoing example, an ordinary cut changes the move. The reason is that the captures are completed in different systems. But exchanges wholly within one system leave the move unchanged. In Fig. 24, White has the move, but cannot win since Black can reach the double corners. But if Black erroneously plays 23-18, White replies 16-11, and after the exchanges in either direction White still has the move, and the remaining Black king is trapped in a single corner.

Black   Black

White   White

Fig. 25. White to move and win.   Fig. 26. White to move and draw.

Piece-down endings. The question who has the move, when one player is a piece down, has no meaning apart from certain piece-down drawing positions. The only position in which one king can draw against two kings is shown in Fig. 25. After 17-22, 30-25, 22-17, 25-21, 17-22, it is clear that Black cannot get out of the corner without sacrificing a piece. But 29-25, 22-29 leaves White with the move, and 25-22, 17-26 lets the White king reach a double-corner. The simplest of king vs. king-and-man draws is shown in Fig. 26. After 18-22, 21-17, 22-18, 17-21, 18-22, it is clear that Black can make no headway without a sacrifice. But 21-25, 22-29 gives White the move and the game, while 17-22, 18-25, 13-17, 25-21 lets the White king get past to the double corner.

All other piece-down draws depend on holding back a single man as in Fig. 26, or on a lock. Useful in this connection to the weaker side is Patterson's Rule: If it is your turn to move, count the pieces in your own system; if the total is even, hold an adverse single man on your double-corner side: if the total is odd, hold an adverse single man on your double-corner side. The reason for this rule is shown in Fig. 27, where White, though a piece down and regardless of whose turn it is to move, can head into a well-known draw.

In Fig. 27, White to move: 19-23, 20-24, 23-26, 24-27, 26-30, 27-31, 30-25, 2-6, 25-30, 6-10, 30-25, 10-14, 25-21, 31-27, 21-25, 27-24, 25-30, 24-19, 30-26, 19-15, 26-23. This position is Payne's Draw. Black can

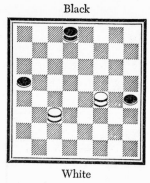

FIG. 27. Either to move, White draws.   FIG. 28. Either to move, White to win.

never force the king off 22, so cannot advance the single man. For example: 14-17, 23-26, 17-21, 26-23, 15-10, 23-26, 10-14, 26-30, 14-17, 22-18, and now to avoid loss (by 17-22) Black has to give up his extra piece by 17-14.

Black to move: 2-7, 22-26, 13-17, 26-31, 17-22, 19-23, 22-25 (see final remarks), 31-27, 25-30, 27-31, 7-10, 23-19, 10-14, 19-23, 14-17, 31-27, 17-22, 27-31. This position is Roger's Draw. The point of it is that if the single man advances, now or earlier, White locks it in the corner, e. g., 20-24, 23-27, 24-28, 27-32. Then the other White king has in effect a "quadruple corner" (31 to 20) along which he can move perpetually without being dislodged or exchanged.

With only kings left on the board, a piece-down player must lose every ending except Fig. 25. For the sake of the beginner, we show the process with two against one and three against two. Take the position: Black king on 5, White kings on 10 and 14. White wins by: 10-6, 5-1, 14-10, 1-5, 6-1, 5-9, 1-5, 9-13, 10-15 (useless is 10-14 because of 13-9), 13-17, 15-18, 17-13, 18-22. With three against two, four against three, etc., the weaker party may huddle all his kings in one double-corner or divide them between the two. In either case, the stronger party can force exchanges and reduce eventually to two against one.

In Fig. 28, White to move: 15-18, 5-1, 14-9, 6-2, 9-5, 2-6, 18-14* (for if Black takes the two-for-one by 6-9, the move is against his remaining king), 6-2, 13-9, 1-6 (or 2-7, 14-10), 5-1, 6-13, 14-9, 13-6, 1-10.

Black to move: 6-2, 15-10, 5-1, 14-9, 1-5, 9-6.

In Fig. 29, White to move: 15-18, 9-5, 10-6, 27-32 (or 5-1, 18-15), 19-23 (threatens 6-9), 5-1, 6-9, 32-28 (or 1-5, 9-14 and White will force a cut next move), 23-27, 28-32, 9-14.

Black to move: 9-5, 15-18, 5-9, 10-14, 9-6, 19-23, 27-24. Now White has in effect reproduced the diagrammed position, with himself to move. He continues 18-15, etc.

Black

White

Fig. 29. Either to move, White to win.

Black

White

Fig. 30. First Position
by William Payne
White to move and win.

The "Positions." Certain endings are of such frequent occurrence and fundamental importance that they are called First Position, Second Position, etc. Besides the six so-called Positions, there are other endings classed with them in importance, such as Payne's Draw, Roger's Draw (both discussed under Fig. 27), Buchanan's Draw (Fig. 17). Not all the authorities would draft the same list of "basic endings," but probably all would agree that the following belong on the list.

First Position may be generalized thus: Two kings win against king and man if (a) they have the move; (b) the single man is forced to advance into the double-corner; (c) the enemy king is held in the same double-corner. If in Fig. 30, the single man is transferred from 12 to 3, White still wins, for if this man heads for the single corner he is trapped on square 10 by a king on 18, while the other White king goes to the rear to attack him. But starting from square 2, the single man would reach 13 and Black would draw. Likewise, with the Black king transferred to square 1 there is no win.

SOLUTION

23-27	24-28 (c)	28-32	28-32
28-32	18-15	27-24	27-31
19-23	28-24 (d)	18-15	32-28
32-28 (a)	32-28	24-28 (g)	11-15
27-32	24-27 (e)	15-11 (h)	19-24
28-24 (b)	15-18	16-19	15-19
23-18	12-16 (f)	32-27	

(a) Or 12-16, 27-24, 16-20, 24-28.

(b) Or 12-16, 32-27, 16-20, 27-32, 28-24, 32-28.

(c) Or 12-16, 18-15, reaching a later position of the trunk line. Or 24-19, 32-28, 12-16, 28-32, 16-20, 32-28, 19-16, 18-23, 16-11, 23-19, 11-8, 28-32, 8-12 (the king cannot reach the double-corner by 8-3, 32-27, 3-7, 19-15), 32-27, etc. This king walks around to bottle up the Black king.

(d) Or 12-16, 15-11, 16-19, 32-27, reaching a later position of the trunk line.

(e) Or 24-20, 15-11, 12-16, 28-32, 16-19, 11-15, 19-24, 32-28, 24-27, 28-32, 27-31, 15-19, 31-26, 19-24.

(f) Or 27-32, 18-23, 12-16, 28-24.

(g) Or 16-19, 32-27.

(h) Beware of 15-18, 16-19, 32-27 (hoping for 28-32, 27-24, 19-28, 18-23), 19-23 and draws.

Black

White

Fig. 31. Second Position
by William Payne
White to move and win.

Black

White

Fig. 32. Third Position
by William H. Avery
Black to move and win.

Second Position may be generalized thus: Three kings win against king and two men when (a) they have the move; (b) the single men are held on squares 20 and 21 (if Black) or 12 and 13 (if White). In Fig. 31, note that the Black king is in his own double-corner. If he were in the White double-corner, White would have a First Position win if he had a second king on the scene; otherwise the man on 20 could be forced down to crown and the game would be a draw.

SOLUTION

Run the man from 29 to the king row. The Black king cannot hold back this man, as White has the move. Bring this king to 22, then run the man on 30 to the king row. Having three kings, post them on 22, 27, and 9. The Black king at this time must be on 1. Black is forced to play 1-5, then 22-17, 5-14, 17-10, and the king is gone.

This cut gives Black the move. The point of holding the man on 20 is to force a second cut, regaining the move for White. Continue: 21-25, 10-15, 25-30, 15-19, 30-26, 27-32, 26-22, 19-24, 20-27, 32-23 and White wins.

Third Position may be generalized as: A single man advancing to the single-corner is accompanied by two kings, and opposed by two kings that have the move (meaning, in this connection, that the stronger party is in turn to move when all the pieces stand in the same system). In Fig. 32, the victory would be easy if it were White's turn to move. As it is, Black has the task of forcing his single man ahead while steering clear of Payne's Draw (Fig. 27) and the draw shown in Fig. 26.

SOLUTION

13-9	6-2 (f)	26-31	11-15	16-12 (j)
22-18	17-14	10-14	25-22	22-26
9-6	25-22	31-27	23-27 (i)	12-8
18-22 (a)	15-10	18-22	22-26	26-22
6-1 (b)	22-26	27-23 (h)	27-24	8-3
22-18 (c)	14-18 (g)	22-25	26-22	14-9 (k)
21-25	5-9	2-7	24-20	15-10
18-15	10-6	25-22	22-26	9-5
1-6 (d)	9-13	7-11	20-16	10-14 (1)
14-17 (e)	6-10	22-25	26-22	

(a) If White moves 18-15, the right answer is 21-25, not 6-1, because of: 18-15, 6-1, 15-10, 21-25, 14-17 and 5-9 would lose the man by 17-13. White would draw by shuttling perpetually 14-17 and 17-14.

(b) Now this is the only move to win. Wrong would be 6-2, 14-10, 5-9, 10-6, 9-13, 6-10, 21-17, 22-18, drawing as in Fig. 26.

(c) Or 14-10, 5-9, 10-15, 21-17. Or 14-10, 5-9, 22-18, 1-5, 10-14, 21-17, 14-21, 9-14.

(d) Not 25-22, 15-10 and draws by the perpetual as in note (a).

(e) Or 15-18, 6-2, 18-15, 25-22 as in the trunk line. Or 14-10, 6-2, 10-14, 25-22 with the same result.

(f) Of course not 5-9, with visions of 17-13, 6-1, because White strikes first with 17-14, 9-18, 15-29.

(g) Or 10-15, 26-23, 15-10, 23-19, 14-17, and Black can play 5-9, since 17-13 is no threat. This is the point of posting the king on 2.

(h) To reach Payne's Draw, White has to march his king from 14 to 25. Black stops this march at the moment by keeping the king on 23 to answer 14-17 with 23-18.

(i) The king on 15 releases 23 to march around to 3, since 14-17 can be answered by 15-18.

(j) A lamentable blunder would be 16-11, for then White could play 14-17, the set reply 15-18 being debarred.

(k) To avoid the cut by 15-10.

(1) Now the king on 22 can be forced away by posting the kings on 15 and 18, after which the single man marches down.

Black

White

FIG. 33. Fifth Position
by John Drummond
White to move and draw.

Black

White

FIG. 34. Sixth Position
by A. Mackintosh
White to move and draw.

Fifth Position is reached from several openings, for example: 10-14, 24-19, 6-10, 28-24, 11-15, 22-18, 15-22, 25-18, 9-13, 18-9, 5-14, 29-25, 8-11, 25-22, 11-15, 23-18, 14-23, 27-11, 7-23, 26-19, 4-8, 22-18, 8-11, 31-26, 11-16, 18-15, 16-23, 15-6, 1-10, 26-19, 3-7, 30-26, 7-11, 24-20, 2-6, 26-22, 10-14, 32-27, 6-10. The White side is repeatedly lost by inexperienced players, through 27-24, 11-15, 20-16, 14-18 or 27-23, 11-15, 20-16, 15-24, 16-11, 10-15.

SOLUTION

20-16, 11-20, 27-23, 20-24, 22-18, 24-27, 18-9, 27-31, 23-18, 10-14, (or 31-27, 18-15 leading to the same position), 18-15, 31-27, 15-11, 27-23, 19-15, 23-19, 15-10 and White saves his men because 19-15 is answered by 11-8.

Sixth Position illustrates one of the constant hazards to which single men are exposed when they have to fight their way to the king row against adverse kings. The great danger is that two single men will be blocked by one king, leaving the player a piece ahead on the rest of the field. In Fig. 34, if White commences with 32-27, Black will play 7-11 and win easily. This king blocks both 12 and 20. After running 3 to the king row, Black will have two kings free to bottle up the one White king. White is compelled to commence with 20-16, so that the two single men cannot be restrained by one king. But then 16 stands exposed, subject to attack by Black kings posted on 7 and 11. White, having the move, can just parry this threat by occupying 20 whenever Black tries 15-11.

SOLUTION

20-16, 6-10, 32-27, 10-15, 27-24, 15-11, 24-20, 11-15, 20-24, 7-10, 24-20, 3-7 (a), 16-11, 15-8, 12-3. (a) Or 10-14, 20-24, 3-7, 12-8, 15-11 (b), 8-3. (b) Or 14-10, 8-3, 15-11, 24-20, 11-15, 16-11, 15-8, 3-12.

CHECKER VARIANTS

Giveaway Checkers. This is played under the same rules as regular Checkers, the sole difference being that the game is won by the first player to get rid of all his pieces. A juvenile favorite, this "losing game" has never gained place in serious competition. Opening tactics are all concerned with luring a Black piece to square 21 or a White piece to square 12. A piece locked on such a square brings sure defeat to the owner, for the opponent can at leisure dispose his entire army so that after the piece is released and forced to jump to the king row the new king will devastate the board. There are no subtleties of end play, for the move is all that matters. The rule for determining who has the move is the converse of that in regular Checkers. For example, two kings of opposite color stand in frontal opposition (equivalent to Fig. 21) when they stand three moves apart, as on 11 and 23. Whoever has to move from this position loses—there is no possible draw in Giveaway.

Eleven-man Ballot. A way of revitalizing Checkers, additional to restriction play, was proposed by Newell W. Banks, a leading American expert, and has received some trial. This is to start with only eleven men on each side. Two corresponding squares (as 1 and 32) are left vacant, the pair being chosen by chance. If the two-move opening, also selected by chance, calls for moving a piece that has been balloted off the board, a man must instead be moved to the vacant square. For example, if 9-14 is required but 9 was balloted off, the move is 5-9; or if 9-13 is required, the move is 6-9; this substitute move must be made in the same direction as the original. The eleven-man plan has been tried out under alternative rules: pieces may be balloted off the second and third rows, but not the king rows; or all three rows are included.

Contract Checkers. Another way to vary Checkers without vitiating all past analysis was suggested by L. S. Stricker of Chicago in 1934. In his variant Contract Checkers, the number of pieces on each side can be extended to thirteen, fourteen, or more, as desired. A game commences with the usual twelve on a side, and single men are added to each side on previously selected pairs of king-row squares (as 4 and 29) as these squares become vacant.

Dammspiel. This is the German name for the earliest variant whose rules are completely known. It is played on the usual 8 x 8 board, with sixteen pieces on each side set up on the first two ranks. The rules are as follows:

(a) The men always remain on the squares of same color as their initial posts.

(b) The simple move is the same as in Checkers—to the adjacent square diagonally forward.

(c) Capturing is compulsory, and serial-captures must be made so long as possible. A single man, however, captures in any of five directions—diagonally forward, or laterally on the rank, or forward on the file.

(d) On reaching the king row, a man must stop to be crowned.

(e) A king moves diagonally in any direction (as in Checkers), but captures in all eight directions.

Black

White

FIG. 35. Dammspiel

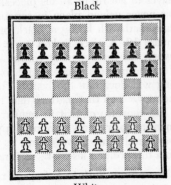

Black

White

FIG. 36. Turkish Checkers.

(f) As in Checkers, there is no restriction on choice of captures.

Polish Checkers. The board is 10 x 10, with 100 squares. All pieces move only on the dark squares. Each player begins with twenty men, set up on the first four ranks. The rules are as follows:

(a) A single man moves only forward (diagonally), but captures in any (diagonal) direction.

(b) Capturing is compulsory, and serial-captures must be made so long as possible. If a single man reaches the king row by a jump, and is able to jump backwards, it must do so, thereby remaining single.

(c) A single man is crowned only when it reaches the king row and can stop there. (In connection with all these variants, we use the term king as in Checkers, but the actual term is dame, woman or queen.)

(d) A king moves like a bishop in Chess—any distance along an open diagonal. The king can (and must) jump an enemy from a distance, and may come to rest on any of the consecutive vacant squares beyond it.

(e) With choice of captures, the player must take the maximum possible number of pieces. (Among equal numbers, he may choose to take kings or single men, as he pleases.) This means that a king, in jumping, must if possible land on a square from which he can make another jump, and his complete tour must be planned to gather the maximum of victims. However, in any such serial capture, the king is debarred from touching or passing over a square from which he has taken an enemy previously during that turn. In other words, the tour is completed before any jumped piece is removed from the board; jumped pieces therefore remain as possible obstructions.

Damespiel. The variant prevalent in Germany and neighboring countries, Damespiel, follows all the rules of Polish Checkers, but uses a board 8 x 8 with twelve pieces on each side, arranged as in Checkers.

Turkish Checkers. The board is 8 x 8. The sixteen men on each side are arrayed on the second and third ranks, leaving the king rows vacant. The rules are as follows:

(a) A single man may move one square in any of five directions— diagonally forward, laterally on the rank, or forward on the file.

(b) A single man captures by jumping, in the same five directions as the simple move.

(c) Capturing is compulsory, and serial-captures must be continued so long as possible.

(d) On reaching the king row, a single man must stop to be crowned.

(e) A king moves any distance on an open line in any direction, and captures by jumping to an adjacent vacant square beyond an enemy piece. Each piece jumped is removed at once from the board and so ceases to be an obstruction to the repassage of the king across the same square.

— BACKGAMMON —

Backgammon (sometimes called by its French name, Trictrac) is a game of blended luck and skill, played with dice and counters ("stones") on a special board. It is one of the most ancient of all games, and one of the most universally played. It was the "twelve-lined game" of the ancient Romans, and before them was played by the Egyptians; in lands bordering the Mediterranean it is still played so seriously that few Europeans and Americans can match the skill of the better Greek and Levantine players. In old England a large group of games was developed to be played "within the tables," that is, on the Backgammon board. There has been no significant change in the rules of the game for 2,000 years, but the element of doubling, introduced into Backgammon in the 1920's, greatly increased its popularity.

Definitions. 1. The following terms are defined as used in Backgammon:

BACKGAMMON. Loss of a game, when the loser has borne off no stone and has a stone on the bar or in the adverse home table.

BAR, ON THE. Said of a stone that has been hit and must be reëntered.

BAR POINT. Either 7-point.

BEARING OFF. The final stage of a game, in which one player is removing his stones entirely from play.

BLOT. A single stone on a point.

BUILDERS. Stones in advantageous position to make valuable points, especially stones in one's own outer table.

CHOUETTE. A way of playing Backgammon (or any two-hand game) with three or more participants.

CLOSED POINT. One that is occupied by two or more adverse stones.

COCKED DICE. The position when any die does not come to rest with one face flat on the table.

COMFORT STATION. Either 12-point.

DOUBLETS. Like numbers on both dice, as 6-6.

ENTER. Move a stone, after it has been hit, from the bar to the adverse home table.

GAMMON. Loss of a game, when the loser has borne off no stones but has advanced all his stones beyond the adverse home table.

HIT. Move a stone so as to touch upon or land upon a point occupied by an adverse blot.

LOVER'S LEAP. The move, on roll of 6-5, from the adverse 1-point to his 12-point.

MAKE A POINT. Occupy it with two or more stones.

MAN. See *stone*.

POINT. Any of the twenty-four marks on the board, usually in shape of elongated triangles.

PRIME. The making of six consecutive points.

OPEN POINT. One that is not occupied by two or more adverse stones.

RUNNERS. The two stones initially posted on the adverse 1-point; any stones back of adverse stones on the adverse side of the board.

SHUTOUT. A prime in the home table, preventing adverse stones from entering.

STONE. Any of the pieces used in playing Backgammon.

Number of players. 2. Only two compete directly, but three or more frequently participate in the stakes (see Chouette, paragraph 31).

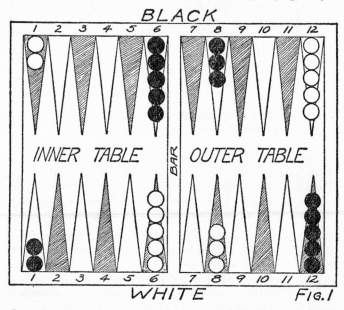

The board. 3. The rectangular board is divided into two halves by a bar extending from the White side to the Black. These two halves are designated arbitrarily as the inner or home table and the outer table. (When the contestants sit down at the board, they agree which table to construe as the inner; traditionally, it was the side nearer the light.) Extending from each side toward the center are twelve triangular marks called points, six in each table. The points are colored alternately light and dark. (See Fig. 1.) The twenty-four points represent what originally were twelve lines across the board (and it may help the beginner in following the rules to consider them as lines).

Stones. 4. Each player has fifteen pieces, commonly called stones. The stones are made in two colors, one for each player, who (as in most board games) are conventionally designated as Black and White. To commence a game, the pieces are arranged as shown in Fig. 1.

Other equipment. 5. Each player has two dice and a cup in which to shake them. A useful accessory is a doubling cube, a large die with faces marked respectively 2, 4, 8, 16, 32, 64. It is used to keep track of doubles (paragraphs 24, 25), the current multiplier of the basic stake being turned uppermost.

Notation. 6. The numbers shown in Fig. 1 are not actually marked on the board; they are added to the diagram to explain the notation. The points on each side are numbered from 1 to 12, beginning at the outside of the inner table. The two points of like number are distinguished by the prefixed W or B (White or Black side of the board). A move is denoted by the point moved from and the point moved to, joined by a hyphen [White, B12-W7, B1-B5, means: White moves one man from Black's 12-point to his own 7-point and one man from Black's 1-point to Black's 5-point.] If more than one stone makes the same move, the number of stones making that move is added in parentheses.

Object of play. 7. In accordance with chance rolls of the dice, each player moves his stones in a fixed course toward the home table on his side of the board. The direction of White movement is from W1 to W12, thence to B12, thence to B1. Black moves in the reverse direction: W1 to W12 and B12 to B1. The two 12-points are consecutive in both cases. From their home table, the pieces are borne off, which is to say, they continue to move as though to a "zero-point" outside the board. The player first to bear off all his fifteen stones wins the game.

The dice. 8. To begin a game, the stones being arranged as in Fig. 1, each player rolls one die. The higher number plays first. If equal numbers are cast, both players must roll again.

9. The first player uses the numbers on the two dice—his own and his opponent's—for his first move. Thereafter, the turn to play alternates, and each player begins his turn by rolling both of his own dice.

10. When the player rolls his own two dice, a doublet (both numbers the same) counts twice over. For example, a roll of 6-6 counts as four sixes, not merely two, a total of 24 instead of 12.

11. The numbers on the dice indicate the number of points by which the player may and must advance his stones. He may apply them to any of his stones, subject to the following provisions, and may apply both dice to the advance of one stone, or the two numbers separately to different stones, or four numbers (in case of a doublet) to one, two, three, or four stones.

12. The player must use both (or all four) numbers if he can. (This

rule sometimes operates to preclude choice.) If he can use one number but not the other, he must if possible use the higher.

The moves. 13. A point is open to a player when it is not occupied by two or more adverse stones. Any number of stones of one color may be massed on one point, and the point remains open to the owner of that color.

14. When two or more stones of one color stand on one point, stones of the opposite color may neither come to rest on that point nor touch upon it in making a compound move. Such a point is *made* by the stones that occupy it. But a point made by one player is not of itself a barrier to the stones of the other; such stones may skip over the closed point provided that they find open landing places.

15. A stone may advance by a number of points corresponding to the number on one die, provided that the landing place is open. A stone may advance the total distance of two (or more) numbers on the dice provided that it can find points open so that each number can be taken separately. [For example, on a roll of 5-4, White can move B1-B10, provided that either B5 or B6 is open, since the stone can first move 4, then 5, or vice versa; but if both B5 and B6 are closed, the White runner on B1 cannot move on this roll.]

Hitting. 16. A single stone on a point is a *blot*. A blot is hit if an adverse stone comes to rest on the same point, or touches on the point in passing, or enters from the bar on that point.

17. When a blot is hit, it is picked up and put on the bar. The owner must enter the stone from the bar to the adverse home table, before he may move any other stone. With several stones on the bar, a player must enter all before these or any other stones may move on the board.

18. To enter from the bar, a player must roll on one die a number corresponding to an open point in the adverse home table. The stone is moved from the bar to this open point, and the number on the other die may be taken in the same turn, by the same or another stone (the player having no other stone on the bar).

19. If all six points in the adverse home table are closed (called a shut-out), a player having a stone on the bar does not roll at all; his opponent continues to roll and move until a point is opened in the home table.

Bearing off. 20. A player may begin to bear off when all fifteen of his stones lie in his own home table. If one of his stones is hit during bearing off, such stone must be entered from the bar, and moved around the board to its home table, before the player may resume bearing off.

21. Stones borne off are removed from the board and never reëntered during that game. A stone may be borne off a point corresponding to a number on one die. [For example, on roll of 4-2 a stone may be removed from the 4-point and another from the 2-point.] One or both numbers may be used, if the player chooses and the position permits, to move stones within the home table. [For example, the roll of 4-2 could be used

to advance one stone from the 6-point to the 2-point and another from the 5-point to the 3-point.]

22. When a number on one die is higher than the highest point on which the player has any stones left (or equal to it), the player has no option but to bear a stone off this point. [For example, there are three stones on the 5-point, none on the 6-point. On roll of 6-6, the player must bear off the three from the 5-point, and one from the next-highest occupied point.]

Gammon. 23. The player first to bear off all his stones wins the game. If the loser has borne off at least one stone, he loses only a single game (though it may have been increased by voluntary doubles). If the loser has not borne off a single stone, he is *gammoned* and loses a double game; or if, in addition to having borne off no stone, he has a stone on the bar or in the adverse home table, he is *backgammoned* and loses a triple game.

Doubling. 24. If equal numbers are rolled for first turn, the basic stake is doubled automatically. Both players must roll again. (The automatic doubles may be waived by agreement, and in any event the number of such doubles per game is usually limited by agreement to one or two.)

25. Either player may offer the first voluntary double. The opponent must agree to continue play at a doubled stake, or resign the game at once. Thereafter the right to offer a voluntary double alternates. Accepted doubles are cumulative, and additional to increases through gammon or backgammon; if the basic stake has been increased to 4, a player who is gammoned loses 8. If any double is refused, the player who offered it wins the game forthwith at the current value of the stake.

Irregularities. 26. *Cocked dice.* The player must cast his dice upon the table at his right. If either die falls outside the table, or fails to come to rest flat on the board, the roll is void and the player must cast both dice again. (In club play, there is often a house rule that a roll stands wherever the dice fall, and if a die is "cocked" an adjudication must be made as to which side is uppermost.)

27. *Completing play.* A player should leave his dice on the board until he has completed all his plays. If he picks them up before completing his plays, his opponent may declare the roll void, require replacement of such stones as were moved, and require a new roll to be made.

28. *Retracting a play.* A correct play is completed and may not be retracted after the player has removed his hand from the stone.

29. *Error in initial position.* If an error is made in placing the stones for the beginning of a game, it may be corrected by either player prior to the completion of his first play. If not corrected in time, the error stands as regular.

30. *Error in play.* If an erroneous move is made, not in accordance with the dice, it may be corrected on demand of either player before the next roll. When such correction is made, a stone that was moved errone-

ously must be moved correctly, if possible. If the error is not noticed before the next roll, it stands as regular.

Chouette. 31. Chouette is a way of playing Backgammon with three or more players. (It is applicable to any two-hand game.) To commence, each participant casts one (or two) dice; the highest roll becames the "man in the box;" the second-highest becomes "captain." The others rank in order below the captain, according to their rolls. Players rolling the same numbers for precedence cast again to determine their rank in relation to each other.

32. The man in the box plays for himself, against the captain, who represents a team comprising all the other players. The captain may consult with and be advised by his teammates; his decision is final in any matter of moves, but each player of the team may decide for himself whether to endorse a double offered by the captain or accept a double offered by the man in the box.

33. When any player of the team refuses to endorse or accept a double, he pays the man in the box at the current value of the stake, and no longer participates in that game. If the captain declines a double offered by the man in the box, any other member of the team (the option going by precedence) may accept the double and continue play as a new captain.

34. If the man in the box wins the game, he continues in the box, and the next member of the team in order replaces the previous captain. If the man in the box loses (including loss by refusal of a double), he joins the team as its lowest-ranking member, and the captain who won the game becomes the man in the box.

35. When a game ends, the man in the box collects from or pays to each remaining active member of the team separately the full value of the stake at that time.

BACKGAMMON FOR FOUR

Four play, in two partnerships. One member of each side plays against a member of the other side, their Backgammon boards placed so closely together that the rolls of the dice at one table are easily seen at the other. On each team, one partner plays White and one plays Black. The members of only one side cast the dice; one casts for White and his casts are used by the White players on both sides, the other casts for Black and his casts are used by both Black players. When any player has borne off all his men, his side wins the game.

BACKGAMMON VARIANTS

Acey-Deucey. The essential idea of Acey-Deucey is that special privileges are attached to the roll of 1-2. In the variant widely played among

U. S. Naval and Marine forces, the roll allows the player to (a) move the 1-2, (b) name any doublet he chooses and move accordingly, and (c) roll the dice again. If unable to use a number, the player loses the balance of the privilege, e.g., if he can move the one but not the two, he loses (b) and (c). He may deliberately choose a doublet of which he cannot use all four numbers, thereby forfeiting (c).

Other differences from regular Backgammon are:

(d) In rolling single dice for first turn, ace is high, and the first player rolls his own two dice for his first numbers.

(e) All the stones are on the bar at the outset. With one or more stones duly entered, the player can use subsequent rolls to enter additional stones or to move those already entered, as he pleases. But blots are hit at usual, and must be entered before the player may make any other move.

Methods of settlement vary in different localities. In some places, the loser pays one point for each stone he has left on the board. Elsewhere, the loser pays for each stone according to the number of points required to bear it off. Some double the stake on every roll of 1-2; others double the stake automatically in this way and also allow voluntary doubling. The increases for gammon and backgammon are usually eliminated.

Other variations are: If a player cannot use all the privileges of an 1-2 roll, the unused ones go to his opponent. If a player rolls a third successive 1-2, it belongs to his opponent, and the player's most advanced man is deemed to be hit and goes on the bar.

European Acey-Deucey. In this variant, the stones are set on the board as for regular Backgammon. The differences from the regular game are:

(a) On roll of 1-2 the stake doubles and the player moves 1-2, names any doublet he chooses, moves this doublet and also the complementary doublet (difference from 7), and rolls again. Of course, if he is unable to use one of the numbers in order, he loses the rest of the acey-deucey privilege.

(b) To bear off, the player must roll the exact number of the point on which he has stones. For example, if he has one stone left, on the 2-point, it may be borne off only by roll of a 2 on one die. With any stone outside his own table, the player may move the stones inside his home table; but with all in the home table, only bearing off is permitted.

Russian Backgammon. All the stones are on the bar at the outset. Both players enter in the same quarter and move jointly in the same direction around the board to the same home table. With two or more stones entered, the player may use subsequent rolls to enter additional men or to move those already entered. But blots, when hit, must enter from the bar before any other move is permitted. The roll of a doublet allows the player to use also the complementary doublet (difference from 7) and to roll again, but if he cannot use one number of the series he loses the rest of the privilege.

Dutch Backgammon. All the stones are on the bar at the outset. Each player must enter his fifteen stones before he may advance any of them. He may not hit an adverse blot until he has moved at least one stone around to his own home table; so at this stage of the game a single man closes a point to the opponent.

Snake. The Black stones are set up as for regular Backgammon. All the White stones are on the bar, except for four or six which are placed so as to make W1 and W2 (and W3). The number of such points given to White at the outset may be varied as a method of handicapping. White must enter all his stones before he can advance any.

POINTERS ON BACKGAMMON PLAY

Opening rolls. Certain rolls are "naturals" for opening moves, and there is no difference of opinion as to what these moves should be. Other rolls are less desirable, and some are positively awkward; players have various ideas how they should be absorbed. In the following tabulation, the first recommendation in each case is that made by Edmond Hoyle in 1746. The alternatives are frequently seen in modern play. (All moves are given as for White.)

6-5 Move B1-B12 ("lover's leap")
6-4 Move B1-B11; or B12-W7 and B1-B5.
6-3 Move B1-B10; or B12-W7 and B1-B4.
6-2 Move B12-W5; or B12-W7 and B12-W11.
6-1 Move B12-W7 and W8-W7.
5-4 Move B1-B10; or B12-W8 and B1-B5; or B12-W8 and B12-W9.
5-3 Move W8-W3 and W6-W3; or B12-W8 and B12-W10.
5-2 Move B12-W8 and B12-W11.
5-1 Move B12-W8 and W6-W5; or B12-W8 and B1-B2.
4-3 Move B12-W9 and B12-W10; or B1-B5 and B12-W10.
4-2 Move W8-W4 and W6-W4.
4-1 Move B12-W9 and W6-W5; or B12-W9 and B1-B2; or B1-B5 and W6-W5.
3-2 Move B12-W10 and B12-W11; or B1-B4 and B12-W11.
3-1 Move W8-W5 and W6-W5.
2-1 Move B12-W11 and W6-W5; or B12-W10.

Early doublets. In Acey-Deucey and other variants, the opening roll can be a doublet. The following moves are recommended for doublets. The same moves, when possible, are usually good when doublets are rolled early in a game of regular Backgammon. (All moves are given as for White.)

6-6 Move B1-B7 (2) and B12-W7 (2). This roll may be very awkward if Black has already made one of the bar-points. Where the excess sixes cannot be absorbed by the runners, it is usually better to move extra stones from B12 to W7 than from W8 to W2.

5-5   Move B12-W3 (2). Repeated fives in the early stages are apt to be awkward: one reason for advancing a runner in the adverse home table is to absorb a succession of fives. After 5-5, split the runners or otherwise make provision for future fives.

4-4   It is said that "there is no wrong way to play double fours." Hoyle recommends B12-W5 (2). A good alternative is B12-W9 (2) and B1-B5 (2). Worth consideration also is W8-W4 (2) and W6-W2 (2). If the White runners are unmoved, and Black has made his bar-point, a plausible move is B1-B9 (2).

3-3   Hoyle recommends W8-W5 (2) and W6-W3 (2). A good alternative is B12-W7 (2). If Black has made his bar-point, it may be advisable to play B1-B4 (2) and W8-W5 (2).

2-2   Usual is W6-W4 (2) and B12-W11 (2). If the 4-point is already made, move B12-W9 (2). If Black has made his bar-point, it may be advisable to play B1-B5 (2).

1-1   Move W8-W7 (2) and W6-W5 (2). If Black has already made either point, and one or two aces have to be absorbed by the runners on B1, split them by advancing one runner to B2 or B3, rather than play B1-B2 (2).

Key points. The most desirable points to make, early in the game, are your own 7-point and 5-point. Which of these, if either, is the more valuable, is moot. The closure of either point tends to impede the egress of the adverse runners. In addition, extra stones placed on these points serve as "feeders" to make additional points inside the home table.

All points on the home table are desirable to make in accordance with their proximity to the 6-point—the nearer, the better. The 4-point is highly desirable even when the 5-point is still open. The 3-point is prized by some players even when the 5- and 4-points are open, and scored by other players. One school plays the opening roll of 5-3 by W8-W3 and W6-W3; the other moves B12-W8 and B12-W10. The 2-point is quite generally ignored unless an additional point between it and the 6-point has previously been made. Thus, few players take an opening 6-4 by W8-W2 and W6-W2. However, each point made in the home table, additional to the 6-point, increases the value of making more points, even of low number.

The object of "making up the home table" is threefold: (a) to impede the egress of adverse runners; (b) to increase the difficulty of entry for adverse blots that are hit; (c) to provide safe landing places for one's own incoming stones. Points in one's own outer table have a certain value, in contribution to (c), which is greatly enhanced if the 7-point is made before the adverse runners have escaped.

Advancing the runners on doublets, to the adverse 5-point or 7-point has defensive value in that it increases their chances of escaping to safety. But making either of these points in itself has little offensive value. For offensive purposes—hitting adverse blots—the runners are best left on the 1-point, though they have fair prospect of hitting at the outer table from the 5-point. But on the adverse 7-point the runners do little but make the roll of 6-6 awkward for the opponent. From this point, the runners are best split at once to bring one around to safety. The remaining stone has maximum chance to be hit, but the hit is less dangerous if it is risked before the adverse home table is "made up" than after.

The prime. The ideal toward which to strive is to establish a prime— six consecutive points made, with one or more adverse runners trapped behind it. From the initial position, the most likely place for the formation of a prime is of course around your own bar-point. If the bar-point is made early, the 9-point is valuable, together with the higher points in unbroken phalanx. In early play, it is therefore advisable to bring stones down from your "comfort station" to your outer table. These stones function not only as builders for points lower than 8, but also look to the making of outer points.

Once a prime is established, it should be "walked" forward in unbroken formation. The process is as follows: Put one of the three extra stones (twelve being needed for the prime) on the point just ahead of the prime. Cover this blot when you can, preferably from the rearmost point of the prime. Thus the prime has walked forward one point.

A walking prime is subject to certain hazards that tend to break it. First, your blot placed ahead of the prime may be hit and may find itself in trouble. The trouble does not lie in entering—so long as the stone is on the bar, your prime stands intact. If your opponent has a shutout, he has to play on and break it. The trouble comes if the stone enters quickly, but then is unable to emerge from the adverse home table quickly, so that it is not available to help the prime. Second, one or more high doublets may be ruinous, especially 5-5. To absorb these numbers, there may be no alternative but to put all the extra men far ahead of the prime, or to make a split in the prime. Third, if two or more runners are trapped by your prime, they may be able to make a point. As they cannot be pushed back, the prime thus walks past them and may release them in time to let your opponent win the race. Avoid this ill, where possible, by trapping only one adverse runner, no more, behind your prime.

The ideal continuation, after making a prime, is to walk it into the home board to become a shutout. The adverse runner or runners are thus sent to the bar, and cannot enter until you have borne off enough stones to open a point. The shutout is a strategical advantage that can overcome a huge deficit in time. For example, suppose your opponent has started to bear off, but you have hit one blot and then trapped it by a prime. If you succeed in walking the prime around to become a shutout, you will almost surely win if he has borne off no more than six stones. You have fair chances to win even if your opponent has borne off more. A shutout has been known to win against a single remaining adverse stone.

Hitting. The question sometimes arises where to place a blot so as to minimize its chances of being hit. The chance of hitting within a distance of six points is always greater than the chance of hitting at a distance of seven points or more. The maximum chance is offered at a distance of six points, and the chances decrease both ways from this interval. The exact figures, assuming that no intervening points are closed, are as follows:

DISTANCE OF BLOT	ODDS AGAINST HITTING
1	25:11
2	24:12
3	22:14
4	21:15
5	21:15
6	19:17
7	30:6
8	30:6
9	31:5
10	33:3
11	34:2
12	33:3

The question whether to risk being hit—where any choice exists as to blotting—depends on the potential gain. For example, on opening roll of 5-1 there are two alternatives not listed in the classical choices: You as White might move B1-B7 or B12-W7. In either case you leave a blot at the distance of six from an adverse stone. If the blot on B7 is hit, you are set back by six points; if the blot on W7 is hit, the loss is eighteen points. But the question of relative "time" is minor. What matters is that in moving B1-B7 you blot on a point which, if you cover, is more of a liability than an asset. The slight chance that the runner will escape is not worth the risk. But in moving B12-W7 you try for one of the two key points, and many players consider that the risk is eminently worth-while taking.

The classical recommendations of Hoyle are to lay a blot on the 5-point when the opening roll is 4-1 or 6-2. The potential gain is worth the risk. On the same grounds, many modern players will use opening rolls of 6-4, 6-3, 5-1, to lay a blot on the bar-point. Similarly, in all early play the expert will blot freely, provided (a) that the potential gain by way of additional points made is worth striving for, and (b) that the adverse home table is still fairly open. The consideration (b) governs early play more than any other factor. So long as your opponent has closed no point in his home table, additional to the 6-point, or possibly no more than one other point, assume that any blot you leave, and which is hit, will enter at once. Considerations of "time" at this early stage are held in the back-ground—much can happen—and early strategic advantages are para-mount.

The importance of holding back the adverse runners is such that an experienced player will often hit and blot in his own home table, provided always that the adverse home table is still wide open. For example, suppose that White has played an opening 4-3 by B1-B5 and B12-W10. Black rolls 3-2. If he brings a builder down from W12, it will be subject to attack from B5. The move W12-B8 is too supine for consideration. Black is forced to blot to make any forward-looking move. That being so, he should hit by B8-B5, and play W12-B11. The blot in his home table, with a White stone entering from the bar, has fair chances to escape being hit; if it is not hit at once, Black can almost surely cover it next roll, making the 5-point.

The possible gain through a double-hit is so great that many players will make it even at the cost of leaving two blots in the home table. For example, White plays an opening roll of 4-3 by B1-B5, and B12-W10. Black rolls 5-3. The "gammon play" is B8-B5 and B6-B1, hitting twice. To get a return hit, White will have to roll a flat 5 or 1. Even if he hits on 1, Black has a fair chance of entering on his next roll and also covering on his 5-point (a flat 3 or 1). The potential advantage of the double-hit is that if White is not lucky on his very next roll, Black will almost surely make his 5-point. Black will not cover the blot on B1, for it is hard to hit, and if hit may actually be an asset. Three runners have better chances of escaping, or of getting worthwhile hits, than two. Once having made his 5-point, Black has some prospect of closing up his board rapidly, repeatedly hitting the White runners as he does so. In this kind of battle— Black making points in his home board even at the risk of leaving blots there, but hitting the White runners repeatedly—only a few of the 36 rolls are bad for Black, while only a few are good for White.

In later stages of the game, e.g., when both home boards are fairly made up (say three points), or when one player is markedly ahead in a running game, do not hit blots on general principle but only for specific cause. If you are well ahead you do not want additional runners back of your lines to harass you. Let the adverse runners escape to safety. Conversely, if you are far behind in the running game, look for hits and take even greater chances to get them than in the early game. When the adverse home board is well made up, calculate the risk in blotting carefully: prudence may dictate ultra-safety play, even if you are somewhat behind. You may do best to leave adverse blots alone, and hope to "outroll" your opponent in a running game.

The back game. The normal policy of playing "wide open" at the beginning of a game, in the effort to make key points, will sometimes go awry. Your opponent hits one or more of your blots, and your effort to impede his runners by making key points is frustrated. He acquires a large lead in a running game. Or, he acquires such a lead early through rolling large numbers while you are rolling small. He gets 6-6, while you get 3-2 and suchlike misfits. You may decide to try to overcome your deficit in time by playing a back game.

The ideal course of a back game is as follows: You leave your runners on the adverse 1-point. You get enough additional blots to secure one or two additional points in his home table. You manage to delay so long that most or all of your stones are no further advanced than his outer table at the time that all his stones are in or near his home table. The blockade of your two or three points compels him to mass all his stones on a few points. He is forced eventually to leave a blot, perhaps after he has borne off a few stones. You hit the blot, and then while he is entering it and bringing it around you form a prime in his outer table. You walk the prime around to become a shutout, keeping his lone runner trapped and finally leaving it on the bar while you start to bear off. You bear off enough stones to acquire a decisive lead, before he can find an open point, enter, bring his runner around, and resume bearing off.

This ideal program is subject to many hazards. Your opponent may be so lucky, even though his stones are jammed on three or four points in his home table, that he never blots. Or he may blot and you may miss the hit. Or you may be forced by your own rolls to scatter your stones, or move some out of play on low points in your home table, so that by the time you get your hit you cannot form a prime or shutout.

In defending against a back game, avoid hitting additional blots after you have acquired a sufficient lead to have an easy victory in a straight running game. Try above all to split the adverse army into two or more parts. Make a blockade in your outer table that hampers or prevents the emergence of extra stones in your home-table points held by the enemy. Then he may have to absorb high rolls by hurrying his outside stones around to his side of the board, where they cannot coöperate later in building a prime.

Bearing off. In a running game, bring as many men as possible into your home table, even if it means piling them all on the 6-point. In early stages of bearing off, remove a stone at every opportunity rather than move within the board. For example, you have four stones on your 6-point, none on the 5-point. You roll 5-1. Remove a stone from the 6-point, rather than move, say, 6-1 and 6-5. This advice is necessary only because in certain ultimate positions, as every experienced player knows, it is better to move down than to bear off. An example is shown in Fig. 2. White rolls 3-1. In taking his move, he has to reckon with the certainty that Black will bear off all his men in 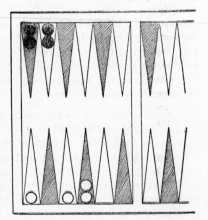 two turns, at most. White therefore will have only one more roll. If he bears off a man from his 4-point, he will need doublet 4, 5, or 6 to win.

But if he moves 4-1 and 4-3, doublet 3, 4, 5, or 6, will suffice if he gets a second turn. Moving two, rather than bearing off one, has thus increased his chances of winning.

Moving down, instead of bearing off, is also advisable in many cases where the opponent still holds a point in your home table. Suppose that you are White, and that Black still has his original runners on W1 when you start to bear off (Black having a "one point" back game). The chief danger to you is a high doublet, 6-6 or 5-5, that would give you no choice of play. Such doublets are dangerous only if you have an odd number of stones on your outermost point, or on the two outermost points together. Thus, if you have five stones together on your 6- and 5-points, either 6-6 or 5-5 will force you to leave a blot. In the earlier play, you should therefore strive to leave an even number of stones on your outermost point, or on the two outermost together.

Doubling. It is easily demonstrated that on mathematical grounds you should accept any double if your chances of winning are no worse than 1 to 3. But it is rarely possible to determine by any formula what your chances of winning are in any given position, since there are intangible factors, such as relative skill. Your accuracy in offering and accepting doubles will be greatly improved, however, if you recognize clearly the differences between advantages that are likely to be enduring and those that are temporary.

Enduring advantages are the making of key points against adverse runners, near or complete primes, shutouts, the early escape of your own runners while the adverse runners have not yet reached safety. Temporary advantages are hits on adverse blots, "misses" by the opponent attempting to enter a fairly open board, an early large doublet (as 6-6), a lead in a running game by a player who still has one or two runners in the adverse home table.

A double should be offered primarily on psychological rather than mathematical grounds. The latter are never very certain. But an opponent who displays a misunderstanding of, or a distaste for, a certain type of position, should be "needled" by a double whenever this position arises. For example, certain players lose heart if the opponent rolls an early 6-6; the opponent should double as a matter of course if he can do so soon afterward. Other players are dismayed by having a blot hit, or by facing a "natural" opening roll, or by having less than an odds-on chance to win.

PACHISI

Pachisi may have been one of the very earliest of sedentary games played by man. Pachisi boards of great antiquity have been found throughout the Orient, and Indian annals carry it back thousands of years. There is ground for the belief that Pachisi is the ancestor of Backgammon, Chess, Checkers, and most other board games. The stages in the development of these games are believed to be as follows: the first gaming implements were dice, in the form of cowrie shells and knuckle bones; tokens were used to mark the accumulation of numbers cast on dice; presently the movement of such tokens on a track became the center of interest, the dice being relegated to the machinery—at this stage Pachisi developed, and later the very similar Backgammon; the opportunity for skill in choice of moves (which exists even in Pachisi) was extended, as in Chaturanga or Shatranj, a kind of four-hand Chess played even today in India and Persia; eventually the dice were entirely abandoned to allow unfettered choice of play, as in Chess and kindred games.

The modern proprietary game Parchesi adheres faithfully to what is known of the rules of ancient Pachisi. Two, three, or four may play. Each player is provided with four tokens, of distinctive color, which he moves around a track in accordance with the rolls of two dice. The first to get his pieces around and then into a common central "home" square wins the game. Through choice of which piece to move the player can to some degree impede his opponents. He may leave two of his pieces on one step of the track, forming a blockade that no enemy can pass. And, as in Backgammon, he can "hit" a lone enemy and compel it to return to the starting line.

THE MILL

The Mill (from the German Mühle) is also known as Nine Men's Morris and Morelles. It is a game of great antiquity, and efforts have been made to prove that it was the ancestor of both Chess and Checkers. In effect, The Mill is an extension of Tit-Tat-Toe, and like that game has been largely a pastime of the juvenile.

The Mill is a board game for two players.

The board. 1. As shown in Fig. 1, the board comprises three concentric squares, crossed by four or eight transverse lines. The earliest sources state that there were diagonal lines connecting the corners, but in modern play these lines are usually omitted. In either case, there are twenty-four points of intersection, which are numbered in the diagram for reference.

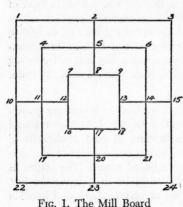

FIG. 1. The Mill Board

The pieces. 2. Each player is supplied with nine counters of his own color. All pieces are alike in form, and similar to the counters used in Checkers and Backgammon.

The play. 3. The play divides into two stages. During the first stage, the players alternately lay counters on the board, one at a time. The pieces are placed on the intersections, and the player is free to occupy any open point.

4. In the second stage, after all the pieces have been placed on the board, each player in turn moves any one of his pieces from one point, along a line, to an adjacent open point.

Object of play. 5. Each player strives to get three of his own pieces in line upon one line of the board. Such a formation is a *mill*. Whenever he completes a mill, the player is entitled to remove one adverse piece from the board, with the proviso that he may not choose a piece that is part of a mill.

6. Having once formed a mill, and provided the second stage of play has begun, a player may open it by moving one piece off the line, and later close it by moving the piece back. Such a maneuver counts as a new mill, even though the same three counters again lie in the same order on the same line.

7. A player wins the game when he reduces his opponent to two pieces or blockades all the adverse pieces so that his opponent cannot move in his turn. (An optional rule is that when a player is reduced to three pieces he may move from one point to any other, regardless of line connections and blockades.)

Irregularities. 8. Any move or removal of a piece that is not in accordance with these laws must be corrected if attention is drawn to it before the opponent has touched a piece for his next move; thereafter, it stands as though regular.

9. In the first stage of play, a move is final when the player removes his hand from the piece. In the second stage of play, a piece (except for apparent or announced purposes of arrangement) must be moved if it legally can be.

Pointers on Mill play. With correct play on both sides, the game is undoubtedly drawn. In the second stage of play, it is fairly easy to calculate how to move so as to "keep the draw in hand." Whenever the opponent has two in line, or can move two pieces upon a line, guard the third point of the line by keeping one piece nearer to it than the nearest adverse piece. Look ahead to see what might happen in a blockading or "squeezing" process. Usually it suffices to note whether, if a contemplated move is made and the opponent blocks its retraction by occupying the vacated square, he will thereby exert any serious threat or open up another safe move.

In this stage, it may be said that no mill can be made without an adverse blunder, and the effort to induce a blunder may run some risk. The tactics here are governed by personal considerations.

Making one mill is not in itself enough to win the game, though if you are first to make a mill you naturally gain a decided advantage. Even if your opponent also makes a mill, you will win out if the game becomes a matter of alternate openings and closings. But whether you are first or second in making a mill, strive to capitalize it with collateral threats.

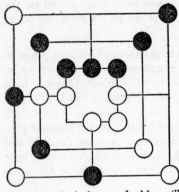

Fig. 2. Black has a double mill
(8-5, 5-8)

The greatest threat of all is to make a double mill. This is a formation where one piece can shuttle back and forth between two lines, closing a mill with each move. A double mill is a sure win. If you are ahead in the game of alternation, open your mill and leave it open while you maneuver for a double mill; if your opponent opens his mill, close your own and destroy his. If you are second in the alternation, maneuver for a second mill or a double mill, the threat of which will force your opponent to close his mill; then seize the initiative by opening your own.

In the first stage, there is scope for trappy play based on timing. Obviously the best play on both sides at the outset is to occupy the points from which radiate the maximum of rays; these are (if the diagonal lines are omitted) 5, 11, 14, 20. These points have four rays: all others have only three rays. Correct opening play is undoubtedly to divide these points two and two. Yet, if the first player occupies, say, 5, he can make a mill by force if the second player fails to occupy an adjacent point (2, 4, 6, or 8). For example,

WHITE	BLACK
5	14
8	2
7	9
12	16
11	10
4	6
19	

The "fork" has gained White a mill, every Black move being forced. Is Black's first move therefore a mistake? Not at all! White has paid too great a price for his mill. Let him remove any Black piece. Black simply replaces it, and the game continues

WHITE	BLACK
21	20

Now, wherever White puts his last piece, Black will put his last piece adjacent to it, and after no more than one move the eight Black pieces will completely blockade the White nine. Black wins.

The second player, through placing the last piece in the first stage, has an advantage that nullifies many of the early threats of the first player. Yet it cannot be said that this is the whole story. Through astute timing, the first player may deliver a threat in a way that carries over into the second stage. For example:

WHITE	BLACK
5	14
20	11
1	24
12	18 (?)
7	16
17	23
22	10
8	9
2	

Black at his fourth move has departed from the generally-sound idea of maintaining symmetry. White has now made a mill by force, and removes the Black piece on 9. The continuation is:

. . .	9
2-3	14-13

Black is compelled to close his mill, else White will close his own and destroy the incipient Black mill. But now what piece can Black remove with hope of salvation? If he takes 1, 3, or 8 White can still close a mill next move, whereupon White removes 16 and wins. If Black removes 5, White continues 8-5, and nothing can stop 5-2, whereupon White removes 16. By leaving this second mill open until Black breaks his mill, White wins easily.

GO

Go, also called I-Go or Wei-ch'i, is the major intellectual game of Japan. It originated probably in China, where historical records carry it back at least a thousand years before the Christian era. Reaching Japan in A.D. 754, it presently achieved the position taken by Chess is Occidental countries (though an Oriental form of Chess is also played). But there is very little recorded analysis of Go, certainly nothing that can compare with the literature of Chess, although the leading Go players have to master a subject equally profound. Efforts have been made by some Western writers to popularize Go in Europe and America, and there is a small but growing number of Go enthusiasts in the United States.

Go is a board game for two players.

The board. 1. As shown on page 404, the board comprises 19 vertical and 19 horizontal lines, making 361 intersections. The pieces are placed on these intersections, not on the squares enclosed by the lines.

Nine of the intersections are emphasized by large dots; these are the *handicap points.*

The notation, whereby the points are designated by letters and numbers, is a Western device, patterned after the "algebraic" Chess notation.

The pieces. 4. The so-called stones are lenticular (disks thicker in the center than at the edge), and are a trifle larger than the squares of the board, so that stones on adjacent points overlap slightly. Black is provided with 181 stones, White with 180 (the exact number is immaterial, since the player almost never uses all of his allotment).

Object of play. 5. Black plays first, and thereafter the players move alternately. Every move consists in placing a stone upon a point, there being no movement of the stones on the board. Under certain circumstances, a player may capture adverse stones, which are then removed from the board in his custody.

6. A player's final score for a game is numerical—the number of vacant points he controls (his territory), less the number of prisoners he has lost. The player with the higher net wins the game, by the difference.

The meaning of territory, and the conditions of capture, are explained in the following paragraphs.

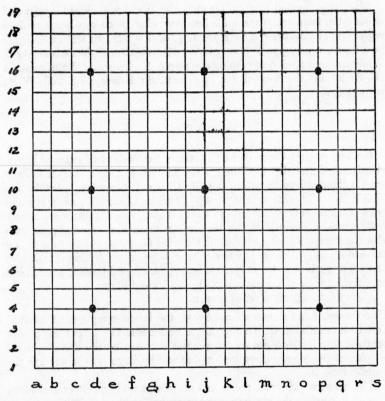

GO Board with notation

Units. 7. Two stones of like color are connected if they stand on adjacent points of the same line. Connection is always horizontal or vertical, never diagonal. A group of stones, each of which is connected to at least one other member of the group, forms an indissoluble unit; it lives or dies as a whole but can never be dismembered.

8. A unit lives so long as any member of it is connected to any vacant point. (In Japanese, such vacant points essential to life are "breathing spaces.") It dies when its last breathing space is occupied by an enemy stone. A dead unit is removed from the board, all the stones being prisoners of the enemy.

A peculiarity of the play is that a player need not actually fill all the breathing spaces to capture an enemy unit. It is sufficient to isolate the unit and enclose it in such a way that he could surely smother it if he chose to do so; the opponent is bound to concede that the unit is doomed, unless he chooses to expend additional stones to try to save it. Such doomed, but not actually killed, units are removed as prisoners at the end of the game.

Eyes. 9. An eye is a single vacant point entirely enclosed by the stones of a unit. The enemy cannot play into an eye, unless he kills the unit by that move, else his stone would have no life and could simply be removed by the owner of the unit. It follows that any unit containing two separate eyes is forever safe, since the enemy cannot play into both eyes at once.

A player does not form eyes within a unit unless forced to do so. Rather, he tries to control enough vacant territory within or near each unit so that he could form the necessary eyes if forced to do so. Or, if a unit encloses insufficient space to form eyes, the player seeks to connect it to a safe unit.

Territory. 10. At the end of a game, the territory that belongs to a player comprises all the vacant points wholly enclosed by stones of his color. That is why eyes, single points, are not enclosed unless absolutely necessary. The player seeks to stake out large areas of vacant points, into which the enemy does not dare play for fear of losing all his invaders. In defending against invasion, a player tries to put as few stones as possible into his own territory, for each stone subtracts one point from the net territory.

Ending play. 11. A game ends by agreement, when each player concedes that he is unwilling to attempt the invasion of territory that *prima facie* belongs to his opponent. In theory, if a player insists on continuation when the other is willing to stop, he cannot gain unless he makes a successful invasion, because for every stone he forces the unwilling opponent to put in his own territory (subtracting therefrom) he risks a potential prisoner. However, obscure situations can arise, to which the application of the traditional rules is not clear even to the Japanese.

12. Common points, connected to stones of both colors, count for neither player. When the game ends, these common points are first

filled up by stones of either color, from the box. Then each player puts the prisoners he has captured into his opponent's territory. The remaining vacant points controlled by each player are then counted and compared.

Rule of the knot. 13. Imagine Black stones on b3, c2, c4, d3; White stones on d2, d4, e3. White to play can lay a stone on c3 and capture the Black stone on d3. If Black were then allowed to play on d3, capturing c3, he could restore the initial position. If both players were unwilling to deviate, the game might continue with perpetual capture and recapture in this corner. To avoid this outcome, this formation (called a knot) is governed by a special rule: when a single stone is captured in a knot, the opponent may not play back immediately into the knot, recapturing a single stone, but must wait at least one turn. The enforced delay gives the first capturer a chance to close the knot, should he desire to do so. White could close the knot by playing on d3, connecting c3 so as to be (singly) unassailable.

Handicapping. Among experienced players, a handicapping system is used that requires a stronger player to defeat a lesser by a minimal difference, say three points. An expert playing against a tyro gives him a handicap by way of from two to seven extra stones on the board at the outset. The tyro, playing Black, puts stones on the handicap points as follows: for handicap of two, on d4 and q16; for three to five, stones also on q4, d16, k10; for six stones, k10 is left vacant and extra stones go on d10, q10; seven stones, the extras go on k4, k16, k10. After the handicap stones are placed, the expert, taking White, moves first. A handicap of four stones is about the same as queen odds in Chess.

Smaller board. Go is sometimes played on a smaller board, 13 x 13. The full-size board may be used for this purpose, by considering the outer lines to be d, q, 4 and 16. The reduced board makes for a simpler and shorter game, helpful in learning the principles of play. It is also used for four-hand partnership play in this country; partners move alternately and must not consult.

GO-MAKU, or GO BANG

This is another game played on the Go board, entirely different from Go and much less profound. The two players put stones of their own color on the board in turn, and the first to succeed in getting five in a row (adjacent) on a vertical, horizontal or diagonal line wins the game. Since it is known that the first player can always force a win, a special rule is invoked to make a game a contest: a player may not place a stone on a point that gives him simultaneously two "open threes." An open three is a row of three stones that might be developed to five in a row. In order to force a win, a player has to establish a row of four open at both ends, or an open three plus a row of four open at one end.

HALMA

Halma was invented and played in England toward the end of the 19th century. The name comes from the Greek, to leap. A modified board allowing the participation of two to six players was popularized in the 1930's under the trade name Chinese Checkers.

Players. Two to four, each playing for himself.

The board. The large square of 16 x 16 small squares (which may or may not be checkered) has a group of 13 squares fenced off in each corner. These pens are used in four-hand play. For two-hand play, pens of 19 squares each are marked off in two diagonally-opposite corners (see Fig. 1).

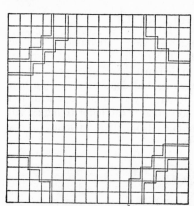
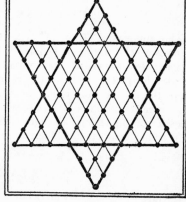

Fig. 1. Halma board   Fig. 2. Chinese Checkers board

The pieces. The counters are like checker men, though smaller in order to fit the smaller square of the Halma board. Each player is supplied with a number of counters of distinctive color, 13 in four-hand play, 19 in two-hand play. To begin a game, each player places his pieces on the squares of a corner-pen.

The play. The players move in turn. The object of each is to move his entire force across the board to a corner-pen diagonally opposite that from which it started, and the first to move all his 13 or 19 pieces into his goal wins the game.

A move may be either a step or a hop, but never a combination of the two. The step move is to an adjacent square in any direction, vertical, horizontal, diagonal; forward or backward. The hop move may likewise be made in any direction. It is like a jump in Checkers—over an adjacent piece to a vacant square just beyond the same line. As in Checkers, the piece may continue jumping so long as it finds others in suitable formation, and may change direction with each separate hop. But the Halma piece may jump over friendly as well as enemy pieces, and the hopping move is not a capture: no pieces are ever removed from the board. Furthermore, the player is under no compulsion to make a hopping move when able; he may instead make a step move. Having started a series of hops, he may terminate them whenever he pleases, though additional hops would be possible.

Pointers on Halma play. The quickest way to reach the goal is to space out part of the force in a "ladder across the board, and advance the remainder by long hops up this ladder. When enemy forces meet in the center of the board, effort should be made to block, or at least to avoid helping, the opponent.

CHINESE CHECKERS

The appellation "Chinese" is a fancy of games manufacturers; the game is an elaboration of Halma, of English origin. The board is shown on page 407. It is usually constructed so that marbles of glass or clay may be used for pieces, each square having a central depression or hole that keeps the marble from rolling about. Each player commences with ten (in larger boards, fifteen) pieces, placed in one of the outer triangles. All rules are as in Halma, the only difference being that as many as six players may compete in Chinese Checkers.

REVERSI

Reversi was published in London about 1888, and a series of articles on its strategy, probably by its inventor, Lewis Waterman, was published in *The Queen,* a periodical devoted to "the affairs of interest to ladies." One gathers that the *fin de siècle* ladies were more mathematically-minded than their descendants.

Reversi is a board game for two players.

The board. A regular checkerboard. (Alternate coloring of the squares is in fact unnecessary, and was omitted in the boards manufactured solely for Reversi.)

The pieces. Each player is supplied with 32 counters, like Checker pieces, except that they are differently colored on the two faces. (The usual colors are red and blue, but they are herein referred to as white and black, in accordance with the custom of designating the players in two-hand board games.)

The play. The players alternately lay pieces on the board, one at a time, each player taking care to turn his color (white or black) uppermost. The first four pieces must be placed on the four center squares, as shown in Fig. 2. Thereafter, the play is governed by the following rules:

I. The piece must be placed adjacent to one of opposite color (on a vertical, horizontal, or diagonal line).

II. The piece must lie on a line with another piece of its own color, so as to enclose without break one or more pieces of opposite color. The enclosed pieces are then reversed (turned over) and so become of the same color as the enclosing pieces.

III. If a piece is played so as to complete the enclosure of adverse pieces on more than one line, the enclosed pieces on all such lines are reversed.

IV. If unable to play anywhere on the board so as to reverse one or more adverse pieces, the player misses his turn, and the opponent continues play until the other can reënter. But neither player may lay down more than 32 pieces.

V. The winner is the player whose color predominates after the last piece is laid down. (The game may end in a tie.)

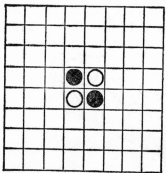

Fig. 1. Oblique opening

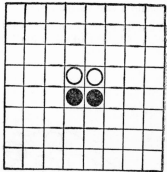

Fig. 2. Square opening

Pointers on Reversi play. The most desirable squares to occupy are the four corners, since pieces so placed can never be reversed. The least desirable are squares adjacent to the corner. Undesirable to occupy are all squares once removed from an edge of the board. Neutral in character are the middle edge squares and the sixteen central squares.

Place as few pieces as possible outside the existing array, until you can reach the edge of the board. Never play in an outside square adjacent to the corner (as b8) when the rest of the row is vacant. It is usually safe to play adjacent to a piece of your own color, or on a line separated by two vacant squares. It is usually safe to play on a line with an adverse piece, with one vacant square intervening. If your opponent plays adjacent to your single piece on the edge of the board, immediately enclose and reverse his attacker. Do not reach a square on the edge of the board by a diagonal move.

The square opening, illustrated in Fig. 2, should always be forced by the second player. If he allows the oblique opening the first player can force him to make the first play outside of the center.

MANCALA

Mancala has been called "the national game of Africa," since it is played by tribes in every part of that continent, but it is by no means confined to Africa. It has been found among primitive peoples the world over—as in Ceylon, Malaya, the Philippines, the West Indies. Every tribe, sometimes every village, has its own name for the game: Abangah, Bau, Chanka, Chongkak, Chungcajon, Gabatta, Kale, Kpo, Madji, Mbau, Mungala, Naranj, Poo, Wa-Wee, Wari, and many others. Preference is here given to the Arabic name Mancala because there is some belief that the game was developed and spread by the Arabs. But nothing certain is known of its origin.

The anthropologists have not undertaken to explain how it happens that the universal game of primitive peoples is one of pure intellectual skill. Mancala is wholly mathematical, akin to the game of drawing pebbles from a pile in an endeavor to win the last, but so complex as to remain a real contest.

Number of players. 1. Two. (Some tribes use boards with three or four rows of holes and allow participation of three or four players.)

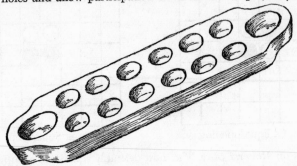

The board. 2. The Mancala board at its simplest contains two parallel rows of six holes or cuplike depressions. Usually some additional holes are provided at each end to contain the pieces removed from the board, and among some tribes the playing rows themselves are extended to eight holes.

3. The board is placed between the two players so that each finds a row of holes along the edge nearest him.

The pieces. 4. Any small counters will serve—cowrie shells, pebbles, etc. are used by primitive peoples. For a home-made set, metal washers are recommended. The usual number of counters used is seventy-two, but this varies with the tribe and the particular game.

The games. Many primitive peoples recognize two or three variant games, and the rules of these games are not the same the world over. There will be described here three variants with rules that are fairly typical.

5. *First game.* (Among the Syrians this is known as the "crazy game."
Western sources state that the result of the play is pre-ordained—but
give neither the result nor the method.)

(a) Ninety-eight pieces are used. The first player, chosen by lot, distributes all the pieces as he pleases in the holes of the board, not less
than two per hole. He then plays first.

(b) Each player in turn lifts all the pieces from the rightmost hole
of his row and distributes them one by one in the holes of the adverse
row, from right to left. If there are more than six pieces, he continues
counter-clockwise, by putting pieces in his own row from left to right,
and so on until all the pieces are distributed.

(c) If the rightmost hole in the player's row is empty, he begins his
turn by taking the pieces from the nearest occupied hole toward the left.

(d) If the last piece of a batch so distributed falls in a hole already
containing two, four, or more pieces, the player continues his turn by
lifting all the pieces from this hole and distributing them one by one
counter-clockwise. His turn ends only as described in paragraphs 5 (e)
and (f):

(e) If the last piece falls in an empty hole, the player's turn ends.

(f) If the last piece falls in a hole containing one or three pieces, his
turn ends, but he first removes as captives:

(1) The two or four pieces now in the final hole; and

(2) All pieces from holes ahead of and consecutive with this hole,
that contain just two or four pieces; and

(3) Pieces in all holes of the other row opposite the holes he was
entitled to empty under the foregoing rules.

[For example, suppose the following distribution of pieces.

PLAYER A

6 5 4 1 2 4

a b c d e f

7 2 3 6 1 3

PLAYER B

[If it is Player B's turn, he distributes the three pieces from hole Bf
in Af, Ae, and Ad. Since Ad now contains two pieces, he may take them,
together with the six in Bd. At the next hole ahead of Ad, namely Ac,
contains four pieces, Player B also takes them together with the three in
Bc. But he may not take the contents of the b-holes: though Bb contains
two pieces, what counts is the contents of the next hole in order, Ab,
where there are five.

[If it were Player A's turn in the diagrammed position, he would lift
the six pieces in Aa and distribute them in Ba, Bb, etc., ending with Bf.
Now he is entitled to remove captives from Bf, Af; as Af was emptied
under the rule of the opposites, Ae counts as the next consecutive hole,
and since it contains two pieces Player A may take them together with
the two in Be.]

(g) Captive pieces are removed permanently from the board.

(h) The game ends when all the pieces have been taken captive, or too few remain to allow further capture. Such residual pieces do not count in the score. The player having the greater number of captives wins by the difference.

6. *Second game.* (The Syrians call this the "rational game." While the outcome of the "crazy game" is wholly dependent on how the pieces are originally placed, the "rational game" allows for significant choice throughout the play.)

(a) Eighty-four pieces are used. To begin a game, seven pieces are placed in each hole.

(b) To begin his turn, a player lifts all the pieces from any one of the six holes on his side of the board. All other rules of play are exactly as in the First Game, paragraph 5 (b), (d), (e), (f).

7. *Third game.* (This is Wari, a West African variant that has achieved some following in America.)

(a) Seventy-two pieces are used, distributed at the outset six per hole.

(b) Each player in turn lifts all the pieces from any one of the six holes on his side and distributes them one by one counter-clockwise around the board (left to right on his side, right to left on the opponent's side). His turn ends when he has placed the last piece of the batch.

(c) If the last piece goes into a hole already containing just one or two pieces, all the pieces are removed from this hole and discarded. (Discarded pieces belong to neither player.)

(d) The player who first is unable to move in turn, because no pieces remain on his side of the board, loses the game.

SOLITAIRE (PEGBOARD)

The name Pegboard is suggested to avoid confusion with patience games played with cards. It is a solo pastime akin to a familiar type of Checker puzzle. Friedrich Anton (1884) states that its rules were formulated by a Frenchman traveling in America, after a game he had observed played by Indians with arrows stuck in the ground; a more widely circulated legend has it the invention of a prisoner in the Bastille, before or during the French revolution.

The board. 1. A square panel is pierced with thirty-seven holes, arranged as shown in the diagram. (A different board is also made, with thirty-three holes, omitting those numbered 4, 8, 30, and 34.) In each hole is placed a peg.

The play. 2. One peg of the thirty-seven having been removed, one peg at a time is jumped over another into a vacant hole, the peg so jumped being removed from the board. All jumps must be horizontal or vertical, never diagonal.

Solitaire problems. 3. The pastime is a puzzle to work out a sequence of jumps that will produce a prefixed pattern or leave the sole remaining peg in a prefixed hole. Many different problems have been propounded, and the reader can readily invent others for himself. Here are some popular puzzles and their solutions (in each case, many solutions are possible).

```
            1   2   3

        4   5   6   7   8

    9  10  11  12  13  14  15

   16  17  18  19  20  21  22

   23  24  25  26  27  28  29

       30  31  32  33  34

           35  36  37
```

First problem. Peg 1 being removed, to leave the last peg in hole 37.

3-1	20-7	18-20
12-2	9-11	20-33
13-3	16-18	33-31
15-13	23-25	2-12
4-6	22-20	8-6
18-5	29-27	6-19
1-11	18-31	19-32
31-18	31-33	36-26
18-5	34-32	30-32
20-7	20-33	26-36
3-13	37-27	35-37
33-20	5-18	

Second problem. Peg 19 being removed, to leave only hole 19 and all outer holes occupied. ("Curate and Flock.")

6-19	26-24	29-27
4-6	35-25	14-28
18-5	24-26	27-29
6-4	27-25	19-21
9-11	33-31	7-20
24-10	25-35	21-19
11-9		

Third problem. Peg 19 being removed, to leave the following occupied: 1, 3, 6, 9, 12, 15, 17, 18, 20, 21, 23, 26, 29, 32, 35, 37. ("Triplets.")

6-19	19-17	8-21
10-12	16-18	32-19
19-6	30-17	28-26
2-12	21-19	19-32
4-6	7-20	36-26
17-19	19-21	34-32
31-18	22-20	

⤙ MAH JONGG ⤚

Mah Jongg is essentially Rummy played with special "tiles" of wood or bone. There is no doubt that the chief fascination of the game to Occidental players is the colorful tiles, for much the same game can be and is played with several packs of cards shuffled together.

History. Chinese folk tales attribute a prehistoric origin to Mah Jongg but historical evidence can carry it back only a few hundred years. The tiles were probably evolved from dominoes, which also were invented by the Chinese and became standardized in their present form about a thousand years ago. Travelers in China during the late 19th century took note of a game played variously in many provinces, and whose name they transliterated variously as ma cheuk, ma chiang, ma chiao, mo tsiah. It remained, however, for Joseph P. Babcock, an American businessman, to make a systematic study of the Chinese rules, codify them, devise English terms, and christen the game Mah Jongg. He began in 1920 to import Chinese Mah Jongg sets to the United States, and found ready sale for them. Mah Jongg quickly became a "fad" on a scale never before achieved by any game. Its popularity faded in 1926, as suddenly as it had arisen. But Mah Jongg continues to be played by many enthusiasts.

The rules here given follow the American Code of Laws for Mah Jong,[*] promulgated in 1925 by a committee comprising Babcock, R. F. Foster, Milton C. Work, Lee Foster Hartman, and John H. Smith. These laws admittedly make concession to American taste as expressed in the then-current practices. The original Chinese game emphasizes skill as does basic Rummy (any four sets and a pair to go out), while the American game emphasizes a slower tempo and huge scores. Other codes (1936 and later) make Mah Jongg akin to Seven-card Stud Poker with all hearts and deuces wild.

Definitions. 1. The following terms are defined as used in Mah Jongg:

ACTORS. The suit Characters.
BAM. A card of the Bamboo suit.
BAMBOOS. One of the three suits.
BOUQUET. All four Flowers drawn by one player.
CHARACTERS. One of the three suits.
CHARLESTON. The passing of unwanted tiles to other players.

---

[*] So spelled because Mah Jongg is a trade name registered by Babcock.

CHOW. A set of three tiles in suit and sequence; to ground such a set.

CIRCLES. One of the three suits.

CLEARED HAND. One in which all the suit tiles are of one suit.

COMPLETE HAND. One of 14 tiles conforming to the requirements to be declared and to win the deal.

CONCEALED (SET). Obtained by drawing from the wall, not by taking a discard.

CRACKS or CRAKS. The suit Characters.

DOG. Make a safe discard.

DOTS. The suit Circles.

DRAGONS. The twelve tiles comprising four duplicates each of Red Dragons, Green Dragons, and White Dragons.

FLOWERS. 1. Four special tiles. 2. Eight or more special tiles, including the Seasons.

GROUNDED. Placed face up on the table (said of a set).

HAND FROM HEAVEN. A complete hand drawn by East before play begins.

HONORS. All Dragons and Winds tiles.

KONG. A set of four identical tiles; to ground such a set, or add a fourth tile to a pung to make a kong. Also quong.

LIMIT HAND. A complete hand that collects the limit in stakes.

LOOSE TILE. One placed on the wall, to be drawn in replacement of a Flower or the fourth of a kong.

PUNG. A set of three identical tiles; to ground such a set.

QUINT. A set of five like tiles (including wild Flowers).

QUONG. Kong.

ROB A KONG. Claim a fourth tile just added to a pung by another player, to complete one's hand.

SEASONS. Four special tiles.

SEXTETTE. A set of six like tiles (including wild Flowers).

SIMPLES. Suit tiles of ranks 2 to 8 inclusive.

STACK. Two superposed tiles, in the wall

STICKS. The suit Bamboos.

SUITS. Bamboos, Circles, Characters; the 36 tiles in each suit, comprising four duplicates each of ranks 1 to 9.

TABLE, FROM THE. (A set) formed by claiming the last discard.

TERMINALS. Suit tiles of ranks 1 and 9.

WALL. The array of tiles as arranged after shuffling.

WALL GAME. Void game, by exhaustion of the wall without any declaration of a complete hand.

WINDS. 1. The sixteen tiles comprising four duplicates each of East Wind, South Wind, West Wind, North Wind. 2. The four compass positions around the table, designated as East Wind, etc. PREVAILING WIND: that in which a set of tiles earns a special bonus.

WOO. Declare a complete hand and so end the play.

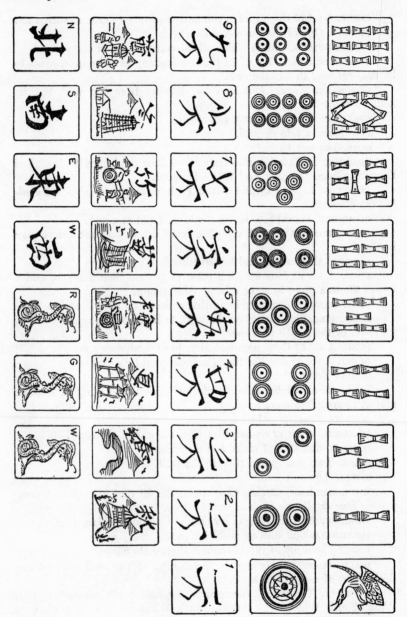

Tiles from a typical Mah Jongg set. In columns left to right: Winds and Dragons, Flowers and Seasons, Cracks, Dots, Bams. For use outside of China, numbers are stamped on the suit tiles, as shown here on the Cracks.

Number of players. 2. Mah Jongg is a game for four, each playing for himself. Two may play, or three, building the usual four walls but having only one hand each. Five or six may play a cut-in game, as in Bridge.

The Mah Jongg set. 3. There are 144 tiles, as follows:

SUITS

Bamboos ("bams")	36
Circles ("dots")	36
Characters ("cracks")	36

(In each suit there are four duplicates each of tiles numbered from 1 to 9.)

HONORS

Red Dragons	4
Green Dragons	4
White Dragons	4
East Winds	4
South Winds	4
West Winds	4
North Winds	4

SPECIAL

Flowers	4
Seasons	4

(Each Flower and Season is marked with one of the four wind designations: E, S, W, N. The eight tiles are usually called Flowers collectively.)

4. A set also includes four racks, two dice, and (usually) a quantity of colored sticks to be used in settlement like Poker chips. Each player uses a rack to hold his tiles upright on the table in front of himself.

Positions. 5. One player is chosen by lot to be East. He has choice of seats. The others sit where they please, and take their designations South, West, North, from the position of East.

6. The East player wins or loses double. If he wins, he holds his position. If he loses, the player at his left becomes East, all other compass designations being shifted to the left accordingly. The position of East is marked by a rack of special color.

7. One of the four winds prevails in each deal. In the first deal East prevails; in the second, South; in the third, West; in the fourth, North; and so on in regular rotation. This rotation is independent of the rotation of the East position at the table, which is intermittent according as East wins or loses. The effect of the prevailing wind is merely to give an increased bonus to the player who obtains a corresponding set on honor tiles. Some Mah Jongg sets include a marker for keeping track of the prevailing wind.

Building the walls. 8. To begin a game, the tiles are shuffled face down, all players assisting. Each player draws tiles at random to build before himself a wall two tiles high and eighteen tiles long, all tiles face down. The four walls are pushed together (with aid of the racks) to form a solid enclosure.

Drawing the hands. 9. East rolls the dice and totals the two numbers. He counts up to this total, beginning with the East wall as 1 and going clockwise, to determine which wall shall be broken. The player whose wall is so selected rolls the dice again, and the numbers are added to the previous total to determine where the wall shall be broken.

10. Beginning at the right end of his wall, the player counts to the left, the number of stacks indicated by the dice. A stack is two superposed tiles. When the dice total more than 18, the player continues counting around the corner upon the wall at his left. The indicated stack is lifted out and the two tiles are placed on top of the wall, to right of the break, with the undermost tile nearer the break.

11. The two tiles so placed are loose tiles. During the play, when both loose tiles have been taken, the stack at the right side of the break is lifted out and placed as loose tiles.

12. The hands are drawn from the continuous wall at the left of the break. Each player in turn, beginning with East, takes two stacks (four tiles) until he has twelve tiles. Then one more tile is drawn all around, and finally East takes a fourteenth tile, all other players having thirteen.

Object of play. 13. There are two objects: (a) To score by forming sets of three or four like tiles; (b) to win the deal by forming a complete hand of four sets and a pair.

Sets. 14. The valid sets that may be formed are of three kinds, as described in the paragraphs below. A set is *concealed* if it was obtained entirely by draws from the wall, or from the table if it was completed by drawing a discard. (This distinction affects scoring values.) Exposing a set face up on the table is called *grounding* it; any set from the table must by rule be grounded.

15. *Chow* is a set of three tiles (no more) of the same suit in sequence, as Bamboos 5-6-7. The chow has no intrinsic scoring value, but may be formed to complete the hand and has value in certain special hands (all chows or no chows).

16. *Pung* is a set of three identical tiles—same suit and rank, or same color of dragons, or same direction of winds.

17. *Kong* is a pung with addition of the fourth like tile. This fourth tile is never counted among the fourteen necessary to make a complete hand (four sets of three and a pair). A player may ground a kong, or add a fourth tile to his own pung; on doing so, he must immediately draw a loose tile from the wall to restore his hand.

Flowers and kongs. 18. Immediately after drawing his hand, each player must ground any Flowers he finds, and replace them by drawing loose tiles. The hands are restored in rotation, beginning with East. Similarly, when at any later time a player draws a Flower, he must ground it and take a loose tile. The Flowers have scoring value, but are never counted as part of the thirteen tiles in the hand.

19. If a player finds a kong in his original hand, he may ground it at once in order to establish his right to a loose tile. The two end tiles of the grounded kong are turned down to mark that it scores as concealed. Similarly, at any later time that a player obtains a concealed kong, he may ground it in his turn to play, mark it as concealed, and draw a loose tile.

The play. 20. East plays first. As he drew fourteen tiles originally, he must begin by discarding one. All hands are thereafter maintained at thirteen tiles, counting unmatched tiles, chows, pungs, but not Flowers and fourth tiles of kongs.

21. The turn to play passes in clockwise rotation except when interrupted by claim of a discard out of turn (paragraph 23). The player begins his turn by drawing the tile at the open end of the wall (left of the break) or by taking the last previous discard. He may then ground as many sets as he wishes, and if he takes the discard he must ground it as part of a set. He ends his turn by a discard.

22. The discards are placed inside the enclosure formed by the walls. Most American players leave them all face up; some follow the Chinese practice of putting them face down. In any event, the custom is to name a tile in discarding it so that other players need not take their eyes from their own tiles.

23. Any player, regardless of position, may claim the last discard if he can use it, and if he makes the claim promptly before the in-turn player draws. If two or more players claim the same tile, precedence goes according to the purpose for which it was wanted: to complete a hand (first priority), to make pung or kong, to make chow. If two players claim for the same purpose, the one whose turn would come first has priority.

24. When a discard is taken out of turn, the claimant grounds the set in which it is used, and discards. The turn then passes to his left neighbor. When the claim was out of turn, intervening players thus lose a turn.

25. The discard may never be taken to be added to a pung already grounded, but may be taken to add to a pung in the hand, making a kong from the table.

Going out. 26. To go out is called *woo*. A player may woo, ending the play, when his hand comprises four sets and a pair. As the complete hand comprises fourteen tiles, his final play must be a draw without a discard.

27. A player may rob a kong in order to woo, i. e., claim the fourth tile that another player has just added to a grounded pung to make a kong.

28. Fourteen tiles must be left untouched in the wall. If all the rest are drawn, play continues only so long as each successive player takes the last discard. If play ends, with no player having wooed, the deal is

abandoned without score and East keeps his position for the next deal.

Scoring. 29. At the end of play (when some player has wooed), the basic value of each hand is determined by totaling the values of the sets, as follows:

SETS	FROM TABLE	CONCEALED
Pung of simples	2	4
Pung of terminals	4	8
Pung of honors	4	8
Kong of simples	8	16
Kong of terminals	16	32
Kong of honors	16	32
Pair of dragons	2	2
Pair of prevailing wind	2	2
Pair of player's own wind	2	2
Pair of player's own wind, when prevailing	4	4
Each flower and season	4	

Simples are suit tiles of ranks 2 to 8 inclusive. *Terminals* are suit tiles of ranks 1 and 9.

30. The winner adds 20 to his basic count, for woo. In addition, he scores 2 if he drew from the wall the tile that completed his hand; and 2 if he filled the only place that would complete his hand.

31. The basic count of a non-winner's hand is multiplied by the sum of all applicable factors, as follows:

FOR HAVING	FACTOR
Pung or kong of dragons (each)	2
Pung or kong of prevailing wind	2
Pung or kong of player's own wind	2
Player's own flower (not season)	2
All four flowers (not seasons)	16

(The last item includes the double for the player's own flower.)

32. The winner applies to his basic count any factors applicable in the table, paragraph 31, and also any applicable in the following:

WINNER HAS	FACTOR
Wooed with last tile of the wall or a subsequent discard	2
Wooed with a loose tile drawn after a kong	2
No chows	2
All chows and a worthless pair	2
All one suit, with honors	2
All terminals, with honors	2
All one suit, without honors	8
All terminals, without honors	Limit
All honors, without suits	Limit

(See paragraph 34 for Limit Hands.)

33. The winning hand is counted first, and each other player pays its value to the winner; if the winner is East, he collects double. Then the other three hands are counted, and each player settles with each other according to the difference of their two hands. When East is one of the three, he pays or collects double.

Limit hands. 34. The players should agree in advance on a limit, the maximum that any player may be required to pay or may collect from another player. The 1925 code suggests a limit of 500 (1,000 for East). It also defines two types of woo hands that collect the limit.

[Various localities in China permit a player to woo with various types of hands that do not agree with the standard definition, four sets and a pair. An example is "The Thirteen Extraordinaries"—fourteen tiles including only one pair. All such fanciful hands collect the limit. In China they affect the game little, as they are about as frequent as royal flushes in seven-hand Draw Poker. But American players in the 1920-1926 heyday of Mah Jongg adopted all the limit hands from all the provinces of China and invented many more of their own; some players went so far as to bar wooing with anything but a limit hand.]

Irregularities. 35. *Imperfect set.* If the set of tiles is found to be incomplete or incorrectly marked in any way, the current deal is void unless a player has wooed, but the scores of previous deals stand.

36. *Exposed tile.* A tile exposed in shuffling or drawing must be shuffled back with the tiles; if the wall has already been built, a section of six adjacent stacks must be shuffled with the exposed tile and rebuilt.

37. *Wrong number of tiles.* If a player has too few tiles, by reason of failure to draw enough originally, he may correct his error before East's first discard; otherwise he must play on with a short hand. If a player fails to draw a loose tile when he should, or discards two tiles, he may correct his error before the next player in turn has discarded; otherwise he must play on with a short hand. If a player draws too many tiles before looking at his hand, he may return the excess (drawn at random from his hand by the opposite player) to the open end of the wall. If a player has too many tiles at any time after he has seen his hand, he must play on with a long hand.

38. *Incorrect set.* If a player grounds tiles that do not form a correct set, he may retract them or correct the set before the next hand has discarded; otherwise he must play on with a foul hand.

39. *Foul hands.* A hand that is foul or incorrect may not woo. A long hand scores as zero; a short or foul hand may score its basic count, but no doubles (factors) may be applied.

40. *Incorrect claim.* If a player takes or claims a discard that he cannot in fact use, he may correct the error without penalty before the next hand has drawn, and the discard becomes available to other claimants; otherwise paragraph 36 applies.

41. *False woo.* If a player calls woo when in fact his hand is incom-

plete, or foul in any way, play ends; the offender, if East, must pay the limit to each other player, or, if not East, must pay the limit to East and half the limit to the other two. In either case, there is no settlement among the other three players. East keeps his position, if he was not the offender, or loses it if he was.

Variations. Of many different ways of playing and scoring in Mah Jongg, the most widely circulated method is that of the National Mah Jongg League, Inc. (One author calls this Mah Jongg variant That's It, with a generic name of Chinese Tiles for the family of games.) The principal differences from the procedure described in the foregoing pages are:

The Flowers are wild; and often the set is increased to include sixteen Flowers. Each player receives one Flower, then draws twelve more tiles to complete his hand (East taking one more).

After the hands have been drawn, but before play begins, there are one or two Charlestons, or passes of tiles: Each player passes three tiles to his righthand neighbor, then (having received and seen the tiles passed to him), three to the player opposite him, then, in the same manner, three to his lefthand neighbor. By agreement of all players there may then be a second Charleston, with the first pass to the left, the second to the player opposite, the third to the right. A "blind pass" is permitted on the last pass of a second Charleston; that is, a player may pass along the three tiles passed to him, without looking at them.

No more than four may play in a game; but a fifth player, after looking at all four hands, and after the Charleston but before the first play, may write on a slip of paper the name of the player he bets on; he then pays in full if another player wins, but collects (from the three losers in equal shares) if his chosen player wins. In the same manner six may participate, there being two "bettors."

The game ends only when a player woos. The winning hand has a pre-determined value, according to the schedule adopted for the game, and is not increased by doubles. The entire wall may be drawn, and if no one goes out the game is void.

A hand may be played concealed or exposed. Any hand may be played concealed; but then a discard may be claimed only to woo. A hand becomes exposed when a discard is claimed to complete a kong, quint, or sextette, whereupon the set must be exposed on top of the player's rack. (A discard may be claimed only to complete these sets or to go out.) Concealed and exposed hands score the same.

A typical list of hands and values (which are doubled for East) follows:

POINTS	HAND
40	Kongs of North and South Winds and an odd-numbered sextette; or of East and West Winds and an even-numbered sextette.

50	Quints of North and South Winds, or of East and West Winds, and a kong of Dragons.
50	Quints of ones and fives, a kong of threes; or quints of fives and nines, a kong of sevens; all in the same suit.
50	Two kongs of Dragons plus two pungs of the same numeral but in different suits.
50	Quints of threes and nines, and a kong of sixes; or of fives and sevens, and a kong of sixes; or of sixes and eights, and a kong of sevens; or of sevens and nines, and a kong of eights; all in different suits.
50	Quints of ones and twos with a kong of threes, etc. (the kong representing the sum of the numerals of the quints, $1 + 2 = 3$), so that the sets may be twos, threes and fives, etc.), all in different suits.
60	Sextettes of North and South Winds, plus one East and one West Wind.
60	Quints of the terminals, or of twos and eights, or of the same numeral, in different suits; plus a kong of Dragons.
70	Kongs of red, white and green Dragons, with a pair of North or South Winds; or two kongs of Dragons and a sextette of threes, sixes, or nines.
70	Sextettes of the same number in different suits, plus two tiles of a third suit representing the square of this number (as, two sextettes of sixes, a three and a six for 36).
80	Sextettes of the terminals, or of twos and eights, in different suits; and a pair of Dragons.
80	Sextettes of consecutive numbers plus two tiles of the suit representing the sum of these numbers (as, sevens, eights, a one and a five, or 15); in three different suits.
100	Quints of red and green Dragons and a kong of whites.

If a player claims to be out when not having a valid combination, his hand becomes dead; the others continue without him and he pays the winner at the end.

⤙ DOMINOES ⤚

A set of dominoes represents all combinations of numbers that can turn up in the cast of two dice. The derivation from dice is abundantly clear from ancient domino sets, which lacked the modern "blanks," and from the traditional games that can be played with either dice or dominoes. On the authority of a Chinese dictionary of the 18th century, it is often said that dominoes were invented in 1120 A.D. during the reign of Siuen-ho. But closer reading of this source, as well as a wealth of other evidence, indicates that what happened at this time was a standardization of the Chinese set. Dominoes certainly must be of much greater antiquity. Since dice are known to be among the first gaming implements ever used by man, the folk tales that attribute dominoes to the remote past may not be far wrong.

The domino set. 1. A domino is a flat, rectangular block. The dimensions of its face are usually in the ratio 2:1, so that the median line divides it into two square *ends*. Each end is marked with dots or pips, or is left *blank*.

2. The modern set comprises twenty-eight pieces, marked as follows: Larger sets are also made, extending up to 9-9 or 12-12, but all the traditional games are based on the 6-6 set.

3. The dominoes are commonly called *bones*. A bone with both ends

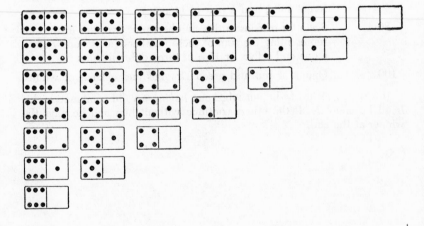

marked alike is a *doublet;* it belongs to one *suit* alone. All other bones belong to two suits, as, 5-3 belongs to the 5-suit and the 3-suit. There are seven bones in each suit, but because of the doublet there are eight *ends* of the same number. The total of all pips on a bone determines its *weight,* leading to the self-explanatory terms *lighter* and *heavier.*

Beginning a game. 4. To begin any game, the bones are shuffled face down. All players may assist, though if only two players sitting opposite shuffle there is less danger of exposing a bone.

5. After the shuffle, each player draws at random enough bones to give him the number proper to the particular game. Any bones not drawn for the original hands remain as the *boneyard.*

6. The player is best-advised to hold the bones in his hand. But most dominoes are made thick enough so that they can be stood on edge on the table. If the player leaves his hand on the table, he does so at his own risk. He has no redress if another player sees the face of any of his pieces or if a piece falls face up through jiggling of the table or any other accidental cause.

7. Before the final shuffle, players draw one bone each and the heaviest plays first. (Some players determine first turn to play by drawing extra bones from the boneyard; the extra pieces are then shuffled back in the boneyard. This practice is manifestly undesirable, as it reveals some of the bones not in play.)

The play. 8. The rotation of the turn to play is to the left, clockwise. Each in turn (if he can) plays one bone, by placing it face up on the table. In real domino games (as distinguished from card games played with dominoes), each bone played must be placed to abut one previously played. The assemblage of all bones played is called the *layout.* The first bone played is usually called the *set.* Various games differ in the restrictions governing the set.

9. The layout always has one or more *open ends,* on which it is legal to play. A bone added to such an end must always *match* according to the rule of the game. The usual rule is that like ends must touch, as 6 against 6, 5 against 5, etc. In some few games the rule is different.

10. A bone may be placed against an open end so as to continue a straight line or make a right-angle turn, as is convenient to keep the layout from running off the table. A doublet is usually placed crosswise, but usually does provide two open ends where there was only one before.

Irregularities. 11. *Wrong number of bones.* If a player draws too few bones for his original hand, he must fill it by drawing from the boneyard whenever the error is discovered. If a player draws and sees the faces of more than enough bones at any time, he must keep them all.

12. *Exposed bone.* A bone exposed face up in drawing the original hands must be shuffled back into the boneyard. If during the play a player exposes a bone in drawing another from the boneyard, he must take the exposed bone into his hand also.

13. *Illegal play*. If a player plays a bone that cannot properly be played under the rules of matching or the set, he must retract and correct the error if demand is made before the next player has played; otherwise the incorrect play stands as regular.

DRAW DOMINOES

Number of players. 1. From two to four may play. The best game is two-hand.

The hands. 2. With two players, each draws seven bones. With three or four players, each draws five.

The set. 3. Various rules are followed as to the set.

(a) Whoever draws 6-6 may set it; if 6-6 is not drawn, 5-5 may be set; and so on through the doublets. If no doublet is drawn the heaviest bone is set (heaviest is 6-5, then 6-4, etc.).

(b) The first player, chosen by lot, may set any doublet. If he lacks a doublet, the turn passes to the first player at his left who has a doublet.

(c) The first player, chosen by lot, may set any bone.

The play. 4. The set, doublet or not, has two open ends and the layout always has two open ends. By custom, doublets are placed crosswise and play is off the longer sides.

5. Matching is by like ends. If unable to play in turn, a player must draw from the boneyard until able. After the boneyard is exhausted, a player unable to play must pass his turn. A player may draw from the boneyard even if able to play (this may be to his advantage in such games as Muggins and All Threes).

6. The player first to get rid of his entire hand wins the deal. If play ends in a block, no player being able to play, the one with the lightest hand (smallest total of pips) is the winner. If two tie for low, there is no score for the deal.

Scoring. 7. The winner scores the total of all bones left in the hands of the losers. There is no deduction for bones left in the winner's hand (when play ends in a block).

8. The player first to reach a total of 50 or 100, as agreed, wins a game. Some players prefer to settle each deal as a separate game.

MUGGINS

Other names for this game are All Fives and Sniff.

Follow all the rules of Draw Dominoes, plus the following:

1. *Set*. The first player, chosen by drawing from the boneyard, may set any bone.

2. *Sniff*. The first doublet played, whether or not it is set, is the *sniff*. It is open four ways.

3. *Fives.* Whenever a player makes the total of pips on the open ends of the layout a multiple of 5, he scores that number of points. [For example, if 6-6 is set and the next player places 6-3 off the side, he scores 15.]

4. The ends countable for scoring may be greater than or less than the number of *open ends*. In the example of paragraph 3, the layout is open four ways as sniff has been played, but there are only three countable ends since no play has yet been made off one side of sniff. When a non-sniff doublet is played, it must be placed crosswise and both its ends must be counted in the total; hence the number of countable ends may be as high as eight. But a non-sniff doublet represents only one open end for subsequent play.

5. Since sniff is open four ways, the player who plays the first doublet may place it crosswise or endwise, as he pleases, on the existing layout. [For example, if the first player sets 6-4 to score 10, the second may add 6-6 endwise to score 10 also. (If he should place it crosswise, the total would be 16.)]

6. *Muggins.* Every fives score must be claimed orally to be recorded. If a player overlooks that he is entitled to a score, any other player may call "Muggins!" and take the score himself.

7. *Scoring.* If play ends in a block, the lighter hand wins only the difference of the hands from each other player. Each difference (including the case when the winner has no bones left) is taken to the nearest multiple of five; for example, 7 points counts as 5 and 8 points counts as 10. The player first to reach a total of 200 points wins a game. Points scored during play by making fives are recorded at once, and if a player reaches 200 during the play the deal is not played out.

AMERICAN DOMINOES

The rules are as in Muggins, except: When two or three play, only a bone whose ends total 7 or 9 may be set. The first player, if having no such bone, must draw till he gets one. "Muggins" (paragraph 6, above) may not be claimed.

HAWAIIAN DOMINOES

The rules are as in Muggins, except: Having played a doublet, a player must play another bone in the same turn. (If the doublet is his last bone, and the boneyard is exhausted, he must pass every succeeding turn.) "Muggins" (paragraph 6, above) may not be claimed.

ALL THREES

Follow all the rules of Muggins, except that scores are earned during play by making the total of open ends a multiple of three. Final differences in scores are recorded exactly.

BERGEN

Follow all the rules of Draw Dominoes except:

The highest doublet drawn, or the heaviest bone if no doublet is drawn, must be set. For making both open ends of the layout alike (*called double-header*), a player scores 2 points, or, if there is a doublet on one end (*triple-header*), 3 points. The winner of a deal scores 1 point. The first to reach a total of 15 wins a game.

MATADOR

Follow all the rules of Draw Dominoes except:

The rule of matching is that ends placed together must total seven. For example, 5 on an open end calls for 2. A doublet counts singly in matching, i.e., 3-3 on an open end calls for 4, not 1, and 2-2 may be played on an open 5. An open 0 calls for any of the four *matadors:* 0-0, 6-1, 5-2, 4-3. The matadors are wild and may be played at any time regardless of matching.

BLOCK DOMINOES

Number of players. 1. From two to four may play. The game is better for three or four than two.

The hands. 2. With three or four players, each draws five bones. With two, each draws seven.

The play. 3. The first player, chosen by lot, may set any bone.

4. Matching is by like ends. If unable to play in turn, a player must pass.

5. A player who gets rid of his entire hand wins the deal. If play ends in a block, no player being able to play, the lightest hand (smallest total of pips) is the winner. If two tie for low, there is no score for the deal.

Scoring. 6. The winner scores the total of all bones left in the hands of the losers. There is no deduction for bones left in the winner's hand (when play ends in a block).

7. The player first to reach a total of 50 or 100, as agreed, wins a game. Some players prefer to settle each deal as a separate game.

DOMINO POOL

Follow all the rules of Block Dominoes except:

Three to five may play. With three, each draws seven bones; with four, five bones; with five, four bones. A pool is formed by equal antes, and the winner takes the pool. If two or more tie (in a block) for lightest hand, they divide the pool equally.

SEBASTOPOL

This is a game for four players. Each draws seven bones, leaving no boneyard. Whoever draws the 6-6 must set it, and play continues in turn to his left. The 6-6 is open four ways, and no other play may be made until all four sides of the 6-6 have been played upon. Thereafter the layout is open four ways. Score and settle as in Domino Pool.

TIDDLY-WINK

This is a game for six to nine players. Each draws three bones. The highest doublet must be set, and the turn then rotates to the left. Anyone playing a doublet, including the set, may play again if able. The layout has only one open end. Matching is by like ends. If unable to play in turn, a player passes. The first to get rid of his hand wins. If game ends in a block, no player being able to play, there is no winner. Before each deal a pool is formed by equal antes and the winner takes it. If the play ends without a winner, the pool is added to the antes for the next deal.

BINGO

This is a card game played with dominoes, based on Bézique. Many such games were developed in the United States during the 19th century, in localities where playing cards were socially taboo but dominoes were acceptable. Most of these games have passed away with the taboo, but a few continue to be popular on their merits.

Number of players. 1. Two.

The hands. 2. Each player draws seven bones.

Trumps. 3. After the opening lead, the other player, before following to the trick, turns up one bone from the boneyard. The higher number on this bone fixes the trump suit for the deal. The trump bone must be left in the boneyard until all other bones have been exhausted.

4. The blank suit ranks highest, above the 6, and each 0 end counts 7.

5. The 0-0, called *bingo,* is always a trump whatever the trump suit. When blanks are trumps, bingo counts 28. When another suit is trump, bingo counts 14; if the owner captures the trump doublet with it, he scores one point.

6. The trump doublet invariably counts 28. The other trumps count the total of their pips (but 0 always counting 7).

Counters. 7. Besides the trumps the following are also *counters,* regardless of what the trump suit is: all doublets, the non-trump doublets counting their total of pips; the 6-4 and 3-0, counting 10 each.

8. The number of counters is fourteen when the trump is 0, 6, 4, or 3; fifteen when the trump is 5, 2, or 1. The total of points on the counters is as follows:

When 0 is trump	143
1	135
2	138
3	131
4	134
5	129
6	140

Early play. 9. The first player, chosen by lot, may lead any bone. Each lead, together with a bone played by the opponent, constitutes a trick. The two bones are taken in by the winner, who leads to the next trick.

10. The winner of a trick draws one bone from the boneyard, and the opponent then draws a bone, so that until the boneyard is exhausted both hands are maintained at seven bones.

11. Until the boneyard is exhausted, the second player to a trick may play any bone—he need not follow suit.

12. A trick containing a trump is won by the higher trump. A trick containing no trump is won by the heavier bone, or by the lead if both are of the same weight. For example, the lead of 3-3 wins 4-2 (6 being trump) but loses to 5-2.

Object of play. 13. The several objects are: (a) to win counters in tricks, particularly to gain a total of 70 or more; (b) to win all the tricks; (c) to gain extra points by capturing the trump doublet with bingo, and by declaring doublets as in paragraph 14.

Declaring doublets. 14. When in the lead, a player holding two or more doublets may lead one of them and announce how many doublets he has at the time of his lead. The form of announcement is traditionally:

"Doublets" to declare two	20 points
"Triplets" to declare three	40
"Double doublets" to declare four	50
"King" to declare five	60
"Emperor" to declare six	1 *game point*
"Invincible" to declare all seven	3 *game points*

15. If the doublet led and announced wins the trick, the player scores the number of points indicated. The same doublets (depleted) may be used as the basis for consecutive announcements and consecutive scores, failing only when the leader fails to win the trick.

Final play. 16. After the boneyard is exhausted (the trump bone going to the player who did not win the last trick of the early play), the rules of play change. Each lead then requires the opponent to follow suit if able: a trump lead calls for a trump; a non-trump lead calls for the higher suit first, then the lower suit; if the second player can follow to neither, he must if able play a trump.

Closing. 17. At any time during the early play, a player who has gained the lead may *close*.

18. Closure is signified by turning the trump bone down. Thereupon no more bones are drawn from the boneyard, and the rules of final play (paragraph 16) come into force.

Scoring. 19. Points earned during play by winning counters and by declaring doublets must be claimed orally, and when so claimed are scored at once (with pencil and paper). A running total is kept of each player's score for that deal only.

20. The points won in play (for counters, etc.) determine certain *game points.* For winning 70 or more in play, a player scores 1 game point, or 2 if his opponent won less than 20 in play, or 3 if his opponent won not a single trick. The scores for *emperor* and *invincible,* being game points, do not count in the total won in tricks but are additional to any game points earned therefrom.

21. A player who closes thereby undertakes to win at least 70 in play. If he succeeds, scoring is as usual. If he fails, the opponent scores 2 game points, or 3 if the opponent had won no trick before the closure. The opponent may also score points due from winning 70 or more himself.

22. The player first reaching a total of 7 game points wins a game. If he correctly claims to have reached this total during play of a deal, the deal is not played out.

Irregularities. 23. *Revoke.* A revoke by failure to follow suit or trump as required by the rules of final play, when the player is able to do so, may be corrected without penalty before the next lead. If it is not corrected, and if the error is discovered before the final score for the deal (in game points) is agreed, the deal is played out and scored as usual, but 1 game point is then deducted from the score of the offender.

24. *Exposed bone.* If a player exposes a bone in the boneyard, in drawing another, the opponent at his next draw may elect to take the exposed bone or to draw another. If the exposed bone is so rejected, it is then shuffled face down in the boneyard.

FORTY-TWO

This is a card game played with dominoes, based on Auction Pitch. Its invention is credited to W. A. Thomas of Garner, Texas, about 1885. It is still played extensively in Texas and neighboring states.

Number of players. 1. Four, in two partnerships.

The hands. 2. Each player draws seven bones, leaving no boneyard.

Bidding. 3. There is one round of bidding. Each player in turn to the left (beginning with a player chosen by lot) must pass or make a bid higher than any previous bid. Each bid must be a number from 30 to 42 inclusive, or 84 or 168.

The play. 4. The high bidder names the trump suit and makes the opening lead. He must lead (*pitch*) a trump.

5. After any lead, each other hand must if able follow suit: a trump lead calls for a trump; a non-trump lead calls for the suit of the higher end. If unable to follow suit, a player may discard or trump as he pleases. A trick is won by the highest trump, or, if it contains no trump, by the highest bone of the suit led. (The 6 suit is highest, blank lowest.) The winner of a trick leads to the next.   •

Object of play. 6. The object is to win tricks, and also to capture counters.

Counters. 7. The five bones whose total is 5 or 10 count accordingly: 5-5, 6-4, 5-0, 4-1, 3-2. The total value of the counters is 35.

Scoring. 8. Each trick counts 1 point. The 7 points for tricks, with the 35 for counters, make up the total of 42 available in every deal.

9. At the end of play, each side totals what it has won. If the side that pitched made at least its bid, both sides score what they won in play. If the bid is not fulfilled, the pitcher's side scores nothing; the opponents score what they won in play, plus the bid. For example, if one side bids 37 but makes only 32, the opponents score 10 plus 37, or 47.

10. Bids of 42, 84, and 168 are to win all the points, and differ only for bidding purposes. If made, all score just 42; but the opponents, if they win any point, score their points plus the bid.

11. The side first to reach a total of 250 points wins a game. All deals are played out, and if both sides reach 250 in the same deal the higher total wins the game.

Irregularities. 12. *Revoke.* A revoke by failure to follow suit when able may be corrected at any time before the next lead, and an opponent who has played to the trick after the revoke may retract his bone and play another after the correction. If a revoke is not corrected and is discovered before the deal is scored, the offending side may score nothing for the deal and the other side scores what it won in play plus the amount of the bid.

13. *Exposed bone.* If a player exposes the face of a bone except in playing it legally, the bone must be left face up on the table and must be played at first legal opportunity thereafter, either in leading or in playing to a lead. This penalty applies to a bone exposed in revoking, when the revoke is then corrected, but not to a bone exposed by the non-offending side in consequence of the revoke.

A mathematical game is one whose outcome, with perfect play by all participants, can be determined in advance. For example, Tit-Tat-Toe or Noughts and Crosses can very easily be demonstrated to be a forced draw, barring a mistake by either player. Many such games have been played since ancient times, despite the certainty of their outcome. Most of them are two-hand and are forced wins for one player. The most prevalent are described below. Full analysis is given where space permits. We may here include also such games as Quadrangles, which must be mathematical in nature but which have not been exhausted by any published analysis. Most of the games and the analyses of them are taken from *Mathematical Puzzles* by Geoffrey Mott-Smith.

TIT-TAT-TOE

The name also appears in many sources as Tic-Tac-Toe, and in England the game is usually called Noughts and Crosses. [See also Go-bang, page 406.]

Two vertical parallel lines are drawn, crossing two horizontal parallels. In effect, the field is a square of nine cells, the border being omitted. The players in turn mark their symbols, X or O, in empty cells, and whoever gets three of his marks in a line, horizontal, vertical, or diagonal, wins.

The cells may be distinguished as center (one), corner (four), and side (four). The strongest opening is play to the center; the second must play to a corner to avoid loss. Similarly, to the corner opening the only reply is to the center. The side opening may be answered safely by playing to center or an adjacent corner. There are two traps that may be attempted by the first player. If the sequence is: center, corner, opposite

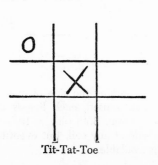

Tit-Tat-Toe

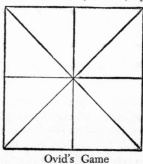

Ovid's Game

corner, the second player must take another corner or he gives his opponent a "fork." If the sequence is: corner, center, opposite corner, the second player must play in a side, as a corner play would allow a fork.

OVID'S GAME

The field is made by drawing a square, then adding diagonals, and horizontal and vertical medians parallel to the sides. There are nine points of intersection. Each player is provided with three counters. The counters are placed on the points one at a time, in alternate turns. After all are down, play continues by alternate moves, a counter being moved along a line to an adjacent point. Whoever gets his three counters in a row, on any one line, wins the game.

The first player can force a win by seizing the center. If play to the center is barred until all the counters are down, correct play forces a draw.

Very similar is The Mill (page 400), which is probably an intrinsic draw, though complete analysis has never been published.

QUADRANGLES

For two players. Mark off a square or rectangle of any agreed size on a sheet of quadrille paper. To avoid drawn games, make the number of cells odd. A square of 25 or 49 cells is ample to bring out the strategy of the game, though most of the players prefer large fields of 100 or more cells. If quadrille paper is not available, unlined paper will do: make a square or rectangle of dots aligned in rows and columns. These mark the corners of small squares.

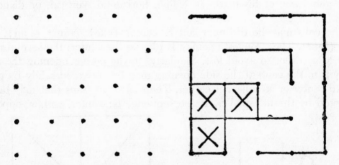

Quadrangles. At left, dots placed for a field of 25 squares. At right, a late stage of the game; "Cross" has captured three cells.

The players alternately draw one line, marking the side of one of the small squares. Where dotted plain paper is used, each line is drawn between two points adjacent in row or column. Both players try so long as possible to avoid drawing the third side of any cell. But eventually a stage is reached when no other move is available.

When a player draws the third side of any cell, his opponent may draw the fourth and put his own mark (X or O) inside the cell. On winning any cell, the same player plays again. If the completion of one cell adds a third side to an adjacent cell, he may complete and win that too. In the final stages of a game, cells are captured in series this way. The same player continues to play so long as he wins a new cell with each line. When he finally draws a line that does not complete a cell, the turn passes.

The player who wins the most cells, as indicated by the symbols (X and O), wins the game.

It is important to note that a player need not complete a cell if he does not wish to do so. (The strategy of the game lies in artful sacrifice.) But when he has completed a cell, he must play again. (Otherwise one player would win every cell of the field.)

Partial analysis of the strategy has been published, but whether either player can force a win against the best play is still unknown.

TRIANGLES

This is the same as quadrangles except that the cells of the field are triangular instead of square. The field is prepared by putting dots on plain paper, to mark the vertices of equilateral triangles (but precision is not essential). The field itself is by custom a large triangle, but to accommodate more cells it can be made roughly rectangular with jagged sides. A player wins a cell by adding its third side.

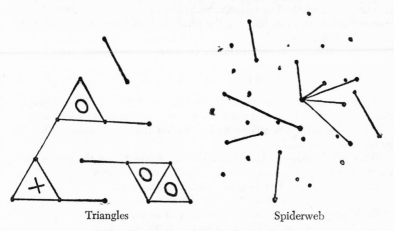

Triangles   Spiderweb

SPIDERWEB

This game is noticed in current German books as Das Nullenspiel.

On a piece of plain paper, the two players mark dots alternately. The total number to be marked is agreed in advance. Each player is free to place his dots where he will, within the limits of the paper. After all the dots are marked, each player in turn connects any two of them by a straight line, with the proviso that no line must ever cross another. Note that if three dots chance to be collinear, they may not be connected by a single line segment, but may be connected by two separate segments. To avoid arguments, the players should agree in advance as to what sets of three or more points are collinear and which are not.

The player who places the last dot can always force a win.

LAST DRAW

There are many games based on drawing counters from piles, in the effort to win the last, to take an odd number, etc. The simplest is One Pile. The players draw alternately from a common stock of counters, being limited to a fixed maximum per draw. The one who draws the last counter wins.

If the maximum allowed per draw is m, and the player must take at least one counter, a player can force a win if at any time his opponent is forced to draw from a number

$$n(m + 1)$$

where n is any integer. For example, if the maximum is three counters, the losing combinations for the player who has to draw are 4, 8, 12, etc. The outcome is thus determined by whether the original number in the pile is or is not of this form.

The object of play can be reversed: the player wins who forces his opponent to take the last counter. Since the pile must be reduced to one counter before this can happen, the series of losing combinations for the player in turn to draw is

$$n(m + 1) + 1$$

ODD AND EVEN

An odd number of counters is placed in a pile, from which the players draw alternately. There is a fixed maximum as to the number that may be taken in one turn. The player wins who has the odd number, after the whole pile is divided.

Where the minimum draw allowed is one counter, and the maximum is m, the losing combinations for the player in turn to draw are:

For a player who has an *odd* number of counters,
$$2n(m + 1) + 1 \quad \text{or} \quad 2n(m + 1) + 1 + m$$
For a player who has an *even* number of counters,
$$2n(m + 1) \quad \text{or} \quad 2n(m + 1) + 2 + m$$

In these formulas, n is any integer. For example, where the maximum is four counters per turn, a player having an odd number loses if he must draw from 1, 11, 21, 31, etc. or from 5, 15, 25, 35, etc. A player having an even number loses if he must draw from 10, 20, 30, etc. or from 6, 16, 26, etc.

MULTIPLE PILES

Counters are placed in three or more separate piles, with a different number in each pile. The players draw in turn, and may take any number from one counter up to a complete pile, but may not draw from more than one pile in a turn. The player who is forced to take the last counter loses.

The analysis depends upon the reduction of the numbers in each pile to the binary scale. That is, every such number must be expressed (as it can be, uniquely), as the sum of 1, 2, 4, 8, 16, etc., with no number of this series repeated. For example, $11 = 8 + 2 + 1$; $26 = 16 + 8 + 2$. A combination is a loser for the player who has to draw if each of the series 1, 2, 4, 8, etc. appears an even number of times when the total in each pile is expressed in the binary scale. The outcome of a game thus depends on whether the original allotment of counters makes or does not make a losing combination.

A prevalent form of this game starts with three piles, respectively containing three, five, and seven counters. These numbers reduce to $2 + 1$, $4 + 1$, and $4 + 2 + 1$. Unity alone is represented an odd number of times. The first player can therefore infallibly win by drawing one counter from any one of the piles.

THIRTY-ONE WITH CARDS

Twenty-four cards from a pack, the A, 2, 3, 4, 5 and 6 of each suit, are laid out in any convenient array. The players alternately draw cards, and a running total of the cards drawn is noted. The object is to draw the last card to make exactly 31. A player wins if he makes 31, or if his opponent in turn cannot draw without exceeding 31.

This game is a favorite of sharpers, against "gulls" who understand the formula for Last Draw (page 436). It might seem that a player can win by making the total 24, 17, 10, or 3 (by successive subtraction of 7 from 31, 7 being the total of the lowest and highest available numbers). But this idea is crossed up by the exhaustion of numbers. If the gull starts with a 3, the sharper takes a 4, and if the gull continues with the series, taking all the threes while the sharper takes all the fours, a total of 28 is reached. Now the threes are all gone; the gull has to draw an ace or a deuce, and the sharper wins.

The win is fairly easy by starting with a 5. If the second player also takes a 5, to make 10 and get into the series 10, 17, 24, the first player should draw a 2 to make 12, and threaten exhaustion of the fives. If the second player keeps to the series, the other will make 26 with all the fives gone. But if the second player does not keep to the series, the first will take it and win because no four-of-a-kind can then be exhausted. The first player can also win by starting with an ace or deuce, but the play is very intricate.

WIT AND REASON

This game is described in Cotton's *Compleat Gamester*, 1674. Each player takes half a pack of cards, one having all the red and the other all the black. Face cards are discarded. Each in turn puts one card in a center pile, and a running total is kept of the played cards. Whoever makes the total 31, or who leaves his opponent unable to play in turn without exceeding 31, wins the game.

On the principle of Last Draw (page 436), a player should win by making the successive totals 9 and 20. But if the first player starts with a nine, and the second plays a deuce, the first will lose if he spends his second nine to make 20. Then the second can play his other deuce to make 22, and the first cannot make 31. After nine-deuce, the first player must continue with a seven, to make 18. If the second spends his second deuce to make 20, the first will make 29 and win. If the second does not make 20, the first wins anyway.

THIRTY-ONE WITH DICE

A die is cast at random, and the uppermost number is noted. Each player in turn then rotates it through 90 degrees in any direction, to expose a new face. A running total is noted of the uppermost faces, and the player who makes it 31, or leaves his opponent unable to play without exceeding 31, wins the game.

Apart from the chance selection of the first number, this game differs from both Last Draw and Thirty-one with Cards in that a player can never turn up the number which at that juncture is on the bottom face. The analysis has recourse to digital roots: the digital root of an integer is the sum of its digits, reduced to a single integer by successive summations. For example, the digital root of 29 is 2, since $2 + 9 = 11$ and $1 + 1 = 2$. The method of winning is as follows:

Make the total a number with digital root 4, that is 4, 13, or 22; or when this is not possible, make a total whose root is 1, 5, or 9 by turning up 3 or 4; or when this is not possible, make a total whose root is 8 by turning up 5 or 2.

⟳ SOLITAIRE ⟳

Solitaires, also called Patience (and, often, "Idiot's Delight"), are card pastimes for one person. To win a Solitaire, the player must bring the cards into some prefixed order, pitting his wits against the chance order of the shuffle. Many Solitaires can be arranged as competitions among two or more players: the most frequent choice for this purpose are Canfield, Klondike, Poker Solitaire, Golf, Pyramid. In the definitive work on Solitaire (*The Complete Book of Solitaire and Patience Games,* by Morehead and Mott-Smith), more than 150 different forms are described.

Definitions. The following terms are defined as used in Solitaire.

PACK. The standard pack contains 52 cards, thirteen cards in each of four suits: spades, hearts, diamonds, clubs.

SEQUENCE. The cards in each suit have a basic rank: K (high), Q, J, 10, 9, 8, 7, 6, 5, 4, 3, 2, A (low). In some games, the sequence is continuous, the king being below the ace. Where there are foundations, the foundation cards are the lowest rank, so that ace-king necessarily form a sequence when the foundations are not aces.

LAYOUT. The cards first dealt, before commencement of actual play. All such cards are placed face up, unless otherwise specified. Component parts of the layout may be foundations, tableau, reserves.

STOCK. The rest of the pack after the layout is dealt. The stock is invariably kept face down, additional cards being brought into play from the top of the pile.

WASTEPILE. A pile in which cards turned from the stock are laid face up, if they cannot at the moment be played elsewhere.

ROW. A line of cards dealt from left to right, parallel to the player. When cards in a row are overlapped, only the one at the right end is available.

COLUMN. A line of cards dealt from the opposite side of the table toward the player, perpendicular to him. When cards in columns are overlapped, only the one nearest the player is available. Overlapping columns are best dealt by dealing one row at a time, with each card of a row resting partly upon a card of the row previously dealt.

FAN. Cards spread face up, fan-fashion.

FOUNDATIONS. Cards of a certain rank (or ranks), which are to form the bottoms of piles on which the rest of the pack is to be built.

TABLEAU. An array of cards on which (usually) some building is allowed, under the rules invariably different from those applying to the foundations.

RESERVE. An array (usually a pile) of cards available for play on foundations and tableau. A player may never build on his reserve cards.

·SPACE. A vacancy made in the tableau by removal of an entire pile, when the rules permit this vacancy to be filled.

BUILDING. Placing one card on another, under rules as to how the cards must match.

BUILD. A batch of cards in correct order of building.

AVAILABLE CARD. One that under the rules may be picked up to be moved elsewhere, usually to be built on foundations or tableau. Unless otherwise specified, every card in the layout that is not covered (in whole or part) by another is available, except that cards once built on foundations are never available for removal to another part of the layout.

Options. With a few exceptions duly noted, the following rules govern the player's exercise of discretion:

1. Foundation cards, if not placed in advance, must be moved to a row or column separate from the tableau, as soon as available.

2. It is always optional whether to build a card on another, either in tableau or foundations.

3. Cards built on foundations may never be retracted, e.g., to aid in tableau-building.

4. Cards built in the tableau may always be "unbuilt" by removal to foundations. They also may usually be transferred from one tableau pile to another, and sometimes into spaces.

5. When cards from the stock are turned over on a single wastepile, the player may "peek" at the next card before deciding whether to play off the wastepile. But "peeking" is barred when there is choice of two or more wastepiles.

ACCORDION

Cards. One pack.

Object of play. To get the entire pack, after it is entirely dealt out, into one pile.

Play. Deal the entire pack in a row, left to right, pausing to make what plays are possible. Whenever a card matches its left neighbor, or the third to its left, in either suit or rank, it may be moved upon that card. It is permissible to deal one additional card, before deciding upon a choice of plays.

After each play, move cards leftward so as to close up the gaps in the row.

ACES UP

Cards. One pack. Ace ranks high, above the king.

Object of play. To discard all cards but the four aces from the tableau.

Play. Deal a row of four cards. Finding two or more cards of the same suit, discard all but the highest, without disarranging the cards that remain. Continue dealing the stock in rows of four at a time, one card to each pile (or space) of the tableau. After the new row is dealt, discard any and all cards lower than a higher card of the same suit, showing on another pile.

A space made by removing an entire pile may be filled by the top card of any other pile, and all spaces must be filled (if possible) before the next row of cards is dealt.

BAKER'S DOZEN

Cards. One pack.

Layout. Deal the whole pack in thirteen overlapping columns of four cards each.

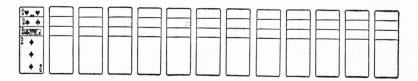

Object of play. To build each suit entire upon its ace.

Play. First transfer every king to the top of its column, i. e., put it under all other cards.

On the tableau, build down in sequence, regardless of suit. Only one card at a time may be lifted from the bottom of a column to be moved elsewhere. A space (made by removing an entire column) is never filled.

Move each ace, as it becomes available, to a row above the tableau. Build up on these foundations in suit and sequence.

BELEAGUERED CASTLE

Cards. One pack.

Layout. Set out the four aces in a column, for foundations. Deal the rest of the pack in a tableau of eight overlapping rows of six cards each, four such rows on each side of the foundations. The tableau is usually dealt by columns.

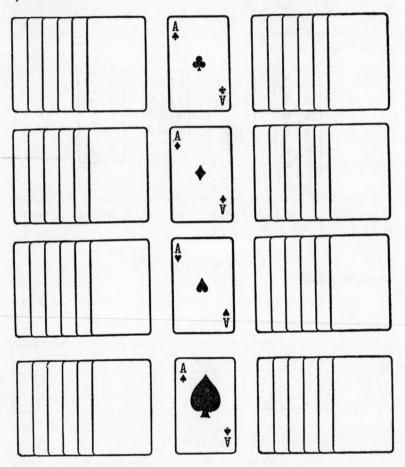

Object of play. To build each suit entire upon its ace.

Play. On the aces, build up in suit and sequence. On the right-end cards of tableau rows, build down in sequence regardless of suit. Only the end card of a row is available. Fill a space (made by removing an entire row) with any available card.

442

BIG BEN

Cards. Two packs.

Layout. Remove from the pack the following cards: ♣2, ♡3, ♠4, ◇5, ♣6, ♡7, ♠8, ◇9, ♣10, ♡J, ♠Q, ◇K. These cards are foundations. Put them in order in a circle corresponding to the hours of a clock, beginning with the ♣6 at "one o'clock." Around the foundations deal a tableau of 36 cards, comprising a fan of three cards opposite each "hour" of the clock. The remaining cards are the stock.

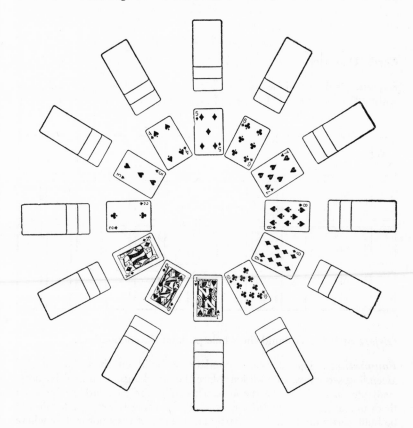

Object of play. To build up every foundation in suit and sequence, until the top card shows the number appropriate to its position in the "clock."

Tableau. Build down in suit, with rank continuous, ace being in sequence with the king. One card at a time (the wholly uncovered card) may be lifted from a tableau fan to be placed elsewhere.

Play. Turn up cards from the stock one by one, putting unplayable cards face up in a single wastepile. The top of this pile is always available for building, on foundations or tableau, but is not available for filling spaces unless the stock is exhausted.

Spaces (made by removal of an entire fan) must be filled from the stock by a new fan of three cards. Each fan must be maintained at a minimum of three cards by the deal of additional cards from the stock; fans may be kept in depleted condition while plays are being made, but when any fan or space is filled, all must be.

BISLEY

Cards. One pack.

Layout. Deal the whole pack in four rows of thirteen cards each, first putting the four aces at the left end of the top row.

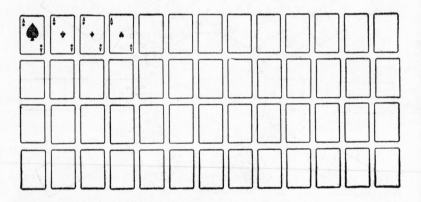

Object of play. To build the whole pack on the foundations.

Foundations. The aces are foundations; build on them in suit and ascending sequence. In addition, place the four kings, each as it becomes available, in a row above the aces. These also are foundations; build on them in suit and downward sequence. If the game is won, each suit will be built partly on its ace and partly on its king: it does not matter where the two foundations chance to meet.

Play. The bottom card of each column is available for play on foundations. The bottom cards may also be built on each other, in suit and sequence either up or down. Only one card at a time may be lifted from a pile in tableau building. A space (made by removal of an entire column) is never filled.

BRITISH SQUARE

Cards. Two packs.

Layout. Deal a tableau of sixteen cards, in four rows of four each. (More convenient is two rows of eight.)

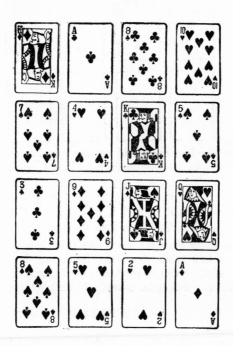

Object of play. To build the whole pack upon the foundations, which are four aces.

Foundations. As they become available, move one ace of each suit to a row above the tableau.

Play. On the foundations, build in suit and ascending sequence, up to kings, then play the duplicate kings on them and build down to aces.

On the tableau cards, build in suit and sequence, up or down. Upbuilds end at the king, down-builds at the ace. When one card is laid on another, it fixes the direction of building for that pile. Only one card at a time may be lifted from a pile for transfer elsewhere. The top cards are available for play on foundations or other piles.

Turn up cards from the stock one at a time, putting unplayable cards face up in a single wastepile.

Fill a space (made by removal of an entire pile) either from wastepile or stock, and it is permissible to look at the next card of the stock before making the decision.

445

CALCULATION

Cards. One pack.

Layout. Put in a foundation row any ace, deuce, trey, and fourspot.

Foundations. The four cards laid out are foundations. They are to be built up as follows, by number alone, regardless of suits:

A, 2, 3, 4, 5, 6, 7, 8, 9, 10, J, Q, K
2, 4, 6, 8, 10, Q, A, 3, 5, 7, 9, J, K
3, 6, 9, Q, 2, 5, 8, J, A, 4, 7, 10, K
4, 8, Q, 3, 7, J, 2, 6, 10, A, 5, 9, K

Play. Turn up cards from the stock one at a time, putting unplayable cards in any of four wastepiles. These piles may be (and should be) spread so that all cards can be read. Any card turned from the stock, and the top card of each wastepile, is available for play to foundations.

CANFIELD

Cards. One pack.

Layout. Deal a reserve of thirteen cards in a pile; a tableau of four cards, dealt in a row to the right of the reserve; and one card above the tableau, for the first foundation.

Object of play. To build each suit entire upon its foundation.

Play. Move the other three cards of same rank as the first foundation to

446

the same row, as they become available. Build on them in suit and ascending sequence. The ace plays on the king if neither is a foundation.

In the tableau, build in downward sequence and alternate color, red on black and black on red. The king plays on the ace, unless either is the foundation rank. A whole pile may be moved as a unit on another pile, if the touching cards are in correct sequence and color. Fill a space at once with the top card of the reserve; after the reserve is exhausted, fill spaces from the stock.

Turn up cards from the stock in batches of three; the top of the batch is available, and so are lower cards when uncovered. Put every batch face up in one wastepile, and when the stock is exhausted, turn over the wastepile to form a new stock. Go through the stock in this way, without limit, until the game is won or comes to a standstill.

Pounce. This is Canfield played by two to seven players. Each has his own pack and makes his own layout, but all foundations are common property, to be played upon by all players alike. The player who first gets rid of his reserve pile wins the game. All packs should have different backs, to facilitate sorting. Play should begin simultaneously on signal, after all players have completed their layouts. A card that reaches a foundation too late must be retracted (or legally moved to another foundation) before the player can resume play.

CLOCK

Cards. One pack.

Layout. Deal the whole pack in thirteen piles of four cards each, all face down. The piles are by tradition arranged in a circle to represent the hours of a clock, with the thirteenth pile in the center.

Object of play. To get all fours-of-a-kind together.

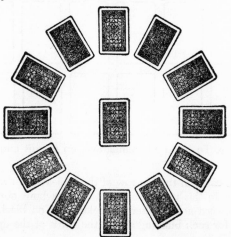

Play. Turn up the top card of the thirteenth pile. Put this card face up underneath the pile of its number. For example, if the card is a five, put it under the pile at "five o'clock." Turn up the top of the pile so increased, and continue in the same way, turning up in each case the top card from the pile of same number as the previous card. If the last face-down card of a pile chances to belong there, take next the top card of the next-higher pile. The game is blocked if the fourth king is turned up before all other fours-of-a-kind are assembled.

CONSTITUTION

Cards. Two packs. Discard all the kings and queens.

Layout. Place the eight aces in a row for foundations. Below them deal a tableau of 32 cards, in four rows of eight cards each (not overlapped).

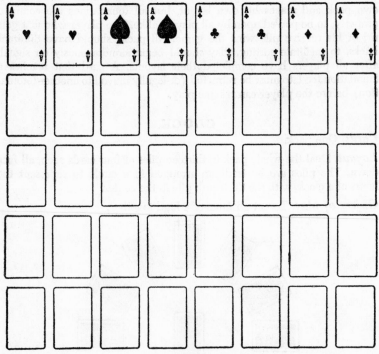

Object of play. To build all foundations up in suit and ascending sequence to jacks.

Play. Only the cards in the top row of the tableau are available for play on foundations. In this row, also, cards may be built on each other, in sequence downward and in alternate colors, red on black and black on red. Available for such building are all the cards of the upper two rows.

A space in any row may be filled only by moving up a card from the row below (not necessarily the card in the same column). Spaces in the bottom row are filled from the stock. One card at a time may be turned from the stock before deciding on a play, but each such card must find place in the tableau before the next is turned. If place cannot be made for it, the game is lost forthwith.

CORNER STONES

Cards. Two packs.

Layout. Deal the whole pack into twelve piles, one card at a time to each pile in order, but interrupting the deal to make plays when possible, as described below. Arrange the piles in two columns of six, with the top and bottom piles turned sidewise or askew. These four outer piles are the corner stones.

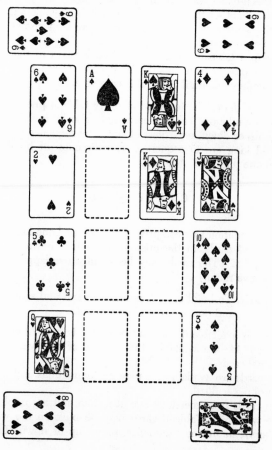

Object of play. To build the whole pack on eight foundations, four aces and four kings.

Foundations. As they are turned in dealing, place one ace and one king of each suit in two foundation columns between the tableau columns. The aces must be in one column, kings in the other, with the ace and king of same suit on the same row; and the central spaces must be filled in strict order (top to bottom) within these rules.

Play during the deal. On the foundations, build in suit and sequence, up on aces and down on the kings. When two foundations of the same suit have been built to the meeting point, either may be reversed upon the other, in whole or part, except for the ace or king at bottom.

Foundation cards can and must be placed in the center as they turn up. Any other card turned from the stock may be laid on a foundation instead of the tableau with this limitation: if the card would have gone on a tableau pile other than a corner stone, it is playable only on a foundation in the same row. Cards that would land on corner stones may instead be placed on any foundation.

Do not skip a tableau pile because of such plays to the center: give every tableau pile in turn an additional card. Cards once laid on the tableau are immovable until the deal is complete.

Play after the deal. The top card of every tableau pile is available for play on any foundation. Tableau cards may also be built on each other, in sequence up or down, regardless of suit. The sequence is here continuous: ace and king are in sequence. The direction of building may be reversed on one pile, as K-A-2-A-K.

CRAZY QUILT

Cards. Two packs.

Layout. A foundation row comprising one ace and one king of each suit. A tableau of 64 cards, in the criss-cross pattern shown by the accompanying diagram. (The cards may be slightly overlapped, from center outward, to save room.)

Object of play. To build each foundation in suit and sequence, upward on aces to kings, and downward on kings to aces.

Play. A card is available if one narrower edge is free. At the outset, four cards on each side are available; the removal of any will release one or two additional cards.

Tableau cards are available for play on foundations and on wastepile. Spaces are never filled.

Turn up cards from the stock one at a time, putting unplayable cards in a single wastepile. Tableau cards may be built on the wastepile (to release others), in suit and sequence, either up or down. The direction

may be reversed, as 4-3-4, and the sequence is continuous, ace being in sequence with king.

After the stock is exhausted, turn over the wastepile to form a new stock. The stock may be thus run through twice.

CRESCENT

Cards. Two packs.

Layout. Eight foundations in two rows, comprising one ace and one king of each suit. The rest of the pack in a tableau of sixteen piles of six cards each, arranged in a semi-circle. (More convenient is two rows of eight piles each, below the foundations.) The top card of each pile should be face up, the other cards face down.

Object of play. To build the whole pack on the foundations, in suit and sequence, upward on aces to kings, and downward on kings to aces.

451

Play. On the tableau, build in suit and sequence. The build may go up or down, and may be reversed on the same pile, as 6-7-6. Sequence is continuous; ace and king are in sequence. Only one card at a time may be lifted from the top of a pile to be moved to another pile or to foundations. When a face-down card is bared, turn it up. Spaces made by clearing away entire piles are never filled.

When two foundations of the same suit have been built to the meeting point, either may be reversed upon the other, except for the ace or king at the bottom.

When play comes to a standstill, move the bottom card of every tableau pile to the top, and resume play. Three such shifts, from bottom to top, are permitted.

CRIBBAGE SOLITAIRE

Cards. One pack.

Object of play. To make the highest possible total score in Cribbage hands.

Play. Deal yourself six cards for your hand, then two cards face down for your crib. Lay away two cards from your hand to the crib. Turn up the next card of the stock for the starter. Score your hand, then turn up and score the crib. Discard the six cards and put the starter at the bottom of the stock.

Continue through the stock in the same way, six cards at a time. When only four cards remain, turn them up and score them without a starter.

You may consider that you "win" the game if your total score after running through the whole stock is 120 or more.

Variant. Turn up sixteen cards from the pack, putting them to best advantage in a tableau four by four. Turn the seventeenth card for a starter. Score each row and column with the starter as a Cribbage hand. A total of 61 wins the solitaire.

452

EIGHT OFF

Cards. One pack.

Layout. A tableau of 48 cards, in eight overlapping columns of six cards each. Spread the remaining four cards below the tableau, starting the reserve.

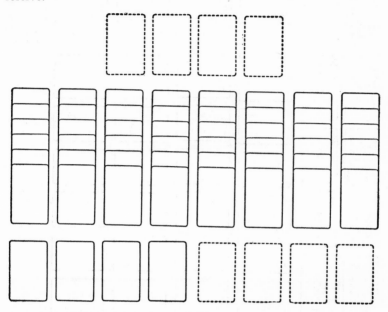

Object of play. To build each suit entire upon its ace. Move each ace, as it becomes available, to a row above the tableau. Build on the aces in suit and ascending sequence.

Play. On the tableau, build in suit and sequence downward. Only one card at a time may be lifted from the bottom of a column for transfer elsewhere. A space made by removing an entire column may be filled only by an available king.

All cards of the reserve are available for building on foundations and tableau. Available cards of the tableau may be removed and placed in the reserve, with the proviso that the reserve may never comprise more than eight cards.

EMPRESS OF INDIA

Cards. Four packs. Discard all the black queens and red jacks.

Layout. Remove and set out two foundation rows, one comprising all eight black aces and the other all eight red kings. Deal a tableau of 48

cards in four rows of twelve cards each. The upper two rows (the army) must contain only red cards; the lower two rows (the navy) only black. Deal cards as they come, putting each card in a row of its own color, and setting aside any excess of one color in a red or black wastepile.

Object of play. To build the whole pack in suit on the sixteen foundations, in the following sequences (columns show corresponding cards):

Black piles: A 2 3 4 5 6 7 8 9 10 J K
                 K Q 10 9 8 7 6 5 4 3 2 A

Play. Tableau cards may be combined with each other and with cards from the wastepiles in couples of corresponding cards (see preceding tabulation; a black 5 may be moved to a red 8, etc.).

A space in the tableau must be filled at once by the top card of the wastepile of appropriate color. Cards may be played on foundations only from the tableau, and then only in pairs of corresponding cards.

Turn cards from the stock one at a time, putting unplayable cards in two wastepiles, one for red cards and one for black. Take note that these cards can reach the foundations only via spaces and builds in the tableau.

FLOWER GARDEN

Cards. One pack.

Layout. A tableau (the garden) of 36 cards, in six overlapping columns of six cards each. A reserve (the bouquet), comprising the remaining 16 cards, spread below the tableau in a fan or any other convenient array.

Object of play. To build up each suit entire on its ace.

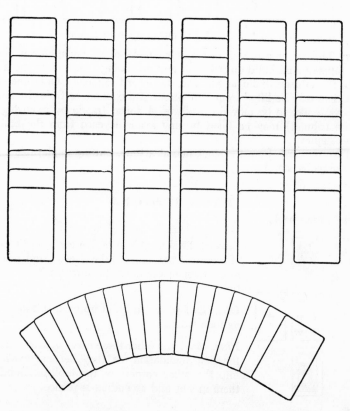

Play. Move each ace, as it becomes available, to a foundation row above the tableau, and build it up in suit and ascending sequence.

On the tableau, build in downward sequence regardless of suit. Only one card at a time is available at the bottom of a garden column. A space (made by removing an entire column) may be filled by any available card.

All cards of the bouquet are available for building on foundations or tableau.

FORTY THIEVES

Cards. Two packs.

Layout. Deal a tableau of forty cards, in ten overlapping columns of four cards each.

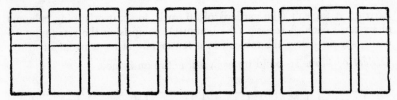

Object of play. To build each suit entire upon its ace.

Play. Move each ace, as it becomes available, to a foundation row above the tableau, and build on it in suit and ascending sequence to the king.

In the tableau, build in suit and downward sequence. Only one card at a time may be lifted from the bottom of a column, or from the top of the wastepile, to be moved elsewhere. A space (made by removing an entire column) may be filled by any available card from the tableau or wastepile.

Turn up cards from the stock one at a time, putting unplayable cards in a single wastepile.

FOUR SEASONS

Cards. One pack.

Layout. Deal a tableau of five cards, in the form of a cross. Deal one additional card, and place it in a corner of the cross, to form the first foundation.

Object of play. To build up each suit entire on its foundations.

Play. Move the other three cards of same rank as the first foundation, as they become available, into the other corners of the tableau. Build on them in suit and ascending sequence.

Turn up cards from the stock one at a time, putting unplayable cards face up in one wastepile.

On the tableau, build in downward sequence, regardless of suit. Only one card at a time may be moved from the top of a pile to be placed elsewhere. A space may be filled with any available card, from the tableau (to aid in consolidating piles) or from the wastepile.

FROG

Cards. Two packs.

Layout. Deal thirteen cards face up in a reserve pile at left, holding out any aces that turn up. Put these aces in a row at the right of the reserve. If no ace turns up, take one ace from the stock and put it in position to start the foundation row.

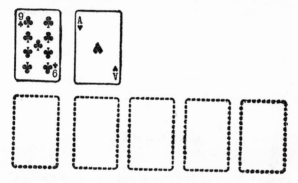

Object of play. To build the eight foundations from ace to king, regardless of suits. As the other aces become available, move them to the row with the first foundation.

Play. Turn up cards from the stock one at a time, putting unplayable cards in five wastepiles. You may put each card in whichever wastepile you wish. The tops of all wastepiles and of the reserve pile are available for play on foundations.

GAPS

Cards. One pack.

Layout. Deal the whole pack in four rows of thirteen cards each (not overlapping). Then take out and discard the four aces, making four gaps.

Object of play. To get each suit entire on one row, in sequence from two to king, left to right.

Play. Into each gap, move the card next-higher in sequence and suit to

the card at left of the gap. Continue so moving until blocked because each gap is closed by a king at its left. When a gap is made in the leftmost column, move any deuce you choose into it.

Further play being blocked, gather all cards that are not part of a regular sequence beginning with a deuce at the left end of the row. Shuffle well, then deal the cards so as to fill each row out to thirteen, but leave a gap at the right of the rightmost card of each row that was left on the table. Continue play as before, until the game is won or is blocked and lost.

GARGANTUA

Cards. Two packs.

Layout. Deal a tableau of 45 cards in nine piles respectively of one, two, three, etc. up to nine cards. The top card of each pile should be face up, all others face down. (This game is, in effect, Klondike played with two packs.) The usual method of dealing is by rows.

Object of play. To build each suit up on its ace.

Play. As they become available, move the aces to a row above the tableau. Build on them in suit and ascending sequence to kings.

In the tableau, build in downward sequence and alternate colors, red on black and black on red. All face-up cards on a pile are moved as a unit in building. When a face-down card is bared, turn it up. A space (made by clearing away an entire pile) may be filled only by an available king, or by a build with a king at the bottom.

Turn up cards from the stock one at a time, putting unplayable cards in a single wastepile. After the stock is exhausted, turn over the wastepile to form a new stock. The stock may be thus run through twice.

GAVOTTE

Cards. Two packs.

Layout. Deal two squares of sixteen cards each (four rows of four cards each), with space between the squares for two additional columns.

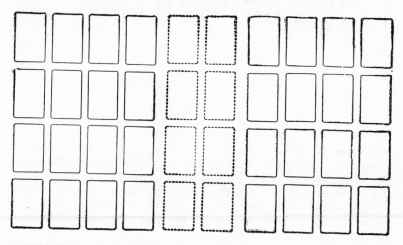

Object of play. To build the whole pack upon eight foundations.

Options. After inspecting the layout, decide which wing is to be the tableau and which the reserve. Also, decide on two consecutive ranks to be the foundations (as, sixes and sevens; or tens and jacks, etc.).

Play. As they become available, move one card of each suit in each foundation rank to the center columns. Build on all foundations in suit and skip-sequence; if foundations are sixes and sevens, the sequences are:

$$6, 8, 10, Q, A, 3, 5, 7, 9, J, K, 2, 4$$
$$7, 9, J, K, 2, 4, 6, 8, 10, Q, A, 3, 5$$

In the reserve, the bottom card of each column is available for play on foundations. Spaces are never filled.

In the tableau, all cards are available for play on foundations. Fill spaces at once from the wastepile.

Turn up cards from the stock one at a time, putting unplayable cards face up in a single wastepile.

GOLF

Cards. One pack.

Layout. Deal a tableau of 35 cards, in seven overlapping columns of five cards each.

Object of play. To remove the entire tableau.

Play. Turn up cards from the stock one by one, putting them face up in a single wastepile. Build uncovered cards in the tableau upon the wastepile, in sequence regardless of suits. The sequence may go up or down, and may reverse, as 5-6-7-6-5. The ace and king are not in sequence, and a king (but not an ace) ends a build. That is, after a build J-Q-K, it is not permissible to build a queen on the king; but a build 3-2-A-2 is allowed.

Tournament Golf. Two players may compete in a Golf "match" each using his own pack and making his own layout. Nine games or "holes" are played. A player's score for a hole is the number of cards left in his tableau after his stock is exhausted. (If he clears away his tableau, any cards remaining in his stock are counted as "minus" strokes, deductible from his total.) The scores are compared hole by hole, and the better score in each wins one match point. Three match points go to the better "medal" score—the final total of all "strokes" taken by a player.

GRANDFATHER'S CLOCK

Cards. One pack.

Layout. Remove from the pack the following cards: ♣2, ♡3, ♠4, ♢5, ♣6, ♡7, ♠8, ♢9, ♣10, ♡J, ♠Q, ♢K. These cards are foundations. Put them in order in a circle, corresponding to the hours of a clock, starting with the ♣10 at "one o'clock." Deal the rest of the pack in a tableau of eight overlapping columns of five cards each.

Object of play. To build up every foundation in suit and ascending sequence, until the top card shows the number appropriate to its position in the "clock."

Play. The bottom card of each tableau column is available for play to a foundation or for building on another available tableau card; in the tableau build in sequence downward regardless of suit. A space made by clearing away an entire column may be filled by any available card. Only one card at a time may be lifted from a tableau column to be transferred elsewhere.

HIT OR MISS

Cards. One pack.

Object of play. To discard the whole pack.

Play. Deal cards one at a time face up in a single wastepile, counting "ace" for the first card, "two" for the second, and so on. After reaching "king," begin again at "ace."

When a card proves to be of the rank called, it is hit. Throw each hit into a separate discard pile. Each time the stock is exhausted, turn over the wastepile without shuffling, to form a new stock, and continue as before, calling the next-higher rank after the one called for the last card of the old stock.

You must abandon the game as lost if you go through the stock two consecutive times without scoring a hit.

INTELLIGENCE

Cards. Two packs.

Layout. A tableau of 54 cards, in eighteen fans of three cards each. If any aces turn up in dealing the tableau, put them in a foundation row and replace them by other cards.

Object of play. To build each suit entire upon its ace.

Play. Move all aces, as they become available, to the foundation row. Build on them in suit and ascending sequence to kings.

On the end cards of fans in the tableau, build in suit and sequence up or down. The direction may be reversed on the same fan, as 10-J-10. One card at a time may be lifted from a fan to be played on another or on foundations. A space made by clearing away an entire fan is filled by a new fan of three cards dealt from the stock. This is the only way the stock can be brought into play.

When play comes to a standstill, gather all cards of the tableau (but not foundation piles) together with the stock, shuffle thoroughly, and deal a new tableau of eighteen fans. During the deal, aces may be held out and replaced by other cards, but no higher cards may be built on foundations until the tableau is complete. The tableau may be thus dealt out three times in all.

KLONDIKE

Cards. One pack.

Layout. Deal a tableau of seven piles, respectively of one, two, three, four, five, six, and seven cards; the top card of each pile face up, the other cards face down. The usual method of dealing is by rows.

Object of play. To build each suit entire upon its ace.

Play. Move each ace as it becomes available to a row above the tableau. These are the foundations; build on them in suit and ascending sequence.

In the tableau, build down in sequence and alternate color, red on black and black on red. All face-up cards on a pile may be moved as a unit upon another pile, if the touching cards are in correct sequence and color. On baring a face-down card, turn it face up. A space (made by clearing away an entire pile) may be filled only by an available king or by a build with a king at the bottom.

Turn cards from the stock one at a time, putting unplayable cards face up in one wastepile. Go through the stock thus only once.

Multiple Klondike. From two to about six may play a common game of Klondike. Each has his own pack and deals his own layout, but all foundations are common property, to be played on by all players alike. The first player to get rid of all his cards upon the foundations wins the game. If none gets rid of all, the player with fewest cards left after play comes to a standstill is the winner. An available ace must be moved to the center, but the player may refrain from playing any higher card to the center, if he wishes.

Double Solitaire. Two play, as described in the preceding paragraph; the first player is decided by lot and each player's turn ends when he lays a card on his wastepile, whereupon the other's turn begins.

LA BELLE LUCIE

Cards. One pack.

Layout. Deal the whole pack in seventeen fans of three cards each, with one card left over.

Object of play. To build each suit entire upon its ace.

Play. Move each ace, as it becomes available, to a foundation row. Build on it in suit and ascending sequence.

Available tableau cards may be built on each other in suit and downward sequence. Only one card at a time may be moved from the top of a fan. Spaces made by clearing away entire fans are not filled.

After play comes to a standstill, gather up all cards left in the tableau (leaving foundation piles untouched), shuffle them, and deal a new tableau in fans of three. The tableau may be dealt three times in all. After the third deal, any one buried card may be drawn out of any one fan (to overcome an impasse).

LITTLE SPIDER

Cards. One pack.

Object of play. To build each suit entire upon its foundation.

Play. Deal the whole pack in batches of eight cards at a time, with a final batch of four. Distribute the cards to eight tableau piles, in two rows of four, leaving room for a foundation row between. The final batch of four cards is dealt to the upper row.

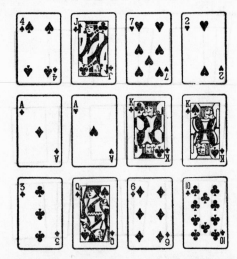

After dealing a batch, pause to play what you can. Move two red aces and two black kings, or two black aces and two red kings (choosing as you will), into the foundation row. These foundations may be taken from either row of the tableau.

Build on the ace-foundations in suit and ascending sequence, on the king-foundations in suit and downward sequence.

Before the deal is complete, a card from the lower tableau row is playable only to the foundation in column above it; after the deal is complete, such a card is playable to any foundation. Cards of the upper row are playable to any foundation throughout the game.

After the deal is complete, available tableau cards may be built on each other, in sequence regardless of suit. The sequence may be up or down, and may reverse, and the ace and king are in sequence. A space (made by removing an entire pile) is never filled.

MONTE CARLO

Cards. One pack.

Layout. Deal twenty-five cards in five rows of five each.

Object of play. To discard the whole pack in pairs.

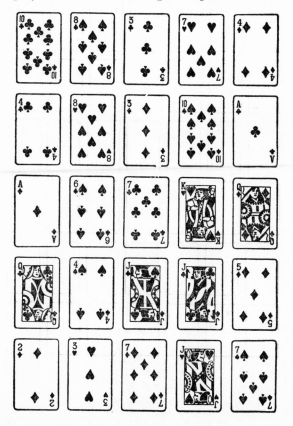

Play. From the layout discard each pair of cards of the same rank that are adjacent, in a row, column, or diagonal line. Having removed all such pairs, move the remaining cards into a solid array by backing them up in order within the 5 x 5 square. That is, push the remaining cards of each row leftward without disturbing their order, and fill each short row by bringing up cards from the left end of the row below.

Restore the layout to 25 cards by dealing additional cards in order to the bottom of the depleted layout. Continue in this way until the stock is exhausted.

OLGA

Cards. Four packs. Discard all deuces, treys, fours, fives, and sixes.

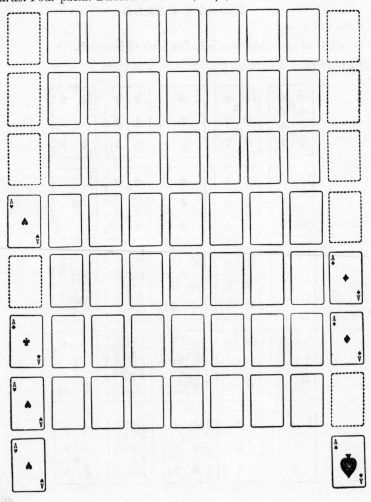

Layout. Deal a tableau of 49 cards, in seven rows of seven cards each. The even rows (2nd, 4th, 6th) should be face down, the odd rows face up.

Object of play. To build the whole pack upon the sixteen aces.

Play. Move each ace, as it becomes available, to a column at either side of the tableau. Build on these foundations in suit and ascending sequence, the next-higher cards to aces being sevens.

Any face-up card in the tableau may be lifted to be built on another tableau pile, and a whole pile is lifted as a unit to be placed on another. Build in sequence downward and in alternate color, red on black, black on red.

Only the bottom card of each tableau column is available for play on foundations. When a face-down card is at the bottom of a column, turn it up. A space made by clearing away an entire column may be filled by any available king, from wastepile or tableau (and in the latter case any build on the king is moved with it as a unit).

Turn up cards from the stock one at a time, putting unplayable cards face up in a single wastepile.

OSMOSIS

Cards. One pack.

Layout. Deal a reserve of four piles of four cards each, in a column at the left. Deal one more card at the right of the top reserve pile; this is the first foundation.

Object of play. To build each suit entire on its foundation.

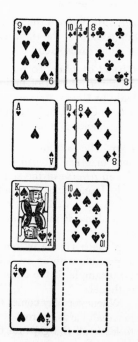

Play. Move the other three cards of the same rank as the first foundation, as they become available, into column with it. Build in suit on all foundations, putting the cards in an overlapping row so that all can be read. Sequence is ignored in building; the only condition is that a card may not be put on a foundation unless another of the same rank has already been built in the row above. On the first foundation, all cards of the suit may be built as soon as available, but the lower rows are limited by those above.

The top card of each reserve pile is available for play on foundations.

Turn up cards from the stock in batches of three. The top card of each batch is available, and so are lower cards when uncovered. Put all batches face up in a single wastepile. After the stock is exhausted, turn over the wastepile to form a new stock. The stock may be thus run through without limit, until the game is won or comes to a standstill.

PAIRING GAMES

Elevens. From one pack of cards, deal three rows of three cards each. Discard each pair of cards that total 11, face cards having no point values. Discard any king, queen, and jack exposed in the layout at the same time. When all possible discards have been made from the nine cards exposed, fill the spaces from the stock and continue. The object is to discard the entire pack.

Thirteens. From one pack of cards, deal two rows of five cards each. Discard each pair of cards that total 13, counting jack as 11 and queen as 12. Each king is discarded singly. Having made all possible discards, fill the spaces from the stock and continue. The object is to discard the entire pack.

PENDULUM

Cards. One pack.

Layout. Remove the four aces from the pack and put them in a foundation column at the right. Deal the rest of the pack in a tableau of six rows of eight cards each.

Object of play. To build each suit entire upon its ace. You may choose whatever interval of building you wish. For example, if the choice is to build by threes, the sequence on each foundation must be: A, 4, 7, 10, K, 3, 6, 9, Q, 2, 5, 8, J. The chosen interval must be followed on all four aces. (The choice is of course made after you see the tableau.)

Play. The bottom card of each column is available for play on foundations or other tableau cards. The builds in the tableau must be in suit, and in reverse of the sequence chosen for the foundations. For example, if the foundations are built up A, 4, 7, etc., tableau builds must go down: J, 8, 5 . . . 7, 4. The bottom of a column may be moved only upon (a) the card above it in column, or (b) either end card of the top row of the tableau.

A space (made by removing an entire column) must be filled as soon as possible with an available card of the rank last-wanted on foundations. For example, if the chosen interval is A, 4, 7, etc., spaces are filled only with jacks.

Whenever play comes to a standstill, swing the pendulum. This means, move all cards, in rows where there are gaps, toward the left (or right) to leave all the gaps on the opposite side of the tableau. Swing to each

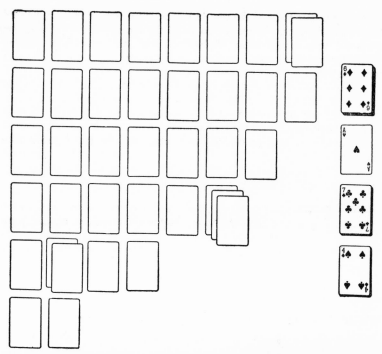

side alternately, toward the right on the first occasion. Each swing discloses some new cards at the bottom of columns. The pendulum may be swung, repeatedly, without limit, until the game is won or ends in a block.

PERPETUAL MOTION

Cards. One pack.

Object of play. To discard the whole pack in fours-of-a-kind.

Play. Deal a row of four cards. These cards fix the position of four piles, on which the remainder of the pack is to be dealt in rows, though some piles will at times be represented merely by spaces.

469

When all four cards of the row just dealt are of the same rank, discard them from the pack. If three or two are of the same rank, move the others upon the leftmost. Continue (when possible) this process of moving cards leftward upon equal cards until all exposed cards are of different rank, then deal the next row.

After the stock is exhausted, gather the piles from right to left, putting each on its left neighbor. Then turn the pack over to form a new stock, and deal it out in the same way. Continue redealing without limit until all fours-of-a-kind are cast out, or until the game is blocked. (A block is detectable by recurrence of the same order, usually when just twelve cards are left.)

POKER SOLITAIRE

Cards. One pack.

Object of play. To make the best possible total score in Poker hands.

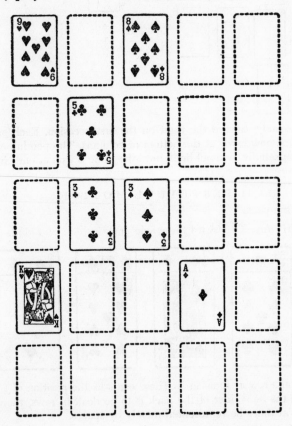

Play. Turn up 25 cards from the stock, one by one, and place them in a 5 x 5 square. You may put each card wherever you wish, within the square, and the whole game consists in placing them to best advantage. Once laid down, a card may not be moved, and it is not permissible to look at the next card of the stock before deciding where to place a card.

Scoring. The square being filled, compute the total score for the ten Poker hands represented by the five rows and five columns. Choose the count you prefer, between the two following:

HAND	ENGLISH	AMERICAN
Royal flush	30	100
Straight flush	30	75
Four of a kind	16	50
Full house	10	25
Flush	5	20
Straight	12	15
Three of a kind	6	10
Two pairs	3	5
One pair	1	2

Average scores are about 50 (English) and 145 (American). You may consider that you have "won" the game if you make 60 (English) or 170 (American).

Poker Squares. Any number of persons may compete at Poker Solitaire in a test of skill. Each has his own pack, which he sorts into suits in order to find each named card quickly. A non-playing "caller" shuffles another pack, turns cards up one by one, and names each card aloud. Every player takes the named card from his own pack and places it where he will in his own square. (Or he may write in that card, in a 5 x 5 grid.) After the 25th card is called, the player having the highest count wins the round.

PRECEDENCE

Cards. Two packs.

Object of play. To build the whole pack on eight foundations.

Foundations. Remove any king from the pack and place it at left for the first foundation. As they become available, move any queen, jack, ten, nine, eight, seven, and six into a row with the king. These foundations must be placed strictly in order; e.g., a jack may not be moved into the foundation row if the queen is not yet in place.

Play. On all foundations, build in sequence downward, regardless of suits, until each pile contains thirteen cards. Sequence is continuous: ace and king are in sequence.

Turn up cards from the stock one at a time, putting unplayable cards face up in a single wastepile. Cards so turned, and the top of the wastepile, are available for play to foundations. After exhausting the stock, turn over the wastepile to form a new stock. The stock must be thus run through three times in all.

PYRAMID

Cards. One pack.

Layout. A tableau of 28 cards, dealt in a pyramid as shown in the accompanying diagram.

Object of play. To throw the whole pack into the discard pile.

Play. Turn cards up from the stock one at a time, putting unplayable cards in an overlapping row (the wastepile). Go through the stock only once.

When any two available cards total 13, remove both to a discard pile. Queens count 12, jack 11, aces 1, other cards their index value. Discard kings singly. The cards available for matching up are wholly uncovered cards in the pyramid, and the right end of the wastepile row. (The wastepile card may be removed with a card newly-turned from the stock, as well as with a tableau card; tableau cards may be removed in couples.)

SALIC LAW

Cards. Two packs. Discard all eight queens. (Traditionally, the queens are placed in an ornamental row about the foundations.)

Layout. Remove any one king and place it at the left. Deal cards on it in an overlapping column until another king appears. With each king, start a new column at the right of the previous column. Deal out the whole pack in this way, in columns on the eight kings.

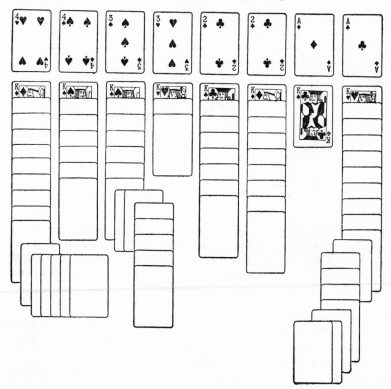

Object of play. To build the whole pack upon the aces, in upward sequence to jacks, regardless of suits.

Play. During the deal, place aces in a foundation row above the tableau. Any card newly-turned from the stock may be built on a foundation instead of laid on the tableau, but a card once laid down is immovable until the deal is complete.

After the whole stock is dealt, the bottom cards of tableau columns are available for play on foundations. A king when bared is the equivalent of a space; any available card may be moved upon it. Except for such utilization of spaces, there is no building in the tableau.

SCORPION

Cards. One pack.

Layout. Deal seven overlapping columns of seven cards each; the upper three cards in each of the first four columns face down, all others face up. The usual method of dealing is by rows.

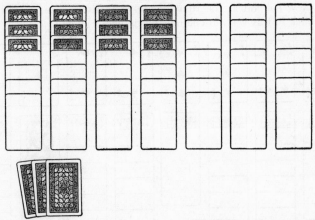

Object of play. To assemble each suit in sequence from ace to king (bottom of column to top).

Play. On the bottom card of a column may be built the next-lower in the same suit. When such card is visible in the tableau, it and all cards on it (below in column) are picked up as a unit, to make a build. But nothing may be built on an ace, and a king may be moved only into a space (made by clearing away an entire column).

When all face-up cards are cleared off one of the four leftmost columns, turn up the top face-down card.

The last three cards of the stock must be dealt on the three leftmost columns. It is entirely optional when to make this final deal: fillable spaces may be held open in order to see what these cards are.

SHAMROCKS

Cards. One pack.

Layout. Deal the whole pack in seventeen fans of three cards each, with one card left over. (See diagram of La Belle Lucie layout.)

Object of play. To build each suit entire upon its ace.

Play. Move each ace, as it becomes available, to a foundation row. Build on it in suit and ascending sequence.

Inspect the tableau, and if any king covers a lower card of the same suit move it under that card. (*Optional rule:* If no ace is uppermost on a fan, any one ace may be drawn out.)

474

On the top card of tableau fans, build in sequence regardless of suits. The sequence may go up or down, and may reverse, as 8-9-8. But no fan may ever comprise more than three cards. Only one card at a time may be lifted from a fan to be built elsewhere. A space (made by clearing away an entire fan) is never filled.

SPIDER

Cards. Two packs.

Layout. Deal a tableau of ten piles: six cards in each of the first four piles, and five cards each in the others. Turn the top card of each pile face up, all other cards face down.

Object of play. To discard all eight suits from the tableau.

Play. On the exposed tableau cards, build in downward sequence, regardless of suit. (But it is advantageous to build in suit when able.) Ace is low; nothing may be built on it. Kings are movable only to spaces or discard. On baring a face-down card in the tableau, turn it face up. A space (made by removal of an entire pile) may be filled by any available card from the tableau.

The top of each tableau pile is always available. In addition, cards of the same suit and in correct sequence with that at the top of a pile may be moved with it as a unit. (Such a build-in-suit may also be broken at any point.)

Whenever play comes to a standstill, deal from the stock a batch of ten cards, one on each tableau pile. All spaces in the tableau must be filled before such a deal.

Whenever thirteen cards of a suit lie on top of a pile, in correct sequence from ace at top to king at bottom, the suit may be lifted off and discarded. It is not compulsory to discard when able (there may be an advantage in breaking the suit to aid in tableau manipulation).

TERRACE

Cards. Two packs.

Layout. Deal eleven cards in an overlapping row, to form the reserve. Look at the next three cards and choose one of them for your first foundation (in accordance with what cards are buried in the reserve). Put the chosen foundation at the left, to start a row of foundations below the reserve. Put the two rejected cards below it to start the tableau row. Complete the tableau by dealing seven more cards, making nine in all (not overlapped).

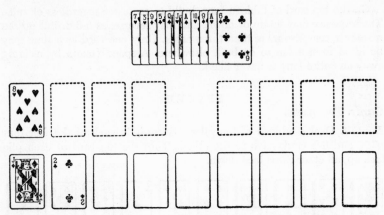

Object of play. To build the whole pack on eight foundations.

Play. All other cards of the same rank as the first foundation are also foundations. As they become available, move them into the same row. (It is helpful to group all red foundations together and all black together.)

Build foundations in ascending sequence and alternate colors, red on black and black on red, until each pile contains thirteen cards. Ace and king are in sequence, when aces are not foundations.

Turn up cards from the stock one at a time, putting unplayable cards face up in a single wastepile. Cards so turned, and the top of the wastepile, are available for either foundation- or tableau-building. The right end of the reserve row is available only for play on foundations.

On the tableau, build down in sequence and alternate color. A build once made is immovable except that the cards can be played off on a foundation. A space in the tableau (made by removal of a whole pile) must be filled at once from the wastepile (never from the tableau or reserve).

TOURNAMENT

Cards. Two packs.

Layout. Deal a reserve of eight cards, in two columns of four each. Shuffle and start the deal again (if necessary) until at least one ace or king appears in the reserve. Between the two reserve columns deal a tableau of 24 cards, in six overlapping columns of four cards each.

Object of play. To build the whole pack on eight foundations, four aces and four kings.

Play. As they become available, move one ace and one king of each suit to two foundation rows above the tableau. Build in suit and sequence up on aces, down on kings. When two foundations of the same suit meet, either can be reversed in whole or part upon the other.

All cards of the reserve are available for play on foundations. Fill

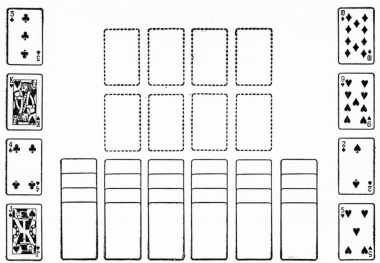

spaces in the reserve from the tableau; a space may be kept open indefinitely until it can be used to best advantage. (The point of assuring that the reserve as dealt contains an ace or king is that the game is virtually impossible without a reserve space at the outset.)

Bottom cards of tableau columns are available for play on foundations and to fill reserve spaces. A space in the tableau (made by clearing away a whole column) must be filled at once by an overlapping column of four cards dealt from the stock. In all other circumstances, the tableau must be dealt by rows.

Each time play comes to a standstill, deal four more rows from the stock upon the tableau columns (as far as the stock lasts).

When the stock is all dealt out and play has again come to a standstill, gather the tableau cards alone, sliding each column together and placing each pile on its left neighbor. Without shuffling, turn over this packet to form a new stock, and continue dealing to the tableau as before. The stock may be thus dealt three times in all.

TRIUMPH

Cards. Two packs.

Layout. Set out a foundation row comprising all eight aces. Deal a row of eight cards below it, starting the reserve. Deal a column of four cards at the left, forming the tableau.

Object of play. To build all eight suits in ascending sequence on their aces.

Play. In the tableau, build in suit and downward sequence, moving a whole tableau pile as a unit to consolidate piles. Fill spaces at once from the stock. Tableau cards may be played off only upon foundations.

The bottom card of each reserve column is available for play on foundations. Spaces must be filled from the stock, but may be held open to make other plays.

Whenever play comes to a standstill, deal another row of eight cards at the bottom of the reserve. All spaces in upper rows must be filled before such deal.

After the stock is exhausted, any four cards may be lifted arbitrarily out of the reserve; this is the draw. The card above each gap thus created becomes available. (Bottoms of columns remain available at all times.) Place must eventually be found for the cards so lifted out, on foundations or tableau, or the game is lost forthwith. Two such draws, of four cards at a time, are permitted.

VIRGINIA REEL

Cards. Two packs.

Layout. Remove from the pack a deuce, trey and fourspot, of different suits. Place these three cards in column at the left, forming the first foundations. Deal seven more cards in a row at the right of each foundation; these 28 cards together form the tableau. Below it, deal a row of eight cards to start the reserve.

Object of play. To build the whole pack up on the foundations.

Foundations. All deuces, treys, and fourspots are foundations, but none may be built upon until it is in the row with the first foundation of the same rank. Build on them in suit, and in sequence of three as follows:

2, 5, 8, J

3, 6, 9, Q

4, 7, 10, K

Play. All tableau cards are available for play on foundations, and aces are discarded to make spaces, but it is not permissible to make a space in either way unless the space can immediately be filled by a foundation belonging in that row. Such foundations may be moved from other tableau rows, but eventually the spaces must be filled with new foundations from the reserve. However, it is permissible to make a cyclic change among two or three foundations, all in different rows not their own. For example, a trey in the deuce-row may change places with a deuce in the trey-row; a deuce, trey, and fourspot shift serially if each thereby reaches its proper row. Such cyclic shifts do not leave a space in the tableau.

Top cards of reserve piles are available for play on foundations and to fill spaces. Do not fill spaces in the reserve except by the ensuing deal.

Whenever play comes to a standstill, deal eight more cards to the reserve, one on each pile. After the deal, discard any aces that show, and continue play.

WEAVERS

Cards. Two packs.

Layout. Set out a foundation row of eight cards, comprising one ace and one king of each suit.

Object of play. To build the whole pack upon the foundations in suit, up on the aces to kings and down on the kings to aces.

Tableau. Deal the stock into a tableau of thirteen piles, one card at a time to each pile in rotation. Imagine the piles to be numbered consecutively: when a card would fall on the pile of its own number (king counting as 13, queen 12, jack 11), put it instead on a separate exile pile,

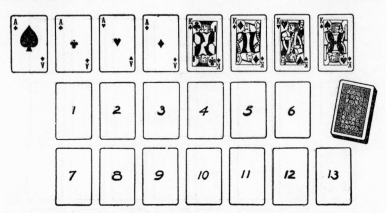

face down. When a card is so exiled, do not skip the tableau pile so deprived—deal the next card to it.

Play. The pack being dealt out, spread the cards of the 13-pile. All these cards are available for play on foundations, together with the top card of every other numbered pile.

When play comes to a standstill, turn up the top card of the exile pile. If this card can be placed on a foundation, it must be, and the next exile turned up. If the exile is unplayable, use it to commence weaving. Put it at the bottom of the pile of its own number, remove the top card of this pile and put it at the bottom of the pile of its own number, and so on. As soon as this weaving process bares a card playable on a foundation, move it up and continue with any other plays thereby made possible. (The card in hand when such a playable card is bared goes under the pile of its own number, but any further weaving must begin with the next exile.)

If an exile card is a king, it must be put under the 13-pile and the next exile turned up.

When two foundations of the same suit have been built to the meeting point, either pile may be reversed upon the other, in whole or part, except for the ace or king at the bottom.

When the exiles are exhausted and play is again at a standstill, pick up the tableau piles in order to form a new stock, with the 13-pile at the top. The stock may be thus run through three times in all.

WINDMILL

Cards. Two packs.

Layout. Remove any ace from the pack; place it in the center of the table for a foundation. Around it deal four radiating lines (the sails) of two cards each; these eight cards are the tableau.

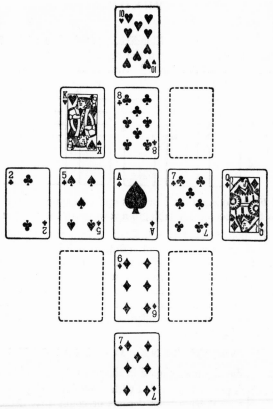

Object of play. To build the whole pack on the foundations, in sequence regardless of suit.

Foundations. On the ace, build up to king, then ace, and so on until the pile contains 52 cards. (Turn kings crosswise to keep track of how many sets of thirteen have been built.) Move any four kings, as they become available, into the spaces between the sails; build each of these foundations down to aces.

From king-foundations, cards may be transferred to the ace-foundation, but only one card at a time from any one king-foundation. After any such move, the next card on the ace-foundation must come from elsewhere.

Play. Turn up cards from the stock one at a time, putting unplayable cards face up in one wastepile. All cards in the sails are available for play on foundations. It is not compulsory to play to foundations when able, or even to move kings into place as foundations. A space in the sails must be filled at once from the wastepile. If there is no wastepile, the space may be filled by the next card turned from the stock.

YUKON

Cards. One pack.

Layout. Deal 28 cards as for Klondike. Deal the remaining 24 cards in four rows of six cards each, upon the six columns other than the single card at the left. Spread the cards downward so as to overlap in column.

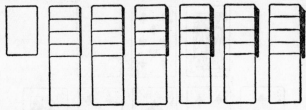

Object of play. To build the four suits up in sequence on the aces. Move the aces, as they become available, to a row above the tableau.

Play. On the bottom card of a tableau column may be laid a card of next-lower rank and opposite color. (But no build may be made on an ace, since available aces must be moved at once to the foundation row.) For purposes of building, a face-up card anywhere may be lifted, together with all covering cards, the whole being moved as a unit.

When a face-down card is bared, turn it up. A space made by clearing away an entire column may be filled only by a king (any cards on the king being moved with it).

RUSSIAN BANK, OR CRAPETTE

This is a two-hand game, played in the manner of a solitaire.

Layout. 1. Each player is provided with a regular pack of 52 cards. The respective packs must have back designs or colors that make them distinguishable from each other.

2. Each player shuffles the pack to be used by his opponent.

3. Each player counts off twelve cards from his pack and places them face down in a pile at his right, forming his reserve. Then he deals a column of four cards face up above his reserve, extending to the opponent's side of the table. The two columns together, eight cards, are the tableau. The player puts the rest of his pack face down at his left, forming his stock (often called hand).

4. The first player is he whose last-dealt tableau card is lower than his opponent's (if they are the same rank, the next-to-last cards govern).

Beginning play. 5. The first player must begin by moving any aces from the tableau to the center, the space between the columns. He must build on such aces, if he can, from the tableau, upward in suit and sequence. Having made all possible plays to the center, he may turn the top card of his reserve face up.

6. The second player, at his first turn, must likewise play first to the

center, if possible. Having done so, he may turn up his top reserve card.

7. After his first turn, a player is always entitled to see the top card of his reserve before making any play, even to the center.

Building. 8. All aces are foundations and must be moved to the center as soon as they become available.

9. The foundations are built up in suit and sequence, to kings.

10. On the uppermost tableau cards, builds may be made in downward sequence and alternating colors. Only one card at a time may be lifted off a tableau pile to be transferred elsewhere.

11. The tableau comprises eight piles. A space made by removing an entire pile may be filled by any available card from the tableau or reserve (subject to rules of precedence below).

12. The cards available for building on foundations and tableau are: uppermost cards of tableau piles, top card of the reserve, a card newly turned from the stock. Tableau builds may be "unbuilt" as the player pleases, to consolidate piles and make additional spaces; but a card once laid on a foundation may not be retracted.

Rules of precedence. 13. The player must make plays in the order given by the following paragraphs. Should he make a play out of order, he may be stopped and forfeits his turn (as explained below).

14. When an available card can be played on a foundation, it must be so played at once. The duty to play to the center overrides all other considerations, except as provided in paragraph 7.

15. If the reserve card is playable to the center, it must be played ahead of any card from the tableau.

16. On playing off his reserve card, to center or tableau, the player must immediately turn up the next reserve card.

17. When no play to the center is possible, the player may manipulate the tableau as he pleases. There is no compulsion to build from reserve to tableau, but it is usually advantageous to do so at every opportunity. But if the reserve card is playable anywhere, it must be so played before a card is turned from the stock. [The reserve card is playable if a space exists in the tableau, but is not so deemed because a space could be made.]

18. The player may turn up the top card of his stock if his reserve card is at the moment unplayable, which necessarily means that there is no tableau space.

19. If the stock card is unplayable, it must be placed face up on the *wastepile,* and the player's turn ends. The exposed card of the wastepile is *never available.* Even should the stock card be playable, the player ends his turn if he inadvertently places it on his wastepile.

20. If the stock card is played, to center or on the tableau, any new plays to center or from the reserve thereby opened up must be completed before the player returns to his stock.

21. Subject to the above rules, the player may return to his stock repeatedly, turning up the top card each time and playing it, until an unplayable card shows and thereby ends his turn.

22. When his reserve is exhausted, the player may fill spaces from his stock.

Loading. 23. A player may build cards on his opponent's reserve and wastepile, in suit and sequence *either up or down.*

24. Loading is legal at any time that tableau-building is legal and the same cards are available for both (paragraph 12).

Stops. 25. If a player makes any play out of order as prescribed by paragraphs 13-22, his opponent may cry "Stop!" On any such call, regardless of its merits, play must be suspended.

26. If the claim of error is agreed to be correct, the turn of the stopped player ends. If the claim is agreed to be false, the player's turn continues and he transfers one card face down from the bottom of his reserve to the bottom of his opponent's reserve.

27. A play is deemed completed only after the player has removed his hand from a card moved. A call of stop is not valid until an erroneous play is completed.

28. A player may touch any cards at any time, except opponent's reserve, stock, and wastepile, for purposes of arranging; if he says "I arrange" or words to that effect, a stop may not be called for the act.

Ending play. 29. When a player's stock is exhausted, he turns his wastepile face down to form a new stock. Play continues until one player wins the deal by getting rid of his entire reserve and stock (and wastepile).

30. The winner scores 2 points for each card left in opponent's reserve, plus 1 point for each card in opponent's stock and wastepile, plus a bonus of 30.

Irregularities. 31. *Incorrect build.* If a player makes an incorrect build, the error must be corrected on demand, but if it is not noticed until the player has completed a following play it stands as regular.

32. *Exposing cards.* If a player sees more than one card at a time from his reserve or stock, as by turning up two cards together, he may complete his current play but then his turn ends.

33. *Reserve card.* If a player is correctly stopped at a time when there is no face-up card on his reserve, his opponent may require him to turn up a card [to give the opponent the opportunity to load it].

34. *Stop moves.* When a player is correctly stopped for moving a card out of order, the opponent may elect whether to let the move stand or retract it.

35. If a player makes a move out of order, but is permitted to complete a following move before stop is called, the call is void without penalty and the previous play stands.

CARD GAMES FOR CHILDREN

The games that follow are particularly easy to learn, having few and simple rules. Some of these games offer astonishing opportunity for skill. For example, few games are less a matter of luck than Authors, Concentration, and I Doubt It, which are often played by professional gamesters in order to train the memory. Even Old Maid can be played as a pure battle of wits: it was so played in the German beer-gardens of the 80's, when a burgher stuck with *schwarze Dame* had to pay for the drinks.

Some games that might have been included in this section, as easy to learn and often played by children, have been placed elsewhere for historical reasons: Casino, Snip Snap Snorem, Slobberhannes, Polignac, Lift Smoke, Catch the Ten, Fan Tan and other Stops games, as Comet. Many of the Rummy games are popular with children.

In all of the following games, the full pack of 52 cards is used. Little is said of shuffling, cutting, etc., because these matters are not important to children. The directions as to dealing are designed to accommodate the greatest possible range in the number of players. The cards may be dealt one at a time or in batches, as the players find convenient. Rules as to playing in turn, following suit, etc., should be strictly enforced, for these are the essence of the game and children quite appreciate the necessity for such rules. In most of the games irregularities should not be penalized; they should be rectified, if necessary, or simply glossed over.

When the nature of the game permits, it is likely to be more enjoyable to children if Poker chips are used for settlement.

HIGHEST CARD

This game is designed for the very youngest age group (five or six), as an introduction to basic principles of card play.

Each player is dealt four cards. The hands are played out in tricks. The highest card wins the trick, suits being ignored. Beginners should be taught the rank of cards as: K (high), Q, J, 10, 9, 8, 7, 6, 5, 4, 3, 2, A. After they are well-versed in the rank, especially as to the face cards, it should be agreed that the ace will be ranked high, above the king. (This change is made to accustom children to the variable rank of the ace.)

The pack need not be shuffled after each deal. The cards of the first deal are set aside, and new hands are dealt from the stock, and so on so far as the stock lasts. After the final deal the cards are all gathered and shuffled.

For beginners, each deal is a game, won by a player that wins a plurality of tricks. Later, a simple plan of cumulative scoring should be introduced: A game lasts until the stock is exhausted. The number of tricks won by each player is recorded on paper, and the highest total wins the game.

After the children have learned to play the suitless game with ease, the suit principles may be introduced. At first, there is no trump suit, but a lead calls upon other hand to follow suit if possible. Later the use of a fixed trump suit, as hearts, may be added.

OLD MAID

One queen is discarded from the pack. The pack is then divided into approximately equal packets, one for each player. (Or the pack may be dealt out, one card at a time, as far as it goes.) Each player spreads his cards face up, picks out pairs of the same rank and discards them face up in a common pile in the center of the table. Players may help one another during this process: there is no necessity for concealment.

When his packet of cards is stripped of all pairs, the player picks it up and shuffles it out of sight of the other players—as, behind his back. Now, there are either three queens or one queen left in play. If one, the first draw is made from the hand holding the queen. If three, the first draw is made from the hand having the most cards, of the three hands holding queens, or the one nearest the left of the dealer if none has a plurality of cards.

The player so elected to give the first draw holds his cards toward his left neighbor—carefully concealing the queen after having shuffled it well in the hand—and the neighbor draws out one card. If this card pairs with one in his hand, he discards the pair. In any case, he then shuffles his hand and allows the player at his left to draw out one card. The play continues in the same way, in rotation. Each pair formed is discarded. Whenever his hand is to be drawn from, a player should shuffle it, then extend it so that his left neighbor cannot see the face of any card—it does not matter if other players sight the cards.

The player left with the odd queen, all other cards having been paired and discarded, is the "old maid" and loses the game.

RANTER GO ROUND

This ancient gambling game is also known as Cuckoo. With the stakes left out, it makes an amusing game for children, and a good introduction to the use of chips. It is best for five to ten players, though as many as twenty may play. Each player is provided at the outset with three chips.

One card is dealt to each player. Beginning with eldest hand (at left of the dealer), each in turn must say "Stand," keeping his card, or "Change," in which case he exchanges cards with the player at his left.

The latter is bound to exchange except when he has a king; in this case he responds to demand "Change" by exposing the king, and the turn passes to his left. On receiving an ace, two, or three by exchange, a player must at once face it on the table.

When the turn reaches the dealer, he may stand on his original card or exchange it for one drawn at random from the undealt remainder of the pack. Then all cards are exposed, and the player having the lowest "loses a life" and must pay one chip to a pool. King ranks high, ace low. But if the dealer has obtained a king by exchange, he alone loses a life. In any other case, if two or more players tie for lowest card, each must pay a chip.

On losing all three of his chips, a player drops out of the game. The others continue, and the lone survivor wins the game.

SLAPJACK

The whole pack is dealt out. It does not matter if some players have one or two more cards than others. With two or three players, the customary method of dealing is therefore to divide the pack into approximately equal packets, one for each player.

Each player must keep his cards in a packet, face down in front of himself. Each in rotation turns the top card of his packet face up and places it on a common pile in the center of the table; he should lift the card by the edge farthest from him, and turn it away from him. When the turned card proves to be a jack, the first to slap it wins the entire center pile. The player turning the card must slap with the same hand. Cards so won are turned face down and put under the winner's packet.

If a player slaps a card that is not a jack, in two-hand play, the center pile is forfeited to his opponent. The same rule may be applied in three-hand, with the opponents sharing the forfeited pile equally. With more players, one who slaps a card not a jack must give one card from the top of his packet to each other player, the center pile remaining to be won regularly.

If a player is unable to play in turn, having no cards left, he drops out and the others continue until one of them has won all 52 cards.

When several players slap a jack simultaneously, the one whose hand is nearest the card wins the pile.

MENAGERIE

Each player selects the name of an animal—the longer the better, as rhinoceros, hippopotamus. The cards are dealt out evenly as far as they will go. Each player puts his cards in a face-down pile in front of him. Each player in rotation turns up one card, putting it on the table in front of his pile; when a turned card matches the top face-up card of another player, each of the two players concerned must say the animal-name of the other three times, as "Hippopotamus, hippopotamus, hippopotamus." The player who first completes saying the other's animal-name takes all the face-up cards of the other. As each player loses all his cards he drops out, and the player who finally has all the cards is the winner.

BARNYARD

This is the same game as Menagerie except that each player selects a barnyard animal or fowl (cow, pig, duck, dog, etc.) and that instead of calling another player's name, one calls the traditional sound made by that player's animal, as, "Quack, quack, quack" for a duck.

WAR

Though it can be adapted for three or four players, War is essentially a two-hand game. The pack is evenly divided between the two. Each player keeps his cards in a packet face down in front of himself. The players simultaneously turn up the top cards of their packets. The higher card wins both cards, which are then put face down under the winner's packet. (Ace ranks high, above the king.) Play continues in the same way, each couple of cards being captured by one player or the other.

When the turned cards are of the same rank, the "war" begins. These two cards are set aside for the moment, each covered by one additional card dealt from the player's packet. (The covering card is dealt face down, in adult games, but face up with children play.) Then two more cards are turned and compared; the higher wins all six cards in question. If again the turned cards are equal, they are set aside together with an extra card from each player, and a new turn is made to decide the ownership of ten cards. And so following—the war is protracted until finally settled by the turn of different cards.

The game is won by the player who captures all 52 cards. But this practically never happens, for an ace can be lost only as the chance victim of a war. The practicable rule is that the game is won by the player first to win three wars.

BEGGAR-YOUR-NEIGHBOR

This is a game for two. The pack is divided into approximately equal halves. Each player keeps his packet face down in front of himself. Cards are turned up alternately and placed face up in a common center pile until a face card or ace appears. An ace calls for four cards, a king for three, a queen for two, and a jack for one. The next player must cover the face card or ace with this number of cards, always provided that only lower cards turn up from his stock. If he turns up a face card or ace himself, before finishing the quota to the previous high card, the obligation switches, and the other must play a due quota on the new card.

Whenever the quota of low cards has been duly placed, the player of the high card wins the whole center pile, which is placed face down under his stock. The winner of the pile then leads to start a new pile.

The game is won by the player who takes in all 52 cards. If a player is left with no high card in his stock he is bound to lose, for he cannot replenish his stock and must simply contribute his cards until all are gone. The outcome of the play is of course a matter of pure chance, determined by the original shuffle.

TWENTY-ONE

Though most "scientific" for two or three players, this game is better played by four or more, so as to reduce the number of cards per hand. The pack is dealt, one card at a time, as far as it will go evenly. Any extra cards are laid aside face up and are not used in that deal.

Eldest hand (at left of dealer) begins by playing one card face up to the center, announcing its value, as "Four." All aces and face cards count one each; other cards count their index value. Each hand in rotation must contribute a card to the center, announcing the new total that it makes with the previous cards. For example, if eldest hand starts with a four and the next player contributes a jack, the latter announces "Five."

The total count of cards played must not exceed 21. It is compulsory to play if able, but if unable to contribute another card without going over 21, a player says "Stop." The player at his right then wins all the cards in the center. The one who called stop leads for a new series of plays, beginning the count again from zero. Play continues thus until all the cards are won. The dealer, playing the last card of all, is always sure of winning at least this one card.

It may be agreed that each deal is a game; the player who captures a plurality of the cards wins. But it is better to keep score on paper and credit each with the cards he wins; the first to reach a total of 50 wins a game.

TWENTY-NINE

Four play, in two partnerships, partners sitting opposite each other. The full pack is dealt, thirteen cards to each. Aces and face cards count 1 each, other cards their numerical value. The player at the dealer's left leads a card, announcing its value; each player in turn then plays one card, announcing the new total, until 29 is reached. The player who made the total 29 takes the trick, and the player at his left makes the next lead. There are eight possible tricks, and the object is to win more cards in tricks than the opponents. If at any time a player is unable to play without putting the total over 29, play ends, the cards taken in tricks are counted to determine the winner of that deal, and the deal passes in rotation.

PIG

From a full pack take as many fours-of-a-kind as there are players in the game. (The game is best for four or more players—the more, the merrier.) For example, with five players, form a special pack of twenty cards, five fours-of-a-kind. Any ranks may be chosen, but with very young children avoid face cards, which are easily confused.

Each player receives four cards, dealt one at a time. The play consists in passing cards one at a time to the left, then picking up the card received from the right. Among adults (for Pig is often played as an ice-breaker at adult parties), the customary rule is that every player must put one card face down on the table at his left, and all the cards so placed are picked up simultaneously. The attempt to enforce this rule with children may spoil the game: Better let the players pass cards ad lib and allow every player to exhort his right-hand neighbor to hurry.

The object of the play is to collect four cards of the same rank. The moment he receives the fourth of a kind, the player lays his hand face down on the table and touches his nose with one finger. This act should be as unobtrusive as possible. Every other player, as soon as he notices that another has ceased play, must likewise lay his cards down and touch his nose. The last to do so is the "pig" and loses the deal.

DONKEY

The deal and passing of cards are as in Pig. Before each deal, a number of chips, matches, or other tokens, one less than the number of players in the game, is placed in the center of the table. A player completing four of a kind calls "Donkey" and takes a chip; each other player must then get a chip, and the one player who does not is the donkey.

MY SHIP SAILS

In principle, this game is the same as Pig, but it is designed for older children who can hold seven cards easily. The play of a deal is also more protracted than in Pig.

With three or four players, use twenty-one or twenty-eight cards respectively, comprising any seven cards of each of three or four suits. With five to seven players, use the full pack. In any case, shuffle the pack well and deal it one card at a time, giving each player seven cards.

Every player puts any one card face down at his left; then all players simultaneously pick up the cards at their right. The passing of cards continues until some player collects seven cards of one suit. He then exposes his hand and announces "My ship sails!" The first to make this announcement validly wins the deal.

AUTHORS

The original game Authors was played with special cards bearing the pictures of famous writers; such cards are still widely available. The name has become attached to the same game played with regular cards.

The whole pack is dealt out, one at a time. It does not matter if some players receive one more card than others. (If the number of players is less than six, some of the ranks may be discarded to reduce the size of the hands.)

Each player in rotation requests another to surrender a specified card. The asker must state both the rank and suit, and must have at least one other card of the same rank in his hand at the time, but may not ask for a card he already has.

The request applies only to the one person addressed. If he has the named card, he must surrender it; if not, he says "No." The same player may continue asking for cards so long as he is successful in obtaining them; on first response of "No" the turn passes to the left.

On collecting four cards of the same rank, the player puts them on the table in front of himself as a "book." The player who has the most books, after all fours-of-a-kind are segregated, wins the deal.

Authors is a game of memory; the player must keep track of who asked who for what, of the ranks in which he himself holds cards. Children who find it too difficult to keep track of suits as well as ranks should play Go Fish instead.

When Authors is seriously played, settlement is usually made with chips. Upon putting down a book, a player collects one chip from each other player; but if he does not put down the book when he makes it (before calling for another card) he may not collect for it. For any violation of procedure, a player pays one chip to each other player, and if he has asked out of turn, or has failed to surrender a card duly, he is barred from making a book of that rank.

GO FISH

Each player receives five cards. (In two-hand, some players prefer to start with seven cards.) The rest of the pack is placed face down on the table to form the stock.

Each player in rotation addresses any other and names a rank. The asker must himself hold at least one card of this rank; the preferable way of asking is to expose this card. If the player addressed has any cards of the named rank, he must surrender all of them. A player's turn continues so long as he succeeds in obtaining the cards named. When the one addressed cannot comply, he says "Go Fish!" and the asker must draw the top card of the stock. If it should chance to be of the named rank, he may show it and continue his turn; in any other case, his turn ends.

On getting four cards of the same rank, a player puts them on the table in front of himself as a "book." The player with the most books when the stock is exhausted, and all fours-of-a-kind are segregated, wins the deal.

Note that when a player completes a book by drawing from the stock, having asked for a different rank, his turn does not continue. But the distinction here is sometimes not clear to younger children and seems unfair; if so, the rule may well be reversed and the turn continued in this case too.

SPADE THE GARDENER

This game [taken from Vernon Quinn's *50 Card Games for Children*] is Authors designed for greater hilarity. Twenty cards are used, K, Q, J, 10, A of each suit. The ♤K is Spade the Gardener, the ♤Q, Spade the Gardener's wife, the ♤J, Spade the Gardener's son, the ♤A, Spade the Gardener's servant, the ♤10, Spade the Gardener's dog. (With six or more players, add the nines and eights to the pack, whereupon the ♤9 will be Spade the Gardener's cat, and the ♤8, Spade the Gardener's canary.) Likewise, the ◊K is Sir Hinkam Funniduster, and the other diamonds are respectively his wife, son, servant, dog (cat, canary); the ♡K is Sir Hearty John, and the ♧K is Club the Constable. Each card must be asked for by its name; the ♧10, for example, must be designated as "Club the Constable's dog." A player who asks incorrectly must give one of his own cards to the player asked. The object is to get an entire suit, not four of a kind. It is not necessary to have a card of the suit asked for.

CONCENTRATION

This is a game for two players. (It is often called Memory, or Pelmanism.) The pack is thoroughly shuffled, then spread face down on the table so that every card is detached from every other. If the space available will not accommodate the full pack, reduce it by discarding some fours-of-a-kind.

The first player, chosen by lot, turns any two cards face up. Having turned them up, he removes his hand so that all may see them. If they are a pair (as, two kings) he removes them from the center and puts them in a pile of his own. If they are not a pair, he turns them face down, and his opponent then plays.

The whole game consists in remembering the position of cards previously exposed, so as to capture a pair whenever the second card of a rank is exposed. The player having the majority of cards, after all cards in the center have been taken, wins the game.

An important rule is that cards must not be moved away from their places on the table, in the course of turning them up and down. To shuffle them about interferes with the visual memory of their respective positions.

A more difficult variant, for players with very good memories, is to turn up four cards at a time and capture them only in fours-of-a-kind.

STEALING BUNDLES

This game is simplified Casino, playable by children who have not yet mastered addition. Follow the rules of dealing for Casino (page 255). Cards may be taken in only by pairing, tripling, or quadrupling cards of the same rank—there is no building. Each player must put the cards he wins in a pile face up, and his pile is subject to capture by his opponent —by pairing the top card with a card from the hand. The deal is won by the player having the majority of cards after the stock is exhausted. Cards left on the table belong to the player who was last to take in.

GO BOOM

Each player receives seven cards. (This number may be reduced to five for small children, in which case the pack should be reduced by discarding all the face cards.) The rest of the pack is placed face down on the table to form the stock.

Eldest hand (at left of the dealer) makes an opening lead. Each other hand in rotation must play a card of the same suit or the same rank. If unable to comply, the player must draw up to three cards from the top of the stock. If unable to play after drawing the third card, the player passes, and the turn goes to the left. Whatever cards have been played to the lead, after the player at the right of the leader has had his turn, constitute the trick. A trick is won by the highest card of the suit led. The winner of a trick leads to the next.

The tricks, of no value in themselves, may be tossed in a common pile in the center of the table. The object of play is to get rid of all the cards in the hand, and the first to do so wins the deal.

The method of scoring should be suited to the age group. For the youngest, each deal is a separate game. For an older group, the winner of a deal is credited with one point for each card left in the losers' hands, and the player first to reach 50 wins a game. For a still older group, the cards left in a loser's hand may be charged against him at their index values, with aces one and face cards ten. The player who has the lowest cumulative score when another reaches 100 wins a game.

I DOUBT IT

With five or fewer players, one pack may be used. With six or more, two full packs should be shuffled together. The two-pack game is better, and the more players, up to about nine, the better. Since a player may at times have thirty cards or more, the game is scarcely playable by children younger than nine or ten. It is most popular among teen-agers; the necessity for bluffing makes for both hilarity and the exercise of real skill.

The whole pack is dealt out. It does not matter if some players have one card more than others. To save time, the cards may be dealt in batches of two or three or more.

Eldest hand (at left of the dealer) begins the play, by placing a number of cards in a packet face down in the center of the table, and announcing the number of cards and their rank, for example, "Two aces." The number of cards in the packet must be stated correctly: often the cards are played in fans, so that all may verify the number. The rank announced is fixed by rotation: eldest hand must begin with aces, the next player must announce twos, the next player threes, and so on in ascending rank. After kings have been played, the next player must announce aces again, and so on continuously. Each must play to the center in turn, playing at least one card, and any number more up to four (with one pack) or eight (with two packs).

But the cards played need not be of the announced rank. In fact, a player must often falsify on this point, for he must play in turn and announce the next rank in rotation, even when he has no cards of that rank.

After each play, any player at the table may cry "I doubt it!" The first to call has precedence. If the last player has put into his packet any card not of the announced rank, he must then pick up the whole of the center pile and add it to his hand. But if his packet was strictly in accord with his announcement, as three jacks when he announced three jacks, the doubter must take the center pile.

The interruptions due to calls of "I doubt it!" do not affect the rotation of rank and of the turn to play.

The player first to get rid of all his cards wins the deal.

Experience shows that a player can often gain by doubting repeatedly during the early play, in order to get desired ranks into his hand. On this account, some limitation on doubting is necessary in sharp company. The usual rule is that the right to doubt passes in rotation to left of the player; some circles enforce the rule that only the player at the left may doubt. As a usual concomitant of any such limitation, successive packets played are laid crosswise so as to remain segregated; when a player is doubted and has actually "cheated," he must expose the actual cards he played before taking them back with the rest of the center pile. Thus the "cheater" is compelled to give some slight information about his hand.

FROGPOND

Two to six may play, using the 52-card pack with such deletions as will provide an equal number of cards for each player plus one hand. (With two, delete one deuce; with four, delete two deuces; with five, delete all four deuces; with six, delete three deuces.) Four may play in two partnerships.

The cards are dealt one at a time to each player and the extra hand.

The object is to win counting cards in tricks, counting 10 for each ten, 5 for each five, 4 for each ace, 3 for each king, 2 for each queen and 1 for each jack. Eldest hand leads first, and each player in turn must follow suit if able; if unable, he may play any card. Each trick is won by the highest card of the suit led, the cards ranking A (high), K, Q, J, 10, 9, 8, 7, 6, 5, 4, 3, 2. The winner of a trick leads to the next. The winner of each trick also draws the top card of the extra hand ("the frogpond"), looks at it, and adds it to his tricks. Game is won by the first player to reach 100 points.

The *tadpole* is an optional feature: The ♠J is the tadpole and counts minus 10 points for the player (or side) taking it.

YUKON

This is a simplified Schafkopf derivative; its name comes from its reputation of having been played by the Klondike miners.

Four play, using the 52-card pack; or three play, deleting the ♠2 from the pack. Four may play in two partnerships. Five cards are dealt to each player, and the remaining cards form a stock from which each player draws a card after each trick, the winner drawing first; when the stock is exhausted, the remaining cards are played out.

The ♠J (Grand Yukon) is the highest-ranking card in the pack; then come the other three jacks (Yukons), which have no relative rank. Other cards rank A, K, Q, 10, 9, 8, 7, 6, 5, 4, 3, 2 in each suit.

Eldest hand always leads first; each player in turn after him must follow suit if he can. If he cannot follow suit, he must play a jack if he has one; and if he has none, he may play any card. A trick containing the ♠J is won by that card; a trick containing any other jack is won by the jack, and if it contains two or more jacks of equal rank, the one played first wins. When a jack is led, it calls for its suit. The winner of a trick leads to the next.

The object is to win counting cards in tricks. Grand Yukon counts 15, other jacks and all tens count 10 each, aces count 5 each, kings 3 each, queens 2 each. The first player (or side) to reach 250 wins the game.

⤙ WORD GAMES ⤚

There are many games based on the formation of words from such letters as are made available by the rules of the particular game. In nearly every such game the following rules apply: Every word formed must be listed in a dictionary selected as the final authority for the game; no proper noun or proper adjective is valid; each word must be of at least four letters, and may not be formed by the addition of "s" to a three-letter root.

Useful equipment for word games of the studious type is a set of Anagram cards or tiles. Each card bears a printed letter, and the set provides the various letters in quantities roughly proportional to the frequency of their use in English. (But there is usually a deliberate excess of lower-frequency letters.) Such cards are useful for Scrambled Words (page 503) and kindred games, and are indispensable for the prime favorite called Anagrams.

ANAGRAMS

Any number may play, up to about eight. With four or more players, there should be from 200 to 400 cards or tiles. They are first shuffled thoroughly by cooperation of several players. Cards are then stacked in one pile face down in the center; tiles are spread over the table with a space cleared in the center. Anagrams is popular in several different forms.

Anagram Tiles   Anagram Cards

Game 1. Each player in turn draws the top card of the stock or any tile at random and puts it face up in the center. After the game is well-started, time must be allowed after every new letter is exposed; a one-minute allowance makes a slow game, preferred by some players, while others prefer a "rapid transit" game with a fifteen-second allowance. The

496

object is first of all to form words out of the letters available in the center. Whoever sees the letters necessary for a word he has in mind utters the word, then withdraws the letters from the center and builds the word in front of himself. The player first to make five or ten words, as agreed, wins the game.

Words must be good English and at least four letters long. The host should keep a dictionary at hand for the settlement of arguments as to the validity of words.

The words in front of a player are subject to capture by the other players. The condition for capture is that the word must be lengthened, by the addition of one or more letters from the center. For example, if a player has made GEAR, another may call RANGE if an N is available in the center; RANGE in turn may be taken with a D to make GARDEN, then with an E to make GRANDEE, then with an L to make ENLARGED, and so on. Some essential change in form and meaning must be made, to validate a capture; adding S to make a plural or D to change the tense of a verb is not sufficient. The owner of a word is usually allowed to make such additions, however, in order to increase the difficulty of capturing it.

If two or more players speak at the same time in claim of letters on the table, or to capture the same word, the longest new word claimed has precedence. As between words of equal length, the first to speak has precedence, and the host must decide which player spoke first.

If a player utters a word that cannot in fact be made out of the available letters (including any word he intended to capture), his claim is void and he must return to the stock the last word he obtained. (Some players charge a debt of "one word owed" when a player with no words in front of him makes such a mistake. In other circles, the penalty is waived.)

Any player may challenge the validity of a word claimed by another. The host or the dictionary must decide. If the challenge is supported, the challenged player loses not only the claim but also the last previous word he obtained; if the challenger is overruled, the challenger must return his last word to the stock.

Game 2. Each player in turn, when he draws the new letter, has sole right to make or capture a word. If he uses the letter newly-turned in either of these ways, or adds it to one of his own words, he draws another letter and his turn continues. If he cannot, his turn ends, even though in the same turn he has made or captured a word with letters available in the center. Any player may challenge a new word; the first to challenge has precedence, and if two challenge simultaneously the one nearer the player's left has precedence. A justified challenge costs the player his next turn; an unjustified challenge costs the challenger his next turn. If a player draws and exposes more than one letter at a time, he must play only with the one first exposed, but the other is available to players after him.

Game 3. Each player draws twenty letters. Time is kept; at a signal from the timekeeper each player may turn up his letters, and after five minutes the player who has used the most letters in word construction is the winner. If two players used the same number of letters the one with more words wins; if they tie in number of words, the one with the longest word wins. Some allow a player to draw additional tiles at will; then from the number of letters he uses in word-construction is deducted the number of additional letters he drew, to determine his net score.

GHOSTS

Any number may play. Each player in turn names a letter, and the letters are visualized as written in order as named. From the fourth letter on, the player must avoid completing any English word, but must be prepared on demand to give a word containing the letters already named. For example, if the first three letters are CAR, the fourth player must avoid calling E or T, thereby completing CARE or CART. He may call O, having in mind CAROM. The fifth player, faced with CARO, calls T having in mind CAROTID. The sixth calls I, and the seventh is stuck, for to avoid making CAROTIN or CAROTID he must call a letter other than T or N, but then he cannot supply a word containing the sequence.

Any player in his turn may, instead of calling a letter, challenge the last previous player. If the latter cannot supply a suitable word containing the letters in the order named, he loses a "life"; but if he does give a correct word, the challenger loses a life. A player also loses a life if he completes a word. Whoever loses a life becomes "a third of a ghost"; on losing a second life, he is "two-thirds of a ghost"; loss of the third life makes him a full ghost. Ghosts no longer participate in the calling of letters; in children's play, they may talk freely to each other and to the active players, and an active player who makes the mistake of speaking to a ghost becomes a ghost himself. The last survivor wins the game.

TWO-WAY GHOSTS

This is Ghosts with the added rule that a player may add his letter either after or before the sequence that comes up to him. For example, if he has to add to PROBABL—which would cost him a life in one-way Ghosts—he can escape by prefixing M, having in mind IMPROBABLE.

WORD CHAIN

This is also called Word Dominoes. The first player states a name—of a bird, river, city, or whatever category he selects and announces. The player to his left must give a name beginning with the terminal letter of the preceding name, and so on in rotation. For example, the first might name a thrush, the second a hawk, the third a kiwi, the fourth an ibis, and so on. A player who cannot supply a name is out of the game, provided the player who follows him can do so, or (if no player following him can) the player who gave the preceding name can. If this player cannot, he must substitute another word for his previous one. The survivor wins.

HANGMAN

This is essentially a game for two, but it may be arranged for more players. One player thinks of a word, having an agreed minimum number of letters. He represents it on paper by a series of dashes. For example, if he selects BLACK, he writes — — — — —. The other player tries to guess the word, by naming letters of the alphabet. Whenever he hits a right letter, the opponent writes it in the appropriate position. Suppose that the first guess is "E"; the answer is no. The second guess is "A", and the opponent writes

A
— — — — —

The game takes its name from the way of counting the wrong guesses. A gibbet is drawn, and on the first wrong guess the head of a man is added; the second wrong guess gives him a neck; the third a body; and so on to arms and legs one by one. If the man is completed before the guesser has recovered the whole word, he is "hung" and loses the round.

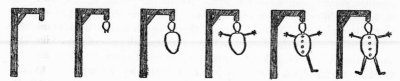

Stages in the process of being "hanged." One part of the man—head, body, etc.—is added for each wrong guess. From six to a dozen wrong guesses may be allowed, according to preference of the players.

Practice differs in the number of wrong guesses allowed. The most prevalent number is eight; some allow only six, and others, especially in playing with children, allow twelve. The man on the gibbet is planned accordingly.

The choice of words naturally falls upon those of uncommon form or containing rare letters. The usual rule is that all repetitions of the same letter (as the P in POLYP) must be written in when this letter is guessed; then only letters without repetitions are chosen. But some players agree to enter only one letter for a correct guess, and the trick is then to choose words with few different letters but many repetitions.

To play Hangman as a round game with three or more players, supply each with paper and pencil. The leader thinks of a word and announces its length. The others all write the appropriate number of dashes on their papers, while the leader draws a gibbet. The players then guess letters in turn, operating as a team against the leader, who keeps track of the misses on his gibbet. The team wins or is hung as a unit. Teammates must not consult, but each may preface his call of a letter with one guess as to the complete word. For example, if the team has guessed the A and L of BLACK, the members in turn may guess BLAND, CLAWS, SLACK, etc. Such tries for the whole word are not counted toward hanging the team, and it therefore becomes the duty of every member to make a guess each turn, even before any letters at all have been placed.

VOCABULARY

Any number may play. Each player is provided with paper and pencil. The host holds a watch with a second hand. He names a letter and simultaneously commences keeping time. Every player must then write as many words as he can think of beginning with that letter. At the end of one minute the host calls time and all writing must stop. The player having the greatest number of words wins the round. Lists should be read aloud, for the elimination of inadmissible words.

Some players may do badly because they are slow writers. To eliminate this defect, allow the words to be spoken instead of written. The host assigns a letter to the first player, and counts the number of words this player supplies in one minute. He then assigns a different letter to another player, and so on by turns around the circle. Each player has to have a different letter, else the later players could repeat lists given by earlier players. The host should therefore write out in advance the letters to be assigned, selected to be of the same degree of difficulty. The rare letters, X, Z, Q, J, K, are usually excluded, though they can well be used as tie-breakers. Next-infrequent as initial letters are N, Y, V, E, perhaps O. Easier are U, H, W, I. All the rest are equally easy: A, B, C, D, F, G, L, M, P, R, S, T.

CATEGORIES

This game is also called Guggenheim. Any number may play. Each participant is provided with paper and pencil. Each in turn may name one category, such as animals, authors, countries, cities, games, etc. Every player lists all the selected categories in a column on his paper. Next a word is selected by agreement, one having no repeated letters, usually no uncommon letters, and not too long. Each player writes the letters of this word at the head of columns to the right of his category list. At a signal to start, each player tries to fill in every space with an acceptable name—a specific item that belongs to the category on the row and has the initial letter assigned to that column. For example, if the selected word is BARON, a completed paper might look like this:

	B	A	R	O	N
Animal	bison	armadillo	rat	ostrich	nyala
Author	Bacon	Alcott	Rabelais	Ouida	Norris
Country	Bolivia	Austria	Romania	Orange Free State	Netherlands
City	Boston	Austin	Richmond	Omaha	Newark
Game	bezique	authors	rummy	oklahoma	nap

A time limit is set, say fifteen minutes. Every player must stop writing at the call of time. The entries in each category are compared and scored. The maximum score, one point less than the number of players, goes to a word that the player was alone in writing. For example, with four players, if no one else wrote "bison" the player scores 3 for this word. For each additional player who wrote the same word, one point is deducted from the maximum score, so that if two players chose "armadillo" each scores 2, or if all four players wrote "rat," the word scores nothing. For each space in which he wrote no word at all, the player must subtract one point (some players prefer to score a blank as zero, without deduction). The player with highest total score wins the round.

The categories should be broad enough to offer a good selection of names for all the common letters of the alphabet, but should not be too broad. For example, "animals" should be restricted in some way, say to mammals; "cities" should be restricted, say to American cities of a minimum size, or state capitals, or capitals of countries; "games" should be restricted to card games, or indoor games, or athletic games. The meaning of the category often calls for definition; for example, "countries" is usually intended to mean sovereign states, not regions such as Bohemia.

The player proposing a category should define his intention as to its restrictions. His category should be subject to veto by majority vote or by a single blackball, according to the temper of the company. A player's natural choice is a category of which he has superior knowledge; but it spoils the fun if a player is allowed to name some obscure category of which he alone has knowledge, such as "minor French poets of the seventeenth century."

Certain rules should be decided arbitrarily by the host and announced in advance. These rules should at the minimum decide whether compound names (as Orange Free State) are admissible; which initial governs in case of compound words and proper names; whether the foreign or the American spelling of geographic names is to be followed. Many players prefer to give less credit for a compound name where a single word is available (giving full credit, e. g., to Newark, but one point less to New York). If a player enters a word that is not admissible under the advance rules, or which fits the category poorly, his entry may be rejected by majority or unanimous vote of the other players. The host, however, should intervene and make all such decisions himself if he finds that majority voting is impracticable or engenders ill feeling.

WORD SQUARES

Any number may play. Each participant is provided with paper and pencil. Each draws a square box divided into 25 cells. Then each player in turn names any letter of the alphabet he chooses, and all players write the letters in cells of their boxes. Each may choose to put a letter in any empty cell. Once placed, a letter may not be moved elsewhere, and all players must write the last-named letter before the next is called. The object is to make as many good English words as possible, on the five rows and five columns of the box. Letter-calling continues in rotation until 25 letters have been called. Then each player in turn reads off his words, for approval, and scores his approved words.

Only one word may be counted on each line of the box. Thus CAPES scores as a five-letter word; it does not score in addition for CAPE, APES, CAP, APE.

The recommended scoring is 10 points for a word of five letters, 5 for a word of four letters, 2 for a word of three letters, nothing for shorter words. The player with the highest total score wins the round.

Approval of the words is the duty of the host. He should state in advance what kinds of words are admissible, e. g., any in the dictionary, or any in the dictionary not marked foreign, etc.

BATTLESHIPS

This game is also called Salvo. It is played by two, each equipped with pencil and quadrille paper. To prepare for the game, each outlines two squares of 100 cells. One is labelled "My Zone" and the other "Opponent's Zone." For reference, the rows and columns of each field are marked with numbers 1 to 10 and letters A to J.

Out of sight of his opponent, each player disposes his "fleet" as he chooses in "My Zone." The fleet comprises four "ships"; a "battleship" of four cells (some players prefer five); a "cruiser" of three cells; two "destroyers" of two cells each. Each ship is marked by outlining or blacking in the appropriate number of cells, adjacent along a row, column, or diagonal. The usual rule is that no two ships may touch each other.

The player chosen by lot to play first fires a "salvo" of seven shots into "Opponent's Zone." He writes the figure 1 (for first salvo) in any seven cells of this zone that he chooses. He names the cells (by row-number and column-letter), and the opponent writes figure 1 in the corresponding cells of his square "My Zone." The salvo ended, the opponent states whether any of his ships have been hit, and if so, what type of ship and the number of hits. But he does not state which of the shots were hits.

The second player now takes his turn, and similarly fires seven shots as his salvo number 1. Play continues by alternate turns, the salvos being numbered from 1 up. The object is to sink the entire enemy fleet, by hitting every cell of every ship. The first to succeed wins the game. For each of his ships that is sunk, a player suffers a reduction of the number of shots he may fire in all subsequent salvos; the battleship costs three shots, the cruiser two, and each destroyer one.

Clues are gained as to the location of enemy ships by the salvo-numbers of the shots that hit them. For example, if a player knows that he hit the enemy battleship on his salvos 1 and 3, he looks in "Opponent's Zone" for places where a 1 and a 3 stand on a line within a space of four (or five) cells, the other two cells being empty. To keep track of the hits, he writes the salvo numbers into "ghost ships" outlined on his paper to represent the enemy fleet.

SCRAMBLED WORDS

Anagram games are perennial favorites. There are many variants on the idea of rearranging jumbles of letters to form words. Three typical games are described below.

Any number may play. Each participant is provided with paper and pencil.

Game 1. Each player selects five words; he may be free to choose any words, but a better plan is for the host to name a subject or category to which all the words must relate. Examples are flowers, geographical features, occupations and professions, descriptive adjectives, etc. The player jumbles the letters of each word as he pleases and writes down the jumbles. When all papers have been completed, they are passed to the left, and each player must then recover the words scrambled by the player at his right. The first to finish wins the round. Or, better, each player writes the answers on separate paper which he keeps; the lists of scrambled words are passed around the circle until everyone has solved all the scrambles. The lists must be left face up on the table, so that a player who finishes a list ahead of his right-hand neighbor can start on the next list immediately.

Game 2. Each player chooses and scrambles one word. It must relate to a category named by the host or chosen by agreement, and it must contain a minimum of letters (usually eight). The scrambling must produce two or more words or pronounceable groups. For example, IMPERTURBABLE may be scrambled as E RUMPLE RABBIT. The object in making other words, so far as practicable, is to facilitate communicating the scrambles. After all the scrambles are prepared, they are read off in turn and every player writes down the scrambles prepared by the others. Then all try to solve the scrambles, and the first to complete the list wins the round. A prize may be given for the scramble judged to be the most amusing or most appropriate.

Game 3. The foregoing game may be played with emphasis on making real anagrams instead of mere scrambles. By a "real anagram" is meant the scrambling of a word into other words that give some clue to the sense of the original. For example, GLINT WINK makes TWINKLING: OPERA OF TIN makes PIANOFORTE. No category should be specified; the players are free to choose words of any kind whatsoever. One or more prizes should be given by majority vote for the most apt anagrams.

LITTLE WORDS

The full title of this game is Little Words from Big Words. To many it is simply the Word Game.

Any number may play. Though each participant may play alone, a better plan is to form two or three teams. Each team is provided with a pad of paper and several pencils. A word is chosen by agreement, or read off by the host from a prepared list. Each team then tries to write down as many words as possible that can be made out of the letters of this word. A time limit is fixed, say fifteen minutes, at the end of which all writing must stop. The lists are then compared, and the team with the longest list wins the round.

The usual rules are that each word must be at least four letters long, must be good English; plurals of three-letter words made by adding "s" are barred; only one form of a word (as, one tense of a verb) may be used; proper names are barred. Unless the Big Word is very short, the four-letter minimum allows so many words to be formed that the principal consideration is speed in writing them down. Inveterate players therefore prefer a five-letter minimum, with a Big Word not too long, so that the imagination plays a part in the game.

Best for Big Words are those eight to twelve letters in length, with at least three different vowels, and not too many repeated letters. For example, (four-letter minimum) CONTUMELY, IMPORTANCE, ARCHITECTURE; (five-letter minimum) FACETIOUS, ORCHESTRATE, OPERATION. Some groups like to choose very opulent words; in a game where five letters was the minimum and the word was CONSEQUENTIAL, the winning list comprised 97 words, and with unlimited time the number was increased to about 600. Other groups prefer short difficult words; for example, BELONGING with a four-letter minimum, ekes out perhaps 35 words in unlimited time.

Team play is better than individual play because it solves the problem of writing down words fast enough. The letters of the word are partitioned among the members of the team, and each writes only the words beginning with his assigned letters. He is responsible also for thinking of the easy words on his list, but is expected to contribute to other lists as he thinks of the words. The teams should work in different rooms so that they can talk freely without contributing to their opponents.

WHO AM I?

Almost uniquely among party games, Who Am I? is best played while the guests are walking about and conversing in groups. It is thus an ideal "ice-breaker."

The host prepares a number of large cards by printing on each the name of some well-known person. The names may be famous authors, statesmen, musicians, etc. of the past, or contemporary celebrities. The important point is to choose persons of whom every guest can reasonably be assumed to have a smattering of knowledge.

As each guest arrives, the host pins one of the cards on his back. None must be allowed to see the card on his own back. He must try to discover "who he is" by questioning other guests. The guests trade questions—each time one asks a question, he must answer one. Any question is allowable if it can be answered with "yes" or "no" or "I don't know," and no one may answer a question in any other way.

A prize is often given to the first gentleman and first lady that guess correctly who they are.

COFFEEPOT

One person chosen to be the Guesser goes out of the room, while the rest of the company agrees on some verb expressing human action, such as dance, sing, walk, fight, etc. The Guesser is recalled and must try to guess the verb by putting questions to each other player in turn. In place of the unknown verb he says "coffeepot," as "Do I coffeepot?" . . . "Is coffeepotting done outdoors?" Every question must be answered truthfully with "yes" or "no" or "I don't know." The Guesser may at any time try for the word directly, as by asking "Is it walking?" When he finally guesses correctly, the player to whom he addressed the last previous question becomes the next Guesser.

TWENTY QUESTIONS

The person chosen to be Guesser is sent from the room, and the others agree on some word, phrase, or sentence. The Guesser is recalled, and allowed to ask no more than twenty questions, which must be answered truthfully by the persons addressed. If he succeeds in guessing the word within twenty questions, the Guesser joins the company and a new Guesser is chosen.

Experienced players often agree to place no restriction whatsoever on what word, etc. may be chosen. Easiest to guess are of course concrete things and events, as London Bridge, the President of the United States, the Blizzard of '88. Somewhat more difficult are adjectives and qualities, as purple, verbose, courage. Often difficult are literary quotations, fictional characters and qualities, general or vague terms, as "the quality of mercy;" Jack Sprat's wife, facism. In some circles, the choice is limited to concrete entities, excluding events, qualities, etc.; in other circles, only persons may be chosen.

Practice also differs in the latitude allowed in answering questions. The Guesser is supposed to ask only questions that can be answered "yes" or "no." But some of his questions are bound to be inapplicable. For example, the time-honored formula is to begin by asking "Is it animal?" "Is it vegetable?" "Is it mineral?" Even if choice is limited to concrete objects, all three questions may be inapplicable, e. g., "the frigate Constitution." In severest circles, an inapplicable question must be answered "no"; elsewhere, it is allowable to reply "not applicable" or "partly."

Twenty Questions is often played as a team game, the members of the guessing team, without consultation, asking questions in turn.

HIDDEN PROVERBS

The Guesser being out of the room, the company agress on a proverb. The Guesser is recalled and told the number of words in the proverb. He must then try to guess it by asking an equal number of questions, each addressed to a different person. The questions may be on any subject whatsoever. The only stipulation is that the answer of the first person must contain the first word of the proverb, the answer of the second person must contain the second, and so on. If the Guesser guesses the proverb, the last person he addressed becomes the next Guesser.

The burden of ingenuity falls on the company rather than on the Guesser. Suppose that the proverb chosen is "A cat may look at a king." The second person, having to include "cat" in answer to some such question as "What did you do today?" may reply weakly "I took my cat for a walk." The Guesser may hit on "A cat . . ." at once. His task is more difficult if the answer is longer and sprinkled with red herrings, as, "I put salt in my coffee, sugar on my eggs; I wound the cat and put out the clock."

MURDER

The host announces that the lights will presently be turned off for one minute. During that time a mock murder will be committed. Everyone is expected to keep his wits about him and note what goes on in the dark, so far as he can, since he will be questioned about it later. The host has previously informed one guest that he is to be the Murderer and another that he is to be the Victim. When the lights go out, the Murderer must approach the Victim and touch him, whereupon the Victim must lie on the floor or sit in a chair and remain there when the lights go up. Sometimes it is required that the Murderer leave a token on the Victim, such as a red handkerchief provided by the host.

After the lights go up, the Victim is pointed out (if not sufficiently obvious), and he takes no further part in the game. The host appoints a District Attorney, who must try to discover the identity of the Murderer. He may ask questions of every other person (except the Victim), and everyone must answer him truthfully except the Murderer. The Murderer may tell the truth or lie as he pleases.

The District Attorney may ask any reasonable question as to what persons were doing, where they stood, what they heard, etc. But he may not ask "Are you the Murderer?" or any such question that cannot be answered truthfully without pointing out the Murderer by elimination. When he believes he has discovered the identity of the Murderer, the District Attorney must charge him directly, "You are the Murderer." If he is right, the Murderer becomes the new District Attorney; if he is wrong, a new murder may be staged with the same or different characters, or the original inquiry may be continued until the Murderer is finally caught. In some circles, the District Attorney is allowed to ask "Are you the Murderer?" and even the Murderer must answer truthfully, but this question may not be asked more than three times. If the true Murderer is not found in three guesses, the District Attorney is impeached and retired.

A version played when the company can wander through several rooms is: the lights are not turned out, but the Murderer and Victim must conspire to get out of sight of the rest of the company for a moment. The Murderer hands over a token and makes his escape, while the Victim lies down with the token in sight and remains until discovered by a witness.

OBSERVATION

The host loads twenty or more small assorted articles on a tray or table. They may include cigarette, pencil, thimble, coin, stamp, key, etc. All the guests are allowed to view this assortment for one minute. The exhibit is then removed, each guest is provided with paper and pencil, and each writes down as many of the articles as he can remember. The one with the longest accurate list wins the round. For every article named in error, not actually in the exhibit, a point is deducted.

A variation is to put only about a dozen articles in the exhibit, but to choose more elaborate items and require some description of each, rather than mere identification.

TESTIMONY

This is a game of observation sprung as a surprise on the guests. The host arranges with one or more confederates to create some kind of scene where all the guests can witness it. The simplest plan is to garb the confederate in some outlandish costume, equip him with all sorts of impedimenta, and have him walk about the room for one minute. Another idea is to stage a sham fight or altercation, with all the words to be uttered carefully written and memorized in advance. Whatever the incident, it should be sufficiently extraordinary to compel the attention of everyone, and it should last not more than about one minute.

The host immediately explains to the company that it was a "put-up job." He requests that every witness write a report of what the intruder wore, or what was said during the altercation, etc. The testimony requested should concern matters that have been planned completely in advance and on which the host has a complete and accurate record. The guests are provided with paper and pencil and given, say, fifteen minutes, to write their reports. Then all the reports are read aloud, and there is often amusing discrepancy among them on essential facts. A prize may be given for the most accurate report.

When the incident is a fight or the like, calculated to excite the guests and so impair their observation, the reports may be given orally. The host acts as a "judge," appoints counsel, and "tries" one of the actors, calling each of the guests in turn to the witness chair.

TREASURE HUNT

The host prepares and secretes a series of written clues that lead in a chain to the hiding place of a prize. A copy of the first clue of the chain is given to each guest, or better, to each pair of guests. Each player or team must try to discover the meaning of each clue in turn and so follow the chain until he reaches the prize, which belongs to the finder.

Each clue, written on a small slip of paper that can be easily secreted, should give veiled hints as to the hiding place of the next clue, without naming it outright. For example, a clue hidden in a piano may be indicated by "Hunt for a note" or "I'm riding the high seas." An alternative especially delightful to children—who dote upon Treasure Hunt—is to make the clues pictorial, simple drawings of the places or objects in which the next clues are hidden.

After reading a clue that he has unearthed, a player must return it to its hiding place so as to make it available to other players. The clues should be scattered over as many rooms or as large an area as possible, so as to give each player a chance to discover the clues without aiding his competitors.

HIDDEN TREASURES

The host secretes a dozen or more different small articles in one or two rooms. A list of the articles is handed to each guest, and the first to discover all of them wins the game. On finding an article, the player must not remove it from its hiding place, but merely note where it is.

Each article should be hidden in a foreign environment. For example, a needle may be put in an ashtray. To put it in a sewing kit would be unfair, because the player would have no way of knowing whether he had found the intended needle. For the same reason, every article should be such that it is probably the only one in the room. For example, to hide a cigarette in a roomful of people is meaningless, for the searcher is bound to find scores of cigarettes. But common articles will serve if they are individualized in some way. For example, if the list includes "an unsmoked cigarette with a lipstick mark at the middle" there is little chance of ambiguity.

The player claiming the prize must satisfy the host that he has actually discovered all the right articles. A verbal report will do, if the player can remember all the hiding places. (The host should of course have a written memorandum for comparison.) The players should be warned in advance that if they do not wish to rely on their memories they must write down the hiding places. But then they must be warned too not to start writing the moment they discover one of the hidden treasures, for then they will direct their competitors to the same spot.

SCAVENGER HUNT

The guests are paired in teams, either by the host or by their own initiative. The host hands each team an identical copy of a list of items. The teams fare forth in search of these items, and the first team to come back with a specimen of every item on the list wins a prize.

The style of Scavenger Hunt that ranges over a whole township and includes such items as "a policeman's hat," "a red ostrich plume," "a Diesel engine" has been widely publicized. But Scavenger Hunts may be conducted on a more modest scale. The indoor Scavenger Hunt is an excellent "ice-breaker." The host should designate in advance the rooms that may be entered in the hunt—and include as many rooms as possible. The items on the list may be articles that are already there in sufficient numbers for all the teams, as "a paper clip," "a stub pen point," "a red-covered book." Or, the host may conceal special articles for the purpose of the Scavenger Hunt, in the style of a Treasure Hunt.

CHARADES

Divide the players into two teams. The teams alternate as Actors and Audience. The Actors withdraw to another room, where they select any word of three or more syllables and plan a pantomime whereby each syllable is to be acted out. For example, if the word is ROMANTIC it may be divided as ROW-MAN-TICK. Then the Actors return and act out the scenes of the pantomime, the last of which conveys the whole word. The Audience must try to guess the word, and is timed from the end of the last scene. The team that averages the best time in guessing words as Audience wins.

The syllable or word to be conveyed should be the focal point of the pantomime. It is always possible to baffle the Audience by introducing the idea in a minor role. For example, ROW might be acted out by an elaborate scene, at one juncture of which the courtiers stand in a row before the king. But such a device is foreign to the spirit of the game, which is to pantomime so well that the Audience cannot miss the idea. A proper plan for ROW would be to pantomime a rowing race.

Since all the fun is in the acting, some part should be provided for every member of the team in every scene. In order to do this, it is not unfair to introduce byplay, sub-plots, and so on.

A variation is to allow spoken dialogue to the scenes, with the requirement that the syllable or word be uttered by one of the Actors at some time.

"THE GAME"

This is a modern version of Charades that has become one of the most popular of all party games. The players are divided into two equal teams that alternate as Actors and Audience. Each member of the Audience writes a phrase or sentence on a piece of paper. Their Captain allots one slip to each Actor, who must not show the slip he receives to any other Actor. A few minutes are allowed for planning; then each Actor in turn must try to convey by pantomime to his fellow Actors the exact words on his slip.

The Actor may divide the sentence as he wishes, acting out each word, or each syllable, or the whole sentence at once.

The Captain of the Audience keeps time on each Actor, from the moment he begins his pantomime until the other Actors guess his message word for word. The team that, as Actors, takes the lowest total time to guess all the sentences wins the game.

The variations in the game found all over the country begin with the sentences. In some circles, these must be well-known in history, fable, or literature. For example, "Don't give up the ship!" would be allowed but not "What time is it?" Elsewhere a single word or short phrase must be chosen, not a sentence, and it must be well-known as an allusion or a cliché. Allowable are "Fifty-four forty or fight," "The bee's knees," "View with alarm," but not "A white chrysanthemum." Some players allow any word, phrase, or sentence whatsoever.

Though it is universal to require the Actor to remain mute, practice differs as to how far he can use prearranged signals. Some of the most prevalent signals are:

Several fingers held up: number of words in the phrase, and number of syllables in a word; also, ordinal number of word or syllable that the Actor will next pantomime.

Two fingers held up, then gesture of closing fist: next two words or syllables will be combined.

Arms clasped over chest in self-embrace: whole phrase will be acted out.

Beckoning: "You are warm!"—continue the same line of guessing.

Pushing away: "Cold"—you are on the wrong track.

Finger to nose: that is the word or syllable exactly.

Twisting motion: guess another form of the same word.

Gesture or rapid counting with index finger: make it plural.

Looking over shoulder: make it past tense.

Hand shading eyes to peer ahead: make it future tense.

Chopping motion: I will cut the word into syllables.

The general practice is to bar the use of any props. A variation is to allow the Actor to use any prop he finds in the room. Usually the Actor is permitted to point to other persons in the room for some significant purpose; as pointing in rapid succession to several women to signify the word "women" or "ladies" or "skirts" or whatever.

At the minimum, the Actor is allowed to indicate "hot" and "cold" and to show that the team has guessed the exact word or syllable. Useful in this connection is to point to the member of the guessing team that is closest to the idea.

Members of the guessing team must help out their fellow Actor as much as possible by speaking aloud all the ideas that his pantomime suggests. They should also state their understanding of each signal he gives, in order that he may confirm or deny it without loss of time. Victory depends as much on imaginative guessing as on clever pantomime.

UP JENKINS

The players are divided into two teams, and the teams are seated on opposite sides of a long table. (The number per team is limited by the length of the table. The top of the table should be wood, and may or may not be veneered; play is too hazardous on a glass or finely polished top.) Each team chooses a Captain. A coin (best is a large coin, like a fifty-cent piece) is given in custody of one team, which will be designated as Team A.

The members of Team A pass the coin from hand to hand below the level of the table, trying to deceive Team B as to its location. To this end, all hands are kept in motion, even though the coin be far away. After an interval, Captain A announces that the team is ready. Captain B then calls "Jenkins says, hands up!" Every member of Team A must then put his elbows on the table, with forearms vertical and fists closed.

Captain B may now direct a series of movements that Team A must execute, as follows:

Umbrellas. The tips of all fingers and thumb must be placed on the table, with fingers separated and elbow high.

Dance. With hand and arm in umbrella position, the fingers must be wiggled.

Down with a slam. All hands slammed down with palms flat on the table.

Down slowly. Palms brought flat to the table from the umbrella position.

Team B must try to spot which hand of Team A holds the coin. If Team B succeeds, it obtains possession of the coin; if it fails, Team A retains the coin.

Members of Team B may advise their Captain, but Team A responds only to orders of Captain B. Furthermore, any order given that is not prefaced by "Jenkins says" is void. If any member of Team A responds to an invalid order—made without "Jenkins says" or uttered by anyone but Captain B—the coin must be surrendered to Team B.

In trying to spot the coin, Captain B may proceed by elimination. He may say "Jenkins says, all left hands away!" or to a specific A player "Jenkins says, your right hand up!" All such orders are construed to mean that he thinks the coin is not there; if he is wrong, Team A keeps the coin. Or, Captain B may say where he thinks the coin is, as "Jenkins says, the coin is there!" pointing to a hand. If he is right, Team B obtains possession; if he is wrong, Team A again passes the coin under the table.

Team A must maintain complete silence after the order "Jenkins says, hands up!" The point of this rule is that the coin is usually spotted by a "clink" when it hits the table; Team A is not entitled to drown out the clink by loud conversation. But Captain A may and should instruct his teammates in procedure, prior to this time. For example, the object of "down with a slam" is to detect the location of the coin by ear; Team A best defeats this object by hitting with all hands simultaneously, so as to make the maximum of noise. Captain A may instruct his players how to count or follow his lead, after such an order, so that all members of the team will hit the table simultaneously.

⟶ BLACKJACK ⟵

Also called Twenty-one, Vingt-et-un (French), Van John (British), this is one of the most ancient of card games, dating back to the 17th century, and is still among the most-played games both as a home diversion and as a gambling game. As to why it is called Blackjack, there is not even a good theory; the jacks of spades and clubs have no particular significance in the play and there is no known connection with any historical personage called Black Jack. One explanation connects the term "Hit me," used in the game, with the idea of a blackjack with which one might be hit.

Number of players. 1. Two to twelve.

The pack. 2. The game may be played with a 52-card pack or with a double pack of 104 cards; a joker or blank card should be placed face up at the bottom of the shuffled pack, to mark the point at which reshuffling is obligatory.

Dealer. 3. There may be a permanent dealer; or the pack may be shuffled and cards dealt face up to the players in rotation until a jack (as some play, a spade or club jack) shows, marking the first dealer.

4. When the dealer is not permanent, each dealer's turn to deal ends, and the new dealer is decided, as provided in paragraph 24. A player privileged to deal may sell his privilege at auction and the highest bidder replaces him as dealer; the auction may be conditioned on a minimum selling price, and unless that price or more is bid the dealer need not sell.

Values of cards. 5. Each face card counts 10, each other card except the ace counts its numerical value, and each ace counts 1 or 11 at the holder's pleasure.

Object of the game. 6. Each player's object is to achieve a count of 21 in two or more cards, or as nearly 21 as possible, without going over 21.

7. A player may change the count of an ace in his hand as often as he wishes, except that an ace is never counted as 11 if it would put the player over 21.

The deal. 8. The dealer gives each player, including himself, one card face down; at this point the deal may be interrupted for the placing of bets, as provided in paragraph 12. The dealer then gives each player one more card, face up. The rotation in dealing is clockwise, beginning with eldest hand (the player nearest the dealer's left).

9. *Optional rules.* All cards, except the dealer's second card, may be

dealt face down; or all cards, except the dealer's first card, may be dealt face up. [The latter method is slightly more advantageous to the player.]

10. Having completed the deal of two cards to each player, the dealer (if he has an ace, face card or ten for his face-up card) looks at his face-down card. If his two cards constitute a count of 21 (ace and face card or ten, called a *blackjack*, or *natural*) he shows them and collects forthwith the bet of each player who does not also have a blackjack. The cards of all players are then discarded and there is a new deal. If the dealer does not have a blackjack, he offers additional cards to each player in rotation, beginning with eldest hand. This begins *the draw* (see below).

Betting. 11. Before the deal begins, each player bets one or more chips that his hand will beat the dealer's. The dealer may place a limit on the amount each player may bet.

12. *Optional rule.* After one face-down card has been dealt to each player, the deal is interrupted for the placing of bets. Each player except the dealer, after looking at his card, may bet any amount up to the limit. The dealer, after looking at his card, may require each player to double his bet. Each player then has the option of redoubling his bet.

The draw. 13. Each player in rotation, beginning with eldest hand, may stand on his first two cards or may draw additional cards, one at a time, dealt face up by the dealer, until the player decides to stand.

14. If a card drawn by a player gives him a count of more than 21, he must show and then turn down all his cards, and forthwith pay the dealer the amount of his bet. This payment is in no case returnable.

15. If a player stands with a count of 21 or less, the determination of his bet is held in abeyance until all other players and the dealer have had a chance to draw or to stand.

16. If a player has a blackjack (ace and face card or ten) the dealer immediately pays him twice the amount of his bet. (*Variant.* In gambling houses, the dealer pays one and one-half times the amount of the bet.)

17. When all other players have drawn, the dealer may either stand or draw, the same as the players. (In many games, the dealer must stand when his count reaches 17 or more, must draw while his count is 16 or less. He must count an ace as 11 if it gives him 17 or more.) If the dealer, in drawing, goes over 21, he pays every player who stood on 21 or less. If the dealer stands on 21 or less, he settles separately with each other player who stood; paying when that player is closer to 21, collecting when he is closer to 21. When the dealer and a player have the same count, 21 or less, their bet is a stand-off. (*Variant.* In informal games, ties pay the dealer; this gives the dealer a tremendous advantage.)

Shuffling. 18. Before the first deal, the dealer shuffles the pack and places the blank card or joker face up at the bottom; or, if such card is not in use, he *burns* a card by exposing it and placing it face up at the bottom. If the card burned is an ace, the pack must be reshuffled and another card burned.

19. As each player's bet is settled, the dealer places that player's cards face up on the bottom of the pack.

20. The pack as originally shuffled is used for successive deals until the first face-up card is reached. All cards not in play are then shuffled, the blank card or a burned card is placed face up at the bottom, and the deal is continued.

Players' options. 21. *Splitting pairs.* A player whose first two cards are a pair may play them as two separate hands, putting the amount of his original bet on each. When his turn comes, the dealer gives him one card face down to each card of the pair. The player may draw to, or stand on, each of the hands, in whatever order he wishes, or alternating as he pleases, until he has stood or gone over on both. A blackjack made after splitting a pair is paid for the same as a blackjack made in the first two cards. (*Variant.* Any pair but aces may be split.)

22. *One down to eleven.* A player whose first two cards total 11 [as, a seven and a four] may double his bet and draw one card face down. He may not thereafter draw, but must stand on the three cards.

Bonuses. 23. A player (but not the dealer) wins his bet forthwith, and at the following increased values:

(a) If he stands on five cards counting 21 or less, double his bet; six cards, four times his bet; and so on, doubling again for each additional card.

(b) If he has three sevens, three times his bet.

(c) If he has 8-7-6, double his bet.

Change of dealer. 24. Except when the dealer is permanent, a player who is dealt a blackjack in his first two cards becomes the dealer at the end of the current deal, provided the dealer does not have a blackjack. If two or more players have blackjacks, and the dealer does not, the deal goes to the blackjack nearest the dealer's left. (*Variant.* The deal rotates as in Poker and other games, after each deal.)

Irregularities. 25. There is no misdeal, as applied to cards already dealt. A player who is dealt too many cards, or is given a card he did not ask for, may accept or reject the extra card. A player who is dealt too few cards may drop out, withdrawing any bet he may have made, or may have additional cards dealt him, when his turn comes, from the top of the pack.

26. *Reshuffling.* If a card is faced in the pack, or if the dealer failed to burn a card, he must reshuffle on demand of any player.

27. *Exposed cards.* If a card dealt to a player is improperly exposed, he must keep that card; but he may have his next card, if any, dealt to him face down. A player may accept or reject a card faced in the pack (or paragraph 25 may apply).

28. *Optional.* If a player is found to have stood on a count of more than 21, he must pay twice the amount of his bet.

29. *Failure to announce a blackjack.* If a player does not show a blackjack at least by the time his turn to draw comes, but instead stands without showing it, he must play it as a count of 21, cannot collect a bonus for it, and merely ties. Another 21.

Pointers on play. Customary terminology in Blackjack is: A player says "Hit me" when he wishes to draw a card; a player is said to "bust" when his count goes over 21. When dealer stands on a count under 21 he announces the lowest count that will beat him; for example, "I'll pay 19."

Chart I. WHEN TO HIT AND WHEN TO STAND

YOUR TOTAL (*in two or more cards*)	STAND *if dealer's showing card is*	HIT *if dealer's showing card is*
3 to 11	Never stand	Always hit—but see below
12	4, 5, or 6	All other cases
13	2 or 3	All other cases
14, 15, or 16	2, 3, 4, 5, or 6	10, 9, 8, 7, or Ace
Hard 17 (such as 9 & 8)	Ace, 2, 3, 4, 5, 6, or 7	10, 9, or 8
Soft 17 (such as Ace & 6)	Never stand	Always hit
Hard 18 (such as 10 & 8)	Always stand (but see Chart II below)	Never hit
Soft 18 (such as Ace & 7)	Ace, 2, 3, 4, 5, 6, 7, or 8 (but see Chart III below)	10 or 9
19, 20, or 21	Always stand	Never hit

Chart II. WHEN TO SPLIT A PAIR

YOU HAVE A PAIR OF	SPLIT *if dealer's showing card is*	DO NOT SPLIT *if dealer's showing card is*
Aces	Always split	
2's or 3's	2, 3, 4, 5, 6, or 7	10, 9, 8, or Ace
4's	5	All other cases
6's	2, 3, 4, 5, 6, or 7	10, 9, 8, or Ace
7's	2, 3, 4, 5, 6, 7, or 8	10, 9, or Ace
8's	Always split	
9's	2, 3, 4, 5, 6, 7, 8, or 9	10, 7, or Ace
5's, 10's or face cards	Never split	Never split

Chart III. WHEN TO TAKE ONE DOWN FOR DOUBLE

YOUR FIRST TWO CARDS TOTAL (*not including an Ace*)	TAKE ONE DOWN FOR DOUBLE only *if dealer's showing card is*
11	Anything but an Ace
10	2 to 9, but not a 10, face card, or Ace
9	2 to 6, but not 7 or higher, or an Ace

HOUSE RULES IN BLACKJACK

In hardly any game are there more variations in practice than in Blackjack; not even the gambling houses are in general agreement, except on the proposition that dealer must hit 16 and stand on 17. Some of the house rules encountered are:

Doubling the bet. A player may take "one down for double" if his first two cards total 9 or 10, as well as 11. If he doubles on 9 and draws a deuce, he may double his bet again and take one down to the 11.

Split pairs. A 21 in two cards after splitting a pair of tens or face cards does not win automatically and does not receive a bonus.

Any two 10-point cards may be split; they need not be a pair.

The two hands produced by splitting a pair must be played in regular rotation, the player first completing play on the one nearer dealer's left before he begins to play the other.

Aces may be split, but the player may then take only one card down to each, as when he has 11 in his first two cards.

Reshuffling. When the dealer reshuffles, he must omit dead cards from the current deal.

Insurance. When the dealer's first card is an ace, the house will bet a player 2 to 1 that dealer will not get a blackjack; the player may not bet more than he previously bet on his hand. (Some houses set a lower, or an arbitrary, limit on an insurance bet.) When the dealer's first card is a face card or ten, the house will bet 4 to 1 against a blackjack. The result of an insurance bet in no way affects the result of the bet on the hand.

Bonuses. Special bonuses are often paid on three sevens or 6-7-8 in the same suit; on making 21 in a hand including three aces; on making a blackjack with A-J of spades, or with any black ace and black jack; on making 21 (exactly) in six or seven cards.

Irregularities. In houses where one or more of a player's cards are dealt face down, a player is often paid his bonus for a blackjack even if he failed to claim it when it was dealt or in his turn.

If a player permits the player at his left to draw ahead of him, he must stand on the cards he has. (But some houses permit a player to reserve his right to draw cards, whether or not he has drawn a card in turn, and then to draw after the last player but before the dealer has had a chance to draw.)

If a player receives too many cards in the original deal, his hand is dead but the bet is a stand-off. If the dealer gives himself too many cards, an extra face-up card is dead, and any face-down card but the one that came from the top of the pack is dead, and play continues.

When the next card to be dealt is faced in the pack (but does not mark the end of the shuffled cards), a player may not take it but the dealer must take it if it would fall to him; except that if the previous card brought the dealer to 17 or over, the card is dead.

Dealer hits a "soft" 17 (one that includes an ace) if the ace is exposed, not if the six is exposed.

GAMES SIMILAR TO BLACKJACK

Farmer, or The Farm. In *The Academy of Play* (1764), The Farm was described as an ancient game. The pack has only 45 cards, all eights and the sixes of spades, clubs and diamonds being deleted from the 52-card pack. Everyone contributes equally to a pool, and then there is an auction to determine who shall contribute additionally (the amount of his high bid) and become the dealer, or farmer.

The object is to reach a count of 16, without going over. Aces count 1 each, face cards 10 each, other cards their numerical value. First one card is dealt to each player, after which each in turn must draw one or more cards and may stand after the draw of any card. A player who goes over must pay the farmer one chip for each point over 16. The pool goes to the player who has 16; if two or more have 16, the six of hearts wins; next in precedence, the hand with the fewest cards; next, the hand nearest the dealer's left. If no one has 16, the pool goes over to the next deal, which is by the same player, and the player closest to 16 collects one chip from each other player (if two or more players tie, precedence is established as stated above). A player who has 16 and wins the pool becomes the farmer for the next deal.

Seven and One-half. This is the same as Blackjack, but played with the Spanish pack of 40 cards (no tens, nines, or eights), with face cards counting ½, aces 1, other cards their numerical value. The object is to reach 7½, or as close as possible, without going over; 7½ in two cards is a natural, but a player has the privilege of standing on his first card.

Macao. This is played like Blackjack, but face cards and tens count zero, ace counts 1. Bets are placed before the deal begins. One card is dealt to each player, and each may draw as in Blackjack; but a nine on the first card immediately collects triple the bet, and eight double, a seven singly, with a nine beating an eight or seven, and an eight beating a seven. Ties are a stand-off. If a player goes over 9, he loses forthwith.

Quinze. (Quince, or Fifteen.) The usual form of Quinze is for two players. They ante equal amounts to form a pool. One card is dealt face down to each; then non-dealer accepts as many more cards face up as he wishes. His object is to get as near as possible—under or over—to a total of 15. An ace counts 1, a face card 10. After he stands (he never busts as in Blackjack), the dealer draws what cards he wishes, face up. After he stands, the two hole cards are turned up, and the hand nearer to 15 but not over wins the pool. A hand that is under wins against one that is over. If the two tie under 15, on 15, or if both are over (regardless of relative excess), the deal is a tie, and the pool remains to be won later, increased by subsequent antes.

A variant played in Europe can be played by any number up to about seven. There is no ante. Each player receives one card face down, then each in turn draws what additional cards he wishes face up. But a hand that goes over 15 must drop out (as in Blackjack). The survivors bet as in Poker, beginning with the one nearest the left of the dealer. The players who stay right through to the showdown expose their hole cards and the best takes the pool, or equal hands divide it.

THIRTY-FIVE (TRENTA-CINQUE)

This popular Italian game has been adopted (in slightly altered form) by many American card-playing groups. Both the original game and some of the popular variations are described in the rules that follow.

Number of players. 1. Four play, each for himself. Two or three may play, in which case not all the cards are dealt; or five may play, using the American instead of the Italian pack.

The pack. 2. 40 cards—the 52-card pack with the tens, nines and eights deleted. If five play, the full 52-card pack should be used.

Values of cards. 3. Each face card counts 10, each ace 1, each other card its numerical value.

The pool. 4. Before each deal, each player contributes 5 chips to a pool.

The deal. 5. After the cards have been shuffled by the dealer and cut by the player at his right, the cards are dealt one at a time in rotation (in the original game, the rotation is to the right); on the first four rounds of dealing, one card is dealt to each player and one is dealt to a widow, and thereafter one is dealt to each player, so that finally each player holds nine cards and there is a widow of four cards.

6. The first dealer is decided by lot; thereafter, the turn to deal rotates (to the right or left, depending on whether foreign or American customs are being followed).

Object of the game. 7. The objects are (1) to have in one's hand cards of a single suit having a point value of 35 or more, (2) to hold and collect bonuses for a hand without a face card (*beggar*), and for K-Q-J of the same suit (*royale*).

Bidding. 8. Each player in turn, beginning with eldest hand (first player to receive a card in the deal) may pass and discard his hand, or may bid one or more chips. Each bid must be higher than the preceding bid. The bidding continues until three players have passed. Having once passed, a player may not bid.

(*Optional rule.* No one may bid more than 5 chips. When a player bids 5, the bidding is ended. The high bidder, whatever his bid, must then announce the point value of the best suit in his hand; each active player in turn after him, excluding players who have passed, may then announce any higher count, but need not if he does not choose to. A player who announces the highest count is deemed to be the high bidder, and his bid is deemed to be the highest bid made.)

Bonuses (optional). 9. When the high bidder has been determined, any player who has not passed may show a hand without a face card, or

K-Q-J of any suit, and collect 2 chips from each other player in the game, including players who passed.

Taking the widow. 10. The high bidder pays into the pool as many chips as he bid. He then takes the widow into his hand. If he can then show a suit whose point value is 35 or more, he takes the pool. If he cannot, the pool remains for the next deal.

11. *Optional rule.* A player who is dealt a suit having a point value of 35 or more may show it and forthwith collect the pool; if two or more players have such a suit, they divide the pool equally. All point values of 35 or more rank alike.

12. *Optional rule.* If the high bidder makes 35, he takes only the amount of his bid from the pool (and if the pool amounts to less than he bid, he takes only the pool); if he does not make 35, he pays the amount of his bid into the pool. Any chips remaining in the pool go over to the next deal.

Irregularities. 13. If a player announces any point value and cannot show it on demand, before or after taking the widow, he must pay into the pool as many chips as there are in it and then discard his hand. (It is the custom for the high bidder immediately to show the cards proving whatever total he announced.) If the hand of the high bidder is invalidated in this way, the previous high bidder becomes the high bidder and the game continues.

STOCK MARKET

There may be any number of players up to eleven. A 52-card pack is stripped so that it includes any four face cards plus one card of each suit for each player, beginning with the ace and ranging upwards through the 2, 3, 4, etc.: In a six-hand game there would be A, 2, 3, 4, 5 of each suit plus four face cards.

The face cards count 0, each ace 1, each other card its numerical value.

Two cards are dealt to each player, face down. The object of the game is to guess the total count of all cards dealt; this is the "market price." In private transactions, the players buy and sell a fictitious stock whose market price is this total. When there is no more trading, all dealt cards are exposed and their values totalled. Each player then pays each other player for the number of shares he bought from that player and collects from each other player for the number of shares he sold to that player, winning or losing on the net according to how well he estimated the market price.

A record is kept of the transactions, and the simplest form of settlement is this: Any player whose transactions resulted in a net sale of shares below the market price, or who bought above the market price, puts into a pool the amount he lost thereby. The successful purchasers take their respective shares from this pool.

⟶ BACCARAT ⟵

Baccarat is the principal card game of European casinos and is played somewhat in British countries, but is almost unknown in the United States. The variant Chemin de Fer (page 524) is more often played everywhere, and is quite popular among American gamblers. Supposedly, Baccarat is played with a fixed banker (in some Riviera casinos, the "Greek syndicate" has traditionally monopolized the bank), but in practice the bank goes to the highest bidder—the person who agrees to put up the largest bank. Chemin de Fer is always played with the right to be banker passing in rotation among the players.

Number of players. 1. The acknowledged players are the banker, or dealer; and two to twenty *punters,* or players against the dealer, seated at a circular or oval table. Any number of bystanders may stand around the table and bet, but they have no prerogatives in precedence.

The pack. 2. From three to ten 52-card packs are shuffled together and toppled over on the table or placed in a dealing box, or *shoe,* which facilitates pulling out one card at a time, face down.

The deal. 3. The dealer deals three hands of two cards each, dealt face down, one at a time: A card to his right, a card to his left, a card to himself; and another card to each hand, in the same order. The deal and play of these hands constitute a *coup.*

Object of the game. 4. Each face card or ten counts zero, each ace counts 1, each other card counts its numerical value.

5. The object is, in two or three cards, to achieve a count (*point*) of 9 or, if not 9, as high as possible. When the count of a hand is over 10, only the final digit counts; a nine and a six count 5, not 15.

Betting. 6. Before any card is dealt, any punter may bet *on the right* (that the hand dealt to the right will beat the dealer's hand); or *on the left;* or *à cheval* (that the dealer will lose both, the bet being called off if dealer neither wins nor loses both).

7. The dealer announces the amount of his bank before the first deal; thereafter, the bank consists of the original sum plus winnings and minus losses. The dealer is not responsible for the payment of bets in excess of the current value of the bank.

8. The dealer's winnings must be added to the bank and become available to cover the bets of punters. The dealer may add to the bank at any time. The dealer may relinquish the bank, but may not withdraw part of it. If the dealer relinquishes the bank, he may not bid in the auction for the next bank.

9. Before each coup, the bank is deemed to be divided in two equal portions, one available to each side (unless there is a banco; see paragraph 11). Any portion of either half not bet by one side may be bet by the other. Any remainder may be bet by the bystanders. Players at the table may bet à cheval only against a remainder of the bank not taken by either side.

10. The player nearest the dealer's right takes what part of the bank he chooses as a bet on the right; then the next player to the right, who is privileged only to bet what part of the bank is left, or any portion thereof; and so on. Similarly, the player nearest the dealer's left may take whatever portion of the bank he chooses as a bet on the left, the remainder being available to the player at his left, and so on around the table. The order of precedence is circular, so that the player first in precedence to the right is last in precedence to the left, and vice versa.

11. If any player (whether or not at the table) calls *Banco*, he undertakes to bet the entire amount of the bank, and takes precedence over all others who would bet, except that any player before him in order of precedence may supersede his banco by betting the entire amount of the bank. At the table, the precedence on banco is: the player at the dealer's right, then the player at his left, then the second player at the right, and so on. Upon call of banco, all lower bets previously placed are withdrawn. If a banco results in three consecutive stand-off coups, it must be withdrawn. There may be only one banco during the tenure of any bank; and on any coup after the first, dealer may refuse it and withdraw his bank.

The players. 12. For the first coup, the first player on the right plays the hand dealt to his side, and the first player on the left plays the hand dealt to his side. The right to play for one's side continues until that side loses a coup, when it goes to the next player in precedence on that side; it never passes to a punter on the other side, but returns to the first player again. A player may forego his right to play, passing it to the next in precedence. The dealer always plays his own hand.

13. A player who bancos may play both hands against the dealer, or may designate others to play one or both of them; he may place his entire bet on either side, or may divide it as he pleases.

Procedure of play. 14. The dealer is first to look at his two cards. Then:

(a) If the dealer's point is 8 or 9 (*natural*), he shows his cards. The right then looks at his cards and shows them; if his point is not 8 or 9, or if his point is 8 and dealer's is 9, the dealer takes the bets on the right; if his point is the same as dealer's, 8 or 9, bets on the right are withdrawn; if his point is 9 and dealer's is 8, the dealer pays bets on the right. The left then looks at and shows his cards; he loses, has a stand-off, or wins, as did the right.

(b) If the dealer's point is 7 or under, he says, "I give." The hand on the right may then show a count of 8 or 9, whereupon the dealer pays bets on the right; or may ask for a card, in which case the dealer gives him one more card and turns it face up; or may stand on his first two cards. The hand on the left may then show and collect on 8 or 9; or draw a card face up; or stand. The dealer may then draw a card, or stand. Then all cards are exposed and the dealer pays a side whose point is higher than his, collects from a side whose point is lower than his, and has a stand-off with a side whose point is the same as his.

15. When there are too few cards in the shoe for another coup, the bank is ended and an auction is held to determine the next dealer. (Seven or fewer cards are deemed insufficient for another coup. Six packs shuffled together produce about thirty-five coups.)

16. If the dealer withdraws the bank, all the cards are reshuffled for the next bank.

Irregularities. [Nearly every casino has its own elaborate house rules governing Baccarat play and irregularities in great detail.] 17. If a card is found faced in the pack before a coup, or after the hands have been dealt, it is discarded; if found during the deal of the hands, a punter may either accept or reject it, but dealer, if it would fall to him, must accept it.

18. If the dealer gives an opponent three cards in the original deal, that hand is dead and bets on that side are withdrawn.

19. If the dealer gives an additional card to a player who did not ask for it, and the card has been shown, it is discarded.

20. The dealer is not required to pay bets in excess of the bank. Bets are settled with the players in order of precedence; if they exceed the bank, the first player to the right is paid first, then the first player to the left, then the second player to the right, and so on.

21. If a punter stands on 4 or under, or draws to 6 or higher, and his side loses, he must pay the losses of all punters who bet on his side but is not responsible to bystanders.

Pointers on play. The player on each side must stand on 6 or 7, draw to 4 or under, and has the option on 5. The dealer's correct play against either player considered separately is: If the player stands, dealer should stand on 6 or 7 and should draw to 5 or under. If the player draws, the dealer's correct play (which is printed on the shoe) depends on what count he has and what card he "gives":

DEALER GIVES	DEALER STANDS ON	DEALER DRAWS TO
0 or 1	4, 5, 6, 7	0, 1, 2, 3
2 or 3	5, 6, 7	0, 1, 2, 3, 4
4 or 5	6, 7	0, 1, 2, 3, 4, 5*
6 or 7	7	0, 1, 2, 3, 4, 5, 6
8	3, 4, 5, 6, 7	0, 1, 2
9	3*, 4, 5, 6, 7	0, 1, 2, 3*

While in effect the dealer always has the option, the plays stated are mathematically sound and any deviation would be losing play, except in

---

* Dealer has the option of standing or drawing when he has 3 and the opponent draws a 9; or when he has 5 and the opponent draws a 4 (though in this case it is advantageous to draw).

one circumstance: when the bets on one side are much larger than the bets on the other side, so that the dealer may sacrifice his chance to win the smaller bets so as to increase his chance of winning the larger bets.

The advantage of the dealer in Baccarat has been estimated at 7% of the sums bet against him. Most casinos charge, as their fee, 5% of the amount of each bank.

The optional plays figure out as follows:

Against the dealer, if you stand on 5 your chance of winning is 51.23%; if you draw to 5, your chance of winning is 50.06%. For this reason, most players stand.

As dealer, holding 3 and giving an opponent a nine: If you stand your chance of winning is about 60%; if you draw, your chance of winning is about 59%. Therefore you are slightly better off if you stand. But these approximate chances are based on the assumption that the opponent will usually stand on 5. Against an opponent whose known practice is to draw to 5, the dealer is slightly better off to draw than to stand. Drawing, his chance of winning is about 58.5%; standing, it is about 57.5%.

As dealer, holding 5 and giving an opponent a 4: Your chance of winning is slightly better if you draw, but by only ⅙ to ½ of 1%—and assuming there is some chance that your opponent has drawn to 5. Against an opponent who always stands on 5, it is about even, with an almost infinitesimal advantage (¹⁄₂₀ of 1%) to dealer if he stands.

All the above is influenced, however, by the cards that have already been dealt, and since the ranks of these cards cannot be foreseen one must either remember them as they fall and make his decisions accordingly, or else assume (as the house rules do) that he has no better than a guess as to his best play when it is "optional."

CHEMIN DE FER

The informal variant of Baccarat is Chemin de Fer (Chemmy, or Shimmy). Only two hands are dealt, one for the banker and one for his opponent. The first banker is the player who is willing to put up the largest bank; each banker retains the bank only so long as he wins or ties on each coup. When he loses a coup the player at his right becomes the banker. A player may always pass the bank voluntarily, but otherwise may not withdraw any part of it. The largest bettor against the bank plays the hand against him. Precedence in betting is to the right, and banco is permitted on any coup. Both the player against the bank and the banker are required to play in accordance with the advice given above (Pointers on play), which is printed on the shoe.

TRENTE ET QUARANTE, or ROUGE ET NOIR

This is a banking game, played in continental casinos; all betting is against the house. Six 52-card packs are used, shuffled together. The lay-out provides places for bets on *rouge, noir, couleur,* and *inverse*—red, black, color, opposite (color). Bets are placed before each deal, or *coup,* begins.

The dealer lays out a row of cards until the count reaches 31 or more, each ace counting 1, each face card 10, each other card its numerical value, so that the count cannot exceed 40. This first row dealt represents noir. Below it the dealer lays out a similar row representing rouge. The row counting nearer 31 wins. If the first card dealt was of the color designating the winning row, a bet on couleur wins; if this card was of opposite color, a bet on inverse wins. When both rows count the same, and the total is anything more than 31, all bets are withdrawn; this is called a *refait.* When there is a refait at exactly 31, all bets are "put in prison" (see page 553) so in effect the house takes half the bets when this occurs.

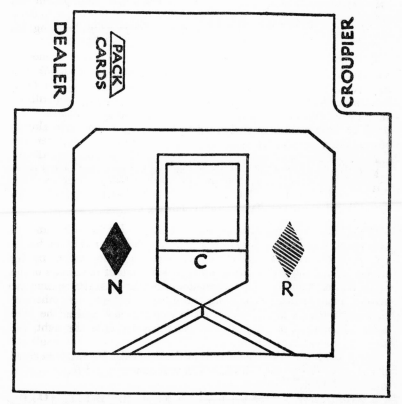

Trente et Quarante Layout. Bets on noir go in the space N, on rouge in the space R, on couleur in the space C and on inverse in the triangle below it.

◄ RED DOG ►

This game is also called High-card Pool.

Number of players. Three to ten.

The pack. 1. A regular pack of 52 cards; plus a joker or blank card to be kept face up at the bottom of the pack.

Rank of cards. 2. A (high), K, Q, J, 10, 9, 8, 7, 6, 5, 4, 3, 2.

The pool. 3. Before the game begins, each player contributes equally to a pool. Thereafter, whenever the pool is depleted the players contribute again.

The deal. 4. The shuffle, cut, and rotation of the turn to play and to deal, are as in Poker. Five cards are dealt to each player, one at a time, face down. (*Variant rule.* Four cards are dealt to each player. This variant must be adopted when there are nine or ten players; or when, with seven or eight players, it is decided to burn a card after each bet, as provided in paragraph 7.)

The play. 5. Each player in turn, beginning with eldest hand (the player at dealer's left), may bet one or more chips that his hand will beat the top card remaining on the pack; or may pay a forfeit of one chip into the pool and discard his hand without showing it.

(*Optional rule.* A player may "copper" his bet—bet that his card will lose. In this case he must bet, to win or to lose; he may not forfeit.)

6. After each player bets, the dealer exposes the top card remaining on the pack. If the player has a higher-ranking card of the same suit, he shows that card and collects the amount of his bet from the pool. If the player cannot do this he shows his entire hand and pays the amount of his bet into the pool. All bets are made with the pool, and no bet may exceed the amount of the pool. No player may bet until the bet of the preceding player has been settled.

7. *Optional rule.* After each bet is made, the dealer *burns* the top card of the pack (discards it, without showing it) and exposes the next card to decide the bet.

8. When every player's bet has been settled, the deal passes to the next player in rotation.

Irregularities. 9. There is no misdeal. A card faced in dealing must be accepted by the player to whom it is dealt; a card found faced in the pack thereafter is discarded and the topmost face-down card decides the next bet. A deal with an incorrect pack stands.

10. *Incorrect hand.* A hand with too many cards is dead, and the holder need not bet or pay a forfeit; if the player has bet he loses his bet, provided the irregularity is discovered before the bet of the next player has been settled, and before the cards have been mixed for the next shuffle.

11. A hand with too few cards may bet or may discard his hand without betting or paying a forfeit, but he may not be dealt additional cards.

12. *Betting errors.* If a player bets more chips than there are in the pool, he must pay the entire amount if he loses and cannot collect more than the pool if he wins. Once a bet is stated by a player in turn, it cannot be changed. Chips once put in the pool may not be removed except to collect for a winning bet.

Pointers on play. The relative numerical ranks of the cards are: ace 14, king 13, queen 12, jack 11, each other card its index number. Subtract your highest card in each suit from 14 and add the differences; for each void suit add 13. The total will be the number of cards you cannot beat.

At the start, when you hold five cards, there are forty-seven cards that may be turned from the pack. If twenty-four or more of them will beat you, the odds are against your winning your bet; if twenty-three or fewer will beat you, the odds are in your favor. The figures must be adjusted as each additional card is exposed. To "bet the pot" (the maximum bet) most players like to have a 3-to-1 advantage, meaning that no more than twelve of the forty-seven cards can beat them.

SLIPPERY SAM

A pool is formed by equal antes from all players. Each player receives three cards, dealt one at a time face down, which he must not look at until the betting interval is over. Then one card is dealt face up to the center of the table; since the center card must be a six or lower (ace ranks high), the dealer turns up cards from the stock until he reaches the first such low card.

Each player in turn to the left may bet any amount, up to the total chips in the pool. He must bet at least one chip—dropping is not allowed. Each bet is against the pool, and is settled at once before the next player bets. Having made his bet, the player turns his three cards face up. Cards rank as in Poker, ace high, deuce low. He wins if one of them is of the same suit and higher rank than the center card; otherwise he loses. Lost bets go into the pool. If a player bets the amount of the pool and wins, the remaining hands have nothing to bet against; the cards are therefore thrown in for the next deal. But there is a new ante at the beginning of each deal, even though the pool already contains chips not won in the previous deal.

BANKER AND BROKER

Also called Beat the Dealer.

The dealer shuffles a 52-card pack and cuts packets of four or more cards off the top, placing one such packet in front of each other player and one in front of himself. Each player then bets any amount up to the limit (which is decided, before the deal, by the dealer) that his card will beat the dealer's. When all bets are placed, each player turns over his packet, and the bets are decided by the bottom cards, the dealer settling separately with each opponent; the cards rank as at Poker, ace high and deuce low. Suits do not count; if the dealer and a player have cards of the same rank, their bet is a stand-off.

Optional rule 1. Ties pay the dealer.

Optional rule 2. Dealer takes half the bet on ties.

[Either of the optional rules gives the dealer such an advantage that it is encountered only in sucker games.]

BINGO WITH CARDS

There are at least two forms of this game, played with the 52-card pack.

(a) Each player, except the dealer, receives five cards face up. The dealer turns up cards from the remainder of the pack, one at a time. Each player having a card of the same rank as the card turned up must place chips on his card equivalent to the numerical value of the card, counting king as 13, queen 12, jack 11, ace 1. A player holding more than one card of the rank turned must put the full number of chips on each. The first player having chips on all five of his cards calls Bingo and wins, and takes all the chips on other players' cards. If two or more players properly call Bingo on the same turn of a card, they share equally in all the chips that have been put up, including the chips on their own cards.

(b) Each player antes equally to a pot. The dealer gives each player, including himself, five cards face up. From a different 52-card pack he turns up the remaining cards of the pack one by one, announcing the rank of each as he does so. When any player's card is called, he turns that card down. (The card turned down must match the card called in both suit and rank.) The first player to turn down all his cards calls Bingo and wins the pot; if two or more properly call Bingo on the same turned card, they share the pot equally.

— FARO —

Faro was once the most popular gambling card game of the world; in the 19th century it was the most-played game in American gambling houses. Before that it had been so much played in England (under the name Pharoah, taken from a face card in a French-designed pack of cards) that in the 17th century there was a Stuart law against gaming on it. It nearly wrecked the young Count Rostof in Tolstoy's *War and Peace*. Dozens of games employ the same principle. But today Faro is almost unknown and little played, and the once familiar sign of the tiger denoting a Faro game inside (whence playing Faro is called "bucking the tiger") is only a nostalgic memory.

Number of players. 1. Faro is a banking game; any number can play, each betting only against the house.

Layout. 2. The thirteen cards of the spade suit (sometimes the diamond or another suit) are represented on a layout; and though the suits have no relative rank or other significance in Faro, every bet is placed on that card of the spade suit representing its rank in the pack.

The pack. 3. 52 cards. Faro cards were once manufactured somewhat oversized, for as the pack became soiled the edges were trimmed.

The deal. 4. The dealer is a representative of the house, and is assisted by a *casekeeper* who keeps track, on a device similar in appearance to an abacus, of what cards have shown; and a *lookout,* who watches, pays and collects bets.

5. The pack having been shuffled and cut to the satisfaction of the players, it is placed in a dealing box, face up, so that its top undealt card is always exposed. The box permits one card at a time to be slid off the pack.

Betting. 6. Players may bet that any rank of card will win; by *coppering* a bet on a card (putting a token on it, the token having originally been a copper penny or disk) they may bet that any rank of card will lose; or they may bet on combinations of cards to win, or to lose, or one to win and the other to lose; and on the last three cards they may bet on the order in which they will come out of the box.

7. There is *action* (determination of bets) every time the dealer takes two cards from the box (called a *turn*). Except when cards are being dealt, players may place any new bets or withdraw any previous bets.

Determination of bets. 8. The first card exposed in the box is called *soda;* there is no action on it, which is to say, it affects no bets. For the first turn, the dealer removes soda from the box and places it to his right;

this founds the pile of cards that win. The next card from the box he places at the left of soda; this card *loses,* and bets on its rank are collected or paid by the house, depending on whether they were bets to win or to lose, respectively. The card left exposed in the box *wins,* and bets on that rank to win are paid by the house, bets on that rank to lose are collected by the house. For the next turn, the dealer puts this last exposed card on top of soda, in the win pile; the next card on the lose pile; and leaves exposed the next win card, in the box. The deal proceeds in this manner until only three unexposed cards remain in the box.

9. When two cards of the same rank come up in a single turn, it is called a *split;* the house takes half of all bets on that rank, the remainder of such bets being withdrawn by the players.

10. When only three unexposed cards remain in the box, players may bet on the order in which they will come up; the house pays 4 to 1 if the player is correct (it is called *calling the turn*). [The player's chance of calling the turn is only ⅙, so the house has an advantage of 16⅔% of the money bet against it.] If two of the last three cards are a pair (which is known by the casekeeper's record) it is called a *cathop;* the house pays 2 to 1. [The player's chance is only ⅓; the house has a 33⅓% advantage.] The last card in the box is called *hock* and there is no action on it, other than the bets described in this paragraph.

The Faro Layout. A bet on a single card to win is placed on that card; if it is a bet to lose, a "copper" is put on top of the chips. Chips placed between any two cards are bet on both cards, the first to show determining the entire bet. In the same way a bet may be made on three cards in a row (as, a bet below the jack would be a bet on 10, J, Q); or on a triangle of cards (as, a bet on the upper right corner of the eight would be a bet on 5, 8, 9); or on four cards, by placing the bet in the center of the four. A bet off the corner of a card bets that card and the one diagonally adjacent to it; a bet on the outside corner of a card bets it and the second card in line with it, skipping the next card. To bet on separated cards, a player may obtain from the dealer a marker that indicates his bet. To bet on two cards, one to win and the other to lose, the player heels his bet—leans one chip against another, the leaning chip pointing toward the second card and representing the card selected to win. The layout may contain space to bet that the next winning (or losing) card will be odd or even, or that it will be higher or lower than the losing (winning) card. A player calling the turn places his bet, with an appropriate marker, on the card he calls to show first, and heels it toward the card he calls to be second.

Pointers on play. Faro is one of the most favorable of gambling-house games, from the player's point of view; but even so, the house advantage, derived from splits, is slightly more than the 1.4% house advantage in Craps, which perhaps (but not surely) has some bearing on the fact that Craps has replaced Faro as the principal gambling-house game in the United States. A player can remove all house percentage by betting only on case cards (the only cards of their rank remaining in the box, so that there can be no splits); but this policy does not make one popular with the proprietors of the game. Many systems have been devised for Faro (see page 554) but none overcomes the basic advantage of the house.

PHAROAH, or PHAROAN

The original game or Pharoah was far more informal than the Faro described above. The dealer gave one card face down to each other player; the other players, after looking at their cards, bet on them, the dealer having the privilege of accepting or requiring reduction of their bets; the dealer then laid out the remainder of the pack in win and lose piles, the bets being settled accordingly.

STUSS

The most-played form of Faro is called Stuss; often it is played without a dealing box, and sometimes without a layout. The differences from Faro are: Any bet on the first card (on which there is no action in Faro) loses to the house; all bets are placed to win, none to lose; the house takes all bets, not merely half the bets, on a card when a split in that rank occurs; the last four cards in the box (or in the pack) are house cards, and all unsettled bets on them are taken by the house. There is no betting on calling the turn, therefore, and the cathop does not exist.

MONTE

The name Monte, or Monte Bank, is applied to various games. There is also a sleight-of-hand routine called Three-card Monte whereby one lays out three cards, face down, on a table and invites spectators to guess (and bet on) the location of one specified card among the three; this is productive of great opportunity for chicanery and so is often encountered at carnivals and near race tracks.

Monte Bank traditionally is played with the Spanish pack of 40 cards (no tens, nines or eights). The dealer takes the shuffled pack and draws two cards from the bottom, laying them out on the table to form the "bottom layout." Beyond them on the table he turns up the two top cards of the pack, the "top layout." Players bet on either layout; bets being placed, the dealer turns up the next card of the pack. This is the "gate." If in suit it matches a card of either layout, the dealer pays bets on that layout; he collects the bets on either layout that has no card of the same suit as the gate. The five cards so dealt are discarded and new layouts and a new gate are dealt from the same pack, the process being repeated without reshuffling while the pack suffices.

Monte in another variation is a game of the Faro type, based on matching the ranks of cards. The dealer lays out the bottom and top layouts; if any two cards in them be of the same rank, there is a new deal. If the four cards are of different ranks, players may bet on any card of the four to be paired (by turning up cards from the pack) before any other card of the four. The dealer then turns the remainder of the pack over, exposing the bottom card; and he pulls cards from the bottom one by one, each time exposing the next card, until all bets on the layout have been determined by the pairing of cards in the layout with the exposed bottom cards of the pack. Players may place new bets as the deal continues.

ZIGINETTE

This is a favorite game of Italian-Americans. The 40-card pack is used (a 52-card pack from which tens, nines and eights have been deleted). There is no rank of cards or suits. Rotation and order of precedence are to the right.

The dealer turns up the first two cards of the pack for the players and the third card for himself. (Often a dealing box is used, in which all cards are face-up as at Faro, whereupon the dealer pulls out the first two cards and leaves the third in the box.) Players bet on either of the first two cards—whether it will be paired before the dealer's card. The dealer continues to turn up cards; any that pairs his own card wins all bets for the players, any that pairs another card wins for the dealer all bets on that card, and any that does not effect such a decision is left on the table and players may bet on it as they could on the first two cards.

If the two first cards are a pair, the matched cards are piled together and additional cards are dealt to provide the second players' card and the dealer's card; in this case, the bet as between the paired cards and the dealer's card is on which will first produce three of a kind. Likewise, if all three cards of the first deal are of the same rank, they are piled together and the bet is on whether that rank or the dealer's card will first produce four of a kind.

SKINBALL

Also called The Skin Game, or Skinning. This is a favorite game of Negro gamblers.

Number of players. 1. Three *principals;* up to ten other players, known as *pikers,* who bet among themselves but not with the principals. The players usually kneel in a ring on the ground or floor.

The pack. 2. 52 cards.

The deal. 3. Only the principals may deal; they take turns in any rotation. The pack, having been shuffled and cut to the satisfaction of all three, is put on the ground and a weight put on it. Each card to be dealt is *skinned* (slid) off the pack, the dealer lifting the weight just enough for this purpose.

4. To start the game, the dealer gives one card face up to each of the three principals; but bets are placed after the deal of each.

Betting. 5. Upon receiving his first card, and thereafter every time a card is turned from the pack, each principal may bet any amount against either of the other principals (or against both) that that other principal's card will lose before his, or that his card will lose before the other's. A principal may bet only with another principal and must accept every bet he is offered, or drop out of the game; except that he need not accept any bet before he has been dealt a card of his own. If two principals have cards of the same rank, they may bet only against the third; if all three principals have cards of the same rank, there is a new shuffle, cut, and deal.

6. The dealer skins cards off the pack one by one and exposes them, then puts them in a discard pile, face up. New bets may be placed after the exposure of each.

7. Whenever a card newly exposed pairs (in rank) the card of a principal, that principal's card loses, and bets pertinent to that card are settled. (Note that a card dealt to or drawn by a principal may cause the card of another player to lose.)

8. When a principal's card has lost, he may either:

(a) Refuse to accept another card, and drop out of the betting until the next deal, without losing his place as a principal; in this case, the deal and betting by the other two principals continues, and the principal who has dropped out may make side bets with pikers.

(b) Have the dealer give him another card from the top of the pack, face up or face down as the principal may specify.

(c) Select from the cards in the discard pile any card that has not been paired.

(d) Cut the pack and skin off the face-down card next below the cut to be his new card, turning it up only if he so chooses.

9. When a principal takes a new card without showing it, he must show it when it or another principal's card loses. [The penalty for failure to show the card promptly is usually a violent one.]

10. No bet may be offered on a card that can no longer lose (that is, when every card that would pair it has already shown).

Betting by pikers. **11.** A piker may withdraw from the discard pile any card to be his card, keeping it in front of him as the principals do theirs, and betting with other pikers as to whether it will lose before the cards of the other pikers or the card of a principal.

12. A piker must select a card that has not been paired, if such a card is available. The discards are always open to inspection.

13. When a principal drops out, any piker may take his place; as between two or more candidates, the earliest arrival has precedence.

Irregularities. **14.** A card faced in the pack is dead and no bets are settled on it. All other irregularities (including those solely concerning the pikers) are rectified by agreement of the three principals. There may be a new shuffle and cut at any time upon agreement of the three principals.

15. A bet once made may not be called off except by mutual consent; but no piker is required to accept a bet.

SKINBALL VARIATIONS

There are many variations of Skinball.

When two play, each cuts a card; unless they are a pair, the dealer merely turns up cards one by one until either card loses. New bets may be placed after each card is exposed.

When Skinball is played indoors, and regulated by a gambling house or operator, the dealer offers the first card to the player at his right; that player may either accept the card and bet on it (the dealer covering his bet) or refuse it, in which case he is out of the game until the next deal and the card he refused is offered to each player in rotation to his right until one takes it. The dealer then takes the next card for himself. He continues to turn up cards, any unmatched ("fresh") card being offered to the players in rotation, any matching card causing its mate to lose and settling bets made on that contingency. The house usually does not participate in the play but charges a fee (2% to 5%) on every winning bet. Players may bet among themselves instead of betting against the dealer, except that a player has no card unless he has made some bet against the dealer.

PUT AND TAKE

"Put and take" games are played with spinning tops; they are played with dice specially marked (two dice, one having three sides marked **P** and three sides marked **T**, the other having 1, 2, 4, 8, 16, 32, or any other numbers, on its six sides); they are played with cards. The only common characteristic is that if chance tells you to put, you put the specified number of chips into the pot; if chance tells you to take, you take out that number. The put-and-take card games described below are only two of many.

Up and Down the River. The dealer gives each player, including himself, five cards face up. He then turns up five cards from the remainder of the pack, one at a time. When the card of any player matches the turned card in rank, he must put into the pot a number of chips representing the numerical value of that card, counting king as 13, queen 12, jack 11, ace 1. The dealer then turns up five more cards, and these are "take" cards: For each such card that matches a card in his hand in rank, the player takes from the pot as many chips as represent the numerical value of that card. The dealer must supply any deficit of the pot, and may take any chips left in the pot at the end.

Put and Take. This is the same game as described above, except that the rank of the card turned does not control the contribution of a player to the pot: On the first card turned by the dealer, the player having a card of the same rank must put in one chip; on the second card 2 chips, on the third 4, on the fourth 8, on the fifth 16. The "take" cards are then dealt, the players taking 1, 2, 4, 8, or 16 in the same manner. The dealer owns the pot, taking the profits and paying its losses.

GAMES BASED ON POKER

The principle of betting in Poker, and the making of combinations in five-card hands, have found expression in several games having no connection with the combinations controlling the values of Poker hands. Some of these games, played in series while one person deals, have been grouped together to form a single game called Garbage; others are selected from time to time in Dealer's Choice games. The principal ones (possible variations are innumerable and inexhaustible*) are as follows:

Red and Black. All bets are placed against the dealer. Each player makes any bet, up to the limit established by the dealer, on red or black. All bets having been placed, the dealer gives each player five cards, face up, one at a time in rotation as in Poker. The pay-off is at even money: the player wins if he named red and has three or more red cards, or if he named black and has three or more black cards; he loses if the dominant color is the one he did not name. If his first four cards are two red and two black, he may double his bet before receiving his fifth card. Some play that four of the color named collect double for the player, four of the opposite color pay double to the dealer; five either way collect or pay quadruple.

Numerical Valuation. [One form of this game is also called Red and Black, because of the counting distinction between red cards and black cards.] The deal, first betting interval and draw are as in Draw Poker, but the object is to make up hands of the best numerical valuation, count-

---

* *Incomprehensible* is a word that springs to mind.

ing face cards 10 each, aces 1 each, other cards their numerical value. There are the following methods of counting:

1. Every card in the hand is counted and the highest count wins.

2. Cards of one suit in a hand only are counted, and the hand with the highest count in a single suit wins. (A hand containing ♠ J 7 4, counting 21, would win from a hand containing ◇ K Q, counting 20.)

3. *(Plus and Minus.)* Every red card counts plus, every black card minus. The highest and lowest counts divide the pot. If there are ties for high or low, the rules of High-Low Poker apply. (For example, a hand is ♠K ♠8 ♣7 ◇J ♡3. The black cards total 25, which is a minus quantity; the red cards 13, which is a plus quantity; the net for the hand is —12.)

Garbage. A game of Garbage is a series of games. Every player except the dealer antes. First, the dealer deals for a game of Red and Black (in any variation; see above). Next each player considers his five cards as a Poker hand; the highest Poker hand takes the antes. The players keep the same hands while the dealer turns up cards for Bingo (page 528). They keep the same hands while the dealer turns up cards for Put and Take in either variation (page 534). Finally the dealer turns up cards for Treize (see below).

Treize is the consummation of the game of Garbage, described above. The dealer turns up thirteen cards from the top of a newly-shuffled full 52-card pack; as he does so he counts "One, two, three," etc., counting the jack as 11, queen 12, king 13, ace 1. If he hits the rank of the number he calls on any turn (as, turning an eight when he says "Eight"), each other player must pay him as many chips as the number called. If the dealer continues through the number 13 without getting a hit, he pays each other player 7 chips. If the dealer hits more than once, each player must pay him each time. The dealer must call the numbers consecutively, one on the first card turned, two on the second, etc. It is better than 2 to 1 that the dealer will get a hit, and this constitutes the dealer's advantage when Garbage is played.

TWO-UP, OR SWY

Based on a similar game called Pitch and Toss, formerly played in England, this is the most popular gambling game of Australia and has spread into other parts of Australasia and into Spain. A gambling house where the game is played is called a *school*. A dealer called a *spinner* places two coins, tails up, on a small, paddlelike piece of wood called a *kip* (about 4″ x 2½″ x ¼″). He "chucks 'em up" and bets are settled, even money, if both land heads or both land tails; no decision if one head and one tail. The game is illegal in Australia but much played.

⊸ DICE GAMES ⊸

Dice may have been the earliest gaming implements, and have emerged independently in nearly every known human society. The earliest dice are believed to have been knucklebones, but dice in substantially their modern form are believed to have existed several hundreds of years B.C. A modern die is a cube, marked with dots (pips) on its six faces, the number of pips on each face being 1 to 6, inclusive, and the sum of pips on opposite faces always being 7. There are in addition Poker dice (on which the faces are marked as the six highest playing cards, A, K, Q, J, 10, 9); Crown and Anchor dice, on which the faces are marked with the suit symbols, ♠, ♡, ◇, ♣, and a crown and an anchor; put-and-take dice, of which one die is marked P (put) on three faces and T (take) on the others, and the other die is marked on each face with a number, so that a cast of the dice determines whether the player shall put chips into the pot or take them out, and how many chips; and dice in various other designs suited to specific games.

By far the most popular dice game in the United States is Craps ("crapshooting"). It is exclusively a gambling game and is played in two principal forms, the private game and the banking game. In the former, players bet among themselves; in the latter, they bet only against the house. The two games are identical in structure, but the house makes certain changes in the rules to maintain its profitable operation, and offers bets on many propositions that are seldom bet upon in private games.

CRAPS

Definitions. 1. The following terms are defined as used in Craps.

ACE. The face of a die having only one spot.

ACTION. A bet made and accepted.

BACK LINE. The section of the betting layout on which is placed a bet that the shooter will not pass.

BANK CRAPS. The game of Craps as played against a gambling house, all bets being laid against the house.

BAR. To rule out any decision on (a certain number); as, when aces are barred on a given bet, there is a stand-off if the shooter's first throw is 1-1. Also, *the bar* is the same as *back line*.

BIG EIGHT, BIG SIX. A bet that neither 8 nor 7, or that neither 6 nor 7, respectively, will be thrown in the next two rolls. The terms big eight, big six, are also applied to the bets that 8 or 6 respectively will be thrown before 7.

CASTER. The player who throws the dice; same as *shooter*.

CENTER. That part of the playing area into which the dice are cast.

CENTER BET. A bet between the shooter and other players on the result of the next series of rolls to be made by the shooter.

COCKED DICE. A die not resting squarely on one of its faces.

COME. To pass, considering the next roll as the first of a series.

COME OUT. To make the first roll of a series.

CRAP. The throw 1-1, 1-2 or 6-6 (2, 3, or 12).

CRAP OUT. Throw a 7 when trying for a point.

DON'T COME. The proposition that the shooter will lose, counting his next roll as the first of a series.

DON'T PASS LINE. The portion of the betting layout on which is placed a bet that the shooter will not pass.

DRAG, OR DRAG DOWN. Remove (part of one's winnings).

FADE. Bet against the shooter's center bet.

FIELD. A group of numbers (2, 3, 5, 9, 10, 11, 12, or 2, 3, 4, 9, 10, 11, 12); a bet may be placed that any of these numbers will come out on the next roll. Sometimes double is paid on 2 or 12.

FRONT LINE. The section of the betting layout on which is placed a bet that the shooter will win; the *pass line*.

GAG. The point 4, 6, 8, or 10 made the *hard way*, that is, 2-2, 3-3, 4-4, 5-5 respectively.

HARD WAY (see *gag*); a hard-way bet is a bet that the shooter will make his point with doubles before he makes it any other way or sevens.

LAY THE ODDS. To bet that the shooter will not make his point (the odds always being against his making it).

LAYOUT. The markings on the surface of the Crap table, indicating where bets are to be placed.

LINE. The *pass line;* the section of the layout on which is placed a bet that the shooter will pass.

MISS. Fail to pass. Also, *missout*.

NATURAL. The number 7 or 11 thrown on the shooter's first roll.

OFF NUMBER. A number that is neither a crap, a natural, nor the shooter's point.

OPEN CRAPS. A Crap game conducted by a house but permitting bets among the players.

PASS. A roll or series of rolls in which the shooter wins, either by throwing a natural on his first roll or by making his point.

PASS LINE. The section of the layout on which is placed a bet that the shooter will pass.

PLACE BET. A bet that the shooter will make his point.

POINT. The number 4, 5, 6, 8, 9, 10, if thrown by the shooter on his first roll.

POINT BET. A bet that the shooter will make his point.

PROPOSITION BET. A bet that a certain number or combination of numbers will or will not appear on a succeeding roll or series of rolls.

RIGHT. About to pass, or to win; a bet that a player is *right* is a bet that he will pass, or "come," or make his point, depending on usage.

ROLL. Throw or cast the dice from one's hand onto the playing surface.

ROLLER. The shooter.

SEVEN. To roll a 7. To *seven out* is to roll a 7 when trying for a point.

SHOOTER. The player whose turn it is to roll the dice.

STICKMAN. The house representative who handles the dice at a Crap table, retrieving them when they have been thrown and returning them to the shooter; he uses a long hooked stick for this purpose.

TAKE THE ODDS. To bet that the shooter will make his point.

WRONG. Antonym of *right;* the expectation that the shooter will lose.

Number of players. 2. Any number may play; they form a ring, leaving space in the center where bets may be put down and into which the dice may be thrown. In a gambling house, this ring forms around the table.

Dice. 3. Two dice are used. They must be of the same size and color, and identically marked. Each die must be practically a perfect cube, marked on its respective sides with one, two, three, four, five, and six spots; if the 2 side is vertical and facing you, and 4 is on top, 1 should be at your right, 6 at your left, 3 on the bottom and 5 on the back.

Betting. 4. Any player may be the first shooter; if necessary all candidates may throw one or two dice and the highest shoots first, two or more players who tie for high throwing again.

5. The right to shoot passes from player to player to the left. A newcomer entering the circle should take his place at the right of the shooter, if space and the convenience of the players permit.

6. The shooter places in the center whatever amount he wishes to bet, announcing its amount. Any other player may fade all or any portion or any remaining portion of it; if two speak simultaneously, a player who faded and lost on the preceding bet has precedence.

7. The shooter may at any time withdraw all his center bet, or any unfaded portion of it; in the former case he relinquishes the dice to the next player in turn. After each pass or loss, the shooter must again announce the amount he is shooting (betting).

8. Any player including the shooter may at any time bet with any other player on any contingency connected with the cast of the dice.

The play. 9. The shooter shakes the dice in his hand and rolls them away from him onto the playing surface. It may be ruled that both dice must strike some vertical surface and bounce back. When the dice both come to rest, the total of the spots on their uppermost faces is the number that has been thrown.

10. If the number is 2, 3, or 12, the shooter loses his center bet. If the number is 7 or 11, the shooter wins his center bet. If the number is 4, 5, 6, 8, 9, or 10, that number is the shooter's point and he must continue to roll the dice until his point appears again, in which case he wins, or until he rolls a 7, in which case he loses. After the shooter has a point, the roll of 2, 3, 11, or 12 is meaningless, as is any other number except the shooter's point and 7. (Such other numbers may, however, have bearing on bets other than the center bet.)

Irregularities. 11. *Cocked dice.* If a die comes to rest so that two or more of its faces are equally upward, the roll is void.

12. When play is on a table or other elevated surface, a roll is void if either die falls off the playing surface.

13. A player may stop a roll before either die has stopped rolling (saying, "No dice"), but only if he can readily capture both dice before the probable result of the roll could be apparent. [The privilege of stopping the roll, while traditional, causes trouble and should not be used except in unusual circumstances.]

14. A bet once made and accepted, whether or not the money has been put up, may be cancelled only by mutual agreement.

15. Once the shooter has rolled the dice, any unfaded portion of his center bet reverts to him and may not be faded.

Pointers on play. Skill at crapshooting (assuming honest play) is exclusively a matter of knowing the proper odds and accepting no less. Calculation of the odds is simple, in most cases; two dice produce thirty-six different combinations, which is not too many to permit one to calculate the number of combinations that will win for him, and the number that will beat him. Those are the odds. (See also pages 567–568.)

In some cases it is necessary or desirable to make a slightly inferior bet: The shooter is at a disadvantage, but suffers it for the pleasure of controlling the dice and his bets. In a gambling house, every bet is advantageous to the house; but without this profit it could not supply the place and equipment for the game.

The odds on the principal bets are:

251 to 244 that the shooter will lose; since all center bets are placed on an even-money basis, this represents a 1.42% expectancy of loss on the part of the shooter, and the same expectancy of gain on the part of the fader.

976 to 949 against a don't-pass bet in a gambling house, with aces or sixes barred; 1.4% advantage to the house. When the house bars ace-deuce, its advantage is increased to 488 to 447, or 4.4%.

6 to 5 against making the point if it is 6 or 8; to bet even money on making either of these points is to surrender 9.09% of the amount bet. Some gambling houses offer the shooter the equivalent of 11 to 10, or 7 to 6, or even as high as 11.60 to 10, against making his point when it is 6 or 8; in the last case, the advantage of the house is under 2%.

3 to 2 against making the point if it is 5 or 9. Laying 7 to 5, the house has an advantage of 4%.

2 to 1 against making the point if it is 4 or 10. Laying 9 to 5, the house has an advantage of 6⅔%.

8 to 1 against making a 4 or 10 the hard way. Laying 7 to 1, the house has an advantage of 11+%.

10 to 1 against making a 6 or 8 the hard way. Laying 9 to 1, the house has an advantage of 9+%.

19 to 17 against the field including the 5; 20 to 18 against the field including the 4 but paying double or double ace and double six; 20 to 19 on the same field if double six pays triple; 20 to 16 against the field including the 4 and not paying doubles. In each case the house lays even money.

5 to 1 against coming out 7; 8 to 1 against any crap; 17 to 1 against 3 or 11; 35 to 1 against any specified double, and 5 to 1 against throwing some double. These are the poorest bets available, at the odds that are usually offered.

The multitude of proposition bets that are offered in Crap games—that the shooter will roll 8 or 7 in the next two rolls, that he will throw 5 or 9 before 7, that he will throw 8 or 9 in three rolls, and so on—these are for those who have figured out the odds in advance and know where the advantage lies. They are easy enough to figure (see page 569) but it might spoil your enjoyment of the game to take time out for the calculation.

Among many layouts for the crap table are the following:

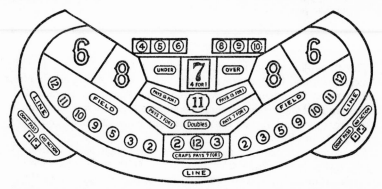

This is one of the less favorable layouts, from the player's point of view. On the don't pass bets, 1-2 is barred. The odds on proposition bets (except the field) are the minimum usually offered: "4 for 1" is equivalent to "3 to 1," for it means that the winning bettor gets 4 chips including the one he bet. On this layout the bettor should limit himself to line bets. (See, also, "Under and Over Seven" on page 544.)

The following layout is considerably kinder to the bettor:

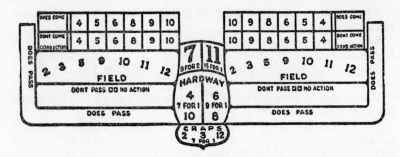

Note that on this layout aces, not 1-2, are barred on don't-pass bets, that a bet on 7 pays 7 to 2, or 3½ to 1 (but most houses offer 4 to 1), and that higher odds are offered on hard-way bets on 6 and 8 (on the layout shown on page 541 these bets—"doubles"—paid the same odds regardless of the point). Either the "does pass" or "don't pass" bet is satisfactory on this layout.

CRAPS WITH CARDS

A special 48-card pack is constructed, containing eight cards each of the ranks A, 2, 3, 4, 5, 6. The ace counts 1. The dealer shuffles, cuts, and turns up the top two cards; they represent a cast of the dice. He shuffles them back in, cuts again, and turns up two more cards, representing another cast of the dice. So the game proceeds, two cards at a time being turned, and always from the full pack. Betting and the rules of the game are otherwise precisely as in Craps.

CHUCK-LUCK

The three-dice game known generally as Chuck-luck (and spelled Chuck-a-luck and in other ways) has grown to be indistinguishable from, and in name interchangeable with, the game known as Hazard. Other names are Bird Cage, taken from the equipment used; Crown and Anchor, taken from the markings on the dice used in some games; Grand Hazard (obsolete); and Sweat.

Chuck-luck is a banking game. Players place such bets as are invited by the layout in use. The dealer then causes the three dice to come up at random, using either of two principal methods—he drops them through a chute in which there are obstructions to trip them, or he turns over a cage ("bird cage") and causes them to tumble over in falling to its new bottom surface—or he even rotates a wheel marked with the 216 combinations possible for three dice.

On the simplest Chuck-luck layout, players may bet only on a single number. If the number does not appear in the three dice, the bank takes the bet. If it appears once, the bank pays even money; twice, the bank pays 2 to 1; three times, the bank pays 3 to 1. (Of every $216 bet against the bank, the player may expect to get only $199 back. This gives the house an advantage of about 8%.

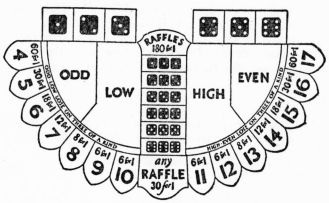

Layout often used for Chuck-luck (though a far simpler layout is often seen).

On the next-simplest Chuck-luck layout, players may bet on a specified three of a kind, or any three of a kind, as well as on the single numbers. The odds against a specified three of a kind showing are 215 to 1 and the house pays 180 or 179 to 1 (the latter being called 180 *for* 1). The odds against any three of a kind are 35 to 1 and the house pays 30 or 29 to 1.

On the most elaborate Chuck-luck layout, the house accepts bets not only on single numbers and on triplets but also on the point totals of the three dice. When this layout is used, the house takes all bets when any triplet (formerly called a *raffle*) shows; a bet on a single number does not pay 3 to 1, but is lost. The only bets paid by the house when a triplet shows are bets on that triplet and bets on any triplet.

The possible bets on the various possible totals, together with the odds against this total, and the odds most often offered by the house, are:

TOTAL	ODDS AGAINST	HOUSE ODDS
4 or 17	71 to 1	60 to 1
5 or 16	35 to 1	30 to 1
6 or 15	23 to 1	18 to 1
7 or 14	13.4 to 1	12 to 1
8 or 13	9.14 to 1	8 to 1
9 or 12	8 to 1	6 to 1
10 or 11	7 to 1	6 to 1
High (11 to 17)	111 to 105	Even
Low (4 to 10)	111 to 105	Even
Any odd number	111 to 105	Even
Any even number	111 to 105	Even

UNDER AND OVER SEVEN

This is played as a separate game and also occupies space on many Crap table layouts. Two dice are thrown, and players may bet at even money that the total will be over 7, or will be under 7; they are offered 3 to 1 (often stated as 4 *for* 1, thus counting the player's bet, which is returned to him) on some layouts, 4 to 1 on others. Since the odds are 21 to 15 against over or under, and 5 to 1 against 7, the bank's advantage is a large one. (See the layout on page 541.)

ODD AND EVEN

Games bearing this name may be played with one, two, three, or four dice. Bets are placed on a layout marked to indicate the various possible combinations.

With one or two dice. The player may roll one die twice, or two dice once, betting that both will be odd-numbered, or that both will be even (in either case the odds are 3 to 1 against him and the house will pay him 2 to 1 if he is right), or that one will be odd and the other even (in which case he must lay 6 to 5 against the house, since this is an even chance).

With three dice. All three dice are cast, or one die is cast three times. It is 7 to 1 against three odds or three evens; it is 5 to 3 against getting two odds and one even, and 5 to 3 against getting two evens and one odd. There are other combinations on which bets are accepted. In each case the house offers somewhat less than the actual odds.

With four dice. It is 15 to 1 against four odds, and the same against four evens; 7 to 1 against any four of a kind; 3 to 1 against a specified three of a kind, odd or even; even money against a pair or odds and a pair of evens. Again, the house offers somewhat less than these odds.

FOUR-FIVE-SIX

This game is also called See-Low, no doubt a corruption of its original Chinese name, Sz' 'ng Luk or Sing Luk. A variant of it, explained below, is called Acey-out.

Three dice are used. The only limit on the number of players is a practical one; with more than ten there is apt to be confusion. One player is the banker; he may be chosen by lot in any way, but usually by rolling for high dice. The banker states the amount of his bank and puts it in front of him; each other player may bet some portion of it, and each other player must be permitted to make some bet.

Bets having been placed, the banker rolls the three dice (usually from a dice cup). If he rolls any triplet, any pair and a six, or 4-5-6, he wins and collects all bets. If he rolls any pair and an ace, or 1-2-3, he loses and pays all bets. If he rolls any pair and a 2, 3, 4, or 5, that single number becomes his point. If he rolls any other number, it does not count and he continues to roll the three dice until one of the stated combinations comes up.

When the banker gets a point, the dice pass from player to player to his left, and each player in turn rolls the dice until his bet against the banker is settled: Like the banker, the player wins if he rolls a triplet, a pair and a 6, or 4-5-6; loses if he rolls a pair and an ace or 1-2-3; and establishes his own point if he gets a pair and any other number. If the player's point is higher than the banker's point, the player wins; if it is lower, the banker wins; if they have the same point it is a stand-off and the bet is withdrawn.

All bets are at even money.

The banker has an advantage, because he rolls first and there are more winning than losing rolls. The player stands to lose 2 chips in each 81 he bets, giving the banker about 2½% advantage.

Acey-out. This is the same game as 4-5-6 except that three aces as an initial roll lose instead of winning; the other triplets win, and all other combinations have the effect described above. The banker's advantage is very slightly reduced by the shift of the three aces.

BARBOOTH

Two dice are used, and two players roll them alternately, across a table to each other; but as many more as please can bet on the two active players. A player who rolls two aces, two deuces, two fours, or ace-deuce, loses; a player who rolls two sixes, two fives, two threes, or six-five, wins; other rolls do not count. When a decisive number is thrown, bets are settled; the player who won retains his position as an active player, and the player who lost loses his position to another. There is no advantage to either side in this game, and when it is conducted in a gambling house the house charges a fee (usually 2½%) for handling the bets.

COUNTER GAMES

Dice games played on cigar-store and other store counters are countenanced and flourish in some parts of the United States, and are seldom if ever encountered in other parts. Most of the counter games are played with dice and are gambling games in which the player tries to win money; others are for sales promotion and the house has little if any advantage, except in that it pays in merchandise on which it makes a profit.

Twenty-six is perhaps the most prevalent of the counter games. The player pays the sum required or permitted, usually 25 cents; the house keeps this. With ten dice and a dice cup, the player makes thirteen casts of the dice. Before the first cast he selects one of the six numbers to be his point. If in the thirteen casts he throws eleven or fewer of this number, the house pays him four times his bet ($1.00, in the case of the 25-cent bet); if he throws the number precisely thirteen times, the payoff is twice his bet; if he throws it twenty-six or more times, he is paid four times his bet; and if he throws it thirty-three or more times, he is paid eight times his bet. The actual payoff is respectively 3 to 1, even money, 3 to 1 and 7 to 1, since part of it is the player's own bet being returned to him.

The game has apparently received scant attention from mathematicians; the only published analysis of which we know, Edward X. Anderson's scholarly *Dice Analysis,* asserts that the player's expectancy is 21⅔ appearances of his number per game, and that the house advantage is slightly less than 25%. That is, for each 25 cents you pay, you figure to get back 20+ cents.

Fourteen is similar to Twenty-six: The player casts ten dice five times. He may select his point after the first cast, and is credited with a minimum of three appearances for that number on the first cast. The player has a 9+% chance of getting fourteen appearances in his five casts, and the payoff is 8 to 1 if he does, so that the house has a 10% advantage. Some houses reduce this slightly by paying higher amounts for more than 15 appearances. Most houses pay 8 to 1 for a "blank out"—failure of the point to show up at all in the last four casts.

Bingo, as a counter dice game, in various forms is called High Dice, Beat the Banker, Two-dice Klondike. Two dice are used, cast from a dice cup. The banker throws first, then the player. The higher number (total of the two dice) wins, but ties pay the banker. The player cannot win, so does not cast, when the banker has 12 (double sixes), but when the player throws double sixes the banker pays him double his bet.

The advantage of the banker depends on which of several house rules are in effect:

(a) In the basic game, as described, with 6-6 paying double, the player figures to lose 111 chips out of every 1,296 he bets.

(b) Sometimes the banker pays off automatically when he throws double aces; the player need not throw to beat him. This increases the banker's advantage infinitesimally; the player now figures to lose 112 chips out of every 1,296 bet.

(c) In a very few games, the banker pays off automatically when he casts either 2 or 3. This decreases the banker's profit; the player figures to lose only 100 chips out of every 1,296 bet.

(d) Instead of conceding defeat on a cast of 2, the banker takes the bet automatically on 2 as well as on 12. This materially increases his advantage; the player figures to lose 182 chips out of every 1,296 he bets.

Klondike. This is a counter game based on Poker dice. The banker drops five dice through a chute similar to the one used for Chuck-luck (page 543). The player then tries to beat the banker's poker hand. Ties pay the banker. The banker's advantage, which is 5+%, is comparatively small for a counter game.

Often an additional bet is offered: The player may bet even money that his hand will beat a pair of aces. The house has an advantage of 11+% on this bet.

Qualify. Five dice are used, and the game is played in two frames. In the first frame the player tries to qualify by casting successively five, four, three, two and one dice, saving and scoring the highest number he throws each time. If the pip total for the five casts is 25 or over, he qualifies and may now cast for prizes.

The cast for prizes is a single cast of all five dice. The pay numbers now are: if he qualified with 25, aces; with 26, deuces; with 27, threes; with 28, fours; with 29, fives; with 30, sixes. For his final cast, the player collects one unit (the amount of his bet) for each pip on the pay numbers showing. For example, if he qualified with 25 and now casts two aces, he collects two times his bet; if he qualified with 28 and now casts three fours, he collects twelve times his bet. Anderson calculates that this game is about even as between banker and player, and so is useful to the banker only to stimulate sales of merchandise.

POKER DICE

Five dice are used, either marked with playing-card designs, ace to nine; or regular dice; in which case the rank is 1 (high, representing the ace), 6, 5, 4, 3, 2. Any number may play, and the object is to make the best Poker hand, in one, two, or three casts. The rank of the hands is: Five of a kind (high); four of a kind; flush (optional), consisting of five dice with no pair and no sequence; straight (optional), consisting of five cards in sequence, Q-J-10-9-A or 5-4-3-2-1 being a sequence; three of a kind, two pair, one pair.

The first player casts five dice. He may stand pat on them, or put any of them aside and cast the others again; after his second cast, he may put aside any of the dice, adding them to the ones previously put aside, and cast the remaining die or dice a third time. Dice put aside after the first cast may not be cast again.

After the first player, each player in turn casts in the same manner.

There is seldom any betting, other than the establishment of a pot, which goes to the highest hand; or the lowest hand pays the check, if that is the purpose of the game.

Among the many forms of Poker Dice and five-dice games are:

Deuces Wild. This is the same as Poker Dice except that deuces are wild.

Battleships, or Ship, Captain, Mate and Crew, or Destroyers. Five dice are used. A player must have a six, a five and a four, otherwise his hand does not count; if he does have these three numbers, his other two dice represent the number of his crew. He has three rolls of the dice, as in Poker Dice. The player with the largest crew wins.

Liar Dice. This form of Poker dice is played with five dice and a dice cup for each of two players, and a screen to be placed on a table between them (a large book, propped open, will do). They roll for high dice, and the higher is the *caller.*

Each player rolls his five dice; then either player, beginning with the caller, may request a recast, but if the other refuses the play must continue. When play continues, the caller must announce a Poker hand, naming every "card" in it (for example, "three fours, a six and a five"). He need not announce his hand truthfully; either player may announce any hand he wishes, regardless of what he holds.

Following an announcement, the other player must either (a) announce a higher hand, or (b) roll some portion of his dice, as in Poker dice, and then announce a higher hand, or (c) say "You're a liar!" and remove the screen.

On claim of "You're a liar," if the player actually has the hand he announced, or better, he wins; if he has less than he announced, he loses.

Only three casts in all are permitted to each player, as in Poker Dice.

Addition. This is played the same as Poker Dice, using five dice and permitting three casts for each player, but the object is to make a hand of the highest numerical valuation, counting aces only 1 each. A player must retain at least one die from each cast.

YACHT

Most popular of the five-dice games is Yacht. Any number may play, each being provided with a scoresheet on which to record the scores of his progressive casts. The scoresheet provides twelve categories of hand, and each player has twelve turns to cast the dice. In each turn, a player may cast the five dice (or such portion of them as he does not retain) three times in all. At the end of this time he must select one of the twelve categories on the scoresheet (a category he has not previously selected) and enter the score to which his five dice entitle him in that category.

The different hands and scores are:

Yacht. Any five of a kind scores 50. (Some play that on his first turn the player must select the category Yacht, and he must continue casting until he gets five of a kind, 5 points being deducted from his score for every cast he requires in excess of three.)

Big straight. 6-5-4-3-2 scores 30.

Little straight. 5-4-3-2-1 scores 30.

Four of a kind. Provided there are any four of a kind in the five dice, the total of the pips on the dice is scored. (The maximum is four sixes and a five, scoring 29; four aces and a two would score only 6.)

Full House (three of a kind and a pair) scores as do four of a kind—the total of pips.

Choice is the free play; any five dice may be entered in this category, scoring the total of their pips. They may be five of a kind, if Yacht has already been scored, and likewise throughout the list.

Sixes, fives, etc., score for the pips on those numbers held when the category is selected. A player who selects sixes when he has five sixes scores 30; if he has only two sixes he scores 12. It is common to waste the ace and deuce categories, when, for example, one has tried for Yacht, straight, or another difficult category, and has failed. The hand may then be scored as aces, even though there is not an ace in the hand, for the maximum score in that category would be only 6 anyway.

The player with the highest score at the end of the game wins.

Player		
MAX. SCORE	HAND	SCORE
50	YACHT	
30	65432	
30	54321	
29	FOURS	
28	FULL HOUSE	
30	SIXES	
25	FIVES	
20	FOURS	
15	THREES	
10	TWOS	
5	ACES	
30	CHOICE	
302	TOTAL	

Yacht Scoresheet

MAX. SCORE	PLAYER	A	B	C	D	E	F
30	FIVE OF A KIND						
28	FULL HOUSE						
30	23456						
21	12345						
30	SIXES						
25	FIVES						
20	FOURS						
15	THREES						
10	TWOS						
5	ONES						
214	TOTAL						

Double Cameroon Scoresheet

CAMEROON

This is a form of Yacht in which the principle of play is the same but the categories are somewhat different, not including *choice* or *four of a kind.* Five dice are used, and may be cast three times each turn as in Yacht. Each player has only ten turns.

DOUBLE CAMEROON

Double Cameroon speeds up the game by using ten dice. In each turn a player must select two categories, using any five of his dice for each. The dice may be cast three times in each turn. The categories are as in Cameroon: Five of a kind, full house, big straight, little straight, sixes, fives, fours, threes, deuces, and aces.

CRAG

This is a three-dice game on the order of Yacht and Cameroon. A player is permitted to cast only twice in a turn. Each player has thirteen turns, and must fill thirteen categories:

Crag—a pair plus a die that brings the pip total to 13 (3-3-7, 4-4-5, 5-5-3, 6-6-1). Scores 50.

Thirteen—any three dice totalling 13. Scores 26.

Three of a kind. Scores 25.

High straight (6-5-4), *low straight* (3-2-1), *odd straight* (1-3-5), *even straight* (2-4-6), score 20 each.

Sixes, fives, fours, threes, deuces, aces, score the pip total of those numbers in the three dice when the category is selected.

⇀ ROULETTE ↽

The Wheel of Fortune as a gambling device may be very ancient; the modern game of Roulette is of relatively recent origin, perhaps not more than 150 years old. There are innumerable variations on the principle of the compartmented wheel that spins then stops at random at a number or symbol, players being invited to bet on the number or symbol at which it may stop. In the form described below it is a fixture in casinos throughout the world.

Roulette is a banking game; any number may play, betting only against the house.

The Roulette wheel. 1. The essential equipment for Roulette comprises a bowl that revolves on a spindle, the bowl ("wheel") being divided into 38 compartments; and a layout on which players may place their bets.

2. The compartments are alternately colored red and black, except for two that are colored green and marked 0 and 00; the red and black compartments are numbered from 1 to 38, as shown on the next page. (In Europe the wheel has only 37 compartments, the 00 being omitted; some wheels, especially in Central America, have 39 compartments, the additional one being marked with an eagle.)

3. The layout is marked with each of the numbers and colors of the wheel, and has additional spaces for bets on various contingencies.

Betting. 4. A player bets by placing chips on the appropriate section of the layout. Betting begins when the representative of the house calls "Place your bets," and ends when the wheel is spinning. [The French announcements are most common: *"Faites vos jeux"* (Place your bets), *"Rien ne va plus"* (No more bets).]

5. The bets permitted are:

(a) Low (that the number will be 1 to 18), high (that the number will be 19 to 36); either pays even money.

(b) Odd, even; either pays even money.

(c) Red, black; either pays even money.

(d) First, second or third dozen (1-12, 13-24, or 25-36, respectively); each pays 2 to 1.

(e) First, second or third column (that is, that the winning number will be in this column on the layout); each pays 2 to 1.

(f) Any of six consecutive numbers, the bet being indicated by placing the chip(s) at the outermost point of the horizontal line dividing these six numbers into rows of three; pays 5 to 1.

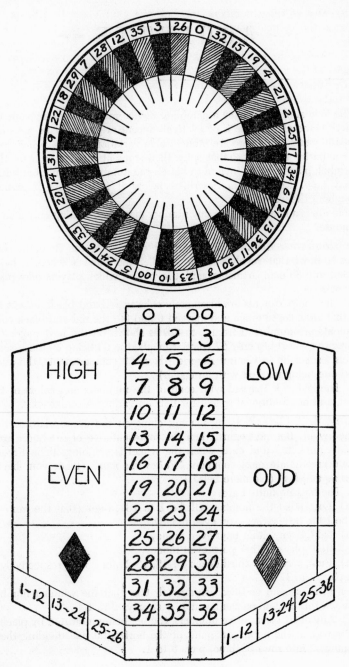

(g) Any of three numbers, the bet being indicated by placing the chips on the vertical line bounding the row of three numbers; pays 11 to 1.

(h) Any of four numbers, the bet being indicated by placing the chip(s) at the point in the center of the four numbers; pays 8 to 1.

(i) Either of two numbers, the chip(s) being placed on the line between the two numbers; pays 17 to 1.

(j) A single number; pays 35 to 1.

Bets (f), (g), (h) and (i) may be made only on combinations of numbers whose position on the layout makes possible the placing of chips as described in this paragraph.

Determination of bets. 6. A representative of the house (the *tourneur*) turns the wheel in one direction and releases into it an ivory ball, which he tosses in the opposite direction. When the wheel stops turning, the ball will be lodged in one of the compartments and the tourneur or another house man (*croupier*) announces the winning number and other factors pertinent to the settling of bets (red or black, odd or even, etc.).

7. If the 0 or 00 comes up, the house collects all even-money bets and all bets on the dozens and columns, as well as all bets on the numbers that did not come up; and pays only bets on the 0 or 00 (as the case may be) at 35 to 1. [On American wheels, this is equivalent to a 5¼% advantage for the house; on European wheels, with only the one 0, the advantage is about 2¾%. Many European casinos increase the inducement to players by merely putting the even-money bets "in prison" when the 0 comes up; that is, the bet remains and if it wins on the next turn the player may withdraw it, but receives no winnings with it. This is equivalent to giving back half the bet when the 0 shows, and most casinos following this policy permit the player, if he wishes, to withdraw half his bet at once and forfeit the remainder.]

Pointers on play. When the Roulette wheel is honest, as it is in most casinos, and when the player is looking for entertainment and not profits (which is usually the case in America, where the houses maintain Roulette to amuse the ladies while the men are at the crap tables), the cost to the player is not exorbitant—not, at least, in comparison with other gambling devices. With both 0 and 00 on the wheel, the player figures to lose $1 out of every $19 he bets. With only one 0 on the wheel, the loss should be only $1 out of every $37 bet, and where the rule of "in prison" applies, by betting only on the even-money bets (odd, even, red, black, high, low) one may reduce the cost to 50 cents in each $37 bet.

No system ever devised has convinced mathematicians that it reduces this expectancy of loss, or increases the player's chance of winning, in any degree. A reasonable system designed to produce small profits on considerable investment may nevertheless be expected to return some income daily for some months or even years until an unusually long series of losses would require a system bet beyond the limit established by the house; at this point the system bettor could lose his entire capital or an amount exceeding his previous profits.

Playing to win, the player should be careful not to bet on mutually exclusive contingencies; as, betting on the first column and on the number 26, when the winning of one bet must mean the loss of the other. The "hedge" bet—a large bet on red and a small bet on 0, for example—is mathematically a worse risk than merely the bet on the even-money proposition.

The other gambling wheels usually reserve such advantage to the operator that any bet on them must be considered in the nature of a contribution.

SYSTEMS AT ROULETTE

All the following systems are based on a progression by which the amount of a bet is increased after a loss; all are based on betting the even-money chances only, and so apply equally to Faro or any other game where such bets are available and the house advantage is moderate.

The Martingale. 1, 2, 4, 8, etc. Start afresh at 1 as soon as a bet is won.

The Great Martingale. 1, 3, 7, 15, 31, etc. (Sum of the Martingale geometrical progression.) Start afresh at 1 as soon as a bet is won.

D'Alembert. Increase 1 unit after a loss; decrease 1 unit after a win. When numbers are equal, you win ½ unit for every coup played.

1.
Labouchere. Write down any number of units—say 2. Bet the top and
3.
bottom numbers. After a win, cross out the numbers involved in the bet. After a loss, write the amount of the bet at the bottom. When all numbers are crossed out, begin again.

Paroli. Bet 1. If win, leave the 2 for a second bet. If win, begin again with 1. If lose on first or second, bet 1 until you have 2 successive wins. After 3 units lost, begin with 2, etc.

Anti-Labouchere. Write down nine 1's. Proceed as in Labouchère except that win is written down and losses crossed off. After a win of 9 units, start over. (It is possible to win 9 units in 3 coups—but takes bank 5 coups.)

Ascot. Progression is 3, 6, 9, 12, 20, 25, 35, 50, 75, 125, 200.

Begin with 25 and go up the scale as long as you win; down the scale, as you lose. Start over after winning or losing 200 bet.

BOULE

The continental casino game La Boule (the bowl) is a wheel game except that the wheel itself is stationary; it is divided into nine compartments numbered from 1 to 9, and the croupier spins a ball around the rim of the bowl, the bets being determined when the ball comes to rest in a compartment. The number 5 is reserved to the house, so that its expectancy is to win 1/9, or 11+%, of all money bet against it. Players may bet on any number (including 5), the pay-off being 7 to 1; or odd (1, 3, 7, 9), or even (2, 4, 6, 8), or on either of two bandes (1, 3, 6, 8 and 2, 4, 7, 9), the pay-off on any of these being at even money. While far less attractive percentage-wise than Roulette, La Boule flourishes in many casinos where Roulette is available; for the minimum bet is far lower, so that one may bet the equivalent of a few cents at a time and thus derive cheap entertainment from the game. The house must in such circumstances reserve a greater advantage, for the cost of maintaining the game and paying the croupiers' salaries is as great as at the games played for higher stakes.

OTHER WHEEL GAMES

Gaming wheels other than Roulette are seldom seen in casinos; they are a specialty of carnivals, amusement parks, and beach resorts. Generally they reserve an advantage to the operator that would make them profitable even if honestly run, but in addition they are so rigged that the operator can control the stopping place. Most of them are simple mechanisms, consisting of a flexible shaft whose tip catches in a circle of pegs, the same principle as a popular type of noise-making toy. Some are more complex.

Horse-race wheel. The layout provides the names of famous race horses; a vertical wheel spins till it stops at the name of one of these horses; a horizontal wheel above it spins until it stops at a figure that indicates the odds, as 2 to 1, 8 to 1, etc. Since the horse selected usually has a 1/10 to 1/12 chance to win, and the pay-off averages 3 or 4 to 1, the operator should retain 50% or more of whatever is bet against him.

Dice wheel. The wheel has 36 compartments, marked with all the possible combinations of two dice. Each spin of the wheel is equivalent to one roll of two dice, so that any two-dice game can be played on this wheel; usually the betting is confined to the place and proposition bets described on pages 540-542.

Other dice wheels are marked with three-dice combinations, permitting the play of such games as Chuck-luck (page 543).

Color wheel. The number of compartments may be as high as 200, each marked with one of five colors. Any type of betting may be invited; but, assuming that a player has a 1/5 chance that the wheel will light on his color, and the pay-off is 2 to 1, the operator should retain 40% of what is bet against him.

Skillo, or Slum. This is the simplest form of carnival wheel, on which there are only six to ten different numbers, each repeated often enough to give the wheel the usual 40 compartments; play is usually for prizes.

Slot Machines. The machine known as the "one-armed bandit" is a fixture in gambling houses, as well as providing income for private clubs and for restaurants, bars, and shops wherever the law allows. Fundamentally it is a wheel game, though a complex one.

Three wheels are mounted on a horizontal axle; they turn independently of each other. The outside of the rim of each wheel is divided into (usually) twenty panels, each bearing a picture: of a cherry, lemon, plum, bell, or bar. The player deposits a coin in the machine. A pull on a handle then spins the wheels by spring action; when all three have stopped, the row of pictures determines whether or not the player has won, and the odds at which he will be paid, if so. The biggest prize is for three bars in a row; this combination pays (usually) 19 to 1 plus a jackpot that brings the total pay-off to about 119 to 1. On most machines, however, the odds against making this combination are 3,999 to 1. Most "one-armed bandits" would return about 65% of the money put into them, retaining 35% as the operator's profit, if no steps were taken by the operator to reduce this pay-off; in fact, however, the machine is usually rigged to retain even more, though on the contrary some gambling houses encourage play by materially reducing the machine's advantage.

⟶ L O T T E R I E S ⟵

There are a myriad methods of distributing prizes by lot, but few of them may properly be classed as games. The following forms, however, are often played as games. Equipment for Lotto, for example, is manufactured under a variety of trade names as a juvenile pastime.

Lotto. Cards are prepared, each card having three to five horizontal rows of five numbers per row, the numbers ranging from 1 to 99, and no two rows of numbers being identical whether on the same or on different cards. One such card is issued to each player. Small balls numbered from 1 to 99 are placed in a bag and mixed, then are withdrawn at random, one by one. As each ball is withdrawn, its number is announced and each player marks wherever that number appears on his card. The first player so to mark a complete row of five numbers on his card wins. The prize is usually a purse made up of equal contributions from all players, less the percentage, if any, taken by the proprietor of the game. A player may have more than one card by contributing in full for each. If two or more cards complete a row on the same number, the purse is divided equally.

Keno. This is a form of Lotto in which the numbered balls are squeezed one by one from the mouth of a leather bag, called a *keno goose,* which has an opening just large enough to permit one ball at a time to escape. Though the derivation of *keno* is the word meaning *five* in romance languages, the pace of the game is sometimes accelerated by having only three numbers in a row on the cards, so that three in a row wins the prize.

Bingo. The modern American form of Lotto employs a 5 x 5 card, the object being to get five numbers in a row horizontally, vertically, or (in some games) diagonally. The center square is usually a "free play"; that is, it is deemed to be a number that has been called. Most Bingo games are conducted as profit-making enterprises; for example, each player pays 10 cents for a card (or gets three cards for 25 cents) and the prize is one dollar; two or more players winning on the same number receive the prize in full. With more than ten players, the proprietor of the game must make a profit (duplication of prizes rarely occurs); with more than thirty players the amount of the prize is usually increased. The first player to fill a row, column or diagonal calls "Bingo!" Bingo is known by a variety of names; a form called Screeno and by other names has been much used for business promotion in motion-picture theatres.

Typical Bingo card. The actual size of the card is about 6 x 4 inches. The caller facilitates the player's finding the number on his card by announcing the column—"B," "I," etc.—in which it will be found. Any five in a row complete the card and end the game.

Baseball pools. The player buys—usually at a cigar-store counter or from a similar outlet—a card that allots to him three, four or five teams playing in that number of baseball leagues. If his teams score an unusually high or low number of runs during the day or week to which his card applies, he wins a prize. He cannot select his teams and so the baseball pool is pure lottery. The prizes on cards selling at 25 cents each run from $10. to $500. Because of the high cost of operating such a lottery (in which the unit sales are so small) the operators retain a large proportion of their receipts, usually paying out no more than 10% to 25% of them; the player therefore figures to lose 75 to 90 cents out of every dollar he spends for "tickets."

Football pools. Unlike the baseball pools, most football pools theoretically permit the exercise of skill. The cards are sold as are those for the baseball pools (see above), but the player may try to select the winners of any number of games from a list of ten or more (up to perhaps thirty) games offered by the card. All his selections must be correct (that is, each of his teams must win, not tie or lose) for him to receive a prize. The operators of the football pool are able to maintain it at full profit (as though it were a matter of pure lot) by excellent handicapping. In every game offered, either the teams are evenly matched or the superior team "spots" some number of points to the inferior. For example, you may be offered "Ohio State vs. Northwestern + 6." So far as the football pool is concerned, the result of this game will be determined after adding 6 points to Northwestern's actual score; on this basis, the player is permitted to select either team. The operators' handicapping has been shown, over the years, to be remarkably accurate.

This being so, every game must be considered an even proposition, whereupon the player has ½ chance of selecting its winner. His chance of selecting three winners out of three is therefore ½ x ½ x ½, or ⅛; the odds are 7 to 1 against him, the pay-off is 4 to 1, so he figures to lose $3. out of every $7. he spends on cards in the football pool—if there is no tie. The probability of ties can be estimated only statistically, but probably increases the operators' advantage by 10% or so. The player has the privilege of picking any number of winners from three to ten, the pay-off increasing accordingly, but the disproportion of the pay-off likewise increasing so that in attempting to select three winners the player surrenders perhaps 40% of his investment; in attempting to pick ten winners, he has a 1/1,024 chance and is paid only 199 to 1, so that the operator's advantage approaches 90% (allowing for ties).

Race-horse Keno. In the Lotto variant most popular in the legal game rooms of Reno, Nevada, each ticket has 80 numbers, each accompanied by the name of a race horse (though this is in no way essential to the game). A player selects ten numbers (horses). Twenty of the eighty numbers are drawn at random.

The pay-off is as follows:

PLAYER HAS		PAY-OFF
5 numbers		Even money
6	"	17 to 1
7	"	179 to 1
8	"	899 to 1
9	"	1,799 to 1
10	"	3,599 to 1

The player figures to lose slightly more than 25% of the cost of each ticket he buys.

Many more types of ticket are sold, providing different groups and combinations that the player may bet will be included in the twenty numbers drawn.

This type of lottery is called the Chinese lottery.

RAFFLES

In modern usage, a raffle is any lottery in which a winner (of a prize of any kind, usually merchandise) is determined by drawing a number at random from all the numbers previously allotted to all contestants.

Raffles were formerly conducted, and sometimes still are, by giving each contestant three casts of three dice (equivalent to one cast of nine dice). The highest total thrown wins. If two or more players tie for high score, there are two solutions, (a) if the contestants are few enough and are readily available, they play off the tie among themselves by three more casts each; (b) if the contestants are not available for this determination of the winner, the prize is divided equally among those who tie for it.

The average total of the spots on nine dice cast once, or three dice cast three times, is 32. It is more than 2,000 to 1 against throwing a total as high as 48. (See *How to Calculate Odds,* on page 569).

SPORTING GAMES
WITH DICE AND CARDS

PLAYING-CARD FOOTBALL*

Two players or sides compete. The "field" must show 100 divisions representing the yards in a football gridiron; it may be made by drawing parallel lines on a long sheet of paper, or by putting holes in a board. One peg or other token is used to represent the ball. A useful accessory is a strip 10 yards long, used as in a regular football game to keep track of the previous position of the ball and determine when a first down has been gained.

One pack of 52 cards is shuffled, then dealt until exhausted, plays being made accordingly. One such deal represents a quarter, and four deals make a game.

Kings count 13, queens 12, jacks 11, aces 1, other cards their index value. The numbers on the cards indicate the distance the "ball" is to be moved, and the colors indicate the direction—red cards favor the offense (side in possession of the ball) and black the defense.

Kick-off. One side is chosen by lot to kick off. The ball is put on its 40-yard line. Five cards are dealt, and the ball is advanced by the total of the numbers (colors being ignored). The pack is then given to the receiving side.

Receiving the kick-off. If the ball has passed the receiver's 10-yard line, he may pick it up where it lands, or announce "Let it roll" and deal one card: if it is red, the ball is put back on his 20-yard line; if it is black, the ball is advanced 5 yards toward receiver's goal.

If the kick-off falls short of the receiver's 10-yard line, he deals one card. (a) If the first card is red, he continues dealing cards so long as reds turn up, and runs the ball back by the total of the red cards. Eight successive reds score a touchdown regardless of their total. (b) If the first card is black, a second is dealt. If the second is red, the player may continue dealing so long as reds appear, and run the ball back by the total, except that a touchdown on this play is barred. If the second card is black, the ball is fumbled, and a third card is dealt to show which side recovers it (red gives it to the receiver). A recovered fumble stays where it landed from the kick-off.

---

* Invented by Lt. Com. Arnold H. Bateman, U. S. N. (ret.)

Carrying the ball. The player having the ball may choose any of the following plays, and the outcome is determined by the cards.

Punt. Five cards are dealt to determine the distance of the punt, as for a kick-off. But if the first three cards are black, the kick is blocked and the fourth card shows who recovers the ball (red for receiver); in either case the ball is moved back toward the kicker's goal the distance of the three black cards. Rules for receiving a punt are the same as for receiving a kick-off.

Line buck. Deal one card. If it is red, advance the ball the indicated distance. If it is black, the play is blocked; deal a second card: red shows no loss on the play; black sets the ball back for a loss of 5 yards maximum.

End run. Deal two cards. If both are red, plays succeed; deal additional cards until first a black appears; the ball is advanced by the total of the reds. Eight successive reds make a touchdown.

First card red, second black, ball stays fixed.

First card black, second red, set ball back by the distance of the black but not more than 5 yards.

Both cards black, set ball back by the total but not more than 15 yards.

Whatever the outcome of the play, one down is counted against the offensive side.

Short forward pass. Deal one card. If it is red, the pass succeeds and the ball is advanced accordingly; deal additional cards, and any additional reds show ground gained by running. If the first card is black, deal a second: if it is red, the pass is incomplete; if it is black, the pass is intercepted, and the pack must be surrendered to the opponent, who then deals for a possible run-back by successive reds.

Long forward pass. Deal three cards. If at least one is red, and the total of all is at least 25, deal a fourth; red completes the pass for a total of all the cards (colors ignored), black makes the pass incomplete. If the total of first three cards is less than 25, the pass is incomplete. If the first three are black, the passer is tackled behind his line the indicated distance but not over 15 yards.

Field goal. The offense may try for a field goal as below. For success the first card must be red, and the total of all cards (colors ignored) must at least equal the distance from ball to goal. If the try fails, the rules for punt and receiving punt apply.

BALL ON	DEAL	BLOCKED IF
7-14	two cards	both black
15-21	three	first two black
22-28	four	first two black
over 28	five	first three black

Point after touchdown. Deal one card; red scores the point, black fails.

Penalties. Each of the following cards involves a penalty when it is dealt as the first card of any play except kick-off and point after touchdown, or dealt as an indicator.

CARD	PENALIZES	DISTANCE
◇2	offense	5
◇J	offense	5
◇Q	offense	15
♤2	defense	5
♤J	defense	5
♤Q	defense	15

HORSE RACE WITH CARDS

One player is chosen by lot to be the first banker. After each "race," the bank rotates to the next player at the left. The banker has absolute right to fix the betting limits during his tenure, also to fix the odds on the "horses." If players do not like the odds quoted, they need not bet.

The four aces are removed from a pack of 52 cards to represent the horses. They are laid, face up, in a row near one side of a table. The rest of the pack is shuffled and cut; six cards are dealt, face up, in a column at one side of and above the aces. These cards represent the track. Each horse has to take six steps up the track to reach the finish line, and the first to get there wins.

Each player who wishes to bet places his stake below the ace that he backs to win. If it were not for the six track cards, the odds against each ace would be 3 to 1. But the track cards are bound to contain more cards of some suit than of others, and so to affect the actual odds. It is up to the banker to quote such odds as will attract bets on all horses.

The remaining 42 cards of the pack being well shuffled, cards are turned up one by one from the top. As each card shows, the ace of the same suit is advanced one step. The race is thus won by the suit in which six cards first appear.

BASEBALL WITH CARDS

This is a game of chance, in which the various plays of a baseball game are determined by turning cards up from the pack. The game is best for two, but can be played by more, the greatest number of runs winning in any case.

To keep track of the position of runners, draw a baseball "diamond" on a sheet of paper, and use coins or other tokens to represent players.

Shuffle together three full packs of 52 cards. (Two packs, or even one, may be used, but three is preferable.) One player then turns cards from the top of the pack, scoring hits, runs, and outs according to the schedule below. After three outs, his turn ends, and the pack is reshuffled for the next player. In the two-hand game, each player has nine turns to make a complete game. With three or more players, the game should be limited by agreement to fewer "innings."

Each card has a meaning as below. The players must of course be familiar with baseball in order to determine the cumulative effect of the sequence of the cards.

♠A—home run

♡A—three-base hit

♢A or ♣A—double, runners score

♠K—double, runners advance 2 bases

Other kings—single, runners advance 2 bases

Any queen—single, runners advance 1 base

♠J or ♡J—base on balls

♢J or ♣J—ball; runner nearest 1st base steals a base, unless occupied

Any 10 or 9—ball

Any 8, 7 or 6—strike

Any 5—batter out, runners advance 1 base

Any 4—batter out, runners hold bases

Any 3—out; with any man on base, runner farthest advanced is out, batter safe at 1st base

♠2—strikeout

♡2—double play, provided man is on base

♢2—batter and all runners out

♣2—triple play, retires the side even with no man on base

CONTINUOUS BASEBALL*

Any number may play, up to about nine. Each in turn rolls five dice simultaneously and repeatedly, until he has made three "outs" or has scored a run to win the game.

Draw a baseball diamond on a sheet of paper and use three blue poker chips to represent the runners. Use red chips to record the outs, and white chips for betting. To begin a game, equal stacks of whites should be distributed to all players. Each antes one white chip to form a pool, which goes to the player first to score a run. After the pool is won, a new pool is formed by equal antes.

The baseball plays are governed by the total of the five dice, which may vary from 5 to 30, according to the following schedule:

5—hit, home run	12—ball and stolen base
6—choice of play	13—out, pitcher
7—out, left field	14—ball
8—strike	15—hit, one base
9—out, center field	16—foul
10—hit, two bases	17—out, first base
11—out, right field	18—strike

---

* Invented by Louis J. J. Taney

19—out, second base

20—hit, one base

21—out, shortstop

22—ball

23—out, third base

24—ball and stolen base

25—hit, two bases

26—foul

27—out, catcher

28—strike

29—choice of play

30—hit, three bases

Straight (either 1-2-3-4-5 or 2-3-4-5-6)—batter goes to first base, but runners already on advance two bases.

Five of a kind (other than five 1's or 6's, which are played normally)— batter takes base to which he is entitled by the hit, but all runners already on advance three bases.

Hit (5, 10, 15, 20, 25, 30)—advance batter and runners all the same number of bases, as indicated in the schedule, except as especially provided for Straight and Five of a Kind.

Infield out (7, 9, 11)—batter is out, but all runners advance one base.

Ball (14, 22)—four balls entitle batter to go to first base. Runners advance only if forced by the walk.

Ball and stolen base (12, 24)—on fourth ball, execute this play as for ordinary ball (14 and 22). On any previous ball, all runners advance one base.

Choice of play (6, 29)—batter may choose any play, usually a home run. He must cast the dice again; if the total is even, he may execute the play; if the total is odd, the play is an out.

FIVE-DICE BASEBALL*

Draw a baseball diamond on a sheet of paper, and use poker chips or other tokens to represent runners. Three chips for each side are enough. The game may be solitaire, or by two sides with one or more players on a side.

Five dice are cast simultaneously and repeatedly by one side until three of its men have been put out. The dice are then given to the opposing side. Team members (with more than one player on a side) roll the dice in turn.

The plays on the baseball diamond are made in accordance with the total on all five dice, which can vary from 5 to 30. A copy of the following schedule must be kept at hand to interpret the rolls.

30—home run, counting 4 runs even with no man on base

29—home run, counting at least 3 runs

28—home run, counting at least 2 runs

27—home run

26—triple, counting at least 2 runs

---

* Invented by Louis J. J. Taney

25—triple, counting at least 1 run

24—triple

23—double, runners score

22—single, runners advance 2 bases

21—single

20—two balls

19—ball

18—strike, runner nearest 1st base steals a base

17—strike

16—strike

15—sacrifice, batter out, runners advance 1 base

14—batter out, runners hold bases

13—strike, runner nearest 1st base out stealing

12—batter out, runners advance

11—batter out, runners hold bases

10—out; with men on, runner nearest home out, batter safe.

9—batter and runner farthest advanced, out

8—double play, two out even with no man on base

7—batter and all runners out

6—triple play, three out even with no man on base

5—triple play, and any runs previously made in that inning called off because the umpire reverses a decision

➤ THE SCIENCE OF BETTING ➤

Anyone afflicted with the gambling fever will take a bet in any of three circumstances: (a—and preferably) when the odds favor him; (b) when the odds are even; (c—for want of anything better) when the odds are against him.

The question always is, What *are* the odds? who has the edge? where does the "percentage" lie?

Everyone talks—and writes—about this esoteric term "percentage." Everyone knows you have a good bet if the percentage is with you, a bad bet if the percentage is against you. But no one seems to know precisely what percentage is. No one bothers to define it.

One thing may be stated flatly: If you figure to win once in every eleven times you bet, and you are offered odds of 10 to 1, then when you have made eleven bets you will have put up one unit eleven times; ten times you will have lost; once you will have gotten back the one unit you bet plus ten units paid you for winning the bet; you will have broken even, and there is no percentage for either side.

If you figure to win once in eleven times and you are offered 9 to 1, or less, the percentage is against you; if you are offered 11 to 1, or more, the percentage is for you.

But exactly what is the percentage for or against you? If it is only 2%, then you can say that an evening in which you bet $100.00 (or bet $10.00 ten times) will cost you only $2.00, and you are willing to spend this much. It is no more than the price of a theatre ticket. But if the percentage against you is 13%, then every time you bet a dollar it costs you 13 cents; a $10.00 bet costs you $1.30; an aggregate of $100.00 bet in an evening's play costs you $13.00. This may be more than you are willing to spend for an evening's entertainment.

To know where you stand, you must know how to calculate the odds for and against any contingency on which you bet; and you must also decide how you choose to define "percentage."

Percentage. There are at least three distinct theories as to how the banker's "percentage" in a house game should be figured. In most games, the percentage is derived from payments at shorter odds than the actual chance of winning. The three theories will therefore be illustrated for the case of a house that pays off at 10 to 1 on a bet that has only a 1-in-12 chance of being won.

(a) *Theorist method.* This is a method advanced by certain writers on chances. The percentage is to be figured by the formula:

$$\text{House advantage} = \frac{\text{House net profits}}{\text{House losses}}$$

Assume that for every 13 times the punter makes the same bet, the probability is that he will lose twelve times and win once, on which occasion he collects 10. The house thus pays out 10 during a period when it collects 12, a net gain of 2. Its percentage is 2/10 = 20%. Whatever the mathematical merits of this formula, it is a far cry from what the house or the punters consider to be "the percentage."

(b) *House method.* As might be expected, gambling houses use a formula for their percentage that gives the lowest possible figure:

$$\text{House advantage} = \frac{\text{House net profits}}{\text{Total purse}}$$

Assume that the punter puts up 13 units, to cover which (at odds of 10 to 1) the house must put up 130; this makes a total purse of 143. On the whole transaction, the house makes a net gain of 2. Its percentage is 2/143 = 1.4%. This method is more valid than may be immediately evident. The house must actually have the 130 in operating funds, and must make capital expenditures in equipment, etc., to entice the punter's 13. Out of this investment it realizes a return of 2. If the percentage of return, figured on this formula, is no greater than the savings bank rate of interest on deposits, obviously there is no more point in maintaining a gambling casino than in depositing in a savings bank.

(c) *Bettor's method.* The gambling-house customer is not concerned with the capital expenditure of the house, but with what portion of his betting money he must expect to lose merely through the discrepancy in the odds. His formula is:

$$\text{House advantage} = \frac{\text{Net loss of punter}}{\text{Amount staked by punter}}$$

Assume that he pays out 13, and collects 11. His net loss is 2, and the percentage against him is therefore 2/13 = 15.4%. This formula is obviously correct from the bettor's point of view.

Consider the case in which a bettor bets that double sixes will come out on the next roll in Craps.

Double sixes should come out only once in 36 rolls. The bettor has a losing bet unless he is offered odds of 35 to 1.

The house offers only 30 to 1. The bettor therefore says justly, "For every $36.00 I put up, at $1.00 per roll for thirty-six rolls, I will get back $31.00—my dollar plus $30.00 from the house on the one time in thirty-six that I win. I figure to lose $5.00 out of every $36.00 I bet. The house has a percentage of nearly 14%."

The house says, "Every time the bettor puts up $1.00, we must put up $30.00 to cover it. By the time he has bet $36.00, we have put up $1,080.00. And what profit do we have on that investment? Only $5.00. Less than ½ of 1%! We'd rather have him bet on the line, where our profit is better than 1.4%." And it is true that gambling houses seem to bend all their efforts to encourage bets on the "pass" and "don't pass" chances, and on the bets on making or not making a point (where the bet is nearer even money) rather than on the long shots such as the bet on double sixes.

In this book percentages are quoted from the bettor's point of view—the percentage of his bet that he may expect the house (or any opponent) to retain.

For those who are willing to spend some time and effort learning how to calculate the precise odds, the following section is appended.

HOW TO CALCULATE ODDS

The Set of Events. 1. What is the chance of rolling an ace with a single die? A die has six faces, numbered from one to six. In the absence of positive knowledge to the contrary, we assume that every face has an equal chance to turn up. The chance for an ace—or any other number—is therefore one in six, that is 1/6.

2. This example illustrates the initial step in calculating any probabilities about games. A set of events is established, one of which must occur, and the occurrence of any of which precludes the others. Due care must be taken to see that the list is complete—overlooks no event that might occur—and to define the events so that they are mutually exclusive. Then, in the absence of knowledge to the contrary, it is assumed that every event in the set is equally probable.

3. This basic assumption can never be proved. The contrary might be proved—it might be known that the die is untrue or loaded. Nevertheless, credence can be given to the assumption if the observed occurrences are in accord with theoretical prediction.

4. By mathematical rules, other probabilities can be deduced from an assumption. But they cannot add to the validity of the assumption; they stand or fall with it. Mistakes are sometimes made by failure to formulate and scrutinize the assumption. For example: Probabilities as to Bridge hands are calculated from the assumption that every possible combination of four hands of thirteen cards each is equally probable. This assumption is valid in form, and certainly as likely as that every face on a die has an equal chance to turn up. Now suppose that a person enters a room where a Bridge deal is in its last stages of play. Each hand contains five cards; this person is told the identity of all twenty cards remaining. Can he calculate the probabilities of their distribution on the premise of a "random deal"? Certainly not; though these cards are the dregs of (presumably) a random deal, the cards already played were not selected by blind chance but by willful act, limited by certain rules of play. The fact is that certain random distributions of the twenty cards could be proved impossible as the result of legal play, whatever the original deal.

5. Given a proper set of events, totalling n items, the basic assumption is that F, the probability FOR any one of them, is

(1)
$$F = \frac{1}{n}$$

A probability of 1 represents certainty that a given event will happen; a probability of 0 means certainty that it will not happen. Every "maybe" probability is expressed by a fraction between 1 and 0.

6. An event must either occur or not occur. The sum of the separate probabilities for the two alternatives must be certainty, 1. Therefore, where A is the probability AGAINST the event.

(2)
$$F + A = 1$$

Sub-sets. 7. What is the chance that a card drawn at random from a pack of 52 will be an ace? The chance that it will be the spade ace is 1/52, that it will be the heart ace 1/52, etc. The chance for any ace as against another rank is the sum of the probabilities for each, 4/52 or 1/13. To generalize, if a sub-set of the *n* events contains *r* of them, the chance that one of the *r* events will occur is

(3)
$$F(r) = \frac{r}{n}$$

8. Similarly, if there are several sub-sets in *n*, such as *r, s,* etc., the chance that one of these will occur is

(4)
$$F [r \text{ or } s \ldots] = \frac{r + s}{n}$$

Due care must be taken to define such sub-sets so that they are mutually exclusive. For example, what is the chance that a drawn card will be a spade or an ace? It would be wrong to say that, since there are 13 spades and four aces, the chance is $(13 + 4)/52$. There are only 16 cards that will satisfy, not 17, since the spade ace is common to both sub-sets.

9. Formula (4) is sometimes written

(5)
$$F [r \text{ or } s] = F [r] + F [s]$$

But the direct addition of probability-fractions is proper only when they concern sub-sets of the same proper set *n*; formula (5) must be understood to mean that *r, s,* etc. are the separate groups that all together make up *n*. Ludicrous mistakes are sometimes made by misapplication of (5). For example, if six dice are rolled simultaneously, what is the chance that at least one ace will turn up? The chance for an ace on each die is 1/6; to add $1/6 + 1/6$ etc. six times gives a sum of 1—which means certainty that an ace will turn up. This answer is of course absurd. The correct method of computation is given later.

Independent events. 10. What is the chance that in tossing a coin I will get heads twice consecutively? The chance for heads each time is 1/2; the chance for both together is $1/2 \times 1/2 = 1/4$. To generalize, if *a, b, c* . . . are independent events, the probability that all of them will occur is

(6)
$$F [a, b, c \ldots] = F [a] \times F [b] \times F [c] \ldots$$

11. Independent events can be conceived as occurring consecutively or simultaneously. Thus, the problem of the six dice cast simultaneously, in paragraph 9, can be conceived as one die cast six times. What is the chance of rolling an ace at least once? One wrong method of solution has been shown: here is another. The chance for an ace each roll is 1/6, hence the chance in six rolls is 1/6 x 1/6 etc. or $(1/6)^6$. The answer is palpably absurd, because it says that the chance dwindles with each successive roll. The method misapplies formula (6). For a correct direct application, it would be necessary to calculate separately the chance of getting an ace on the first roll, not on the first roll but on the second, etc., and then add all these separate chances.

12. But this problem and many like it can much more simply be solved through negative probability. The chance of not getting an ace on any given roll is 5/6. The probability that not one of six rolls will produce an ace is 5/6 x 5/6 etc. or $(5/6)^6 = 16,625/46,656$. Then formula (2) gives the positive probability for at least one ace, 30,030/46,656 or about 2/3.

Dependent events. 13. What is the chance that two cards drawn at random from a pack of 52 will be an ace and a king? By misapplication of (6) it might be argued that the chance of drawing an ace is 4/52, of drawing a king 4/52, of the two together 4/52 x 4/52. This is a misapplication because the two events are not independent. If the cards are conceived to be drawn consecutively instead of simultaneously (and the formula applies only when either conception can be adopted with indifference to the result), it becomes obvious that after the first card is drawn, the second comes from 51, not 52. The chance for the second card is 4/51. The chance for the two together is a little better than the erroneous method gives. (The true answer is 8/52 x 4/51 = 8/663 for on the first draw either an ace or king will serve).

14. Events are dependent, among several that must occur to create a single "favorable" case, if the success or failure of one affects the probabilities of another. One way of dealing with dependent events is shown in paragraph 13: due account is taken of the alteration in the proper set after one favorable event has occurred. Another way—and usually the simpler—is to form the proper set in such a way as to include all the separate events that must occur together to make a "favorable" case.

15. As applied to the problem of drawing an ace and king together, this means that the set of events should be composed of all possible two-card draws. This number is 1326 (the method of calculation is given later). Of these, 16 are "favorable"—any of 4 aces combined with any of 4 kings. The probability 16/1326 reduces to 8/663, as found in paragraph 13.

Permutations and combinations. 16. How many distinct pairs are there in a double pair royal at Cribbage? A double pair royal is four cards of the same rank. The answer may be found simply by writing out all the possible combinations of two suits: ♠ and ♡, ♠ and ♢, ♠ and ♣, ♡ and ♢, ♡ and ♣, ♢ and ♣. There are six. But many of the proper sets that have to be formed are far too extensive for such a direct count; methods are needed for computing the total without writing out the actual items. The methods fall under the general head of permutations and combinations.

17. Seven known cards remain to be turned up at Faro; in how many different orders can they appear? The first card can be any of seven; after the first is fixed, the second can be any of the six remaining; and so on. The available choices for each successive card are 7, 6, 5, 4, 3, 2, 1, and the answer to the problem is the product of these integers, 5,040.

18. *Factorial symbol.* A standard shorthand way of expressing the product of a series of consecutive integers, from 1 up, is to put the symbol ! after the highest. Thus 4! (read "four factorial") means 1 x 2 x 3 x 4 = 24. When it is necessary to know the absolute value of a large factorial, e. g., 52! the number should be looked up in a standard table of factorials. Convenient also for practical computation is a table of the logarithms of factorials; for most purposes, the evaluation of probability-fractions with five-place logarithms is close enough.

19. A permutation is an arrangement of a set, where the order as well as identity of the members is relevant. The Faro problem in paragraph 17 asks for the permutations of seven cards. By generalizing the solution:

(7) $$P [n] = n!$$

The symbol P denotes permutations, and the set is specified in the following parentheses.

20. One card is dealt face down to each player to start a five-hand Blackjack game; how many different arrangements of such "hole cards" can there be? Different orders of dealing the same five cards will be counted as "different arrangements." This problem is a little more complex than the Faro problem of paragraph 17. Here, we have to take account of the fact that five cards are selected at random from a pack of 52. But the same method can be applied. The first card can be any of 52; after it is fixed, the second may be any of 51; and so on. The answer is evidently a product that begins 52 x 51 . . . But the problem concerns only five cards, so the product must extend only to five terms: 52 x 51 x 50 x 49 x 48.

To express this in factorial notation we can write 52!/47! (This is equivalent to the foregoing five-term product, since the denominator cancels out all but the first five terms of the numerator.) The factorial form condenses actual computation, since the values (or logarithms) of 52! and 47! can be found in tables.

To generalize, if r is a subset of n, then

(8) $$P [r/n] = \frac{n!}{(n - r)!}$$

By (r/n) is meant, not a fraction, but "r members out of a total set n."

21. How many different two-card draws are there from a pack of 52? (This number was wanted in paragraph 15.) By formula (8) the number of permutations is $\frac{52!}{50!} = 52 \times 51 = 2,652$. But the problem asks for combinations. A combination is a group in which the identity of the members is relevant, but not their order. A two-card draw of ♡7 then ♣4 is the same as ♣4 and then ♡7, so far as concerns the outcome. It is evident that in the permutations 2,652, each combination is counted twice over. The number of combinations is therefore 2,652/2 = 1,326, as previously stated.

22. The general formula for combinations is derived by taking the formula for permutations, then dividing by a factor that is the number of times each combination is repeated in the list of permutations. This number is equal to the number of ways any one combination can be shuffled about to make a different permutation. If there are *r* individuals in a combination, it can be permuted in *r*! ways—as stated by formula (7). Therefore

(9) $C \ [r/n] = P \ [r/n] \ / \ r! = \dfrac{n!}{(n - r)! \ r!}$

23. In Cribbage, how many different hands are there of type 9-8-8-7-7? (The differences must be in the suit designations of the individual cards.) There is a choice of 4 ninespots; 6 different pairs out of the four eightspots; 6 different pairs of sevenspots. The answer is $4 \times 6 \times 6 = 144$. If each combination must be made up of *r* members chosen from a set *r'*, and *s* from a set *s'*, etc. then the number of combinations

(10) $C \ [s/s', \ r/r' \ldots] = C \ [r/r'] \times C \ [s/s'] \ldots$

For the case where one member is to be chosen from each set, this reduces to

(11) $C \ [1/r, \ 1/s \ldots] = r \times s \ldots$

24. The seven cards remaining to be turned from a Faro box comprise three jacks, two nines, an ace, and a four. In how many different orders can they appear? In paragraph 17 the total number of permutations of seven cards was found to be 5,040. What is wanted here is the lesser number when cards of the same rank are considered identical. The answer is found in the same way that combinations are calculated from permutations (paragraph 22). Consider any one of the sequences of the cards, say J-J-J-9-9-A-4. If suits are ignored, this pattern represents just one permutation. If suits are taken into account, the pattern represents as many different permutations as the ways in which the three jacks and two nines can be permuted among themselves. For the jacks the ways are 3! and for the nines 2! For the two together the ways are $3! \times 2! = 12$. Every suit-ignoring pattern is therefore counted 12 times over in the full list of 5,040. The answer to the problem is 5,040/12 = 420.

25. The foregoing method may be generalized as follows: The permutations of n objects, when r of them must be construed identical, s of them identical, etc. are

$$(12) \qquad P\ [n/r,\ s\ \ldots = n] = \frac{n!}{r!\ s!\ \ldots}$$

26. It is easy to make systemic errors in calculating permutations and combinations, and even easier to err in relating them to probabilities. Much depends on how a particular problem is construed so as to take account of all relevant possibilities. It is often necessary to fix a pattern (or list of patterns) and calculate each part of it by the applicable formula. For example: How many different hands of three-of-a-kind can be formed in Poker? The pattern by rank is 3-1-1. For the block of three, there is choice of 13 ranks, and choice of 4 triplets in each rank, making 13 x 4 = 52 possible triplets. After the triplet is fixed, the two other cards must be chosen from 12 remaining ranks, and must be different (to avoid full house). The combinations of two out of twelve ranks are 12 x 11/2 = 66. In each chosen rank there is choice of 4 cards, so that the choices for the two odd cards are 66 x 4 x 4 = 1,056. Combining the triplet with the odd cards gives 52 x 1,056 = 54,912 as the answer to the problem.

Odds. 27. Chances are often stated in form of odds instead of probability-fractions; as, the odds against a certain horse to win are 8 to 3. What this means, in effect, is that if the horse ran 11 races it would probably win 3 times and lose 8. The 11 forms a set of events as defined in paragraph 1 *et seq.* The set is divided into sub-sets f and $a,$ of successful and unsuccessful cases. A statement of odds against gives the ratio $a{:}f$; of odds for, the ratio $f{:}a.$ In bookmaking, it is usual to state the odds always in form $a{:}f$, and if a happens to be less than f it is called an "odds on" quotation.

28. The relationship between odds and probability is simply stated. Where F and A mean respectively probability for and probability against,

$$(13) \qquad F = \frac{f}{f + a\ (= n)} \qquad\qquad A = \frac{a}{f + a\ (= n)}$$

The bookmaker who "lays odds" of 8 to 3 against a horse thus bets that its chance of winning is no better than $\dfrac{3}{3 + 8}\ =\ \dfrac{3}{11}$.

HORSE-RACE BETTING

All race tracks in the United States today use the pool or mutuel system of betting. Tickets are sold on each horse in amounts of 2, 5, 10, 20, 50 and 100 units. At the larger tracks, a totalizator is used. This machine prints the ticket as it is sold, and records each sale as the betting is in progress.

In the infield across from the grandstand a large electrically operated board records the total amounts bet on each horse for win, place and show. It also shows the changes in the odds on winning.

At tracks where no totalizator is used, the tickets are printed in advance. Calculation of the amounts sold and the effect of these sales on the shifting odds is done manually by staffs of trained men. The odds are posted every ten minutes up to the start of the race. The "tote" board shows changes every three minutes. All betting ceases when the horses are in the starting gate, and the sellers' windows close at that time.

At tracks that allow "daily doubles," these are calculated as a separate pool. The bettor selects two horses, one in the first race and one in the second (at some tracks, in the second and third races). If both horses win, he and the other holders of the winning double tickets receive the monies bet on the other combinations in proportion to the size of their bet.

The largest daily double payoff in the United States occurred on August 14, 1939, at Washington Park, when the return for a $2 ticket was $10,772.40.

The total yearly attendance at American tracks since the end of the war approximates 25,000,000, and the total of monies bet has averaged close to $1,800,000,000 per year. Between 75 and 80 meetings are held each year, for an aggregate of more than 2,400 racing days. Total purse distribution to horsemen is close to $50,000,000 per year.

Calculation of odds is illustrated by the following example. Suppose that the totalizator board shows:

STRAIGHT		PLACE		SHOW	
Total	24,000	*Total*	12,000	*Total*	12,000
1	10,000	1	5,000	1	5,000
2	6,000	2	3,000	2	3,000
3	4,000	3	2,000	3	2,000
4	2,000	4	1,000	4	1,000
5	2,000	5	1,000	5	1,000

The pools on straight, place, and show are calculated separately.

The Straight or Win Pool. From the total monies bet on all entries to win (24,000) deduct the percentage (called "take") which goes to the track and state. This is from 10% to 15%. In addition, the "breakage" to the nearest nickel or dime is also deducted, so that if the final odds on a winning horse should be 1.28 to 1.00, or $2.56 to $2.00, the 6 cents is kept by the track and the payoff is $2.50 to $2.00, or 1.25 to 1.

The net after deduction of 10% take is 21,600. From this deduct the amount wagered on the horse you are figuring. If horse 1, deduct 10,000 from 21,600. The difference of 11,600 will be paid to those who bet on horse 1, if he wins. The odds would be 11,600 to 10,000, or 1.15 to 1.

The odds on horse 5 work out thus: from 21,600 (net pool) take 2,000, leaving 19,600; then 19,600 to 2,000, or 9.80 to 1, gives the odds.

As the payoff prices are shown and paid out on the basis of a $2 bet, the mutuel price on horse 1 would be $4.30, on horse 5, $21.60. These figures are derived by doubling the odds to $1 (horse 5: $9.80 to $1, $19.60 to $2) and adding the price of a $2 win ticket.

The win mutuels and odds to $1 on the five horses are:

	TOTAL BET	MUTUEL PRICE	ODDS TO $1
1	10,000	4.30	1.15
2	6,000	7.20	2.60
3	4,000	10.80	4.40
4	2,000	21.60	9.80
5	2,000	21.60	9.80

The Place Pool. The place, or second horse, calculation is somewhat different as there is a place payoff on two horses—that which finished first and that which finished second. Proceed as follows:

Deduct the take from the total place pool (10% of 12,000 or 1,200) leaving 10,800. From this deduct the totals wagered on the two horses finishing first and second—say horse 1: 5,000; horse 4: 1,000; or 6,000 in all. Deducting 6,000 from 10,800 leaves 4,800. Half of this net, or 2,400, will be paid to ticket holders on Number 1, and the other half to holders of Number 4.

The odds to place on Number 1 would therefore be 2,400 to 5,000 or 48 cents to $1. This becomes 96 cents to $2, but the track takes the odd 6 cents and pays off at 90 cents to $2. Adding the price of the mutuel ticket, the payoff would show as a mutuel price of $2.90.

On horse 4 the odds are 2,400 to 1,000, or 2.40 to 1. Doubling this and adding the $2 mutuel price makes the payoff $6.80.

As can be seen from this example, the payoff on place horses cannot be calculated until after the race. Had horses Numbers 4 and 5 run first and second the place mutuel would have been 11.60 on each, or 4.80 to 1.

The Show Pool. To figure the odds on the show horses (i. e., horses finishing as good as third), proceed as follows:

From the total show pool deduct the 10%. Add the monies bet on the three horses that figure in the payoff (the winner, second and third horses), and deduct this sum from the net pool. Divide the remainder in three equal parts and apportion one part to each of the three horses.

On our example "tote" board, the show pool is 10,000; 10% from 10,000 leaves 9,000 net pool. Assume that horses 1, 4, 5 finished in the money. Deduct the total bet on these three, 6,000, from 9,000, leaving 3,000 to be divided three ways. Hence the odds on horse 1 for show are 1 to 5, or 20c to $1.00; on horse 4 and horse 5, 2 to 1. Mutuel payoffs would be: on No. 1, $2.40; on Nos. 4 and 5, $6.00.

Larger mutuel tickets, as $5, $10, $50 and $100, are simply multiples of the $2 ticket. A $50 ticket on horse 1 above would pay off at $60.00, that is, a $10 profit on the $50 invested.

As with the place prices, you cannot determine the odds for show until you know which horses have finished in the money.

Bets with bookmakers. In betting through a mutuel machine there is one thing to keep in mind. Every dollar you bet helps to depress your return. The loss is microscopic to the $2.00 bettor, but a sizable bet makes a noticeable difference, even at one of the larger tracks where large amounts are wagered.

To illustrate, let us turn again to the example "tote" board, where 10,000 of a pool of 24,000 is bet on horse 1, making the straight odds $1.15 to 1. Assume that you were willing to take these odds and bet $6,000 on horse 1. The pool will now total 30,000. Taking 10% off leaves 27,000 net pool, of which there is now 16,000 on No. 1. Deducting 16,000 from 27,000 leaves 11,000 for the ticket holders (of which you are one) and a payoff of 11 to 16 or about 70c to $1. Due to the breakage, you might get only 60c to $1. Because of this, all really big bettors bet through bookmakers.

The bookmaker who takes your bet will limit you to certain odds for payoffs regardless of what the horse actually pays at the track. The usual limits are 20-8-4, that is, 20 to 1 to win, 8 to 1 to place, 4 to 1 to show. Although many bettors decry this limit, in practice it is a fair one; if the money were placed at the track, it would materially lower the price.

The bookmaker sets a limit so as not to be put out of business by any single bet at huge odds. Occasionally a book will give odds up to 30-12-6 for limited amounts. A few books in Nevada will pay full track odds up to a $10 bet.

Parlays. On parlays, most books pay a maximum of 50 to 1; a few pay 75 to 1. If you wish to insure your bets by paying a 10% bonus, many books will give you double the above limits. Hence you give the book $11 and get $10 worth of action.

A parlay operates as follows: The player selects two horses and makes a $2 bet. If either horse loses, he loses the $2. If both win, the amount won on the first horse is added to the $2 bet and the total goes on the second horse. For example, horse A wins and pays 3 to 1; the player wins $6; this, plus his original $2, making $8, goes on horse B, who wins and pays 2 to 1. The player receives $24, of which $22 is profit.

A player can make three-horse parlays, four-horse or up. However, the total payoff is always restricted by the bookmaker's limit of 50 or 75 to 1. If a player happened to pick two long shots, one at 10 to 1 and one at

20 to 1, and parlayed them for a $1 bet, he would theoretically be entitled to collect $230. But the bookmaker would pay only the limit, $50 or $75.

Percentage against the bettor. The track take (assumed in our example to be 10%) actually produces a greater percentage (more than 10%) of reduction in the payoff to each winning bettor. The reason is that the track takes its share from the total amount bet, before any calculation of payoff. The difference will be seen by comparing the payoff in the preceding example with what it would be if there were no take.

		MUTUEL PRICE		ODDS TO 1		
Horse	Bet	If no take	10% take	No take	10% take	Difference
1	10,000	4.80	4.30	1.40	1.15	17%
2	6,000	8.00	7.20	3.00	2.60	13%
3	2,000	12.00	10.80	5.00	4.40	12%
4	1,000	24.00	21.60	11.00	9.80	11%
5	1,000	24.00	21.60	11.00	9.80	11%

When these calculations are applied to place and show betting, the differences rise to very large percentages amounting to as high as 60% in the show price returns on a heavily backed horse. That is, 60% less than if there were no take. It is apparent that these differences fall most heavily on the shortest priced horses—those with the most money bet on them, and more lightly on the horses with smaller amounts bet on them. As many states have a take, as high as 15%, and as the breakage figures another 2% on the average, it is easy to see that backing heavily played horses puts the bettor up against an enormous percentage. A study of place and show betting brings out this factor in startling manner. The very smallest decrease to the show bettor of heavily played horses is close to 25%—running to 60% and over.

— THE IMPLEMENTS OF GAMES —

The oldest gaming implements, probably, are dice, though it may be surmised that the implements for the drawing of lots (a long and a short straw, an odd and an even number of pebbles) may have preceded them. By the 15th century, gaming implements had come to be represented in four main subdivisions, playing cards, dice, wheels of fortune, men of war. The men of war are the pieces or "men" in such games as Chess (where they have individuality) and in Checkers, Backgammon, and other games where they have not; the wheels of fortune are those used at Roulette and other games described on pages 551 to 555; playing cards and dice merit more elaborate descriptions, which follow.

PLAYING CARDS

Any of several peoples may independently have created playing cards, but the earliest known reference is A.D. 969, and the place is China. The early Chinese cards were almost indistinguishable from Chinese paper money. They established the pattern that has prevailed since: The pack of cards consists of four "suits," which is to say, one quarter of the pack consists of cards bearing identical markings in some design or being identical in color, no other card of the pack bearing that design or color. In each suit there is a number of cards distinguished from one another by different numerical or pictorial designs.

So, for example, in the pack of cards that is standard in the United States there are four suits marked essentially by the symbols ♠ (spade), ♡ (heart), ◊ (diamond), ♣ (club)—that the spade and club symbols happen always to be printed in black, and the heart and diamond symbols always in red, is not essential to the recognition of the suits, despite its traditional importance. Each suit of this pack contains thirteen cards. Three are face cards, also called picture cards, or court cards, or coat cards—the king (K), queen (Q), and jack or knave (J). Ten are number cards, each bearing as many large suit-symbols or pips as the number of the card, 10, 9, 8, 7, 6, 5, 4, 3, 2, or 1; the card bearing only one large pip is called the ace (A). Since there are four suits of thirteen cards each, the total number of cards in the United States pack is fifty-two. When one buys a pack of cards, however, he receives in addition an extra card called the joker, another extra card bearing rules of popular card games or an advertisement of the maker, and sometimes two additional cards used by the manufacturer for advertising purposes; all such extra cards may be used as jokers in games where they are required.

579

The pack of cards sold in the United States was originally the "French pack." This 52-card pack was adopted in England, imported when the law permitted, smuggled in when it did not. The French pack and various other packs of cards grew out of the development of card playing in Europe after the 14th century.

At some unknown time (but probably no earlier than the 13th century) there arose in Italy an indigenous pack of twenty-two cards called *tarots*. Not many decades later, the oriental pack of "number cards" was introduced into Europe, and perhaps this introduction too came first through Italy. The Italians thereupon developed a pack of 78 cards—the 22 tarots, and 56 number cards, consisting of cards numbered 1 to 10 in each of four suits, plus four picture cards, a king, a queen, a knight or cavalier, and a knave (jack). This pack is still used for the ancient and basic European game Tarok (page 335). It was varied in other countries, and no doubt for practical reasons: because the printing press would take a sheet ample for 32, or 36, or 40, or 52 cards, but not for more; or because the papermakers in that country made a sheet too small for more than the number of cards that came to be the national standard; or because a printer had managed to obtain plates for the number cards but not for the tarots; or for any similar reason.

In any event, there evolved certain standard packs of playing cards identified with the countries of their origins. The suit symbols so identified are:

English	*French*	*German*	*Spanish*	*Italian*
spade	pique	Grün	espada	spada
heart	coeur	Herz	copa	coppa
diamond	carreau	Schelle	oro	denare
club	trèfle	Eichel	basto	batone

The Germans retained four face cards, including the cavalier. The French dropped him. The Germans had a 36-card pack—king, queen, cavalier, knave, ten, nine, eight, seven, and ace in each suit—and also a 32-card pack ("the Piquet pack," better attributed to the French) lacking the knaves or cavaliers. The Spanish and Italians used a 40-card pack, the king, queen, knave, 7, 6, 5, 4, 3, 2, and ace in each suit. The French, British and United States packs of 52 cards have been noted. To any of these packs might be added the 22 tarots (also called *attutti,* or trumps, and *naibes,* or playing cards), of which a typical list is:

I.	The juggler	IX.	The hermit
II.	Juno	X.	The wheel of fortune
III.	The empress	XI.	Fortitude
IV.	The emperor	XII.	The hanged man
V.	Jupiter	XIII.	Death
VI.	The lovers	XIV.	Temperance
VII.	The chariot	XV.	The devil
VIII.	Justice	XVI.	The hospital

XVII. The stars   XX. The Last Judgment
XVIII. The moon   XXI. The end of the world
XIX. The sun

Unnumbered, considered **XXII.** The fool—precursor of the joker

Cavalier, from an
old German pack
of cards

LE MONDE   LE BATELEVR

Typical Tarots

The manufacture of playing cards has progressed from the earliest stages of hand illumination through the successive developments of the graphic arts, and has been important to each. Printing, which began with wood cuts, might have been delayed by decades had it not been for playing cards; the public demand for cards made it a profitable trade.

The first European cards were hand-painted. Then they were printed from woodcuts and the colors put in by stencil. This method survived for centuries. In the 19th century they began to be printed or lithographed, as they are today, and then too began the practice of using pasteboard—most important in playing-card manufacture, for paper is translucent but an opaque paste between sheets of paper makes the whole opaque, and a player with his back to a light need not fear that an opponent can see through his cards and so identify them. Modern machinery puts a knife-edge on playing cards and delays the fraying of their edges when they are shuffled. In the last two decades, washable plastic coatings have been put on the faces of the cards, and cards have been manufactured of cellulose plastics and vinyl resins.

The design of playing cards has been influenced by the superstitions of card players. The face cards still show costumes of the time of Henry VII and Henry VIII of England. Efforts to change the designs of the cards have been generally unsuccessful. The printing of index numerals and pips in the corners became general only in the late 19th century; before then, the card could be read only by looking at its full face. Reversible designs, reading the same from top or bottom, were adopted some years earlier; so were "picture backs," or any other uniform back design, players having previously preferred plain white backs on the assumption that they could not so easily be marked.

By the end of the 19th century, the size of the playing card had been standardized at 3½ x 2½ inches. The spread of the Bridge games influenced the introduction of a narrower card, 3½ x 2¼, for now the player had to hold thirteen cards in his hand rather than five cards as in Euchre and Poker, and besides more women were playing cards and their hands are smaller. In 1949 manufacturers began to reduce the thickness of the pasteboard used, because of the popularity of double-pack games such as Canasta.

Many playing cards not conforming to the standard designs have been produced and constantly appear. Some redesign the pips and use four different colors for the four suits; some introduce fifth and even sixth suits; some replace the kings, queens and jacks with historical figures (as, in revolutionary France and Russia, and in the United States after the Revolutionary War, heroes of the revolutions replaced them). Church opposition to card playing caused a large market to exist, and it still exists though in diminished volume, for playing cards unlike standard playing cards in appearance but serving a similar purpose; outstanding among such packs have been Rook cards, for playing the game of that name and other games.

Between 65 and 70 million packs of cards were sold in the United States each year as of 1949; this figure had fallen as low as 40 million during the early 1930's and risen as high as 100 million during the second World War.

The packs of playing cards generally available are:

52 cards—the standard pack, but with two jokers

48 cards—the Pinochle pack

32 cards—the pack used in Skat; usually three are packed together, to save tax.

DICE

It was remarked on page 537 that dice are undoubtedly the oldest of gaming implements. They must have emerged independently in nearly every society. But the origin of cubical dice with spot markings, as we know them, was probably oriental—Korea and China—and in this form dice must have existed for millennia.

The modern form of dice is as shown in the illustration. No more than three faces of a cube can be seen at one time; the illustration shows both the obverse and reverse of a single die.

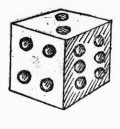

The combinations possible on a single cast of two to five dice are as follows. The column headed "total" gives the sum of all the spots on the uppermost faces of the dice cast: if two dice are cast, and one comes up 5, the other 2, the total is 7. The column headed "number of rolls" gives the number of combinations that will produce this total: on a cast of two dice there are six rolls that total 7, 1-6, 2-5, 3-4, 4-3, 5-2, 6-1. The column headed "probability" gives the percentage that will yield this total out of the total number of possible rolls: if you cast three dice 216 times, there will be 27 times, or 12½%, when the total will be 10, and 27 times, or 12½%, when the total will be 11.

TWO DICE

Probabilities of totals on casts of TWO dice

TOTAL	NUMBER OF ROLLS	PROBABILITY
2	1	.028
3	2	.055
4	3	.083
5	4	.111
6	5	.139
7	6	.167
8	5	.139
9	4	.111
10	3	.083
11	2	.055
12	1	.028
Possible rolls	36	

THREE DICE

Probabilities of totals on casts of THREE dice

TOTAL	NUMBER OF ROLLS	PROBABILITY
3 or 18	1	.004
4 or 17	3	.014
5 or 16	6	.028

TOTAL	NUMBER OF ROLLS	PROBABILITY
6 or 15	10	.046
7 or 14	15	.070
8 or 13	21	.097
9 or 12	25	.116
10 or 11	27	.125
Possible rolls	216	

FOUR DICE

Probabilities of totals on casts of FOUR dice

TOTAL	NUMBER OF ROLLS	PROBABILITY
4 or 24	1	.0008
5 or 23	4	.0031
6 or 22	10	.0077
7 or 21	20	.0155
8 or 20	35	.0270
9 or 19	56	.0432
10 or 18	80	.0618
11 or 17	104	.0804
12 or 16	125	.0965
13 or 15	140	.1080
14	146	.1130
Possible rolls	1296	

FIVE DICE

Probabilities of totals on casts of FIVE dice

TOTAL	NUMBER OF ROLLS	PROBABILITY
5 or 30	1	.0001
6 or 29	5	.0006
7 or 28	15	.0019
8 or 27	35	.0045
9 or 26	70	.0090
10 or 25	126	.0162
11 or 24	205	.0264
12 or 23	305	.0392
13 or 22	420	.0540
14 or 21	540	.0695
15 or 20	651	.0840
16 or 19	735	.0946
17 or 18	780	.1000
Possible rolls	7776	

GENERAL RULES OF CARD GAMES

The following describes procedure common to most card games. The rules should be accepted as binding in the absence of any special rules to the contrary.

The Draw. 1. All matters of precedence, as entry to a table, seating, partnerships, first deal, may be settled as the players see fit, but if there is no general agreement on another method, precedence is decided by drawing cards from a pack.

2. One pack is shuffled, then spread face down on the table. Each candidate or player draws one card and turns it face up.

3. No card may be drawn from the four at each end of the spread pack, and if a player exposes more than one card all such cards are void and he must draw again.

4. The rank of the cards drawn determines the order of precedence, first precedence going to the player with the highest card, second to the player with the second-highest, etc. The rank of cards in drawing is the same as in the game (in the absence of special rule). If the game has no relative ranking of suits, players drawing cards of the same rank must draw again to break the tie between them.

5. The player drawing the highest card deals first. He may choose his seat at the table. The other players may choose among the remaining seats, in order of precedence, so far as the game permits. If there are to be two partnerships, the two, three, or more players at the top of the precedence are partners against the others.

The Shuffle. 6. Any player has the right to shuffle the pack, but the regular duty of shuffling is usually delegated to one, the player at the dealer's left. The dealer has the right to shuffle last.

7. The cards must be shuffled so that none is exposed; if a card is exposed, a reshuffle may be demanded at any time before the deal has begun.

The Cut. 8. The dealer puts the shuffled pack face down at his right, and the player on that side cuts it, by lifting a packet from the top and laying it beside the lower portion.

9. The cut must divide the pack into two portions, neither of less than four cards. If this rule is violated, or if a card is exposed in cutting, there must be a new shuffle and cut.

10. The dealer closes the cut by placing the former bottom portion of the pack on top of the other.

Rotation. 11. The rotation of dealing, bidding, playing, is from player to player to the left, or clockwise. The first to receive cards is *eldest hand,* the player nearest the dealer at his left. (Special rules invariably fix who bets or bids first and who makes the opening lead.)

The Deal. 12. The dealer distributes cards in rotation, beginning with eldest hand. In the absence of special rule, the cards must be dealt face down and one at a time. The rules of some games provide for dealing in batches of two or more cards at a time. If all players receive the same number of cards (as is usually the case), the last card of the deal goes to the dealer.

13. If a widow or extra hand is dealt, this is usually placed in the center of the table after the first round of cards is dealt to the players.

14. Any departure from correct procedure in dealing, as by giving too many or too few cards, exposing a card, etc., entitles any player at the table to demand a redeal. In this event, there must also be a new shuffle and new cut. (In some few games, a *misdeal* costs the player his right to deal at that time, and the new deal is made by the player at his left.)

15. The position of dealer rotates to the left after the hands are played out.

Bidding, Betting. 16. Where there is bidding or betting, the first to act is fixed by special rule; thereafter the turn to bid or bet rotates. Any active player may in his turn ask and receive full information about all previous bids or bets.

17. In betting games, the dealer has the duty of seeing that due antes are made, of indicating the first bettor, and otherwise keeping the game in orderly progress.

The Play. 18. In any game where the cards are played in tricks, special rules fix the opening leader. Thereafter, the winner of a trick leads to the next.

19. A *trick* is a batch of cards, one contributed by each active player. The first card played to a trick is the *lead.* Each trick is gathered (usually) by the hand that wins it, and is left face down on the table. In partnership games, all the tricks won by one side are usually gathered by one member.

20. In playing to a trick after the lead, a hand is constrained by certain obligations, e.g., to follow suit, that are invariably stated in the special rules. To *follow suit* is to play a card of the same suit as the lead.

21. Where the number of tricks won is relevant to the scoring, the tricks must be kept separate, though they may be overlapped to save space.

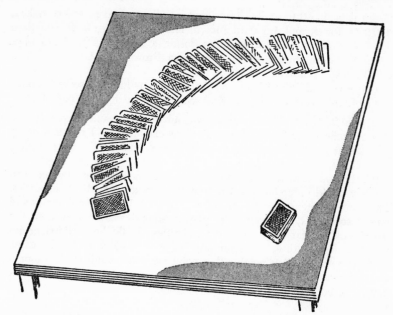

A pack of cards spread for drawing cards (see paragraphs 1-5).

Scoring. 22. The scores accruing from play are recorded and settled by one of three alternative methods—whichever is most convenient to the particular game:

   (a) By writing the scores on paper.
   (b) By a special scoring device, e.g., a Cribbage board.
   (c) By tokens, e.g., Poker chips.

Settlement. 23. The use of Poker chips is a method of making settlement of monetary stakes as the game progresses. When the score is recorded on paper or by a scoring device, settlement is made at the end of a game, rubber, or session. In two-hand play, the net on which the settlement is based is simply the differences of the final total scores. With three or more players, a round-robin settlement is made in either of two ways:

   (a) Each player settles with every other according to the difference of their scores. For example, suppose that the final scores are

Smith	5,170
Jones	3,940
Brown	1,780
Green	430

Green pays 4,740 to Smith (translated into the agreed monetary stake), 3,610 to Jones, and 1,350 to Brown, losing 9,700 in all. Brown pays 3,390 to Smith and 2,160 to Jones, losing a net of 4,200. Jones pays 1,230 to Smith, but the collections from Brown and Green put him 4,540 ahead. Smith wins 9,360 in all.

(b) Each player collects or pays according as his final score is above or below the average of all the final scores. See example on page 321.

Irregularities. 24. Special rules cover all of the common irregularities that may be committed. These rules are elaborate and detailed as to games that support national governing bodies, such as Contract Bridge, Skat, Chess, Checkers.

24. In tournament competition, the players and the referee can scarcely avoid enforcing the letter of the law as regards irregularities. The same stringency is often found in club play. But in home games and purely social play generally, the players should avoid recourse to the "rule book" so far as possible. Irregularities should be rectified or ignored or dealt with in whatever way is best calculated to let the game proceed normally. It is notable that point penalties—equivalent to monetary fines—are quite generally eliminated whenever players authorize a governing body to write rules for their game.

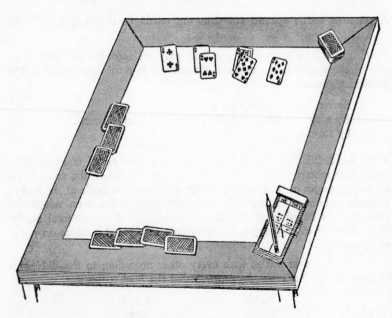

Tricks taken in and stacked (in this case, the game is Contract Bridge and the dummy is shown exposed on the table).

DICTIONARY OF GAMES AND TERMS

Bold face is used for the names of games.

SMALL CAPITALS are used for terms.

All numbers refer to pages in the Encyclopedia.

A

A: abbr. of ace.

ABANDON THE DEAL: discontinue the play and throw the cards together to be shuffled.

Abangah = Mancala, 410

ABOVE THE LINE: place on the scoresheet where premiums are scored (Bridge).

ABSOLUTE: a declaration to win 82 points at a trump or 62 at no trump (Alsós).

A-B, Y-Z: letters formerly used to designate the players in a Whist game. Now supplanted by compass designations: N-S, E-W.

Academy of Play, The: from the French of Abbé Bellecour, London, 1768. A book of games rules.

Accomodez-Moi, variant of Commerce (= Help Me, Neighbor).

Accordion, 440

ACE: 1. The one-spot in a pack of cards. 2. The face of a die having only one spot. 3. One dollar.

Ace-Deuce-Jack, a card game of betting (even money) that no ace, 2 or jack will be among three cards cut from a 52-card pack.

ACE-HIGH: a hand with no pair or better, having an ace (Poker).

Ace in the Pot, two-dice game in which a chip is put in the pot for each ace cast.

ACE-KICKER: an ace held with a pair in a two-card draw (Draw Poker).

Acepots, 70

ACES: 1. Cast of 1-1 (Craps). 2. The count of 1 point for each ace won (Casino).

Aces Up, 441

ACES UP: a hand of two pairs including aces (Poker).

Acey-Deucey, 391

Acey-Out, 545

A CHEVAL: placing a bet on a line of a banking layout, so as to bet on both sides at once.

ACOL: see page 151.

ACTION: betting; opportunity to bet; a bet made and accepted.

ACTIVE PLAYER: 1. One who receives cards in the current deal (as in Skat). 2. One who has not withdrawn from the betting and abandoned his hand (as in Poker).

ACTORS: the suit Characters (Mah Jongg).

ADA FROM DECATUR: the roll of 8 (Dice).

Addition, 546

ADJUSTED SCORE: an arbitrary score assigned by the referee, when regular play is not feasible (Duplicate Bridge).

ADVERSARY: any opposing player; especially in two-hand games; an opponent of the contractor.

ADVERSE: pertaining to an adversary, as *adverse lead*, one made by an opponent. (*Note:* this term usually carries no implication of ill-fortune.)

ADVERTISE: 1. Make a bluff intended to be exposed (Poker). 2. Discard a card to induce an opponent to discard another of same or near rank (Rummy).

AFFRANCHIR (Fr.): establish a suit.

AGAINST: same as WITHOUT (Skat).

AGE: player to the dealer's left; eldest hand.

Agnes, a card Solitaire.

AHEAD: more advanced toward bearing off (Backgammon).

ALBANY LEAD: a lead that shows a hand of four trumps and three of each plain suit (Whist).

ALBIN COUNTER GAMBIT: a Chess opening.

ALEKHINE'S DEFENSE: a Chess opening.

Alexander the Great = La Belle Lucie, 463

ALFIL: obsolete Chess piece, precursor of the bishop.

All Fives (cards), 232

All Fives (dominoes) = Muggins, 426

All Fours, 229

Alliance, obsolete card game similar to Frog.

ALL THE TRUMPS: a declaration to win all the trumps (Alsós).

All Threes, 427

ALMA: a Checkers opening.

ALONE: a bid to play without help of a partner (Euchre).

Alsos, 283

Alternates, a card Solitaire.

ALTERNATE STRAIGHT: = skip straight.

Amazons, The, a card Solitaire.

A MA ZU A LAT: Eskimo name for dominoes ("standing upright side by side").

Ambigu, 80

AMBSACE: cast of two aces (Dice).

American Brag, variant in which a raiser and caller show each other their hands immediately, the inferior hand dropping out (see Brag).

AMERICAN BRIDGE ASSOCIATION: national organization of Negro players of Bridge.

AMERICAN CONTRACT BRIDGE LEAGUE: national organization of Bridge players, founded in 1927.

American Dominoes, 427

American Hoyle, The: published by Dick & Fitzgerald, New York, 1864.

AMERICAN LEADS: a system of length-showing by leads (Whist).

American Whist, see Whist, 180

AMERICAN WHIST LEAGUE: national organization of Whist players, founded in 1891.

AMES ACE: cast of two aces (Dice); also *Ambsace.*

L'AMOUREUX (Fr.): the tarot VI ("lovers").

Anagrams, 496

ANCHOR: player who retains his seat in a pivot or progressive game.

Ancient Schafkopf, 315

ANDERSON, EDWARD X. (pseudonym Hugh Payne), author of *Dice Analysis.*

Angehen, variant of Tarok popular in Germany and Austria during World War I.

ANGLE: a situation favorable to a bet.

Animal, Vegetable or Mineral = Twenty Questions, 506

Anna, a card Solitaire.

Anno Domini, a card Solitaire.

ANNOUNCE: 1. Meld. 2. Name the trump suit. 3. Predict schneider or schwarz.

ANNOUNCED BET: one made orally without putting up chips or money.

ANTE: chips required to be put into the pot before the deal; to put in such chips.

ANTI-LABOUCHERE, 554

ANTON, FRIEDRICH, author of *Encyklopädie der Spiele,* Leipzig, 1884.

ANZAMIA (Burmese): dice.

APPROACH BID: one made for information of partner rather than with intention to play the named declaration (Bridge).

APRES: dealer's announcement that bets are off because of a tie (Trente et Quarante).

Arlington = Oklahoma.

Army Pinochle, four-hand partnership variant with an 80-card pack.

ARROSER (Fr.): to be compelled to undertrump.

Art of Memory, a Quodlibet game in which players name cards previously memorized, the first to err paying for the drinks.

As, 79

AS (Sp.): playing-card ace.

ASCOT, 554

ASK: 1. Inquiry by eldest hand whether the next player wishes to bid against him (as in Skat). 2. Signal partner to lead trumps (Whist). 3. Inquire "May I go out, partner?" (Canasta). 4. Make any bid or inquiry that requires another player to respond as provided by the rules of the game.

ASKING BID: one that systemically asks partner to make a control-showing response (Contract Bridge).

As Nas, 79

Assembly, a card Solitaire.

ASSIST: 1. Increase partner's bid; raise (Bridge). 2. Order partner to take up the trump (Euchre).

ATARI: Japanese "I attack," warning that a stone is threatened with capture (Go).

ATOUT (Fr.): a trump card; the trump suit; a tarot.

ATTACK: in the name of an opening, a White choice of moves (Chess).

ATUTTI: a tarot (see page 576).

AUCTION: the period of the bidding.

Auction Bid Whist, 184

Auction Bridge, 171

Auction Cinch, 239

Auction Euchre, 206

Auction Forty-five, 191

Auction Gin Rummy = Manhattan

Auction Hearts, 243

Auction Pinochle, 291

Auction Pinochle FOR 1,000 POINTS (the club game), 299

Auction Pinochle FOR 1,000 POINTS (the home game), 300

Auction Pitch, 233

Auction Sixty-six, variant in which the players bid for the right to name the trump.

AUF DIE DORFER GEHEN (Ger.): Cash high cards instead of leading trumps.

Auld Lang Syne, a card Solitaire.

Australian Poker = Blind Opening, 71

Authors, 491

AUXILIARY CARDS: reserve cards (Solitaire).

AVAILABLE CARD: one that under the rules may be picked up to be moved elsewhere, usually to be built on foundations or tableau (Solitaire).

AVONDALE SCHEDULE: recommended scoring table for Five Hundred.

AX: 1. The house cut, as in a dice game. 2. Double (Bridge slang).

AYRESHIRE LASSIE: a Checkers opening.

B

B: abbr. of bishop (Chess).

Babette, a card Solitaire.

Baccarat, 521

BACK DOOR: a sequence in a plain suit (Bézique).

BACKER: 1. Non-player who finances an active player. 2. Banker.

BACK GAME: the policy of holding one or more points in the adverse home table, with a view to hitting blots when the opponent begins to bear off (Backgammon).

Backgammon, 386

BACKGAMMON: loss of a game, when the loser has borne off no stone and has a stone on the bar or in the adverse home table (Backgammon).

Backgammon Variants, 391

Backgammon for Four, 391

BACK IN: come into the betting after checking (Poker), or into the bidding after passing (Bridge).

BACK LINE: section of the betting layout on which is placed a bet that the shooter will not pass (Craps).

BACK TO BACK: said of the hole card and first upcard when they are a pair (Stud Poker).

BACKWARD PAWN: one that is subject to attack from an enemy pawn if advanced, especially if the advance is difficult to enforce without loss (Chess).

BAGGAGE: a hanger-on who does not play or cannot pay his own way. (Often with *excess*.)

BAIT: 1. A card discarded to advertise (Rummy). 2. A card discarded from a combination or set in the hope of getting the discard pile with it (500 Rum). 3. Bête.

BAKER, ELWOOD T.: inventor of Gin Rummy.

Baker's Dozen, 441

BALANCED HAND: one that contains no void or singleton (Bridge).

BALKING CARDS: cards given to the crib by non-dealer because they have little chance of making a score (Cribbage).

BAM: a card of the Bamboo suit (Mah Jongg).

BAMBOOS: one of the three suits (Mah Jongg).

BANCO: a bet for the entire amount of the bank (Baccarat).

BANDE: even-money bet on odd or even numbers, so-called because the bet is placed on a long rectangular space or band of the layout.

Bango, variant of Bingo with Cards, 531

BANK: common gambler; gambling house; the dealer in a gambling house.

Bankafalet, obsolete card game.

BANK CRAPS: the game of Craps as played in a gambling house, all bets being laid against the house.

BANKER: 1. Dealer in a gambling house. 2. The person (usually a player) who sells and redeems chips.

Banker and Broker, 527

BAR: 1. Rule out a decision on a certain number, as to *bar double aces* (Bank Craps). 2. Back line (Craps). 3. Dividing line between the inner and outer tables (Backgammon).

BARAJA (Sp.): pack of cards.

Barbooth, 545

Barbudi = Barbooth, 545

Barnyard, 488

Baroness, a card Solitaire.

BAR, ON THE: said of a stone that has been hit and must be reëntered (Backgammon).

BAR POINT: either 7-point (Backgammon).

BARRED: 1. Estopped from bidding by a legal penalty, as in Bridge. 2. Not permitted (as a move) in tournament play (Checkers). 3. Not affecting the bet (Craps).

Baseball (Five-Card Stud), 88

Baseball (Seven-Card Stud), 90

BASEBALL BUM: cast of nine (Dice).

Baseball Pools, 558

Baseball With Cards, 564

BASE COUNT, BASIC: the total of all bonuses (Canasta).

BASE: Four natural matching cards—a base for a canasta (Canasta).

BASE, or BASIC, COUNT: the point value of bonuses, as distinguished from card values (Canasta).

BASE VALUE: 1. A constant factor in computing the value of a game (Skat). 2. Value of an odd trick (Bridge).

Basket Rummy = Canasta, 18

Bassadewitz, Bassarowitz, obsolete card game of four-hand nullo play without a trump.

Basset, Bassette, obsolete card game similar to Faro.

BASTO, BASTA, DIE BASTE: the third-highest trump, as the club ace in Tarok, the spade queen in Ombre.

BASTOS: in the Spanish pack, the suit clubs, represented by heavy truncheons or tree-trunks.

BATE: bête.

BATELEUR, LE (Fr.): one of the names for the lowest tarot trump, the I ("juggler").

BATH COUP: the play of the low card from A-J-x when an opponent leads the K (Whist).

Batsford, a card Solitaire.

Battle Chess, 360

Battle Royal, 41

Battleships (pencil and paper), 500

Battleships (dice), 547

BATTRE (Fr.): to shuffle.

Bau = Mancala, 410

BAUER (Ger.): 1. A Chess pawn. 2. A playing card jack (whence the English *bower*).

BAZA (Sp.): trick (playing cards).

Beast, 189

BEAST: a forfeit, = bête.

BEAR OFF: remove stones from the board in the final stage of play (Backgammon).

Beat the Banker = Bingo, 546

BEAT THE BOARD: have a higher Poker combination than the exposed cards of any other player (Stud Poker).

Beat the Dealer = Banker and Broker, 527

Beat Your Neighbor, 89

BEDIENEN (Ger.): to follow suit.

Bedsprings, 75

Beer Skat: a variant in which the first to score a fixed number of points wins a game; Bierspiel.

BEG: proposal by eldest hand that a new card be turned for trump (All Fours).

BEGGAR: a hand without a face card (Thirty-Five).

Beggar-Your-Neighbor, 488

BEHIND THE SIX: broke, short of funds. (*Note*: derived from Faro, the money-drawer usually being located behind the six of the layout)

BEKOMMEN (Ger.): to win.

BEKENNEN (Ger.): to follow suit.

BELA: the king and queen of trumps, when held by one player and announced as played (Alsós, Klaberjass).

Beleaguered Castle, 442

BELLA: the king and queen of trumps, when held by one player and announced during play (Klaberjass).

BELLE (Fr.): 1. The last game of a rubber. 2. = bella.

Belle, 1. Obsolete game of chance like Lotto. 2. Obsolete game of chance with collections for highest card, flush, and count nearest 31 (= Flux, Thirty-One).

BELLECOUR, ABBE, editor of *Académie des Jeux*, 1668 (*The Academy of Play*, translated from the French, London, 1768).

Belotte, 282

BELOW THE LINE: place on the score-sheet where trick scores are entered (Bridge).

Bergen, 428

Besieged City, a card Solitaire.

— - BEST: ranking in the ordinal position specified, from the top of the suit, as *third-best*.

BEST BOWER: the joker, when it ranks as the highest trump.

BEST CARD: highest card of a suit remaining unplayed; master card.

Bester Bube, obsolete card game similar to Loo.

Best Flush, 96

BET: 1. Any wager on the outcome of a deal or game; any chips put in a pot; to put chips in a pot. 2. The first bet in a betting interval.

BET BLIND: bet without looking at one's hand.

BET BOTH WAYS: bet either right or wrong (Craps).

BET CARD: = case card (Faro).

BETE: 1. Failure to make a contract. 2. Concession of defeat without play. 3. The penalty for failure to make a contract, or for an irregularity (Also *bate, bait*). *Double —*: a doubled penalty, usually for failure to make a contract after electing to play out the cards.

Betrothal, The, a card Solitaire.

Betsy Ross, a card Solitaire.

BET THE DICE TO WIN: bet that the shooter will pass; bet right.

BET THE POT: bet an amount equal to that in the pot.

BET THE RAISE = previous bet limit.

BETTING INTERVAL: period during which each active player in turn has the right to bet or to drop out.

Betting, The Science of, 563

BETTLI: a declaration to win no trick (Alsós).

Betty, a card Solitaire.

Bezique, 269

BEZIQUE: a scoring combination, usually the spade queen and diamond jack (Bézique).

Bezique Panache, variant of Bézique in which four of a kind must comprise one card of each suit.

BICYCLE: the lowest possible hand in Lowball, consisting of A-2-3-4-5, so called from a former design of Bicycle brand playing cards.

BID: an offer to contract to win a minimum number of points or tricks, for the privilege of naming the trump suit or game; to make a bid.

BIDDABLE SUIT: a holding that meets the systemic requirements for a bid (Bridge).

BIDDER: 1. Any player who bids. 2. The highest bidder, who becomes the contractor, as in Auction Pinochle.

BIDDING: the auction; the period in which bids are made; competing in the auction.

BIDDING, CONTINUOUS: bidding without limit as to the number of bids one player may make, until the highest bid stands unchallenged.

Bid Euchre = Auction Euchre, 206

Bid Whist, 184

Bierspiel, 1. Variant of Skat in which the first to score a fixed number of

points wins a game. 2. Any fast game played to decide who shall pay for the drinks; a quodlibet.

Big Ben, 443

BIG CASINO: the diamond ten (Casino).

BIG CAT = Big Tiger.

BIG DOG: a hand having ace-high and nine-low with no pair (Poker).

BIG EIGHT: 1. A bet that neither 8 nor 7 will be cast in the next two rolls. 2. A bet that 8 will be cast before 7 (Craps).

Big Forty = Forty Thieves, 456

BIG SIX: 1. A bet that neither 6 nor 7 will be cast in the next two rolls. 2. A bet that 6 will be cast before 7 (Craps).

BIG STROKE: a certain opening trap in Checkers.

BIG TIGER: a hand containing king-high and eight-low with no pair (Poker).

Bingo (lottery), 557

Bingo (dice), 544

Bingo (dominoes), 429

Bingo with Cards, 528

BINGO: the 0-0 at Bingo (Dominoes).

Binocle = Pinochle, 284

Bird Cage = Chuck-Luck, 543

Biribi, obsolete game of chance like Lotto (= Cavagnole).

Biritch, 187

BISHOP: a Chess piece.

Bisley, 444

BLACK: conventional designation of one of the players in a two-hand board game.

BLACK DOCTOR: a Checkers opening.

Blackjack, 513

BLACKJACK: the combination of an ace and a face card or ten, counting 21 (Blackjack).

Black Jack Hearts, variant in which the spade jack counts 10 against the player winning it.

Black Lady, 243

BLACK MARIA: the spade queen (Black Lady).

Blackout = Oh Hell, 248

BLACKWOOD CONVENTION, 149

BLANK: a domino-end having no pip; the 0 (zero) suit (Dominoes).

BLANK A SUIT: discard all cards of that suit from one's hand.

BLANK SUIT: a suit of which one holds no cards; a void.

BLAETTER (Ger.): playing cards.

BLAZE: a hand composed entirely of face cards.

BLIND: 1. A compulsory bet or ante made before the cards are dealt. 2. Widow.

Blind All Fours, 235

Blind Cinch, variant in which each player is dealt a widow of four cards which he looks at after the auction ends.

BLINDEN (Ger.): a widow.

Blind Euchre, variant of Auction Euchre in which the high bidder picks up a two-card widow.

Blind Hookey, card game of chance like cutting for highest card.

BLIND LEAD: one made before certain cards are disclosed; the opening lead.

BLIND OPENING: compulsory opening of the pot by a blind bet, as in one form of Draw Poker.

Blind Tiger, 71

BLITZ: shut-out (Gin Rummy).

BLOCK: 1. Position in which all the pieces of one color are immobilized (checkers). 2. Ending of play because no one can make a further play (Dominoes, Rummy).

Blockade, a card Solitaire.

BLOCK A SUIT: cash high cards in such a way that partner, with a longer holding, cannot keep the lead (Bridge).

Block Dominoes, 428

Block Eleven, a card Solitaire.

BLOCK SYSTEM: Blind Opening Draw Poker in which the dealer antes 19 chips, eldest hand opens blind for

2, next player raises blind to 4, the limit before the draw is 2 and after the draw is the largest bet made before the draw.

Block Rummy, 6

Block Ten, a card Solitaire.

Blondes and Brunettes, a card Solitaire.

BLOT: a single stone on a point (Backgammon).

Bluchern, obsolete game of chance based on Treize (= Dreizehnern, sept-huit-neuf).

BLUE PETER: a signal asking partner to lead trumps (Whist). It consists of the play of an unnecessarily high card and then a lower card of the same suit. The term is derived from a flag signal in yachting.

Bluff = STRAIGHT POKER, 79

BLUFF: bet on a hand that one does not believe is actually the best.

BOARD: 1. The field of squares or lines on which certain games are played, as Chess, Go. 2. The exposed cards of all active players (Stud Poker).

BOARDS: raised edges of a table against which the dice must be thrown (Craps).

Boathouse Rum, 7

BOBTAIL: a four-card flush or four cards in sequence except A-K-Q-J and A-2-3-4 (Poker).

Bobtail to Open, 71

BOHN, HENRY G., editor of *The Handbook of Games,* London, 1850.

Bohnenspiel, das = Mancala, 410

BOLAND CLUB: see page 150.

BOLD STAND: a deal in which all must play, the pool containing only the dealer's ante (Loo).

BOLT: = drop (Brag).

BON-AIR: a hazard at Ombre, incurred by playing Sans prendre with four matadors.

BONE: 1. Any of the pieces of a Domino set. 2. A die.

Bone-Ace, Bonne-Ace, obsolete game of chance similar to Belle.

BONEYARD: the reserve of bones left after the original hands are drawn (Dominoes).

BONUS: a scoring item, especially one that is not necessarily awarded in every deal.

BONUS PAYMENTS: see pages 298, 299.

BOOBY PRIZE: prize for the poorest score.

BOOBY TABLE: in progressive play, the one of highest number, to which losers move from table No. 1.

Boodle, 219

BOODLE: a prize or pool won by playing a specified card, as in Poque, Michigan.

BOODLE CARD: one that is part of the layout on which bets or antes are placed, as in Michigan.

BOOK: the tricks that a side must win before it can score for additional tricks (Bridge).

BOOKIE, BOOKMAKER: houseman who collects and pays off bets (slang, from *bookmaker*, a professional common bettor).

Boomerang, a card Solitaire.

BOOST: 1. Bet high. 2. Raise.

BORDERLINE: barely meeting the systemic minimum requirements (Bridge).

BORROW: take extra cards from one's previous melds to complete new melds, as in Panguingue.

Boston, 185

(Boston). 2. A Checkers opening.

Boston de Fontainebleau, 187

BOSTON: 1. The winning of five tricks

BOTH ENDS AGAINST THE MIDDLE: nonsense phrase used by Faro players, as to explain to a kibitzer what they are playing.

Boudoir, The, a card Solitaire.

Bouillotte, 80

Boule, 554

BOUQUET: all four Flowers drawn by one player (Mah Jongg).

BOWER: 1. Any jack (from German *Bauer*). 2. The jack of trumps

(right −) or jack of the other suit of same color as the trump (left −), as in Euchre. 3. One of the high trumps; a matador.

BOX: 1. A case in which the shuffled pack is placed so as to expose only one card at a time (Faro). 2. One deal; the score for winning a deal (Gin Rummy). 3. Bowl in which the dice are kept (Craps).

BOX CARS: the roll 6-6 (Craps).

Box Kite, a card Solitaire.

BOXMAN: change-maker in a gambling house.

BOX NUMBERS: spaces in the layout on which a bet may be placed that any given number will be cast before 7 (Craps).

BOX-UP: shuffle a batch of dice preparatory to selecting a pair (Craps).

BRACE, BRACED GAME: crooked gambling house (Faro).

BRACE GAME: method of cheating in Faro by collusion between dealer and case-keeper; any crooked game.

BRACKET: in a knockout tournament, a group of two, four, eight, etc., contestants scheduled together for a series of elimination matches.

Brag, 81

BRAGGERS: jacks and nines, which are always wild, in Brag.

Brandeln, obsolete card game similar to Commerce.

BRAUN (Ger.): the suit clubs.

BREAK: 1. discard from a combination. (Rummy.) 2. See Rummy, p. 1.

BREAK A GAME: terminate a game by winning all or most of the money, as in Craps.

BREAK EVEN: 1. Bet on a card equal number of times to win and lose (Faro). 2. Win or lose nothing on net. 3. (Of outstanding cards) be found equally divided between the opponents.

BREAK OFF: said of a streak when it changes, as of a rank in Faro that loses after winning two or three times.

BREAKS: 1. Chance occurrences. 2. Division of crucial unplayed cards between two hands.

BREAK THE BANK: exhaust the quota of funds supplied to the dealer in a house. (*Note:* the term does not imply that all of funds available to the house have been won.)

BREAK THE BANK: after winning heavily, to propose a bet so large that the bank terminates play rather than accept it.

BREATHE: check the bet (Poker).

BREATHER: opportunity to check, rather than call or bet, in a betting interval (Poker).

BREATHING SPACE: any open point to which a unit is connected (Go).

Brelan, 80

BRELAN: (Fr.): Three of a kind. — CARRE, four of a kind.

BRETT, DAS (Ger.): the board (Chess, etc.).

BRETTSPIEL (Ger.): any board game.

BRICK: a die so cut that it is not a true cube.

Bridge, 176

BRIDGE: two pieces on the first row that oppose the crowning of adverse men. *Black —,* pieces on 1 and 3. *White —,* pieces on 30 and 32. (Checkers.)

BRIDGE, AT THE: having a score of 4 when the opponents have no more than 2 (Euchre).

BRIDGE IT: 1. Make it no trump. 2. Pass the make to partner (Bridge-Whist).

Bridge Keno, variant of Keno in which the player is provided with a panel representing 25 playing cards in a square.

BRIDGE THE CARDS: bend part of the pack so that a confederate can cut it at a desired point.

BRIDGE THE MAKE: pass, by dealer (Bridge-Whist). (*Note:* said by Foster to be a vulgarism.)

Bridge-Whist, 176

BRIDGEWORK: A compromise between Auction and Contract Bridge, proposed by Milton C. Work and Walter F. Wyman, which did not become popular.

BRIDGE WORLD: A monthly magazine founded October, 1929, in New York; a Contract Bridge team (1930) representing it, composed of Ely Culbertson, Josephine Culbertson, Waldemar von Zedtwitz, Theodore A. Lightner.

Bridgit, name given to several variants of Bridge.

BRILLIANT: the diamond six (Pächter).

BRING IN A SUIT: establish or cash a suit, especially after taking out adverse trumps (Whist, etc.)

Brisca, La, Spanish game, to win majority of points in counting cards.

Briscan, obsolete card game like two-hand Pinochle (= Briscon, Brisque).

Briscola, four-hand partnership game with Italian pack, to win counting cards in tricks.

Briscon = Briscan.

Brisque = Briscan.

BRISQUES: aces and tens (Bézique).

Bristol, a card Solitaire.

BRISTOL: a Checkers opening.

BRITISH BRIDGE LEAGUE: national organization of Bridge players in Great Britain.

British Square, 445

BRULER (Fr.): to burn a card.

Brusquembille, obsolete card game similar to Sixty-Six.

BRUSQUEMBILLE: the ace-ten of a suit.

BUBE (Ger.): jack (playing card).

BUCHE (Fr.) non-counting cards.

BUCK: a token used as a reminder of which player is to deal or perform other duties (originally a buckhorn-handled knife).

Buck Dice, three-dice game.

Buck Euchre, variant for four to six players, each for himself.

BUCK IT: repeat a number previously cast (Craps).

BUCK THE GAME: bet against the house.

BUCK THEM: continue rolling the dice after missing out (Craps).

BUCK THE TIGER: play Faro (from the old-time sign of a Faro house, a tiger's head).

BUDAPEST DEFENSE: a Chess opening.

BUG: the joker when it may be used only as an ace or a wild card to fill a flush or straight (Poker).

BUILD: 1. Put one card on another as permitted by the rules; a batch of cards formed by building (Solitaire). 2. Put together two or more cards, to be taken in by a card of their numerical total; a batch so put together (Casino). *Duplicate a —:* put together two or more sets of cards having the same numerical total. *Increase a —:* add a card to a single build to increase its numerical total.

BUILDERS: stones in advantageous position to make valuable points, especially stones in one's own outer table (Backgammon).

BULL: ace (playing card).

Bull-Frog = Frog, 457

BUMBLEPUPPY: inferior play, especially in defiance of partnership systems (Whist).

BUMPER: a rubber won by two games to none (Whist).

BUNCH: 1. Gather the cards for shuffling. 2. Abandon a deal: propose such abandonment (see page 235).

BUNCO CARDS: a special pack of numbered cards different from conventional playing cards.

BURIED CARD: one not immediately available (Solitaire, Rummy).

BURN A CARD: 1. Place a card face up at the bottom of the pack, to mark the limit of cards available to be dealt without reshuffling. 2. Discard one card from the top of the pack before dealing the next.

Burro, El, Spanish game similar to Loo.

BURY A CARD: 1. Put it in the pack or discards so that it is not readily located. 2. Discard it, after taking the widow (Auction Pinochle).

BUSINESS DOUBLE: one made for the purpose of collecting an increased penalty (Bridge).

BUST: 1. A very poor hand. 2. Go over 21, losing one's bet immediately (Blackjack). 3. Take too many or too few tricks (Oh Hell).

Busy Aces, a card Solitaire.

Butcher Boy, 89

BUY-IN (Poker): Same as stack or takeout.

BUY: draw cards from the widow or stock; the cards so received.

BUY THE CONTRACT: win the right to name the trump or game by making the highest bid.

BUY THE POT: put in the pot as many chips as are already there, to buy a privilege (in certain Poker variants).

BY CARDS: won in tricks (Whist).

BYE: a round of a tournament in which a contestant is not scheduled to play.

BY ME: declaration meaning "I pass" or "I check."

C

CABALLO: in the Spanish pack, a knight, numbered 11.

CABARET: a holding of J-10-9 in the same suit (Guinguette).

CABARET: three of a kind, jack or lower (Guinguette).

Caesar, a card Solitaire.

Calabrasella, 332

CALAMITY JANE: the spade queen (Black Lady).

Calculation, 446

California Jack, 231

California Loo = California Jack, 231

California Lowball, 95

CALL: 1. Declare; bid or pass; any such declaration during the auction.

2. Put in the pot just enough chips to stay in, but not raise (Poker). 3. Make legal demand for a card held by another player (Call-Ace Euchre, Authors, etc.). 4. Ask partner if he has one trump honor (permitted by ancient rules of Whist). 5. Signal for a trump lead by playing high-low (Whist).

Callabra, card game resembling Casino. (See page 255)

Call-Ace Euchre, 208

CALL THE TURN: predict correctly the order of the last three cards in the box (Faro).

CALL SOLO: a bid to win all the points in play, the bidder being privileged to call any card not in his hand and receive it in exchange for a discard (Six-Bid Solo).

CAMBRIDGE SPRINGS DEFENSE: a Chess opening.

Camelot, proprietary board game combining principles of Checkers and Halma.

Cameroon, 549

Campaign, a card Solitaire.

CAN: the Faro box.

Canasta, 18

CANASTA: a meld of seven or more cards. *Natural* —, one using no wild cards, as distinct from *mixed* —. (Canasta.)

Cancellation Hearts, 244

CANE: the stick used by a houseman to retrieve the dice (Craps).

Canfield, 446

Canister, a card Solitaire.

CAN YE: The form of a question asking partner if he holds at least one trump honor (permitted by the ancient rules of Whist).

CAPOT: winning of all the tricks by one player; the bonus therefor (Piquet, etc.).

CAPPED DICE: crooked dice more resilient on one side than another.

CAPPED PAWN: one marked by a token, with which the stronger player undertakes to checkmate in giving extreme odds to a weak opponent (Chess).

Capricieuse, a card Solitaire.

CAPTAIN: the team member who has final decision, as in chouette and in certain partnership bidding systems.

Captain, Mate and Crew = Battleships (Dice), 547

Captive Queens, a card Solitaire.

CAPTURE: remove an enemy piece from the board, as in Chess, Checkers.

Card Dominoes = Fan Tan, 224

CARDS: 1. Playing cards; dominoes or other implements of play. 2. The count of 3 points for winning 27 or more cards (Casino). 3. The number of tricks won over six (Whist).

CARO-KANN DEFENSE: a Chess opening.

CAROLINA: cast of 9 (Dice). *Also Nina-from-Carolina.*

Carousel, 43

Carpet, The, a card Solitaire.

CARRE (Fr.): fourfold, four-square.

CARREAU (Fr.): diamond (the suit).

CARTE (Fr.): card; player's request for an additional card, as in Baccarat.

CARTE BLANCHE: a hand without a face card.

CARTE ROI (Fr.): highest card of a suit remaining unplayed; master card.

CASE: an abacus or counting rack used to record the cards as they show (Faro).

CASE CARD: the last of its rank left in the box (Faro); the last of its rank remaining unplayed or undealt.

CASEKEEPER: houseman who keeps track of the cards as they show (Faro).

CASH: lead and win tricks with (established cards).

CASH POINTS: scores for the aces and casinos (Casino).

CASING: method of altering the cards to cheat.

Casino, Cassino, 255

Casino Variations, 259

CASSA: a declaration to win majority of the points (Alsós).

CASTER: the player who throws the dice; shooter.

CASTLE: 1. Make the move castling. 2. = rook. (Chess.)

CASTLING: a certain compound move of the king and one rook. — *on K-side* or — *short,* is designated by 0-0; — *on Q-side* or — *long* is designated by 0-0-0. (Chess.)

Castle of Indolence, a card Solitaire.

CAT: a Big Tiger or Little Tiger.

CATALAN OPENING: a Chess opening.

CATCH: obtain valuable cards from the widow or stock.

Catch the Ten, 247

Categories, 500

CAT-HOP: two cards of the same rank among the last three (Faro).

Cavagnole, obsolete game of chance like Lotto (= Biribi).

CAVALIER: 1. A face card in certain packs of cards, ranked immediately above or below the jack. 2. The knight in Chess (Fr.).

CAVE (Fr.): the amount a player places in front of him at the beginning of play; table stakes.

CAVENDISH: a London club whose name was adopted as a pseudonym by Henry Jones (q.v.) and by several later Bridge clubs, especially that in New York where leading Bridge experts play.

Cayenne, 187

Cent, le, card game akin to Piquet. (See page 261)

CENTER: 1. The central squares, specifically d5, d4, e5, and e4 (Chess). 2. The foundation piles (Solitaire). 3. That part of the playing area where the dice are cast (Craps).

CENTER BET: one between the shooter and other players on the result of the next series of rolls to be made by the shooter (Craps).

CENTER GAME: a Chess opening.

Centennial, dice game with the object of getting the numbers 1 to 12 in succession in a minimum of casts.

CENTRE: a Checkers opening.

Chak T'In Kau, Chinese two-dice game ("throwing heaven and nine").

CHALLENGE: a call proposed to be substituted for "double" when the intent is informatory, but never incorporated in the laws (Bridge).

Chameleon, The, a card Solitaire.

Chanka = Mancala, 410

CHARACTERS: one of the three suits (Mah Jongg). Also *Cracks.*

Charades, 510

CHARIOT: the tarot VII.

CHARIVARY: a hazard at Ombre, incurred by holding four queens.

CHARLESTON: the passing of unwanted tiles to other players (Mah Jongg).

Chatelaine, a card Solitaire.

CHATTO, WILLIAM ANDREW, author of *Facts and Speculations on the History of Playing Cards,* London, 1848.

Chaturanga, see Chess History, 399.

CHECK: 1. A Poker chip; any token. 2. A declaration that a player elects to remain in the pot without betting, or by making the minimum bet when it is one chip (Poker). 3. A threat to capture the enemy king (Chess).

CHECKER: a piece in Checkers; any disk used in a board game; draughtsman.

CHECKERBOARD: the field of light and dark squares used in Checkers; any similar board.

Checkers, 363

CHECKMATE: situation of a king threatened with capture, when no parry of the threat is possible (Chess).

Check Pinochle, 311

CHECK-RACKED: denied one's winnings in a gambling house, because cheating is suspected or because one has broken the bank.

Cheeseboxes = Quadrangles, 434

CHELEM (Fr.): slam, winning of all the tricks by one player or side.

CH' E ME: Chinese teetotum used for gambling.

Chemin de Fer, 524

Chemmy = Chemin de Fer, 524

Chess, 341; (history), 399.

Chessboard, a card Solitaire.

CHESSBOARD: the field of light and dark squares used in Chess; any similar board.

Chester Game, a card Solitaire.

Chicago, 134, 217

Chicago, two-dice game in which the players try to cast the numbers 2 to 12 in succession.

CHICAGO PELTER: = kilter (Poker).

CHICANE: a hand void of trumps.

CHICO: a solo game with any suit but hearts as trumps (Frog).

CHICOREE: a hazard at Ombre, incurred by holding three or four false matadors.

Children, Card Games for, 485

China = Pounce, 447

China, multiple Klondike, played by several players, each with his own pack; the common foundations are sometimes built up regardless of suit.

Chinaman = Klondike, 462

CHINESE: adjective frequently applied to a bizarre variant of any game: few of the games so-called originated in China or are even played there.

Chinese Bezique = Six-Pack Bézique, 272

Chinese Bridge, (four-hand) 175; (two-hand) 180

Chinese Checkers, 408

Chinese Fan Tan, gambling game in which the players bet on 0, 1, 2 or 3 as the remainder when a handful of beans is counted out by fours.

Chinese Lottery, see Race-Horse Keno, 559

CHINESE TILES: Mah Jongg tiles.

Chinese Whist, variant for two to four players, in which six cards of each hand are exposed and dealer names the trump.

CHIP: a token used in place of money; the unit of currency in betting; to put chips in the pot.

CHIP ALONG: stay in a pot without raising; make the smallest possible bet.

CHIPPING: putting chips in the pot.

CH'IU P'AI: Chinese dominoes made of bamboo.

Chong Un Ch'Au: Chinese six-dice game.

CHISELER: one who tries to obtain undue odds in betting.

Chongkak = Mancala, 410

CHOPS: a system of betting at Faro.

Chouette (Gin Rummy) 40, Backgammon) 391

CHOW: a set of three tiles in suit and sequence; to ground such a set (Mah Jongg).

Chuck-A-Luck = Chuck-luck, 541

Chuckle, a card Solitaire.

Chuck-Luck, 541

Chungcajon = Mancala, 410

Cientos = le Cent. (See page 261)

Cinch, 236

CINCH: play a trump higher than the five, to prevent an opponent from winning with a pedro (Cinch).

CINCH HAND: one that no other player can beat in the showdown, regardless of his hole card (Stud Poker). Any hand sure to win.

Cincinnati, 75

Cincinnati Liz, 75

Cinq Cents, 273

CIRCLES: one of the three suits (Mah Jongg). Also *Dots*.

Cirulo, El, Spanish card game like Hearts, the undesired suit being *oros,* corresponding to Diamonds.

Citadel, a card Solitaire.

Clabber, 282

CLEAR: 1. Establish a card or suit by forcing out adverse higher cards or stoppers. 2. Having taken no hearts or other minus cards (Hearts, etc.).

CLEARED HAND: one in which all the suit tiles are of one suit (Mah Jongg).

CLIP: cheat. *Clip-joint,* crooked gambling house.

Clob = Klaberjass, 278

Clock, 447

CLOSE: 1. Call for a showdown, thus limiting each other player to one more draw (Whisky Poker). 2. Turn the trump card face down to inaugurate the final period of play (Sixty-Six).

CLOSE CARDS: those near in rank (Cribbage). Also *near cards.*

CLOSED POINT: one that is occupied by two or more adverse stones (Backgammon).

CLOSE THE BOARD: establish a shut-out (Backgammon).

Clover = Big Ben, 443

Clover Leaf = La Belle Lucie, 463

Club Piquet, 264

CLUBS: the suit denoted by the symbol ♣; also called trèfle (Fr.), Treff, Eicheln, Eckern, Kreuz (Ger.).

CLUB STAKES: limitations of stakes and betting that apply in a club.

Coan Ki, Chinese backgammon as described by Hyde.

COAT CARDS: face cards (obsolete).

COCKED DICE: a die not resting squarely on one of its faces.

COCK-EYES: the cast of 3 (Dice).

CODILLE, CODILL, CODILLIO: defeat of the contractor (Ombre, etc.).

COEUR (Fr.): the suit hearts.

Coeur D'Alene Solo, variant of Frog in which each deal is a game.

COFFEE HOUSING: talking and acting so as to mislead opponents as to one's cards.

Coffeepot, 505

COGGING DICE: turning dice over with the fingers after they have been cast.

COLD DECK: prearranged pack switched for the fairly-shuffled pack in a crooked game.

Cold Hands, 96

COLLE SYSTEM: a Chess opening.

Colonel, a card Solitaire.

Colonel, two-hand variant of Coon-Can.

COLOR: 1: Suit. 2. In Solo, etc., a suit ranking above others in the bidding and scoring. 3. Red or black (Solitaire).

Colorado, a card Solitaire.

COLORS: a system of betting at Faro.

Color Wheel, 553

COLUMN: a line of cards extending away from the player (Solitaire).

COMBINATION: 1. Group of cards of scoring value (Cribbage); any group of cards. 2. Two cards that can become a meld by addition of a matching third card (Rummy). 3. A precisely calculated series of moves and alternatives (Chess). 4. A syndicate of gamblers.

COMBINE: 1. Take in cards by pairing (Casino). 2. Consolidate piles; build (Solitaire). 3. Combination.

COME: to pass, considering the next roll as the first of a series (Craps).

COME IN: enter the betting or bidding.

COME-ON: 1. Signal to partner to lead or continue a suit; echo (Bridge). 2. A discard selected for purpose of advertising (Rummy).

COME-OUT: to make the first roll of a series (Craps).

Comet, 200

COMET: a wild card, usually the diamond nine (Stops).

COMFORT STATION: either 12-point (Backgammon).

COMMAND: best card of a suit; control a suit with the best card.

Commerce, 81

Commercial Pitch, 235

Commit, 223

COMMON MARRIAGE: the king-queen of a plain suit.

COMMON SUIT = plain suit.

COMPASS GAME: a tournament with separate contests among North-South and East-West pairs (Duplicate Bridge).

Compleat Gamester, The: by Charles Cotton, London, 1674. Revised and enlarged by Richard Seymour; sixth edition, London, 1739.

COMPLETED TRICK: one to which every hand has played a card.

COMPLETE HAND: 1. One of 14 titles conforming to the requirements to be declared and to win the deal (Mah Jongg). 2. One with no unmatched cards (Rummy).

CONCEALED HAND: one that goes out in a single turn, having previously melded no cards (Canasta, etc.).

CONCEALED SET: one obtained by drawing from the wall, not by taking a discard (Mah Jongg).

Concentration, 492

CONDITIONAL MATE: form of Chess problem in which special conditions are stipulated, not applying in actual play, e.g., mate on a certain square or with a certain piece.

CONDITIONS: certain melds for which the owner collects chips immediately (Panguingue).

CONDONE: legalize or waive penalty for an irregularity.

Congress, a card Solitaire.

Connexions, obsolete card game to win counting cards in tricks.

CONNEXIONS: certain scoring combinations, the spade and club aces,

the spade and heart kings, the club ace and heart king (Connexions).

Conquian, 50

¿Con Quien? = Conquian, 50

CONSOLATION: 1. Payment due the winners from the losers, as in Ombre. 2. A hazard at Ombre. 3. Payment to a player who does not win but still has cards at the end of play (Papillon). 4. A special contest open to players knocked out of a main tournament.

Constitution, 448

CONTENTMENT: a hazard at Ombre, incurred by holding five matadors.

CONTESTANT: any player in a game, whether or not active at the moment; any group entered in a contest as a partnership or team.

Continental Rum, 28

Continuous Baseball, 564

CONTINUOUS BIDDING: the rule that a player may bid repeatedly until unwilling to go higher.

CONTRACT: the obligation to win a minimum number of points or tricks.

Contract Bridge, 114

Contract Checkers, 384

CONTRACTOR: 1. The player who assumes the contract; the high bidder. 2. Declarer or dummy (Bridge).

Contract Pinochle, 310

Contract Poker, 94

Contract Rummy, 26

Contract Whist, 172

Contra-Dance, a card Solitaire.

CONVENTIONAL: 1. Orthodox; in accordance with common practice. 2. Systemic; in accordance with an agreed system.

CONVENTIONS: common practices in partnership bidding and play; advance agreements between partners on systemic procedure.

COOK: 1. An improvement or deviation from published analysis, especially when reserved by a tournament competitor to spring as a

surprise upon his opponents.
(Checkers). 2. An alternative solution to a problem, rendering it
unsound (Chess).

Coon-Can, 6

Cootie, dice game similar to Yacht.

COPAS: in the Spanish pack, the suit
cups, corresponding to *hearts.*

COPPER: a cent or other token placed
on a bet indicating that it is a bet
on a card to lose (Faro).

CORAZONES (Sp.): the suit hearts.

Corner Stones, 449

Corona, a card Solitaire.

Costly Colours, obsolete card game
similar to Cribbage.

Cotillion, a card Solitaire.

COTILLON: the stock, after the hands
are dealt (obsolete).

COTTON, CHARLES, author of *The
Compleat Gamester,* London, 1674.

COULEUR (Fr.): 1. Suit; color. 2. A
bet that the winning row will be
of same color as the first card dealt
(Trente et Quarante).

COUNT: 1. Score; determine or total
the score. 2. Numerical total of
certain cards, as deadwood in Gin
Rummy, cards played in Cribbage.
3. Base values. 4. Oral accumulation of scores, as in Piquet.

COUNTER: 1. A token used in place of
money; chip. 2. A piece used in a
board game; checker. 3. In the
name of an opening, a Black choice
of moves (Chess). 4. Counting card
or bone.

Counter Games, 545

COUNTING CARD (or bone): One that
has intrinsic scoring value when
taken in a trick.

COUNT OUT: claim to have accumulated enough points for game, during play, thereby ending the play;
go out during the play.

COUP: 1. One deal, or the determination of one bet or result of one
event, in a banking game. 2. A
brilliant play.

COUPER (Fr.): 1. Cut the pack. 2.
Ruff a plain-suit lead.

COURT CARD: face card; a king, queen,
or jack.

COURTENAY, F. DUDLEY: prime mover
in the promulgation of the Official
System of Contract Bridge (q.v.).

Court-Yard, a card Solitaire.

COVER: play a higher card of the same
suit than any previously played to
the trick.

CRAB: A losing cast in Hazard, 2, 3
or 12. Later, *craps.*

Crabapple, a card Solitaire.

CRACK: abandon a policy of waiting
or attrition; meld first, discard a
dangerous card, as in Rummy.

CRACKS, CRAKS: the suit Characters
(Mah Jongg).

Crag, 548

CRAG: cast of 3-3-7, 4-4-5, 5-5-3, or
6-6-1 (Crag).

CRAMP: restraint exerted upon a whole
group of enemy pieces, usually in
a corner (Checkers).

CRAP: cast of 1-1, 1-2 or 6-6 (2, 3, or
12) (Craps).

Crapette, 482

Crapless Craps, variant of Craps
in which 2, 3 and 12 are allowed as
point-numbers.

CRAP OUT: throw a 7 when trying
for a point (Craps).

Craps, 537

Craps with Cards, 542

Crazy Eights = Eights, 225

Crazy Jacks = Eights, 225

CRAZY JOKER: the joker when used as
a completely wild card (Poker).

Crazy Quilt, 450

Crescent, 451

CREVE (Fr.): busted, as by over-
drawing at Blackjack.

CRIB: the extra hand belonging to the
dealer, formed by discards (Cribbage).

Cribbage, 250

CRIBBAGE BOARD: a scoring device
used in Cribbage and other games.
(See page 250.)

Cribbage Solitaire, 452

Cribbage Variations, 254

Cribbidge = Cribbage, 250

CRIMPING: method of bending cards for cheating.

Criss-Cross, 76

CROCKFORD'S: former London club and gaming rooms; several later Bridge clubs have adopted the name.

CROSS: a Checkers opening.

Crosscards Poker, duplicate tournament form of Poker Solitaire, 470

CROSS COLORS: a system of betting at Faro.

CROSS-EYES: cast of 1-2 (Dice).

CROSS-RUFF: alternate trumping of each other's plain-suit leads by two partners (Bridge, Whist).

CROSS THE SUIT: name as trump a suit of opposite color from that of the rejected turn-up (Euchre). *Cross-suit,* one of opposite color.

CROUPIER: houseman who collects and pays bets, as in Roulette.

CROWN: promote a single man to a king by moving it to the eighth rank; place a second checker on a single man to mark it a king (Checkers).

Crown and Anchor = Chuck-Luck, 543

CROWNS: English name of the fifth suit, blue or green in color, at one time added to the standard pack.

CSALAD: a declaration to win the A, K, Q of trumps (Hungarian, "all the family") (Alsós).

CUADROS (Sp.): the suit diamonds.

Cuckoo = Ranter Go Round, 486

CUE-BID: one that systemically shows control of a suit, by possession of the ace or a void (Contract Bridge).

Cul-Bas, obsolete card game like Casino.

CULBERTSON: 1. Ely Culbertson, authority on Contract Bridge and other games. 2. Josephine Culbertson, Contract Bridge author. 3.

— System, the bidding system once used by the majority of Contract Bridge players.

CULIN, STEWART: author of *Chinese Games with Dice and Dominoes* (1893); *Chess and Playing Cards* (1896), and other historical inquiries.

CUMULATIVE SCORING: method of scoring by determining the net total of the plus and minus scores made on all boards played by a partnership (Duplicate Bridge).

CUP: receptacle in which dice are shaken up before casting.

CURSE OF SCOTLAND: the diamond nine.

CUT: 1. Divide the pack into two parts in completion of the shuffling; such division. 2. Draw cards from a spread pack to determine dealer, etc. 3. An exchange of captures (Checkers). 4. House share of a pot.

CUT IN: gain entry to a table by drawing cards for precedence.

CUT THE POT: take a percentage from the pot, as to defray expenses or admission charges.

CUT UP JACKPOTS: boast about previous winnings.

CUTTHROAT: any game in which each plays for himself, especially as applied to variants of partnership games.

Cutthroat Bridge, 177

Cutthroat Contract, 174

Cutthroat Gin, 40

Cutthroat Euchre, 205

D

D: abbr. of *dame* (= queen).

D'ALEMBERT, 554

Dama, Dame, Damm = Checkers, 363

DAMESPIEL, DAMENSPIEL, 385

DAMMSPIEL, 384

DAME: 1. Queen (Fr. and Ger.) (Chess, playing cards.) 2. = king

605

(Checkers). 3. Common points (Go).

DANISH GAMBIT: a Chess opening.

DAUS (Ger.): playing-card ace.

DEAD CARD: 1. One already played or discarded. 2. One ruled unavailable by a legal penalty. 3. One of the layout on which there is no further action because all four cards of the rank have shown (Faro).

DEAD HAND: 1. One that must be abandoned in penalty for an irregularity. 2. Extra hand dealt to create stops (Stops); widow. 3. A player who has bet all his chips and may bet no more.

DEAD MAN'S HAND: a hand of two pairs, aces and eights, said to be the hand held by Wild Bill Hickok when he was shot (Poker).

DEADWOOD: 1. Unmatched cards remaining in a hand (Rummy). 2. The pile of discarded cards (Poker).

DEAL: 1. Distribute cards to the players; draw bones from a common stock, as in Dominoes; such distribution or draw; the turn to deal. 2. The period from one distribution or draw to the next, including all such sub-periods as the auction, play, melding, betting, showing, scoring.

DEALER: 1. The player who distributes the cards. 2. The banker.

Dealer's Choice, any Poker game in which the dealer has the right to name the variant to be played in that deal.

DEAL OFF: terminate a session by giving each player one more turn to deal.

DEAL OUT: omit giving a card or a hand to a player.

Decade, a card Solitaire.

DECAVE (Fr.): broke; having lost all one's money.

DECK: pack (of cards).

DECLARE: 1. Bid; make the trump. 2. Announce; predict schneider or schwarz. 3. Meld; show. 4. Count out. [This term, because of its ambiguity, is usually avoided in favor of a specific term.]

DECLARATION: 1. Announcement of melds or scoring combinations, as in Piquet. 2. The game or trump or no trump at which a deal is played.

Declarations, 94

DECLARER: the player who for his side first bid the denomination named in the contract, and who thereupon plays both hands of the partnership (Bridge).

DECLARING OUT: claiming, during play of a deal, to have won enough points to win the game; counting out.

DECKHEAD: card turned for trump; turn-up.

DEFAUSSER (Fr.): to discard.

DEFENDER: an opponent of declarer, or of the first bidder (Bridge).

DEFENSE: 1. In the name of an opening, a Black choice of moves (Chess). 2. The opponents of declarer (Bridge).

DEFENSIVE BID: 1. One made by an opponent of the opening bidder. 2. One made to boost the opponents. (Bridge).

DEFENSIVE STRENGTH: cards expected to win tricks against an adverse contract (Bridge).

DEFIANCE: a Checkers opening.

DEGOUT: a hazard at Ombre, incurred by losing the last game of a party.

DEMAND BID: one that systemically requires partner to respond or assure that the auction is kept open (Bridge).

D'EMBLEE (Fr.): on the first deal; before the draw.

Demon = Canfield, 446

Demon Patience = Klondike, 462

Demon Fan, a card Solitaire.

DENIAL BID: One showing lack of support for partner's declaration (Bridge).

DENNY: a Checkers opening.

DENOMINATION: 1. Rank. 2. The suit or no trump named in a bid (Bridge).

Denver Progressive Solo, variant of Frog.

DESPATCHERS: improperly marked dice used by cheats.

Desperation, a multiple Solitaire game.

Destroyers = Battleships, 547

DEUCE: two-spot, in cards and dice.

Deuces, a card Solitaire.

Deuces Wild (Poker), 73

Deuces Wild (Dice), 547

DEVELOPMENT: the initial phase of a game, particularly the moving of other pieces off the first rank and castling so as to "unite the rooks" (Chess).

Devil and Tailors, The, = Fox and Geese.

DEVIL'S BED POSTS: the club four.

DEVOLE: loss of all the tricks by the contractor, as in Ombre.

DIABLE, LE (Fr.): the tarot XV ("devil").

DIAGONAL: a line of squares parallel to a diagonal of the board (Chess).

Dial, a card Solitaire.

DIAMANTES (Sp.): the suit diamonds.

DIAMONDS: the suit denoted by the symbol ◇; also called carreau (Fr.), Schellen, Eckstein, Ruthen (Ger.).

Dice (history), 578

DICE: cubes having faces numbered from 1 to 6, used in many games. (*Singular,* die.)

Dice Games, 537

Dice Wheel, 555

DIE: singular of *dice.*

Diplomat, a card Solitaire.

DIRECT MATE: form of Chess problem in which White must mate Black against his resistance.

DIS = dix, the nine of trumps.

DISCARD: 1. Lay aside excess cards in exchange for others from the stock or widow; a card so discarded. 2. Play a plain-suit card not of the same suit as the lead to a trick; a card so played.

Discard Hearts = Black Lady, 243

DISCARD PILE: the common pile of discarded cards (Rummy).

Discard Pinochle = Auction Pinochle, 291

DISCORD: a hazard at Ombre, incurred by holding four kings.

DISCOURAGING CARD: one that indicates no desire to have partner lead or continue the suit (Bridge).

DISCOVERED CHECK: one delivered by a queen, rook, or bishop by moving a piece off its line of attack (Chess).

DISPATCHERS: improperly marked dice used by cheats.

DISTRIBUTION: 1. Deal. 2. Division of cards among the hands, especially as to the number of cards of each suit dealt to each hand.

Division Loo = Loo, 192

DIX: the lowest trump, as the 7 in Klaberjass, the 9 in Pinochle. Also *dis.*

DOG: 1. Big Dog or Little Dog (Poker). 2. Make a safe discard (Mah Jongg).

DOGGING: saving tiles of several suits instead of clearing the hand (Mah Jongg).

DOMINO GAME: 1. Any game with dominoes. 2. Any card game in which the hands are replenished, after each trick, by drawing from the stock, as Gin Rummy.

Dominoes, 424

DOMINOES: tiles used in many games; the usual set contains tiles marked with each possible combination of 0, 1, 2, 3, 4, 5, 6, taken two at a time and including repetitions [28 tiles].

Domino Euchre, a game with dominoes based on Euchre.

Domino Hearts, 243

Domino Pool, 428

Domino Whist = Five or Nine, 225

Dom Pedro, 236

Donkey, 490

DON'T COME: the proposition that the shooter will lose, counting his next roll as the first of a series (Craps).

DON'T PASS THE LINE: the part of the betting layout on which is placed a bet that the shooter will not pass (Craps).

Doppelmuhle = Mill, 400

DORMITZER: a kibitzer of low intelligence or limited privilege (jocular). Also dorbitzer, daubitzer.

DOTS: the suit Circles (Mah Jongg).

Dots Game = Quadrangles, 434

DOUBLE: 1. A voluntary doubling of the basic stake, as in Backgammon. 2. A call that increases the scoring items in case the last preceding bid becomes the contract (Bridge).

Double and Quits = Monte Carlo, 465

Double-Barreled Shotgun, 89

DOUBLE BETE: 1. Loss suffered by a Bidder who has elected to play and has lost (Auction Pinochle). 2. Doubled penalty for certain irregularities.

Double Calculation, a card Solitaire.

Double Cameroon, 550

DOUBLE CHECK: check by each of two pieces simultaneously (Chess).

DOUBLE CORNER: 1. The squares 1 and 5 or 28 and 32. 2. One of the openings. (Checkers.)

DOUBLE DOUBLETS: a holding of four doublets (Domino Bingo).

DOUBLED PAWN: two pawns of the same color on the same file (Chess).

Double Dummy, 179. Also Double Dumby.

DOUBLE-DUMMY PROBLEM: one in which all four hands are shown to the solver (Whist, Bridge).

DOUBLE-ENDED STRAIGHT: four cards in sequence, except A-K-Q-J and A-2-3-4 (Poker).

Double Fives, a card Solitaire.

Double Hasenpfeffer, 210

DOUBLE-HEADER: 1. A pool increased by addition of a prior pool not won in the prior deal. 2. Same numbers on both ends of the layout (Bergen).

Double Hearts = Cancellation Hearts, 244

Double Klondike, variant played by two, each having his own pack and layout, but with foundations pooled.

DOUBLE MILL: a formation in which a player can open one mill and close another at every turn (Mill).

DOUBLE NINGRE: a hand of two pairs (Romestecq).

Double or Quits, a card Solitaire.

DOUBLE-OUT: a system of betting on the case card at Faro.

Double-Pack Pinochle, 310

DOUBLE PAIR ROYAL: four of a kind (Cribbage).

Double Pedro = Cinch, 236

DOUBLE ROME: a hand of one pair, aces or kings (Romestecq).

Double Rum, 6

DOUBLE RUN: a run of three cards with one rank duplicated, as 9-8-8-7 (Cribbage).

DOUBLE SOLITAIRE: any Solitaire game when played by two; usually, each has his own pack and layout, but foundations are pooled.

DOUBLET: 1. A cast of like numbers on two dice (Dice). 2. A bone having the same number on both ends (Dominoes).

DOUBLETON: a holding of exactly two cards in a suit (Bridge).

DOUBLE UP: bet twice as much as was previously bet and lost.

DOUBLE VALUATION: a valuation method advocated by Wilbur C. Whitehead, whereby the estimated trick-winning power of a hand was twice its quick tricks (Auction Bridge).

DOUBLING CUBE: large die with faces marked 2, 4, 8, 16, 32, 64, for keeping track of double applied to the basic stake.

Doubling Gin, 42

Doubling Limit (Poker), 61

DOUGLAS: a Checkers opening.

DOWN: defeated; having failed to make contract; set; gone bete.

DOWN AND OUT: the play of two cards, higher first, the show no more of the suit (Bridge).

Down the River = Seven-Card Stud, 87

Down the Stairs, a card Solitaire.

DRAG, DRAG DOWN: remove part of one's winnings from the center (Craps).

DRAGONS: the twelve tiles comprising four duplicates each of Red Dragons, Green Dragons, and White Dragons (Mah Jongg)

Draughts = Checkers, 363

DRAUGHTSMAN: checker piece; any piece of disk shape used in a board game.

DRAW: 1. Pull cards from a spread pack, to determine dealer. etc. 2. Receive cards from the stock to replace discards; receive additional cards after the original deal; cards so received. 3. Drawn game.

Draw Bridge, 180 (Under Honeymoon Bridge, 179.)

Draw Casino, 259

Draw Dominoes, 426

Draw Hearts, 243

DRAWN GAME: one abandoned without victory for any player, as in Chess, Gin Rummy, etc.

Draw Poker, 52

Dreiblatt = Three-Card Loo, 192 (also called Tippen, Zwicken).

DREIER = THREESOME: a bid in Tarok.

Dreizehnern, obsolete game of chance based on Treize (= Blüchern, sept-huit-neuf).

Dress Parade, a card Solitaire.

DRIB: unskillful player (*slang*).

Drive Bridge, Drive Whist, obsolete names for Progressive Bridge, Progressive Whist.

DRIVER'S SEAT, IN THE: said of a player who holds what is sure to be the best hand (Poker).

DRIVE THE HEARSE: keep cases at Faro.

DROP: withdraw from the current deal; discard one's hand, rather than put enough chips in the pot to remain an active player.

Drop Dead, five-dice game to score highest total in a series of rolls, those in which 2 or 5 is cast being nullified

Dr. Pepper, 91 (under Woolworth, 90).

DRY: broke; having lost heavily.

Dubblets, obsolete Backgammon game.

DUCK: fail to cover when able (Bridge).

Duel, two-hand variant of Honeymoon Bridge, with the stock face up as in California Jack.

DUFFER: unskillful player.

DUKE: hand of cards (*slang*).

DUMBY = DUMMY

Dummy, 188

DUMMY: declarer's partner; the hand he lays on the table (Bridge).

Dummy Whist, variant in which the hand of dealer's partner is faced on the table and played by the dealer together with his own hand.

DUNDEE: a Checkers opening.

DUPLICATE: a form of Whist or Bridge play in which all contestants play the same series of hands; a contest in any game, conducted in form analogous to Duplicate Bridge.

DUPLICATE A BUILD: see BUILD.

Duplicate Backgammon, a contest in which a referee rolls and calls the dice, the contestants using these common rolls being paired together in knockout matches.

DUPLICATE BOARD: a device for holding separate the four hands of a deal, for Duplicate play.

Duplicate Contract Bridge, 162

Dutch Backgammon, 393

Dutch Bank = Blind Hookey

DUTCH DEFENSE: a Chess opening.

Dutchess, a card Solitaire.

DUTCH IT: 1. Make it next (Euchre). 2. Each player to settle for himself.

DUTCH STRAIGHT = skip straight.

DYKE: a Checkers opening.

E

E: abbr. of East.

EAGLES: American name of the fifth suit, green in color, at one time added to the standard pack.

Eagle Wing, a card Solitaire.

Earl of Coventry = Snip Snap Snorem, 227

EAST: conventional designation of one of the players in a four-hand game.

EAST WIND: 1. The player having first turn and who pays or collects double. 2. One of the Honors tiles (Mah Jongg).

EASY ACES: two-two division of the aces between the two sides, with no honor score for the deal (Auction Bridge).

Ecarte, 197

Ecarte Nap, 197

ECARTER (Fr.): to discard.

Echecs, le jeu d' (Fr.): Chess.

ECHIQUIER (Fr.): chessboard.

ECHO: a signal, the play of a higher and then a lower card of the same suit, made to request a lead or continuation of that suit (Bridge) or to request a trump lead (Whist); to signal in this way.

ECKERN, ECKSTEIN (Ger.): the suit clubs.

EDGE: 1. = age, eldest hand; the player at left of the dealer. 2. Advantage (from the advantage of being eldest hand, in many games).

EDINBURGH: a Checkers opening.

EICHELN (Ger.): the suit clubs.

Eight-Card Stud, 91

Eight-Day Clock = Perpetual Motion, 469

Eighteens, a card Solitaire.

EIGHTER FROM DECATUR: cast of 8 (Dice).

Eight-hand Pinochle = Double-pack Pinochle, 310

Eight Off, 453

Eight-Pack Bezique, 273

Eights, 225

80 KINGS: a meld of four kings, one of each suit (Pinochle).

Elective Contract, 175

Eleven-Man Ballot Checkers, 383

Elevens, 468

Elfern, two-hand game to win a majority of the twenty high cards (Ger. *elevens*).

Elf Hoch: three-dice game, "eleven high."

ELDER: sitting at the left (when the rotation is clockwise); non-dealer in two-hand play.

ELDEST HAND: player at left of the dealer (when the rotation is clockwise); the first to receive cards, and (usually) the first to bid or declare.

L'EMPEREUR (Fr.): the tarot IV ("emperor").

Emperor, a card Solitaire.

EMPEROR: a holding of six doublets (Domino Bingo).

Emperor of Germany, a card Solitaire.

Empress of India, 453

L'Emprunt, obsolete card game similar to Hoc.

ENCOURAGING CARD: one played to show a desire to have the suit led or continued by partner, or to show strength in the suit.

END: 1. The number on one half of a bone. 2. An open end of the layout, on which a legal play may be made (Dominoes).

ENDHAND: the dealer in three-hand play; the last active player to receive cards (Skat, etc.).

END GAME: the final phase of a game in which many pieces have been captured; a posed problem embodying principles of end play (Chess, Checkers).

END HOLE: extra hole at one end of a Cribbage board; game hole.

ENDPLAY: any of several stratagems (especially *throw-in*) that can usually be executed only in the last phase of play (Bridge).

Enfle, 228

ENGLISH OPENING: a Chess opening.

English Poker = Blind Opening, 71

English Whist, see Whist, 180

EN PASSANT: special form of pawn capture (Chess). Abbreviation, *e. p.*

EN PLEIN: placing a bet on a single number (Roulette).

EN PRISE: attacked, liable to capture (Chess).

ENTER: move a stone, after it has been hit, from the bar to the adverse home table (Backgammon).

ENTRY: a card with which a hand can win a trick and so gain the lead.

E. O., obsolete betting game similar to Roulette, so-called because each space of the betting layout was marked E or O.

E. P. = EN PASSANT

EQUAL: statement by a player that he can tie a scoring combination announced by opponent, as in Piquet.

EQUALS: cards in sequence or which have become sequential by the play of all cards intervening in rank.

L'ERMITE (Fr.): the tarot IX ("hermit").

ESPADAS: in the Spanish pack, the suit *swords*, corresponding to *spades*.

ESPAGNOLETTE: four of the six top cards, the aces and quinolas (Reversis).

Esperance, obsolete two-dice game.

ESTABLISH: make cards the best by forcing out adverse higher cards; clear.

ESTABLISHED SUIT: one that can be cashed in its entirety without loss of a trick.

L'ESTOILE: the tarot XVII ("star").

ESTRAPADE: a hazard at Ombre, incurred by playing sans prendre and making beast.

Euchre, 201

EUCHRE: failure of the making side to win three tricks (Euchre).

Euchre Loo = Penalty Euchre, 205

European Acey-Deucey, 392

EUROPEAN BRIDGE LEAGUE: federation of national Bridge organizations of most of the western European countries.

EVANS GAMBIT: a Chess opening.

Even Up, a card Solitaire.

Everest, dice game similar to Yacht.

EXCESS BAGGAGE: a hanger-on who does not play or cannot pay his own way.

EXCHANGE: capture and counter-capture of pieces (Chess, Checkers). *Win the* —, capture pieces of greater value than those lost (Chess).

Exchange Dummy, see **Three-Hand Bridge,** 177

Exiled Kings = Beleaguered Castle, 442

EXIT: get out of the lead; compel another hand to win a trick.

EXPOSED CARD: one shown inadvertently, especially in partnership play, and therefore subject to penalty for giving information illegally.

EXPOSED HAND: 1. One laid down in *open* play for a greater score, as in Solo. 2. The dummy hand (Bridge).

EYE: an open point entirely enclosed by stones on one color (Go).

F

FACE CARD: any king, queen, or jack. (Also the obsolete *cavalier*.)

611

FACED HAND: 1. One laid down in *open* play for a greater score, as in Solo. 2. The dummy hand (Bridge).

FADE: bet against the shooter's center bet (Craps).

FADING GAME = OPEN CRAPS.

FAIRE LES CARTES (Fr.): shuffle the cards.

FAIRY CHESS: name given to the domain of Chess problems depending on pieces or rules not found in the actual game.

FAITES VOS JEUX (Fr.): "Place your bets," croupier's call in Roulette.

FALKBEER COUNTER-GAMBIT: a Chess opening.

FALL OF THE CARDS: identity and order of cards played, especially as it gives clue to the location of unplayed cards.

FALSE CARD: one selected for play so as to mislead the opponents. *False-card*, to play such a card.

FALSE MATADORS: a sequence of high trumps lacking spadille, the highest (Ombre).

FALSE MOVE: One that is illegal, as in Chess.

FALSE OPENERS: a hand with which a pot has been opened, but which is not so good as the rules require (Poker).

FAMILY: the entire sequence or group of cards to be built on a foundation; a suit (Solitaire).

FAMILY OF GAMES: a group associated by superficial resemblances or common ancestry.

Fan = La Belle Lucie, 463

FAN: cards spread face up, fan-fashion (Solitaire).

FANATIQUE: a hazard at Ombre, incurred by holding four jacks.

Fanny, a card Solitaire.

Fan Tan, 224

Fan Tan, Chinese, gambling game in which the players bet on 0, 1, 2, or 3 as the remainder after a handful of beans is counted out by fours.

FARBE, DIE (Ger.): suit (playing cards).

FARO BANK: gambling house that banks a Faro game.

Farmer, The Farm, 517

FARMER: an opening trap in Checkers. (See page 374.)

Faro, 529

Fascination = Canfield, 446

Fascination = Klondike, 462

Father Time = Grandfather's Clock, 460

FATTEN (a trick): smear a high card on it (Pinochle). — the pot: ante again to a jackpot not opened on the previous deal (Poker).

FAT TRICK: one rich in counting cards.

Favorite Whist, variant in which each suit has a different trick value and every deal is played out to decide the score.

FEED: contribute to. — the kitty: set aside a percentage of each pot to defray expenses, as in Poker. — a player: discard a card he can use, as in Rummy.

FEHLKARTEN (Ger.): non-counting cards.

FEIND, DER (Ger.): enemy; opponent.

Felsos, 283

Ferris Wheel, a card Solitaire.

FERS: obsolete Chess piece, precursor of the queen.

FIANCHETTO: develop a bishop at N2 (Chess).

FICHE (Fr.): a chip.

FIELD: numbers from 2 to 12 on the layout, for placement of bets on the next roll (Craps).

FIFE: a Checkers opening.

Fifteen = Quinze, 518

Fifteen, a card Solitaire.

FIFTEEN: a combination of cards totaling 15; the score of 2 points therefor (Cribbage).

Fifteen Hundred, variant of Five Hundred for game of 1,500, with a graduated count for cards won in tricks.

Fifty, two-dice game.

FIFTY-FIVE: a scoring combination, A-7-6 of one suit (Primiera).

FIGURE: face card.

FILE: a vertical column of squares (Chess).

FILL: draw cards that improve the hand.

FILLE (Fr.): widow; extra hand.

Financier, a card Solitaire.

FINESSE: an attempt to win a trick with a card that is lower than a card of the same suit held by an opponent (Whist, Bridge).

Firehouse Pinochle, 311

Firing-Squad = Aces Up, 441

FIRST HAND: 1. The leader to a trick. 2. Eldest hand.

FISH: 1. A chip (from Fr. *fiche*). 2. Draw cards from the stock.

Fish-Bone, a card Solitaire.

Fish, Go, 491

FISH-HOOK: any seven (playing cards).

Fission, a card Solitaire.

Five and Ten = Forty-five, 191

Five-Card Cribbage, 254

Five-Card Loo, 195

Five-Cards = Spoil Five, 189

Five-Deal Klondike, a card Solitaire.

Five-Dice Baseball, 565

Five Fingers = Spoil Five, 189

FIVE FINGERS: the five of trumps (Spoil Five).

Five-Hand Five Hundred, 216

Five Hundred, 210

Five Hundred (Cinq Cents), 273

5-POINT CARD: any 7, 6, 5, 4 or black 3, each valued at 5 points (Canasta).

500 Rummy, 12

Five or Nine, 225

Fives, a card Solitaire.

FIVE-SUIT PACK: a pack of 65 cards at one time made by adding a fifth suit, Crowns or Eagles, to the regular 52-card pack.

FIXED LIMIT (Poker): see page 60

FLAG-FLYING: bidding for more tricks than can be won, to prevent the opponents from assuming the contract (Bridge).

FLASH: 1. Expose a card, as in dealing. 2. A hand containing cards of all five suits (Poker with the five-suit pack).

FLAT: a die shaved down so that it is not a true cube, used by cheats.

FLAT BET: 1. One that the shooter will or will not pass, made between players other than the shooter (Craps). 2. An equal amount bet on each of several horses.

Flat Poker, variant of Blind Opening.

FLECHES (Fr.): points on a Backgammon board ("arrows").

Flinch, proprietary card game manufactured by Parker Bros.

Flip, 90

FLOAT: hollowed dice used by cheats.

FLOORMAN: supervisor in a gambling house.

Florentini, variant of Landsknecht.

Flower Garden, 455

FLOWERS: certain special tiles, used like wild cards in modern Mah Jongg.

FLUSH: 1. A hand or combination comprising cards of only one suit. 2. A meld of A-K-Q-J-10 of trumps (Pinochle).

FLUSS, FLUX = flush (obsolete).

Fly, obsolete card game similar to Loo (= La Mouche).

Fly, a card Solitaire.

FOLD: drop; turn one's cards face down to signify withdrawal from the deal.

FOLLOW SUIT: play a card of the suit led.

FOOL: the diamond jack (Guimbarde).

FOOL'S MATE: the checkmate by 1. P-KB4, P-K3; 2. P-KN4, Q-R5 (Chess).

FOOT: bottom portion of the pack, set aside until needed (Panguingue).

Football, 90

Football Pools, 558

— FOR —: statement of odds offered, as in "7 for 1," equivalent to odds of 6 to 1; the first number given is what the bettor will receive if he wins and so includes what he must bet, the second number.

FORCE: 1. Compel a player to trump if he wishes to win a trick. 2. Make a bid that systemically compels partner to respond (Contract Bridge). 3. Discard a card which the next player is compelled by the rules to pick up (Canasta, etc.)

FORCED: 1. Legally compulsory. 2. Imperative for strategical reasons.

FORCEE: compulsory bid in certain games, as Ombre.

FORCE, LA (Fr.): the tarot XI ("fortitude").

FORCING BID: one that systemically requires partner to respond or assure that the auction is kept open (Contract Bridge).

FORCING PASS: one that systemically requires partner to overcall or to double an adverse bid (Bridge).

FORDERN (Ger.): lead trumps.

FOREHAND: eldest hand, especially in three-hand play.

FORK: simultaneous attack on two enemy pieces (Chess).

Fortress = Sebastopol, 429

Fortune's Favor, a card Solitaire.

Forty-five, 191

FORTY-FOUR: a declaration to win all four aces (Alsós).

40 JACKS: a meld of four jacks, one of each suit (Pinochle).

Forty Thieves, 456

Forty-two, 431

Forwards and Backwards, a card Solitaire.

FOSTER, R. F.: author of many books on intellectual games; died 1945.

FOUL HAND: one of more or less than five cards, therefore compelled to drop (Poker).

FOUNDATIONS: cards of a certain rank on which the rest of the pack is to be built (Solitaire).

FOU, LE (Fr.): 1. Bishop (Chess). 2. One of the names for the highest tarot trump, the XXII. 3. Joker.

FOUR ACES: a Contract Bridge team (1934–) composed of Oswald Jacoby, Howard Schenken, Michael T. Gottlieb, David Burnstine, Richard L. Frey, later M. D. Maier and others; see page 150.

FOURCHETTE: a tenace, when the hand on the right is known to hold the missing card, as A-Q held by a defender over the K in dummy (Bridge).

Four Continents, a card Solitaire.

Four Corners = Corner Stones, 449

Four-Five-Six, 544

FOUR-FLUSH: four cards of the same suit.

Fourflush Beats a Pair, 88

FOUR-FLUSHER: a man who falls short of his pretensions.

Fourflush to Open, 70

Four Forty-four, 91 (under Woolworth, 90)

Four Forty-two, 91 (under Woolworth, 90)

Four-Hand Bezique, 271

Four-Hand Chess, 361-2

Four-Hand Cribbage, 254

Four-Hand Five Hundred, 216

Four-Hand Jass, 278

Four-Hand Gin Rummy = Partnership Gin Rummy, 39

Four-Hand Sixty-Six, 276

FOUR HORSEMEN: a Contract Bridge team (c. 1932) composed of P. Hal Sims, Oswald Jacoby, David Burnstine, Willard Karn.

Four Intruders, a card Solitaire.

Four Jacks = Polignac, 246

Four Kings, a card Solitaire.

Four-Leaf Clover, a card Solitaire.

Four Marriages, a card Solitaire.

Four of a Kind, 89

Four of a Kind = Clock, 447

FOUR OF A KIND: four cards of the same rank.

Four Seasons, 456

FOUR SIGNAL: a method of showing four trumps, by withholding the lowest until the third round.

Fourteen, 544

Fourteens, a card Solitaire.

Four Weddings, a card Solitaire.

Fox and Geese, puzzle game on the checkerboard, in which four pieces moving only forward have to trap one piece free to move in any direction.

Frage = Frog, 327

FRAGE: 1. Inquiry by forehand (Ger. *ich frage*, I ask) whether any other will bid against him. 2. The lowest-counting game in Skat, now obsolete.

FREAK: wild card.

FREAK HAND: 1. One of unusual pattern or content. 2. One that contains eleven or more cards in two suits, or one suit longer than seven cards (Bridge).

Freak-Pots = Deuces Wild, 73

FREDON: 1. Four of a kind (Ambigu). 2. Three of a kind (Hoc).

FREE BID: one made voluntarily, not under any systemic compulsion (Bridge).

FREE DOUBLE: double of an adverse bid that is sufficient for game even if made undoubled (Bridge).

FREE RIDE: opportunity to play in a pot without chipping.

Freezeout, 97

FREEZEOUT: any game in which losers retire, leaving winners to continue play until only one survives.

FREEZER: an anticipatory short call when two or more other players are raising; further raises then go to a side pot (Poker).

FREEZE THE PACK: discard a wild card, thereby increasing the difficulty of taking the discard pile (Canasta).

French Boston, 187

FRENCH DEFENSE: a Chess opening.

French Dummy = Mort, 188

French Euchre = Auction Euchre, 206

French-Ruff = Trumps. (See page 189.)

French Whist = Catch the Ten with the proviso that the diamond ten always counts 10, whatever the trump suit.

Frog (Solitaire), 457

Frog (three-hand game), 327

FROG: one of the games in Frog, Solo, Ombre, etc.

Frogpond, 494

FRONT LINE: pass line; part of the betting layout on which are placed bets to win (Craps).

FROZEN OUT: retired from play because: 1. One has lost one's original stake. 2. One has lost a round or deal in a freezeout game.

FROZEN PACK: the discard pile at a time when it can be taken only by matching the top card with a natural pair in the hand (Canasta).

FULL HAND = FULL HOUSE.

FULL HOUSE: three cards of one rank and two cards of another rank (Poker).

FULL PACK: the pack of 52 cards. (See *Standard Pack*.)

Funfzehnern, a game of no-trump play to win 15 or more points in counting cards.

FUZZING: shuffling the pack by drawing cards simultaneously from top and bottom.

G

Gabatta = Mancala, 410

GAG = HARD WAY (Craps).

GAFF: any secret device used in cheating.

Gaigel, variant of Bézique for two to eight players.

GAIN THE LEAD: get entry or opportunity to lead by winning a trick.

GALLERY: non-playing spectators.

GALLOPING DOMINOES: dice (slang).

GAMBIT: a sacrifice in the opening, usually of a pawn (Chess).

GAMBLER'S POINT: 1. The count for the ten of trumps (All Fours). 2. The point for *game* (All Fours).

Gamblers' Rummy, four-hand variant with seven cards dealt to each.

GAME: 1. A pastime in general, as Poker, Chess. 2. A variant of a basic game, as Seven-Card Stud Poker. 3. A bid or declaration, as club solo, grand tournee, in Skat. 4. A period in a session of play, from which emerges a winner, as a game of Chess. 5. The number of points, accumulation of which wins a game, as the game of 100 in Piquet. 6. Fulfillment of contract; the number of points necessary to fulfill contract, as, the Player makes game at Skat by winning 61 or more points. 7. The ten of trumps; a point awarded for winning a majority of the count in counting cards (All Fours). 8. A style or system of play, as the forward game in Backgammon.

GAME HOLES: extra holes at one end of a Cribbage board, from which pegs start and finish to mark a game.

GAMMON: loss of a game, when the loser has borne off no stones but has advanced all his stones beyond the adverse home table (Backgammon).

GANO: demand by a player that his card be allowed to win a trick (Ombre).

Gaps, 457

Garanguet, obsolete three-dice game.

Garbage, 534

Garden = Flower Garden, 455

Gargantua, 458

Gate, a card Solitaire.

GATE: the pay-off card (Monte Bank).

Gathering of the Clans, a card Solitaire.

Gato, El, Spanish card game.

Gavotte, 459

GE: the highest pair; chips won therefor (Gillet).

GEBEN (Ger.): to deal ("give").

GEGNER (Ger.): opponent.

GELB (Ger.): the suit diamonds ("yellow").

Gelber Zwerg, gambling game similar to Michigan (Ger., *yellow dwarf,* after a figure depicted on the layout).

Gentleman's Agreement, 172

Ghosts, 496

GIFT: 1. The point scored by eldest hand when he begs and dealer decides to play (All Fours). 2. Good score on a board in consequence of adverse error (Duplicate Bridge).

Gile, Gilet, Gillet, 80

Gimmi 88, Japanese card game.

GIMMICK: any secret mechanical device; gaff; cheating stratagem.

Gin, Gin Rummy, 31

GIN: a complete hand with no unmatched cards (Gin Rummy).

Gingham, a card Solitaire.

Girdle, a card Solitaire.

Giveaway Checkers, 383

Giveaway Chess, 361

GLASGOW: a Checkers opening.

Gleek, 82

GLEEK: three of a kind.

Glencoe, a card Solitaire.

GLUCKSPIEL, DAS (Ger.): any game of chance.

Go, 403

GO BACK: to redouble (Bridge Whist).

Go Bang, 406

Go Boom, 493

GO DOWN: end the play by placing the remainder of one's cards face up on the table (Rummy).

Go Fish, 491

GO IN: take a batch of cards from the discard pile (500 Rum).

Going to Boston, three-dice game.

Golf, 460

Golfo, El, Spanish card game.

Go-Maku, 406

GOOD: concession by a player that he cannot beat a scoring combination announced by opponent, as in Piquet.

Good Measure, a card Solitaire.

GOOSEWALK: an opening trap in Checkers (See page 374)

GO OUT: get rid of the last card in the hand (Rummy).

GO OVER: 1. Bid higher. 2. Play a higher card.

GOREN SYSTEM, 143

GO RUMMY: go out by melding the whole hand in one turn, having made no previous meld (Rummy).

Goulash (Pinochle), 290

Goulash (Bridge), 172

GRAND, GRANDO: 1. A game in which jacks only are trumps (Skat). 2. A solo game with hearts trumps (Frog).

GRAND COUP: the trumping of an own winning card, to shorten for a trump pick-up (Bridge).

Grand Duchess, a card Solitaire.

Grandfather, a card Solitaire.

Grandfather's Clock, 460

Grand Hazard: See Chuck-Luck, 543

GRAND SLAM: the winning of thirteen tricks by one side (Bridge).

Grant's Reinforcement, a card Solitaire.

GREAT MARTINGALE, 552

Great Thirteen, a card Solitaire.

GREC = GREEK.

GREEK: any card cheat.

GRIFTER: a cheat; confidence man; blackleg.

GROUNDED SET: one placed face up on the table (Mah Jongg).

GROUP: matched set; especially a set of three or four cards of the same rank, as distinguished from a sequence (Rummy).

GRUGED: beaten by a higher hand (obsolete).

GRUN (Ger.): the suit spades.

GUARANTEE SOLO: a bid to win more than a simple majority of the points in play (Six-bid Solo).

GUARD: 1. A low card accompanying a high card, saving the latter from having to be played on adverse higher cards, as Q-x-x, the low cards falling on the ace and king if led. 2. To defend one piece with another; a piece that defends another (Chess).

GUCKI: a game in which the high bidder picks up the widow, making jacks trumps (Skat).

GUCKSER = GUCKI.

Guggenheim = Categories, 498

Guimbarde, obsolete game of chance like Matrimony. (= La Mariée, The Bride.)

GUIMBARDE: the heart queen (Guimbarde).

Guinguette, obsolete card game of chance.

GUINGUETTE: 1. A hazard at Ombre, incurred by winning the hand without a black ace. 2. The diamond queen (Guinguette).

GUIOCO PIANO: a Chess opening.

GUN TURN: two fives showing in one turn at Faro. (*Note:* from an old pickpocket saw
"Two fives together
What the mark had in his
leather . . .")

GUT-PULLER: a Faro dealer.

617

H

Half and Half, a card Solitaire.

Halma, 407

Hamburgern, variant of Elf Hoch.

HAND: 1. The cards originally dealt to a player; any portion thereof remaining unplayed. 2. Same as DEAL, sense 2. 3. A player (holder of a hand). 4. Stock; remainder of the pack after the layout is dealt (Solitaire).

HAND FROM HEAVEN: a complete hand drawn by East before play begins (Mah Jongg).

HANDPLAY: a game in which the high bidder does not pick up the widow; = solo (Skat).

HANETON: capture of three cards of the same rank with the fourth; the bonus therefor (Papillon).

Hangman, 499

HANGMAN'S TURN: a jack and king showing in one turn at Faro. (*Note:* supposedly after Jack King, a dealer who was hanged for murder.)

HARD WAY: roll of an even total by a doublet, as 8 by 4-4 (Craps).

Harp, a card Solitaire.

Harvest = Hit or Miss, 461

Hasenpfeffer, 209

Haufeln, obsolete card game similar to Faro.

Havana, game of chance played with a 32-card pack plus a joker.

HAVE THE MOVE: in Chess and Checkers, have the advantage in the opposition. (*Note:* does not mean having the next turn to play.)

Hawaiian Dominoes, 427

Hazard: 1. See Chuck-Luck, 543. 2. An obsolete dice game on which Craps is based. Also, *Hazzard.*

HAZARD: a circumstance (usually a special hand together with the outcome of the play) that by rule requires special payments (Ombre).

HEAD: top portion of the pack, from which the hands are dealt and cards are drawn during the play (Panguingue).

HEAD A TRICK: play a card higher than any previously played to the trick.

HEARSE-DRIVER: the case-keeper at Faro.

HEART CONVENTION: a Bridge-Whist agreement that if third hand doubles a no-trump make his partner's opening lead must be a heart.

HEARTS: the suit denoted by the symbol ♡; also called coeur (Fr.), Herz, Roth, Rot (Ger.).

Hearts, 240

Heartsette, 242

Heart Solo = Frog, 327

HEAVIER: having a larger total of pips (Dominoes).

HEAVY PIECE: = major piece, queen or rook (Chess).

HEDGE: Bet against a contingency formerly bet on, to reduce or limit possible losses.

HEEL, or HEELED BET: a bet on one card to lose and another to win (Faro).

Heinz, 90

HELP: 1. Raise, assist. 2. Hold helpful cards (in support of partner).

HELP-MATE: form of Chess problem in which both sides must co-operate to mate one of the kings.

Help Me, Neighbor, variant of Commerce (= Accomodez-moi).

Help Your Neighbor, three-dice game.

Hemispheres, a card Solitaire.

Herring-Bone, a card Solitaire.

HERZ (Ger.): the suit hearts.

Hidden Aces, a card Solitaire.

Hidden Cards = Clock, 447

Hidden Declarations, 94

Hidden Proverbs, 506

Hidden Treasures, 509

HIGH: 1. Best, master (card). 2. Having the best score. 3. The ace of trumps, or the highest trump dealt;

the score for having this card (All Fours).

—— HIGH: headed by the card named, as *ace-high*, a Poker hand.

High-Card Pool = Red Dog, 526

HIGH-CARD TRICK: one that is won by rank in the suit led, not by a trump or a long card.

High Dice = Bingo, 546

Highest Card, 485

High Five = Cinch, 236

High-Low Five-Card Stud, 93

High-Low-Jack = All Fours, 229

High-Low Poker, 92

High-Low Seven-Card Stud, 93

Hi-Lo, 96

Hilo-Picalo, 93 (under Freak High-Low Games).

HINTERHAND (Ger.): last hand; the last to receive cards in the deal; = endhand.

HIS HEELS: the turn of a jack as the starter; the score of 2 points therefor (Cribbage).

HIS NOBS: a jack of same suit as the starter, in hand or crib; the score of 1 point therefor (Cribbage).

HIT: 1. Move a stone so as to touch or land upon a point occupied by an adverse blot (Backgammon). 2. Turn of a card of same rank as that called in order (Treize). 3. Discard a card that the next player can use (Rummy games). 4. Deal another card to (a player) (Blackjack).

HIT ME: player's request to dealer for an additional card (Blackjack).

Hit or Miss, 461

Hoc, obsolete card game similar to Piquet.

HOC: 1. Any of the six highest cards in Hoc (four kings, spade queen, diamond jack). 2. The last card left in the box, on which there is no action (Faro). Also *hock, hocly, hockelty.*

Hoca, obsolete lottery game.

Ho-Hpai, Korean domino game ("barbarian tablets").

Hoi T'Ap, Chinese domino game ("open the pagoda").

HOLDING, HOLDINGS: the hand or any part thereof; —— *in a suit,* the cards of that suit held in the hand.

HOLD UP: refrain from playing (a high card).

HOLE: See *in the hole, take a hole.*

HOLE CARD: first face-down card dealt to a player (Stud Poker).

HOLLANDAISE = GOULASH.

Hollywood Gin, 38

Hombre = Ombre, 330

HOME: up to average expectation in total score (Cribbage).

HOME TABLE = inner table (Backgammon).

Honey-Bee, a card Solitaire.

Honeymoon Bridge, 179

HONORS: 1. The five highest trumps, or the four aces at no trump (Bridge). 2. The four highest trumps (Whist). 3. The K, Q, J, A and 7 of trumps (Imperial). 4. All Dragons and Winds tiles (Mah Jongg).

HONOR-TRICKS: units in the Culbertson high-card valuation system (Bridge).

HOOK: finesse (Bridge slang).

Hooligan, five-dice game much-played in taverns.

Hope Deferred, a card Solitaire.

HORSE AND HORSE: score of 1-1 in games.

Horse-Race Wheel, 555

Horse Race with Cards, 563

HOUSE: a casino where gambling games are operated; the dealer or supervisor for such a casino.

House in the Wood, a card Solitaire.

House on the Hill, a card Solitaire.

HOWELL MOVEMENT: a method of progression in Duplicate Bridge (see page 170).

HOWELL SETTLEMENT: a method of scoring in Hearts (see page 241).

HOYLE: common term for any book on intellectual games. *According to —,* in conformance with traditional rules or strategical precepts.

HOYLE, EDMOND (1672-1769): English writer whose *Short Treatise on Whist* (1742) stimulated wide interest in intellectual games.

HUFF OR BLOW: the (now obsolete) rule that if a player fails to capture when able, making a simple move instead, the opponent may either enforce the capture or remove from the board the piece that should have captured (Checkers).

Humbug Whist, two-hand variant.

Hundertspiel, card game for three or four similar to Sixty-Six.

Hurricane, 93

Hussars, a card Solitaire.

HUSTLER: minor gambler; one who seeks advantage through the ignorance of his victims.

HYDE, DR. THOMAS: author of *De Ludis Orientalibus* (Concerning Oriental Games), 1694.

I

ICE = cold deck.

Idiot's Delight, pejorative name given to Solitaire generally and to some Solitaires specifically.

Idle Aces, a card Solitaire.

Idle Year = Accordion, 440

I Doubt It, 491

I-Go = Go, 403

IMMORTAL GAME: one of special brilliance, such as a famous game won by Anderssen against Kieseritzki (Chess).

IMMORTAL HAND: one that is sure to win; = cinch hand.

IMPAIR (Fr.): odd; a bet on the odd numbers at Roulette.

IMPASSE: 1. A play in Quadrille. 2. A formation in which both a black and a white unit are safe, but neither side can add a stone with-

out losing its unit (Go). 3. (Fr.) = finesse.

L'IMPERATRICE (Fr.): the tarot III ("empress").

IMPERFECT PACK: one so worn that some cards are identifiable from the back.

Imperial, 266

IMPERIALS: certain scoring combinations (Imperial).

IMPERIAL TOMBEE: the score for winning the four highest trumps in tricks (Imperial).

IMPLEMENTS OF GAMES, 575

IMPROVE: draw cards that better one's hand.

IN CHEVILLE: sitting between eldest hand and the dealer (Ombre).

INCORRECT PACK: one from which cards are missing or which contains unwanted duplicates.

INCREASE A BUILD: see BUILD.

INDEPENDENCE: a bid for more than five tricks (Boston).

INDEX: the number or letter printed in the corner of a playing card, so that it may be read when held in a fan.

Indian, a card Solitaire.

INDIAN DEFENSE: a Chess opening.

Indian Dice, five-dice game.

INDIFFERENT CARDS: those whose rank need not be specified in posing a problem; equals; low plain cards; non-counters; a poor hand.

INDIVIDUAL: a type of Duplicate Bridge contest in which partnerships change and score is kept for individuals instead of pairs.

Indolence, a card Solitaire.

INFORMATION: disclosure of holdings, intentions, and desires between partners through the legitimate channels of bidding or play.

INFORMATORY DOUBLE: a systemic double made primarily to give information to partner (Bridge).

IN HOCK: liable to capture; = *en prise* (Chess). See also *hoc.*

INITIAL BID: 1. First bid made by a side. 2. First bid of a deal, = opening bid.

INITIAL MELD: the first made by a side (Canasta).

Inn and Inn, obsolete dice game mentioned by Cotton.

INNER TABLE: that half of the board toward in which the stones enter and from which they bear off (Backgammon).

INSIDE CORNER: Faro bet on three cards, so-called from the placement of the bet on the layout.

INSIDE STRAIGHT: four cards in sequence needing a card of interior rank to form a straight, as 8-7-6-4 (Poker).

INSTALLMENT BETS: see page 64

INSUFFICIENT BID: one that is not high enough to supersede the last previous bid.

INSURANCE: 1. In Blackjack, a bet that dealer will not get a natural, when he has an ace showing. 2. In horse-racing, a fee paid to a bookmaker for giving parti-mutuel odds without the usual limit.

Intelligence, 462

INTERMEDIATE CARDS: those middling in rank between the highest and lowest, as tens and nines in Bridge.

INTERPOSE: parry attack from an enemy queen, rook, or bishop by placing a piece on the line (Chess).

INTERVAL OF BETTING: period during which bets are made and players may drop.

IN THE BOX: in Chouette, playing alone against the other participants as a team.

IN THE HOLE: 1. having a minus score, so-called from the practice of marking a score negative by drawing a ring around it. 2. Dealt face down (Stud Poker).

IN THE MITT: received in the deal, as 100 aces in the original hand (Pinochle).

INTRICATE SHUFFLE: = RIFFLE SHUFFLE.

Intrigue, a card Solitaire.

INVERSE: a bet that the winning row will be of opposite color from the first card dealt (Trente et Quarante).

INVINCIBLE: a holding of all seven doublets (Domino Bingo).

INVITATION: a bid that invites but does not command partner to make a response (Bridge).

Irish, obsolete Backgammon game.

Irish Loo, 195

IRONCLAD HAND: one that is sure to win.

IRREGULARITY: any departure from a rule of correct procedure (always in the sense of inadvertent error, not intentional misdeed).

IRREGULAR OPENING: one that is little-played, or little-analyzed, or considered to be inferior (Chess).

ISOLATED PAWN: one not accompanied by another of the same color on either adjacent file (Chess).

I STAY: 1. Declaration by a bidder that he will meet another bid, when the rules permit him to do so without overcalling. 2. See *stay* (Poker).

Italian Casino = Scopa, 259

Italian Checkers, variant similar to Spanish Checkers, but a king is immune from capture by a single man.

J

J: abbreviation of *jack*.

JACK: 1. One of the face cards (playing cards); knave. Also called valet (Fr.), Bube, Wenzel (Ger.). 2. The jack of trumps; the score for winning it (All Fours). 3. A pool increased by the pool left from the previous deal, not won (Hearts). 4. Jackpot.

JACKPOT: a deal of Draw Poker in which every player antes and a pair of jacks or better is required to open.

Jackpots, 52

Jacks Back, 96

JACK UP: raise, boost.

JACOBY, OSWALD, American expert on Contract Bridge and other games, author of "Oswald Jacoby on Poker," "Gin Rummy," "Oklahoma," "How to Win at Canasta."

Jacquet, obsolete Backgammon game.

J'ADOUBE (Fr.): "I adjust," said when a player does not wish to make a move with the piece he touches (Chess).

JAMBONE: a game in which a lone player exposes his hand and allows the opponents to play his cards (Railroad Euchre).

JAMBOREE: a hand of the five highest trumps (Railroad Euchre).

Japanese Rug = Crazy Quilt, 450

Jass, 277

JASS, JASZ: the jack of trumps (Klaberjass).

JETONS (Fr.): chips, counters.

JETTISON: discard unwanted cards, especially to resolve a block (Bridge).

JEU (Fr.): game; hand; system of play.

JEUX DE REGLE (Fr.): regulation hands, those on which it is mathematically correct to stand and play (Ecarté).

Jig, 228

Jigsaw, a card Solitaire.

JINK IT: play on for all five tricks, after winning three tricks (Spoil Five).

JINX: the suppositious cause of bad luck.

Jo-Jotte, variant of Belotte, introduced by Culbertson in 1936 but little played.

JOKER: an extra card furnished with the standard pack, used in some games as a wild card or as the highest trump. See also *bug*.

Joker Hearts, 243

Joker Pitch, 235

Joker Poker, 73

Joker Rummy, see Contract Rummy, 26

Joker Stud, 88

JONAH: an unlucky partner.

JONES, HENRY: English authority on the rules of games who wrote under the pseudonym "Cavendish."

JUGEMENT, LE (Fr.): one of the names for the tarot XX ("judgment day").

Julepe, El, Spanish game similar to Loo.

JUMP BID: an overcall naming more tricks than legally necessary (Bridge).

JUNIOR: partner of senior.

JUSTICE: the tarot VIII.

Juvenile, a card Solitaire.

K

K: abbreviation of king.

KABAT: cubical dice used in India.

Kalaber, see Kalabriás, page 283

Kalabrias, 283

Kale = Mancala, 410

Kaluki, 46

KANGAROO CARD: a system of betting on the first card at Faro.

Kankakee, 90

K'Ap Tai Shap, Chinese domino game ("grasp many tens").

KARTENSPIEL, DAS (Ger.): pack of cards.

KARTEN (Ger.): cards.

KEEP: a declaration of *the color* as trump, as "I keep" (Boston).

KEEP CASES, KEEP TAB: record the cards as they come out of the box (Faro).

KELSO: a Checkers opening.

KEM CARDS: playing cards made of plastics instead of pasteboard. (Trade name.)

Keno, 557

Ke-Pouk-Hpai, Korean Solitaire with dominoes ("tortoise tablets").

Ketch-Dolt, obsolete Backgammon game.

KIBITZER: a non-playing spectator, especially one who criticizes. (Pronounced kib' itzer.) Also *kibbitzer, kiebitzer;* from Ger. *kiebitz* (pewit), a bird that protects its eggs by annoying those who approach them.

KICKER: an extra card held with a pair for a two-card draw (Draw Poker).

KILTER: a hand with no card higher than a nine, no pair, and no four-flush or four-straight (Poker).

Kimberly Solo, variant of four-hand Solo Whist.

KING: 1. One of the face cards (playing cards). Also called roi (Fr.), König (Ger.). 2. The principal Chess piece, capture of which is the object of play. 3. A piece entitled to move both backward and forward (Checkers). 4. A holding of five doublets (Domino Bingo).

KING CARD: highest card of a suit remaining unplayed; master card.

Kingdom, a card Solitaire.

KING ROW: the first rank, on which single men are crowned, either 1-2-3-4 or 29-30-31-32 (Checkers).

King Rummy, see Contract Rummy, 26

Kings, a card Solitaire.

King's Audience, a card Solitaire.

Kings Back, 96

KING'S GAMBIT: a Chess opening.

KITTY: 1. A percentage taken out of the stakes to pay expenses or admission fees. 2. A pool to which betes are paid and from which royalties are collected; a pool that shares like a player in winnings and losses of certain Pinochle bids. 3. Widow.

Kko-Ri-Pouk-Tchi-Ki, Korean domino game ("tail-joining").

Klab = Klaberjass, 278

Klaberjass, 278

Kleine Muhle, die = Tit Tat Toe, 433

Klob = Klaberjass, 278

KLOBBED: tied or beaten, as in Klaberjass.

Klondike (Solitaire), 462

Klondike (dice), 546

KN: abbreviation of *knave.*

KNAVE: jack (playing card).

KNAVE KNOCHER: the club jack (Queen Nazarene).

KNAVE NODDY = HIS NOBS (Cribbage).

KNIGHT: a Chess piece.

KNOCK: 1. Rap on the table to signify check (Poker) or pass or waiver of cutting the pack. 2. End the play by laying down one's hand (Rummy).

Knockout, a card Solitaire.

KNOCKOUT TOURNAMENT: one that is a series of matches between two contestants at a time, the loser being eliminated.

Knock Poker, 77

Knock Rummy, 44

KNOT: a formation in which immediate recapture of a single stone is prohibited (Go).

KOL-HPAI, Korean domino pieces ("bone tablets").

Kol-Ye-Si, Korean domino game.

KONG: a set of four identical tiles; to ground such a set, or add a fourth tile to a pung to make a kong (Mah Jongg). Also *quong.*

Kong Poh, Chinese gambling game played with *pò tsz'.*

KONIG, DER (Ger.): 1. King (Chess, playing cards, etc.). 2. An inactive playeer.

KONIGIN, DIE (Ger.): queen (Chess). More common is *die Dame.*

Kon Min Yeung, Chinese six-dice game ("pursuing sheep").

Kontraspiel, see Trumps, 189

Kpo = Mancala, 410

Kreutz-Mariage, variant of Sixty-Six.

KREUZ, KREUTZ (Ger.) = the suit clubs ("cross").

Kriegspiel, 360

KT: abbreviation of *knight*.

Kukuk = Ranter Go Round, 486 ("Cuckoo").

KWAT P'AI: Chinese domino pieces.

L

LABOUCHERE, 554

La Belle Lucie, 463

Labyrinth, a card Solitaire.

LADONS: non-counting cards.

Lady of the Manor, a card Solitaire.

LAIRD AND LADY: a Checkers opening.

Lamebrain Pete, 75

Lamebrains = Cincinnati, 75

La Mouche, see Trumps, 189

L'AMOUR: a meld of A-10 in the same suit (Marriage).

Landsknecht, Lansquenet, obsolete card game like Faro.

LANE: space (Solitaire).

Lanterloo = Loo, 192

LANZAS (Sp.): the suit spades.

LAPS: the carrying forward of excess points from one game to the next.

La Ronfle = Piquet (see page 261).

LARRY: player who has the last turn (Craps).

LAST: 1. The point for playing the last card (Cribbage). 2. The score for winning last trick, as in Pinochle. 3. Obligatory warning by dealer that the last eight cards of the pack are reached (Casino).

Last Chance, a card Solitaire.

Last Draw, 436

LAST TURN: the play when only three unknown cards are left in the box (Faro).

LAUB (Ger.): the suit spades.

LAUFER, DER (Ger.): bishop (Chess).

LAY AWAY: 1. Discard after picking up the widow, as in Skat. 2. Give cards to the crib (Cribbage).

LAY CARD: plain card.

LAY DOWN: 1. Meld a set. 2. Knock (Rummy).

LAYDOWN: cinch hand.

LAY ODDS: offer a bet of a larger amount against a smaller amount.

LAY OFF: 1. Meld separate cards by adding them to sets already on the table (Rummy). 2. Bet money previously accepted as the bet of another person.

LAYOUT: 1. A table marked with compartments for bets on various propositions in a banking game. 2. The array of cards first dealt to begin a Solitaire game. 3. The array of all bones played on the table (Dominoes).

LAY SUIT: plain suit.

LAY THE ODDS: bet that the shooter will not make his point (Craps); or against any contingency that is apparently unlikely to occur.

Lazy Men, a card Solitaire.

LEAD: 1. Play the first card to a trick; the card so played. 2. Willingness to make the voluntary bet in Poker (see *take the lead*).

LEAD THROUGH (a player): lead to a trick to which that player must be the second and not the last to play.

LEAD UP TO (a player): lead to a trick to which that player will play last.

LEAST: a game to take as few points as possible (Schafkopf).

Le Cent = Piquet (see page 261).

LEFT BOWER: the jack of the other suit of same color as the trump (Euchre).

LEFT PEDRO: the five of the other suit of same color as the trump (Cinch).

LENZ, SIDNEY S., author of *Lenz on Bridge*; noted Whist and Bridge player.

Leoni's Own = Weavers, 479

LEVEE (Fr.): trick.

L. H. O.: left-hand opponent (Bridge).

Liar Dice, 548

Lift Smoke, 246

Light and Shade, a card Solitaire.

LIGHT: in debt to the pot.

LIGHTER: having a smaller total of pips (Dominoes).

LILIES: spades, when declared for trumps at an increased value (Bridge-Whist).

LIMIT: the maximum amount by which any player may increase the previous bet (Poker).

Limited, a card Solitaire.

LIMIT HAND: a complete hand that collects the limit in stakes (Mah Jongg).

Limits (Poker), 60

Lindy Bridge, 179

LINE: 1. The pass line; the section of the layout on which is placed a bet that the shooter will pass (Craps). 2. The score for a box (Gin Rummy). 3. Squares or points in a line on the board, as in Chess, Mill.

Linger Long = Lift Smoke, 246

LITTLE CASINO: the spade deuce (Casino).

LITTLE CAT: = Little Tiger.

LITTLE DOG: a hand of seven-high and deuce-low but no pair (Poker).

Little Packets = Blind Hookey.

LITTLE SLAM: the winning of twelve tricks by one side (Bridge).

Little Spider, 464

LITTLE TIGER: a hand of eight-high and three-low but no pair (Poker).

Little Words, 504

LIVE CARD: one still in the hands or stock and therefore available, not dead.

Liverpool Rummy, see Contract Rummy, 26

L. O.: opponent at one's left.

LOADED DICE: incorrectly balanced dice used by cheats.

LOCK: a position in which all pieces of one color are blocked and immobile (Checkers).

LONG GAME: one in which the entire pack is put into play, as Bridge.

LONE HAND, LONE PLAYER: one who elects to play without help of his partner's hand.

LONG CARD: one left in a hand after all opponents are exhausted of the suit.

LONG SUIT: a holding of four or more cards of a suit (Bridge); the longest holding in any suit in a hand.

Long Whist, Whist when game is 10 points (see page 180).

Loo, 192

LOOK: call, see (Poker).

LOOKOUT: houseman who watches, deals, and pays bets (Faro).

LOOSE CARD: one that can be discarded as useless (Whist, Rummy).

LOOSE TILE: one placed on the wall, to be drawn in replacement of a Flower or the fourth of a kong (Mah Jongg).

LOSE OUT: a rank that loses four times in one deal (Faro).

LOSING CARD, LOSER: a card that cannot be expected to win a trick or to fall on a trick won by partner.

Losing Checkers = Giveaway Checkers, 383

Lotteries, 557

Lottery, obsolete card game of chance.

Lotto, 557

Louis, a card Solitaire.

LOVE: score of zero. —— game, one in which the loser scores nothing.

LOVER'S LEAP: the move, on roll of 6-5, from the adverse 1-point to 12-point (Backgammon).

LOW: 1. The deuce of trumps or the lowest trump dealt; the score for winning it (All Fours). 2. One's lowest card that can legally be played.

Lowball, 95

Low Hole Card Wild, 91

Low Poker, 92, 96

Low Poker With the Ace Low. 92

Low Poker With the Bug. 92

Lu, Lue = Loo, 192

Lucas, a card Solitaire.

Lucky Thirteen, a card Solitaire.

LUMBER: 1. Useless cards; deadwood. 2. A spectator or player out of funds (Craps). 3. Chess pieces. *Chopping* ——, exchanging pieces.

LUNE, LA (Fr.): the tarot XVIII ("moon").

LURCH: the winning of a game when the opponent has not passed the halfway mark (Cribbage).

Lustige Sieben, two-dice game (Ger. "merry seven").

M

Macao, 518

Ma Cheuk, Ma Chiang, Ma Chiao = Mah Jongg, 414

Madji = Mancala, 410

Mah Jongg, Mah Jong, 414

MAID OF THE MILL: a Checkers opening.

MAIN: 1. The pass line (Craps). 2. A bet in Hazard.

MAIN POT: the first pot formed in a deal, as distinct from later side pots (Table Stakes Poker).

MAISON DIEU, LA (Fr.): the tarot XVI ("hospital").

MAJEUR, MAJOR: the non-dealer in a two-hand card game.

MAJOR PIECE: a queen or rook (Chess).

MAJOR SUIT: spades or hearts (Bridge).

MAJOR TENACE: the A-Q of a suit, or equivalent combination when some of the high cards are dead (Bridge).

MAKE: 1. The contract; the denomination or game named in the contract. 2. To name the trump suit or game. 3. To fulfill the contract.

Make a Million, proprietary game of Parker Brothers.

MAKE A POINT: 1. Cast the point number before casting 7 (Craps). 2. Occupy a point with two or more stones (Backgammon).

MAKE GOOD: add enough chips to the pot to meet the previous bet or raise.

MAKE IT: name the trump suit or game.

MAKER: player who names the trump suit or game.

MAKE THE PACK, MAKE UP: gather and shuffle the pack for the next deal.

MALDONNE (Fr.): misdeal.

MALILLA, MALLILLIO: = manille

Malilla, La, Spanish card game.

MAN: piece, in any board game.

Mancala, 410

Man D'Auvergne, see Trumps, 189

Manhattan, variant of Gin Rummy with bidding.

Manille, card game like Comet, with the diamond nine wild.

MANILLE, MANILL, MENEL: the 7 or 9 of trumps, when elevated to second-highest rank.

MANNA FROM HEAVEN: cast of 11 (Craps).

MAN OFF: simplify the position by exchanges (Checkers).

MANQUE: low; the numbers 1 to 18 inclusive (Roulette).

MARCH: the winning of all the tricks by one player or side; the score therefor (Euchre).

Marguerite, a card Solitaire.

Maria, a card Solitaire.

MARIA: the spade queen (Black Lady).

Mariage, variant of Sixty-Six.

Marked Twelve, a card Solitaire.

MARKER: 1. Token or chip used in place of money, especially at Faro. 2. Device for keeping record of the score. 3. Score-keeper. 4. Promissory note.

MARK THE GAME: score the final point necessary to win a game.

Marriage, 276

MARRIAGE: 1. A meld, the K-Q of a suit, as in Pinochle. 2. A build of two matching cards (Solitaire).

Martha, a card Solitaire.

MARTINGALE, 554

MASTER CARD: the highest card of a suit still in play; best card.

MAT (Fr.): 1. Mate (Chess). 2. One of the names for the highest tarot trump, the XXII.

Matador, 428

MATADOR: 1. Each high trump held in an unbroken sequence with the highest (Skat). 2. Any high trump. 3. Any of the bones 0-0, 6-1, 5-2, 4-3 (Domino Matador).

MATCH GAME = SET MATCH (Bridge).

MATCHED, MATCHING: corresponding in kind, said of cards or bones that may legally be melded (Rummy) or played (Dominoes) or built (Solitaire).

MATCHED CARD: one that forms part of a valid set. *Matched set,* three or more cards forming a valid meld, as three aces or 8-7-6 of hearts. (Rummy).

MATCH-POINT SCORING: a system of scoring used in Duplicate Bridge. (See page 170.)

Mathematical Games, 433

Mathematics, a card Solitaire.

Matrimony, 220

Matrimony, a card Solitaire.

MATT (Ger.): mate (Chess).

MAURER (Ger.): an excessively conservative player, one who bids only on ironclad hands.

Maw, see Trumps, 189

MAXIMATE: form of Chess problem in which Black (and sometimes White also) is restricted to the geometrically longest move.

MAX LANGE ATTACK: a Chess opening.

MAYONNAISE = GOULASH

Mbau = Mancala, 410

MECHANIC: a card cheat; a crooked dealer.

MEDIATOR: player who assumes the contract (Mediatore).

Mediatore, 339

MEDICINE TURN: queen and nine showing in one turn at Faro. (*Note:* supposedly a pun on "quinine.")

MEET A BET: call; add enough chips to make a total contribution equal to the maximum made by any previous player (Poker).

Meine Tante, Deine Tante, variant of Landsknecht, similar to Faro (= Tempeln).

MELD (Ger., announce): place one or more cards face up on the table as provided by the rules, whether in a set or in laying off; any card or cards melded; a valid set.

MELER (Fr.): to shuffle.

Memory = Concentration, 490

Memory Duplicate = Replay Duplicate, 166

Menagerie, 487

MENEL: the 9 or 7 of trumps, often elevated to second rank.

Merry Men, a card Solitaire.

Mexicana, 25C

Mexican Stud, 90

Michigan, 217

MICHIGAN BANKROLL: a large roll of bills, consisting mostly of ones (Craps)

Michigan Rum, see 500 Rum, 12

MIDDLEHAND: player at right of the dealer, in three-hand play; second active player in order.

MIDDLE STRAIGHT = INSIDE STRAIGHT

MID-GAME: in a board game, the period of play that follows completion of the opening.

Midnight Oil = La Belle Lucie, 463

Midshipman, a card Solitaire.

Mike, 76

MILITARY: progressive; applied to a tournament in which the winners of each round receive flags, and the player with the most flags at the end wins the tournament.

MILKING: a method of shuffling, by drawing cards simultaneously from the top and bottom of the pack.

Mill, a card Solitaire.

Mill, The, 400

MILLE: an ivory token formerly used, worth ten fish.

Milton, a card Solitaire.

MINES: the tableau (Canfield). See *nuggets, rockpile.*

MINEUR, MINOR: the dealer in a two-hand game.

MINOR PIECE: a bishop or knight (Chess).

MINOR SUIT: diamonds or clubs (Bridge).

MINOR TENACE: the K-J of a suit, or equivalent combination when some of the high cards are dead (Bridge).

Minoru, game of chance similar to Horse Race with Cards, 563

MIRLIRO: a hazard at Ombre, incurred by holding the two black aces without other matadors, or the two red aces with basto.

MISCHEN (Ger.): to shuffle.

MISDEAL: any irregularity in dealing that requires a new shuffle and deal. (*Note:* this term is sometimes reserved to an irregularity that by rule forfeits the player's turn to deal, as distinct from *redeal* or *new deal* by the same player.)

MISE (Fr.): 1. The layout. 2. The pool.

MISERE, MISERY: a bid or game to win no tricks; = nullo.

Misery Bridge, two-hand variant in which a player may bid to avoid winning tricks at no trump.

Misery Nap, variant in which a player may bid misery (to win no trick at no trump), the bid ranking between three and four.

MISS: 1. Fail to draw a helpful card (antonym of *fill* or *improve*); fail to cast a desired number with dice. 2. Fail to pass. Also *miss-out* (Craps). 3. Fail to cast a number that will allow entry (Backgammon). 4. The widow (Loo).

Miss Milligan, a card Solitaire.

Mistigri, see Joker Poker, 73; Trumps, 189.

MISTIGRI: 1. The joker (Joker Poker). 2. The club jack, = pam (Loo).

Mitchell Pair Games, 168

MITTELHAND (Ger.): middlehand; the second to receive cards in a three-hand game.

MIXED CANASTA: a meld of seven or more of a kind, including wild cards (Canasta).

MIXED PAIR: in tournament play, a partnership of a man and a woman.

Mnemonic Duplicate = Replay Duplicate, 166

Modern Ombre = Solo, 330

Modern Schafkopf, 316

Mona, La, Spanish card game, same as Old Maid

MOND: the second-highest trump, the XXI (Tarok).

MONDE, LE (Fr.): the tarot XXI ("world").

MONKEY FLUSH: three cards of a suit, not in sequence (Poker)

Montana, a card Solitaire.

Monte, 77, 93

Monte, Monte Bank, 531

Monte Carlo, 465

Montreal Draughts, variant of Polish Checkers.

Moojub, a card Solitaire.

Moon Game, card-game derivative played with dominoes, similar to Forty-Two.

MORELLE (Fr.): checker piece, counter. Also *morel.*

Morelles = Mill, 400

MORNING LINE: in horse-racing, the probable final odds, estimated before the actual betting begins.

Mort, 188

MORT, LA (Fr.): 1. The tarot XII ("death"). 2. = Dummy.

Mo Tsiah = Mah Jongg, 414

Mouche, La, obsolete card game similar to Ombre.

MOUCHE: a flush, in La Mouche.

Mount Olympus, a card Solitaire.

MOURNIVAL: four of a kind, as in Gleek.

MOUTH BET: one made orally, without putting up chips or money.

MOVE: 1. In a board game, one play; the turn to play. 2. Advantage in the opposition of the pieces, determinable by a precise formula (Checkers).

Muchas Grazias, Spanish card game, same as Authors.

Muerto, El, Spanish card game.

Muggins, 426

MUGGINS: the rule that a player may score for himself points earned but not claimed by his opponent (Cribbage, Sniff).

Muhle = Mill, 400

Multiple Piles, 437

MULTIPLIERS: factors by which the base value of a declaration is multiplied to determine the value of a game (Skat).

Multiple Solitaire, any Solitaire when played by two or more persons, each with his own pack, but with common foundations.

Multiplication, three-dice game.

Mungala = Mancala, 410

Murder, 507

Mus, El, Spanish game similar to Pochen and Ambigu.

MUZIO GAMBIT: a Chess opening.

My Bird Sings, My Ship Sails, variant of Commerce in which each player receives three cards and tries to get a flush by exchanging cards with other players.

My Lady's Patience, a card Solitaire.

My Ship Sails, 490

N

N: abbr. of 1. North. 2. Knight (Chess).

Nada, four-hand partnership card game of bidding to win the least number of tricks.

NAILOR: a Checkers opening.

NAIPES (Sp.): playing cards.

Nap, Napoleon, 195

NAP: 1. A bid to win all the tricks (Napoleon). 2. The A-2-3 of a suit (Tresette)—from Napolitano.

Napoleon at St. Helena = Forty Thieves, 456

Napoleon's Favorite, a card Solitaire.

Napoleon's Flank, a card Solitaire.

Napoleon's Square, a card Solitaire.

Nap Pool, 197

Naranj = Mancala, 410

Nation, a card Solitaire.

NATIONAL LAWS COMMISSION: body that promulgates Contract Bridge laws in the United States.

Nationale, a card Solitaire.

NATURAL: 1. Without use of a wild card. 2. The cast of 7 or 11 on the shooter's first roll (Craps). 3. The combination of an ace and a ten or face card, counting 21 (Blackjack). 4. Point of 8 or 9 in two cards (Baccarat). 5. A build in suit, when builds not in suit are allowed (Solitaire).

NATURAL CANASTA: a meld of seven or more cards, none wild (Canasta).

NATURAL CARD: any that is not wild.

NATURAL POINTS: those scored necessarily in every deal, as big casino, high.

Naughty Knaves, a card Solitaire.

Nau T'In Kau, Chinese domino game ("turning heavens and nines").

Necklace, a card Solitaire.

NEGATIVE DOUBLE: one made chiefly for information of partner (Bridge).

Negra, La, Spanish card game.

NELL: the nine of trumps; = menel (Jass).

Nestor, a card Solitaire.

NEUTRAL SCORE: an arbitrary score assigned by the referee, when regular play is not feasible (Duplicate Bridge).

Newmarket = Michigan, 217

Newmarket, three-dice game.

Newport, a card Solitaire.

New York Stud = Fourflush Beats a Pair, 88

NEXT: the other suit of same color as the turn-up (Euchre).

NGA P'AI: Chinese domino pieces.

NICK: cast of 7 or 11 on the shooter's first roll; = natural (Hazard, Craps).

Nim, a general term for mathematical games of drawing counters from piles. (See Mathematical Games, 433.)

NIMZOWITSCH DEFENSE: a Chess opening.

NINA: cast of 9. Also *Nina-from-Carolina* (Craps).

Nine Men's Morris = Mill, 400

Nines, a card Solitaire.

NITS AND LICE: two small pairs (Poker).

Nivernaise, a card Solitaire.

NO: declaration meaning "I pass."

NODDY-BOARDS: see Cribbage, 250

NOIR (Fr.): black.

Nojacks, variant of Polignac.

NON-COMOQUERS: aces and kings, so called from their special privilege in forming groups (Panguingue).

Norwegian Whist, 184

NOTATION: a system of recording the moves or plays of a game.

NO TRUMP: a bid or game to play out the hands without a trump suit.

Noughts and Crosses = Tit-Tat-Toe, 433

N-S, E-W: compass points, used to designate the four players in a game, as Bridge. (*Note*: compass designations are often used also in three-hand and two-hand games.)

NUGGETS: the reserve (Canfield). See *mines, rockpiles.*

NULL, NULLO: 1. A bid to win not a single trick, or not more than a specified number of tricks. 2. A non-counting card.

Nullenspiel = Spiderweb, 435

Number Ten, a card Solitaire.

NUMERICAL OVERCALLING: sufficiency of bids determined by the scoring values rather than by the number of odd-tricks (see page 177).

O

OBER (Ger.): a playing card queen. (*Note*: when this term is used, the jack is called *unter*.)

Observation, 507

Octagon, a card Solitaire.

Octave, a card Solitaire.

Octopode, a card Solitaire.

Odd and Even, 436 (mathematical); 544 (dice)

Odd and Even, a card Solitaire.

Oddity, a card Solitaire.

ODDS: a statement of probability in the form of a ratio, as "the odds against casting a seven with two dice are 5 to 1."

Odds Chess, 360

ODDS, HOW TO CALCULATE, 569

ODDS-ON: odds at less than even money.

ODD TRICK: a trick won by declarer in excess of six (Bridge); the seventh trick won by a side (Whist).

OFF, see *playing off.*

OFF CARD: one that is not part of a meld or a combination (Rummy).

OFFENSIVE STRENGTH: cards that are expected to win tricks at one's own declaration (Bridge).

OFFICIAL: validated by having won a trick (Pinochle)—said of a meld.

OFFICIAL SYSTEM: a Contract Bridge bidding system introduced in 1931 by Work, Lenz, and others.

OFF NUMBER: one that is neither a crap, a natural, nor the shooter's point (Craps).

Oh Hell, Oh Pshaw, 248

Oklahoma, 16

Oklahoma Gin, 42

O-Koan, Korean fortune-telling with dominoes ("five gateways").

OLD FOURTEENTH: a Checkers opening.

Old Maid, 484

Old Patience, a card Solitaire.

Old Sledge = Seven-Up, 229

Olga, 466

Ombre, 330

OMBRE: "the man," the player who undertakes a game; the contractor (Ombre).

Omnibus Hearts, 245

ON: 1. Having placed a bet. 2. See *playing on.*

ONCE AROUND: game fixed at 61, when scored on a Cribbage board.

ONE-ENDED STRAIGHT: four cards in sequence, either ace-high or ace-low (Poker).

ONE-EYES: face cards on which the picture shows only one eye; in the standard pack, these are the ♠J, ♡J, and ◇K.

ONE HUNDRED: a declaration to win 100 at a trump or 80 at no trump (Alsós).

100 ACES: a meld of four aces, one of each suit (Pinochle).

ONE PAIR: a hand containing two cards of the same rank, with three unmatched cards (Poker).

ONE-ROLL BET = Come-out bet (Craps).

One-Two, a card Solitaire.

ON THE BAR: 1. Said of a blot that has been hit and is awaiting entry (Backgammon). 2. Said of a bet that the caster will lose (Craps).

Onze et Demie, banking game like Blackjack ("eleven and one-half").

OPEN: 1. Make the first bid, declaration, or move. 2. Make the first bet in the first betting interval (Draw Poker). 3. Make the first lead of a suit. 4. Face-up on the table, as a card in Stud Poker. 5. Meld (Double-pack Pinochle).

OPEN BET: a bet on a card to win (Faro).

OPEN CRAPS: a game in which players may bet among themselves as well as with the house or banker.

OPEN END: a branch of the layout on which it is legal to play (Dominoes).

OPENERS: a hand with which the pot may legally be opened, usually a pair of jacks or better (Draw Poker).

Open Gin, 42

OPENING: in a board game, the first phase of play; an established line or variation of early play.

OPENING BID: the first bid of a deal; a hand strong enough for such a bid (Bridge).

OPENING LEAD: the first lead of a deal.

OPEN PLAY: exposure of his hand by the high bidder, to earn increased score if he makes contract.

OPEN POINT: one that is not occupied by two or more adverse stones (Backgammon).

Open Poker = Stud Poker; a Poker game in which some cards are dealt face up.

OPERA: the play of one's entire hand in a single turn; the bonus therefor (Comet).

OPPONENT: 1. A player of the other side. 2. An adversary of the high bidder or contractor, especially when two or more adversaries combine against him.

OPPOSITION: relation of the kings such that one can prevent the other from reaching a desired square (Chess).

ORDER IT UP: declaration by an opponent of the dealer, accepting the turn-up for trump (Euchre).

Order of Precedence = Precedence, 471

ORIGINAL BID = OPENING BID.

631

ORIGINAL HAND: a hand as dealt, before its alteration by draw, discard, meld, or play.

OROS: in the Spanish pack, the suit *gold* or *coins*, corresponding to *diamonds*.

ORTHODOX: a Checkers opening.

ORTHODOX DEFENSE: a Chess opening.

Osmosis, 467

OUTER TABLE: the other half of the board from the inner table, *q.v.* (Backgammon).

OUTSIDE: applied to the players in a house game, as distinct from the housemen.

OUVERTE = OPEN PLAY.

OVERBID: 1. A bid of more than the value of the game named by the bidder (Skat). 2. Overcall. 3. A bid for more than the player can expect to win.

OVERCALL: 1. A bid or declaration legally sufficient to supersede the last previous bid. 2. Such a bid when made by a defender (Bridge). 3. To make such a declaration.

OVERHAND SHUFFLE: one executed by holding the pack in one hand and dropping batches of cards into the other.

OVER-RUFF, OVERTRUMP: play a trump higher than one previously played to the trick.

OVERS: the count of 1 point for each card won in excess of thirty. *Spade* ——: the count of 1 point for each spade won in excess of eight. (Casino.)

OVERTRICK: a trick won by declarer in excess of his contract (Bridge).

Ovid's Game, 434

P

P: abbr. of pawn (Chess).

Pachisi, 399

Pachter, obsolete card game similar to Blackjack, with a special bonus for the ♥6, called *brillant*.

PACK: 1. Deck; all the cards used in a game, collectively. See also STANDARD PACK. 2. Discard pile, as in Canasta.

PACKET: a portion of the packet, less than the whole.

PACK UP: withdraw permanently from a game.

PAGAT: the lowest trump, the I (Tarok).

PAINT: 1. Any face card. 2. Discard a heart on a trick won by another player. *Painted,* having taken a heart in a trick. (Hearts.)

PAINT SKIN: any face card.

PAIR: 1. Two cards of the same rank. 2. Two players in partnership. 3. (Fr.) Even; a bet on even numbers at Roulette.

Pairing Games, 468

PAIR ROYAL: three of a kind (Cribbage).

Pairs, a card Solitaire.

PAISLEY: a Checkers opening.

PALO (Sp.): suit (playing cards).

PALOOKA: a mediocre player (slang).

PAM: the club jack (Loo).

PAM BE CIVIL: player's request that pam be withheld so that he can win the current trick (Pam-Loo).

PAM-BLAZE: a hand of five face cards including pam (Loo).

PAM-FLUSH: a hand of four cards of the same suit and pam (Loo).

Pam-Loo, 195

Pamphilius, see Trumps, 189

Pan, Panguingue, 47

PAPE, LE (Fr.): the tarot V ("pope" or Jupiter).

PAPESSE, LA (Fr.): the tarot II ("female pope" or Juno).

Papillon, see Casino, 255

Parallels, a card Solitaire.

Parchesi, 399. (*Note:* also *Parcheesi,* a proprietary game manufactured by Selchow and Righter.)

Parejas, Las, Spanish card game, same as Concentration.

Parisienne, a card Solitaire.

PARKER BROTHERS: manufacturers of intellectual games, located at Salem, Mass.

Parliament = Fan Tan, 224

PAROLI, 554

PARTIAL: a trick-score less than is necessary for game; also, PART-SCORE (Bridge).

PARTIE (Fr.): a game in the sense of a session of play; encounter, contest. Anglicized as *party*.

PARTIE CARREE: a hazard at Ombre, incurred by holding three kings and a queen.

PARTNER: another player with whom one shares a common score, and with whom one therefore coöperates in the bidding and play.

Partnership Auction Pinochle, 308

Partnership Auction Pinochle with a Widow, 309

Partnership 500 Rum, 15

Partnership Gin Rummy, 39

Partnership Pinochle, 304

PART-SCORE: a total trick score less than is necessary for game (Bridge).

PARTY: 1. A session of play; a contest (= partie). 2. One deal; one turn of a wheel (= coup).

Party Bridge, 155

PASE: prism dice used in India.

PASS: 1. A declaration signifying that the player at that turn does not wish to bid, or that he withdraws from the deal. 2. A roll or series of rolls in which the shooter wins, either by throwing a natural on his first roll or by making his point (Craps). 3. Cards exchanged among the original hands (Black Lady).

PASS AND BACK IN: enter a pot after having passed (Poker).

Pass and Out = Blind Opening, 71

PASS AND OUT: the rule that a player who once passes must drop out of the deal (Poker).

Passe: three-hand game in which the object is to advance a token from one end of a layout to the other, in accordance with cards taken in tricks.

PASSE: the numbers 19-36 inclusive; high (Roulette).

PASSED PAWN: one not opposed by an enemy pawn on either adjacent file (Chess).

Passing Goulashes: variant of Contract Bridge in which, after a goulash deal, partners exchange one, then two, then three cards.

PASS LINE: the section of the layout for bets that the shooter will pass (Craps).

PASS OUT A DEAL: abandon the deal after all players pass.

PASST MIR NICHT (Ger.): the game of second turn in Skat ("suits me not").

PAT: 1. Without drawing (Poker). 2. (Fr.) Drawn game (Chess).

Pat Cha, Chinese eight-dice game ("grasping eight").

PAT HAND: one that is held intact, the player refusing to draw or discard, as in Draw Poker; a straight, flush, or full house.

Patience = Solitaire, 439

Patience Poker = Poker Solitaire, 470

Patriarchs, a card Solitaire.

PATT (Ger.): drawn game (Chess).

PATTERN: the distribution of a suit to the four hands, or the division of one hand into four suits, expressed by four numbers, as 4-4-3-2 (Bridge).

PAY IN CARDS: said of a punter when his point is tied by the banker.

PAYNE, HUGH, pseudonym of Edward X. Anderson.

PAWN: a Chess piece.

P. C. = PERCENTAGE.

Pea-Knuckle = Pinochle, 284

Pedro, 236

PEDRO: the five of trumps, as in Pedro.

Pedro Sancho, 236

Peek Poker = Seven-Card Stud, 87

Peep-and-Turn = Mexican Stud, 90

Peep Nap, 197

PEG: a marker used in scoring on a Cribbage board; to score, especially during the play (Cribbage).

Pegboard, 412

Pelmanism = Concentration, 490

PELTER = KILTER.

PENALTY CARD: an exposed card that must be played at first legal opportunity (Bridge).

PENALTY DOUBLE: one that is not systemically informatory; one made with the expectation of defeating the adverse bid (Bridge).

Penalty Euchre, 205

Penchant, variant of Bézique.

PENDU, LE (Fr.): the tarot XII ("hanged man").

Pendulum, 468

Peneech, obsolete card game similar to Sixty-Six.

PENEECH: the diamond seven (Peneech).

Penelope's Web, a card Solitaire.

Pennies from Heaven, 25C

PENNY ANTE: a game in which the ante or limit is one cent (Poker); hence, any game for insignificant stakes.

Penuchle = Pinochle, 284

Percentage, 567

Percentage Bridge, 173

Perejila, La, Spanish card game.

PERFECT DICE: dice are so deemed when they are true cubes within a tolerance of .0001-inch.

PERPETUAL CHECK: unending attack on a king, leading to a drawn game (Chess).

PERPETUAL DRAW: drawn game achieved by repetition of the same series of moves, deviation from which is impossible or fatal to the opponent (Checkers).

Perpetual Motion, 469

Perro, El, Spanish card game.

Perseverance, a card Solitaire.

Persian Rummy, 15

Petits Chevaux, game of chance similar to Horse Race with Cards, 563. (Fr. "little horses.") Superseded by Boule in French Casinos.

PETROFF DEFENSE: a Chess opening.

Phalanx, a card Solitaire.

Pharaoh, Pharoan, 531

PHILIDOR'S DEFENSE: a Chess opening.

PHILOSOPHER: European term for a card cheat.

PHOEBE: cast of 5 (Craps).

PIANO HAND: one that offers little opportunity for loss or gain (Whist).

PIANOLA: a hand that plays itself; cinch hand (Bridge).

PIC: the bonus of 30 for scoring 30 in declarations and play before opponent scores a point (Piquet).

Picket, Picquet = Piquet, 261

PICKPOCKET TURN = Gun Turn.

PICK-UP: the capture of an adverse trump that would otherwise win a trick, by plain-suit leads through the adverse hand (Bridge); commonly called *coup* or *grand coup.*

PICTURE CARD: = face card; any king, queen, or jack.

Pig, 488

PIGEON: a card drawn that greatly improves the hand (Poker).

Pig in the Poke = Wild Widow, 74

PIK = PIQUE (1).

PIKER: 1. A cheapskate; a player who bets or bids too little. 2. A player other than a principal (Skinball).

Pike's Peak, a card Solitaire.

PILLSBURY ATTACK: a Chess opening.

PIN: immobilization of a piece through the fact that a move of the piece off a line would expose its own king to check (Chess).

PINK (slang): of the same color—"they're all pink," signifying a flush (Poker).

Pinochle, 284

PINOCHLE: a meld of the ♠Q and ♦J; a meld of Q-J with the suits variable according to the trump suit (Pinochle).

Pinochle Rum = 500 Rum, 12

Pinocle = Pinochle, 284

PION, LE (Fr.): pawn (Chess).

PIONEER: a Checkers opening.

PIP: 1. Any of the suit symbols on a playing card. 2. Any of the dots on dice or dominoes.

PIQUE (Fr.): 1. The suit spades. 2. = pic.

Piquet, 261

Piquet au Cent, 264

Piquet Normand, 266

Piquet Variations, 266

Piquet Voleur, 266

Pirate Bridge, 174

Pirate Gold, a card Solitaire.

Pistol Pete = Pistol Stud, 90

Pistol Stud, 90

Pit, proprietary card game of Parker Brothers.

Pitch, 235

PITCH: make the opening lead; the card so led, which fixes the trump suit (Pitch).

PIVOT: player who retains his seat while the others move (Pivot Bridge).

Pivot Bridge, 156

PLACE BET: a bet that the shooter will make his point (Craps).

PLACES OPEN: the outstanding cards, drawing any of which will improve the hand.

Plafond, 172

Plain Dealing, obsolete card game.

PLAIN SUIT: any that is not trumps.

Plait, a card Solitaire.

Planet, a card Solitaire.

PLAY: 1. Contribute a card to a trick, add a bone from the hand to the layout (Dominoes); make a move in a board game or in Solitaire. 2. The card or bone played; the move made. 3. In a card game, the period during which the hands are de-

pleted by plays to tricks, to a common pile, etc. 4. Betting in general.

Playback = Replay Duplicate, 166

PLAYBOY: the jack of trumps (Spoil Five).

PLAYED CARD: 1. One legally construed to be played, and so nonretractable. 2. Any dead card.

PLAYER: 1. Any participant in a game. 2. An active participant, as distinct from one dealt out of the current deal. 3. The high bidder, contractor, as in Skat (often capitalized). 4. A card that can be laid off on a meld (Rummy).

Playing-Card Football, 561

PLAYING CARDS (history), 579

PLAYING TO THE SCORE: modifying normal tactics of bidding or play when one side has an excessive lead or is close to game.

PLAYING TRICKS: cards, not necessarily high or trumps, expected to win tricks in actual play (Bridge).

PLAY OFF: play a card that will not enable opponent to make a run (Cribbage).

PLAY ON: play a card that may enable opponent to make a run (Cribbage).

Play or Pay, 225

PLAY OVER: play a higher card, cover.

Plot, a card Solitaire.

PLUS VALUES: elements of strength in a hand not directly countable under an arithmetic system of hand valuation (Bridge).

Poch, Pochen, 81

POINT: 1. A unit of scoring. 2. The score for holding the longest or highest suit (Piquet, etc.). 3. The digit signifying the numerical total of one's cards (Baccarat). 4. Cast of 4, 5, 6, 8, 9, or 10 on the shooter's first roll (Craps). 5. Any of the 24 marks on the board, usually elongated triangles (Backgammon).

POINT BET: a bet that the shooter will make his point (Craps).

POINT COUNT: a method of valuing a Bridge hand by assigning relative numerical values to the high cards (see page 143).

POINT VALUE: the assigned value, for scoring purposes, of a counting card.

Pokeno, proprietary game of the United States Playing Card Co., based on Keno; the object is to get five cards in a row.

Poker, 52

Poker Dice, 547

Poker, Games Based on, 535

Poker Rum = Knock Rummy, 44

Poker Solitaire, 470

Poker with the Buck, 79

Poker with the Bug, 73

Polignac, 246

Polish Bezique, 273

Polish Checkers, 385

Pollack, obsolete game of the Pinochle type.

POLLACK: the A-10-9 of a suit (Pollack).

PONE: the non-dealer in a two-hand game; the player at dealer's right.

PONTE (Fr.): punter; one who plays against the bank.

PONTO, PUNTO: the fourth-best trump, the ◇A or ♡A (Quadrille).

Pontoon, occasional name for Vanjohn = Blackjack, 513

Poo = Mancala, 410

POOL: pot; an accumulation of chips from antes, bets, forfeits, etc., to win which is the object of the game.

Pool Ecarte, variant for three players in which the first to win two consecutive games wins a pool.

Pool Game, variant of Block Dominoes in which the first player to get rid of his hand wins a pool.

Pool Nap = Nap Pool, 197

POPE: the diamond nine (Pope Joan).

Pope Joan, 220

Poque, obsolete card game with betting on hands, similar to Poker. (See Poch, page 52).

POQUE (Fr.): compartment of a betting layout.

PORTLAND CLUB: old London club that promulgates Contract Bridge Laws in Great Britain.

POSITION: 1: One of the end-game studies deemed to be of basic and far-reaching importance, as First Position (Checkers). 2. The relative seating of the players, a factor of tactical importance.

POSITIVE DOUBLE: one made with expectation of defeating the adverse bid (Bridge).

Post and Pair, obsolete card game similar to Blackjack.

POST-MORTEM: discussion of the merits of the bidding and play of a past deal.

POT: pool; an accumulation of chips from antes, bets, forfeits, etc., to win which is the object of the game.

Pot Limit, see page 60.

PO TSZ': Chinese gambling cube fitted with a cover.

Pounce, 447

POVERTY POKER: the rule that a player's losses are limited to one or two stacks; thereafter he may draw chips from the banker and his further losses are shared by the other players.

Precedence, 471

PREDICT: announce intention to make schneider or schwarz (Skat).

PREEMPT: a high opening bid, made to shut out adverse competition (Bridge).

Preference, 188. See also Frog, 327.

PREFERENCE: a suit that has bidding precedence over the other three suits, as in Boston; a bid in the preferred suit.

PREMIUMS: 1. Royalties; bonuses paid for certain exceptional hands. 2. All scores other than for odd tricks (Bridge).

PREVIOUS BET LIMIT: see page 61

PRIME: 1. The closure of six adjacent points (Backgammon). 2. = primiera.

Primero, one of the oldest known card games, possibly of Spanish origin, stated by an early writer to be like Ambigu and by Seymour to be like Ombre. Also *Prime, Primavista.* Primiera may be a descendant.

Primiera, 340

PRIMIERA: a scoring combination, one card of each suit (Scopa).

PRINCIPAL: 1. Active player. 2. Backer.

PRISON, IN: said of bets not settled by the current coup, but held in abeyance for the next coup (Roulette).

Privileged Four, a card Solitaire.

PRIZE PILE: the discard pile when frozen (Canasta).

Problem, a card Solitaire.

PROBLEM: a position in Chess, Checkers, Bridge, etc., posed as a puzzle to be solved on the stipulation that both sides must make the best possible moves.

PROGRESSION: the movement of players or boards from table to table in a Duplicate or Progressive tournament.

PROGRESSIVE: 1. A form of tournament in which players progress according to their scores, the cards being shuffled and dealt at every table. 2. Accumulating from deal to deal.

Progressive Bridge, 157

Progressive Jackpots, 71

Progressive Rubber Bridge, 162

Progressive Rummy, see Contract Rummy, 26.

PROIL, PRIAL: contraction of *pair royal.*

PROMOTION: 1. Replacement of a pawn that has reached the eighth rank by a queen or other piece (Chess). 2. Improvement in relative rank through the fall of cards originally higher.

Propeller = Windmill, 480

PROPOSAL: request by the non-dealer that additional cards be dealt, in Ecarte. Also *proposition.*

PROPOSITION BET: a bet that a certain number or combination of numbers will or will not appear on a succeeding roll or series of rolls (Craps).

PROTECTION: 1. Cards by which others are guarded. 2. Guard of one piece by another (Chess). 3. Act of cinching (Cinch). 4. A bid made in the belief that partner has passed a strong hand (Contract Bridge).

Prussian Whist, variant in which the trump is determined by cutting the still pack, to avoid exposure of a card in dealer's hand.

PSYCHIC BID: one made without cards to support it, for purpose of misleading the opponents (Contract Bridge).

Puff, obsolete Backgammon game.

PULL DOWN: remove all or part of one's winnings from the pool.

PUNG: a set of three identical tiles; to ground such a set (Mah Jongg).

Pung Chow = Mah Jongg, 414

PUNTER: one who plays against the bank in a banking game.

PUNTO, PONTO: the fourth-best trump, the diamond or heart ace (Quadrille).

PUPPYFOOT: the club ace; any club.

Purchase Nap, 197

PURE CANASTA = natural Canasta.

PUSH = stand-off.

Puss in Corner, a card Solitaire.

Put, Putt, obsolete card game to win two out of three tricks.

Put and Take, 534

Pyramid, 472

Q

Q: abbr. of queen.

Quadrangle, a card Solitaire.

Quadrangles, 434

Quadrille: 1. An Ancient card game, no longer played; see Ombre, 330. 2. A card Solitaire.

Qualify, 545

Quart: sequence of four cards (Piquet). *Quart major,* the A-K-Q-J of a suit; *quart minor,* the K-Q-J-10.

QUATORZE: four of a kind, tens or higher, counting 14 (Piquet).

Quatre Valets = Polignac, 246

Quebec Draughts, variant of Polish Checkers.

QUEEN: 1. A Chess piece. 2. Equivalent of *king* in European Checkers.

QUEENING: replacement of a pawn that has reached the eighth rank by a queen (Chess).

Queen City Rum, 6

Queen Nazarene, obsolete card game of the Stops type.

QUEEN NAZARENE: the diamond queen (Queen Nazarene).

Queen of Italy = Terrace, 475

Queens, a card Solitaire.

Queen's Audience, a card Solitaire..

QUEEN'S GAMBIT: a Chess opening.

QUEEN'S PAWN GAME: a Chess opening.

QUICK TRICKS: units in a system of valuation of high cards; aces, kings, and queens in combination (Bridge).

Quilt = Crazy Quilt, 450

Quince, 518

Quinella, 25C

QUINOLA: a privileged card in Reversis. *Great* ——, the heart jack; *Little* ——, the heart queen.

Quinquenove, obsolete dice game.

QUINT: 1. A sequence of five cards (Piquet). *Quint major,* the A-K-Q-J-10 of a suit; *quint minor,* the K-Q-J-10-9. 2. A set of five like tiles, including wild Flowers (Mah Jongg).

Quintille, five-hand variant of Ombre.

Quintract, a name given to Five-suit Bridge.

Quinze, 518

QUITTED TRICK: one that has been turned face down; one that no longer may legally be inspected.

Quodlibet, 1. An old German pastime, a sequence of thirteen simple games. 2. A name often given to a game played to decide who shall pay for the drinks.

QUONG = KONG.

R

R: 1. Abbr. of rook (Chess). 2. (Fr.) Abbr. of *roi, rey* (king).

Rabouge, Rapousse, two-hand card game of the Stops type.

Race-Horse Keno, 559

Radio Pinochle, 311

Radmuhle, German board game similar to Mill.

RAFFLE: three like numbers cast on three dice.

Raffles, 560

RAIL: raised edge of the table against which the dice must be cast (Craps).

Railroad Euchre, 205

Rainbow, a card Solitaire.

RAINBOW HAND: one that can win only by very lucky improvement.

RAISE: 1. Bet more than is necessary to call; the amount by which a bet exceeds the amount necessary to call (Poker). 2. Bid higher in a denomination previously bid by partner; such a bid (Bridge).

RAKE-OFF: the percentage of the stakes taken as a fee by a house or club.

Rams, Rammes, see Trumps, 189.

RAMSCH: nullo; a game to take as few points as possible (Skat).

Ramy, El, Spanish card game like Rummy.

Rana = Frog, 327

RANGDOODLES = ROODLES.

RANK: 1. The ordinal position of a card in its suit, determining what card wins or beats another; the precedence of suits in bidding or showing. 2. A horizontal row of squares (Chess).

Rank and File, a card Solitaire.

Ranter Go Round, 484

Rauber Skat, 327

Razzle Dazzle, 239

REARHAND = ENDHAND.

REBID: a second bid by the same player in the same denomination; a second bid by the same player in any denomination; make such a bid (Bridge).

Red and Black, 535

Red and Black = Rouge et Noir, 524

Red Dog, 526

REDEAL: 1. A new deal by the same player, after an irregularity in dealing. 2. A new deal of some of the cards, usually the wastepile, sometimes the tableau (Solitaire).

REDOUBLE: a call that has the effect of further increasing certain scoring quantities in case the bid redoubled becomes the contract (Bridge).

REDSKIN: any face card.

REDUCE: lower the count of one's deadwood by discarding high cards. *Reducer,* a low card. (Rummy.)

REENTRY: a card with which a hand can gain the lead after having lost it.

REFAIT: the same count in both rows (Trente et Quarante).

REFLEX MATE: form of self-mate Chess problem in which a player able to give mate on the move must do so.

REFUSE: 1. Reject a proposal (Ecarté). 2. Accept a beg, thereby refusing gift to eldest hand (All Fours).

REGLE (Fr.): rule of a game.

REGULAR OPENING: one that is considered to be strong and has been much-analyzed (Chess).

Reinforcements, a card Solitaire.

REJECT: nullo; a game to take as few points as possible (Skat).

RELEASED CARD: one made available by the removal of covering cards (Solitaire).

REMIS (Fr.): drawn game.

REMISE: loss of the game by the contracting side, through failure to win more tricks than the opposing side (Ombre).

RENEGE, RENIG: 1. The privilege of withholding a high trump, discarding instead, when a lower trump is lead, as in Spoil Five. 2. Revoke.

RENOUNCE: fail to follow suit because void of the suit led; a void.

RENTRANT (Fr.): player who takes the place of the loser of the previous game, as in Chouette.

RENVIER (Fr.): raise the bet; improve.

REPIC: the bonus of 60 for scoring 30 in declarations before opponent scores a point. Also, *repique.* (Piquet.)

Replay Duplicate Bridge, 166

REPUESTO = CODILLE.

REQUIREMENTS: the minimum holdings deemed systemically necessary for a bet, bid, or declaration, as in Bridge.

RESERVE: a part of the layout, cards available to be built elsewhere but not themselves to be built on until moved (Solitaire).

Reserves, a card Solitaire.

RESPONSE: 1. A bid made in reply to a bid by partner. 2. A card selected to be played to partner's lead so as to give him information (Bridge).

RESTRICTION PLAY: competition in which the first two or three moves are fixed by the chance selection from an admitted list of sound openings (Checkers).

RETI SYSTEM: a Chess opening.

RETOURNE (Fr.): turn-up card; any faced card.

RETRACTOR: form of Chess problem in which one or more moves are to be retracted and superior moves substituted.

Reunion, obsolete three-hand card game to win counting cards.

Reversal, a card Solitaire.

Reverse, Reversis, see Hearts, 240

Reverse Bridge, 173

Reversi, 408

Revertier, obsolete Backgammon game.

REVOKE: play a card of another suit when able to follow suit; fail to adhere to a legal requirement as to trumping, heading, going over.

REVOLUTION: a null ouverte game in which the opponents pool their hands and redivide the cards as they please (Skat).

REVY, REVIE: raise a bet (*obsolete*).

REY: in the Spanish pack, a king, numbered 12.

Rickey de Laet, 90

RIEN NE VA PLUS (Fr.): "No more bets," croupier's call in Roulette.

RIFFLE SHUFFLE: one executed by butting the ends of two packets together and interlacing the cards while riffling them with the thumbs.

RIGHT BET: a bet that the shooter will pass; or, depending on usage, that he will make his point, or that the dice will win on a series of rolls beginning with the next (Craps).

RIGHT BOWER: the jack of trumps (Euchre).

RIGHT PEDRO: the five of trumps (Pedro).

Rising Sun, a card Solitaire.

R. O.: opponent at one's right.

ROB: exchange a card in hand for the turn-up (All Fours).

ROB A KONG: claim a fourth tile just added to a pung by another player, to complete one's hand (Mah Jongg).

ROB THE PACK: select any desired cards from the stock to replace discards (Cinch).

ROCHADE (Ger.): the move castling (Chess).

ROCK: a domino; = bone.

ROCKPILE: the stock (Canfield). See *mines, nuggets.*

ROI (Fr.): king (Chess, cards, etc.).

ROI RENDU: a game in Quadrille ("king surrendered").

ROLL: throw dice from one's hand or a dice-cup upon a plane surface; the numbers that show on the uppermost faces of dice after they are cast.

Roll Call = Hit or Miss, 461

ROLLER: one who rolls dice; shooter.

Rolling Stone = Enflé, 228

ROME: a hand of one pair, jacks or lower (Romestecq).

Romestecq, obsolete partnership card game of melding.

Ronda, Spanish game similar to Comet.

Ronfle, card game akin to Piquet (see page 261).

ROODLES: see page 68.

Rook, proprietary card game of Parker Brothers.

ROOK: a Chess piece.

ROOKING: defrauding a victim; cheating.

ROPE: a set in sequence (Rummy).

ROTATION: the progress of the turn to deal, bid, bet, play, etc., which is from player to player to the left, clockwise. (*Note:* Clockwise rotation is standard for all American and English games. Many games originating in Italy, Spain, China, and elsewhere are traditionally counter-clockwise.)

ROT, ROTH (Ger.): the suit hearts.

ROUE DE FORTUNE, LA (Fr.): the tarot X ("wheel of fortune").

ROUGE (Fr.): red.

Rouge et Noir, 524

Rouge et Noir, a card Solitaire.

ROUGH: relatively poor, as "a rough seven" (7-6-5-4-2) in Lowball.

Roulette, 551

Rounce, variant of Rams.

ROUND: 1. One series of consecutive turns, one turn to each active player, in receiving cards during the deal, in bidding, betting, playing (= trick), or in duty of dealing. 2. Period of a tournament during which there is no progression.

Round Dozen, a card Solitaire.

ROUND GAME: one in which there are no partnerships, and, usually, the number of players can vary.

ROUND HOUSE: a meld of one K-Q in each suit (Pinochle).

Round the Clock, a card Solitaire.

ROUND-THE-CORNER: circular sequence of rank in a suit, K-A-2 being sequential.

Round-the-Corner Gin, 41

Round the World, 75

ROUND TRIP: a meld of one K-Q in each suit (Pinochle). Also, *round house.*

ROW: a horizontal line of cards (Solitaire) or squares on a board, as in Checkers.

Rows of Four, a card Solitaire.

Royal Aids, a card Solitaire.

Royal Auction, 177

Royal Casino, 258

Royal Cotillion, a card Solitaire.

ROYALE: a sequence of K-Q-J of the same suit (Thirty-Five).

Royal Family, a card Solitaire.

Royal Flush, a card Solitaire.

ROYAL FLUSH: an ace-high straight flush, the highest possible hand barring wild cards (Poker).

Royal Marriage, a card Solitaire.

ROYAL MARRIAGE: a meld, the K-Q of trumps (Pinochle).

Royal Parade, a card Solitaire.

Royal Rendezvous, a card Solitaire.

ROYALS: 1. = Lilies; see page 177. 2. English name of the fifth suit at one time added to the standard pack.

ROYAL SEQUENCE: a meld, the A-K-Q-J-10 of trumps, = flush (Pinochle).

ROYALTIES: see page 68; also *bonus payments,* pages 298-299

Royal Widows, a card Solitaire.

RUBBER: the winning of the first two out of three games by one side.

Rubber Bridge, a form in which rubbers are played, as distinguished (usually) from Progressive and Duplicate Bridge.

RUBBER POINTS: points given for winning a rubber — see page 181 (Whist).

RUBICON: failure of the loser of a game to reach a certain minimum score, as 100 in Piquet; lurch.

Rubicon Bezique, 272

Rubicon Piquet, 264

RUFF: play a trump on a plain-suit lead.

Ruff and Honours, a precursor of Whist; see page 114.

RULE OF ELEVEN: the fact that when a player leads the fourth-best of a suit the difference of its rank from 11 is the number of higher cards of the suit in the other three hands (Whist, Bridge).

RULE OF THE FOURTH-BEST: 1. The conventional practice of leading the fourth-best of a long suit. 2. The fact that such a lead shows that if the leader has more than four cards, the additional cards are lower in rank than the lead. (Whist, Bridge.)

Rum, Rummy, 1

Rumjin, a card Solitaire.

RUMMY: 1. A complete hand with no unmatched card; get rid of the last card in the hand. 2. Call made by a player in claiming a discard when more than one may claim. (Rummy.)

RUN: 1. A sequence of three or more cards (Cribbage, Rummy). 2. Try to get all runners to safety; play a running game (Backgammon).

RUNNERS: the two stones initially posted on the adverse 1-point; any stones back of adverse stones (Backgammon).

RUNNING GAME: 1. The policy of trying to advance as quickly as possible and avoid leaving blots. 2. A position in which all the White stones have passed all the Black stones, so that hits are no longer possible. (Backgammon.)

RUNT: 1. Any hand less than one pair. 2. The hand 7-5-4-3-2 in two or more suits, the lowest possible, except in Lowball (Poker).

RUN THE CARDS: deal additional cards and turn a new trump card, after a beg is accepted (All Fours).

Russian Backgammon, 392

Russian Bank, 482

Russian Boston, 187

RUTHEN (Ger.): the suit diamonds.

RUY LOPEZ: a Chess opening.

'**Ryong-Hpai,** Korean Solitaire with dominoes ("dragon tablets").

S

S: abbr. of 1. South. 2. Knight, from Ger. *Springer* (Chess).

SACRIFICE: 1. Voluntary loss of one or more pieces for positional advantage, in a board game. 2. Make a sacrifice bid.

SACRIFICE BID: one made without expectation of fulfilling contract, to prevent the opponents from assuming the contract (Bridge).

SAFE DISCARD: one that the next player surely or probably cannot use or pick up (Rummy).

SAFETY ZONE: a step on a Pachisi board from which no counter may be hit and sent back.

Saka, Siamese Backgammon.

Salic Law, 473

SALT THE PACK: discard from a meld or combination, in order later to retrieve the card together with others above it (500 Rum).

Salvo = Battleships, 502

Samba, 25

SANDBAG: withhold action on a good hand, in order to trap an opponent into greater loss.

SANS APPELLER: a game at Quadrille played without calling a king.

Sans Prendre = Frog, 327

SANS PRENDRE (Fr.): a declaration in which the high bidder does not pick up the widow ("without taking").

Sant, Saunt = le Cent. (See page 261.)

Saratoga = Michigan, 217

SAUTERELLE: sweep (Papillon).

SAY: turn to declare (*colloquial*).

SCAT = SKAT.

Scavenger Hunt, 509

Schach, Schachspiel (Ger.) = Chess, 341

SCHACH-MATT (Ger.): checkmate (Chess).

Schafkopf, 315

SCHELLEN (Ger.): the suit diamonds.

SCHIPPEN (Ger): the suit spades.

SCHMEISS: proposal to abandon the deal, on refusal of which the opponent becomes the trump maker (Klaberjass).

SCHMIER, SCHMEER = SMEAR.

Schnautz, card game similar to Whiskey Poker (= Thirty-One).

SCHNEIDEN (Ger.): to finesse.

SCHNEIDER: 1. Failure to win more than half the points necessary to make or defeat a contract, by one player or side, as in Skat. 2. Loss of the game with zero score; shutout (Gin Rummy).

Schnipp-Schnapp-Schnurr-Burr-Basilorum, variant of Snip-Snap-Snorem.

Schnitt, obsolete card game like Faro.

SCHNITT (Ger.): a finesse.

SCHOLAR'S MATE: the mate after 1. P-K4, P-K4; 2. B-B4, B-B4; 3. Q-R5, N-KB3; 4. QxBP (Chess).

SCHUPPEN (Ger.): the suit spades.

SCHWARZ (Ger.): 1. Black. 2. Loss of all the tricks by one player or side, as in Skat.

S c h w a r z e Dame, Schwarzer Peter = Old Maid, 486

Schwellen = Enflé, 228

Scopa, Scoop, 259

SCOOP: sweep; the count of 1 point for taking all the cards on the table (Scopa).

Scopone, 260

SCORE: 1. Counting value of specific cards or tricks. 2. The accumulated total of points won by each player. 3. Scoresheet. 4. Mark or record the score.

Scorpion, 474

SCOTCH GAME: a Chess opening.

Scotch Whist = Catch the Ten, 247

Scrambled Words, 503

SEASONS: four special tiles (Mah Jongg).

Sebastopol, 429

SECOND BUTTON: a system of betting on case cards in Faro.

SECOND DOUBLE CORNER: a Checkers opening.

SECOND HAND: the second player in turn to call or play.

SECOND TURN: a game in which trump is fixed by the second card turned from the widow (Skat).

SECTION: in a tournament, a group of tables playing as a unit.

SEE: meet a bet, call a bet.

SEEDING: in a knockout tournament, the placement of the strongest players in different brackets so that they will meet in late rounds.

See-Low = Four-Five-Six, 544

SEE-SAW = CROSS-RUFF.

Seisillo, El, Spanish partnership game, to win majority of six tricks.

SELCHOW AND RIGHTER: manufacturer of intellectual games, located at New York City.

Selective Canfield, a card Solitaire.

SELF-MATE: form of Chess problem in which White is to force Black to mate the White king, against Black's resistance. Also *suimate.*

Sell Out, see Pitch, 235

Semi-Exposed Dummy, 180

SEMI-SET: a cut-in game where two of the players are always partners when both are playing (Bridge).

SEMI-TWO-SUITER: a hand with one suit of four cards and another longer suit (Bridge).

Senate, a card Solitaire.

SENIOR: eldest hand; adversary who leads to the first trick.

Senior Wrangler, a card Solitaire.

SEPTET: a sequence of seven cards (Piquet).

SEQUENCE: 1. Two or more cards of adjacent rank, as 8-7. 2. A set or meld of three or more cards of adjacent rank, as 8-7-6 (and of the same suit if the rules so require).

Serpent Poker, a card Solitaire.

SERVE: deal cards, especially in replacing discards.

SET: 1. Defeat the contract; defeated. 2. A valid meld; three or more cards of the same rank, or of the same suit in sequence (Rummy). 3. The first bone played (Dominoes).

Set-Back = Auction Pitch, 233

SET-BACK: scoring in which the value of a bid is deducted from the contractor's score if he fails to make it.

Setback Bid Whist, 184

Set-Back Euchre, 204

SET MATCH: play with unchanging partnerships (Bridge).

SETTANTA: the count of 1 point for winning the highest group of four cards (Scopa).

SETTLEMENT: payment of losses and collection of winnings; redemption of chips in money.

SEVEN: to cast a 7. —*out,* cast a 7 when trying for a point (Craps).

Seven and One-Half, 518

Seven-Card Flip, 90

Seven-Card Stud, 87

Sevens = Fan Tan, 224

Seven-Toed Pete = Seven-card Stud, 87

Seven-Up, 229

SEXTET, SEXTETTE: 1. A sequence of six cards (Piquet). 2. A set of six like tiles, including wild Flowers (Mah Jongg).

SEYMOUR, RICHARD: editor of *The Compleat Gamester* (Cotton's book amplified), London, 1739.

SEWED IN: unable to exit (Bridge).

Shah, a card Solitaire.

Sham Battle = Beleaguered Castle, 442

Shamrocks, 474

SHARK: 1. An expert player. 2. A cheat.

Shasta Sam, see California Jack, 231

Shatranj, see Chess History, 399

SHED: to discard.

Sheepshead = Schafkopf, 315

Shemmy = Chemin de Fer, 524

Sheung Luk, Chinese Backgammon ("double sixes").

Shifting Sands, 90

SHIK TSZ': Chinese dice.

SHILL: confederate of the dealer, who pretends to play against him.

Shimmy = Chemin de Fer, 524

Shing Ku T'o, Chinese dice game ("table of officials").

Ship, Mate and Crew = Battleships, 547

SHOE: the dealing box in Baccarat.

SHOOTER: player whose turn it is to roll the dice (Craps).

Short Bridge, 172

Short Faro, variant that moves faster and gives the house a greater advantage.

SHORT GAME: any in which not all the cards of a pack are put into play during a deal, as Euchre.

SHORT PAIR: in Jackpot Poker, any pair lower than jacks.

SHORT SUIT: a holding of less than one's average share of a suit; a suit of two or fewer cards in Bridge.

Short Whist, Whist when game is 5 points (see page 180).

SHOT: a forced series of exchanges, especially when it results in advantage to the player that forces it (Checkers).

Shotgun, 76

Shove 'Em Along, 88

SHOW: 1. Expose; meld; showdown. 2. Count the scores in hand and crib (Cribbage).

SHOWDOWN: comparison of the full hands of all active players, to determine which wins the pot (Poker).

Showdown Poker = Cold Hands, 96.

SHUFFLE: mix cards, bones or tiles together preparatory to dealing or drawing the hands. (See page 134.)

SHUT-OUT: 1. Failure of the loser of a game to score a single point. *Shut out,* defeated with zero score. 2. A high bid made to prevent the opponents from bidding cheaply (Bridge). 3. A prime in the home table, preventing adverse stones from entering (Backgammon).

Shuttle, a card Solitaire.

Shweck, a form of Three-Card Division Loo with double pool, popular among Slavic-Americans.

SHY: short, as said of a pool to which some player owes chips.

Sice-Ace, obsolete Backgammon game.

SICILIAN DEFENSE: a Chess opening.

Sickle, a card Solitaire.

SIDE: a competing unit; two or more persons playing for a common score and therefore coöperating in the play of a game.

SIDE BETS: 1. Bets on propositions other than who will win a game; bets additional to the regular stakes. 2. Bets among the players other than the shooter, as in Craps.

SIDE CARD: 1. Any in a suit other than a bidder's intended trump suit; plain card. 2. The highest card held outside of one pair or two pairs, referred to in deciding the higher hand between two hands otherwise tied (Poker).

SIDE MONEY, SIDE POT: a pot separate from the main pot, formed by continued betting after one player has put all his chips into the main pot (Table Stakes Poker).

SIDE STRENGTH: high cards in suits other than the bidder's intended trump.

SIDE SUIT: one other than the bidder's intended trump; plain suit.

SIGHT: showdown; the right to compete in the main pot at the showdown (Poker).

SIGNAL: any convention of play whereby opponents of the contractor properly give each other information, as in Whist, Bridge.

SIGN-OFF: a bid that asks partner to pass or to close the auction as soon as possible (Bridge).

Simple Addition, a card Solitaire.

SIMPLE GAME: 1. The lowest declaration that may be bid; = frage or frog (Skat, etc.). 2. Single pool (Loo).

SIMPLE HONORS: the score of 30 for three trump honors held by one side (Auction Bridge).

SIMPLES: suit tiles of ranks 2 to 8 inclusive (Mah Jongg).

Simplicity, a card Solitaire.

SIMS, P. HAL: a leading card player and writer on Contract Bridge, died Feb., 1949.

SIMS SYSTEM: see page 150.

SINGLE BETE: a forfeit paid by a bidder who concedes loss of the hand, without play (Auction Pinochle).

SINGLE CORNER: 1. Square 4 or 29 on the checkerboard. 2. One of the openings. (Checkers.)

Single Dummy, 180

SINGLE GAME: one won at the minimum stake, without increase by shutout, doubles, etc.

SINGLE MAN: a piece entitled to move only forward (Checkers).

SINGLE POOL: one containing no chips left over from a previous pool.

SINGLETON: an original holding of one card in a suit.

Sing Luk = Four-five-six, 544

SINK: omit announcement of a scoring combination, to gain possible advantage in play (Piquet).

Sin-Syo-Tyen, Korean fortune-telling with dominoes.

Sir Garnet, 197

Sir Tommy, a card Solitaire.

SISTER: cast of six (dice).

Six-Bid Solo, 328

Six-Card Stud, 91

SIXIE FROM DIXIE: cast of 6 (Craps).

Six-Hand Five Hundred, 216

Six-Pack Bezique, 272

Sixte, obsolete card game like Loo, with six cards per hand and game of 6 points (= Sechsern).

SIXTY DAYS: point of 6 (Craps).

64-four-Card Pinochle, 290

60 QUEENS: a meld of four queens, one of each suit (Pinochle).

Sixty-Six, 274

Sixty-Three, variant of Cinch in which the card values are increased so that the maximum bid is 63.

Sizette, obsolete six-hand partnership card game to win three tricks.

Skat, 318

SKAT, SCAT: widow; extra cards dealt to the table.

SKATMEISTER: director of a Skat tournament.

SKEET: a hand containing 2, 5, 9 and two cards lower than 9, but no pair (Poker).

Skillo, 555

Skinball, Skin Game, Skinning, 533

SKINNING: dealing cards by sliding them off the top of the pack without lifting them.

SKIP BID = JUMP BID.

SKIP STRAIGHT: a hand comprising five odd or five even cards in sequence, as K-J-9-7-5 (Poker).

SKIS, SKUS: the highest trump, the XXII (Tarok).

SKUNKED = SHUT OUT.

SLAM: 1. The winning of all the tricks by one player or side. 2. *Grand slam*, thirteen tricks. *Little slam*, or *Small slam*, twelve tricks (Bridge).

Slamm, see Contract Bridge, 114

Slapjack, 487

SLAV DEFENSE: a Chess opening.

SLEEPER: a dead or unclaimed bet left in the layout.

SLIPPERY ANNE: the spade queen (Black Lady).

Slippery Sam, 527

Slobberhannes, 245

SLOT: dealer's position, in a game conducted by a gambling house.

Slot Machines, 556

Sluff, Slough = Frog, 327

SLUFF, SLOUGH: to discard.

Slum, 555

Sly Fox, a card Solitaire.

SMEAR: play a high-counting card on a trick won by partner.

SMOKE OUT: compel play of the spade queen, by repeated leads of the suit (Black Lady).

SMOOTH: relatively good, as "a smooth seven" (7-4-3-2-A) in Lowball.

SMOTHERED MATE: checkmate by a knight, the king being largely or wholly confined by his own pieces (Chess).

SMOTHER PLAY: the pick-up of a guarded high trump by a less-guarded master trump (Bridge).

Smudge, 235

Snake, 393

Snake, a card Solitaire.

SNAKE-EYES: cast of 1-1 (Dice).

Snap, variant of Slapjack.

SNEAK: the lead of a plain-suit singleton (Whist).

Sniff = Muggins, 426

SNIFF: the first doublet played (Muggins).

Snip Snap Snorem, 227

Snoozer, 236

SNOOZER: the joker, as in Snoozer.

SNOWBALL THE LAYOUT: distribute white chips all over the layout (Faro).

SNOWING = MILKING.

SODA: the uppermost card of the pack when it is put in the box (Faro).

SOFT 17: a count of 17 including an ace counted for 11 (Blackjack).

SOLEIL, LE (Fr.): the tarot XIX ("sun").

Solid Square, a card Solitaire.

SOLID SUIT: 1. A suit holding composed all of winning cards. 2. A suit that can be established by straight leads, as Q-J-10-9-8 (Bridge).

Solitaire (cards), 439

Solitaire (Pegboard), 412

Solo (Ombre), 330

Solo = Frog, 327

SOLO: 1. A bid to play without a partner. 2. A bid or game in which the high bidder does not pick up the widow.

Solo, El, Spanish game based on Quadrille.

Solo Whist, 185

Somerset, a card Solitaire.

SOTA: in the Spanish pack, a knave, numbered 10.

Sotas, Las, Spanish card game, same as Polignac.

SOUTER: a Checkers opening.

Southern Cross, 76

SPACE: 1. A vacancy made in the tableau by removal of an entire pile, when the rules permit this vacancy to be filled (Solitaire). 2. Vacant points collectively (Go).

Spade Casino, 259

SPADE OVERS: the score of 1 point for each spade won over eight (Casino).

SPADES: 1. The suit denoted by the symbol ♤; also called pique (Fr.), Grün, Schippen (Ger.). 2. The count of 1 point for winning seven or more spades (Casino).

Spade the Gardener, 492

SPADILLE, SPADILLA, SPADILL: the highest trump; the spade ace in Tarok; the club queen in Schafkopf.

Spanish Bridge, 173

Spanish Checkers, variant in which a king moves any distance along an open line in order to capture, and must make the maximum number of captures possible.

Spanish Monte = Monte Bank, 531

Speculation, obsolete gambling game; the pool goes to the holder of the highest trump after a progressive auction sale of trumps that turn up.

Speculation, a card Solitaire.

Spider, 475

Spiderette, a card Solitaire.

Spiderweb, 435

Spin, Spinado, 221

Spit in the Ocean, 74

Spitzeln, obsolete card game similar to Ombre.

SPLIT: 1. The turn of two cards of the same rank (Faro). 2. Discard a card from a combination or set (Rummy). 3. Play, second hand, one of equal honors, as K-Q or Q-J (Bridge).

SPLIT A PAIR: divide two equal cards originally received, to make two separate hands (Blackjack).

SPLIT OPENERS: discard part of a combination that qualified the hand to open the pot (Draw Poker).

Spoil Five, 189

SPOT: 1. = PIP. 2. Give a handicap to.

SPOT CARD: any of rank 10, 9, 8, 7, 6, 5, 4, 3, or 2. ——*spot*, suffix added to the number of a card for clarity, as *fourspot, eightspot.*

Spot Hearts, 243

Sporting Games, 561

SPREAD: 1. Expose, display. 2. A contract that can be fulfilled without playing. 3. Melded set; to meld. 4. = open play.

SPRINGER (Ger.): knight (Chess).

Spry-Pal, two-hand card game to win counting cards.

Square, a card Solitaire.

SQUEEZE: 1. Fan one's hand very slightly, so as to uncover only the corner indices. 2. Lead a suit that compels adverse hands to discard; an end-play based on this principle (Bridge). 3. Attack an enemy piece, especially when it is thereby forced to advance (Checkers).

SQUEEZERS: playing cards that have indices in the corner, so that they can be read by squeezing. (*Note:* prior to this century, most cards manufactured did not have corner indices.)

Ssang-Ryouk, Korean Backgammon ("double sixes").

STACK: 1. Pile of chips; the quota of chips purchased at one time by a player. 2. Two superposed tiles in the wall (Mah Jongg). 3. Prearrange (the pack, or cards in it) for purposes of cheating.

Stag Party, a card Solitaire.

STAKE: 1. The money or chips with which a player enters a game. 2. The agreed amount to be paid for each point, game, or rubber, in play for money.

Stalactites, a card Solitaire.

STALEMATE: drawn game in which the player in turn has no legal move but is not checkmated (Chess).

STAND: 1. Accept the turn-up for trump. 2. Refuse to draw additional cards (= stand pat). 3. Stay in the current deal or pot, not drop.

STANDARD PACK: 1. *Bridge.* 52 cards; 13 of each suit: spades, hearts, diamonds, clubs; in each suit A, K, Q, J, 10, 9, 8, 7, 6, 5, 4, 3, 2. 2. *Piquet, Skat.* 32 cards; the Bridge pack with all sixes and lower cards discarded. 3. *Pinochle.* 48 cards; equivalent to two Bridge packs with all eights and lower cards discarded. (*Note:* at least one joker is included with each pack manufactured; it is used only in certain games.)

STAND-OFF: tie; cancellation of a bet because of an indecisive result.

Star, a card Solitaire.

STAR MOVE, STARRED MOVE: the only correct move to win or to hold the draw, indicated by an asterisk (Checkers).

Star, The = Sebastopol, 429

STARTER: the card turned up from the stock prior to the play (Cribbage).

STAY: 1. Remain in the current deal or pot; meet a bet; call, see. 2. Refuse to draw additional cards (= stand).

Stay Away = Polignac, 246

STEAL A PIECE: win one that is isolated from its fellows, so that it can neither be defended nor advanced in safety (Checkers).

Stealing Bundles, 493

STECHEN (Ger.): to ruff.

STECQ: last trick, in Romestecq.

STENOGRAPHER: a playing card queen.

STICH, DAS (Ger.): 1. Trick. 2. Last trick.

STICKMAN: houseman who handles the dice, retrieving them with a long hooked stick (Craps).

STICKS: the suit Bamboos (Mah Jongg).

STIFF CARD = LONG CARD.

STILL PACK: the one temporarily out of use, when two packs are used alternately.

St. Helena, a card Solitaire.

St. Louis, a card Solitaire.

STOCK: the rest of the pack, after part of it is dealt in hands or layout.

Stock Market, 520

STONE: any of the pieces used in playing Backgammon, Go, and other board games.

STONEWALL DEFENSE: a Chess opening.

STOP: 1. Interruption of a series of plays through absence of the next card in sequence (Stops). 2. A call upon opponent to cease play because of a violation of a rule of order (Russian Bank).

STOP-CARD: any wild card or black trey, so-called because when discarded it stops the next player from taking the discard pile (Canasta).

Stoppa, Italian card game with betting on combinations held, and play as in Stops.

Stops, 217

STOPPER: a holding with which a hand can eventually win a trick against adverse leads of the suit.

Storehouse, a card Solitaire.

Stormy Weather, 74

STRADDLE: 1. The blind raise of a blind bet (Poker). 2. = fork (Chess).

STRAIGHT: a hand of five cards in sequence, including two or more suits (Poker).

STRAIGHT FLUSH: five cards of the same suit in sequence (Poker).

Straight Poker, 79

Strategy, a card Solitaire.

STREAK: a run of good or bad luck.

Streets and Alleys, a card Solitaire.

STRING: a wire or cord stretched across and a few inches above a crap table; the dice are thrown over it.

STRING BETS: see page 65.

STRINGER: the meld of a sequence (Panguingue).

STRIP: exhaust the cards of a suit in one or more hands, in preparation for an end-play (Bridge).

STRIP BRIDGE: see Honeymoon Bridge, 179.

STRIPPED PACK: one from which some cards are permanently discarded for a particular game.

STRIP POKER: Poker (any form) in which each loser in a pot must remove an article of clothing: a jocular, lewd game.

STRIPPERS: cards cut on the bias, used by cheats.

STROKE: a series of forced exchanges, especially when it results in advantage to one player (Checkers).

Stud Poker, 83

Stuss, 531

SUB-ECHO: a trump signal in a plain suit (Whist).

SUB-SNEAK: a lead from a plain-suit doubleton (Whist).

Sudden Death, a card Solitaire.

SUFFICIENT BID: one that is high enough legally to supersede the last previous bid.

Sugoruku, Japanese Backgammon ("double sixes").

SUIT: 1. Any of the four sets of thirteen cards each in the standard pack: spades, hearts, diamonds, clubs. 2. Any of the three sets of thirty-six tiles each in Mah Jongg: Bamboos, Dots, Characters. 3. Any of the groups of seven Domino bones having the same number on one end.

SUITABLE CARD: one that may be built on another or put in a space (Solitaire).

Sultan, a card Solitaire.

Summer Bridge, 172

Super Contract Bridge, 174

SUPPORT: 1. Raise. 2. Cards that may be of assistance to partner.

Surprise Party, a card Solitaire.

SUSSMILCH, obsolete card game like Faro.

Sweat = Chuck-Luck, 543

Swedish Rummy = Eights, 225

SWEEP: the count of 1 point for taking in all the cards on the table (Casino).

SWEEPSTAKE: a method of settling in Hearts (see page 241).

SWEETEN THE POT: ante again to a pot not opened on the previous deal (Poker).

SWING: 1. Lead (the master card of a suit). 2. See SWINGS (2).

SWINGS: 1. Cards in unbroken sequence from the top of the suit down. 2. Differences of scores on the same board played at various tables (Duplicate Bridge).

SWITCHER: a Checkers opening.

SYSTEM: 1. A series of agreements between partners as to tactical procedure in various bidding situations (Bridge). 2. One of the two groups of sixteen playing squares on four alternate files (Checkers). 3. A schedule of bets successively to be placed at Roulette, Faro, or other betting games.

SYSTEMS AT ROULETTE, 554

SYSTEMS, BIDDING (Contract Bridge), see pages 142-151.

Sz' 'Ng Luk = Four-Five-Six, 544

T

T: abbr. of ten, rarely used.

TAB = CASE-KEEPER.

Tabal, Malayan Backgammon.

TABLE: 1. The plane surface on which a game is played. 2. The group of players who compete together, including both active and inactive. 3. One of the quarters of a Backgammon board.

TABLEAU: 1. A part of the layout or of the later deal on which (usually) some building is allowed (Solitaire). 2. = layout (Dominoes).

TABLE, FROM THE: 1. Applied to a set filled by claiming the last discard (Mah Jongg). 2. = from the dummy (Bridge). .

Table Stakes, 61

TAILOR = SCHNEIDER.

TAKE: accept the turned card for trump; such acceptance (Klaberjass).

TAKE A HOLE: concede bete without playing (Pinochle).

TAKE-ALL: the winning of all the counting cards by one player (Hearts).

Take Fourteen, a card Solitaire.

TAKE IN: capture cards from the table with a card from the hand (Casino).

Take It or Leave It, 88

TAKE ODDS: bet a smaller amount against a larger amount.

TAKEOUT: 1. The bid of a different denomination from that bid by partner (Bridge). 2. = rake-off. 3. = stack (1).

TAKEOUT DOUBLE = INFORMATORY DOUBLE.

Take Ten, a card Solitaire.

TAKE THE LEAD: make the first bet in a betting interval (Stud Poker).

TAKE THE ODDS: bet that the shooter will make his point (Craps).

TAKE UP: 1. Accept the turn-up for trump, said only of the dealer (Euchre). 2. Draw from the discard pile, especially when additional cards are thereby obtained (Rummy).

Talkative = Hit or Miss. 461

TALLY: scoresheet, especially of the type used in progressive play.

TALON (Fr.): 1. The stock; any special array of cards, as the eight reserve cards in Piquet. 2. The wastepile in Solitaire.

Tam o' Shanter, a card Solitaire.

TAP: 1. Rap on the table to signify a pass or a waiver of the cut. 2. Bet the whole amount of chips in front of a player (Table Stakes Poker).

Tapp = Frog, 327

Tapp-Tarok, variant of Tarok prevalent in Germany (see page 336).

Tarock, Taroky, Tarocchini = Tarok, 335

Tarok, 335

TAROT: a playing card (see page 576).

Ta T'in Kau, Chinese domino game ("play heavens and nines").

Tatteln: obsolete card game combining features of Piquet and Mariage.

TAU TEM: Siamese dominoes.

TEAM: in tournament Bridge, four or more players competing as a unit.

Team Chess, 361-362

TEAM-OF-FOUR CONTESTS, 168

TELL-BOX: crooked Faro box.

Tempeln, variant of Landsknecht, similar to Faro.

TEMPERANCE: the tarot XIV.

TEMPO: a gain of time (Chess).

Ten, a card Solitaire.

TENACE: a combination of high cards, not in sequence. *Perfect* ——, two high cards in alternate sequence, as A-Q. *Major* ——, the A-Q, or equivalent in a depleted suit. *Minor* ——, the K-J, or equivalent in a depleted suit. *Double* ——, the A-Q-10, A-J-10, or equivalent in a depleted suit. (*Note:* the term may derive partly from the A-10, an *imperfect* tenace, but this term is rare). (Bridge, Whist.)

Tenderete Robado, Spanish game similar to Comet.

Tennessee, 75

10-POINT CARD: any K, Q, J, 10, 9, or 8, each valued at 10 points (Canasta).

Tens High, 96

TENTH CARD: one that counts 10, a face card or ten (Cribbage).

TERMINALS: suit tiles of ranks 1 and 9 (Mah Jongg).

Terrace, 475

TERRITORY: open points controlled by one player (Go).

Testimony, 508

TETES (Fr.): face cards.

Texas Tech = Double Barreled Shotgun, 89

"The Game" (Charades), 510

THIRD HAND: third in turn to call or play.

Thirteen and the Odd, two-hand Whist variant.

Thirteen Down, a card Solitaire.

Thirteens, 468

Thirteen Up, a card Solitaire.

Thirty-Five, 519

Thirty-one, card game similar to Whiskey Poker, to get three cards of a suit totaling 31 or more. (*Note:* this name is also given to many other games in which 31 is the crucial count, *e.g.,* Belle, Trente et Quarante.)

Thirty-one with Cards, 437

Thirty-one with Dice, 438

Thirty-six, one-die game.

Thirty-six Square, a card Solitaire.

THREAT: a specific move, play; or series of plays that impends in a given position, where the first concern of the defending side must be to parry this threat.

Three-Card Division Loo, 192

THREE-CARD ECHO: a signal to show a holding of three cards in a suit (Whist, Bridge).

Three-Card Poker, 77, 93

Three Forty-five, see Woolworth, 90.

Three-Hand Bezique, 271

Three-Hand Bridge, 177

Three-Hand Cribbage, 254

Three-Hand Euchre, 205

Three-Hand Jass, 278

Three-Hand Pinochle, 290

Three-Hand Sixty-six, 276

THREE OF A KIND: three cards of the same rank.

THREE-ONE: a system of betting at Faro.

Threes in the Corner, a card Solitaire.

THREESOME: a game in which the high bidder takes the first three cards of the widow (Tarok).

Three-Up, a card Solitaire.

THROW-IN: the stratagem of forcing an opponent in the lead, in order to compel him to lead to his disadvantage.

THROW OFF: 1. Discard. 2. Smear.

Thumb and Pouch, a card Solitaire.

Tick-Tack = Backgammon, 386

Tic-Tac-Toe = Tit-Tat-Toe, 433

Tiddly-Wink, 429

TIERCE: a sequence of three cards in the same suit (Piquet). *Tierce major,* the A-K-Q; *tierce minor,* the K-Q-J.

Tiger = Blind Opening, 71

TIGER: 1. A Poker hand. See Big Tiger, Little Tiger. 2. Traditional symbol of a Faro game; see *buck the tiger.*

TILE: any of the pieces used in Mah Jongg, Anagrams, etc.

TILLICOULTRY: a Checkers opening.

—— TIMER, as SIX-TIMER: a hand that has the specified number of *places open* (Poker).

TIM TSZ' P'AI: Chinese domino pieces.

Tippen = Dreiblatt.

Tit-Tat-Toe, 433

Tiu U, Chinese domino game ("to angle").

Tjak-Ma-Tchi-Ki, Korean domino game ("pair-making").

Tokkadille, obsolete Backgammon game.

Tomate, El, Spanish game similar to Loo.

Toni, a card Solitaire.

Tontine, obsolete game of chance, single cards dealt to each player determining how much he must pay or collect.

TOP, GOING ON: paying a forfeit to drop out of a deal (Panguingue).

TOTAL-POINT SCORING: a method of scoring in Duplicate Bridge in which the net scores of each pair on each board are totaled.

TOUCH: cheat; money obtained by cheating.

TOUCHING CARDS: cards in sequence.

TOUR (Fr.): 1. A period of play, usually one deal. 2. A rook in Chess.

651

DICTIONARY OF GAMES AND TERMS

Tournament, 476

TOURNAMENT: a contest among a large number of entrants to determine a winner, often with the element of luck eliminated so far as possible.

TOURNEE: a game in which trumps are decided by turning up a skat card (Skat).

TOURNEUR: houseman who spins the wheel (Roulette).

TOUS LES TROIS: a declaration to win the J, 9, 7 of trumps (Alsós).

TOUT: a bid to win all the tricks.

Tower of Babel = Accordion, 440

Tower of Hanoi, a card Solitaire.

Tower of Twenty-eight = Pyramid, 472

Towie, 178

TRAIL: lay a card from the hand on the table, without building or taking in (Casino).

Transformation, a card Solitaire.

TRANSVERSALE: a bet on three numbers (Roulette).

Trappola, one of the earliest card games known. (See page 335.)

TRASH: 1. To discard. 2. Useless cards.

Travelers = Clock, 447

Treasure Hunt, 508

TREBOLES (Sp.): the suit clubs.

TREFF, TREFLE (Fr.): the suit clubs.

Trefoil, a card Solitaire.

Treize, 536

Trenta-Cinque = Thirty-five, 519

Trente et Quarante, 524

Tresette, 338

Tresillo, El, the leading Spanish card game, based on Ombre.

Tres Sietes, Los, Spanish card game.

TREY: any three-spot (playing cards, dice).

Triangle = Klondike, 462; Pyramid, 472

Triangle Contract, 178

Triangles, 435

TRIC (Fr.): a trick, especially the odd trick in Bridge.

TRICHE: three of a kind (Romestecq).

TRICK: a batch of cards formed during the play by the contribution of one card from each hand.

TRICK SCORE: points earned by declarer for odd tricks (Bridge).

TRICON: three of a kind.

Trictrac = Backgammon, 386

TRIO: three of a kind.

TRIOMPHANTE: a hazard at Ombre, incurred by the opening lead of spadille.

Triomphe, see Trumps, 189

Trionfetti, 80

TRIPLE-HEADER: like numbers on both ends of the layout, one of them being the doublet (Bergen).

TRIPLET: three of a kind.

TRIPLETON: a holding of three cards of a suit.

TRIPS: triplets, three of a kind (Poker).

Triumph, see pages 114, 189

Triumph (Solitaire), 477

TRIUNFOS (Sp.): trumps.

Truco, El, Spanish card game.

Trump, see page 114

TRUMP: 1. A privileged card or suit, the privilege being that in the current deal every such card ranks higher than any plain (= nontrump) card. 2. Play a trump on the lead of a plain suit. 3. Any heart, in Hearts (colloquial).

TRUMP CARD: 1. Any card that is a trump. 2. The turn-up.

Trumps, 189

Try Again, a card Solitaire.

Ts'ung Shap, Chinese domino game ("dispute for tens").

Tu Mientes, Spanish card game.

Tunk, 44

Turkish Checkers, 385

TURM (Ger.): rook (Chess).

TURN: 1. A player's opportunity, in due rotation, to bid, declare, play,

652

etc. 2. One period of the play, the drawing of two cards from the box (Faro).

TURN IT DOWN: reject the turn-up for trump (Euchre).

TURN-UP: a card faced after the deal, to fix or propose the trump suit, or (in Rummy games) to found the discard pile.

Tute, El, Spanish card game.

Twenty-nine, 487

Twenty-one (juvenile), 489

Twenty-one = Blackjack, 513

Twenty Questions, 506

Twenty-six, 545

Twenty-three, a card Solitaire.

TWICE AROUND: game of 121 points, when scored on a Cribbage board.

Twin Beds, 75

Twin Queens, a card Solitaire.

TWIST THE TIGER'S TAIL: play Faro.

Two-Card High-Low Poker, 93

Two-Card Poker, 76

Two-Dice Klondike = Bingo, 546

Two-Hand Bridge Games, 179

Two-Hand Euchre, 205

Two-Hand Five Hundred, 216

TWO HUNDRED: a declaration to win 200 at a trump or 180 at no trump (Alsós).

TWO PAIRS: a hand comprising a pair of one rank, a pair of a second rank, and a fifth card unmatched (Poker).

Two Rings, a card Solitaire.

TWO-SUITER: a hand containing two suits each of five or more cards (Bridge).

Two-Ten-Jack, game of the Hearts family.

Two-up, 536

U

UHU: a declaration to win the penultimate trick with the ♦A (Alsós).

ULTIMO: the winning of last trick with the lowest trump; a declaration to win ultimo (Tarok, Alsós, etc.).

UNBALANCED HAND: one that contains a singleton or void (Bridge).

UNBLOCK: avoid or resolve a block, by cashing the high cards of the shorter holding first or by discarding cards that block the suit (Bridge).

Uncle Sam, a card Solitaire.

Under and Over Seven, 542

UNDERCUT: defeat of the knocker by a hand with equal or lower count; show such a hand (Gin Rummy).

UNDERPLAY: lead or follow suit with a lower card when holding a higher card; hold up; refuse to cover.

UNDER THE GUNS: said of the first player in turn to bet (Poker).

UNDERTRICK: a trick by which declarer falls short of his contract (Bridge).

UNITED STATES PLAYING CARD CO.: the largest manufacturer of playing cards, located at Cincinnati, Ohio, manufacturers of Congress, Bicycle, Bee and other brands.

Unlimited Loo, 195

Unlimited Poker, any Poker game in which there is no limit on the amount of bets and raises.

UNLOAD: reduce the count of one's hand by melding and by discarding high cards (Rummy).

UNMATCHED CARD: one not included in a set; deadwood (Rummy).

UNTEN, UNTER (Ger.): a playing card, jack. (*Note:* when this term is used, the queen is called *ober.*)

——UP, as ACES UP: a hand of two pairs, the higher pair being specified (Poker).

Up and Down the River, 534

UPCARD: 1. One dealt to a player properly face up (Stud Poker). 2. The first card of the stock turned up to start the discard pile; the top of the discard pile at any time (Rummy).

Up Jenkins, 511

Usk, a card Solitaire.

Utah = Cincinnati, 75

V

v: abbr. of valet (Fr. = knave, jack).

VADE (Fr.): the pool to be played for.

VALET (Fr.): a playing card jack.

VALLE CARDS: threes, fives, and sevens (Panguingue).

VALSE, WALTZ: proposal to abandon the deal, on refusal of which the opponent becomes the trump maker (Belotte).

VALUE OF CARDS: 1. The arbitrary count assigned to each card, for scoring purposes. Also *point-value*. 2. The strength or worth of various holdings, estimated for purpose of bidding, declaring, etc . 3. Rank (*rare*).

VANDERBILT CLUB CONVENTION: see page 150

VANDERBILT, HAROLD S.: bridge authority who introduced modern Contract Bridge; see page 115.

Van John = Blackjack, 513

VELVET: money won from a house or bank.

VERLEUGNEN (Ger.): to revoke.

Vienna, a card Solitaire.

VIENNA GAME: a Chess opening.

VIENNA SYSTEM: see page 151.

Vierzig Vom Konig, four-hand partnership game to meld and win counting cards in tricks.

VIGORISH: the fee or percentage collected by a gambling house; perhaps from *vicarage*.

VILLAGE: a hand containing two sequences of Q-J or 10-9 (Romestecq).

Vingt-Et-Un = Blackjack, 513

Vingt-Quatre, variant of Imperial.

Vint, 188

VIRADE: the turn-up (*obsolete*).

Virginia Reel, 478

VIRLICQUE: four of a kind (Romestecq).

VISITING THE HAMLETS: cashing aces and tens (Skat).

Vive L'Amour, card game similar to Pig.

Vocabulary, 498

VOID: a holding of no cards in a suit.

VOLAT: a declaration to win nine tricks (Alsós).

VOLE: winning of all the tricks by one player.

VORHAND (Ger.) = FOREHAND.

VULNERABLE: said of a side having won a game toward rubber (Contract Bridge).

VYE, VIE: bet (*obsolete*).

W

w: abbr. of West.

WAGRAM: a Checkers opening.

WALL: the array of tiles arranged after shuffling (Mah Jongg).

WALL GAME: void game, by exhaustion of the wall without any declaration of a complete hand (Mah Jongg).

WALTZ = VALSE (Belotte).

War, 488

Wari = Mancala, 410.

Washington's Favorite, a card Solitaire.

WASTEPILE: a pile in which cards turned from the stock are laid face up, if they cannot at the moment be played elsewhere (Solitaire).

WATERLOO: a Checkers opening.

Wa-Wee = Mancala, 410

Weavers, 479

Weddings, a card Solitaire.

Wei-Ch'I = Go, 403

WEISS (Ger.): white.

Wendish Schafkopf, 316

WENZEL (Ger.): a playing card jack, especially of the trump suit.

Westcliff, a card Solitaire.

WHANGDOODLES = ROODLES.

Wheel, a card Solitaire.

WHEEL: 1. The spinning bowl into which the ball is tossed (Roulette).

2. The lowest possible hand, 5-4-3-2-A; = bicycle (Lowball).

Wheel Games, 555

WHEEL OF FORTUNE = the Roulette wheel; any wheel similarly used for gambling.

WHILTER: a Checkers opening.

WHIPSAW: 1. Loss of two bets on the same turn, one a bet to lose and the other a bet to win (Faro). 2. A method of collusion between cheats, both raising to freeze out a victim that only one can beat (Poker).

Whisk, see Contract Bridge, 114.

WHISKEY HOLE: a score one point short of game.

Whiskey Poker, 77

Whist, 180

WHIST CLUB OF NEW YORK: club that from 1909 to 1948 promulgated laws of Auction and Contract Bridge in the United States.

Whist De Gand = Solo Whist, 185.

WHITE: conventional designation of one of the players in a two-hand board game.

WHITE DOCTOR: a Checkers opening.

WHITEHEAD, WILBUR C.: author of books on Auction Bridge, died 1930.

Whitehead, a card Solitaire.

WHITESKIN: a card other than a face card; antonym of *redskin*.

WHITEWASHED: beaten without having scored a point; = shut out.

Who Am I?, 505

WIDE CARDS: two cards twice or more separated in rank, as 8-5 (Cribbage).

WIDOW: an extra hand or lesser number of cards dealt face down, belonging at the outset to no player. Also *skat, scat, miss, blind,* and (incorrectly) *kitty.*

Widow Nap, 197

WILD CARD, WILD BONE, WILD FLOWER: 1. One that may be designated by the holder to represent any other card for purpose of filling a meld, completing a hand, etc. 2. A card,

the discard of which is completely unsafe so far as the player can infer (Rummy).

Wild-Card [Poker] Games, 73

WILD DISCARD: dangerous discard; one that may be used by the next player (Rummy). (*Note:* seldom used to mean the discard of a wild card.)

Wild Widow, 74

Will-o'-the-Wisp, a card Solitaire.

WILL-O'-THE-WISP: a Checkers opening.

WIMMELN (Ger.): to smear.

Windmill, 480

WINDS: 1. The sixteen Winds tiles. 2. The four compass positions around the table; hence, the four players. *Prevailing wind:* that in which a set of tiles earns a special bonus. (Mah Jongg.)

WINNER: a card that wins a trick; one that may be expected to win a trick.

WINSLOW SYSTEM: see page 151.

Wipe-off, 310

Wish, a card Solitaire.

Wit and Reason, 438

WITH: having the specified number of matadors, as *with two* (Skat).

WITHOUT: 1. Lacking the specified number of matadors, as *without two* (Skat). 2. A call meaning *no trumps.*

With Whom? = Conquian.

WOO: declare a complete hand and so end the play (Mah Jongg).

WOODPUSHER: a routine player (Chess).

Woolworth, 90

Word Chain, 498

Word Dominoes = Word Chain, 498

Word Game = Little Words, 504

Word Games, 496

Word Squares, 502

WORK, MILTON C.: The principal authority on Auction Bridge, died 1934.

WRONG BET: one that the shooter will not pass; see also *right bet* (Craps).

WURFELN (Ger.): dice.

Wurfelspiel (Ger.), any dice game.

Wurttembergischer Tarok = Frog, 327

X, Y, Z

X: a symbol representing an indifferent low card, as ♡Kx, meaning the heart king accompanied by any other lower heart.

X Marks the Spot, 76

Xerxes, a card Solitaire.

Yacht, 548

YACHT: a cast of like numbers on all five dice (Yacht).

YANKEE NOTION CARDS: special playing cards manufactured in the United States in the 19th century and widely used among people prejudiced against the standard European cards.

YARBOROUGH: a hand containing no card higher than a nine (Whist).

(After the Earl of Yarborough, who offered to bet 1,000 to 1 against a player's next being dealt this hand.)

YEUX: a hazard at Ombre, incurred by holding the two red aces. (The term in full is *les yeux de ma grand'mère,* "my grandmother's eyes.")

YOUNGER: the dealer in a two-hand game; = mineur.

Yukon (Solitaire), 482; (card game), 495

ZAHLKARTEN (Ger.): counting cards.

ZARSE, WALTER L.: author of *Zarse on Skat and Schafkopf.*

Ziginette, 532

Zingara, a card Solitaire.

Zioncheck, see Contract Rummy, 26.

Zodiac, a card Solitaire.

ZUG (Ger.): a move, as in Chess.

ZUGZWANG (Ger.): the compulsion to move, especially when this is a disadvantage (Chess).

Zwicken = Dreiblatt.